Microsoft® Visual C#® .NET 2003

DEVELOPER'S COOKBOOK

Microsoft® Visual C#® .NET 2003

DEVELOPER'S COOKBOOK

Mark Schmidt
Simon Robinson

DEVELOPER'S LIBRARY

S800 East 96th Street, Indianapolis, Indiana 46240

Microsoft® Visual C#® .NET 2003 Developer's Cookbook

International Standard Book Number: 0-672-32580-2

Library of Congress Catalog Card Number: 2003110397

Printed in the United States of America

First Printing: December 2003

06   05   04   03   4   3   2   1

Trademarks

All terms mentioned in this book that are known to be trademarks or service marks have been appropriately capitalized. Sams Publishing cannot attest to the accuracy of this information. Use of a term in this book should not be regarded as affecting the validity of any trademark or service mark.

Warning and Disclaimer

Bulk Sales

Sams Publishing offers excellent discounts on this book when ordered in quantity for bulk purchases or special sales. For more information, please contact

U.S. Corporate and Government Sales
1-800-382-3419
corpsales@pearsontechgroup.com

For sales outside of the U.S., please contact

International Sales
1-317-428-3341
international@pearsontechgroup.com

Associate Publisher
Michael Stephens

Acquisitions Editor
Neil Rowe

Development Editor
Mark Renfrow

Managing Editor
Charlotte Clapp

Project Editor
Andy Beaster

Copy Editor
Kris Simmons

Indexer
Bill Meyers

Proofreader
Leslie Joseph

Technical Editors
Ralph Arvesen
Dan Maharry

Team Coordinator
Cindy Teeters

Interior Designer
Gary Adair

Cover Designer
Gary Adair

Page Layout
Kelly Maish
Plan-it Publishing

Contents at a Glance

Table of Contents

About the Authors

Mark Schmidt is a software engineer at Hewlett-Packard. His current research is in the area of advanced custom user interfaces. Part of this work was the topic of a talk he gave at the 2001 VSLive! Conference in San Francisco. Mark has written articles on C# for *Visual Studio Magazine* and *Visual Basic Programmer's Journal*. Mark also coauthored *Sams Teach Yourself Visual C++ .NET in 24 Hours*. At HP, Mark has used C# in many areas from quick user-interface prototypes to fully functional ASP.NET-enabled Web servers. His breadth of knowledge is the result of a constant search for information that leads him down several different technology avenues. More information about Mark Schmidt and this book appears at `http://www.csharpcookbook.com` and `http://www.samspublishing.com`.

Simon Robinson is a well-known author, specializing in .NET programming, and is editor of ASP Today, the leading ASP and ASP.NET-related Web site. Simon's first experience of commercial computer programming was in the early 1980s when his computer project at college became the college's student time-tabling program, running on the BBC Micro. Later, he studied for a PhD in physics and subsequently spent a couple of years working as a university physics researcher. A large part of this time was spent writing programs to do mathematical modeling of certain properties of superconductors. Somewhere around this time, he realized there was more money to be had in straight computer programming and ended up at Lucent Technologies doing mostly Windows COM programming, before finally becoming self-employed, combining writing and free-lance software development. He has an extremely broad experience of programming on Windows. These days, his core specialism is .NET programming, and he is comfortable coding in C++, C#, VB, and IL and has skills ranging from graphics and Windows Forms to ASP.NET, directories, data access, Windows services, and the native Windows API.

Simon lives in Lancaster, UK. His outside interests include theatre, dance, performing arts, and politics. You can visit Simon's personal Web site at `http://www.SimonRobinson.com`.

Christian Nagel offers training and consulting with development and designing of Microsoft .NET solutions. He looks back to more than 15 years experience as a developer and software architect. Christian started his computing career with PDP 11 and VAX/VMS platforms, covering a variety of languages and platforms. Since the year 2000 he has been working with .NET and C#, developing and architecting distributed solutions. While doing this, he has also written several .NET books: among them are *Professional C#*, *Professional .NET Network Programming*, and *C# Web Services*. As a Microsoft Regional Director he speaks at international conferences and is the leader of INETA Europe (International .NET User Group Association). You can contact Christian via Web site `http://www.christiannagel.com`.

❖

To my mother, for never doubting what I can do, for always pushing me to give it my all, and for not getting too upset when I told her I wasn't going to law school.

—Mark Schmidt

❖

Acknowledgments

So many people were involved or touched in one way or another by my time spent on this book, but unfortunately, I can't list you all.

To my wife, Cher, and children, Jordan, Jake, Jonah, and Mallorie. You are my life and the reason I strive to succeed. I love you all more than words can convey.

To my Dad, who instilled in me the principle of working hard so you can play hard later.

To the many editors and people at Sams Publishing and especially to Neil Rowe. You all know how to make a hard job fun and worthwhile, and I will always treasure the relationship Neil and I started.

Damon, Mike, and Byron, you guys put the fun in my life. Thanks for pulling me out of my hole once in a while and for being the close friends you guys are.

Charlie, thanks for making me look good in front of my peers.

To my extended family at River Rock Church, thank you for showing so much love and support. It brings me comfort and peace to see the love of our Lord in all your faces.

Finally, I'd like to especially acknowledge my two brothers, Daron and Scott, who have stuck by my side and each other's through all of life's trials. Brothers until the end, I love you guys.

—Mark Schmidt

We Want to Hear from You!

As the reader of this book, *you* are our most important critic and commentator. We value your opinion and want to know what we're doing right, what we could do better, what areas you'd like to see us publish in, and any other words of wisdom you're willing to pass our way.

As an associate publisher for Sams Publishing, I welcome your comments. You can email or write me directly to let me know what you did or didn't like about this book—as well as what we can do to make our books better.

Please note that I cannot help you with technical problems related to the topic of this book. We do have a User Services group, however, where I will forward specific technical questions related to the book.

When you write, please be sure to include this book's title and author as well as your name, email address, and phone number. I will carefully review your comments and share them with the author and editors who worked on the book.

Email: `feedback@samspublishing.com`

Mail: Michael Stephens
                Associate Publisher
                Sams Publishing
                800 East 96th Street
                Indianapolis, IN 46240 USA

For more information about this book or another Sams Publishing title, visit our Web site at `www.samspublishing.com`. Type the ISBN (excluding hyphens) or the title of a book in the Search field to find the page you're looking for.

Introduction

When Visual C# .NET first arrived on the scene, developers everywhere were hit with a vast wave of documentation and tutorials from magazine articles, books, and Web sites. The obligatory "Hello World" programs were popping up left and right as developers began their path to understanding this new language created by Microsoft. Those days of learning this exciting new technology are now gone for some developers, and they now need more in-depth material—material that corresponds to the tasks you need to accomplish while developing your application. *Microsoft Visual C# .NET 2003 Developer's Cookbook* will help you make that transition from learning to doing.

Microsoft Visual C# .NET 2003 Developer's Cookbook is divided into parts corresponding to the technology within Visual C# .NET. These parts each contain several different recipes to help you understand a single task without having to read several pages of introductory material. Each recipe is carefully constructed to first show you how to accomplish a task using a certain technique and then to follow with comments that provide a closer inspection of the solution.

Along with the immense array of task-specific recipes is a large collection of source code, which is freely available on the Sams Web site, `http://www.samspublishing.com`. Most recipes in this book utilize source code contained within an application developed for the task it is explaining. Even though some of the source code might be terse and to the point, some of the applications would make a great stepping stone to larger, more involved solutions. For instance, Chapter 10, "Programming Graphics with GDI+," uses the source code from an image-editing application with full support for image scaling, cropping, rotation, and even a print preview dialog. Chapter 8, "Windows Forms Controls," contains the source code for an autohiding docked tool window, similar to that used within the Visual Studio .NET 2003 Integrated Development Environment (IDE). Additionally, Chapter 13, "XML in .NET," contains a full XML editor, and Chapter 16, "Building ASP.NET Applications," contains a clever Web application that acts as a remote command-line shell for ASP.NET-capable Web servers.

Visual C# .NET is an exciting technology that allows you to create feature-rich applications while shortening the development cycle. Because the technology itself has a large scope, keeping tabs on all the information is a daunting if not impossible task. *Microsoft Visual C# .NET 2003 Developer's Cookbook* provides the help you need when you just want to know how to perform a single task, and it offers real-world, application-specific information. The companion Web site for this book, `http://www.csharp-cookbook.com`, provides additional material and a way to contact the authors for more information.

Part I, The C# Language

One of the more subtle defects that occur in code is failure to recognize the various rules related to operators, expressions, and control structures. Chapter 1, "Operators, Expressions, and Control Structures," details those rules and how best to utilize them, including topics such as operator precedence and associativity, data type conversions, and understanding logical expressions.

C# is an object-oriented programming language and as such places a strong emphasis on the use of objects within the .NET Framework and the code that you write. Chapter 2, "Objects and Components," starts with basic recipes concerning object creation and ends with advanced topics such as polymorphism, abstract classes, and multiple interface inheritance.

As you see in Chapter 3, "Strings and Regular Expressions," strings play a major role in any programming language. The .NET Framework contains a rich set of classes that aid the developer when working with this data type. Furthermore, regular expressions allow you to take string data and perform input validation and substring replacement.

Very rarely will you work with single bits of data when creating an application. More often than not, you need to utilize collections to store several items of a similar type. Chapter 4, "Creating and Using .NET Collections," covers the fundamental collection types in the .NET Framework, including searching and sorting those collections, as well as recipes that aid in creating your own collection type.

Delegates and events form the eventing system within the .NET Framework. Although a majority of event handlers respond to user-interface interaction, the model used in the .NET Framework allows any object to fire or receive events. Chapter 5, "Delegates and Events," contains several recipes that cover the intricacies of delegates and events.

Application errors are an everyday occurrence. Not to be confused with regular defects, exceptions and errors are used extensively within the .NET Framework to respond appropriately when something doesn't work correctly. In Chapter 6, "Exceptions in Error Handling," you'll see various techniques outlining the proper way to catch and throw exceptions as well as pass exceptions on to other objects.

Part II, User Interface and Graphics

Windows Forms is the technology responsible for client-side user interfaces. Coupled with this technology is the rich design support built into Visual Studio .NET 2003. Chapter 7, "Windows Forms," begins with several recipes aimed at creating basic Windows Forms applications and ends with more advanced topics, such as Multiple Document Interface (MDI) user interfaces.

Without controls, a Windows Form is just a window. The .NET Framework contains an extensive list of controls that you can add to a Windows Form with a simple drag and drop from the designer. Several recipes in Chapter 8, "Windows Forms Controls," demonstrate various ways to control certain common controls, whereas others show methods to harness the Windows Forms designer to create compelling user interfaces.

Although the .NET Framework contains an exhaustive list of controls, there will always be room for more. Chapter 9, "User Controls," shows different techniques you can utilize to create our own .NET Windows Form control and how to plug the control into the Visual Studio .NET 2003 Windows Forms designer seamlessly.

Chapter 10, "Programming Graphics with GDI+," shows different ways to harness the capabilities of GDI+ and the technology responsible for various rendering technologies, such as vector graphics, typography, and images. Some of the recipes include such topics as creating flicker-free animation, rendering anti-aliased text, and displaying animated GIFs.

Localizing an application is a task that should be solidified during an application's design. Without a game plan and without a toolset to enable that plan, you might be playing catch-up during the localization phase. As shown in Chapter 11, "Localization and Resources," Visual Studio .NET 2003 contains several different tools that you use in conjunction with the localization and resource classes of the .NET Framework to make localization easier.

Part III, Data Access

For data to remain persistent, it must be written to a long-term storage medium such as a hard disk. Chapter 12, "File I/O and Serialization," looks at various techniques involved with file input and output. Furthermore, it also covers serialization, the act of saving an object's state, by looking at the various serialization options available within the .NET Framework.

The Extensible Markup Language (XML), discussed in Chapter 13, "XML in .NET," is playing a major role in almost every technology being used or developed. At its most basic level, it's a simple text-based file format, but the different ways in which you can apply rules makes it a good fit for everything from application configuration files to method invocation on remote objects.

Databases have transformed the Internet from static Web pages to truly dynamic information systems. You see in Chapter 14, "Database Programming with ADO.NET," that ADO.NET is the .NET solution for interacting with different database technologies, from Microsoft Access to more industrial-level database systems such as SQL Server.

Part IV, Internet and Networking

Sockets form the underlying layer of network programming. Chapter 15, "Network Programming with Sockets," looks at different ways of programming sockets as well as discusses methods to formulate your own communication protocol. Some of the advanced techniques include accessing data through a proxy server and performing asynchronous Web transfers.

The successor to Active Server Pages (ASP), ASP.NET transforms dynamic Web pages into feature-laden Web applications. In Chapter 16, "ASP.NET," you will see techniques demonstrating everything from creating, manipulating, and responding to Web Forms to specific techniques explaining how to control page output caching and saving session state.

Web Services bring the notion of remote applications as a service to the programming world. Comprising standard protocols, XML-centric data, and programming language independence, Web Services facilitate data sharing across network boundaries. Chapter 17, "Web Services," explores the vast support for Web Services provided by Visual C# .NET and Visual Studio .NET 2003.

In the past, communication between disparate objects across a network was a lesson in perseverance for most developers. Remoting in the .NET Framework was created not only to make this communication much easier but also to provide great flexibility and power for creating distributed applications. Chapter 18, "Remoting," covers various aspects of remoting, including server-activated singleton objects and custom channel sinks for logging.

Part V, Deployment and Security

The main deployment unit of a .NET application is the assembly. Assemblies were created to combat the inconsistent deployment of class libraries and version incompatibilities. Chapter 19, "Assemblies," shows that the .NET Framework contains a vast array of processes to follow when working with assemblies, including strongly named assemblies, and techniques to follow when creating subsequent versions of existing assemblies.

Sometimes regarded as the last step in application design, installation is also one of the most important items to plan and implement. In Chapter 20, "Installation," you'll see the techniques needed to create a robust installation of your application, starting with the creation of installation packages and followed by more advanced techniques, including installation of assemblies into the Global Assembly Cache (GAC).

Security issues within the development community have seen a focused increase. Chapter 21, "Securing Code," covers several different facets of programming, including authentication, code execution permissions, and licensing.

Part VI, Advanced Topics

Threading gives you the ability to run two or more simultaneous programming tasks. However, it also opens the possibility for data corruption if those tasks attempt to manipulate the same area of memory. You use synchronization to prevent this possibility from happening. Chapter 22, "Threading and Synchronization," discusses several different techniques you can use to create multithreaded applications.

The ability to programmatically inspect objects at runtime is known as *reflection*. Reflection allows you not only to view the contents of assemblies, modules, and data types but also to dynamically create assemblies at runtime. Chapter 23, "Reflection," shows different techniques for reflection, such as creating a plug-in architecture and performing dynamic method invocation.

The Component Object Model (COM) is one of the oldest but most widely used Windows technologies. Because a vast array of libraries and controls utilize COM, the .NET Framework contains the necessary toolset to use COM objects in .NET applications as well as .NET objects within COM-based applications. Chapter 24, "COM Interoperability," discusses this toolset.

Using custom attributes allows you to extend the C# language by adding information and functionality to your objects. Chapter 25, "Custom Attributes," contains techniques ranging from creating your own custom attribute to inspecting custom attributes at runtime using reflection.

Smart Device Extensions is a new technology introduced in Visual Studio .NET 2003. These extensions allow you to use C# to create .NET applications that can run on any Compact .NET Framework device, including pocket PCs and Windows SmartPhones. Chapter 26, "Smart Device Extensions," explains some of the key differences you'll encounter when creating device applications, including techniques related to installation, data retrieval, and Compact .NET Framework classes.

I

The C# Language

1

Operators, Expressions, and Control Structures

1.0. Introduction

For several generations, the most widely sold toys have been those that allow you to take small simple objects and combine them to create a replica of some real-world object. Initially starting out as a large pile of plastic blocks with varying shapes and colors, they can transform into a multistage ignition rocket ship or an elegant mansion without a roof.

Toys aren't the only place we see this sort of design. Almost everywhere you look, this piecewise refinement is evident in many facets of everyday life. Cars aren't built using a myriad of non-connecting objects but rather are assembled from smaller pieces to form the engine, for instance, which is then used as a component in the final automobile. Using another example, a company contains employees who form a team. These teams combine to form a section or business unit, and these units group together to form the corporation. In fact, this type of organization doesn't just make sense in the physical realm but is prevalent in many natural things as well.

Based on this concept, it comes as no surprise that software is logically divided into smaller pieces that contribute to a solution when assembled. At the lower levels of the programming language construct hierarchy are the operator, the expression, and the control structure. An expression is any group of operators and operands that are combined to perform some type of computation, such as setting a variable, calling a function, or performing a system-related task.

In this chapter, we look at all the various C# language elements that are available to construct an application. From the basic layout of a small console application to using overloaded operators to change the semantic meaning of objects, this chapter points out the various options you have at your disposal to efficiently design your next Visual C# .NET application.

1.1. Understanding Visual C# .NET Program Layout

You want to create a simple Visual C# .NET console application and inspect the generated code.

Technique

In the Visual Studio .NET IDE, click on File, New, Project (Ctrl+Shift+N) and select Visual C# Projects from the list of project types. In the list of templates, select the Console Application template and type in a name for the project.

Comments

For most of this chapter and in several projects throughout this book, you'll find yourself working with console-based applications. Their minimalist nature allows you to concentrate on the topic being discussed without having to traverse through extraneous, potentially distracting code.

Even though it is just a simple console-based application that currently provides no functionality, it does serve as a good illustration for some of the various pieces that make a C# application. Once you create your project, the Visual Studio .NET IDE opens the application's main program file, which should look similar to Listing 1.1.

Listing 1.1 **A Simple Visual C# .NET Console Application**

```
using System;

namespace _1_ProgramLayout
{
    /// <summary>
    /// Summary description for Class1.
    /// </summary>
    class DateTimePrinter
    {
        /// <summary>
        /// The main entry point for the application.
        /// </summary>
        [STAThread]
        static void Main(string[] args)
        {
            Console.WriteLine( "Today is {0}", DateTime.Now );
        }
    }
}
```

The first couple of lines relate to an organizational construct known as the namespace. Namespaces convey a sense of relationships between like objects. For instance, if you have some objects with such names as *Frame*, *Engine*, *Wheel*, *Light*, and *Seat*, you immediately see the relationship these objects possess in that they all belong on an automobile. In this example, the namespace could be *Automobile*.

On the first line, the program is letting the compiler know that it wants to use some of the objects within the `System` namespace. Therefore, anytime you want to use one of these objects, you do not need to preface the object name with the namespace name. For instance, the `WriteLine` statement prints out a small message in the console. The `Console` object is a class within the `System` namespace. Without the `using` directive, you have to qualify each type you want to use with the namespace it is declared in. In this instance, the line in Listing 1.1 would be

```
System.Console.WriteLine( "Today is {0}", DateTime.Now );
```

In the listing, you can see a namespace declaration, which is simply the name you gave the project when you initially created it. Although the wizard placed an initial type in a namespace for you to use, the namespace declaration itself is purely optional. However, we recommend that you do get into the habit of using namespaces to enhance code organization and readability.

Within the automatically generated namespace is a class called `Class1`, which was renamed to `DateTimePrinter` to more accurately describe the type's functionality (albeit somewhat limited). A class is best described as a data type that can contain various associated methods to interact with it. Whenever an instance of that class is created or instantiated, it becomes a usable object to which you can get or set various properties, receive notification of certain events, and tell it to perform some action using one of its member functions. Chapter 2, "Objects and Components," delves deeper into the many ways classes are used within C# and the .NET Framework.

The last important component of our simple console application is the application's entry point, denoted by the static member function `Main`. Each application must contain an entry point so that the Common Language Runtime (CLR) can effectively start the application by handing control over to you. Once the `Main` function exits, the application ends. Just before the `Main` method declaration is the `STAThread` attribute. This attribute denotes the threading model your application uses. However, it is only applicable if you plan to use COM Interop, discussed in Chapter 24, "COM Interop," and is ignored if you do not.

1.2. Parsing Command-Line Arguments

You want your application to support command-line argument parsing.

Technique

Use a string array as a parameter in your application's entry point, the static `Main` function.

```
using System;

namespace _2_CommandLineArgs
{
    class Class1
    {
        static void Main(string[] args)
        {
            foreach ( string arg in args )
                Console.WriteLine( arg + "\n" );
        }
    }
}
```

Comments

The `Main` function in an application has the option of accepting a string array as a parameter. This array contains the command-line arguments passed to it by the system where each element in the array corresponds to a string on the command line delineated by quotation marks or whitespace.

1.3. Creating Multiple Application Entry Points

You want your application to contain several entry points.

Technique

For each entry point you want to add, create a separate class containing a static `Main` member function. To change which entry point is run by the CLR, go to the project properties (Alt+P,P) and select Common Properties, General. Select the function you want to use as the application entry point in the Startup Object field. You must then recompile your project any time you change the application entry point because you can only change the entry point at compile time, not at runtime.

Comments

There are several reasons why creating several application entry points is advantageous. One key advantage is that it allows you to control the flow of your application to test different avenues of functionality. For instance, you can create an entry point that serves to display a tremendous amount of debugging information at runtime. When you are confident that the unit tests you created are working correctly, you can create a final application entry point that removes most of the debugging information. However, in the past, you might have had to comment out or remove the critical debugging information. By creating a separate entry point, you gain the advantage of preserving your unit tests that you can run simply by changing a property within your project. With a little clever command-line compiling, you can even create an automated test harness that compiles your application, specifying one of your unit-test application entry points; verify that the results are satisfied; and repeat that process for each entry point.

To compile a C# program from the command line and specify which startup object to use as the application entry point, use the `/main` command-line argument for the compiler. Listing 1.2 contains a project source file that contains three different application entry points. To compile this file on the command line and specify an application entry point, you invoke the C# compiler using the following:

```
csc.exe Class1.cs /main:_3_MultEntryPoints.EntryPointTest.Main3Entry
```

Listing 1.2   **A C# Application Containing Multiple Application Entry Points**

```csharp
using System;

namespace _3_MultEntryPoints
{
    class EntryPointTest
    {
        class Main1Entry
        {
            [STAThread]
            static void Main(string[] args)
            {
                Console.WriteLine( "Running in Main" );
            }
        }
        class Main2Entry
        {
            [STAThread]
            static void Main(string[] args)
            {
                Console.WriteLine( "Running in Main2" );
            }
        }
```

Listing 1.2 **Continued**

```
    class Main3Entry
    {
        [STAThread]
        static void Main(string[] args)
        {
            Console.WriteLine( "Running in Main3" );
        }
    }
  }
}
```

1.4. Referencing Assemblies and Namespaces

You want to use a class, but the compiler says that the class cannot be found.

Technique

Add a reference to the assembly that defines the class by clicking on the Project, Add Reference from the main menu. Select the .NET tab, locate the assembly that contains the type you want to use, and double-click it.

Comments

The .NET Framework uses information in an assembly to resolve type information when you want to use a class. An assembly is simply the file that is created when you compile a project such as an .exe or dynamic link library (.dll) file. When you perform the steps of referencing an assembly, the compiler knows to look in each referenced assembly during compilation to resolve any types that are encountered within the source file.

1.5. Creating Valid Identifier Names

You want to ensure that the identifier follows the rules of valid identifier naming.

Technique

Your identifier cannot be the same as that of a C# keyword. You are free to use any combination of letters, numbers, and underscore characters as long as the identifier does not start with a number. Furthermore, you can use the @ symbol as the first character in your identifier. Listing 1.3 shows several valid and invalid identifier names.

Listing 1.3   **Demonstrating Valid and Invalid Identifier Names**

```
namespace _5_Identifiers
{
    class Class1
    {
        [STAThread]
        static void Main(string[] args)
        {
            int i;          // valid
            int @int;       // valid but confusing
            int INT;        // valid since C# is case sensitive
            int 4_Score;    // Not valid. Cannot begin with a digit
            int in@t;       // not valid. @ symbol not at beginning
            int int;        // not valid. Cannot use keywords
        }
    }
}
```

Comments

Identifiers name certain programming elements within a program. They include such items as namespace names, classes, and variables. It is good programming practice to create identifiers that convey important information about the element it is defined as. In the days before .NET, Hungarian notation was used as the de facto standard for identifier naming, at least for those using the C++ language within a Windows program. Although some people argue for or against its suitability as a standard, the fact remains that it was a standard which could alleviate some of the issues that go along with reading someone else's source code. With the release of .NET, Microsoft dropped the Hungarian-notation guideline due to the cross-language support within the .NET Framework. Some of these identifier guidelines include using a combination of Pascal and Camel case for character capitalization within an identifier as well as using semantics in the identifier name. If you want to learn more about the guidelines Microsoft uses for the .NET Framework, search MSDN using the phrase "naming guidelines."

1.6. Working with Numeric Types

You need to store data in a variable as an integral type.

Technique

Choosing the correct data type can almost be considered an art. Keep in mind the range of possible values for the data you need to store in memory and whether you need a signed or unsigned data type.

Comments

There are eight types designed to work with numerical data. Each of the types is designated based on its size and whether it is signed. The smallest integral types available to C# are the 8-bit byte with a range of 0 to 255 and the 8-bit sbyte, a signed data type with a range of –128 to 127. At the far end of the spectrum are the 64-bit ulong and the signed version, the long. Table 1.1 shows the possible numerical data types as well as their sizes in bits and range.

Table 1.1   Integral Data Types and Their Associated Sizes and Ranges

Data Type	Size (Bits)	Range
sbyte	8	–128 to 127
byte	8	0 to 255
short	16	–32,768 to 32,767
ushort	16	0 to 65,535
char	16	0 to 65,535
int	32	–2,147,483,648 to 2,147,483,647
uint	32	0 to 4,294,967,295
long	64	–9,223,372,036,854,775,808 to 9,223,372,036,854,775,807
ulong	64	0 to 18,446,744,073,709,551,615

When working with integral data types, you have to weigh two options. First of all, even though we live in an age where memory is in abundance, you should still attempt to keep memory usage to a minimum. Sometimes, your application might need to run in a low-memory environment, and by choosing a design that optimizes memory usage, you can benefit from this strategy. Secondly, you must ensure that the data type you choose is large enough to hold any value you assign to it. If you inadvertently assign a number outside of a data type's range, your application will encounter a situation that it is not prepared to deal with. Based on your project properties and whether you are using exception handling, which is explained later in this book, the CLR will do one of two things. First, your application will throw an OverflowException. It is then your responsibility to handle this exception or face the consequences of an application crash.

By default, your project is created with overflow checking turned off. This default means that the CLR does not check whether a value being assigned to a data type causes an overflow. Rather, it takes a safer approach, which is either to flip the bits of the data type, thereby causing it to change sign, or to simply roll the value back to 0 in the case of unsigned data. As you might guess, this process can have undesirable side effects in your application and can lead to subtle defects that might be hard to find.

To turn on overflow checking in your project, open the property pages of your project by choosing Project, Properties (Alt+P). Select Configuration Properties, Build. Set the property labeled Check for Arithmetic Overflow to True so that data types are checked for overflow, as shown in Figure 1.1. If you believe that once you thoroughly test your code with all possible inputs your data types will not overflow, you can consider setting this property to `False`. The safest and most advantageous route is to enable this property when you build in debug mode and turn it off, as an optimization technique, during release builds.

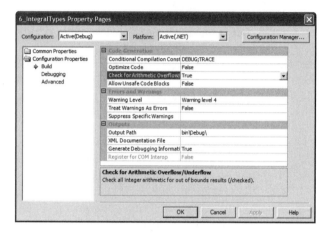

Figure 1.1   Changing project properties to check for arithmetic overflows.

1.7. Working with Floating-Point Numbers

Your application needs to work with floating-point values and you need to determine the correct type to use.

Technique

If memory is your primary concern and the range of possible values isn't too large, use the `float` data type. If you need very large values knowing that you need to sacrifice precision, use the `double` data type. If you need accurate and precise data, use the `decimal` data type.

Comments

Just as with integral types, choosing the proper floating-point number is essential to creating a robust application. There are two main points to consider when deciding which floating-point data type to choose: size and precision.

The .NET floating-point data types allow you to use exponential notation. For instance, the `float` data type has a range of $+/- 1.5 \times 10^{-45}$ to $+- 3.4 \times 10^{38}$. Although this range is certainly large, the precision of the `float` only allows for a maximum of seven digits. Any digits after the seventh digit are simply changed to a 0. For financial applications, this change could result in the improper calculation of money, which could have harsh repercussions from the clients who use your software. If, however, you are programming a video game, you might not need precision greater than seven digits. You might have small side effects but nothing like the side effects a loss of precision on a financial calculation would yield.

The `double` data type has the largest range of all the floating types. It can contain values in the range of 5.0×10^{-324} to 1.7×10^{308}. Its precision is limited to just 15 to 16 digits. Although the precision is larger than that of a `float`, it still might not be suited for financial calculations.

The `decimal` data type is the only floating type not based on an IEEE specification; it is an exclusive .NET Framework type. This 128-bit number contains a precision of 28 to -29 digits, which makes it the most precise floating-point type. However, its range isn't as widespread as the `double` data type. It can contain values in the range from 1.0×10^{-28} to 7.9×10^{28}.

To resolve ambiguities when working with floating-point numbers, C# contains a suffix for each type. For instance, if you want to assign a number to a `double` type, use the suffix d as in `3.14d`. To designate a `float` data type, supercede the number with a `f`. Finally, to use a decimal number, use the `m` suffix.

1.8. Creating Value Types with `struct`

You want to create a new data type that behaves more like a value than a class.

Technique

Define a structure using the `struct` keyword. A `struct` behaves similar to a class in that it can contain any number of member variables, methods, properties, and indexers, but memory for it is allocated on the stack rather than the heap, which also implies that it is passed by value rather than by reference. The following code demonstrates a temperature value type that performs a conversion if the `Fahrenheit` property is accessed:

```
struct TemperatureStruct
{
    public double Celsius;

    public double Fahrenheit
    {
        get
        {
```

```
        return ((9d/5d)*Celsius)+32;
    }
    set
    {
        Celsius = (5d/9d)*(value-32);
    }
  }
}
```

Comments

Sometimes, a language's built-in data types just aren't sufficient to use as a data-storing mechanism. Although using them would most certainly work, you generally need several related variables to describe all the pieces of pertinent information about a single object or abstract value type. Structures, or *structs*, were designed to organize and group built-in data types to create user-defined types that could emulate values.

One of the most prominent distinguishing differences between structs and classes is that you do not have to instantiate a struct using the new operator. You don't have to declare a default constructor because the compiler will ensure that all members are initialized by using a process known as *static flow analysis*. Sometimes, however, the analysis is unable to determine whether a member can be initialized. You can make the determination by declaring a private member variable within your struct. In this case, you have to create a custom parameterized constructor, and clients using your struct must create it using the new operator. Based on this information, you might make the assumption that using new on the struct would then allocate it on the heap. We can in fact verify that it does not by looking at the intermediate language (IL) code generated by the compiler using a tool, ILDasm, which is perfect when you want to investigate a certain behavior.

To run the ILDasm tool, you need to navigate to the bin directory of the .NET Framework SDK. You can double-click on the file to run it, but there are some advanced options available if you run the executable and specify the command-line argument /ADV. For this exercise, you can simply run it without the advanced options. Listing 1.4 shows an application that contains a class called TemperatureClass and a struct named TemperatureStruct. When you build this application, open the assembly in ILDasm. Expand the tree item of the namespace that contains the class and struct definition, which in this case is _8_ValueTypes. You should see three data types defined in the assembly: the main entry point, the temperature class, and the temperature struct. Expand the tree item that denotes the class where the entry point is located. Finally, double-click on the Main function to display the disassembled IL code shown in Figure 1.2.

Figure 1.2   ILDasm is a good tool to understand the inner workings of your
application and how it interacts with the CLR.

Listing 1.4   Comparing Differences Between a Class and a Struct

```
using System;

namespace _8_ValueTypes
{
    class EntryPoint
    {
        [STAThread]
        static void Main(string[] args)
        {
            TemperatureStruct ts = new TemperatureStruct();
            TemperatureClass tc = new TemperatureClass();

            Console.Write( "Enter degrees in Celsius: " );
            string celsius = Console.ReadLine();
            ts.Celsius = Convert.ToDouble(celsius);

            Console.WriteLine(
"Temperature in Fahrenheit = {0}", ts.Fahrenheit );
        }
    }

    class TemperatureClass
```

Listing 1.4   **Continued**

```
    {
        private double degreesCelsius;
        public double Fahrenheit
        {
            get
            {
                return ((9d/5d)*degreesCelsius)+32;
            }
            set
            {
                degreesCelsius = (5d/9d)*(value-32);
            }
        }
        public double Celsius
        {
            get
            {
                return degreesCelsius;
            }
            set
            {
                degreesCelsius = value;
            }
        }
    }

    struct TemperatureStruct
    {
        public double Celsius;

        public double Fahrenheit
        {
            get
            {
                return ((9d/5d)*Celsius)+32;
            }
            set
            {
                Celsius = (5d/9d)*(value-32);
            }
        }
    }
}
```

One particular portion of the IL for the `Main` function in Listing 1.4 is the four lines following the declaration of the locals that are used within the function:

```
IL_0000:  ldloca.s   ts
IL_0002:  initobj    _8_ValueTypes.TemperatureStruct
IL_0008:  newobj     instance void_8_ValueTypes.TemperatureClass::.ctor()
IL_000d:  stloc.1
```

The first two lines initialize the struct. The important piece of information here is the instructions `ldloca` and `initobj`. Compare these two instructions with the two that are used for initialization of the temperature class, `newobj` and `stloc`. When you use the `new` operator on the class, it generates the `newobj` instruction using the class constructor as the operand. However, when you use `new` on the struct, it performs a `ldloca.s`, which is an instruction used to fetch an object from the stack. Based on this information, even though you use the `new` keyword on a struct, it still follows the rules in that it is a stack-allocated rather than a heap-allocated object.

> **Note**
>
> Most of the built-in C# data types are structs themselves. For instance, the `int` is simply an alias for the `System.Int32` structure.

1.9. Converting Data Types

> You need to convert a value of one type to an equivalent value of another type.

Technique

```
long l = 0;
int i = 0;
l = i;
```

If however you need to convert a data type from a larger to a smaller size, you need to explicitly convert the value using the `System.Convert` class or through a technique known as *casting*:

```
long l = 0;
int i = 0;
i = Convert.ToInt32( l );
i = (int) l;
```

For any objects you want to convert to a string, simply use the `ToString` method, which is defined for all .NET value types:

```
int i = 0;
string s = i.ToString();
```

```
Every value type defined in the .NET Framework contains a static method named
Parse. It allows you to convert a string value to that value type. The string
itself must be formatted correctly or a FormatException will occur
"string sNum = "3.1415936535";
double dNum = Double.Parse( sNum );
```

Comments

Data conversion is a process that tends to occur frequently. The most frequent case is when you need to call a function whose parameters are different types than what you have been using in your application. Regardless of how different those two types are, an implicit or an explicit conversion will take place.

Implicit conversion occurs when the data type you want to convert to is a larger size than the data type you are converting from. For example, if a method needs a long data type (64 bits in C#) and your variable is an int, then the compiler will perform the necessary implicit conversion for you. In other words, you can simply pass the int variable into the method that is expecting a long parameter, and it will work without any conversion necessary on your part. The high 32 bits of the long will simply be all zeros.

If you need to convert a larger value to a smaller value, you have to perform an *explicit* conversion. The easiest way to determine whether you need to do so, other than memorizing all the conversion rules, is receiving an error from the compiler indicating that it could not perform an implicit conversion. To explicitly convert one data type to another, you can use the System.Convert class. This class contains several methods and several overloads of those methods to effectively perform explicit conversions. For example, to convert a long variable to an int, use the System.Convert.ToInt32 method, passing the long variable as the parameter. Looking at this class, you'll see most of the data conversions you need.

A shorthand way of performing an explicit conversion is through a technique known as *casting*. You perform casting by prefacing the variable you want to convert with the data type to convert to within parenthesis. To cast a long to an int, you use the following:

```
long l;
int i = (int) l;
```

1.10. Performing Relational Operations

You need to perform a relational comparison on two values or objects.

Technique

C# relational operators compare the actual values of value types but compare references to objects rather than what those objects contain. The format of a relational operation in C# is *expr1 operator expr2* as in x == y. Listing 1.5 demonstrates different relational operations by comparing both value types and objects.

Listing 1.5   **Using Relational Operators on Value and Reference Types**

```
using System;

namespace _10_Relations
{
    /// <summary>
    /// Summary description for Class1.
    /// </summary>
    class ComparingRelations
    {
        /// <summary>
        /// The main entry point for the application.
        /// </summary>
         [STAThread]
        static void Main(string[] args)
        {
            // compare 2 values for equality
            int a = 12;
            int b = 12;
            Console.WriteLine( a == b );
            Console.WriteLine( (object)a == (object)b );

            // compare 2 objects which contains overloaded == operator
            string c = "hello";
            string d = "hello";
            Console.WriteLine( (object) c==(object) d );

            // compare 2 objects for equality
            ClassCompare x = new ClassCompare();
            ClassCompare y;
            x.val = 1;
            y = x;
            Console.WriteLine( x == y );

            // changing 1 object also changes the other
            x.val = 2;
            Console.WriteLine( y.val.ToString() );
        }
    }
    class ClassCompare
    {
        public int val = 0;
    }
}
```

Comments

Testing relationships between values or objects is an important concept in programming. It provides the foundation for program flow and is used extensively in human/computer interaction. You use relational operations for determining how two values or objects relate to one another to decide what the next step in your program flow will be. Some of these include testing to see whether two values are equal, testing whether one value is greater than another, or testing whether one object is the same as another object, a process known as *type-testing*.

One key thing you need to keep in mind when creating relational operations is the difference between testing two value types and testing two objects. When you test value types, such as two `int` values, you are testing the value that those two types contain. Compare it to testing two different objects, shown later in the code, in which testing them means you are testing to see whether they are the same objects. In other words, when you are comparing two objects, you are comparing their locations in memory. If they both point to the same location, then they are considered equal. To test this equality, the last test in the code changes the value in one object and the next line prints a member variable in the second object. When you run this code, you'll notice that even though the variable was changed in one object, the other changed as well because you modified the same memory location that the second one pointed to. Additionally, when creating classes, you might want to overload the `Equals` method so that any comparisons done on your object will compare its internal values rather than the object references.

One particular thing to watch for is a reference type overloading a relational operator. Overloading an operator, discussed later in this chapter, is a technique to change the behavior of a built-in operator so that it makes better sense given the context of the objects you are working with. As an example, code in Listing 1.5 evaluates to `true` even though the two objects being compared are different. The `string` class within the .NET Framework has overloaded the relational operators so that the comparison happens on the internal string rather than the objects themselves. Comparing the strings of two `string` objects makes more sense than comparing two actual `string` objects themselves.

1.11. Using Logical Expressions

You want to evaluate an expression to see whether it is true.

Technique

Use a combination of logical operators on each relational expression you want to test. Logical operations consist of the logical and operator (`&&`), the logical or operator (`||`), and the logical exclusive-or operator (`^`). The following example demonstrates the logical operators as applied to Boolean values:

```
static void Main(string[] args)
{
    Console.WriteLine( "true==true: {0}", (true==true).ToString() );
    Console.WriteLine( "true==false: {0}", (true==false).ToString() );
    Console.WriteLine( "false==false: {0}", (false==false).ToString() );

    Console.WriteLine( "true||true: {0}", (true||true).ToString() );
    Console.WriteLine( "true||false: {0}", (true||false).ToString() );
    Console.WriteLine( "false||false: {0}", (false||false).ToString() );

    Console.WriteLine( "true^true: {0}", (true^true).ToString() );
    Console.WriteLine( "true^false: {0}", (true^false).ToString() );
    Console.WriteLine( "false^false: {0}", (false^false).ToString() );
}
```

Comments

Logical operations test the results of two or more relational expressions. In the last recipe, you used relational operators to test the relationship of two values or objects with each other. This evaluation results in a Boolean value, `true` or `false`, which you can then act upon in some manner. One action is to compare the results from two or more of these relational expressions by using *logical* operations.

Logical operations belong to a larger family of operators known as bitwise operators. The term *bitwise* applies because these operators use the actual bits of a value to determine the result. For instance, a Boolean value of `true` is a single bit (at least in theory), which is "turned on" or equals 1. The Boolean value `false` is "turned off" or set to 0. By using this information, you can generate a table to see the result based on the logical or bitwise operator used on these two values, as shown in Table 1.2.

Table 1.2   **Using Logical Operations**

Operand 1	Operand 2	Operator	Result	Rule
True	True	&&	True	Both operands must be true.
True	False	&&	False	
False	True	&&	False	
False	False	&&	false	
True	True	||	True	At least one operand must be true.
True	False	||	True	
False	True	||	True	
False	False	||	False	
True	True	^	False	At least one operand is true, but not both.
True	False	^	True	
False	True	^	True	
False	False	^	False	

The logical and, and the logical or operators are also known as short-circuit bitwise operators. If you are using a && operator, it makes sense that if the first operand is false, there is no need to test the second operand because you know that the logical statement will still evaluate to false. Furthermore, when using the || operator, it makes no sense to test the second operand if the first is already true because that would automatically make the statement true. The exclusive-or operator cannot use any type of short-circuit evaluation because you must test both operands regardless of the value of the first. This difference is why you see two characters for && and || but only one character for ^. Furthermore, if you want to evaluate both operands and not short-circuit, each operator has a single bitwise operator implementation. However, you generally use these operators for bitwise manipulations of data.

1.12. Determining Operator Precedence and Associativity

> You want to change the order in which your expression is evaluated by modifying operator precedence.

Technique

Our rule of thumb is to parenthesize the expression being evaluated to prevent any possible operator-precedence defects. Determining whether one operator has precedence over another requires understanding all precedence rules for the language you are using.

Comments

Operator-precedence rules are one of those things you just have to keep in the back of your head no matter how boring it is. As we said earlier, the rule of thumb is to just use parentheses around certain parts of the expression so that we know the order of evaluation. Parentheses are at the top of the food chain, so to speak, for operator precedence.

Operator precedence isn't entirely a programming concept. Back in grade-school arithmetic, you learned that multiplication and division is performed from left to right through the expression, followed by addition and subtraction using the result of the multiplication and division expressions as new operands. For instance, the expression 2 + 4 × 6 equals 26 because you perform the multiplication first, with a result of 24, followed by the addition of 2. If you want to change the order of this evaluation, use parentheses around the parts of the expression you want to perform first. So if we want to perform the addition followed by the multiplication, we use the expression (2 + 4) × 6 to get a result of 36. Table 1.3 shows the available C# operators and the corresponding precedence and associativity. An operator has precedence over another if it appears higher in the table (closer to the top) than the other. For instance, the == operator has a higher precedence than the & operator. If both operators appear on the same level, then you must refer to the associativity of those operators. If the associativity is left, then the expression with the operator that appears leftmost in the table is evaluated first.

Table 1.3   **C# Operator Precedence and Associativity**

Operators	Associativity
(x), x, y, f(x), a[x], x++, x--, new, typeof, sizeof, checked, unchecked	Left
unary +, unary --, ~, ++x, --x, (type)x	Left
*, /, %	Left
+, --	Left
<<, >>	Left
<, >, <=, >=, is, as	Left
==, !=	Left
&	Left
^	Left
|	Left
&&	Left
||	Left
?: (ternary)	Right
=, *=, /=, %=. +=, --=, <<=, >>=, &=, |=, ^=	Right

1.13. Using `if` Statements

You want your application to perform a certain action based on the result of evaluating an expression.

Technique

Using a combination of relational operations on variables, you can execute a body of code if the expression evaluates to `true` or evaluate a different body of code if not. Use the `if/else` statement to control program flow.

Comments

One of the most widely used conditional statements is the `if/else` statement. The format of an `if/else` statement follows:

```
if( expr )
{
}
else
{
}
```

You read this code as "If `expr` is true, then perform these actions; else, perform these actions." In the previous recipe, you used relational operators to compare values and objects with one another. You can then combine the result of these relational expressions using logical expressions. You use the results of these comparisons within the `if` statement, which is known collectively as a *conditional statement*.

A shorthand way of creating an `if` statement is to use a ternary operator. The format of a ternary operator is

```
(conditional)? true_expression : false_expression
```

As an example, if you want to test whether a variable is equal to a certain number, you write the following:

```
Console.Write(( i==42 )? "Meaning of life" : "I don't know");
```

A common technique is to create multiple `if` statements to further refine the conditional comparisons of variables. For example, the following is perfectly legal and you'll notice that it can perform one of several different actions based on the conditions that are present. Listing 1.6 demonstrates how to create multiple `if` statements.

Listing 1.6   Creating Multiple `if` Statements to Control Several Actions

```
using System;

namespace _13_IfStatement
{
    /// <summary>
    /// Summary description for Class1.
    /// </summary>
    class Class1
    {
        /// <summary>
        /// The main entry point for the application.
        /// </summary>
        [STAThread]
        static void Main(string[] args)
        {
            string input;
            Console.Write( "Enter your name: " );
            input = Console.ReadLine();
            if( input.ToLower() == "jordan" )
            {
                Console.WriteLine( "{0}, have you cleaned " +
                    "your room yet?", input );
            }
            else if( (input.ToLower() == "jake") ||
                    (input.ToLower() == "jonah") )
            {
```

Listing 1.6   **Continued**

```
        Console.WriteLine( "{0}, clean your room!", input );
    }
    else if( input.ToLower() == "mallorie" )
    {
        Console.WriteLine( "{0}, you may do anything you " +
            "want.", input );
    }
    else
    {
        Console.WriteLine( "Sorry {0}, I don't know you",
            input );
    }
}
}
}
```

1.14. Using Looping Control Structures

You need to continuously perform a set of actions a certain number of times or until a certain condition becomes false.

Technique

C# contains several different looping control structures to handle different cases. You use a for statement if you need to run a loop a set number of times. If you need to execute a block of statements while an expression remains true, use a while loop. Choose a do/while statement if you need to execute a block of statements at least once regardless of any pre-existing conditions and then continuously while an expression remains true.

Comments

In the last recipe, you saw how you can use if statements to execute blocks of code based on certain conditions. However, you could only execute that block of code one time. Looping control structures allow you to execute blocks of code several times and stop either when an expression finally evaluates to false or when you explicitly break out of the loop somewhere within the body of the loop using the C# keyword break. Using loops requires care because the conditional statement to test whether the loop should continue might never become false, which means the program gets stuck in an endless loop. All three of the looping statements covered here have the possibility of continuing forever.

You generally use the `for` loop when you want to execute a block of code a certain amount of times. An index variable associated with the loop keeps count of the iterations that have occurred and if you tested it to see whether the loop should finish executing. The `for` statement contains three sections as shown in Listing 1.7. The first part is for initialization. In most cases, you initialize the variable used to control the `for` loop. However, you are free to initialize other variables or even call methods as long as they are separated by commas. The second component of the `for` statement is the conditional expression you want to evaluate. If the expression remains true, the `for` loop body executes. Finally, the last field of the `for` loop is for changing the variables associated with the conditional statement by either incrementing or decrementing the loop counter, for example.

Listing 1.7 **Using a `for` Statement to Loop and Calculate the Factorial of a Number**

```
static void ComputeFactorial()
{
    ulong loopCount = 0;
    ulong factorial = 1;
    Console.Write( "Enter an integer between 1 and 50: " );
    loopCount = UInt64.Parse( Console.ReadLine() );
    for( ulong i = loopCount; i > 0; i-- )
    {
        factorial *= i;
    }
    Console.WriteLine( "{0}! = {1}", loopCount, factorial );
}
```

The `while` and `do/while` statements are quite similar in that both loop while a certain condition holds true. Once that condition evaluates to false, the loop is exited and the next statement following the loop block is executed. The major difference between the two loop structures is that the `do/while` statement's code block is guaranteed to execute at least once. The `while` statement appears at the end of the code block, as shown in Listing 1.8, instead of at the beginning as with the `while` statement.

Listing 1.8 **Using the `do/while` Statement to Control Program Flow**

```
static void NumberGuessGame()
{
    int guess, number, guesses = 0;
    number = new Random((int)DateTime.Now.Ticks).Next( 0, 10 );

    do
    {
        ++guesses;

        Console.Write( "Enter a number between 1 and 10: " );
        guess = Int32.Parse( Console.ReadLine() );
```

Listing 1.8   **Continued**

```
            if( guess < number )
                Console.WriteLine( "Too low. Pick a higher number" );
            else if ( guess > number )
                Console.WriteLine( "Too high. Pick a lower number" );

        } while (guess != number );

        Console.WriteLine( "You are correct and it only took you "+
          "{0} guesses!", guesses );
    }
```

A `while` statement might never run if the condition is always `false` during the execution of a program because the condition is evaluated before the code block is entered. If the initial condition is `false`, then the block is skipped and the program continues after that point. Listing 1.9 shows a `while` loop being used to create a countdown timer.

Listing 1.9   **The `while` Statement**

```
using System;

namespace _14_Looping
{
    class Game
    {
        [STAThread]
        static void Main(string[] args)
        {
            WaitForNewMinute();
            NumberGuessGame();
        }

        static void WaitForNewMinute()
        {
            int sec = -1;

            Console.Write( "The game will start in " );
            while( DateTime.Now.Second != 0 )
            {
                if( sec != DateTime.Now.Second )
                {
                    sec = DateTime.Now.Second;
                    Console.Write( "...{0}", 60-DateTime.Now.Second );
                }
            }
        }
```

Listing 1.9   **Continued**

```
            Console.WriteLine();
        }
      }
}
```

1.15. Breaking Out of a Loop Control Body

You need to repeatedly execute statements in a block but break out of the loop based on a certain event.

Technique

There are two ways to break out of a loop statement in the middle of a loop body. The first is by using the `break` keyword. Using it will break out of the loop entirely, and execution will begin at the statement following your loop block. The second way is to use the `continue` keyword, which will cause your application to skip the rest of the loop body but then reevaluate the loop conditional and possibly enter the loop again.

Comments

Although the `break` and `continue` keywords are rarely used, sometimes they might prove to be the only alternative. As mentioned earlier, use a `break` statement when you are within the loop body and need to exit the loop entirely. You simply exit the loop, and the program continues execution at the statement following the loop body. An example is a modification of the game in Listing 1.9 in which the loop will exit if the user enters a number that is one less than the randomly generated number.

Listing 1.10   **Using the `break` Keyword to Make the Number-Guessing Game a Little Easier**

```
static void NumberGuessGame()
{
    int guess, number, guesses = 0;
    number = new Random((int)DateTime.Now.Ticks).Next( 0, 10 );

    do
    {
        ++guesses;

        Console.Write( "Enter a number between 1 and 10: " );
        guess = Int32.Parse( Console.ReadLine() );
```

Listing 1.10   **Continued**

```
        if( guess-1 == number )
            break;  // close enough

        if( guess < number )
            Console.WriteLine( "Too low. Pick a higher number" );
        else if ( guess > number )
            Console.WriteLine( "Too high. Pick a lower number" );

    } while (guess != number );

    Console.WriteLine( "You are correct and it only took you "+
    "{0} tries!", guesses );
}
```

If you want to instead make the game a little harder, you could set a difficulty value and use the `continue` keyword to bypass the statements that tell the user whether her guess is too high or too low. Yes, using an `if` statement for these cases seems like a more logical choice, which is a reason why we said the `break` and `continue` statements are rarely used.

2

Objects and Components

2.0. Introduction

Procedural or structured programming languages such as C are designed to manipulate data and control program flow through the various functions that are written for an application. Such a language uses a verb metaphor in which the main programming logic is performed through a series of actions on the data. Object-oriented programming languages, on the other hand, still use actions but place the objects at a higher place level. Rather than work within an action- or verb-oriented environment, it uses an object- or noun-based model. So rather than say something like, "Do this action first, and with the result, do this other action," object-oriented programs prefer, "Take this object and tell it to do this action, and based on what that object does, notify a different object so it can react accordingly.

This chapter takes a look at how Visual C# .NET uses object-oriented programming principles coupled with the design and implementation of the .NET Framework to create a rich set of objects that you can create or further expand to solve myriad programming tasks. The first concept to discuss is the cornerstone of objects, the class. Later you'll see how to manipulate the behaviors of these objects to conform and interact with whatever programming problem you face.

2.1. Creating Classes

You want to use a class to design an object to encapsulate its data and behaviors.

Technique

To create a new class using the Visual Studio .NET IDE, click select Project, Add Class (Alt+P,C). In the Name field, change the default filename, which is something similar to

`Class1.cs`, to a more suitable name. The name you put in this field will be the name of the class you want to create.

Comments

Listing 2.1 shows the class that was generated for a `Television` object. Currently, the television is broken because we haven't added any type of behavioral aspects to it; that comes later. One of the first things you'll notice is that the wizard placed the class within the same namespace as the class that was generated for the entry point. For this example, you can leave the namespace as it is, but in the future, you might want to change it to accurately reflect the organizational structure of your project.

Listing 2.1   **Creating the C# Television Class**

```
using System;

namespace _1_Classes
{
    /// <summary>
    /// Summary description for Television.
    /// </summary>
    public class Television
    {
        public Television()
        {
            //
            // TODO: Add constructor logic here
            //
        }
    }
}
```

Following the declaration of the namespace your class belongs to are three lines used for automatic code-report generation, which is covered elsewhere in this book. Next you see the actual class declaration. A simple class definition consists of an access modifier, the `class` keyword, and the name given to the class by the programmer. Access modifiers control the accessibility of classes or who can use the class. In Listing 2.1, the `Television` class is a top-level type, which means that other than the namespace, it is not nested within another type. Therefore, the only access modifiers that are allowed are `public` and `internal`.

Public access to a type means that any code that wants to access that type is free to do so, ignoring code security issues for now, of course. The code that uses this class can be within the same project or even within a different project or assembly.

> **Note**
>
> An assembly in the .NET Framework is a dynamic-link library or executable file that contains a related group of files packaged together for deployment. Each assembly also contains a manifest file, which lists the contents of the assembly. Whenever you build your project, the IDE creates a .NET assembly and its associated manifest file for you.

Internal access to a class only allows projects contained within the same assembly to use that type. Because your entry-point method is contained within the same assembly, marking the class you just created as `internal` will still allow you to work with that class.

Classes can be nested, which means that you are free to declare another class type within the body of your outer class declaration. Because this new class isn't a top-level type, you have many more choices to use for access modifiers. To determine which access modifiers are available for a given class, select the class in the Class View window. If you cannot find the Class View window, which by default is on the right side of the Visual Studio .NET IDE, select View, Class View from the main menu or by using the Ctrl+Shift+C keyboard shortcut. Once you click on the class name, you see a list of available access modifiers for this class by expanding the Access property drop-down box in the Properties window, as shown in Figure 2.1. Furthermore, Table 2.1 lists the available access modifiers as well as the level to which access is granted for a nested type.

Table 2.1   **Accessibility Modifiers for Nested Types**

Access	Access Permissions
public	No restrictions on who uses the class.
protected	Only classes that derive from the containing class may use the nested class.
private	The containing class has exclusive access to the nested class.
internal	Only code within the same assembly may use the nested class.
protected internal	All code within the same assembly or any class within an external assembly that derives from the containing class may use the nested class.

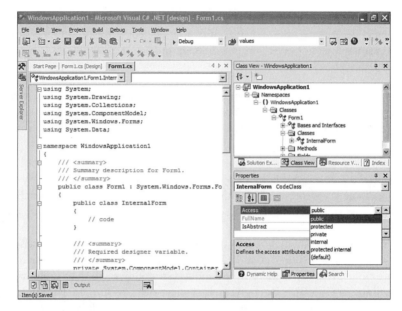

Figure 2.1   You can view and change any class properties by using the
Properties window.

2.2. Defining Class Fields

You want to add a field to your class.

Technique

Right-click on the class name within the Class View window (Ctrl+Shift+C). Select
Add Field (Alt+P,L). In the Add Field dialog box, set the desired access level using Table
2.1 as a guide. Select the data type and name of your field. Additionally, if your field
needs to be static or constant, select the appropriate field modifier radio button.

Comments

A *field* is simply a variable within your class that is available to store a value of a certain
data type. In the past, a field has been traditionally called a *variable*, so we tend to inter-
change the two terms, but the semantics are still the same.

   Fields are useful for internal state information about your object. One of the good
programming practice rules to follow when designing a class is to use data encapsulation
by never exposing internal class variables with a public access modifier. Take care when
designing your class and specifically adding fields to make sure you never allow external
clients who are using your class to modify a member variable. Later in this chapter, you'll

see different ways you can allow clients to change member variables without giving them access to the variable itself, thereby allowing you to first validate that the data they want to send is valid and will not disrupt the current state of your object.

A field can be any data type. You might have noticed that when you created the field using the Add Field dialog, the data type drop-down list contained the C# built-in value types. This list does not contain any of your project's user-defined value types or any other classes. If you need to use a data type not listed in the drop-down list, you have to change the wizard-generated code after you create the field or simply write out the whole declaration yourself to save time.

When creating a field, you can choose to add an access modifier. The `static` access modifier designates that a member variable belongs to the type itself rather than a specific instance of an object. If the value of a static variable is changed, it changes for every instance of the class currently in existence. Nonstatic member fields within a specific instance are simply copies of the type's member fields, whereas a static field is shared across all instances of that type.

A `const` modifier denotes that a field is constant throughout the lifetime of that instance. It cannot be modified. Furthermore, you must define a constant using a value type so that it can be evaluated at compile time. The only exception to this rule is that you can use a string object as a constant.

2.3. Constructing Class Methods

You want to add a new method to your class.

Technique

Select the class within the Class View window and click on Project, Add Method (Alt+P, M). Specify the correct access modifier, return type, and name of the method in the dialog. For each parameter in the method, set any applicable parameter modifiers, such as the type and name of the parameter. Click on the Add button to add the parameter to the parameter list. Finally, click the check box for any method modifier you need.

Comments

Adding a new method to a class can be quite involved given the sheer number of options you have available to you. The required elements of a method include the return type, the name of the element, and a parameter list, which can be empty if your method doesn't require them. All of the other fields in the Add Method dialog are optional, but it is important to understand how they affect the behavior of your method.

Looking at the available method modifiers, you can see the same `static` keyword that you used for fields earlier. Although the effect of creating a static method isn't as noticeable as a static field, meaning that no value is changed as a result of accessing it directly, it still designates the field as a member of the type and not a direct instance of a class. The semantics of the `static` keyword are the same, whereas the behavior is slightly different.

`extern` designates that the method is defined elsewhere and not within the class itself. It is primarily used to interact with system DLLs in conjunction with the `DllImport` attribute.

The `virtual` keyword figures in class inheritance, which is covered later in this chapter. A virtual method means that the method can have its behavior changed by overriding it in a derived class. In other words, if someone wants to change how a class works, he can use the class you created as a base and redefine any methods that are declared virtual. Furthermore, when you declare a method using the `override` modifier, you are redefining a method that was declared `virtual` in the base class you are deriving from. You might in fact hide this overridden method from the person using your derived class by using the `new` modifier. If you do so, the base class's method will be called rather than the overridden method unless the client who uses the derived class fully qualifies the method name with the derived class name.

The method itself can also specify modifiers on each parameter. By default, a value parameter is passed by value, which means a copy is created and placed on the stack. Any changes that your method makes to that value do not affect the original instance that was passed because you are only working with a copy of that variable. If you use the `ref` modifier on a parameter, any changes to that parameter change the variable that the client passed to the method. In Listing 2.2, you can see two versions of a method. The first version does not contain the `ref` modifier on the parameter, so any changes to that parameter do not affect the original variable. In the second version, however, the original variable changes.

Listing 2.2   **Reflecting Parameter Changes by Using the `ref` Modifier**

```
namespace _3_Methods
{
    public class Television
    {
        // current channel tv is set to
        private static int channel = 2;
        private const int maxChannels = 200;

        // changes the channel to a specified channel
        public bool ChangeChannel(int newChannel)
        {
            // only supports 200 channels
            if( newChannel > maxChannels )
                return false;

            // set private channel variable
            channel = newChannel;
```

Listing 2.2   **Continued**

```
            return true;
        }

        public void GetChannel( int param )
        {
            param = channel;
        }

        // overloaded version. Note ref parameter
        public void GetChannel( ref int param )
        {
            param = channel;
        }
    }

    class Class1
    {
      [STAThread]
      static void Main(string[] args)
      {
            // create Television object
            Television tv = new Television();
            int refChan = 0;
            int chan = 0;

            // chan remains 0 after call
            tv.GetChannel( chan );

            // refChan's value will change
            tv.GetChannel( ref refChan );

            Console.WriteLine( "noref={0} ref={1}", chan, refChan );
      }
    }
}
```

The out modifier is similar to ref. It is also passed by reference rather than value, which means it also changes the original value passed into it. The key difference is that you do not use it to pass data from the client to the method, which means there is no guarantee that the parameter is initialized when it is used within the called method. If you pass a variable using the ref keyword without first initializing it to a value, the compiler generates an error. However, if the parameter is an out parameter, then you need not initialize it. Using out is advantageous as it allows a method to return multiple values because you might have more than one out parameter in a single method.

2.4. Instantiating and Using Objects

You want to use a class and access its methods.

Technique

Define a variable with the name of the class you want to use as the type name. To create a new instance of that class, use the new keyword followed by the name of the class and a parentheses parameter list. Assign the result of this to your original variable.

Once an object is created, you are free to call its public methods and properties, as shown in Listing 2.3. You do so using the dot (.) operator on the object followed by the name of the method and its associated parameters. However, if the method you want to call is a static method, recall that that method belongs to the type and not a specific instance of an object. Therefore, you must use the dot operator on the name of the class rather than the variable name of the object.

Listing 2.3   **Creating and Using a Class**

```
using System;

namespace _4_UsingObjects
{
    public class Television
    {
        public Television(){}

        private int channel = 2;
        private static bool on = false;

        // increments channel if tv is on
        public void ChannelUp()
        {
            if( on == false )
                return;

            ++channel;
        }

        // decrements channel if tv is on
        public void ChannelDown()
        {
            if( on == false )
                return;

            --channel;
        }
```

Listing 2.3   **Continued**

```csharp
        // gets or set current channel
        public int Channel
        {
            get
            {
                return channel;
            }
            set
            {
                channel = value;
            }
        }

        // get status of TV and allows you to
        // turn it on or off
        public static bool On
        {
            get
            {
                return on;
            }
            set
            {
                on = value;
            }
        }
    }
    class Class1
    {
        [STAThread]
        static void Main(string[] args)
        {
            Television tv = new Television();

            // turn television on
            Television.On = true;

            // change channel
            tv.Channel = 42;
            Console.WriteLine( "Channel = {0}", tv.Channel );

            tv.ChannelUp();
            Console.WriteLine( "Channel = {0}", tv.Channel );

            tv.ChannelDown();
```

Listing 2.3   **Continued**

```
            Console.WriteLine( "Channel = {0}", tv.Channel );
        }
    }
}
```

Comments

If you have been following the code for this book, you might have already noticed how to instantiate a new object using the new keyword. However, a few things have gone unsaid up to this point.

When you use the new keyword to create a new instance of a class, the class name following the keyword is not just the name of the class but also signifies which constructor you want to call to create that class. Because overloaded constructors appear later in this chapter, you have been using the default constructor, which does not have any additional parameters. With an overloaded constructor, you pass in additional values to initialize the object.

2.5. Overloading Operators

Rather than use methods, you want clients using your class to manipulate your object using built-in C# operators.

Technique

Create a new public static method in your class with any return type. For the method name, use the operator keyword followed by the actual operator you want to overload. Finally, for a unary operator, create a single parameter of a specified type; for a binary operator, create two parameters of a specified type; and for a conversion operator, create a parameter of the type you want to convert from. Listing 2.4 shows how to overload the unary operator ++, which causes an internal member variable to be incremented.

Listing 2.4   **Overloading the ++ Operator to Increment an Internal Member Variable**

```
public class Television
{
    /// <summary>
    /// current channel tv is set to
    /// </summary>
    private static int channel = 2;
    private const int maxChannels = 200;

    /// <summary>
```

Listing 2.4   **Continued**

```
/// changes the channel to a specified channel
/// </summary>
public bool ChangeChannel(int newChannel)
{
    if( newChannel > maxChannels )
        return false;

    channel = newChannel;

    return true;
}

public static Television operator ++( Television tv )
{
    tv.ChangeChannel(++channel);
    return tv;
}

public int GetChannel()
{
    return channel;
}

static void Main(string[] args)
{
    Television tv = new Television();

    for( int i = 0; i < 20; ++i )
    {
        tv++;
        Console.WriteLine( "{0}", tv.GetChannel());
    }
}
}
```

Comments

Operator overloading allows users of your code to interact with the objects it creates by using a syntax that's familiar to them and undoubtedly more natural. However, one of the main design tenants with operator overloading is to ensure that the operator you are overloading makes sense and feels natural. In Listing 2.4, choosing to overload the ++ operator for the Television class is probably not a good idea. Ambiguity is the most common design error when overloading an operator. Although the intention was to change the channel when using the increment operator, it's not clear because you are incrementing the actual television object and not a channel object for instance. However, because the listing was simply for illustration purposes, this sort of design is fine.

There are three available types of operators that you can overload, each with its own set of actual defined operators. Unary operators are designed to work with a single operand. They include the negation operator (-), the increment and decrement operators (++ and --), and the logical negation operator (!). Because there is only a single operand, the overload function only needs one parameter, whose type is the same as the operand the operator is applied to. In the operator overload function in Listing 2.4, you see that a `Television` object is passed as the parameter, which then allows someone to apply the increment operator to any `Television` object. Determining the method signature for unary operators is simple because all unary operators must contain the same type for its return value and single parameter. Furthermore, this type is the same as the containing class, which is overloading the operator.

Binary operators such as operators for addition and subtraction and relational and logical operators, to name a few, must contain two parameters in their method signature. Furthermore, at least one of these parameters must be the same type as that of the containing class. The return value, on the other hand, can be any type. When using binary operators, you must ensure that your object still obeys commutative laws. If you add your object to some number, you should get the same result if you reverse the order of the operands and instead add some number to your object. Using the `Television` class of Listing 2.4, you would need to create two methods for the addition operator. The signatures for these would be the following:

```
static Television operator + ( Television operand1, int operand2 );
static Television operator + (int operand1, Television operand2 );
```

The last operator type is the conversion operator. You use it when converting a value from one type to another, and it consists of the implicit and explicit conversion operators. An *implicit* conversion means that the conversion occurs transparently from the programmer performing the conversion. An *explicit* conversion requires a cast of the original type using the resultant type to convert to. Both of these operators require that the same type as the containing class be either the type you are converting from or the type you are converting to. The format is a little different than that of previous operator overloading methods. Instead of specifying a result type following the `static` keyword, you specify either `implicit` or `explicit`, depending on which type conversion you want to perform. Also, instead of using a predefined operator following the `operator` keyword, you use the type name of the type you want to convert to. To implicitly convert an integer to a new `Television` type from Listing 2.4, the implicit conversion function would be

```
public static implicit operator Television( int from )
{
    Television tv = new Television();
    tv.ChangeChannel( from );
    return tv;
}
```

By doing this conversion, you are enabling someone to use the following syntax on a Television object:

```
static void Main(string[] args)
{
    Television tv = 5;
}
```

2.6. Overloading Class Constructors

You want to change the way an object is created by overloading its default constructor.

Technique

Create a new method within your class with public access that has the same name as your class and at least one parameter. You must create the method within the source code window because the Add Method dialog does not let you create overloaded constructors.

Comments

Overloaded constructors offer a convenient way for users of a class to initialize an object without having to call a number of methods or properties after the class is created. Overloading a constructor is similar to overloading any other method with the exception, of course, being the lack of a return value. You can easily distinguish different constructors within a class by noting their different signatures.

You are free to have as many constructors for a class as you want. However, you can also have no callable constructors for a class by creating a private constructor, which prevents any object instance being created from that class. You might find it advantageous if your class, for example, emulates a data type and only contains static methods. In this instance, by using a private access modifier on the constructor, you only allow any client to gain access to the class through the type and not an instance of an object. If you want the benefit of having a constructor to initialize internal data within your class, while still preventing instances of the class from being created, you can create a static constructor. A *static* constructor is called before any instance of the class is created and before any static members are accessed. Any client can call a static method within the class, and the Common Language Runtime (CLR) first calls the static constructor to allow you to perform any initialization steps. To declare a static constructor, use the `static` keyword followed by the name of the class. A static constructor does not contain an access modifier, and it also does not contain any parameters because it is called by the CLR and never directly from a client.

You might need to call other constructors from within a different constructor to ensure member variables are properly initialized. Listing 2.5 contains the Television class used throughout this chapter. You can see that in addition to a default constructor, an overloaded constructor initializes the private channel member variable. You can also see how the channel member variable can be initialized if you use the default constructor by calling the overloaded constructor with the default channel for the class.

Listing 2.5   **Overloading a Constructor Is Similar to Overloading a Regular Class Method**

```
using System;

namespace _6_Constructors
{
    public class Television
    {
        public Television() : this(2)
        {
        }

        public Television( int initChannel )
        {
            channel = initChannel;
        }
        private int channel;

        public int GetChannel()
        {
            return channel;
        }
    }
    class Class1
    {
        [STAThread]
        static void Main(string[] args)
        {
            Television tv = new Television(42);
            Console.WriteLine( "TV Channel = {0}", tv.GetChannel() );
        }
    }
}
```

2.7. Constructing Class Properties

You want to allow access to a member variable from client code without allowing direct access.

Technique

Right-click on the class you want to add the property to in the Class View window, and select Add, Add Property. Select the correct access modifier and data type and enter a property name in the corresponding fields in the Add Property dialog. If you want read-only access to the property, select the `get` accessor radio button while the `set` accessor allows write access. Choose one or both as appropriate. You might also make the property `static` or `virtual` by clicking the available property modifiers.

Comments

Properties are designed to properly enforce data hiding through encapsulation. If you were to just give public access to a member variable, the stability of your object could be compromised because you don't have control over the values placed in that variable. By using a class property, it appears that you are giving transparent access to a class member variable when in actuality you are routing the request to a member accessor method. Within this method, you can validate the value being assigned to a private member variable.

There can be two methods associated with any given property. If you are providing a read-only property accessor, then you are using a `get` method. Likewise, if you are allowing the variable to change based on the value being passed in, you are using a `set` method. You are free to do anything within these methods, which traditionally is to validate the data being passed in and to set or return the value of a private member variable.

The `get` method, as shown in Listing 2.6, simply returns the value of a private member variable. Because this method requires no data validation, the method body is simply a `return` statement.

The `set` method contains an implicit parameter that corresponds to the value of the code accessing the property used in the assignment statement. This parameter is named `value`. In Listing 2.6, you can see the `set` method for the `Television` class first validates that the value passed in isn't larger than the number of available channels and finally sets the internal channel member variable to the implicit parameter value.

Listing 2.6 **Defining Properties to Provide Validating Member Variable Access Using Data-Hiding Techniques**

```
using System;

namespace _6_Properties
{
```

Listing 2.6   **Continued**

```
public class Television
{
    private int channel = 1;

    // this tv only has 255 channels
    private const int maxChannels = 255;

    // changes the channel on the tv
    public int Channel
    {
        get
        {
            return channel;
        }
        set
        {
            // check value's range
            if( value > maxChannels )
                return;

            // set private variable
            channel = value;
        }
    }
}
}
```

2.8. Inheriting from Other Classes

You want to use a new class that is similar to another class and inherit some of the original base class's implementation.

Technique

Following the class declaration, insert a colon followed by the name of the class whose behavior your new class will inherit. Finally, override any of the base class's virtual functions to change any behaviors to more appropriately model your class. Any method in the base class that can be overridden should be marked `virtual`. Likewise, when overriding a method, use the `override` keyword in the derived class, as shown in Listing 2.7.

Listing 2.7   **Using Inheritance to Define a Related Set of Objects**

```
using System;

namespace _8_Inheritance
{
    // base class definition
    public class MediaDevice
    {
        protected bool on = false;

        virtual public void TurnOn()
        {
            on = true;
        }

        virtual public void TurnOff()
        {
            on = false;
        }
    }

    public class Television : MediaDevice
    {
        private int curChannel = -1;

        // turn on tv and set to channel 2
        public override void TurnOn()
        {
            base.TurnOn ();
            curChannel = 2;
        }

        // turns tv off
        public override void TurnOff()
        {
            base.TurnOff ();
            curChannel = -1;
        }

        public int Channel
        {
            get
            {
                return curChannel;
            }
            set
```

Listing 2.6   **Continued**

```
            {
                // can't change channel if tv is off
                if( on == false )
                    return;

                curChannel = value;
            }
        }
    }
    class Class1
    {
        [STAThread]
        static void Main(string[] args)
        {
            Television tv = new Television();
            tv.TurnOn();
            tv.TurnOff();
        }
    }
}
```

Comments

Inheritance is a fundamental feature of Visual C# .NET and appears everywhere within the .NET Framework. It allows you to extend the capabilities of an object by inheriting the implementation of some other base object. Object-oriented programming uses inheritance to further refine an abstract object by defining more specialized objects until a complete hierarchical system of objects is created. The .NET Framework, for instance, defines a System.Object type, which in itself is a rather abstract entity. Every object within the Framework is ultimately derived from this single object. When designing a system of objects, find the object traits that are the same throughout and create a base class from those traits. Continue organizing new objects based on this base class and further extract similar information until what you have left is a collection of derived objects that share the same commonality but are specialized based on their implementation details.

Listing 2.7 demonstrates creating a base class that you can use as a stepping stone to more specialized classes. A MediaDevice is something that provides some sort of electronic information delivery. It can be a radio; a computer; or, as shown in Listing 2.7, a television. Within the MediaDevice class, you can see two methods both marked with the virtual keyword. By using this keyword, you are allowing a derived class to override the implementation of this method. This step allows the more specialized class to further refine and add additional functionality for that method. The Television class uses the TurnOn and TurnOff methods to control the current state of the channel variable.

To override a virtual method, create a method with the same signature as the method you are overriding, but replace the `virtual` keyword with the `override` keyword. Furthermore, if you also need to call the base class's implementation of an overridden method, you can use the implied `base` member that exists within your class. Whereas the `this` keyword represents the current instance of a class, the `base` keyword represents the current instance of the base class a class is derived from.

A simple way to override a method is to begin typing the method signature within the source code window. When you finish the `override` keyword, an IntelliSense window lists all the possible virtual methods within the base class that you can override. Using the arrow keys, select the method you want to override and press Enter. The method signature will then be created, and a call to the base class implementation will be added to the method body.

2.9. Preventing Object Inheritance

You don't want your class to be used as a base class for other classes.

Technique

Use the `sealed` keyword within the declaration of your class:

```
public sealed class HDTV : Television
{
}
```

Comments

When you seal a class, no other class can derive from it. The most common reason you might want to consider doing so is if you feel the class is as specialized as you can get within the hierarchy of derived classes that you created. For instance, if I expanded the `MediaDevice` derivation further and created an `HDTV` class that derives from `Television`, then `HDTV` would be a good candidate for a sealed class.

You might be thinking that sealing a class doesn't add much value because all it does is prevent derivation, which itself limits the expandability of a class. Sealing a class also carries with it the added benefit of performance optimization. The runtime can call any of the virtual functions of that object using nonvirtual function-call techniques. However, if you disassemble an assembly containing a sealed class, you will notice that even though you call methods contained within the sealed class, the intermediate language (IL) instruction to call a virtual function, `callvirt`, is still emitted. The instruction for a nonvirtual method is the `call` IL instruction. Even though it sounds like it, there is no contradiction here. When the IL is just-in-time (JIT) compiled, which happens when the assembly is first executed, the `callvirt` instruction is optimized to call the method using a nonvirtual call. The only performance hit, which itself is negligible, is a simple check to ensure the `this` pointer is not null.

2.10. String Representation of Objects

When creating a new class, you want to add the ability to return a readable string that represents your object.

Technique

Create an overridden method named ToString that returns a string data type, as shown in Listing 2.8.

Listing 2.8 **Overriding the** ToString **Method to Associate Your Class with a Human-Readable String**

```
using System;

namespace _10_ObjectString
{
    public class MediaDevice
    {
        public override string ToString()
        {
            return "a generic media device";
        }
    }
    public class Television : MediaDevice
    {
        public override string ToString()
        {
            return "a Television";
        }
    }
    class Class1
    {
        [STAThread]
     static void Main(string[] args)
     {
         Television tv = new Television();
            MediaDevice md = new MediaDevice();
            MediaDevice mdtv = (MediaDevice) new Television();

            Console.WriteLine( "tv is {0}\nmd is {1}\nmdtv is {2}", tv.ToString(),
                md.ToString(), mdtv.ToString() );
        }
    }
}
```

Comments

Every class that you create in Visual C# .NET is transparently derived from the `System.Object` class, regardless of any other base class you derive from. The class inherits the method from the `Object` class. `ToString` is a method in the `System.Object` class used to return a human-readable string that represents whatever object the method is called on. For instance, within the `Int32` class, which is a class that represents a 32-bit integer, the `ToString` method converts the internal integer member variable to a string and returns that conversion result. It is up to you to determine how you want to define the `ToString` method for your class. If you do not override this method, the default method simply returns the namespace-qualified name of the class.

2.11. Abstract Classes and Interfaces

> You want to create a set of methods and properties that a derived class must implement.

Technique

To enforce the requirement that only some methods or properties need to be implemented, add the `abstract` keyword to the class and each method and property that must be implemented as shown in the `VolumeLevel` property in Listing 2.9.

Listing 2.9   **Abstract Classes Requiring Implementation public abstract class**
`MediaDevice`

```
{
    bool on = false;
    virtual public void TurnOn()
    {
        on = true;
    }

    virtual public void TurnOff()
    {
        on = false;
    }

    public abstract int VolumeLevel
    {
        get;
        set;
    }
}
```

If all methods and properties need to be implemented by a derived class, design and create an interface declaration. An *interface declaration* is similar to a class declaration, but instead of using the `class` keyword, use the `interface` keyword as shown in Listing 2.10. Furthermore, methods and properties cannot use accessibility modifiers and cannot contain a definition.

Listing 2.10   **Interfaces Are Purely Abstract**

```
public interface IMediaDevice
{
    void TurnOn();
    void TurnOff();
    int VolumeLevel
    {
        get;
        set;
    }
}
```

Comments

When you derive from a base class, you are not required to override any of the virtual methods of the base class. A derived class can expand on the functionality of a base class while still defaulting to the base-class implementation of virtual methods and properties. When designing a base class, you might need to create a requirement that derived classes must contain an definition of some or all of the methods or properties of a base class. Depending on the level of requirement, you can do so using an abstract base class or using an interface.

An *abstract* class is a class that contains some methods or properties that must be implemented by a derived class. In Listing 2.9, you can see that the `MediaDevice` class is an abstract class. It contains an implementation for the two methods `TurnOn` and `TurnOff`. A class that derives from this class is not required to override these methods. However, the class contains an abstract property named `VolumeLevel`. Because this property is abstract, there is no definition for it in the base class, and any derived class must implement it.

One thing to understand when creating an abstract base class is that it cannot be instantiated itself. In other words, you cannot use the `new` keyword to create an object of that type. Because an abstract method does not contain a definition, attempting to call that method would undoubtedly have undesirable results. It is still possible to create a reference to an abstract base class by instantiating a derived class and casting that object to the same type as the base class. Calling the abstract method on this base class, however, will result in a call to the method implementation of the derived class due to polymorphism.

```
MediaDevice md = (MediaDevice) new Radio();
md.VolumeLevel = 2;
```

You use interfaces when you require that all methods and properties be overridden. You can almost think of an interface as a contract. If a class derives from an interface, it must honor the contract and implement all methods and properties. One area where you will see interfaces pervasively within the .NET Framework is the *collection* class. A class that wants to act as a container or collection of objects must support the required collection interfaces. This requirement allows someone unfamiliar with the actual class itself to still access it using the known collection-interface methods.

Another area where interfaces play a major role is in various plug-ins for different technologies. If you want to create an application that allows plug-ins to extend the behavior of your application, you can require that anyone wanting to create a plug-in must implement certain interfaces. You can then access those plug-ins using an API that you know about, regardless of the implementation details.

There are two ways to implement an interface with a class. The first is when you initially create the class using the Add Class dialog. As shown in Figure 2.2, you can choose to have your class implement an interface by selecting the Inheritance tab within the dialog and selecting the interface you want to inherit. Unfortunately, using this method to implement an interface can be cumbersome because the generated code does not contain stubs of the methods you must override. Immediately attempting to compile your code after creating a class will result in an error for each method or property that is not implemented from the interface.

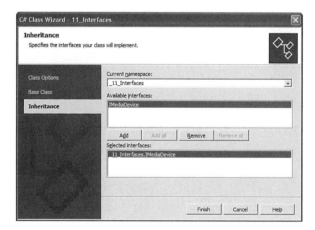

Figure 2.2   Select the Inheritance tab within the Add Class dialog to implement an interface.

You might find it easier to simply use the source code window after you create your class to implement an interface. The reason is that IntelliSense is able to create the necessary method and property stubs that you must implement. This feature can be a real time-saver for large interfaces. Figure 2.3 shows the result of using the source code window to implement an interface, and Listing 2.11 shows the result of the generated code.

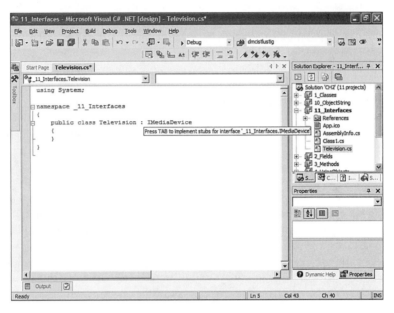

Figure 2.3 Using the source code window to implement an interface allows you to easily create the method and property signatures you must implement for an interface.

Listing 2.11 **Stubs Can Be Generated Automatically**

```
using System;

namespace _11_Interfaces
{
    public class Television : IMediaDevice
    {
        #region IMediaDevice Members
        public void TurnOn()
        {
            // TODO:  Add Television.TurnOn implementation
        }

        public void TurnOff()
        {
            // TODO:  Add Television.TurnOff implementation
        }

        public int VolumeLevel
```

Listing 2.11   **Continued**

```
    {
        get
        {
            // TODO:  Add Television.VolumeLevel getter implementation
            return 0;
        }
        set
        {
            // TODO:  Add Television.VolumeLevel setter implementation
        }
    }
    #endregion
    }
}
```

2.12. Multiple Inheritance Using Interfaces

You want your class to inherit more than one interface.

Technique

For each interface you want your class to support, add the interface name to the derivation list of your class, separating it from the other interfaces with a comma.

Comments

The C# specification states that classes must use single inheritance when deriving from base classes. You can only specify a single base class when creating a new class. However, you are free to multiply inherit from interfaces, meaning you can inherit from several. If you recall from the earlier discussion, an interface by itself does not contain an implementation. It is simply a declaration of methods and properties that a class must define.

With multiple interface inheritance, it is possible to implement two interfaces that contain a method with the same signature. Although it might be rare, it can happen. If this occurs, you have one of two choices. You can simply create a single method that will then be called regardless of the type of the reference to your class a client is using. Listing 2.12 demonstrates how to do so. It declares 2 interfaces, IVolumeControl and IChannelControl, and each of them contain the same property, Current. The Radio class implements these two interfaces, and any time the Current property is accessed, it calls the only Current property defined within the Radio class, regardless of which interface the client is referencing.

Listing 2.12   **Declaring 2 Interfaces,** `IVolumeControl` **and** `IChannelControl`

```
using System;

namespace _12_MultipleInterfaces
{
    interface IVolumeControl
    {
        int Current
        {
            get;
        }
    }

    interface IChannelControl
    {
        int Current
        {
            get;
        }
    }

    public class Radio : IVolumeControl, IChannelControl
    {
        public int Current
        {
            get
            {
                return 5;
            }
        }
    }

    class Class1
    {
        [STAThread]
        static void Main(string[] args)
        {
            // create new radio object and get interface
            IChannelControl radioDial = (IChannelControl) new Radio();

            // output current radio's channel
            Console.WriteLine( "Current Channel = {0}", radioDial.Current );
        }
    }
}
```

You can also create two methods to separate the implementations. To do so, remove the accessibility modifier from each method signature and qualify the name of the method with the name of the interface to which it belongs. You can see this step in Listing 2.13. A client using this class will then have to cast the object instance to one of the interface types to correctly call the property methods.

Listing 2.13   **Implementing Multiple Interfaces**

```
using System;

namespace _12_MultipleInterfaces
{
    // interface declarations omitted

    public class Radio : IVolumeControl, IChannelControl
    {
        int IVolumeControl.Current
        {
            get
            {
                return 1;
            }
        }
        int IChannelControl.Current
        {
            get
            {
                return 2;
            }
        }
    }

    class Class1
    {
        [STAThread]
        static void Main(string[] args)
        {
            IChannelControl radioDial = (IChannelControl) new Radio();
            Console.WriteLine( "Current Channel = {0}", radioDial.Current );
        }
    }
}
```

2.13. Creating and Using Class Libraries

You want to create a class and package it within a dynamic-link library rather than an executable file.

Technique

Create a new project by choosing New, Project from the main menu. Select Visual C# Projects from the list of project types. In the list of project templates, select the Class Library template.

To use an object within a class library, right-click on the client project name in Solution Explorer and select Add Reference. Select the .NET tab in the Add Reference dialog, shown in Figure 2.4, and then click the Browse button. Locate the class library that contains the classes you want to use.

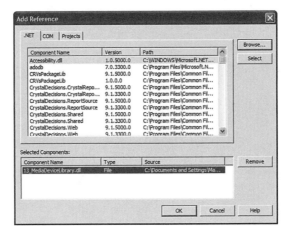

Figure 2.4   To use a type defined in a class library, you must create a reference to it in your project.

Comments

Class libraries allow you to put into a single shared package code that many different modules can use. By itself, a class library cannot run because it is not an executable. It is simply a container of resources and types that can be referenced. The .NET Framework contains several class libraries known collectively as the FCL, or Framework Class Libraries. Up to this point in the book, you have been using types defined within the System library, which is contained within the System.dll assembly. The .NET Framework has many more class libraries, which you will no doubt be familiar with by the end of this book.

3

Strings and Regular Expressions

3.0. Introduction

It would be very rare to create an entire application without using a single string. Strings help make sense of the seemingly random jumble of binary data that applications use to accomplish a task. They appear in all facets of application development from the smallest system utility to large enterprise services. Their value is so apparent that more and more connected systems are leaning toward string data within their communication protocols by utilizing the Extensible Markup Language (XML) rather than the more cumbersome traditional transmission of large binary data. This book uses strings extensively to examine the internal contents of variables and the results of program flow using Framework Class Libraries (FCL) methods such as `Console.WriteLine` and `MessageBox.Show`.

In this chapter, you will learn how to take advantage of the rich support for strings within the .NET Framework and the C# language. Coverage includes ways to manipulate string contents, programmatically inspect strings and their character attributes, and optimize performance when working with string objects. Furthermore, this chapter uncovers the power of regular expressions and how they allow you to effectively parse and manipulate string data. After reading this chapter, you will be able to use regular expressions in a variety of different situations where their value is apparent.

3.1. Creating and Using String Objects

You want to create and manipulate string data within your application.

Technique

The C# language, knowing the importance of string data, contains a `string` keyword that simulates the behavior of a value data type. To create a string, declare a variable using the `string` keyword. You can use the assignment operator to initialize the variable using a static string or with an already initialized string variable.

```
string string1 = "This is a string";
string string2 = string1;
```

To gain more control over string initialization, declare a variable using the `System.String` data type and create a new instance using the `new` keyword. The `System.String` class contains several constructors that you can use to initialize the string value. For instance, to create a new string that is a small subset of an existing string, use the overloaded constructor, which takes a character array and two integers denoting the beginning index and the number of characters from that index to copy:

```
class Class1
{
    [STAThread]
    static void Main(string[] args)
    {
        string string1 = "Field1, Field2";
        System.String string2 = new System.String( string1.ToCharArray(), 8, 6 );

        Console.WriteLine( string2 );

    }
}
```

Finally, if you know a string will be intensively manipulated, use the `System.Text.StringBuilder` class. Creating a variable of this data type is similar to using the `System.String` class, and it contains several constructors to initialize the internal string value. The key internal difference between a regular string object and a `StringBuilder` lies in performance. Whenever a string is manipulated in some manner, a new object has to be created, which subsequently causes the old object to be marked for deletion by the garbage collector. For a string that undergoes several transformations, the performance hit associated with frequent object creation and deletions can be great. The `StringBuilder` class, on the other hand, maintains an internal buffer, which expands to make room for more string data should the need arise, thereby decreasing frequent object activations.

Comments

There is no recommendation on whether you use the `string` keyword or the `System.String` class. The `string` keyword is simply an alias for this class, so it is all a matter of taste. We prefer using the `string` keyword, but this preference is purely aesthetic. For this reason, we simply refer to the `System.String` class as the `string` class or data type.

The `string` class contains many methods, both instance and static, for manipulating strings. If you want to compare strings, you can use the `Compare` method. If you are just testing for equality, then you might want to use the overloaded equality operator (==). However, the Compare method returns an integer instead of Boolean value denoting how the two strings differ. If the return value is 0, then the strings are equal. If the return value is greater than 0, as shown in Listing 3.1, then the first operand is greater alphabetically than the second operand. If the return value is less than 0, the opposite is true. When a string is said to be alphabetically greater or lower than another, each character reading from left to right from both strings is compared using its equivalent ASCII value.

Listing 3.1   **Using the Compare Method in the** String **Class**

```
using System;

namespace _1_UsingStrings
{
    class Class1
    {
        [STAThread]
        static void Main(string[] args)
        {
            string string1 = "";
            String string2 = "";

            Console.Write( "Enter string 1: " );
            string1 = Console.ReadLine();
            Console.Write( "Enter string 2: " );
            string2 = Console.ReadLine();

            // string and String are the same types
            Console.WriteLine( "string1 is a {0}\nstring2 is a {1}",
                string1.GetType().FullName, string2.GetType().FullName );

            CompareStrings( string1, string2 );
        }

        public static void CompareStrings( string str1, string str2 )
        {
            int compare = String.Compare( str1, str2 );

            if( compare == 0 )
            {
                Console.WriteLine( "The strings {0} and {1} are the same.\n",
                    str1, str2 );
            }
            else if( compare < 0 )
            {
                Console.WriteLine( "The string {0} is less than {1}",
                    str1, str2 );
```

Listing 3.1   **Continued**

```
            }
            else if( compare > 0 )
            {
                Console.WriteLine( "The string {0} is greater than {1}",
                    str1, str2 );
            }
        }
    }
}
```

As mentioned earlier, the `string` class contains both instance and static methods. Sometimes you have no choice about whether to use an instance or static method. However, a few of the instance methods contain a static version as well. Because calling a static method is a nonvirtual function call, you see performance gains if you use this version. An example where you might see both instance and static versions appears in Listing 3.1. The string comparison uses the static `Compare` method. You can also do so using the nonstatic `CompareTo` method using one of the string instances passed in as parameters. In most cases, the performance gain is negligible, but if an application needs to repeatedly call these methods, you might want to consider using the static over the non-static method.

The `string` class is immutable. Once a string is created, it cannot be manipulated. Methods within the `string` class that modify the original string instance actually destroy the string and create a new string object rather than manipulate the original string instance. It can be expensive to repeatedly call `string` methods if new objects are created and destroyed continuously. To solve this, the .NET Framework contains a `StringBuilder` class contained within the `System.Text` namespace, which is explained later in this chapter.

3.2. Formatting Strings

Given one or more objects, you want to create a single formatted string representation.

Technique

You can format strings using numeric and picture formatting within `String.Format` or within any method that uses string-formatting techniques for parameters such as `Console.WriteLine`.

Comments

The `string` class as well as a few other methods within the .NET Framework allow you to format strings to present them in a more ordered and readable format. Up to this point in the book, we used basic formatting when calling the `Console.WriteLine` method. The first parameter to `Console.WriteLine` is the format specifier string. This string controls how the remaining parameters to the method should appear when displayed. You use placeholders within the format string to insert the value of a variable. This placeholder uses the syntax {n} where n is the index in the parameter list following the format specifier. Take the following line of code, for instance:

```
Console.WriteLine( "x={0}, y={1}, {0}+{1}={2}", x, y, x+y );
```

This line of code has three parameters following the format specifier string. You use placeholders within the format specification, and when this method is called, the appropriate substitutions are made. Although you can do the same thing using string concatenation, the resultant line of code is slightly obfuscated:

```
string s = "x=" + x + ",y=" + y + ", " + x + "+" + y + "=" + (x+y);

Console.WriteLine( s );
```

You can further refine the format by applying format attributes on the placeholders themselves. These additional attributes follow the parameter index value and are separated from that index with a `:` character. There are two types of special formatting available. The first is numeric formatting, which lets you format a numeric parameter into one of nine different numeric formats, as shown in Table 3.1. The format of these specifiers, using the currency format as an example, is Cxx where xx is a number from 1 to 99 specifying the number of digits to display. Listing 3.2 shows how to display an array of integers in hexadecimal format, including how to specify the number of digits to display. Notice also how you can change the case of the hexadecimal numbers A through F by using an uppercase or lowercase format specifier.

Table 3.1   **Numeric Formatting Specifiers**

Character	Format	Description
C or c	Currency	Culturally aware currency format.
D or d	Decimal	Only supports integral numbers. Displays a string using decimal digits preceded by a minus sign if negative.
E or e	Exponential/scientific notation	Displays numbers in the form $\pm d.dddddE\pm dd$ where d is a decimal digit.
F or f	Fixed point	Displays a series of decimal digits with a decimal point and additional digits.

Table 3.1   **Continued**

G or g	General format	Displays either as a fixed-point or scientific notation based on the size of the number.
N or n	Number format	Similar to fixed point but uses a separator character (such as ,) for groups of digits.
P or p	Percentage	Multiplies the number by 100 and displays with a percent symbol.
R or r	Roundtrip	Formats a floating-point number so that it can be successfully converted back to its original value.
X or x	Hexadecimal	Displays an integral number using the base-16 number system.

Listing 3.2   **Specifying a Different Numeric Format by Adding Format Specifiers on a Parameter Placeholder**

```
using System;

namespace _2_Formatting
{
    class Class1
    {
        [STAThread]
        static void Main(string[] args)
        {
            double[] numArray = {2, 5, 4.5, 45.43, 200000};

            // format in lowercase hex
            Console.WriteLine( "\n\nHex (lower)\n-----------" );
            foreach( double num in numArray )
            {
                Console.Write( "0x{0:x}\t", (int) num );
            }

            // format in uppercase hex
            Console.WriteLine( "\n\nHex (upper)\n-----------" );
            foreach( double num in numArray )
            {
                Console.Write( "0x{0:X}\t", (int) num );
            }
        }
    }
}
```

Another type of formatting is *picture* formatting. Picture formatting allows you to create a custom format specifier using various symbols within the format specifier string. Table 3.2 lists the available picture format characters. Listing 3.3 also shows how to create a custom format specifier. In that code, the digits of the input number are extracted and displayed using a combination of digit placeholders and a decimal-point specifier. Furthermore, you can see that you are free to add characters not listed in the table. This freedom allows you to add literal characters intermixed with the digits.

Table 3.2   **Picture Formatting Specifiers**

Character	Name	Description
0	Zero placeholder	Copies a digit to the result string if a digit is at the position of the 0. If no digit is present, a 0 is displayed.
#	Display digit placeholder	Copies a digit to the result string if a digit appears at the position of the #. If no digit is present, nothing is displayed.
.	Decimal point	Represents the location of the decimal point in the resultant string.
,	Group separator and number scaling	Inserts thousands separators if placed between two placeholders or scales a number down by 1,000 per , character when placed directly to the left of a decimal point.
&	Percent	Multiplies a number by 100 and inserts a % symbol.
E±0, e±0	Exponential notation	Displays the number in exponential notation using the number of 0s as a placeholder for the exponent value.
\	Escape character	Used to specify a special escape-character formatting instruction. Some of these include \n for newline, \t for tab, and \\ for the \ character.
;	Section separator	Separates positive, negative, and zero numbers in the format string in which you can apply different formatting rules based on the sign of the original number.

Listing 3.3 shows how custom formatting can separate a number by its decimal point. Using a `foreach` loop, each value is printed using three different formats. The first format will output the value's integer portion using the following format string:

```
0:$#,#
```

Next, the decimal portion is written. If the value does not explicitly define a decimal portion, zeroes are written instead. The format string to output the decimal value is

`$.#0;`

Finally, the entire value is displayed up to two decimal places using the following format string:

`{0:$#,#.00}`

Listing 3.3   **Using Picture Format Specifiers to Create Special Formats**

```
using System;

namespace _2_Formatting
{
    class Class1
    {
        [STAThread]
        static void Main(string[] args)
        {
            double[] numArray = {2, 5, 4.5, 45.43, 200000};

            // format as custom
            Console.WriteLine( "\n\nCustom\n------" );
            foreach( double num in numArray )
            {
                Console.WriteLine( "{0:$#,# + $.#0;} = {0:$#,#.00}", num );
            }
        }
    }
}
```

3.3. Accessing Individual String Characters

You want to process individual characters within a string.

Technique

Use the index operator (`[]`) by specifying the zero-based index of the character within the string that you want to extract. Furthermore, you can also use the `foreach` enumerator on the string using a `char` structure as the enumeration data type.

Comments

The string class is really a collection of objects. These objects are individual characters. You can access each character using the same methods you would use to access an object in most other collections (which is covered in the next chapter).

You use an indexer to specify which object in a collection you want to retrieve. In C#, the first object begins at the 0 index of the string. The objects are individual characters whose data type is System.Char, which is aliased with the char keyword. The indexer for the string class, however, can only access a character and cannot set the value of a character at that position. Because a string is immutable, you cannot change the internal array of characters unless you create and return a new string. If you need the ability to index a string to set individual characters, use a StringBuilder object.

Listing 3.4 shows how to access the characters in a string. One thing to point out is that because the string also implements the IEnumerable interface, you can use the foreach control structure to enumerate through the string.

Listing 3.4   Accessing Characters Using Indexers and Enumeration

```
using System;
using System.Text;

namespace _3_Characters
{
    class Class1
    {
        [STAThread]
        static void Main(string[] args)
        {
            string str = "abcdefghijklmnopqrstuvwxyz";

            str = ReverseString( str );
            Console.WriteLine( str );

            str = ReverseStringEnum( str );
            Console.WriteLine( str );
        }

        static string ReverseString( string strIn )
        {
            StringBuilder sb = new StringBuilder(strIn.Length);

            for( int i = 0; i < strIn.Length; ++i )
            {
                sb.Append( strIn[(strIn.Length-1)-i] );
            }
            return sb.ToString();
```

Listing 3.4   **Continued**

```
    }

    static string ReverseStringEnum( string strIn )
    {
        StringBuilder sb = new StringBuilder( strIn.Length );
        foreach( char ch in strIn )
        {
            sb.Insert( 0, ch );
        }

        return sb.ToString();
    }
  }
}
```

3.4. Analyzing Character Attributes

You want to evaluate the individual characters in a string to determine a character's attributes.

Technique

The System.Char structure contains several static functions that let you test individual characters. You can test whether a character is a digit, letter, or punctuation symbol or whether the character is lowercase or uppercase.

Comments

One of the hardest issues to handle when writing software is making sure users input valid data. You can use many different methods, such as restricting input to only digits, but ultimately, you always need an underlying validating test of the input data.

You can use the System.Char structure to perform a variety of text-validation procedures. Listing 3.5 demonstrates validating user input as well as inspecting the characteristics of a character. It begins by displaying a menu and then waiting for user input using the Console.ReadLine method. Once a user enters a command, you make a check using the method ValidateMainMenuInput. This method checks to make sure the first character in the input string is not a digit or punctuation symbol. If the validation passes, the string is passed to a method that inspects each character in the input string. This method simply enumerates through all the characters in the input string and prints descriptive messages based on the characteristics. Some of the System.Char methods for inspection have been inadvertently left out of Listing 3.5. Table 3.3 shows the remaining methods and their functionality. The results of running the application in Listing 3.5 apper in Figure 3.1.

Listing 3.5   **Using the Static Methods in** `System.Char` **to Inspect the Details of a Single Character**

```
using System;

namespace _4_CharAttributes
{
    class Class1
    {
        [STAThread]
        static void Main(string[] args)
        {
            char cmd = 'x';

            string input;
            do
            {
                DisplayMainMenu();
                input = Console.ReadLine();

                if( (input == "" ) ||
                    ValidateMainMenuInput( Char.ToUpper(input[0]) ) == 0 )
                {
                    Console.WriteLine( "Invalid command!" );
                }
                else
                {
                    cmd = Char.ToUpper(input[0]);

                    switch( cmd )
                    {
                        case 'Q':
                        {
                            break;
                        }

                        case 'N':
                        {
                            Console.Write( "Enter a phrase to inspect: " );
                            input = Console.ReadLine();
                            InspectPhrase( input );
                            break;
                        }
                    }
```

Listing 3.5   **Continued**

```
            }
        } while ( cmd != 'Q' );
    }

    private static void InspectPhrase( string input )
    {
        foreach( char ch in input )
        {
            Console.Write( ch + " - " );

            if( Char.IsDigit(ch) )
                Console.Write( "IsDigit " );
            if( Char.IsLetter(ch) )
            {
                Console.Write( "IsLetter " );
                Console.Write( "(lowercase={0}, uppercase={1})",
                    Char.ToLower(ch), Char.ToUpper(ch));
            }
            if( Char.IsPunctuation(ch) )
                Console.Write( "IsPunctuation " );
            if( Char.IsWhiteSpace(ch) )
                Console.Write( "IsWhitespace" );

            Console.Write("\n");

        }
    }
    private static int ValidateMainMenuInput( char input )
    {
        // a simple check to see if input == 'N' or 'Q' is good enough
        // the following is for illustrative purposes
        if( Char.IsDigit( input ) == true )
            return 0;
        else if ( Char.IsPunctuation( input ) )
            return 0;
        else if( Char.IsSymbol( input ))
            return 0;
        else if( input != 'N' && input != 'Q' )
            return 0;

        return (int) input;
    }

    private static void DisplayMainMenu()
    {
```

Listing 3.5   **Continued**

```
            Console.WriteLine( "\nPhrase Inspector\n------------------" );
            Console.WriteLine( "N)ew Phrase" );
            Console.WriteLine( "Q)uit\n" );
            Console.Write( ">> " );
        }
      }
}
```

Table 3.3   `System.Char` **Inspection Methods**

Name	Description
IsControl	Denotes a control character such as a tab or carriage return.
IsDigit	Indicates a single decimal digit.
IsLetter	Used for alphabetic characters.
IsLetterOrDigit	Returns true if the character is a letter or a digit.
IsLower	Used to determine whether a character is lowercase.
IsNumber	Tests whether a character is a valid number.
IsPunctuation	Denotes whether a character is a punctuation symbol.
IsSeparator	Denotes a character used to separate strings. An example is the space character.
IsSurrogate	Checks for a Unicode surrogate pair, which consists of two 16-bit values primarily used in localization contexts.
IsSymbol	Used for symbolic characters such as $ or #.
IsUpper	Used to determine whether a character is uppercase.
IsWhiteSpace	Indicates a character classified as whitespace such as a space character, tab, or carriage return.

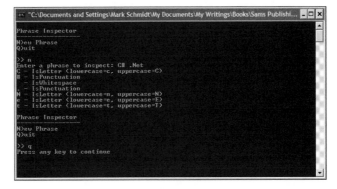

Figure 3.1   Use the `static` method in the `System.Char` class to inspect character attributes.

The `System.Char` structure is designed to work with a single Unicode character. Because a Unicode character is 2 bytes, the range of a character is from 0 to 0xFFFF. For portability reasons in future systems, you can always check the size of a `char` by using the `MaxValue` constant declared in the `System.Char` structure. One thing to keep in mind when working with characters is to avoid the confusion of mixing `char` types with integer types. Characters have an ordinal value, which is an integer value used as a lookup into a table of symbols. One example of a table is the ASCII table, which contains 255 characters and includes the digits 0 through 9, letters, punctuation symbols, and formatting characters. The confusion lies in the fact that the number 6, for instance, has an ordinal `char` value of 0x36. Therefore, the line of code meant to initialize a character to the number 6

```
char ch = (char) 6;
```

is wrong because the actual character in this instance is ^F, the ACK control character used in modem handshaking protocols. Displaying this value in the console would not provide the 6 that you were looking for. You could have chosen two different methods to initialize the variable. The first way is

```
char ch = (char) 0x36;
```

which produces the desired result and prints the number 6 to the console if passed to the `Console.Write` method. However, unless you have the ASCII table memorized, this procedure can be cumbersome. To initialize a `char` variable, simply place the value between single quotes:

```
char ch = '6';
```

3.5. Case-Insensitive String Comparison

You want to perform case-insensitive string comparison on two strings.

Technique

Use the overloaded `Compare` method in the `System.String` class which accepts a Boolean value, `ignoreCase`, as the last parameter. This parameter specifies whether the comparison should be case insensitive (`true`) or case sensitive (`false`). To compare single characters, convert them to uppercase or lowercase, using `ToUpper` or `ToLower`, and then perform the comparison.

Comments

Validating user input requires a lot of forethought into the possible values a user can enter. Making sure you cover the range of possible values can be a daunting task, and you might ultimately run into human-computer interaction issues by severely limiting what a user can enter. Case-sensitivity issues increase the possible range of values, leading to greater security with respect to such things as passwords, but this security is usually at the expense of a user's frustration when she forgets whether a character is capitalized. As with many other programming problems, you must weigh the pros and cons.

To perform a case-insensitive comparison, you can use one of the many overloaded `Compare` methods within the `System.String` class. The methods that allow you to ignore case issues use a Boolean value as the last parameter in the method. This parameter is named `ignoreCase`, and when you set it to `true`, you make a case-insensitive comparison, as demonstrated in Listing 3.6.

Listing 3.6   **Performing a Case-Insensitive String Comparison**

```
using System;

namespace _5_CaseComparison
{
    class Class1
    {
        [STAThread]
        static void Main(string[] args)
        {
            string str1 = "This Is A String.";
            string str2 = "This is a string.";

            Console.WriteLine( "Case sensitive comparison of" +
                " str1 and str2 = {0}",  String.Compare( str1, str2 ));

            Console.WriteLine( "Case insensitive comparison of" +
                " str1 and str2 = {0}", String.Compare( str1, str2, true ));
        }
    }
}
```

3.6. Working with Substrings

You need to change or extract a specific portion of a string.

Technique

To copy a portion of a string into a new string, use the `SubString` method within the `System.String` class. You call this method using the string object instance of the source string:

```
string source = "ABCD1234WXYZ";
string dest = source.Substring( 4, 4 );
Console.WriteLine( "{0}\n", dest );
```

To copy a substring into an already existing character array, use the `CopyTo` method. To assign a character array to an existing string object, create a new instance of the string using the `new` keyword, passing the character array as a parameter to the string constructor as shown in the following code, whose ouput appears in Figure 3.2:

```
string source = "ABCD";
char [] dest = { '1', '2', '3', '4', '5', '6', '7', '8' };

Console.Write( "Char array before = " );
Console.WriteLine( dest );

// copy substring into char array
source.CopyTo( 0, dest, 4, source.Length );

Console.Write( "Char array after = " );
Console.WriteLine( dest );

// copy back into source string
source = new String( dest );

Console.WriteLine( "New source = {0}\n", source );
```

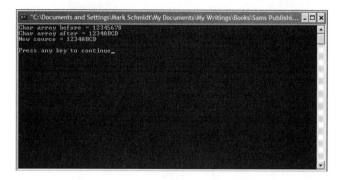

Figure 3.2   Use the `CopyTo` method to copy a substring into an existing character array.

If you need to remove a substring within a string and replace it with a different substring, use the `Replace` method. This method accepts two parameters, the substring to replace and the string to replace it with:

```
string replaceStr = "1234";
string dest = "ABCDEFGHWXYZ";

dest = dest.Replace( "EFGH", replaceStr );

Console.WriteLine( dest );
```

To extract an array of substrings that are separated from each other by one or more delimiters, use the `Split` method. This method uses a character array of delimiter characters and returns a string array of each substring within the original string as shown in the following code, whose output appears in Figure 3.3. You can optionally supply an integer specifying the maximum number of substrings to split:

```
char delim = '\\';
string filePath = "C:\\Windows\\Temp";
string [] directories = null;

directories = filePath.Split( delim );

foreach (string directory in directories)
{
    Console.WriteLine("{0}", directory);
}
```

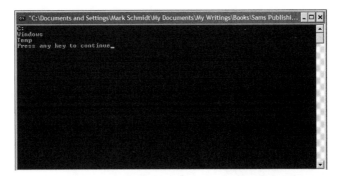

Figure 3.3   You can use the `Split` method in the `System.String` class to place delimited substrings into a string array.

Comments

Parsing strings is not for the faint of heart. However, the job becomes easier if you have a rich set of methods that allow you to perform all types of operations on strings. Substrings are the goal of a majority of these operations, and the `string` class within the .NET Framework contains many methods that are designed to extract or change just a portion of a string.

The `Substring` method extracts a portion of a string and places it into a new string object. You have two options with this method. If you pass a single integer, the `Substring` method extracts the substring that starts at that index and continues until it reaches the end of the string. One thing to keep in mind is that C# array indices are 0 based. The first character within the string will have an index of 0. The second `Substring` method accepts an additional parameter that denotes the ending index. It lets you extract parts of a string in the middle of the string.

You can create a new character array from a string by using the `ToCharArray` method of the `string` class. Furthermore, you can extract a substring from the string and place it into a character array by using the `CopyTo` method. The difference between these two methods is that the character array used with the `CopyTo` method must be an already instantiated array. Whereas the `ToCharArray` returns a new character array, the `CopyTo` method expects an existing character array as a parameter to the method. Furthermore, although methods exist to extract character arrays from a string, there is no instance method available to assign a character array to a string. To do this, you must create a new string object using the `new` keyword, as opposed to creating the familiar value-type string, and pass the character array as a parameter to the string constructor.

Using the `Replace` method is a powerful way to alter the contents of a string. This method allows you to search all instances of a specified substring within a string and replace those with a different substring. Additionally, the length of the substring you want to replace does not have to be the same length of the string you are replacing it with. If you recall the number of times you have performed a search and replace in any application, you can see the possible advantages of this method.

One other powerful method is `Split`. By passing a character array consisting of delimiter characters, you can split a string into a group of substrings and place them into a string array. By passing an additional integer parameter, you can also control how many substrings to extract from the source string. Referring to the code example earlier demonstrating the `Split` method, you can split a string representing a directory path into individual directory names by passing the \ character as the delimiter. You are not, however, confined to using a single delimiter. If you pass a character array consisting of several delimiters, the `Split` method extracts substrings based on any of the delimiters that it encounters.

3.7. Using Verbatim String Syntax

You want to represent a path to a file using a string without using escape characters for path separators.

Technique

When assigning a literal string to a string object, preface the string with the @ symbol. It turns off all escape-character processing so there is no need to escape path separators:

```
string nonVerbatim = "C:\\Windows\\Temp";
string verbatim = @"C:\Windows\Temp";
```

Comments

A compiler error that happens so frequently comes from forgetting to escape path separators. Although a common programming *faux pas* is to include hard-coded path strings, you can overlook that rule when testing an application. Visual C# .NET added verbatim string syntax as a feature to alleviate the frustration of having to escape all the path separators within a file path string, which can be especially cumbersome for large paths.

3.8. Choosing Between Constant and Mutable Strings

You want to choose the correct string data type to best fit your current application design.

Technique

If you know a string's value will not change often, use a `string` object, which is a constant value. If you need a mutable string, one that can change its value without having to allocate a new object, use a `StringBuilder`.

Comments

Using a regular `string` object is best when you know the string will not change or will only change slightly. This change includes the whole gamut of string operations that change the value of the object itself, such as concatenation, insertion, replacement, or removal of characters. The Common Language Runtime (CLR) can use certain properties of strings to optimize performance. If the CLR can determine that two string objects are the same, it can share the memory that these string objects occupy. These strings are then known as *interned* strings. The CLR contains an intern pool, which is a lookup table of string instances. Strings are automatically interned if they are assigned to a literal string within code. However, you can also manually place a string within the intern pool by using the `Intern` method. To test whether a string is interned, use the `IsInterned` method, as shown in Listing 3.7.

Listing 3.7 **Interning a String by Using the** `Intern` **Method**

```
using System;

namespace _7_StringBuilder
{
    /// <summary>
    /// Summary description for Class1.
    /// </summary>
    class Class1
    {
        /// <summary>
        /// The main entry point for the application.
        /// </summary>
```

Listing 3.7   **Continued**

```
        [STAThread]
        static void Main(string[] args)
        {
            string sLiteral = "Automatically Interned";
            string sNotInterned = "Not " + sLiteral;

            TestInterned( sLiteral );
            TestInterned( sNotInterned );

            String.Intern( sNotInterned );
            TestInterned( sNotInterned );
        }

        static void TestInterned( string str )
        {
            if( String.IsInterned( str ) != null )
            {
                Console.WriteLine( "The string \"{0}\" is interned.", str );
            }
            else
            {
                Console.WriteLine( "The string \"{0}\" is not interned.", str );
            }
        }
    }
}
```

A `StringBuilder` behaves similarly to a regular string object and also contains similar method calls. However, there are no static methods because the `StringBuilder` class is designed to work on string instances. Method calls on an instance of a `StringBuilder` object change the internal string of that object, as shown in Listing 3.8. A `StringBuilder` maintains its mutable appearance by creating a buffer that is large enough to contain a string value and additional memory should the string need to grow.

Listing 3.8   **Manipulating an Internal String Buffer Instead of Returning New String Objects**

```
using System;
using System.Text;

namespace _7_StringBuilder
{
    class Class1
    {
        [STAThread]
```

Listing 3.8 **Continued**

```
static void Main(string[] args)
{
    string string1 = "";
    String string2 = "";

    Console.Write( "Enter string 1: " );
    string1 = Console.ReadLine();
    Console.Write( "Enter string 2: " );
    string2 = Console.ReadLine();

    BuildStrings( string1, string2 );
}

public static void BuildStrings( string str1, string str2 )
{
    StringBuilder sb = new StringBuilder( str1 + str2 );
    sb.Insert( str1.Length, " is the first string.\n" );
    sb.Insert( sb.Length, " is the second string.\n" );

    Console.WriteLine( sb );
}
}
}
```

3.9. Optimizing `StringBuilder` **Performance**

Knowing that a `StringBuilder` object can suffer more of a performance hit than a regular string object, you want to optimize the `StringBuilder` object to minimize performance issues.

Technique

Use the `EnsureCapacity` method in the `StringBuilder` class. Set this integral value to a value that signifies the length of the longest string you may store in this buffer.

Comments

The `StringBuilder` class contains methods that allow you to expand the memory of the internal buffer based on the size of the string you may store. As your string continually grows, the `StringBuilder` won't have to repeatedly allocate new memory for the internal buffer. In other words, if you attempt to place a larger length string than what the internal buffer of the `StringBuilder` class can accept, then the class will have to allocate additional memory to accept the new data. If you continuously add strings that increase in size from the last input string, the StringBuilder class will have to allocate a new buffer size, which it does internally by calling the GetStringForStringBuilder method defined in the System.String class. This method ultimately calls the unmanaged method FastAllocateString. By giving the StringBuilder class a hint using the EnsureCapacity method, you can help alleviate some of this continual memory reallocation, thereby optimizing the StringBuilder performance by reducing the amount of memory allocations needed to store a string value.

3.10. Understanding Basic Regular Expression Syntax

You want to create a regular expression.

Technique

Regular expressions consist of a series of characters and quantifiers on those characters. The characters themselves can be literal or can be denoted by using character classes, such as \d, which denotes a digit character class, or \s, which denotes any nonwhitespace character.

Table 3.4   **Regular Expression Single Character Classes**

Class	Description
\d	Any digit
\D	Any nondigit
\ws	Any word character
\W	Any nonword character
\s	Any whitespace character
\SW	Any nonwhitespace

In addition to the single character classes, you can also specify a range or set of characters using ranged and set character classes. This ability allows you to narrow the search for a specified character by limiting characters within a specified range or within a defined set.

Table 3.5   **Ranged and Set Character Classes**

Format	Description
.	Any character except newline.
\p{uc}	Any character within the Unicode character category uc.
[abcxyz]	Any literal character in the set.
\P{uc}	Any character not within the Unicode character category uc.
[^abcxyz]	Any character not in the set of literal characters.

Quantifiers work on character classes to expand the number of characters the character classes should match. You need to specify, for instance, a wildcard character on a character class, which means 0 or more characters within that class. Additionally, you can also specify a set number of matches of a class that should occur by using an integer within braces following the character class designation.

Table 3.6   **Character Class Quantifiers**

Format	Description
*	0 or more characters
+	1 or more characters
?	0 or 1 characters
{n}	Exactly n characters
{n, }	At least n characters
{n, m}	At least n but no more than m characters

You can also specify where a certain regular expression should start within a string. Positional assertions allow you to, for instance, match a certain expression as long as it occurs at the beginning or ending of a string. Furthermore, you can create a regular expression that operates on a set of words within a string by using a positional assertion that continues matching on each subsequent word separated by any nonalphanumeric character.

Table 3.7   **Positional (Atomic Zero-Width) Assertions**

Format	Description
^	Beginning of a string or beginning of a newline
\z	End of the string, including the newline character
$	End of a string before a newline character or at the end of the line
\G	Continues where the last match left off
\A	Beginning of a string
\b	Between word boundaries (between alphanumeric and nonalphanumeric characters)
\Z	End of the string before the newline character
\B	Characters not between word boundaries

Comments

Regular expressions use a variety of characters both symbolic and literal to designate how a particular string of text should be parsed. The act of parsing a string is known as matching, and when applied to a regular expression, the match will be either true or false. In other words, when you use a regular expression to match a series of characters, the match will either succeed or fail. As you can see, this process has powerful applicability in the area of input validation.

You build regular expressions using a series of character classes and quantifiers on those character classes as well as a few miscellaneous regular-expression constructs. You use character classes to match a single character based either on what type of character it is, such as a digit or letter, or whether it belongs within a specified range or set of characters (as shown in Table 3.4). Using this information, you can create a series of character classes to match a certain string of text. For instance, if you want to specify a phone number using character classes, you can use the following regular expression:

```
\(\d\d\d\)\s\d\d\d-\d\d\d\d
```

This expression begins by first escaping the left parenthesis. You must escape it because parentheses are used for grouping expressions. Next you can see three digits representing a phone number's area code followed by the closing parenthesis. You use a \s to denote a whitespace character. The remainder of the regular expression contains the remaining digits of the phone number.

In addition to the single character classes, you can also use ranged and set character classes. They give you fine-grain control on exactly the type of characters the regular expression should match. For instance, if you want to match any character as long as it is a vowel, use the following expression:

```
[aeiou]
```

This line means that a character should match one of the literal characters within that set of characters. An even more specialized form of single character classes are Unicode character categories. Unicode categories are similar to some of the character-attribute inspection methods shown earlier in this chapter. For instance, you can use Unicode categories to match on uppercase or lowercase characters. Other categories include punctuation characters, currency symbols, and math symbols, to name a few. You can easily find the full list of Unicode categories in MSDN under the topic "Unicode Categories Enumeration."

You can optimize the phone-number expression, although it's completely valid, by using *quantifiers*. Quantifiers specify additional information about the character, character class, or expression to which it applies. Some quantifiers include wildcards such as *, which means 0 or more occurrences, and ?, which means only 0 or 1 occurrences of a pattern. You can also use braces containing an integer to specify how many characters within a given character class to match. Using this quantifier in the phone-number expression, you can specify that the phone number should contain three digits for the area code followed by three digits and four digits separated by a dash:

```
\(\d{3}\)\s\d{3}-\d{4}
```

Because the regular expression itself isn't that complicated, you can still see that using quantifiers can simplify regular-expression creation. In addition to character classes and quantifiers, you can also use positional information within a regular expression. For instance, you can specify that given an input string, the regular expression should operate at the beginning of the string. You express it using the ^ character. Likewise, you can also denote the end of a string using the $ symbol. Take note that this doesn't mean start at the end of the string and attempt to make a match because that obviously seems counterintuitive; no characters exist at the end of the string. Rather, by placing the $ character following the rest of the regular expression, it means to match the string with the regular expression as long as the match occurs at the end of the string. For instance, if you want to match a sentence in which a phone number is the last portion of the sentence, you could use the following:

```
\(\d{3}\)\s\d{3}-\d{4}$
My phone number is (555) 555-5555 = Match
(555) 555-5555 is my phone number = Not a match
```

3.11. Validating User Input with Regular Expressions

You want to ensure valid user input by using regular expressions to test for validity.

Technique

Create a RegEx object, which exists within the System.Text.RegularExpressions namespace, passing the regular expression in as a parameter to the constructor. Next, call the member method Match using the string you want to validate as a parameter to the method. The method returns a Match object regardless of the outcome. To test whether a match is made, evaluate the Boolean Success property on that Match object as demonstrated in Listing 3.9. It should also be noted that in many cases, the forward slash (\) character is used when working with regular expressions. To avoid compilation errors from inadvertently specifying an invalid control character, use the @ symbol to turn off escape processing.

Listing 3.9   **Validating User Input of a Phone Number Using a Regular Expression**

```
using System;
using System.Text.RegularExpressions;

namespace _11_RegularExpressions
{
    class Class1
    {
        [STAThread]
        static void Main(string[] args)
        {
            Regex phoneExp = new Regex( @"^\(\d{3}\)\s\d{3}-\d{4}$" );
```

Listing 3.9 **Continued**

```
            string input;

            Console.Write( "Enter a phone number: " );
            input = Console.ReadLine();

            while( phoneExp.Match( input ).Success == false )
            {
                Console.WriteLine( "Invalid input. Try again." );
                Console.Write( "Enter a phone number: " );
                input = Console.ReadLine();
            }

            Console.WriteLine( "Validated!" );
        }
    }
}
```

Comments

Earlier in this chapter I mentioned that you could perform data validation using the static methods within the System.Char class. You can inspect each character within the input string to ensure it matches exactly what you are looking for. However, this method of input validation can be extremely cumbersome if you have different input types to validate because it requires custom code for each validation. In other words, using the methods in the System.Char class is not recommended for anything but the simplest of data-validation procedures.

Regular expressions, on the other hand, allow you to perform the most advanced input validation possible, all within a single expression. You are in effect passing the parsing of the input string to the regular-expression engine and offloading all the work that you would normally do.

In Listing 3.9, you can see how you create and use a regular expression to test the validity of a phone number entered by a user. The regular expression is similar to the previous expressions used earlier for phone numbers except for the addition of positional markers. The regular expression is valid if a user enters a phone number and nothing else. A match is successful when the Success property within the Match object, which is returned from the Regex.Match method, is true. The only caveat to using regular expressions for input validation is that even though you know the validation failed, you are unable to query the Regex or Match class to see what part of the string failed.

3.12. Replacing Substrings Using Regular Expressions

> You want to replace all substrings that match a regular expression with a different substring that also uses regular-expression syntax.

Technique

Create a `Regex` object, passing the regular expression used to match characters in the input string to the `Regex` constructor. Next, call the `Regex` method `Replace`, passing the input string to process and the string to replace each match within the input string. You can also use the static `Replace` method, passing the regular expression as the first parameter to the method as shown in the last line of Listing 3.10.

Listing 3.10   **Using Regular Expressions to Replace Numbers in a Credit Card with xs**

```
using System;
using System.Text.RegularExpressions;

namespace _12_RegExpReplace
{
    class Class1
    {
        [STAThread]
        static void Main(string[] args)
        {
            Regex cardExp = new Regex( @"(\d{4})-(\d{4})-(\d{4})-(\d{4})" );
            string safeOutputExp = "$1-xxxx-xxxx-$4";
            string cardNum;

            Console.Write( "Please enter your credit card number: " );
            cardNum = Console.ReadLine();

            while( cardExp.Match( cardNum ).Success == false )
            {
                Console.WriteLine( "Invalid card number. Try again." );
                Console.Write( "Please enter your credit card number: " );

                cardNum = Console.ReadLine();
            }

            Console.WriteLine( "Secure Output Result = {0}",
                cardExp.Replace( cardNum, safeOutputExp ));
        }
    }
}
```

Comments

Although input validation is an extremely useful feature of regular expressions, they also work well as text parsers. The previous recipe used regular expressions to verify that a particular string matched a regular expression exactly. However, you can also use regular expressions to match substrings within a string and return each of those substrings as a group. Furthermore, you can use a separate regular expression that acts on the result of the regular-expression evaluation to replace substrings within the original input string.

Listing 3.10 creates a regular expression that matches the format for a credit card. In that regular expression, you can see that it will match on four different groups of four digits apiece separated by a dash. However, you might also notice that each one of these groups is surrounded with parentheses. In an earlier recipe, I mentioned that to use a literal parenthesis, you must escape it using a backslash because of the conflict with regular-expression grouping symbols. In this case, you want to use the grouping feature of regular expressions. When you place a portion of a regular expression within parentheses, you are creating a numbered group. Groups are numbered starting with 1 and are incremented for each subsequent group. In this case, there are four numbered groups. These groups are used by the replacement string, which is contained in the string safeOutputExp. To reference a numbered group, use the $ symbol followed by the number of the group to reference. This sequence represents all characters within the input string that match the group expression within the regular expression. Therefore, in the replacement string, you can see that it prints the characters within the first group, replaces the characters in the second and third groups with xs, and finally prints the characters in the fourth group.

One thing to note is that you can use the RegEx class to view the groups themselves. If you change the regular expression to "\d{4}", you can then use the Matches method to enumerate all the groups using the foreach keyword, as shown in Listing 3.11. In the listing, the program first checks to make sure at least four matches were made. This number corresponds to four groups of four digits. Next, it uses a foreach enumeration on each Match object that is returned from the Matches method. If the match is in the second or third group, the values are replaced with xs; otherwise, the Match object's value, the characters within that group, are concatenated to the result string.

Listing 3.11 **Enumerating Through the** Match **Collection to Perform Special Operations on Each Match in a Regular Expression**

```
static void TestManualGrouping()
{
    Regex cardExp = new Regex( @"\d{4}" );
    string cardNum;
    string safeOutputExp = "";

    Console.Write( "Please enter your credit card number: " );
    cardNum = Console.ReadLine();
```

Listing 3.11   **Continued**

```
    if( cardExp.Matches( cardNum ).Count < 4 )
    {
        Console.WriteLine( "Invalid card number" );
        return;
    }

    foreach( Match field in cardExp.Matches( cardNum ))
    {
        if( field.Success == false )
        {
            Console.WriteLine( "Invalid card number" );
            return;
        }

        if( field.Index == 5 || field.Index == 10 )
        {
            safeOutputExp += "-xxxx-";
        }
        else
        {
            safeOutputExp += field.Value;
        }
    }

    Console.WriteLine( "Secure Output Result = {0}", safeOutputExp );
}
```

3.13. Building a Regular Expression Library

You want to create a library of regular expressions that you can reuse in other projects.

Technique

Use the `CompileToAssembly` static method within the `Regex` class to compile a regular expression into an assembly. This method uses an array of `RegexCompilationInfo` objects that contain any number of regular expressions you want to add to the assembly.

The `RegexCompilationInfo` class contains a constructor with five fields that you must fill out. The parameters denote the string for the regular expression; any options for the regular expression, which appear in the `RegexOptions` enumerated type; a name for the class that is created to hold the regular expression; a corresponding namespace; and a Boolean value specifying whether the created class should have a public access modifier.

After creating the `RegexCompilationInfo` object, create an `AssemblyName` object, making sure to reference the `System.Reflection` namespace, and set the `Name` property to a name you want the resultant assembly filename to be. Because the `CompileToAssembly` creates a DLL, exclude the DLL extension on the assembly name. Finally, place all the `RegexCompilationInfo` objects within an array, as shown in Listing 3.12, and call the `CompileToAssembly` method. Listing 3.12 demonstrates how to create a `RegexCompilationInfo` object and how to use that object to compile a regular expression into an assembly using the `CompileToAssembly` method.

Listing 3.12 **Using the** `CompileToAssembly` `Regex` **Method to Save Regular Expressions in a New Assembly for Later Reuse**

```
using System;
using System.Text.RegularExpressions;
using System.Reflection;

namespace _12_RegExpReplace
{
    class Class1
    {
        [STAThread]
        static void Main(string[] args)
        {
            CompileRegex(@"(\d{4})-(\d{4})-(\d{4})-(\d{4})", @"regexlib" );
        }

        static void CompileRegex( string exp, string assemblyName )
        {
            RegexCompilationInfo compInfo =
                new RegexCompilationInfo( exp, 0, "CreditCardExp", "", true );
            AssemblyName assembly = new AssemblyName();
            assembly.Name = assemblyName;

            RegexCompilationInfo[] rciArray = { compInfo };

            Regex.CompileToAssembly( rciArray, assembly );
        }
    }
}
```

Comments

If you use regular expressions regularly, then you might find it advantageous to create a reusable library of the expressions you tend to use the most. The `Regex` class contains a method named `CompileToAssembly` that allows you to compile several regular expressions into an assembly that you can then reference within other projects.

Internally, you will find a class for each regular expression you added, all contained within its corresponding namespace, as specified in the `RegexCompilationInfo` object when you created it. Furthermore, each of these classes inherits from the `Regex` class so all the `Regex` methods are available for you to use. As you can see, creating a library of commonly used regular expressions allows you to reuse and share these expressions in a multitude of different projects. A change in a regular expression simply involves changing one assembly instead of each project that hard-coded the regular expression.

Creating and Using .NET Collections

4.0. Introduction

Variables are well suited for holding a single piece of data, but more often than not, you need a mechanism that can store more than one piece of data of a certain type. *Collections* allow you to place data within a single containing object and retrieve individual elements within that container using a consistent retrieval method. This chapter looks at how collections are used within the C# language and .NET Framework. Because several different collection types are built into the .NET Framework, you'll see how to select the appropriate container based on your application design. Furthermore, you will also learn how to create your own collection types if no other suitable container is available.

4.1. Declaring and Using Arrays

You want to create a simple array of objects, and you know exactly how many elements the collection needs.

Technique

Use a single dimension array if you want a collection of objects that can be accessed in a linear fashion. The `array` data type is the data type of the objects you want to insert into the array, followed by left and right brackets. To initialize the array with a set of values, assign the array variable to a comma-delimited list of values surrounded by left and right braces.

```
int[] arr1 = {1,2,3,4,5,6,7,8,9,10};
```

If you don't want to initialize the elements in the array but would rather set the individual elements later, use the `new` keyword on the collection data type, specifying the array size in brackets.

```
int[] arr2 = new int[10];
```

To access a single element in the array, place the index of the element you want to access—relative to the beginning of the array element, which has an index of 0—in brackets following the array variable name:

```
static void TestSingleDimensionArray()
{
    int[] arr1 = {1,2,3,4,5,6,7,8,9,10};
    int[] arr2 = new int[10];

    for( int i = 0; i < arr1.Length; i++ )
    {
        arr2[i] = arr1[i];
        Console.WriteLine( arr1[i] + "=" + arr2[i] );
    }
}
```

If you want to create an array with more than one dimension, declare the variable using the data type to place in the array, followed by brackets containing a comma to separate each dimension within the array. For instance, a two-dimensional array used to hold data in rows and columns, as shown in the `TestMultiDimensionArray` listing, would contain one comma. To create the array without initializing the individual elements, use the same technique for a single-dimension array but use a comma-separated list denoting the number of elements each dimension can hold:

```
static void TestMultiDimensionArray()
{
    string[,] arr1 = new string[10,10];

    // assign values
    for( int row = 0; row < 10; row++ )
    {
        for( int col = 0; col < 10; col++ )
        {
            arr1[row,col] = row + "," + col;
        }
    }

    // print values
    for( int i = 0; i < 10; i++ )
    {
        for( int j = 0; j < 10; j++ )
        {
```

```
        Console.Write( arr1[i,j] + "\t" );
    }
    Console.WriteLine();
    }
}
```

To create an initialized multidimensional array, place each dimension's value within left and right braces similar to the initialization of a single-dimension array, and place each dimension's element list within braces also.

```
int[,] identity = { {0,1},{1,0} };
```

Comments

Arrays are simple collections whose elements you access using indices. Because their use is widespread in a variety of different programming scenarios, C# created special syntactical elements to aid in their creation, initialization, and element access.

The declaration of an array consists of the data type of the elements you want to place into the array followed by a set of brackets and the variable name of the array. These brackets specify how many dimensions an array has. A dimension in an array is the same as its mathematical counterpart. A two-dimensional array, for instance, contains a group of elements that in turn each contain a group of elements. A real-world example is a spreadsheet that contains two dimensions, a row and a column. Although it might be hard to think of dimensions in the fifth or higher degree, you can easily create them in a programming language like C#.

To access an individual element within an array, you use an *indexer*, which is an integer value between brackets specifying the number or index of the element you want to access. For a single-dimension array, there is one index value per array element. For a multidimensional array, the indices specified within a comma-separated list correspond to the element at each location of the dimension in which the index is placed. For instance, an element within a two-dimensional array uses the format $[x, y]$, where x is an index into the first dimension and y is the index into the second dimension. This line in turn returns the value at that location.

A major advantage to using an array over any other collection type is the fast performance when retrieving an element. When you create an array, the memory is allocated as a single contiguous block of memory, regardless of the number of dimensions within the array. Therefore, given an index value, the Common Language Runtime (CLR) can easily find the corresponding element by multiplying the index by the size of the element's data type and using that value as an offset from the beginning of the array's memory block. The performance of accessing an element within an array given an index value runs in constant or 0(1) time.

Although the performance of element access within an array is certainly fast, it still requires that you know the index of the element you want to access. In some cases, this requirement might be acceptable, but once you start needing features such as finding an element, the performance of using an array drops. Searching an array for a specific value requires that the program access every element, beginning with the first index and continuing until it finds the element or reaches the end of the array.

Due to its simple nature, arrays also have a few more drawbacks. Once you create an array, you cannot add elements past the sizes declared for each dimension. In other words, an array cannot increase in size nor can it insert elements into the middle. Additionally, a single-dimension or multidimension array can consume large amounts of memory, even if you do not place values in the array. For small arrays, this point is a moot, but large multidimensional arrays reserve large portions of memory, even if you don't place values into the array elements.

4.2. Defining Jagged Arrays

You want to create an array of arrays, each with different dimensions.

Technique

To create a jagged array, use separate brackets for each dimension in the array. For instance, to create an array of three elements where each element contains another array of a certain size, the code would appear as follows:

```
int [][] jaggedArrayA = new int[3][];
jaggedArrayA[0] = new int[3];
jaggedArrayA[1] = new int[4];
jaggedArrayA[2] = new int[2];
```

In the example, each element in the created arrays is initialized to 0. You can also explicitly initialize the jagged array by using an array initializer list, as shown in the following example:

```
int [][] jaggedArrayB = new int[3][];
jaggedArrayB [0] = new int[]{0,1,2};
jaggedArrayB [1] = new int[]{0,1,2,3,4};
jaggedArrayB[2] = new int[]{0,1};
```

Comments

A multidimensional array is a rectangular dimensioned collection. If you were to take each element and place it in row-column format, the elements would form a rectangle because each row has the same number of columns as all the other rows, assuming a two-dimensional structure, of course. A jagged array, however, can contain any number of elements, each of which contains an array of differing dimensions. The term *jagged* is used because placing the values in a row-column format, again assuming only two dimensions for simplicity, would create a jagged appearance along the right side of the table. It is because of this characteristic that a jagged array is also known as an "array of arrays."

4.3. Enumerating Arrays with the `foreach` Operator

> You want to access all the elements within an array without requiring the use of index values.

Technique

To enumerate an array, use the `foreach` iteration statement, specifying the data type of an individual element within the array, the variable name for the element returned as a result of the enumeration, and the `in` keyword and variable name of the array:

```
static void TestSingleDimensionArray()
{
    int[] arr1 = {1,2,3,4,5,6,7,8,9,10};

    foreach( int elem in arr1 )
    {
        Console.WriteLine( elem );
    }
}
```

Comments

In the previous recipes' code listings, the contents of each array were enumerated using `for` loops. For single-dimension arrays, the format was simple. However, as soon as you begin adding extra dimensions in the array, using `for` loops starts to seem less attractive. To enumerate a multidimension array using `for` loops, you have to create a `for` loop for each dimension that is nested within the `for` loop preceding it. For an array with even a small number of dimensions, this process can get quite tedious.

Luckily, the C# language has a built-in enumeration keyword designed for this specific purpose. `foreach` allows you to easily access every single item within a collection in a linear fashion. You can therefore replace each `for` loop for a multi-dimension array with a single `foreach` statement. However, when you do so, you are losing the benefit of knowing exactly which index is being accessed within the loop because you no longer use index variables to access each individual element. For a single-dimension array, you can simply create an integer variable and increment it each time within the body of the `foreach` statement, but for multidimension arrays, this step is not possible without using an algorithm to figure out the index of the current element being accessed within the `foreach` loop. The next recipe shows one possible solution.

4.4. Determining the Current Element Index Within a `foreach` Loop

You want to avoid using a series of `for` loops to iterate the elements of an array, but you also need to know the location (index values) of an element in multiple dimensions of an array.

Technique

The `System.Array` class that serves as the base object for all arrays contains a few properties and methods to help you examine various attributes about an array. They include the `Rank` property, which tells you how many dimensions an array has, and the `GetUpperBound` method to determine the maximum number of elements within a certain dimension. Using this information, you can create an algorithm that calculates the index of each dimension given a single flat index value:

```
static int[] GetDimensionIndices( int flatIndex, Array array )
{
    int[] indices = new int[ array.Rank ];

    int p = 1;
    for( int i = array.Rank-1; i >= 0; i-- )
    {
        indices[i] = (((flatIndex/p)) % (array.GetUpperBound(i)+1));

        if( i > 0)
        {
            p *= array.GetUpperBound( i )+1;
        }
    }
    return indices;
}
```

Comments

This challenge wasn't a trivial thing to figure out. If there were ever an ultimate interview question, this problem is it. Given a multidimensional array that has been flattened out into a single-dimension array, determine the indices of each dimension given only the single-dimension array index. Let's take a look at the algorithm.

The first thing you see is the creation of an integer array that contains the amount of elements as specified by the rank of the array being passed in. In other words, if a three-dimensional array is passed in, a separate array that holds three values is created. This array corresponds to the indices of each dimension the element belongs to and is used as the return object.

Next, you see the declaration of a variable named p, which is initialized to 1. This variable is known as the *period* of a certain dimension. A period is how long it takes a single dimension's index to change when the lower indices are enumerated. You can find a dimension's period by multiplying the upper bounds of the dimensions following it. For instance, given an array such as

```
int[,,] array[3, 2, 3]
```

the third dimension's period is 1 because no dimensions follow it. The second dimension's period is 3, and the first dimension's period is 2 × 3, which is 6. In effect, this means that for every six elements, the index of that dimension will change.

A `for` loop loops based on the number of dimensions. As mentioned earlier, you can retrieve the number of dimensions using the `Rank` property of the `Array` object. For a three-dimensional array, the loop body will execute three times. Also, the `for` loop counter is initialized to the rightmost dimension and decrements upon each subsequent iteration of the loop, working back toward the leftmost dimension.

Next is the calculation of the index of the element in the current dimension. Using the information about periods and the upper bound of the current dimension, you can create an equation to calculate the index of that dimension. This equation takes the original single-dimension index variable and divides that by the current period. The resultant value is used with the modulus operator on the current upper bound of that dimension (plus 1 to compensate for the zero-based array index). The process is then repeated for the remaining dimensions after the new period value for that dimension is calculated. Figure 4.1 shows the result of using a `foreach` loop to print out an array and also calculating the dimension indices for each element. The array is a three-dimensional string array, where each string is simply initialized to the value of the indices of the corresponding dimension.

Figure 4.1   Using the `foreach` operator to print an array of values and their corresponding dimension indices.

4.5. Using `ArrayLists`

You want to use an array but want the array to grow if elements go past the initial array size.

Technique

Declare an `ArrayList` variable and instantiate an object of that type. You can optionally use two overloaded constructors. One constructor allows you to pass an integer to specify the initial size or capacity of the internal array, and the second overloaded constructor allows you to pass in a collection object whose values are copied into the new `ArrayList` object:

```
static void CreateArrayLists()
{
    ArrayList al1 = new ArrayList();
    ArrayList al2 = new ArrayList( 10 );

    int[] intArr = new int[10];
    ArrayList al3 = new ArrayList( intArr );
}
```

To adjust the size of the `ArrayList`, use the `Capacity` property. This value must be greater than the value of the `Count` property. In other words, you can make the array larger but not smaller:

```
ArrayList myArrayList = new ArrayList();
myArrayList.Capacity = 10;
```

To add objects to the end of the `ArrayList`, use the `Add` or AddRange method. `Add` allows you to add a single object to the array, whereas `AddRange` allows you to add an entire collection. If the number of elements exceeds the size of the array, the `ArrayList` class will allocate additional memory to make room:

```
int[] intArr = {2, 3, 4, 5};
myArrayList.Add( 1 );
myArrayList.AddRange( intArr );
```

You can also use `Remove`, which removes a specified object from the array; `RemoveAt`, which removes an object given an index into the array; and `RemoveRange` to remove a specified number of objects beginning at a certain index into the array:

```
myArrayList.Remove( 1 );
myArrayList.RemoveRange( 1, 2 );
```

To insert elements in the middle of the array, use the `Insert` method, which inserts an object at a specified index within the array, and `InsertRange`, which inserts the contents of a collection at a specified index within the array:

```
myArrayList.Insert( 1, 3 );
myArrayList.InsertRange( 0, intArr );
```

Comments

In the previous recipe, you saw how to initialize an array of a certain data type and set the values of that array using indexers. These arrays were fixed in size. If you attempt to set a value using an index value that is greater than the size of the array, an IndexOutOfRangeException is thrown and the application prematurely exits. The ArrayList, on the other hand, allows you to increase the size of the internal array to make room for more objects.

One important thing to note is that although the ArrayList also has the ability to get or set values using an indexer, as with a regular array the index value cannot be greater than the size of the internal array. You can find the size of the internal array by accessing the Count property. If you need to set a value at an index that is greater than the Count property, set the Capacity property to a larger value. Internally, the ArrayList does a few things when the Capacity property is changed. First of all, a new array is created using the new value of the Capacity property. The values of the original array are then copied over to the new array. Finally, because the original array is no longer needed, it is marked for removal.

One major difference between the Array and ArrayList class is that the ArrayList class can only work with generic objects. An Array allows you to create an array using a specified data type. Therefore, when accessing an element from the ArrayList, you might have to perform a data-type conversion to work with that value, as shown in the following code:

```
static void Main(string[] args)
{
    ArrayList al = new ArrayList();
    for( int i = 0; i < 10; i++ )
    {
        al[i] = i;
    }

    // compilation error
    int fifthElement = al[5];

    // compiles fine
    int fourthElement = (int) al[4];
}
```

4.6. Choosing Between an Array and an `ArrayList`

> When designing your application, you need to store data in a collection and you are unsure about whether to use a regular array or an `ArrayList`.

Technique

Use an `ArrayList` if

- You need to add elements passed to the end of the array during runtime.
- You want more methods that allow you to manipulate the `ArrayList`'s values.
- You want synchronized access to elements but want the collection to take care of the details.
- You want the ability to create read-only or fixed-size arrays.

Use a regular array if

- You know exactly how many values you need to store in the array.
- You need to use multiple dimensions.
- You want the performance advantage that using an array provides.

Comments

It's tempting when choosing between an `ArrayList` and an `Array` to simply choose the `ArrayList` due to its greater support for object manipulation. However, you have to take a close look at how your data needs to be stored and how it will be accessed while also taking a look at the performance impact.

If the number of items to store is unbound or unknown, then using an `ArrayList` might be a good idea. One of the primary features of the `ArrayList` class is that it can grow internally as you place more items within it. Once you add an item at an index greater than the current capacity of the internal array, a new larger array is created, the contents of the original array are copied over, and that array is subsequently destroyed. By default, the internal array size has a capacity of 16 items. Once you add an item past that capacity, the array grows to support 16 additional items. By setting the `Capacity` property, you adjust the size of the internal array, but furthermore, you also adjust how many additional items are created when the array is expanded to accommodate additional items. For instance, if you set `Capacity` to 32, an additional 32 blocks of memory are created each time the `Count` of the internal array goes beyond the current `Capacity`. If you plan to use an `ArrayList` and you know that it will have to grow substantially, set the `Capacity` value to a larger number to decrease the number of memory allocations, copies, and deallocations that occur as a result of creating a new internal array.

A major disadvantage of using an `ArrayList` is that it acts as a list rather than an array. An `ArrayList` is in essence a single-dimension array. Now that's not saying you couldn't emulate a multidimensional array using an `ArrayList`. Items within an `ArrayList` must derive from `System.Object` as all classes do. You can place any class within the .NET Framework within an `ArrayList`, and because `System.Array` derives from `System.Object`, you can add an entire array reference to a single item within an `Array`. This technique is the same technique you use to create a jagged array in which items at a certain index contain additional arrays, creating arrays within arrays.

One area of concern is performance. As mentioned earlier, an `ArrayList` has to allocate memory for an additional array, copy the memory of the original array to the new array, and then destroy the original array. If this process happens over and over again, you see an impact on performance. Additionally, when an item is added to an `ArrayList`, that item is converted to a `System.Object`. For .NET classes, this conversion isn't a problem because all classes ultimately derive from `System.Object`. For value types, however, the value must first be boxed. *Boxing* refers to the process of converting a value type into a class that is derived from `System.Object`. For instance, if you add an integer (data type `int`) to an `ArrayList`, it is first packaged as a `System.Object`, which means memory is allocated from the heap and type information is created for that integer. Furthermore, when you need to retrieve the item from the `ArrayList`, you must unbox it, which, as its name implies, is the reverse process of boxing; an object is converted back to its original value type using the type information associated with that object. If the items within the `ArrayList` are continually boxed and unboxed, this process too will have an impact on performance.

4.7. Using Stacks and Queues

> You want to use a data structure that orders items based on when they are added to the collection.

Technique

If you want to use a last-in-first-out structure (LIFO) in which the last item in the collection is the first item that is removed, then use a stack. To add an object to a stack, use the `Push` method defined in the `System.Collections.Stack` class. To remove an item from the stack, use the `Pop` method. This object is the same object that was added with the last `Push` method call.

A queue is similar to a stack, but it uses a first-in-first-out (FIFO) method. The first element removed from the queue was the first element initially added to the collection. To add an object to a queue, use the `Enqueue` method defined in the `System.Collection.Queue` class. Likewise, to remove an object from the queue, use the `Dequeue` method.

Comments

The previous recipes in this chapter looked at arrays and `ArrayLists`, which allowed you to randomly access any element within the array using an indexer. These data structure act as simple collections without any type of data-organizing structure to them. Stack and queues, on the other hand, don't allow indexers to randomly access the elements in the collection but rather use methods that allow you to add or remove elements from the beginning or end of the collection.

As mentioned earlier, a stack is a LIFO data structure. To use a metaphor for visualization purposes, imagine stacking blocks on top of each other. Each time you add a block to the top, you are doing the equivalent of the `System.Collections.Stack`'s `Push` method. When it's time to remove the blocks one at a time, it makes sense to remove them from the top working your way to the bottom because removal of the bottom block isn't possible without breaking the structure. Removing the top or last block that was added to the structure is the equivalent of the stack method `Pop`, as demonstrated in Figure 4.2.

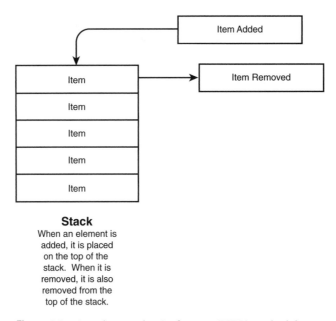

Stack
When an element is
added, it is placed
on the top of the
stack. When it is
removed, it is also
removed from the
top of the stack.

Figure 4.2   A stack uses a last-in-first-out (LIFO) methodology.

Listing 4.8 shows a simple application that uses a stack. The `Main` method asks the user to enter a list of names separated by a space. These names are placed within a simple string array, and that array is then passed to the `TestStack` method. This method then enumerates through the string array and pushes each string onto the stack, visually displaying the progress, as shown in Figure 4.2. Finally, the user is prompted to enter an integer value specifying how many objects to pop off the stack. Again, as the items are removed, the application shows the contents of the stack.

Listing 4.1   **Pushing and Popping Objects from a Stack**

```
using System;
using System.Collections;

namespace _6_StacksQueues
{
    class Class1
    {
        [STAThread]
        static void Main(string[] args)
        {
            string input;
            Console.Write( "Enter a list of names separated by a space: " );
            input = Console.ReadLine();

            // place names into a string array
            string[] names = input.Split( ' ' );

            // print out string array
            PrintCollection( "Input", names );

            TestStack( names );
        }

        static void PrintCollection( string name, ICollection coll )
        {
            Console.Write( name + ": " );
            foreach( object elem in coll )
            {
                Console.Write( elem.ToString() + ' ' );
            }
            Console.WriteLine("\n");
        }

        static void TestStack( string[] names )
        {
            Stack nameStack = new Stack();

            // enumerate through the array
            foreach( string name in names )
            {
                // push name onto stack and display new stack contents
                nameStack.Push( name );
```

Listing 4.1   **Continued**

```
                Console.WriteLine( "Pushed value: {0}", name );
                PrintCollection( "New Stack", nameStack );
        }

        // let user choose how many items to remove
        Console.Write( "Pop how many items? " );
        int pops = Int32.Parse( Console.ReadLine() );
        for( int i = 1; i <= pops; i++ )
        {
            // Pop value. Note that Pop also
            // returns the value that was removed
            Console.WriteLine( "Popped value: " + nameStack.Pop());

            // display the new stack contents
            PrintCollection( "Stack after " + i.ToString() + " pops",
                nameStack );
        }

        Console.WriteLine();
    }
  }
}
```

Figure 4.3   The objects on a stack that were added last are the
first to be removed.

A queue is quite similar to a stack, which is the reason they are both mentioned in this recipe. As with the stack, you cannot randomly access or remove items using an indexer into the queue. The equivalent of a stack's Push method is called Enqueue. However, rather than add that the object to the beginning of the list as a stack does, the queue adds the item at the end of the list. This process ensures that the first item added to the queue is at the beginning of the collection, which results in it also being the first item removed when you call the Dequeue method. To visualize a queue, you can use the classic example of a line of people waiting for an attraction. The first person who entered the line will be the first person who gets into the attraction.

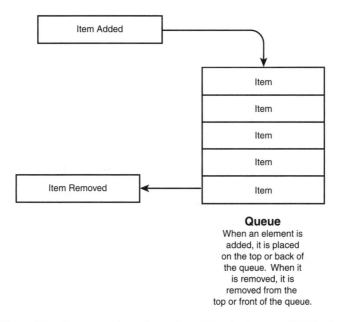

Queue
When an element is added, it is placed on the top or back of the queue. When it is removed, it is removed from the top or front of the queue.

Figure 4.4   Queues work on the notion of first-in-first-out (FIFO) when adding and removing objects.

Listing 4.2 expands on the application presented in Listing 4.1. It adds a new method called TestQueue, which is quite similar to the TestStack method. What is different is the output that you see in Figure 4.5. If you compare this figure with Figure 4.3, you can see how the LIFO and FIFO data structures compare.

Listing 4.2   **Using** Enqueue **and** Dequeue **Instead of** Push **and** Pop

```
static void TestQueue( string[] names )
{
    Queue nameQueue = new Queue();
    foreach( string name in names )
    {
        nameQueue.Enqueue( name );
        Console.WriteLine( "Enqueued value: {0}", name );
        PrintCollection( "New Queue", nameQueue );
    }
```

Listing 4.2   **Continued**

```
    Console.Write( "Dequeue how many items? " );
    int dequeues = Int32.Parse( Console.ReadLine() );
    for( int i = 1; i <= dequeues; i++ )
    {
        Console.WriteLine( "Dequeued value: " + nameQueue.Dequeue());
        PrintCollection( "Queue after ", nameQueue );
    }
}
```

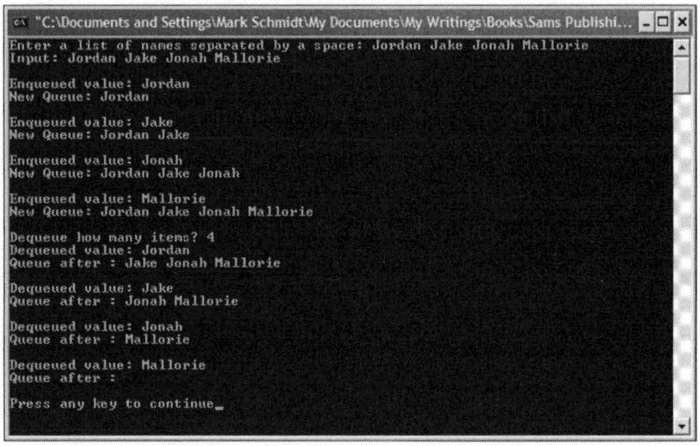

Figure 4.5   The objects in a queue that were added first
are also the first to be removed.

4.8. Using Hashtables

You want to use a data structure that allows you to associate a key object with
a value object.

Technique

Create a HashTable object, which is a class in the System.Collections namespace.
Each value added to the collection needs to be associated with a key object, which you
do by calling the Add method, passing the key and value objects. To remove a item, call
the Remove method, passing the key object as the parameter. To remove all the items
within the entire hash table, you can use the Clear method:

```
using System;
using System.Collections;
```

```
namespace _7_HashTable
{
    class Class1
    {
        [STAThread]
        static void Main(string[] args)
        {
            Hashtable dir = new Hashtable();
            dir.Add( 'N', "You travel north." );
            dir.Add( 'S', "You are now travelling south." );
            dir.Add( 'W', "You are facing west." );
            dir.Add( 'E', "You run towards the east." );
            dir.Add( 'Q', "Goodbye" );

            char input;

            do
            {
                Console.Write("Enter a direction (N,S,E,W) or Q to quit: ");
                input = Char.ToUpper(Console.ReadLine()[0]);
                Console.WriteLine( dir[Char.ToUpper(input)]);

            } while( input != 'Q' );

            PrintHashtable( dir );

            dir.Remove( 'Q' );

            dir.Clear();
        }
    }
}
```

To enumerate a hash table, declare a IDictionaryEnumerator object and assign it the result of calling the GetEnumerator method on an instance of a hash table. Next, create a loop that breaks when the MoveNext method of the IDictionaryEnumerator returns false. If successful, the Key property and the Value property of the IDictionaryEnumerator object contain a key and value from the associated hash table respectively:

```
static void PrintHashtable( Hashtable ht )
{
    IDictionaryEnumerator htEnum = ht.GetEnumerator();
```

```
Console.WriteLine( "\nHashtable Contents\n-----------------" );
while( htEnum.MoveNext() )
{
    Console.WriteLine( "Key: {0}\tValue: {1}",
        htEnum.Key, htEnum.Value );
}
}
```

Comments

Up to this point, all of the collections have been linear in nature, meaning the elements are arranged in a list. Hash tables, on the other hand, use a *dictionary* arrangement, which means each value added to the collection is placed based on an associated key. One of the methods in System.Object is GetHashCode. This method, which all classes within the .NET Framework contain, generates a unique integer based on information about the key object. For example, a String object can use an algorithm that uses information about each individual character to produce the hash code. Although you are not guaranteed to receive a different hash code for every differing object, the algorithms within the .NET Framework are robust enough to minimize hash-table collisions. By using a hash code for each key object, the hash table can find the corresponding area of memory that the hash code belongs to. You might also hear the term "buckets" when referring to this method. Using a hash code and finding its corresponding bucket, the hash table can retrieve or place an object at that location. Furthermore, if it uses a good hash function, meaning a hash function that minimizes the number of collisions, the performance of a hash table rivals that of using an index lookup on a single-dimension array. A hash table is capable of performing a lookup in constant, O(1), time. Once you throw collisions into the equation, however, you start to see performance drop to linear, O(n), time, which is equivalent to searching for a value in a single-dimension array by starting at the beginning and enumerating through the array until the value is found.

There are a couple of ways to retrieve values from a hash table. The most common way is to use the Hashtable indexer. The value used for the indexer is the key object used to find the corresponding value. You can also retrieve all the values at one time and manipulate them using a different collection class by accessing the Values property of the Hashtable class. This step returns an ICollection interface, which you can use in the constructor when you create an instance of any collection class. Furthermore, if you change a value in this collection, you are changing the value in the hash table because you are working with the actual values in the original hash table. In fact, you can also perform the same type of manipulations to the Keys collection in the hash table. Changing the value of a key also means you change the value of a key within the hash table.

4.9. Working with BitArrays

You want to create an array of Boolean values and manipulate them using Boolean logic.

Technique

Create a BitArray object using one of its six constructors. By passing a single integer value into the constructor, you can create a BitArray with a bit count equal to that integer. By default, these bits are initialized to false. You might also pass an additional Boolean value if you want to override the default bit initialization:

```
BitArray bt = new BitArray( 32, true );
```

You can also pass an array of values into the constructor. The size of the BitArray is equal to the number of items within the array passed into the constructor multiplied by the size of that array's data type. An integer array therefore would add 32 bits to the bit array for each integer in the integer array. Furthermore, the bits in the BitArray are initialized based on the bits of the values passed in the array via the constructor:

```
int[] intArray = {1,2,3,4,5};
BitArray bt = new BitArray( intArray );
```

Comments

BitArrays are useful when you need to store a larger number of Boolean values to designate certain states and configuration parameters in your object. One of the more common uses of bits to store this information is objects that use flags to control their behavior. A BitArray behaves similarly to a single-dimension array, but rather than store integers or other data types, which consequently would consume more memory than is needed, the BitArray creates an array of Boolean values. You can then access these values as you do any other array through the use of an indexer. Each index value corresponds to a certain bit or Boolean value in the BitArray. Listing 4.3 shows how you can use a BitArray to create flags within your class. In this example, the Coffee class contains a private BitArray corresponding to the possible ingredients you can add to a cup of coffee. A user using the class can then add ingredients using a value from the defined enumerated type. The value of that ingredient is then used as the index into the BitArray, and the corresponding bit is set to true, as shown in the AddIngredient method. Imagine what it would be like if you didn't use this method. You would have to create either a property for each ingredient or a method that performed a lengthy switch of if/then/else statements. BitArrays allow you to save some of the hassles associated with simple Boolean configuration values.

Listing 4.3   **Representing Configuration Flags Within Your Class**

```
using System;
using System.Collections;

namespace _8_BitArrays
{
    enum Ingredients
    {
        ice, sugar, cream, chocolate, milk, syrup, cinnamon, decaf
    }

    class Coffee
    {
        private BitArray ingredientFlags;

        public Coffee()
        {
            ingredientFlags = new BitArray(8);
        }

        public void AddIngredient(Ingredients Ingredient)
        {
            ingredientFlags[(int) Ingredient] = true;
        }
    }

    public void ListIngredients()
    {
        Console.WriteLine( "Coffee Ingredients\n------------------");
        for( int i = 0; i < ingredientFlags.Count; i++ )
        {
            if( ingredientFlags[i] )
            {
                Console.WriteLine( "-" +
                    Enum.GetName(typeof(Ingredients), i) );
            }
        }
    }

    class Class1
    {
        [STAThread]
        static void Main(string[] args)
        {
            Coffee latte = new Coffee();
```

Listing 4.3   **Continued**

```
        latte.AddIngredient( Ingredients.sugar );
        latte.AddIngredient( Ingredients.cream );
        latte.AddIngredient( Ingredients.decaf );

        latte.ListIngredients();
    }
  }
}
```

As you saw earlier, the `BitArray` class contains several useful constructors that allow you to create bit arrays of different sizes as well as control how the individual bits are initialized. The simplest way is to pass a single integer into the constructor and a Boolean value specifying what each bit should be initialized to. Traditional methods of using bit arrays or bit fields required you to use, for instance, an integer. They would give you 32 bits to work with even though you might only use a fraction of them. A `BitArray`, on the other hand, lets you create as many or as few bits as needed. Although on the outside it might seem that you are saving memory, don't forget that the `BitArray` is a .NET Framework class derived from `System.Object` and as such consumes more memory than a single integer because it is a class and not a value. However, the ability to create only a few bit fields instead of a greater amount of unused fields might seem like a good tradeoff.

A few of the constructors of the `BitArray` class allow you to pass in an array of values, such as an array of integers, bytes, or Booleans, which each correspond to 32 bits, 8 bits, and 1 bit, respectively. The behavior of passing in an array instead of a single integer changes the behavior of the `BitArray` object creation. For each value in the array passed in, the `BitArray` creates a number of bits equal to the size of the data type passed in. If you pass in an integer array with five values, 32 bits are created for each of those five values, giving a total of 160 bits. Those bits are then initialized based on the actual values of the passed-in array. The first 32 bits are set to the value of the bits in the first value of the integer array; the second 32 bits are initialized to the same value as the bits of the second value of the integer array; and so on. Passing an array of values into the constructor of a `BitArray` not only allows you to specify how many bits to create (in multiples of the array data type size) but also allows you to initialize the individual bits in one method call.

The `BitArray` class also contains methods that allow you to manipulate the internal bits using Boolean logic. Due to the fact that the `BitArray` can contain any number of bits, you are limited to either performing Boolean logic on a single bit or passing in a different `BitArray`. In other words, you cannot perform a Boolean logic operation using a value such as an integer or byte because you cannot guarantee the *BitArray* contains the same number of bits of that data type. The available logic operations are `and`, `or`, `xor`, and `not` in addition to the regular Boolean logic operators that work with a single bit. The following code shows how you can easily clear or set each bit to 0 by using the `Xor` method. `Xor` will set a bit to `true` if either bit is set to `true` but not both. Therefore, if you `xor` a set of bits with itself, it sets all of the bits to `false` or `0`. Take note, however, that the `BitArray` class also contains a `SetAll` method, which can also set all the bits to `false`.

```
public void Drink()
{
        ingredientFlags.Xor( ingredientFlags );
        Console.WriteLine( "\nDrank Coffee" );
        ListIngredients();
}
```

4.10. Enumerating Collections with `IEnumerator`

You want to create a function that can enumerate the items of a collection regardless of the collection data type.

Technique

The `IEnumerator` interface allows you to enumerate the contents of collections that implement that interface, which you can retrieve by calling the `GetEnumerator` method on an instance of a collection. To begin enumeration, call the `MoveNext` method from the `IEnumerator` interface. Next, create a loop that breaks when `MoveNext` returns `false`. Within the loop body, retrieve the current value by calling the `ToString` method defined on the `Current` property. However, if the collection is a dictionary-based collection, check the type of the `Current` property; if it is a `DictionaryEntry` type, you have to cast the `Current` property to a `DictionaryEntry` object and access the `Value` property, as shown in Listing 4.4.

Listing 4.4   **Printing Collections That Implement the `IEnumerator` Interface**

```
using System;
using System.Collections;

namespace _9_IEnumerator
{
    class Class1
    {
        [STAThread]
        static void Main(string[] args)
        {
            int[] intArr = {1, 2, 3, 4, 5};

            ArrayList al = new ArrayList( intArr );

            bool[] baVals = { true, true, false, false, true };
            BitArray ba = new BitArray( baVals );
```

Listing 4.4   **Continued**

```
        Hashtable ht = new Hashtable();
        ht.Add( 1, "one" );
        ht.Add( 2, "two" );
        ht.Add( 3, "three" );
        ht.Add( 4, "four" );
        ht.Add( 5, "five" );

        PrintCollection( "Integer Array", intArr.GetEnumerator() );
        PrintCollection( "ArrayList", al.GetEnumerator() );
        PrintCollection( "BitArray", ba.GetEnumerator() );
        PrintCollection( "Hashtable", ht.GetEnumerator() );
    }

    static void PrintCollection( string name, IEnumerator collEnum )
    {
        Console.WriteLine( collEnum.GetType().ToString() );
        Console.WriteLine( name );
        while( collEnum.MoveNext() )
        {
            if( collEnum.Current.GetType() ==
                Type.GetType("System.Collections.DictionaryEntry") )
            {
                DictionaryEntry di = (DictionaryEntry) collEnum.Current;
                Console.Write( di.Value.ToString() + " " );
            }
            else
            {
                Console.Write( collEnum.Current.ToString() + " " );
            }
        }
        Console.WriteLine("\n");
    }
  }
}
```

Comments

One of the major advantages of object-oriented programming lies in the fact that objects can share some of the same characteristics, thereby allowing similar access to their data. Collections within the .NET Framework are no exception. Each collection implements two known interfaces, ICollection and IEnumerable, in addition to the interface that is implemented based on the type of collection (IList for list-based collections and IDictionary for dictionary-based collections like the Hashtable). Because collections implement these interfaces, you can create generic methods that can operate on differing collection types without having to create methods for each type of collection.

IEnumerable contains only a single method named GetEnumerator. This method returns a different interface named *IEnumerator*. Because collections implement the IEnumerable interface, you can retrieve the enumerator for each collection and use methods that allow you to traverse the items in the collection one at a time.

Although synchronization isn't covered until a later chapter, it's important to note that an enumerator is valid only if the collection never changes. In other words, if you are enumerating a collection and another thread changes a value in the collection, the enumerator is invalid and any calls to MoveNext or Reset throw an exception. You should therefore either lock the collection or handle the exception so you can recover should this event happen. Chapter 6, "Exceptions and Error Handling," discusses exceptions.

4.11. Sorting Collections

You want to sort the items in a collection.

Technique

The Array class contains a static Sort method. There are several overloaded versions of this method. To simply sort an array, pass the array as a parameter. If you need to sort a dictionary-based collection, create two arrays by converting the Keys and Values collections. Pass these two arrays into the Sort method. It will sort the Keys array and place each value associated with each key at the same index within the Values array. The additional Sort methods allow you to sort a range of items within the array.

The ArrayList contains three overloaded Sort methods. This nonstatic method works on a current instance of an ArrayList object. It too allows you to sort the array or a smaller range of items within the array.

The Array and ArrayList Sort methods also allow you to define your own comparison method. Create a class or struct that implements the IComparer interface. This interface contains one method, Compare, which accepts two objects as parameters. It returns an integer less than 0 if the first object is less than the second object, an integer greater than 0 if the first object is greater, and 0 if the two objects are the same:

```
struct Person : IComparer
{
    public string firstName;
    public string lastName;

    // a Person is identified by a first and last name
    public Person( string first, string last )
    {
        firstName = first;
```

```
        lastName = last;
    }

    // compares 2 Person objects
    public int Compare( object a, object b )
    {
        int lNameCmp;
        int fNameCmp;

        Person pa = (Person) a;
        Person pb = (Person) b;

        // compare last names first
        lNameCmp = String.Compare( pa.lastName, pb.lastName );

        // if names are not equal, return the result
        if( lNameCmp != 0 ) return lNameCmp;

        // last names were equal, check the first names
        fNameCmp = String.Compare( pa.firstName, pb.firstName );

        return fNameCmp;
    }
}
```

Comments

Whether it's a set of integers, a list of names, or records in a database, sometimes you need to sort a group of values. Sorting makes it easier to both manually and program-matically search for an individual item within a large group of values. The Array and ArrayList collection classes allow you to sort a group of values for this purpose. One thing to note is that these are the only collection classes that allow sorting. Fortunately, you can easily sort a group of values from a different collection class by converting its keys and values into an array. Furthermore, if you want to keep a sorted list of values at all times, even when new items are added, you can use the SortedList class.

At the simplest level, the Array and ArrayList can perform a default sort on the val-ues by simply either passing the array to sort to the Sort method if using the Array class or calling the Sort instance method in the ArrayList class, which doesn't need any parameters. This method works well for data types that are defined within the .NET Framework, but when you need to sort a custom data type, you need to help the Sort method by creating a custom comparison method.

In the code listing earlier, you can see a struct that represents a person. A Person sim-ply contains fields denoting first and last names, which are string objects. If you pass an array of Person values into a Sort method without any type of custom comparison method, you get unexpected results or at least results that are undesirable. Therefore, you create a custom comparison method named Compare, which is declared in the IComparer interface. The method defined in the Person struct compares two Person objects based on their last names. If the last names are equal, then it makes a comparison on the first names. When sorting an array of these objects, repeatedly calling the Compare method, which the Sort method can do, will result in a list of names sorted by last names in ascending order and first names in ascending order for those objects with equal last names.

To use the Compare method defined here, you have to pass a created object of this type into the Sort method. The Sort can accept an IComparer object as the last parameter, and because the Person struct implements that interface, an implicit cast occurs. Listing 4.5 shows how to use the Person struct defined earlier by first allowing the user to input a list of first and last names. When the user is finished, the unsorted array is printed to the console. You then call the Sort method of the ArrayList class, passing an instance of a Person to use the Compare method of that object.

Listing 4.5 **Sorting Names by Last Name and First Name Using the** Compare **Method in the** Person **Object**

```
using System;
using System.Collections;

namespace _11_Sorting
{
    class Class1
    {
        [STAThread]
        static void Main(string[] args)
        {
            string input;
            ArrayList alPeople = new ArrayList();
            Console.Write( "Enter first and last name or 'q' to quit: " );
            input = Console.ReadLine();

            // get list of names from user
            while( input.Length != 1 || Char.ToUpper(input[0]) != 'Q' )
            {
                string[] name = input.Split( new char[]{' '}, 2 );
                alPeople.Add( new Person( name[0], name[1] ));

                Console.Write( "Enter first and last name or 'q' to quit: " );
                input = Console.ReadLine();
            }

            // output unsorted names
            Console.WriteLine( "\nArray before sort" );
```

Listing 4.5   **Continued**

```
        foreach( Person p in alPeople )
        {
            Console.WriteLine( "    {0} {1}", p.firstName, p.lastName );
        }

        // sort arraylist using custom IComparer
        alPeople.Sort( new Person() );

        // output sorted array
        Console.WriteLine( "\nArray after sort" );
        foreach( Person p in alPeople )
        {
            Console.WriteLine( "    {0} {1}", p.firstName, p.lastName );
        }
    }
}

// person definition here...
}
```

4.12. Binary Searching with Arrays

You want to search an array for a specific item using a binary search method.

Technique

The `Array` and `ArrayList` classes each contain a method named `BinarySearch`. This method contains several overloads, which allows you to choose the best method to perform the search. To search an entire array for a specified object, call the static `BinarySearch` method, passing a single-dimension array and the object to search for:

```
Array.BinarySearch( myArray, "my value" );
```

You can also limit the search to a specific range by specifying a starting index and the number of items to search in:

```
Array.BinarySearch( myArray, 2, 3, "my value" );
```

You can also control how the comparison between objects is performed by passing an object in the last parameter that implements the `IComparer` interface. This interface contains a single method named `Compare` with two objects as parameters. This comparer can be either a .NET Framework comparer such as the `CaseInsensitiveComparer` class or one created by you. The previous recipe contains an example showing how to create your own comparer:

```
Array.BinarySearch( myArray, "My Value", new CaseInsensitiveComparer() );
```

Comments

Performing a linear search is a time-consuming process. Linear searching starts at the first index of a collection and checks the value of each index until the value you are searching for is found. For large arrays, this type of search can take a considerable amount of time. Binary searching drastically cuts the time it takes to search for a value. Binary searching works only on a sorted array. Therefore, when you want to perform a binary search using the BinarySearch method, you must ensure that the array is sorted. You can do so by calling the static method Sort, which takes the array to sort as a parameter.

Binary searching works well because it reduces the number of elements it takes to find a value. It begins by finding the middle element of the array. If the value it is searching for is less than that middle value, you are guaranteed that the value is not in the upper half of the array, which means you don't have to search any of those values. The search then finds the middle index of the lower half and compares it with the target value. Again, if the value is lower than the middle index, it searches the lower subarray; otherwise, it searches the upper subarray. This process repeats until the value is found. Because you effectively cut the search space in half each time, which is why it is called a binary search, the performance runs in $O(\log_2 n)$ time. Listing 4.6 shows how to create a simple number-guessing game utilizing a binary search to determine whether the user has made successful matches.

Listing 4.6 **Performing a Binary Search on an Array of Integers**

```
using System;
using System.Collections;

namespace _12_BinarySearch
{
    class Class1
    {
        [STAThread]
        static void Main(string[] args)
        {
            int[] lottoNumbers = new int[3];

            // generate the random numbers
            GenerateNumbers( lottoNumbers );

            // start the game
            PlayGame( lottoNumbers );
        }

        static void GenerateNumbers( int[] numbers )
        {
            // initialize random number generator with current ticks
            Random rand = new Random((int)DateTime.Now.Ticks);
```

Listing 4.6   **Continued**

```
        // fill array with random numbers from 1 to 10
        for( int i = 0; i < numbers.GetUpperBound(0)+1; i++ )
        {
            numbers[i] = rand.Next( 1, 10 );
        }

        // sort the final array
        Array.Sort( numbers );

    }

    static void PlayGame( int[] numbers )
    {
        int[] playerNumbers = new int[3];
        char[] space = {' '};
        string input;
        int matches = 0;

        // get user input and quit if 'q' is entered
        Console.Write( "Enter 3 digits between 1 and 10 (q to quit): " );
        input = Console.ReadLine();
        while( input.Length != 1 || Char.ToUpper( input[0] ) != 'Q' )
        {
            // split the input into a string array
            string[] temp = input.Split( space, 3 );

            // make sure 3 numbers were entered
            if( temp.Length < 3 )
            {
                Console.WriteLine( "You did not enter 3 digits." );
                Console.Write( "Enter 3 digits between 1 and 10 " +
                    "(q to quit): " );
                input = Console.ReadLine();
                continue;
            }

            // convert string values and place into integer array
            for ( int i = 0; i < 3; i ++ )
                playerNumbers[i] = Int32.Parse( temp[i] );

            // count how many matches occured
            matches = NumMatches( playerNumbers, numbers );
            if( matches == 3)
            {
                Console.WriteLine( "You won!" );
```

Listing 4.6   **Continued**

```
                return;
            }
            else
            {
                Console.WriteLine( "You have {0} matches. Try again.",
                    matches );
            }
            Console.Write( "Enter 3 digits between 1 and 10 " +
                "(q to quit): " );
            input = Console.ReadLine();
        }
    }

    static int NumMatches( int[] playerNumbers, int[] numbers )
    {
        int matches = 0;

        // arraylist to hold current numbers to compare
        ArrayList al = new ArrayList( numbers );

        foreach( int number in playerNumbers )
        {
            // search for current user number in arraylist
            int result = al.BinarySearch( number );
            if( result >= 0 )
            {
                // since matched, remove it so it isn't counted again
                al.RemoveAt( result );
                matches++;
            }
        }

        return matches;
    }
}
```

Listing 4.6 shows how binary searching works with an array of integers. The application is a number-guessing game that uses an array of three integers from 1 to 10. The numbers are generated randomly using the Random class, which itself is seeded based on the current date and time. Once the array is created, the game begins. The user must enter three digits. Those three digits are then placed in an array, which is enumerated. For each value in that array, the program performs a binary search on the target numbers and keeps a count of matches. If there are three matches, the user guessed the numbers and the game is over. Figure 4.6 shows an example of running this application.

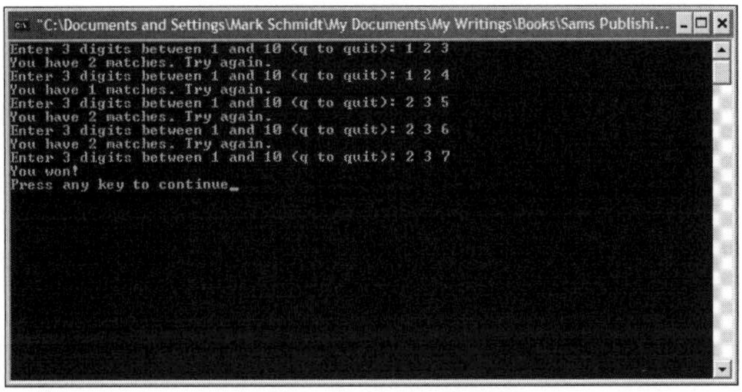

Figure 4.6 An array of integers is searched using a binary search to determine whether a successful match occurs.

4.13. Creating New Collection Types

None of the .NET Framework collection classes will work for the type of data
you want to store. You want to create your own collection class.

Technique

Determine which collection class is similar to what you want to accomplish and create a
derived class from that collection class. Overload any item-manipulation methods necessary for your new collection. You might also choose to implement a collection that isn't
based on a predefined collection, or you might want to create a strongly typed collection. In either case, for a list-based collection, create a class derived from
CollectionBase, and for a dictionary-based collection, create a class derived from
DictionaryBase.

Comments

Due to the design of the collection classes within the .NET Framework, implementing a
collection class of your own is much simpler because you can borrow implementation
details from the built-in collection classes. Depending on your needs, there are a couple
of ways to go about implementing your own collection.

    If you want to alter the behavior of a collection but keep a majority of the imple-
mentation details intact, you can use inheritance to your advantage. This process saves
you from a lot of the bookkeeping tasks associated with collection classes while still giving you control of how objects are manipulated within your collection. Let's take the
example from the previous recipe, which worked with a list of first and last names. You
can create a class that derives from ArrayList and overload some of the methods to validate the values that are added to the collection. For instance, by overloading the Add

method, you can ensure that the object passed in is a string object and that it contains a first name and a last name separated by a space:

```
class NameCollection : ArrayList
{
    public override int Add( object value )
    {
        if( value.GetType() == Type.GetType("System.String" ))
        {
            string[] name = ((string)value).Split( new char[]{' '});
            if( name.Length == 2 )
                return base.Add( value );
        }

        return -1;
    }

    public int Add( string value )
    {
        string[] name = ((string)value).Split( new char[]{' '});
        if( name.Length == 2 )
            return base.Add( value );
        return -1;
    }
}
```

Deriving from a .NET collection class can be a real time-saver and allows you to slightly alter the behavior of a collection class. However, you might need an even finer grain of control over your collection. The NameCollection example would benefit more if you created a strongly typed collection. A strongly typed collection is one that uses a certain data type for its values rather than generic object instances.

To create a strongly typed collection, derive from either CollectionBase if your collection is list based or DictionaryBase if your collection needs to be dictionary based like a hash table. These classes implement the appropriate interfaces for a .NET collection. Furthermore, they also provide protected methods and properties that you can use to add objects to the collection.

We'll take a look at an example of creating a strongly typed list collection that represents a hand of cards. The definition of a Card is similar to the example shown in the sorting recipe, which means it contains fields for data and properties to access those fields and implements the IComparable interface to compare two cards. The comparison checks the suit of a card first, and if they are equal, it compares the actual value of the card. Listing 4.7 shows the implementation of the Card class.

Listing 4.7   **Card Type Containing a Card Value and Suit Defined with Enumerated Types**

```
public enum CardSuits
{
    Hearts = 1, Clubs, Diamonds, Spades
}
public enum CardValues
{
    Two=2, Three, Four, Five, Six, Seven, Eight, Nine, Ten,
    Jack = 11, Queen, King, Ace
}

public class Card : IComparer
{
    int number;
    CardSuits suit;

    public Card() : this( CardValues.Two, CardSuits.Hearts )
    {
    }

    public Card( CardValues cvalue, CardSuits csuit )
    {
        // ensure values fall within range
        if( (int) cvalue > 1 && (int)cvalue < 15 )
            number = (int) cvalue;
        else
            number = 2;

        // ensure suits fall within range
        if( (int) csuit > 0 && (int) csuit < 5 )
            suit = csuit;
        else
            suit = CardSuits.Hearts;
    }
    public override string ToString()
    {
        string ret;

        // get face card name if card is greater than 10
        if( number > 10 )
        {
            ret = Enum.GetName( typeof(CardValues), number );
        }
        else
        {
```

Listing 4.7 **Continued**

```
            ret = number.ToString();
        }

        ret += " of ";

        // get suit name from CardSuits enum
        ret += Enum.GetName( typeof(CardSuits), suit );

        return ret;
    }

    public CardSuits CardSuit
    {
        get
        {
            return suit;
        }
        set
        {
            // make sure suit falls within range
            if( (int) value > 0 && (int) value < 5 )
                suit = value;
        }
    }

    public CardValues CardValue
    {
        get
        {
            return (CardValues) number;
        }
        set
        {
            // make sure value is within range
            if( (int) value > 1 && (int) value < 15 )
            {
                number = (int) value;
            }
        }
    }

    public int Compare(object x, object y)
    {
        Card a = (Card) x;
        Card b = (Card) y;
```

Listing 4.7   **Continued**

```
        // check card suits
        if( (int) a.CardSuit < (int) b.CardSuit )
            return -1;
        if( (int) a.CardSuit > (int) b.CardSuit )
            return 1;

        // check card values since suits are the same
        if( (int) a.CardValue < (int) b.CardValue )
            return -1;
        if( (int) a.CardValue > (int) b.CardValue )
            return 1;

        return 0;
    }
}
```

If you were to create a class that simply derived from ArrayList, a person using the class might add a different object, an integer for example, to the collection. This class obviously doesn't work for what you want to do. Listing 4.8 shows the CardHand class. This class is a strongly typed collection class derived from CollectionBase and only allows you to place Card objects into the collection. The reason it works is that the CollectionBase class uses explicit interface implementation to "hide" the interface methods of the collection interfaces. It allows you to restrict the types of objects added to the collection. However, you can still cast your collection object to one of the collection interfaces, thereby allowing you to add an object not designed to work with your collection. To circumvent this, the CollectionBase class contains several events that you can handle to prevent the addition of data types not consistent with your collection. (Events are covered in Chapter 5, "Delegates and Events.")

During implementation of your collection, because the CollectionBase base class contains a protected ArrayList member variable, you are free to use that as the internal collection and route any method calls on your object to that internal collection, a process known as *containment*. Figure 4.7 shows the result of running the application in Listing 4.8.

Listing 4.8   **Implementing a Strongly Typed Collection by Deriving from**
CollectionBase **and Storing Card Objects**

```
using System;
using System.Collections;

namespace _13_CardCollection
{
    //
```

Listing 4.8   **Continued**

```
// Card implementation from Listing 4.7 here
//

public class CardHand : CollectionBase
{
    public CardHand()
    {
    }

    public override string ToString()
    {
        string ret = "";

        // print out name of each card in hand
        foreach( Card c in base.InnerList )
            ret += c.ToString() + "\n";

        return ret;
    }

    public void GenerateRandomHand( int numCards )
    {
        // initialize random number generator using tick count
        Random rand = new Random( (int)DateTime.Now.Ticks );

        // copy to array and sort
        ArrayList sortedCards = (ArrayList) base.InnerList.Clone();
        sortedCards.Sort( new Card() );
        for( int i = 0; i < numCards; i++ )
        {
            Card newCard;

            do
            {
                int val = rand.Next( 2, 15 );
                int suit = rand.Next( 1, 4 );

                // create new random card
                newCard = new Card( (CardValues) val, (CardSuits) suit );

                // make sure card doesn't already exist
                // by searching current hand
            } while( sortedCards.BinarySearch(newCard, newCard ) > 0);

            // add to sorted cards array
```

Listing 4.8   **Continued**

```csharp
                sortedCards.Add( newCard );
                Add( newCard );

                // resort the sortedCards collection
                sortedCards.Sort( new Card() );
            }
        }

        public int Add( Card value )
        {
            // add to base class list
            return base.InnerList.Add( (object)value );
        }

        public void Remove( Card value )
        {
            // remove from base class list
            base.InnerList.Remove( value );
        }

        public void Sort()
        {
            base.InnerList.Sort( new Card() );
        }
    }

    class Class1
    {
        [STAThread]
        static void Main(string[] args)
        {
            CardHand hand = new CardHand();

            hand.GenerateRandomHand( 5 );

            Console.WriteLine( "Random Hand\n" + hand.ToString() );

            hand.Sort();

            Console.WriteLine( "\nSorted Hand\n" + hand.ToString() );

            Console.WriteLine( "Total of {0} cards", hand.Count );
        }
    }
}
```

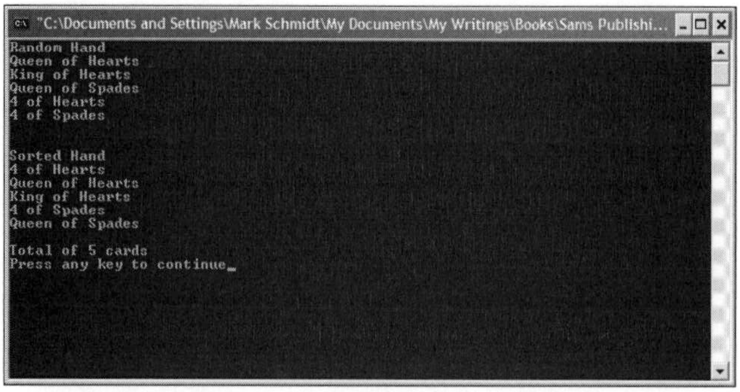

Figure 4.7   The `CardHand` collection works with `Card` objects to simulate a collection of cards.

It is important to note that if your collection is not list or dictionary based, the method of creating the collection is still similar. Rather than derive from a class such as `CollectionBase` or `DictionaryBase`, you instead implement a number of interfaces and their associated methods. Generally, you implement `ICollection` and, if you allow enumeration, the `IEnumerable` interface. Even if you decide to store the objects differently within your class—using a red-black tree, for example—you might still want to implement the same method signatures shown in other collections. List-based collection classes implement the `IList` interface, and dictionary-based collections implement the `IDictionary` interface.

4.14. Creating Indexers

You want to allow users of your class to use an indexer to retrieve individual elements from your collection.

Technique

Indexers allow users to access items within a class in the same way items within an array are accessed. To create an indexer for a custom collection class, rselect the class within ClassView that you want to add an indexer to and select Project, Add Indexer from the main menu. Select the data type from the Indexer Type field that is the data type of the value used to get or set an individual item in your collection, as shown shown in Figure 4.8. Next, add any parameters within the brackets of the indexer. Implement the `get` and `set` methods for the indexer within your class.

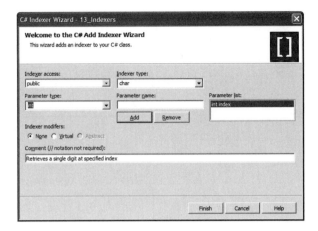

Figure 4.8   Add an indexer to your class by using the Add Indexer dialog.

Comments

Creating an indexer is similar to creating a regular class property. Like a property, it uses `get` and `set` procedures to manipulate an internal value within your class. Listing 4.9 shows an indexer for a class that allows you to change an individual digit within an integer. Although the class itself isn't a full .NET collection, it does serve to show how you can use an indexer to set an individual item within a collection.

Listing 4.9   **Creating an Indexer**

```
using System;
using System.Text;
namespace _13_Indexers
{
    class Class1
    {
        [STAThread]
        static void Main(string[] args)
        {
            IntegerString val = new IntegerString();
            val.num = 12345;
            for( int i = 0; i < 2; i++ )
            {
                int swap;
                swap = val[i];
                val[i] = val[4-i];
                val[4-i] = swap;
            }

            Console.WriteLine( val.num );
        }
```

Listing 4.9   **Continued**

```
    }

    class IntegerString
    {
        public int num = 0;

        public int this[int index]
        {
            get
            {
                return Int32.Parse(num.ToString()[index].ToString());
            }
            set
            {
                StringBuilder sValue = new StringBuilder(num.ToString());
                sValue[index] = Char.Parse(value.ToString());
                num = Int32.Parse(sValue.ToString());
            }
        }
    }
}
```

5

Delegates and Events

5.0. Introduction

Behavior largely consists of responding to events. Something occurs, and it is our investigation and response to that event that determines what to do next. For instance, when we're assembling some new toy for the kids and a piece breaks, we adjust our behavior accordingly to respond to that event, whether it is to fix it or find some other mechanism to get the job done. With the advent of graphical user interfaces, event-driven programming added a layer on top of procedural programming. That's not saying that procedural programming was entirely replaced because some of its characteristics are in place today. Event-driven programming modifies the behavior of a program due to some internal or external change in state that requires special processing to handle that event.

This chapter looks at how events and their supporting constructs, delegates, work within the .NET Framework. Initially, you'll learn how to define and use delegates to lay the groundwork necessary to understand how events and event receivers work. You'll also see how you can propagate events to multiple receivers by using multicast delegates.

5.1. Defining and Using Delegates

You want to define a delegate and allow the use of that delegate within a member function.

Technique

A delegate is similar to a member method but does not contain a method body. Define a member method using the `delegate` keyword following the access modifier. Because there is no body associated with the delegate, place a semicolon instead of braces at the end of the method header. For member methods that will use an instance of that delegate, add a parameter whose data type is the name of the delegate method name followed by a parameter identifier:

```
class StringPrinterDelegate
{
    public delegate void PrintString( string s );

    // delegate passed as parameter
    public static void PrintWithDelegate( PrintString psDelegate, string s )
    {
        psDelegate( s );
    }

    // internal delegate implementation
    public static void InternalImp( string s )
    {
        Console.WriteLine( s );
    }
}
```

To use a delegate within a client application, create an instance of the delegate method whose data type consists of the name of the class, the dot (.) operator, and the name of the delegate. The constructor expects the name of the function that implements this delegate as a parameter. You can locate this delegate implementation within the class that implements the delegate or within a different class, as shown in the code example via the `InternalImp` method, as long as the method header is identical. Listing 5.1 shows how to create a client application that instantiates two instances of the delegate shown earlier. Each delegate uses a different method implementation using either the static method in the same class as the delegate or the method within the client application class itself. Additionally, the listing also shows how to pass a delegate instance to a method. The output of Listing 5.1 appears in Figure 5.1.

Listing 5.1   **Defining Delegates**

```
using System;

namespace _1_Delegates
{
    class Class1
    {
        [STAThread]
        static void Main(string[] args)
        {
            // instantiate delegates
            StringPrinterDelegate.PrintString internalPrint =
                new StringPrinterDelegate.PrintString
                    ( StringPrinterDelegate.InternalImp );
```

Listing 5.1   **Continued**

```
            StringPrinterDelegate.PrintString firstCharPrint =
                new StringPrinterDelegate.PrintString( FirstCharPrint );

            // get string from user
            Console.Write( "Enter a string: " );
            string input = Console.ReadLine();

            // call delegates directly
            internalPrint( input );
            firstCharPrint( input );

            // pass delegates as parameter
            StringPrinterDelegate.PrintWithDelegate( internalPrint, input );
            StringPrinterDelegate.PrintWithDelegate( firstCharPrint, input );
        }

        // external delegate implementation
        static void FirstCharPrint( string s )
        {
            string[] splitStrings = s.Split( new char[]{' '} );
            foreach( string splitString in splitStrings )
            {
                Console.Write( "{0}", splitString[0] );
                for( int i = 0; i < splitString.Length; i++ )
                    Console.Write( " " );
            }
            Console.WriteLine();
        }
    }
}
```

Comments

To delegate means to transfer the care or management of something to a different person or other object. A delegate within the .NET Framework acts like a method whose implementation is provided or delegated to some other object. In other words, an object declares that it supports a certain method but relies on different objects or methods to provide the actual implementation.

Looking at the syntax of a delegate, it's perfectly reasonable to assume that a delegate is a method because it resides in an object and it is declared much like other methods. However, a delegate is actually converted to a class when the source is compiled to (MSIL). This class name is the name you give to the delegate when you declare it, and the class itself is derived from System.MulticastDelegate, as shown in Figure 5.2, which shows the code listing earlier in the ILDasm tool. In the client application shown earlier, you can see that you use the new keyword on a delegate. Because a delegate is in actuality a class, the new keyword is creating an instance of that class.

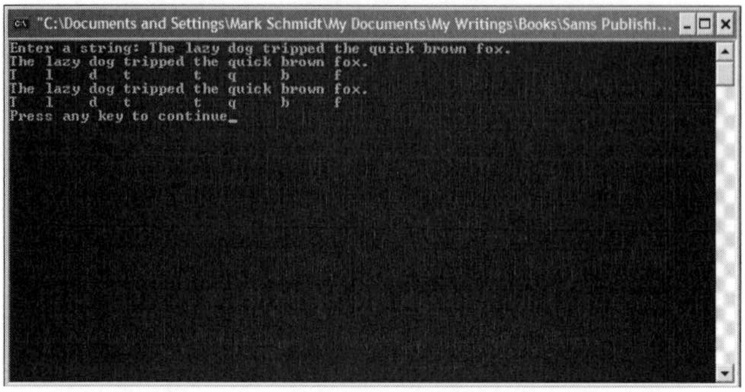

Figure 5.1   Delegates can be associated with different implementations, and you can define those implementations in different classes.

Figure 5.2   A delegate is actually a class nested within its containing class.

Delegates have been compared to function pointers, and in some cases they are quite similar. The pointer in the delegate sense of the word is a managed pointer to the method, which provides the implementation for the delegate. Because this pointer is managed by the Common Language Runtime (CLR), it is secure, type safe, and verifiable, unlike its unmanaged counterpart. This pointer is passed into the constructor of the delegate when you use the new keyword. If you look at the intermediate language (IL) that is generated when an instance of a delegate is created, you see the instruction ldftn, which places a managed function pointer onto the runtime stack. So the question is now, how does the delegate class that is created call the method using the unmanaged pointer?

Looking at the delegate class in ILDasm, you can also see three methods within the class. The first two, BeginInvoke and EndInvoke, are used for asynchronous delegates, which are explained later in this chapter. The third method, Invoke, is where the implementation of the delegate is called. However, double-clicking on the method name in ILDasm shows the method signature with an empty body, as shown in Figure 5.3. When you see this sort of behavior, you will also usually see the attribute "runtime managed" on the method. When Invoke is called, the CLR retrieves the function pointer that was placed on the runtime stack (with the IL instruction ldftn mentioned earlier), and that is now a member variable within the delegate class, and uses it to call the actual method. The reason no IL shows up in the method is that the act of calling the actual delegate implementation happens within unmanaged code contained within the runtime.

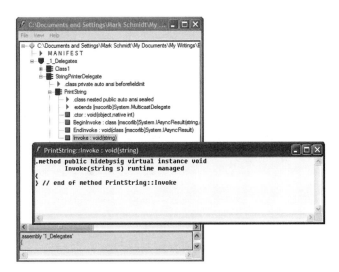

Figure 5.3   A delegate's Invoke method is runtime managed.

To summarize the steps involved when the CLR creates a delegate, the first step is to convert the delegate into a class derived from System.MulticastDelegate during the compilation process. A client then creates an instance of that class passing a method, either static or nonstatic, to the constructor of that object. This step results in the IL instruction ldftn, which places a managed pointer to the method onto the stack. The delegate constructor places that managed pointer into a member variable within the delegate class. When the actual method is called, the runtime-managed Invoke method is called instead, and unmanaged code within the runtime finds the correct method, via the managed method pointer, and calls its implementation.

5.2. Combining Delegates to Form Multicast Delegates

You want to use a single delegate but allow it to bind to multiple methods.

Technique

The generated delegate class is derived from System.MulticastDelegate, which means you are free to use any methods defined in that class for your delegate. To bind to multiple implementations, use the static method Combine, either passing an array of instantiated delegates bound to methods or passing two delegates you want to bind together to create a new delegate:

```
static void Main(string[] args)
{
    // create delegate array
    StringPrinterDelegate.PrintString[] printDelegates = new
        StringPrinterDelegate.PrintString[3];

    // main delegate
    StringPrinterDelegate.PrintString stringPrinters;

    // create 3 delegates with 3 different implementations
    printDelegates[0] = new StringPrinterDelegate.PrintString( NormalPrint );
    printDelegates[1] = new StringPrinterDelegate.PrintString( FirstCharPrint );
    printDelegates[2] = new StringPrinterDelegate.PrintString( LastCharPrint );

    // combine the 3 delegates into the main delegate
    stringPrinters = (StringPrinterDelegate.PrintString)
        Delegate.Combine( printDelegates );

    // get string from user
    Console.Write( "Enter a string: " );
    string input = Console.ReadLine();

    // print with main delegate which causes all 3 to be invoked
    StringPrinterDelegate.PrintWithDelegate( stringPrinters, input );
}
```

Comments

Sometimes, you might want a single delegate to bind to several different implementations, thereby causing each implementation to be invoked when the delegate is called. This premise is behind the multicast delegate. A multicast delegate allows you to create several delegate implementations and bind them to only one delegate. Therefore, when the delegate is called, each method within the delegate's invocation list is called one after the other.

In the code listing earlier, you can see a collection of `PrintString` delegates being created and placed into an array. Each of them are bound to a certain delegate implementation whose purpose is to simply print a string in a certain way. Once the collection is created, the static method `Combine` in the `System.Delegate` class is called, passing the collection as the only parameter. This method enumerates the entire collection and creates a multicast delegate. Because the generated delegate class derives from `System.MulticastDelegate`, you can assign a variable of that type from the result of the `Combine` method. However, because `Combine` returns a generic multicast delegate object, you have to cast the return value to the type you declared. Now any time the multicast delegate is called, each method that it is bound to is called. The `PrintWithDelegate` method is the same method shown in the previous recipe. No special programming is needed because the `Invoke` method that is generated for the delegate class will enumerate each method.

One thing to keep in mind when creating multicast delegates is order. Unless you are calling a delegate asynchronously, which is discussed in a later recipe, order can be important. The order of method invocations on a multicast delegate is determined based on the order in which the method implementations were bound to it. For the example earlier, the first method invoked is the lowest indexed method within the collection used to create the multicast delegate.

5.3. Removing Individual Delegates from Multicast Delegates

You want to remove an individual delegate from the invocation list of a multicast delegate.

Technique

Use the subtraction assignment operator to remove a delegate that appears at any point within the invocation list of a multicast delegate. You can use the same object that you used to add the delegate and allow the delegate class to find the corresponding delegate within the multicast delegate:

```
StringPrinterDelegate.PrintString[] printDelegates =
    new StringPrinterDelegate.PrintString[3];
StringPrinterDelegate.PrintString stringPrinters;
```

```
printDelegates[0] = new StringPrinterDelegate.PrintString( NormalPrint );
printDelegates[1] = new StringPrinterDelegate.PrintString( FirstCharPrint );
printDelegates[2] = new StringPrinterDelegate.PrintString( LastCharPrint );
stringPrinters = (StringPrinterDelegate.PrintString)
    Delegate.Combine( printDelegates );

// remove index 1 from invocation list
stringPrinters -= printDelegates[1];
```

You can also access the invocation list directly and use an individual delegate with the subtraction assignment operator to remove the delegate:

```
Delegate[] delegateList = stringPrinters.GetInvocationList();
stringPrinters -= (StringPrinterDelegate.PrintString)
    delegateList[delegateList.Length-1];
```

To remove a range of delegates, you must use another multicast delegate whose invocation list contains the delegates you want to remove. When you use the static `Remove` method defined in `System.Delegate`, you remove the last occurrence of a list of delegates within a source multicast delegate. The list of delegates to remove is contained within the second parameter to the function:

```
Delegate.Remove( delegateSource, delegateList );
```

If you, however, want to remove all occurrences of an invocation list from a multicast delegate, you can use the `RemoveAll` static method. Whereas the `Remove` function only removes the last occurrence of an invocation list, `RemoveAll` removes any and all occurrences of that list within a multicast delegate. The parameters of this method are the same as those for the `Remove` method.

Comments

As in physics where every action has an equal and opposite reaction, every addition should have an equal and opposite subtraction within an API. In the recipes leading up to this one, you looked at different ways to add delegates to form multicast delegates. This recipe takes the opposite approach and shows you how to remove individual delegates.

The process of removing delegates is essentially the same but, of course, uses different operator and method names. The easiest way to remove a delegate from a multicast delegate is to use the subtraction assignment operator. If the variables that were used to create the initial delegate objects are still within scope, you can use those as the operands to the subtraction assignment operator. When you do so, the delegate class uses object equality methods to find the correct delegate within its invocation list and remove that delegate. If however those variables are no longer in scope, you can still remove them by accessing the invocation list directly via the `GetInvocationList` method. It simply returns an array of delegate objects, which you can then index to retrieve the delegate you want to remove.

One thing we haven't mentioned up to this point is that you can combine multicast delegates with other multicast delegates. The previous samples showed how to combine single delegates to form a multicast delegate, but the process is the same if you want to then take the resultant multicast delegate and combine it with the invocation list of another multicast delegate. This process results in a merge of the two invocation lists of those multicast delegates to form yet another object. Likewise, you can remove the invocation list of one multicast delegate from the invocation list of another, as mentioned earlier. If you call the Remove method defined in System.Delegate, the delegate class finds the matching list of delegates in a source multicast delegate and removes the last occurrence of that list in its invocation list.

In other words, just as you can add the list of delegates from one multicast delegate to another, you can also turn around and remove that list. If a certain invocation list was added multiple times, then only the last occurrence of that list is removed from the multicast delegate. In other words, you have to call Remove for each associated Combine. If you would rather remove all invocation lists from a multicast delegate given another list, you can call the RemoveAll method. Therefore, any time a matching invocation list appears in the source multicast delegate, it is removed regardless of its location in the entire list.

5.4. Accessing Delegate Names Within a Multicast Delegate

You want to view which methods are attached to a multicast delegate.

Technique

To retrieve an array of delegates that are attached to a multicast delegate, call the GetInvocationList method from the multicast delegate instance. You can access the method name and additional method information on each delegate by using the Method property defined in the delegate. This step returns a MethodInfo object, and you find the name of the method bound to that delegate by accessing the Name property of that object:

```
class StringPrinterDelegate
{
    public delegate void PrintString( string s );

    // delegate passed as parameter
    public static void PrintWithDelegate( PrintString psDelegate, string s )
    {
        Console.Write( "Invocation List Method Names: " );
```

```
        // enumerate through each delegate in invocation list
        foreach( Delegate dg in psDelegate.GetInvocationList() )
            Console.Write( dg.Method.Name + " " );

        Console.WriteLine();

        // call delegate
        psDelegate( s );
    }
}
```

Comments

Whenever you start programming anything that is dynamic in nature, you lose any pre-defined knowledge about objects or methods or anything else that you normally know before you compile. In other words, when you want to call a method, you know what the method name is and you can use that information to output tracing or debug information. However, once you enter the dynamic realm where objects are attached during runtime, or the invocation of methods occurs dynamically based on the running state of the application, you don't always know what object is being accessed or what method is being called at any given point in time. That is, you don't know unless you have some sort of runtime type information or reflection capabilities built into the language or your application.

The .NET Framework is a very dynamic environment and as such has rich support for runtime type information and the ability to inspect an object and its methods at any point. The multicast delegate class is no exception. There are a few reasons why you would want to inspect the methods that a multicast delegate is bound with, the most probable reason being debugging.

You saw earlier how to use the GetInvocationList to access individual delegates within a multicast delegate so you can remove them from the invocation list. One thing that wasn't pointed out was that you can also enumerate this list to gather information about each delegate. The invocation list is simply an array of delegate objects whose type is System.Delegate. Within that class is a Method property that contains any information you need about the method to which the delegate is bound. Although this recipe singles out the Name property to determine the name of the bound method, there are other properties that you might find useful.

5.5. Calling Delegates Asynchronously

A delegate can take a long time to return; you want to invoke the delegate asynchronously so that it returns immediately and notifies you when it has finished.

Technique

In addition to the delegate and the method to bind to that delegate, create a method that is used to process the results of the asynchronous method call. This method takes a single IAsyncResult parameter. This method is called when the delegate method has finished, and you can obtain results by calling the EndInvoke method obtained from the IAsyncResult object.

```
class TearCallback
{
    public void PrintTearResult( IAsyncResult ar)
    {
        TearWebPage tear = (TearWebPage)((AsyncResult)ar).AsyncDelegate;
        Console.WriteLine( "TearPage returned {0}", tear.EndInvoke( ar ) );
    }
}
```

Before invoking the delegate, create an AsyncCallback object by passing the method name of the result method mentioned earlier. If this method is not static, use an instance of the object that implements this method followed by the dot operator (.) and the method name.

Listing 5.2   **Asynchronous Delegates**

```
using System;
using System.Threading;
using System.Runtime.Remoting.Messaging;
using System.Net;
using System.IO;
using System.Text;

namespace _5_AsynchronousDelegate
{
    public delegate bool TearWebPage( string url );

    class Class1
    {
        [STAThread]
        static void Main(string[] args)
        {
            // create delegate attached to DoAsynchSleep method
```

Listing 5.2   **Continued**

```
            TearWebPage tear = new TearWebPage( new WebTear().TearPage );

            // create result class and create callback object
            TearCallback result = new TearCallback();
            AsyncCallback ascb = new AsyncCallback( result.PrintTearResult );

            // invoke the delegate asynchronously
            IAsyncResult ar = tear.BeginInvoke (
                "http://www.samspublishing.com", ascb, null );

            // long operation here
            Thread.Sleep(10000);
        }
    }

    // Insert TearCallback implementation here

    class WebTear
    {
        public bool TearPage( string url )
        {
            // final web page text variable
            StringBuilder pageText = new StringBuilder("");

            // create URI and a web request
            Uri HttpSite = new Uri(url);
            HttpWebRequest wreq = (HttpWebRequest)WebRequest.Create(HttpSite);
            wreq.AllowAutoRedirect = true;

            // get the stream associated with the web request
            Stream webStream = wreq.GetResponse().GetResponseStream();

            // create byte array for chunked data
            byte[] webResponse = new byte[1024];
            int bytesRead = 0;

            do
            {
                // read first 1024 bytes
                bytesRead = webStream.Read( webResponse, 0, 1024 );

                // append current chunk to final result
                if( bytesRead > 0 )
                {
                    pageText.Append( Encoding.ASCII.GetString
                        ( webResponse, 0, bytesRead ));
```

Listing 5.2   **Continued**

```
            }

            // continue until no more bytes are being read
        } while( bytesRead > 0 );

        // output final result
        Console.WriteLine( pageText.ToString() );
        return true;
    }
  }
}
```

To invoke the delegate asynchronously, call the `BeginInvoke` method defined in the delegate, passing the necessary delegate parameters followed by the `AsyncCallback` object and an optional object used to hold state information, as shown in Listing 5.2.

Comments

As fast as computers are nowadays, sometimes fast still isn't fast enough. Whether the lag occurs due to disk I/O, network traffic, or long computations, you can use this lag to your advantage by performing additional work until an operation finishes. Asynchronous method calls allow you to invoke a method and not wait for it to complete before you begin other tasks. As you work through the .NET Framework, you will see that you can perform asynchronous method calls in a variety of different ways. This recipe shows how to invoke a delegate asynchronously.

The initial code for the delegate is the same as the previous recipes in this chapter. The delegate is the same as well as its implementation and the code used to bind the two together. The difference is at the point where the actual work needs to happen, the point of delegate method invocation. The first recipe in this chapter mentioned that the delegate class generated upon using the `delegate` keyword contains three methods: `Invoke`, `BeginInvoke`, and `EndInvoke`. Up to this point, the `Invoke` method was called transparently anytime the delegate was used. `Invoke` performs a classic synchronous method call. In other words, `Invoke` does not return until the method has finished to completion. You use `BeginInvoke` and `EndInvoke`, however, when you want to call the delegate asynchronously.

The code listing for this recipe creates a class that contains a method implementation for the `TearWebPage` delegate. This method, `TearPage`, uses classes within the .NET Framework to open a connection with a remote Web server and request a page. If called synchronously, this method might not return for a while if network traffic is high, so we made the decision to call it asynchronously.

The first step, other than actually creating the delegate method implementation, of course, is to create a method used as the callback method. When the delegate method finishes, this method is called to notify the user of the delegate. The method itself accepts a single parameter whose data type is `IAsyncResult`. Before looking at the implementation of this method, you first have to understand how `BeginInvoke` works.

After you bind a method to a delegate, you have to set up the necessary objects used for the delegate callback. To do so, create an instance of the class that contains the callback method if this method isn't static. Next, create an `AsyncCallback` object passing the callback method name as the parameter. You can then call the `BeginInvoke` method. `BeginInvoke` is dynamically created based on the parameters. When you call `BeginInvoke`, as shown in the listing earlier, you provide each parameter necessary similar to the way you do if you were performing a synchronous method call. However, you need two additional parameters after the delegate parameter list. The first is the `AsyncCallback` method created earlier; the delegate class uses it when the method finishes. The final parameter can be any object that you want to create to hold state information. Because this parameter is optional and not used within the implementation of the `BeginInvoke` method itself, this parameter can be `null`. Once the `BeginInvoke` method is called, it returns immediately even though the method to which the delegate is bound has not finished. You can then perform additional processing as you wait for the delegate method to finish.

Once the delegate method finishes, your callback method created earlier is called. If you recall, this method receives a `IAsyncResult` parameter, which you can use to access the delegate instance that has finished. To do so, cast the `IAsyncResult` to an `AsyncResult` object and then cast the `AsyncDelegate` property of that object to your delegate class, as shown in the `PrintTearResult` method earlier. To access the return value, call the `EndInvoke` method defined in the delegate class. The `EndInvoke` is also dynamically created using the return value of the delegate method as its return value. Figure 5.4 shows the result of running Listing 5.2.

Figure 5.4 You download a Web page using an asynchronous delegate and access its result using the delegate callback method.

5.6. Return Values for Multicast Delegates

You want to access individual return values for each delegate method within a multicast delegate.

Technique

If you want to use the return value from one delegate method as the input to another delegate method within the same multicast delegate, create a parameter prefaced with the ref keyword for value types. If an object is passed as a parameter, note that any change to that object is passed onto the next delegate method within the invocation list:

```
public void Factorial( ref int op1, ref int op2 );
```

If you want to obtain individual return values for each single delegate within a multicast delegate, you can create a collection as a parameter in the delegate list that method implementations can use to place return values as demonstrated in Listing 5.3.

Listing 5.3   Allowing Individual Delegate Return Values by Using a Collection

```csharp
using System;
using System.Collections;
using System.Text;

namespace _6_ReturnValues
{
    public delegate bool PrintString( string s, ArrayList retVals );

    class Class1
    {
        [STAThread]
        static void Main(string[] args)
        {
            ArrayList retVals = new ArrayList();

            // instantiate delegate
            PrintString[] printDelegates = new PrintString[2];
            PrintString stringPrinters;

            printDelegates[0] = new PrintString( NormalPrint );
            printDelegates[1] = new PrintString( FirstCharPrint );

            stringPrinters = (PrintString) Delegate.Combine( printDelegates );

            // get string from user
            Console.Write( "Enter a string: " );
```

Listing 5.3   **Continued**

```
            string input = Console.ReadLine();

            stringPrinters( input, retVals );

            foreach( string ret in retVals )
            {
                Console.WriteLine( ret );
            }
        }

        static bool NormalPrint( string s, ArrayList retVals )
        {
            retVals.Add( s );

            return true;
        }

        static bool FirstCharPrint( string s, ArrayList retVals )
        {
            StringBuilder retVal = new StringBuilder();

            string[] splitStrings = s.Split( new char[]{' '} );
            foreach( string splitString in splitStrings )
            {
                retVal.Append(splitString[0]);
                for( int i = 0; i < splitString.Length; i++ )
                    retVal.Append( " " );
            }
            retVals.Add( retVal.ToString() );

            return true;
        }
    }
}
```

Comments

One of the limitations of using a multicast delegate is the lack of information based on a return value from the individual methods bound to that multicast delegate. The return value from a multicast delegate is the result of the last delegate method called within the invocation list. You are therefore unable to access the previous delegate method return values without resorting to the special programming methods presented here.

Although not necessarily capturing the return value of each delegate, using the ref keyword on a parameter allows you to carry changes to a value type to each subsequent delegate. This move can be useful, for instance, if you need a value that each delegate must change and that change must be carried over. In the `Factorial` method header declared earlier, you can create a factorial function that multiplies the first parameter by the last result and then decrements the first parameter by one. The multicast delegate would contain a instance of that delegate equal to the initial value of the original first parameter. Of course, this process is highly inefficient, but it does a good job of showing how to carry value types across multiple delegates within a multicast delegate.

If you would rather obtain information individually from each delegate, then you can create an array to store that information. Although it's not the most elegant solution, there aren't many other choices to solve this problem. Listing 5.3 uses an `ArrayList` as a parameter to the delegate. As each delegate method is invoked, it places its result at the end of the list. You can then access each delegate's result after the multicast delegate has finished calling each method within its invocation list. We used an `ArrayList` due to its ability to grow if the size of the array is unknown, but you can just as easily use a regular system array. Furthermore, you can pass multiple return values by using a structure that contains the return values as the item data type within the array. Finally, it's worth noting that because `ArrayList` is an object and not a value type, you do not need the `ref` keyword because objects are passed by reference by default.

5.7. Declaring Events

You want to create an event within your class.

Technique

First, create a delegate that is used for the event, as shown in the previous recipe. Next, create a member variable of the type within your class placing the keyword `event` after the variable's access modifier:

```
class ConsoleMenu
{
    public delegate void MenuEventHandler( object sender, string[] args );

    public event MenuEventHandler OnMenuEvent;
}
```

Comments

Delegates allow flexibility within a program that otherwise wouldn't be available, or at least would be difficult to implement, to alter the flow of control dynamically while an application is running. Because delegates provide an inherent connection between two disparate objects, it seems only natural to utilize this design when creating an event infrastructure, which is exactly the case with the .NET Framework.

The first step in the process to add events to your object is to give the event you want to fire a name and to declare the method signature for that event. You declare the method signature for an event using a delegate. In the previous recipe, you saw that a delegate is simply a method declaration using the `delegate` keyword. Furthermore, because a delegate is bound to a different implementation, it does not contain an implementation of its own, which means there is no method body associated with that method. A delegate associated with an event is used as the event handler for the object that has requested to be notified for that event. The process of requesting notification or subscribing to an event is covered in the next recipe.

Events have an associated name to distinguish them from the actual delegates they are bound to. You declare events by creating a member variable within your class whose data type is that of the delegate to which it is bound. Unlike with regular variables, however, you must use the `event` keyword to allow special processing by the compiler. When you do so, the compiler generates additional information, in IL, which creates the necessary information to control how that event is connected to handlers and how the event is fired. Just like the `delegate` keyword, the `event` keyword generates a nested class. However, this class is private and is used internally by methods that the compiler has also emitted. Listing 5.4 shows the code used in this and the following two recipes. The class that supports events is `ConsoleMenu`, and as you can guess by the name, it supports a console-based menu system, albeit somewhat rudimentary. The event fired is `OnMenuEvent`, which is bound to the `MenuEventHandler` delegate.

Listing 5.4   ConsoleMenu **Class Fires the** OnMenuEvent **Event**

```
using System;
using System.Collections;

namespace _7_AddingEvents
{
    class Class1
    {
        static void Main(string[] args)
        {
        }
    }

    class ConsoleMenu
    {       ArrayList menuItems = new ArrayList();
        bool quitMenu = false;

        // menu item event handler delegate
        public delegate void MenuEventHandler( object sender, string[] args );

        // event fired when user selects a menu item
        public event MenuEventHandler OnMenuEvent;
```

Listing 5.4   **Continued**

```
// adds a menu item to the internal ArrayList
public void AddMenuItem( string text )
{
    menuItems.Add( text );
}

public void QuitMenu()
{
    quitMenu = true;
}

public void DisplayMenu()
{
    string input;
    do
    {
        int idx = 1;
        int choice = 0;

        // display each menu item string prefaced by its index value
        foreach( string menuChoice in menuItems )
            Console.WriteLine( "{0}: {1}", idx++, menuChoice );

        Console.Write( "Enter choice: " );

        // get users input and convert to integer
        input = Console.ReadLine();
        choice = Int32.Parse( input[0].ToString() );

        if( choice > 0 && choice <= menuItems.Count )
        {
            // build event arguments
            string[] args = new string[2];
            args[0] = input[0].ToString();
            args[1] =
              menuItems[Int32.Parse(input[0].ToString())-1].ToString();

            // fire event to be handled by client using this class
            OnMenuEvent( this, args);
        }
        else
        {
            Console.WriteLine( "Invalid choice!\n" );
        }
```

Listing 5.4   **Continued**

```
        } while ( quitMenu == false );

        quitMenu = false;
    }
  }
}
```

You can add new menu items by using the `AddMenuItem` method, which uses a string as the name of the menu item when it is displayed. To display the menu and accept user input, you use the `DisplayInput` method. This method continually loops until the `quitMenu` private variable is set to `true`. The actual firing of the event occurs after the user has entered her input value and after that value is validated.

Firing an event is slightly different from the method used to call a delegate method. When you used a delegate, you could simply call it like any other method, and the runtime would invoke the actual method implementation it was bound to. However, the event itself is just a variable and not an actual method even though the preceding code uses a method-calling syntax. To fire an event, use the event name as the method name, but use the parameter list of the delegate that the event is bound to. In this case, the event name `OnMenuEvent` is the method name, and the parameter data types are those of the `MenuEventHandler` delegate. Once you call it, any clients that have subscribed to that event will be notified.

5.8. Defining and Registering Event Handlers

You want to consume the events that are fired from an object.

Technique

Define a method that has the same method signature as the delegate to which an event is bound to. It becomes the event handler. To register this handler to receive events when they are fired, use the addition assignment operator (+=) on the event name of the object instance you want to subscribe to and assign that to an instance of a bound delegate passing the event-handler name to the delegate constructor, as shown in the `Main` method of Listing 5.5.

Listing 5.5   **Creating Event Handlers**

```
class Class1
{
    [STAThread]
    static void Main(string[] args)
    {
```

Listing 5.5   **Continued**

```
        ConsoleMenu menu = new ConsoleMenu();
        menu.AddMenuItem( "Item 1" );
        menu.AddMenuItem( "Item 2" );
        menu.AddMenuItem( "Item 3" );
        menu.AddMenuItem( "Quit" );

        menu.OnMenuEvent += new
            ConsoleMenu.MenuEventHandler(MenuItemHandler);

        menu.DisplayMenu();
    }

    static void MenuItemHandler( object sender, string[] args )
    {
        switch( Int32.Parse( args[0].ToString() ))
        {
            case( 1 ):
            case( 2 ):
            case( 3 ):
            {
                Console.WriteLine( "You selected the item {0}\n", args[1] );
                break;
            }
            case( 4 ):
            {
                Console.WriteLine( "Goodbye!" );
                ((ConsoleMenu)sender).QuitMenu();
                break;
            }
        }
    }
}
```

Comments

Listing 5.5 shows how to subscribe to the events that are fired from the `ConsoleMenu` class in Listing 5.4. When binding a method implementation to a delegate, you create the method using the same signature as the delegate, and with events, this process is the same. The delegate in Listing 5.4 contains two parameters, an object and an array of strings, and the method `MenuItemHandler` in Listing 5.5 follows that same convention.

Instead of binding a method to a delegate, however, event handlers are bound to the actual event name defined within the class that fires that event. You do so using the addition assignment operator (`+=`), which assigns the event to an instance of its delegate class.

If you compare this step to the delegate recipe earlier in this chapter, you should see some peculiar similarities. Earlier, a variable whose data type was that of the generated delegate class was created within the client who was using the delegate. In Listing 5.4, that variable is declared within the class that fires the event, and the event keyword is added to it. Furthermore, just as you bind a method to a delegate using the new keyword passing the name of the method within the constructor, the same process occurs with events and the name of the event handler is passed as the delegate constructor.

At this point, the event communication between a class and a client is set. The event that is implemented by the class which fires it is bound to an event handler. Therefore, when the class that fires the event calls the corresponding event method, the runtime routes the call to the method handlers that have subscribed to that event. It is there that processing can occur based on the arguments passed into the event handler. Within the event handler of Listing 5.5, you can see that the menu is dismissed by calling the QuitMenu method on the ConsoleMenu instance. This method sets the Boolean value quitMenu that is used to control the display of the menu. Figure 5.5 shows the result of running the ConsoleMenu class and its associated client code.

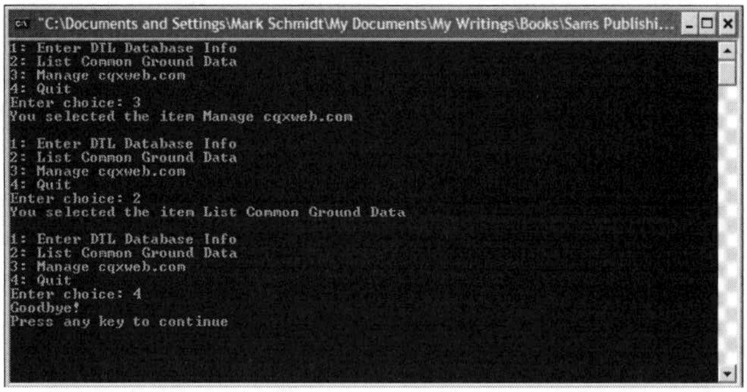

Figure 5.5   Using events to create a simple console-based menu system.

5.9. Packaging Event Arguments

You want to package state information into a class that you can use as arguments to an event handler.

Technique

Create a new class derived from System.EventArgs. Add any public member variables to the class that the event handler can then access. The event delegate should use this class as a parameter in its parameter list. When the event is fired, create an instance of this class, ensuring that its member variables have been properly set to reflect the current event information:

```
public class MenuItemEventArgs : EventArgs
{
    public int id;
    public string displayString;

    public MenuItemEventArgs( int id, string displayString )
    {
        this.id = id;
        this.displayString = displayString;
    }
}
```

Comments

Packaging event arguments into a class derived from `EventArgs`, believe it or not, is purely for aesthetic reasons. If you look at the `EventArgs` class, you'll see that it doesn't add any additional functionality beyond the methods and properties contained in `System.Object`. That said, you are free to forego this procedure of argument-packing altogether and simply pass parameters normally when you fire an event. However, it is recommended, just as coding and naming guidelines are recommended, that you create a consistent method for event arguments by using the steps shown here.

Exceptions and Error Handling

6.0. Introduction

This recipe covers the various topics associated with exceptions and error handling. As you will undoubtedly find out, exceptions are prevalent throughout the .NET Framework, and the .NET documentation does a good job of telling which exceptions are thrown where. We encourage you to become as intimately familiar with exceptions and error-handling diagnostics as possible and to put the techniques in this chapter to use as you code, not later. If you do decide to put it off until later, realize that more often than not you will miss some key coverage points for error handling within your application.

6.1. Using `try`/`catch` blocks

You realize that a certain block of code might throw an exception, so you want to create a handler to catch the exception if it is thrown.

Technique

Wrap the code that might throw an exception within a `try` block. A `try` block consists of the `try` keyword and a body within curly braces. If an exception is thrown within that body, the `catch` handler will execute. The `catch` block contains the keyword `catch` followed by the exception type you want to catch and an optional variable identifier for that exception. The body of the `catch` block contains the code necessary to respond to that exception, as shown in Listing 6.1.

Listing 6.1   **Using a** `try/catch` **Block to Handle Exceptions**

```
using System;

namespace _1_TryCatch
{
    class Class1
    {
        [STAThread]
        static void Main(string[] args)
        {
            try
            {
                // ask for and read a number from the user
                Console.Write( "Enter a number: " );
                int input = Int32.Parse( Console.ReadLine() );

                // the last iteration in this loop will attempt to
                // divide by zero
                for( int i = 5; i >= 0; i- )
                    Console.WriteLine( "{0}/{1}={2}", input, i, input/i );
            }
            catch( Exception e )
            {
                // display exception message
                Console.WriteLine( "An error occurred: {0}", e.Message );
            }
        }
    }
}
```

Comments

In Listing 6.1, you can see an obvious error. As the counter for the loop reaches 0, the program attempts to divide using that value. Naturally, you just want to change the code rather than use exception handling in this case, but sometimes such errors aren't easy to discover.

When you wrap a block of code within a `try` block, you cover every method that is capable of throwing an exception. If any of the method calls or operations within this code block throw an exception, they all share the same `catch` block. You can, however, fine-tune the `catch` block to catch different exceptions and react accordingly. To do so, simply create multiple `catch` blocks. To catch the divide-by-zero exception in Listing 6.1, for example, create a second `catch` block whose parameter is `DivideByZeroException`. Note that by using `Exception` as the exception class to catch, you will catch any exception that occurs regardless of the type that is thrown.

Furthermore, if an exception is caught within a `catch` block, the remaining `catch` blocks do not execute. When the exception is thrown within the code listing that follows, it is caught in the first `catch` block and not the `catch` block that follows:

```
try
{
    // divide by zero code here
}
catch( DivideByZeroException )
{
}
catch( Exception )
{
}
```

If the exception is not handled, the Common Language Runtime (CLR) exception dialog appears, as shown in Figure 6.1. When you close the dialog, the runtime accesses the `Message` and `StackTrace` properties of the exception object and displays that information within the console, assuming it is a console application. Furthermore, because the exception was not handled using the techniques described in this recipe, the runtime will prematurely abort the application. If, on the other hand, you do handle the exception using a `catch` block, your program continues at the next instruction following the last `catch` block. This behavior allows your application to continue even though an error was detected. For instance, in the example shown earlier, if the results of the computation are placed into an array, you can simply skip the computation that caused the divide-by-zero error and continue processing those results, perhaps logging an error along the way.

6.2. Using a `finally` Block

You want to execute a body of code whether or not an exception is thrown.

Technique

You can use a `finally` block to execute a block of code after executing the corresponding `try`/`catch` blocks. Immediately following a catch block or multiple catch blocks, use the keyword `finally` followed by a code block within curly braces. Listing 6.2 shows a `try` block followed by two `catch` blocks. The `finally` block in the code runs whether an exception is thrown or not.

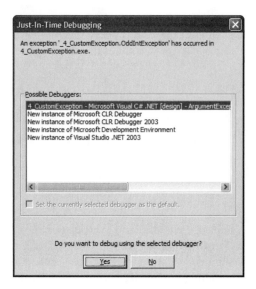

Figure 6.1   Unhandled exceptions result in the display of the CLR exception dialog.

Listing 6.2   **Adding a** `finally` **Block**

```csharp
using System;

namespace _1_TryCatch
{
    class Class1
    {
        [STAThread]
        static void Main(string[] args)
        {
            try
            {
                // retrieve number from user
                Console.Write( "Enter a number: " );
                int input = Int32.Parse( Console.ReadLine() );

                // last iteration attempts to divide by zero
                for( int i = 5; i > 0; i-- )
                    Console.WriteLine( "{0}/{1}={2}", input, i, input/i );
            }
            catch( DivideByZeroException )
            {
                Console.WriteLine( "Program attempted to divide by zero" );
            }
```

Listing 6.2   **Continued**

```
        catch( Exception e )
        {
            Console.WriteLine( "An error occurred: {0}", e.Message );
        }
        finally
        {
            Console.WriteLine( "Program has finished." );
        }
    }
    }
}
```

Comments

When an exception is thrown, the remainder of a `try` block does not execute, and control is transferred to a `catch` block. Any extra processing you have along the lines of cleaning up resources, ensuring out parameters are set correctly, or manipulating any internal variables is skipped. If you were to put that information within a `catch` block instead of a `try` block, then of course it wouldn't execute if an exception were never thrown. You could place duplicate code within the `try` and `catch` blocks, but this solution obviously isn't clean. The `finally` block executes common code that needs to be executed following either the end of a `try` block or the end of a `catch` block.

It is a fair question to ask why you even need a `finally` block in the first place. After all, the lines of code following the `try` and `catch` blocks is executed anyway. That is true, and you are free to use that to your advantage. However, using a `finally` block keeps any variables declared within the `try` block in scope. Once the exception-handling blocks are exited, any variables that were declared within the `try` block are no longer valid and cannot be used. Therefore, you want to free any resources that were created within the `try` block, which can include any open streams or database connections, for example.

6.3. Displaying Exception Information

> You want to display information about an exception to aid in tracking down why it occurs.

Technique

Every exception that you can catch is derived from the `System.Exception` class. Within that class are several properties that you can access to acquire more information. The most frequently used property is `Message`, which returns a readable string detailing the error. Additional properties include Source, which displays the name of the application where the exception occurred, and TargetSite, which displays the name of the method that was currently executing when the exception was thrown.

To view the methods currently in scope, you can view the call stack by accessing the StackTrace string. Finally, if you want to determine whether an exception was thrown by an application, catch the ApplicationException exception object, and if you want to determine whether the exception being thrown is from the CLR, catch the SystemException object. Listing 6.3 demonstrates how to display exception information by throwing a variety of exceptions based on a user's input.

Listing 6.3   **Displaying Exception Information**

```
using System;

namespace _3_ExceptionInfo
{
    class Class1
    {
        // outputs information about an exception
        static void DisplayExceptionInformation( Exception e )
        {
            Console.WriteLine( "Application: {0}", e.Source );
            Console.WriteLine( "Method: {0}", e.TargetSite );
            Console.WriteLine( "Message: {0}", e.Message );
            Console.WriteLine( "Call Stack: {0}", e.StackTrace );
            if( e.HelpLink != null )
                Console.WriteLine( "Help Link: {0}", e.HelpLink );
        }

        // displays a menu and asks user for input
        static int DisplayMenu()
        {
            int input = 0;

            Console.WriteLine( "1) Throw a system exception" );
            Console.WriteLine( "2) Throw an application exception" );
            Console.WriteLine( "3) Quit" );

            Console.Write( "Enter command: " );

            try
            {
                // get input from user
                input = Int32.Parse( Console.ReadLine() );
            }
            catch
```

Listing 6.3   **Continued**

```
        {
            Console.WriteLine( "Invalid Input. Try again.\n" );
            return DisplayMenu();
        }
        return input;
    }

    [STAThread]
    static void Main(string[] args)
    {
        int input = DisplayMenu();

        while( input != 3 )
        {
            // throw exception and display exception information
            try
            {
                switch( input )
                {
                    case 1:
                    {
                        throw new SystemException();
                    }
                    case 2:
                    {
                        throw new ApplicationException();
                    }
                    default:
                }
            }
            catch( ApplicationException e )
            {
                Console.WriteLine( "An application exception occurred:" );
                DisplayExceptionInformation( e );
            }
            catch( SystemException e )
            {
                Console.WriteLine( "A system exception occurred:" );
                DisplayExceptionInformation( e );
            }
            catch( Exception e )
            {
                Console.WriteLine( "An unknown error occurred:" );
                DisplayExceptionInformation( e );
            }
```

Listing 6.3   **Continued**

```
                    input = DisplayMenu();
            }
        }
    }
}
```

Comments

One of the primary purposes of exceptions, other than preventing an application from prematurely exiting, is providing rich information about the error. Compare this information to the generic "This application has performed an illegal operation," followed by a list of the values currently in the processor registers and a hexadecimal dump of the current application stack—a situation so often experienced with applications built without the exception support of the .NET Framework.

All of the exceptions within the .NET Framework are ultimately derived from the `System.Exception` class. In fact, most exceptions only override the `Exception` properties without defining additional properties or methods of their own. You can create a simple method that accepts an `Exception` object and rest assured that it will work with any exception passed to it. Additionally, you can use the class hierarchy of exceptions to your advantage to determine whether the exception is being thrown from an application or from the runtime itself. Listing 6.3 filters the exceptions by creating a `catch` block to catch any `ApplicationException` exceptions and any `SystemExceptions`. When an exception is thrown, the runtime accesses the application's exception-handling table to determine the correct catch handler. It does so by looking for a catch handler for the exact type of the exception. If it doesn't find one, the runtime then looks for a catch handler for that exception's base class. This process continues until the runtime finds a catch handler containing a base class of the exception object. The result of running the application in Listing 6.3 appears in Figure 6.2.

6.4. Creating and Throwing Custom Exceptions

You want to create a new exception type that is more informative and applicable to an object within the application that throws it.

Technique

Create a new class derived from `System.ApplicationException`. Override any applicable properties to customize the exception information, such as `Message` and `HelpLink`, as shown in Listing 6.4.

To throw a custom or predefined exception, use the keyword `throw` followed by an instance of the exception you want to throw.

Figure 6.2   You can use the System.Exception class to display information about an exception when it occurs.

Listing 6.4   **Creating a Custom Exception Class**

```
using System;
using System.Collections;

namespace _4_CustomException
{
    class Class1
    {
        [STAThread]
        static void Main(string[] args)
        {
            OddIntCollection oddValues = new OddIntCollection();

            int input = 0;

            do
            {
                // get input from user
                Console.Write( "Enter an odd number or -1 to quit: " );
                input = Int32.Parse( Console.ReadLine() );

                // add it to the collection
                if( input != -1 )
                    oddValues.Add( input );
```

Listing 6.4 **Continued**

```
        } while( input != -1 );
    }
}

class OddIntCollection : CollectionBase
{
    public void Add( int value )
    {
        // check if value is odd by using a logical & on first bit
        if( (value & 0x1) == 0 )
        {
            // value isn't odd, throw the custom exception
            throw new OddIntException();
        }
        else
        {
            // add value to inner collection
            InnerList.Add( value );
        }
    }
}

class OddIntException : ApplicationException
{
    // override Message property to display custom message
    public override string Message
    {
        get
        {
            return "Value is not an odd number";
        }
    }

}
}
```

Comments

There are two classifications of exceptions. The most common exception is a system exception, which is any exception derived from the `System.SystemException` base class. There are 70 direct descendants of `System.SystemException` defined within the .NET Framework, each of which may have 0 or more derived classes themselves. Some of these exceptions include arithmetic exceptions such as `DivideByZeroException`, I/O exceptions such `FileNotFoundException`, and argument exceptions such as `ArgumentOutOfRangeException`.

Even though there are many available system exceptions that you are free to throw within your application as necessary, you might need to eventually create one of your own. Creating a custom exception is simply a matter of creating a new class derived from `ApplicationException` and overriding a few key properties. The most important property is the string `Message`, which allows you to return a readable string detailing why the exception occurred. In Listing 6.4, the `OddIntCollection` will only accept odd integers. If a user attempts to place an even integer, an `OddIntException` is thrown.

The `Add` method of the `OddIntCollection` class first checks the integer parameter to see whether it's odd. It does so by performing a simple bit check on the least significant bit. If that bit is 1, then you know the number is odd. When an even number is encountered, an `OddIntException` is thrown by using the C# keyword `throw` followed by the creation of an `OddIntException` object. If the exception is not handled, the CLR accesses the `Message` and `StackTrace` property of the exception object and displays that information within the console, if the application is running within the console. If a developer has created an exception handler, she might or might not access those properties.

6.5. Accessing Inner Exceptions

You want to throw an exception within an object if the object encounters an exception itself.

Technique

When creating a new exception class, create an overloaded constructor that accepts an `Exception` object. Initialize the base class constructor by passing the exception message and the exception object passed into the constructor:

```
class TrafficMonitorException : ApplicationException
{
    public TrafficMonitorException() : this(null){}
    public TrafficMonitorException( Exception e )
        : base("A capacity value is set incorrectly", e ){}
}
```

When an exception within the class is handled, throw an instance of the exception class created earlier, passing the exception that is being handled to the overloaded constructor:

```
class TrafficMonitor
{
    private int limit = 0;
    private int current = 8;

    public override string ToString()
    {
        try
```

```
            {
                return ((decimal)current/(decimal)limit).ToString("p",null);
            }
            catch( Exception e )
            {
                throw new TrafficMonitorException( e );
            }
        }

        public int CapacityLimit
        {
            get
            {
                return limit;
            }
            set
            {
                limit = value;
            }
        }

        public int CurrentCapacity
        {
            get
            {
                return current;
            }
            set
            {
                current = value;
            }
        }
    }
```

A client using the class that has thrown the exception can access the exception information as usual using the Message, HelpLink, and StackTrace properties. To access the information about the exception that caused the current exception, use the InnerException property. It returns a System.Exception object:

```
class Class1
{
    [STAThread]
    static void Main(string[] args)
    {
        TrafficMonitor tm = new TrafficMonitor();

        // loop until user enters a valid value
```

```
        for(;;)
        {
            try
            {
                Console.Write( "Enter traffic capacity limit: " );
                tm.CapacityLimit = Int32.Parse( Console.ReadLine() );

                // at this point a valid value has been entered
                break;
            }
            catch( Exception )
            {
                Console.WriteLine( "You must enter a valid value" );
            }
        }

        // loop until user enters a valid value
        for(;;)
        {
            try
            {
                Console.Write( "Enter current traffic capacity: " );
                tm.CurrentCapacity = Int32.Parse( Console.ReadLine() );

                // valid value entered, break out of loop
                break;
            }
            catch( Exception )
            {
                Console.WriteLine( "You must enter a valid value" );
            }
        }

        try
        {
            Console.WriteLine( tm.ToString() );
        }
        catch( Exception e )
        {
            for( Exception cur = e; cur.InnerException != null;
➥cur = cur.InnerException )
                Console.WriteLine( "Exception: {0}\nInner Exception: {1}",
                    cur.Message, cur.InnerException.Message );
        }
    }
}
```

Comments

Due to the hierarchical nature of classes, it is entirely possible for a class to throw a custom exception if it encounters an exception itself. However, without a mechanism in place to filter and pass exceptions down the call stack, you won't be able to access the root cause of the exception being thrown. Fortunately, you can chain exceptions by utilizing the `InnerException` property, which is defined in the `System.Exception` class.

The code listings for this recipe define a `TrafficMonitor` class, which allows you to set how many cars are allowed on a stretch of road. You can then set how many cars are currently on the road and call the `ToString` method to retrieve a string representing the current capacity relative to the limit expressed as a percentage of that limit. This percentage is computed by dividing the current capacity by the limit. Obviously, if a mistake is made and the limit is never set, a divide-by-zero exception will be thrown. The `ToString` method creates an exception handler for this case, and if an exception occurs, it throws a custom exception. However, unlike the last exception, which threw a custom exception, this custom exception wraps the `DivideByZero` exception to add information, thereby allowing anyone using the class to find the root cause that threw the exception.

Based on the complexity of an application, an exception might be thrown within a method that must then be propagated several times as methods are removed from the stack back to the original caller. This complexity could mean that several exceptions are chained together. The `System.Exception` class initializes the `InnerException` property to `null` so you can create a simple loop that follows the exception chain until a `null` value is encountered:

```
catch( Exception e )
{
    for( Exception cur = e; cur.InnerException != null; cur = cur.InnerException )
        Console.WriteLine( "Exception: {0}\nInner Exception: {1}",
            cur.Message, cur.InnerException.Message );
}
```

6.6. Overflow Detection Using Checked and Unchecked

You want to allow or disallow overflows of integral types to occur.

Technique

Overflow detection works by placing an expression to evaluate within parentheses prefixed with the `checked` or `unchecked` keyword. If you specify `unchecked`, an integral value will overflow without an exception being thrown. If you specify `checked` and an integral type overflows, a `System.OverflowException` is thrown. If you use neither of the keywords, overflow detection is based on the current project build settings. Listing 6.5 demonstrates the use of the `checked` and `unchecked` keyword, as shown in the overloaded multiplication operator defined in the `Counter` class.

Listing 6.5   **Overflow Detection Using the** `Checked` **Keyword**

```
using System;

namespace _6_CheckedUnchecked
{
    class Class1
    {
        [STAThread]
        static void Main(string[] args)
        {
            // create 2 counters. One is checked, the other is not
            Counter counter1 = new Counter( 1, false );
            Counter counter2 = new Counter( 1, true );

            // overflow detection disabled
            for( int i = 1; i < 15; i++ )
            {
                // overflow will occur
                counter1 *= i;
                Console.WriteLine( counter1.Value );
            }

            try
            {
                // overflow detection enabled
                for( int i = 1; i < 15; i++ )
                {
                    // an exception is thrown when overflow occurs
                    counter2 *= i;
                    Console.WriteLine( counter2.Value );
                }
            }
            catch( Exception e )
            {
                Console.WriteLine( "Exception caught: {0}", e.Message );
            }
        }
    }

    class Counter
    {
        public int Value = 0;
```

Listing 6.5   **Continued**

```
    public bool EnableCheck = false;

    // passing true in second parameter will enable overflow detection
    public Counter( int val, bool enableCheck )
    {
        this.Value = val;
        this.EnableCheck = enableCheck;
    }

    public static Counter operator * ( Counter op1, int op2 )
    {
        int newVal;

        if( op1.EnableCheck )
            newVal = checked( op1.Value * op2 );
        else
            newVal = unchecked( op1.Value * op2 );

        return new Counter( newVal, op1.EnableCheck );
    }
  }
}
```

To enable overflow detection without using the `checked` keyword on each expression, select Project, Properties from the main menu. Navigate to the Configuration Properties, Build property page and set "Check for Arithmetic Overflow/Underflow" to `true` to enable checking or `false` to disable checking. By default, this setting is `false`, as shown in Figure 6.3.

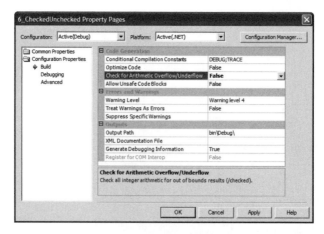

Figure 6.3   Change project-wide overflow detection by changing your project's build settings.

Comments

A variable that overflows can be a subtle defect that can have very undesirable side effects. It can be hard to track down without the aid of a debugger or programmatic debugging techniques. However, the C# language coupled with the C# compiler makes overflow detection an easy task.

You use the `checked` and `unchecked` keywords to check the result of an expression that works with integral types. In Listing 6.5, you can see a simple class named `Counter` that has an overloaded multiplication operator. This operator simply multiplies the current value of a `Counter` instance by a specified integer. If the Boolean value `EnableCheck` is `true` within the instance of the class, then overflow detection is enabled when the multiplication is performed. Likewise, if `EnableCheck` is `false`, then overflow detection is disabled. The `Main` method creates two loops that repeatedly multiply the value of two instances of the `Counter` class, with one instance checking for overflow conditions and the other not. Furthermore, because an overflow throws an exception if it is being checked, an exception handler is used to catch the exception. The results of running Listing 6.5 appear in Figure 6.4.

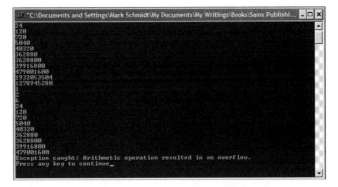

Figure 6.4   The `Counter` value will overflow if unchecked, as shown in the last value of the first set, but an exception occurs in the second set.

II

User Interface and Graphics

7

Windows Forms

7.0. Introduction

Windows Forms is the technology within the .NET Framework that allows you to create and display user interfaces, which include everything from a simple message box to a feature-rich multiple document interface (MDI) application. Windows Forms is a radical departure from user-interface toolkits in earlier versions of Visual Studio, such as the Microsoft Foundation Classes (MFC) and Visual Basic form editor. In those technologies, you saved the user-interface definitions using a proprietary file format known only to those languages. Windows Forms, however, takes a different approach. Rather than create a resource file, your source files generate actual code as you add new controls and change various properties.

This chapter covers the different facets of Windows Forms that make it such an exciting technology. Some of the basics are covered such as creating a Windows Forms project, changing a form's properties, and seeing how events are generated within Windows Forms. Parts of this chapter look at some of the more traditionally advanced topics within Windows user-interface programming, such as drag and drop and creating MDI applications.

7.1. Creating a Dialog-Based Windows Form

You want to create a simple Windows Form application.

Technique

Create a new Windows Forms application by selecting New, Project from the main menu. Select the Visual C# Projects item in the project types list and select the Windows Application project template.

Comments

One of the first things you'll see after creating a Windows Forms project is the Windows Form designer. The designer is a user-interface editor that allows you to change various aspects of the user interface, including changing form properties, adding and manipulating controls, and adding various event handlers.

One aspect of Windows Forms that is different from previous Microsoft user-interface technologies is the absence of a separate resource file containing the user-interface definition. Rather than create a special file format to describe a user interface, the Windows Form editor directly changes the underlying code within your application. To see the code that was generated when you created the project, select View, Code from the main menu while in the designer, right-clicking on `Form1.cs` in the Solution Explorer or on the forms designer itself and selecting the View Code menu item.

You create a Windows Form simply by deriving a class from the `System.Windows.Forms.Form` base class, as shown in Listing 7.1. When you create a Windows Form application, the code generates this class with a default constructor, an overridden method, and a private method named `InitializeComponent`, which is called within the constructor. Due to the outlining features of the Visual Studio Integrated Development Environment (IDE), you cannot initially see the `InitializeComponent` method. This method is to appear only in the designer, and as such it is collapsed within an outline region. To view the `InitializeComponent` method, expand the outlined region named Windows Form Designer Generated Code by double-clicking it. Whenever you make a change to the user interface within the designer, the designer makes the corresponding changes within this code region. That said, you must be aware that any changes you manually make within this method might be overwritten by the designer itself.

Listing 7.1   **A Basic Windows Form**

```
using System;
using System.Drawing;
using System.Collections;
using System.ComponentModel;
using System.Windows.Forms;
using System.Data;

namespace _1_BasicForm
{
    public class Form1 : System.Windows.Forms.Form
    {
        private System.ComponentModel.Container components = null;

        public Form1()
        {
            InitializeComponent();
```

Listing 7.1   **Continued**

```
        }

        protected override void Dispose( bool disposing )
        {
            if( disposing )
            {
                if (components != null)
                {
                    components.Dispose();
                }
            }
            base.Dispose( disposing );
        }

        #region Windows Form Designer generated code
        private void InitializeComponent()
        {
            this.AutoScaleBaseSize = new System.Drawing.Size(5, 13);
            this.ClientSize = new System.Drawing.Size(292, 266);
            this.Name = "Form1";
            this.ShowInTaskbar = false;
            this.Text = "My Windows Form";
        }
        #endregion

        [STAThread]
        static void Main()
        {
            Application.Run(new Form1());
        }
    }
}
```

The class contains a single overridden method named Dispose. You use this method to release any resources your class is holding and to perform any type of processing necessary before closing the form. The parameter for this method is a Boolean value named disposing, which at its surface seems a little misleading. When this parameter is true, you should release any managed resources that your class is holding. When this parameter is false, the semantics lead you to believe that the class does not need to dispose or release any resources, but that is not true. When disposing is false, you are to free any unmanaged resources, which is a subject covered in Chapter 24, "COM Interoperability." Also, the runtime does not guarantee that the Dispose method will be called only once when the form is closed, so you must ensure that you don't inadvertently release a resource that has already been released, thereby resulting in an exception.

7.2. Changing a Form's Properties

You want to change certain properties of the form within your application.

Technique

Select the form within the designer by clicking on it. The available properties for the form appear in the Properties windows, which by default is located at the bottom right of the IDE window, as shown in Figure 7.1. If the Properties window is not visible, click on View, Properties from the main menu.

Each property has a designer control associated with it, which means that each property has a different way to change its value. The Text property, which changes the main title of the form, uses an edit box to change its value. To change the form's title, type a new string into the edit box for the Text property. Some controls use a drop-down box listing all possible values the property contains. For instance, to remove the taskbar button that is displayed when your application runs, click on the ShowInTaskbar property drop-down box and select False.

Figure 7.1   Visual Studio .NET Property Browser.

Comments

Properties define an object's characteristics, whereas you use methods on an object to define its behavior. You can declare properties using any data type, which means creating a visual property editor is no trivial task. The property editor within the Visual Studio .NET IDE is an advanced control that provides a default set of suitable controls you use to set the value or values of a property. Furthermore, the property editor is extendable, which means you are free to create property controls that work better with the property data type you created. For more information on custom property editors, see Chapter 9, "User Controls."

One thing you'll notice as you work within the IDE is the versatility of the property browser. In this chapter, you just change the properties of a Windows Form, but you can also use the property browser to change properties on the controls within a Windows Form, solution and project properties, and even properties on an individual file. Additionally, you can control how you see the properties by using the view buttons at the top of the property browser window. The first button groups the properties based on their category. A Windows Form contains categories such as `Accessibility`, `Appearance`, and `Window Style`. You can also arrange properties alphabetically by using the `Alphabetic` toolbar button on the property browser.

7.3. Creating Modal Dialog Boxes

You want to create a form and make it modal.

Technique

Add a new form to an existing Windows Forms project by selecting Project, Add Windows Form from the main menu. Because dialog boxes do not contain maximize and minimize buttons, change the `MinimizeBox` and `MaximizeBox` properties to `False`. To display the dialog box modally, create an instance of the Windows Form you created and call the `ShowDialog` method:

```
private void Form1_Load(object sender, System.EventArgs e)
{
    this.Visible = true;
    ModalForm newForm = new ModalForm();
    newForm.ShowDialog( this );
}
```

Comments

A modal dialog box displays information to a user requiring the user to close the dialog before proceeding. This box is helpful if you need to gather information from the user before your application proceeds or if you want to guarantee the user sees an informative message.

The technique shown earlier shows how to create a modal dialog box by changing the properties of a new form and displaying it with the `ShowDialog` method. One thing it doesn't explain is when the modal dialog appears. Of course, this factor depends on the requirement of your application. In most instances, the display depends on some event happening, likely fired as the result of user interaction. Chapter 5, "Delegates and

Events," demonstrated how to create event handlers to handle events that are fired from an object. It comes as no surprise that Windows Forms use the same procedure to utilize event handling. However, because you are now able to use a visual editor, the process of creating event handlers is trivial. Recipe 7.5, "Handling Form Events," shows how to handle events in a Windows Form application.

7.4. Displaying Message Boxes

You want to display a message to a user using a message box.

Technique

Use the static method Show defined within the MessageBox class. This method is over-loaded several times, allowing you to customize the display of the message as you see fit. The simplest message box contains a single string parameter denoting the message to display. To add a caption to the message box, insert an additional string parameter. You can control which buttons are displayed in the third parameter by using the MessageBoxButtons enumerated data type. You can use a fourth parameter to display an icon. You specify this icon using a value from the MessageBoxIcon enumerated data type. To specify the default button, use a value from the MessageBoxDefaultButton enumerated data type as the fifth parameter. Finally, you specify additional options in the sixth parameter by using the logical or operator (|) on values within the MessageBoxOptions enumeration. Table 7.1 shows the possible values for the enumerated data types discussed in this recipe.

Table 7.1   MessageBox **Enumerated Data Types**

Data Type	Value	Description
MessageBoxButtons	AbortRetryIgnore	Message box containing three buttons labeled Abort, Retry, and Ignore
	OK	A single button labeled OK
	OKCancel	Displays an OK button followed by a Cancel button
	RetryCancel	Shows two buttons labeled Retry and Cancel
	YesNo	Displays a Yes button and a No button
	YesNoCancel	Displays Yes, No, and Cancel buttons
MessageBoxIcon	Asterisk	Displays a lowercase *i* inside a circle in the corner of the message box

Table 7.1   **Continued**

Data Type	Value	Description
	`Error`	Icon is a white X inside a red circle
	`Exclamation`	Shows an exclamation point within a yellow triangle
	`Hand`	Shows same icon as `Error` value
	Information	Uses the same icon shown when using the `Asterisk` value
	`None`	Does not display an icon
	`Question`	Icon consists of a question mark within a circle
	`Stop`	Same as `Error` value, a white X inside a red circle
	`Warning`	Icon is the same as the `Exclamation` value
`MessageBoxDefaultButton`	`Button1`	Gives the first button the initial focus and renders a focus rectangle around the button
	`Button2`	Makes the second button, if one exists, the default button
	`Button3`	Makes the third button the default button
`MessageBoxOptions`	`DefaultDesktopOnly`	Displays the message box on the current desktop
	`RightAlign`	Aligns the text along the right edge of the message box
	`RtlReading`	Renders the text in the message box in right-to-left order
	`ServiceNotification`	Message box is displayed on the active desktop and will be shown even if a user is not logged on

Comments

Sometimes, all you need to do is display a simple message to the user or ask her a simple question. Message boxes handle this task, freeing you from having to create new forms. The `MessageBox` class contains a single static method, as well as the standard `System.Object` methods, named `Show`. There are 12 overloaded versions of this method corresponding to the level of customization you want to perform on the message box. In its most basic form, a message box can contain a single message and an OK button to close the message box. To show a message box with a single message, use the `Show` method with a single string parameter, and if you want to display a caption on the message box, create a second string parameter for that purpose:

```
MessageBox.Show( "Simple Message Box" );
MessageBox.Show( "Simple Message Box", "With a caption" );
```

As mentioned earlier, you can customize the message box further by controlling the types of buttons and icons displayed, controlling which button is the default button, and specifying different message-box options. Based on the buttons that you elected to display on the message box, the value returned will be a value from the `DialogResult` enumerated data type. You can compare the value returned from the `Show` method with a value from the `DialogResult` type to determine the action performed by the user. The following code listing displays a message box using all the available customization options. Figure 7.2 shows the resulting message box:

```
if( MessageBox.Show( "Simple Message Box",
    "With a caption, default button, icon and RTL reading",
    MessageBoxButtons.OKCancel,
    MessageBoxIcon.Information,
    MessageBoxDefaultButton.Button2,
    MessageBoxOptions.RtlReading |
    MessageBoxOptions.RightAlign ) == DialogResult.Cancel )
    {
        return;
    }
```

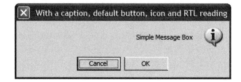

Figure 7.2 The `MessageBox.Show` method contains several overloaded methods to customize the display of the message box.

7.5. Handling Form Events

You want to create event handlers for different Windows Forms events.

Technique

Select the form in the Visual Studio .NET IDE form editor and click the lightning bolt toolbar button in the property browser, which you can see in Figure 7.1. To create an event handler for an event, double-click the event name in the event list in the property browser.

An event can provide additional information using parameters. This information varies based on the event being fired. An event that does not contain additional information will always contain two parameters, a `System.Object` parameter named `sender`, which is a reference to the object that fired the event, such as a control, and a `System.EventArgs` parameter named `e`. The `System.EventArgs` class is used by events that do not require event data. It is also used as the base class for objects that create custom event arguments which do contain data. Listing 7.2 shows the code for a windows form with event handlers for several different form events.

Listing 7.2   **Creating a Handler for a Windows Form's Events**

```
using System;
using System.Drawing;
using System.Collections;
using System.ComponentModel;
using System.Windows.Forms;

namespace _5_FormEvents
{
    public class EventForm : System.Windows.Forms.Form
    {
        private System.ComponentModel.Container components = null;

        public EventForm()
        {
            InitializeComponent();
        }

        protected override void Dispose( bool disposing )
        {
            if( disposing )
            {
                if(components != null)
                {
                    components.Dispose();
                }
            }
            base.Dispose( disposing );
        }

        #region Windows Form Designer generated code
        private void InitializeComponent()
        {
            this.AutoScaleBaseSize = new System.Drawing.Size(5, 13);
            this.ClientSize = new System.Drawing.Size(292, 266);
            this.Name = "EventForm";
```

Listing 7.2 **Continued**

```csharp
        this.Text = "EventForm";
        this.MouseDown += new System.Windows.Forms.MouseEventHandler
            (this.EventForm_MouseDown);
        this.Load += new System.EventHandler(this.EventForm_Load);
    }
    #endregion

    private void EventForm_Load(object sender, System.EventArgs e)
    {
        Console.WriteLine( "Form Loaded: {0}", e.ToString() );
    }

    private void EventForm_MouseDown(object sender,
        System.Windows.Forms.MouseEventArgs e)
    {
        Console.WriteLine( "Mouse Down - Button: {0} X: {1} Y: {2}",
            e.Button.ToString(), e.X, e.Y );
    }


    }
}
```

Comments

We believe you can never have too much information. Fortunately, Windows Forms fire quite a few events, allowing you to know exactly what is going on at any certain moment. Additionally, the events that are fired are not only the result of user interaction but also include events that are fired when certain properties change, such as a system color or font.

Explaining each and every one of the possible events a form can fire would, of course, be superfluous, a restatement of documentation that already exists. Therefore, this recipe focuses on handling form events in the general sense rather than each event in its entirety.

The key to understanding and using Windows Forms events lies in each event handler's associated parameters. It is through the parameters that you know whether there is additional information and whether you can control the outcome of the event using that parameter. Some events merely act to indicate that something has occurred. In Listing 7.2 you can see the event handler for the Load event. This event handler has two parameters, a System.Object type, which all events handlers contain, and a generic EventArgs parameter. When an event handler contains an EventArgs parameter, you will be unable to glean additional information about the event because it doesn't make sense to provide any more information. In the Load event, the only bit of information you know is that the form is being loaded.

Events that provide additional information pass a data type derived from the
`EventArgs` class. This data type contains any additional information for that form. For
instance, events that fire as a result of user interaction using the mouse might pass a
`MouseEventArgs` object. This object contains information such as the X and Y coordinates of the event relative to the upper-left corner of the form, the button on the mouse
that was clicked, the number of clicks that occurred, and how many detents or notches
the mouse wheel rotated. In Listing 7.2, you can see event handlers for several mouse-
related events. Some of these events, such as `MouseEnter` and `MouseLeave`, do not contain additional information. If you want to know the coordinates of the mouse when the
mouse enters or leaves, you can create an event handler for the `MouseMove` event. The
`MouseMove` as well as the `MouseUp` and `MouseDown` events pass a `MouseEventArgs` parameter to provide additional information. Figure 7.3 shows the results of running the application in Listing 7.2. To avoid a constant flow of information, it does not handle the
`MouseMove` event.

Figure 7.3   Some Windows Forms events can contain additional information
about the event details.

Event-handler arguments are not exclusively for providing additional information. Event
arguments can also control the outcome of a certain event. For instance, the `Closing`
event is fired when a form is about to be closed. It is still visible, however, and you can
create an event handler to cancel the closing process. To create an event handler for the
`Closing` event, set the `Cancel` property of the `CancelEventArgs` object passed in as an
event parameter to `false`. Doing so then prevents the form from closing. An event handler for the `Closing` event follows:

```
private void EventForm_Closing(object sender,
System.ComponentModel.CancelEventArgs e)
{
    if( MessageBox.Show("Are you sure you want to quit?","Quit?",
        MessageBoxButtons.YesNo) == DialogResult.No)
```

```
    {
        e.Cancel = true;
    }
    else
    {
        e.Cancel = false;
    }
}
```

7.6. Designating the Initial Windows Form

You have several defined forms in your application and you want to change the form that is initially displayed to the user.

Technique

Modify the static `Main` method, which was created when your project was initially created. Change the `Application.Run` method by creating an object instance of the form you want to initially display.

Another way to specify the initial form is to change a project property. First, create a static `Main` method in each form class. Within each of these `Main` methods, call the `Application.Run` method, passing an object instance of that form. Next, click on Project, Properties from the main menu (Alt+P, P) and select the General property page. Change the `Startup Object` property by selecting the name of the form you want initially displayed from the drop-down box.

Comments

In the technique for this two ways were presented to control the initial startup form when an application is launched. There's a specific reason why we did this: you need to choose the option that best fits your application.

The first option is simply going to your application entry point, the `Main` function, and changing the code that creates and displays your initial Windows Form. If you know that the initial form will not change often, then this is the best route to take.

The second option lets you set the initial form by changing a property in the project's property pages. You might be thinking, why would I ever want to do this? One advantage is that you open the possibility of using automation tools for user-interface validation. You could theoretically create a tool that enumerates the forms within a project and changes the `StartupObject` property to each one of those forms. An additional advantage is being able to specify different forms for either debug or release mode. For instance, you could create a form that captures debug trace information from your main user-interface form while release mode simply displays the main form and bypasses the debug trace form.

7.7. Changing a Windows Form Icon

You want to change the icon displayed in the upper-left corner of a Windows Form.

Technique

Select the form whose icon you want to change and click the browse button in the `Icon` properties value field. Select the icon you want to use. Figure 7.4 shows a Windows Form with a specified icon.

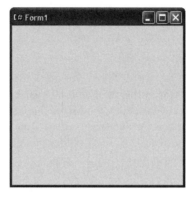

Figure 7.4   You can change the icon associated with a Windows Form by setting the `Icon` property.

You can also programmatically set a form's icon by creating an `Icon` instance and passing the path to an icon file in the constructor. Set the `Icon` property of the form to the icon object you created:

```
this.Icon = new Icon( "NewIcon.ico" );
```

Comments

Icons, whether on individual windows or an application icon, serve not only to provide a little visual flair but can also provide information. When setting the icon on a form, you have two choices. You can set a form's icon by using the form editor by clicking on the browse button on that form's icon property in the property browser. A standard file browser dialog appears, allowing you to select an icon file (`.ico`). When you do so, the icon is placed into the resource table of your application. When the form appears, the `ResourceManager` class loads the icon from your application's resource table and sets the icon on the form using that icon resource. An advantage to using this method other than its obvious simplicity is that you don't have to deploy the icon file with your application.

You can also programmatically change the icon during runtime by creating an Icon object and assigning the Icon property of your Windows Form to that object. Using this dynamic process of changing an icon, you are able to, for instance, create an animated icon for a form to give a visual indication about the state of the application or form at that time. One caveat is that you might be required to deploy the icon file or files with your application. However, Chapter 11, "Localization and Resources," demonstrates how to embed resources in your application similar to the automatic way the form editor does when you set the Icon property within the property browser.

7.8. Assigning Custom Data to a Windows Form

You want to dynamically change a form's properties using a custom configuration file.

Technique

Select the form you want to edit in the form editor. Expand the Dynamic Properties property in the property browser and click the browse button in the Advanced field. Place checkmarks next to the form properties that you want to dynamically configure using a configuration file, as shown in Figure 7.5. This process creates a .config file that will be deployed with your application. Each property that this file dynamically configures will be listed in the appSettings element using attributes for a key and its associated value. Changing a value attribute has the effect of changing that form's corresponding property when the application runs.

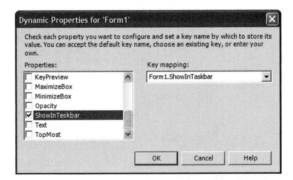

Figure 7.5   Use the Dynamic Properties dialog to select the properties whose values are read from the application configuration file.

You can also use the configuration file to control custom properties of your Windows Form, although you are unable to do so using the form editor. To create a dynamic property that is mapped to a property you created, add a new element in the .config file named `add` whose `key` attribute corresponds to the name of the property you want to control and whose `value` attribute is the value to set on the property. The following configuration file sets the property named `DisplayWelcome` to `false` when the form is displayed:

```
<?xml version="1.0" encoding="utf-8" ?>
<configuration>
    <appSettings>
        <add key="Form1.DisplayWelcome" value="False" />
    </appSettings>
</configuration>
```

In the constructor for your Windows Form, create a new `System.Configuration.AppSettingsReader` object. Set the property that you are dynamically controlling equal to the value returned from the `GetValue` method defined in the `AppSettingsReader` method. This method accepts two parameters. The first parameter denotes the name of the property whose value you want to retrieve, and the second parameter is a `System.Type` object corresponding to the data type of the property. You can create a `System.Type` object by using the `typeof` operator and passing the actual data type of the property to that operator. Finally, because the `GetValue` property returns a generic `System.Object`, cast the return value to the proper data type when setting your property:

```
public Form1()
{
    InitializeComponent();

    System.Configuration.AppSettingsReader configurationAppSettings =
        new System.Configuration.AppSettingsReader();

    this.DisplayWelcome =
        ((bool)(configurationAppSettings.GetValue("Form1.DisplayWelcome",
            typeof(bool))));

}
```

Comments

Configuration files let you alter the behavior of an application without having to rebuild the application's binary files. To circumvent overpopulating the system registry and to facilitate platform independence in the future, applications built using the .NET Framework can take advantage of application-setting configuration files. A configuration file is generated automatically when you use the form editor in Visual Studio .NET to create a dynamic property. In the first example given in the technique recipe, when you enable a standard Windows Form property to be dynamically read from a configuration file, the form editor does two things. First of all, it creates a configuration file, which is named based on the name of the executable with a `.config` file extension. The form editor then adds a new element named add in that XML-based configuration file. Finally, the form editor generates the code necessary to read the value from the configuration file and sets the corresponding property within your class.

The form editor works well for properties already defined within the System.Windows.Forms.Form class but does not have the ability to create dynamic properties for any extra properties you have added. This, of course, doesn't mean it can't be done. All you have to do is emulate what the form editor does and add the necessary plumbing yourself. However, the form editor generates the dynamic property code within your class's InitializeComponent method. When you create your own dynamic properties, take note that if you follow that pattern, it is entirely possible that the form editor will overwrite your code if placed within that method. Therefore, place any dynamic-property configuration code within your class constructor or another method that is not used for code generation, such as your form's Load event handler.

7.9. Changing Form Opacity

You want to change the opacity of a form to make it more transparent when it appears.

Technique

Set the Opacity property of a Windows Form to a value between 0% and 100%. At 100% opacity, the Windows Form is entirely opaque, but at 0%, the form is completely transparent. When programmatically changing the opacity of a form, you must use a double data type between 0.0 and 1.0:

```
private void Form1_MouseEnter(object sender, System.EventArgs e)
{
    this.Opacity = 1;
}

private void Form1_MouseLeave(object sender, System.EventArgs e)
{
    this.Opacity = 0.80;
}
```

If you only want portions of the form to be transparent, use the TransparencyKey property. You define this property using a color. If any portion of the form matches that color, it will be transparent. Figure 7.6 shows a form with 80% opacity. We placed a Panel control on the form and set its background color to a specific color. This color is also the form's TransparencyKey, which means the form is transparent where the Panel control is located.

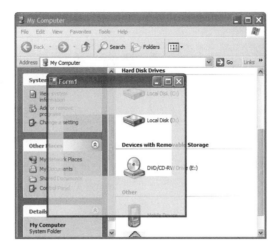

Figure 7.6   A Windows Form with 80% opacity and a `Panel` control whose background color is the same as the form's `TransparencyKey` property.

Comments

When Windows 2000 was released, a big user-interface innovation was the ability to create transparent or layered windows. The `Opacity` property of a Windows Form controls how opaque or transparent a window is. At 100%, the form appears in its default state, which means there are no transparent areas on the form. At 0%, the form is entirely transparent, which also means that you cannot interact with the form at all.

You can also create transparent regions within your form by using the `TransparencyKey` property. Although the `Opacity` property uses a numerical value to control how transparent or opaque a form is, the `TransparencyKey` property uses a `Color` value. When the form encounters that color, it does not draw the corresponding pixel. You might have seen some applications that use bitmaps to display their user interfaces, most notably several types of media players. You can easily create this type of user interface by creating a bitmap with certain portions set to a predefined color you want to use as the transparency key. Next, change the `BackgroundImage` property on the Windows Form to the bitmap file you created. Finally, change the `TransparencyKey` property of the Windows Form to the same color as the color you want to be transparent in the background bitmap. You might also want to remove the form's title bar by setting the `FormBorderStyle` to none. Figure 7.7 shows a Windows Form that uses a background bitmap and transparency key to create an irregularly shaped Windows Form.

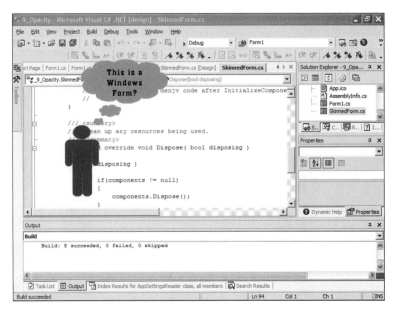

Figure 7.7 You can create irregular shaped Windows Forms using a bitmap and transparency key.

7.10. Supporting Drag and Drop Operations

You want to be able to drag and drop certain items onto your Windows Form.

Technique

Using the property browser for your form, set the `AllowDrop` property to `true`. Drag and drop uses the event system to control how a drag and drop is performed, which means you need to create a few event handlers. Click on the event button in the property browser toolbar and create event handlers for the `DragDrop`, `DragEnter`, `DragLeave`, and `DragOver` events.

The `DragEnter` and `DragOver` event handlers allow you to customize the display of the cursor as a drag operation occurs. Using the `DragEventArgs` parameter, you can query the data type of the object being dragged by calling the `GetDataPresent` method defined in the `Data` object of the event arguments. This method uses a value from the `DataFormats` enumerated data type as a parameter that denotes the type of data which is being dragged by the user. If the user is dragging a group of files, for instance, use the `DataFormats.FileDrop` value. If the object being dragged is supported by your application, set the `Effect` property in the `DragEventArgs` to a value defined in the `DragDropEffects` enumeration. This move changes the cursor to accurately reflect what your application plans to do with the objects. Furthermore, you can also determine whether the user is pressing a system key such as Ctrl or Alt by examining the KeyState property of the event argument's object:

```
private void Form1_DragEnter(object sender, System.Windows.Forms.DragEventArgs e)
{
    if( e.Data.GetDataPresent(DataFormats.FileDrop, false) == true )
    {
        if( (e.KeyState & 8) == 8 )
            e.Effect = DragDropEffects.Copy;
        else if( (e.KeyState & 32) == 32 )
            e.Effect = DragDropEffects.Link;
        else
            e.Effect = DragDropEffects.Move;
    }
}
```

When the user releases the mouse button, the DragDrop event handler is called. This handler uses the same DragEventArgs, as shown earlier. To retrieve the actual data, call the GetData method defined in the Data object of the event arguments using the same data type specification used when querying for the type of data being dragged. Because the GetData method returns a generic System.Object, you have to cast the return value to the appropriate data type. For a FileDrop object, the return value is an array of strings denoting the filenames being dropped:

```
private void Form1_DragDrop(object sender, System.Windows.Forms.DragEventArgs e)
{
    string[] files = (string[])e.Data.GetData("FileDrop", false);
    StringBuilder fileList = new StringBuilder();

    foreach (string s in files)
    {
        fileList.Append( s + "\n" );
    }

    MessageBox.Show( fileList.ToString() );
}
```

Comments

Graphical user interfaces introduced metaphors. A user-interface metaphor acts to associate a common task or command in the operating system with a common and easily recognizable object in the physical world. The classic metaphor example is the Recycle Bin. Its purpose is to act as a holding place for objects that might potentially be deleted by using a trash-can metaphor. Likewise, directories containing files use a folder-based metaphor. The metaphor of this recipe is drag and drop. In the physical world, a person will take a folder that potentially contains a group of files and drop it into a trash can or drop it into a different folder. By using concepts that are prevalent within the physical world, you dramatically increase the ease of use for your user interface.

You add drag and drop by setting the `AllowDrop` property of a form to `true`. When you do this, your form class will be notified via events of any drag and drop operations that a user performs. The first event that occurs when a user drags an item over your form is the `DragEnter` event. In the handler for this event, you should make a check using the `GetDataPresent` method defined in the `Data` object within the `DragEventArgs` parameter. This check determines the cursor that is displayed to give a visual indication to the user about the type of drag and drop support there is for the item being dragged. If your form does not support that item, set the `Effect` property from the `DragEventArgs` parameter to `DragDropEffects.None`. If your form does support the data type of the item, you can further refine the cursor display by checking to see what system keys the user presses. Table 7.2 shows the numerical values of the system keys in the `KeyState` property of the event arguments. To check whether a key is pressed, perform a bitwise and (`&`) with the `KeyState` property and the numerical value of the system key you are checking against. If the value of the bitwise and is the same value as the key you are checking, then that key is pressed. Note also that even though the `KeyState` property appears to only check the keyboard state, it also determines the state of any of the mouse buttons.

Table 7.2   **Bit Values of** `KeyState` **Property for System Keys**

Bit	Key/Button
1	Left mouse button
2	Right mouse button
4	Shift key
8	Ctrl key
16	Middle mouse button
32	Alt key

The `DragOver` event occurs after the `DragEnter` event. When the `DragOver` event handler is called, the user is dragging an item within the form. You will use this event handler more extensively when working with form controls. However, you still need to perform the same data-type check and set the corresponding `DragDropEffect` within this event handler. This step allows the user to press a system key while dragging and allows you to update the cursor based on that key press.

At this point, the user can either cancel the drag and drop or perform the drop by releasing the mouse button. When a user cancels the operation, either by pressing the Esc key or dragging the item off the form, the `DragLeave` event is fired. This event allows you to perform any cleanup associated with the previous drag and drop event handlers that were called. If the user does in fact drop the item, you now have to access the data being dropped.

When the `DragDrop` event handler is called, you can access the associated item data by calling the `GetData` method defined in the `Data` object of the event arguments. The data type that you retrieve should be the same data type you used when performing data-type checks in the initial drag and drop events. The `GetData` method returns a `System.Object`, which means you have to cast the value to the appropriate data type. The final data type depends on the actual data type of the item being dropped. The code for the `DragDrop` event handler presented earlier called the `GetData` method, specifying that `FileDrop` data is requested. The `FileDrop` data item returns a string array consisting of filenames. The next chapter goes into detail about creating and using custom drag and drop scenarios. Even though the process mentioned utilizes controls for drag and drop, the process is similar to using forms.

7.11. Creating MDI Forms

You want to create a Windows Form that acts as a container for several child forms.

Technique

Using the property browser, set the `IsMdiContainer` property to `true` on the form you want to act as the parent form. Create an additional form used as the child form by clicking Project, Add Windows Form from the main menu. To add a new child form within the parent form, create a new child form object and set its `MdiParent` property equal to the parent object. Because you do so within the parent form class, you can use the `this` keyword. Finally, call the `Show` method of the child form to display it:

```
ChildForm[] childForms = new ChildForm[3];

public Form1()
{
    InitializeComponent();

    for( int i = 0; i < 3; i++ )
    {
        childForms[i] = new ChildForm();
        childForms[i].MdiParent = this;
        childForms[i].Show();
    }
}
```

Comments

An MDI application supports several child windows within a main window. MDI applications traditionally allow the editing of several documents within a single main application window. A user can navigate to each document and edit it without having to open and close windows repeatedly. You create an MDI container form, also known as the parent, by setting the IsMdiContainer property to true. When you do this, the form's main area is drawn using a sunken display style with a raised border.

Creating a child window is similar to creating the parent to which it belongs because all you need is a single property change. In the case of the child window, you use the MdiParent property, and its value is a reference to the parent object. Because the creation of child windows occurs within the parent object itself, either through a menu event or some other event, you can simply use the this keyword, as shown in the code listing earlier. In the next few recipes, you'll see how ownership rules apply to forms as well as how parent forms can interact with the child forms they contain.

7.12. Accessing MDI Child Windows

You want to manipulate the child forms from a parent form in a MDI application.

Technique

To access the currently active MDI child form, use the ActiveMdiChild property defined in the parent form. To enumerate all MDI children, you can use a foreach enumeration on the MdiChildren collection. Listing 7.3 demonstrates how to change the title bar of each MDI child. The application also shows how to access individual controls within each MDI child. Figure 7.8 shows the result of running the application in Listing 7.3.

Listing 7.3   **Changing MDI Child Title Bars**

```
using System;
using System.Drawing;
using System.Collections;
using System.ComponentModel;
using System.Windows.Forms;
using System.Data;
using System.Text;

namespace _12_MDIChild
{
    public class Form1 : System.Windows.Forms.Form
    {
        private System.ComponentModel.Container components = null;

        ChildForm[] childForms = new ChildForm[3];
```

Listing 7.3 **Continued**

```
public Form1()
{
    InitializeComponent();

    for( int i = 0; i < 3; i++ )
    {
        childForms[i] = new ChildForm();
        childForms[i].MdiParent = this;
        childForms[i].Show();
    }
}

protected override void Dispose( bool disposing )
{
    if( disposing )
    {
        if (components != null)
        {
            components.Dispose();
        }
    }
    base.Dispose( disposing );
}

#region Windows Form Designer generated code
private void InitializeComponent()
{
    //
    // Form1
    //
    this.AutoScaleBaseSize = new System.Drawing.Size(5, 13);
    this.ClientSize = new System.Drawing.Size(292, 266);
    this.IsMdiContainer = true;
    this.Name = "Form1";
    this.Text = "Form1";
    this.MdiChildActivate +=
        new System.EventHandler(this.Form1_MdiChildActivate);
}
#endregion

private void Form1_MdiChildActivate(object sender, System.EventArgs e)
{
    StringBuilder childTitle = new StringBuilder();
    foreach( Form child in this.MdiChildren )
    {
```

Listing 7.3 **Continued**

```
                childTitle.Append(child.Text);
                childTitle.Replace( "- Active", "" );

                if( this.ActiveMdiChild == child )
                {
                    child.ActiveControl.Text = "Active Child";
                    child.Text = childTitle.ToString() + "- Active";

                }
                else
                {
                    child.Controls[0].Text = "Not Active Child";
                    child.Text = childTitle.ToString();
                }
                childTitle.Remove(0, childTitle.Length);
            }
        }

        [STAThread]
        static void Main()
        {
            Application.Run(new Form1());
        }
    }
}
```

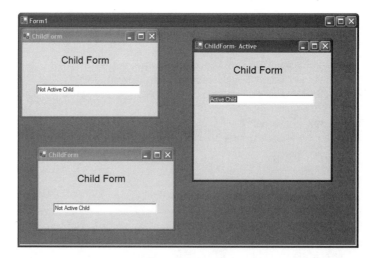

Figure 7.8 Each MDI child's title bar changes based on its active state.

Comments

In Listing 7.3, you can see how to handle the event that is fired whenever a new MDI child is activated. The event, MdiChildActivate, does not have any associated event arguments, but you can determine which child was activated by accessing the ActiveMdiChild property from the parent form. If you look at the result in Figure 7.8, you can see that the main form can change each MDI child's window caption. Furthermore, the parent can also manipulate each child form's control collection by enumerating all child forms using the MdiChildren collection.

7.13. Arranging MDI Child Forms

You want to programmatically arrange the MDI child forms within an MDI application.

Technique

Use the LayoutMdi method and pass a value from the MdiLayout enumerated data type. You can arrange MDI child forms in a cascading fashion, tile them vertically, or tile them horizontally, as shown in Listing 7.4.

Listing 7.4   **Arranging MDI Children**

```
private void Form1_VisibleChanged(object sender, System.EventArgs e)
{
    this.Visible = true;

    this.LayoutMdi( MdiLayout.Cascade );
    MessageBox.Show( "Cascading MDI Child Windows" );

    this.LayoutMdi( MdiLayout.TileVertical );
    MessageBox.Show( "Vertically Tiled MDI Child Windows" );

    this.LayoutMdi( MdiLayout.TileHorizontal );
    MessageBox.Show( "Horizontally Tiled MDI Child Windows" );
}
```

Comments

Whenever an overabundant amount of child windows are active within an MDI application, requiring the user to organize them manually is asking too much. Fortunately, Windows Forms allow you to perform the layout of MDI child windows using the

`MdiLayout` method. The code listing in this recipe simply enumerates through each of the MDI layouts. In most cases, the automatic arrangement of child windows occurs within an event handler for a control within the parent window. Generally, automatic child window layout happens within the event handler for a menu item on the parent form's main menu or a toolbar button on the application's toolbar.

8

Windows Forms Controls

8.0. Introduction

This chapter looks at several different facets of Windows Forms controls. Some of the techniques explore the different controls available to you as you design and implement your user interface. Some of the techniques are similar for all controls, whereas other techniques focus on a certain solution for a single control.

8.1. Displaying Text with a `Label` Control

You want to use a `Label` on your Windows Form.

Technique

You use a `Label` control to display a string of text. Create a new Windows application and within the form designer, drag and drop a `Label` control from the toolbox onto the Windows Form. Next, type in the new text that you want displayed.

Comments

The `Label` control is also known as a static control because its only job is to display information to a user without any interaction. It primarily provides additional information regarding the function of a different control. For instance, a Windows Form that acts as an order form might have a `Label` control with the text "Address" followed by a `TextBox` control. The `Label` control in this instance provides immediate feedback to the user so there is no confusion about what to enter in that `TextBox`.

You can also programmatically create a Label control within your text. The previous chapter mentioned that Windows Forms technology isn't tied to a specified resource file format for user-interface definitions but rather uses dynamic code generation in real time as you define the user interface in the Windows Forms editor. Just as code is generated when defining the attributes of a Windows Form, the Integrated Development Environment (IDE) also generates the code necessary to associate a control with the Windows Form it is placed on. To view the code for a Label control, open the source code file associated with the Windows Form and expand the hidden source-code region named Windows Form Designer Generated Code. In the InitializeComponent method, you see the code necessary to create a label. In Listing 8.1, you can see the InitializeComponent method that is generated by the forms designer. A Label control is created and assigned to a private class member variable. After the label's properties are set, it is associated with and placed on the form by inserting the control into the form's Controls collection.

Listing 8.1   **Code Generated by the Forms Designer for Controls on a Windows Form**

```
private System.Windows.Forms.Label label1;

private void InitializeComponent()
{
    this.label1 = new System.Windows.Forms.Label();
    this.SuspendLayout();
    //
    // label1
    //
    this.label1.Location = new System.Drawing.Point(88, 104);
    this.label1.Name = "label1";
    this.label1.Size = new System.Drawing.Size(120, 23);
    this.label1.TabIndex = 0;
    this.label1.Text = "This is a label control";
    //
    // Form1
    //
    this.AutoScaleBaseSize = new System.Drawing.Size(5, 13);
    this.ClientSize = new System.Drawing.Size(292, 266);
    this.Controls.Add(this.label1);
    this.Name = "Form1";
    this.Text = "Form1";
    this.ResumeLayout(false);
}
```

8.2. Changing Control Properties

You want to alter the appearance of a Windows Form control.

Technique

Change the properties of a Windows Form control by opening the associated Windows Form in the form designer and selecting the control you want to change. The property browser tool window displays all the properties available for that control. To change a property, select the input box located to the right of the property name. Based on the data type of that property, a UI Type Editor control appears. For standard text properties, you can simply enter the new text. For property types that accept a predefined set of values, you see a drop-down arrow. Clicking that arrow displays a drop-down list of possible values. Other UI Type Editors include browse buttons for file-based properties such as the `Image` property, color-chooser controls for color-based properties such as `BackColor`, or a layout-based editor for properties that alter the layout of a control, as with the `Anchor` property. Additionally, as each property field obtains focus, a short description of the property appears at the bottom of the property browser window.

Comments

One of the fascinating features of Windows Forms is the ability to drastically design and alter the appearance of a user interface without ever having to write custom code. If you do get to the point of having to write code to change a property on a form, the names of the properties within the property browser are the same as the property defined in the class, allowing you to immediately see the effects before committing your changes to code. Each property within the control class uses a data type that maps to the type editor used during the design phase. For instance, the `Text` property on a `Label` control uses a `string` data type. The `BackColor` property, however, uses the `System.Drawing.Color` data type. Therefore, the code to change the properties of a `Label` control contains varying data types, as shown in Listing 8.2. In this listing, the `Label` control uses a different font from the font used as a default and also takes advantage of control colors to change the `ForeColor` and `BackColor` properties.

Listing 8.2   **Defining Control Properties Using a Variety of Data Types**

```
private void InitializeComponent()
{
    this.mylabel = new System.Windows.Forms.Label();
    this.SuspendLayout();

    // label properties
    this.mylabel.BackColor = System.Drawing.SystemColors.ControlDark;
    this.mylabel.BorderStyle = System.Windows.Forms.BorderStyle.FixedSingle;
```

Listing 8.2 **Continued**

```
this.mylabel.Font = new System.Drawing.Font("Team MT", 24F,
    System.Drawing.FontStyle.Bold,
    System.Drawing.GraphicsUnit.Point, ((System.Byte)(0)));

this.mylabel.ForeColor = System.Drawing.Color.FromArgb(((System.Byte)(0)),
    ((System.Byte)(0)), ((System.Byte)(192)));

this.mylabel.Location = new System.Drawing.Point(24, 64);
this.mylabel.Name = "mylabel";
this.mylabel.Size = new System.Drawing.Size(232, 120);
this.mylabel.TabIndex = 0;
this.mylabel.Text = "This is a label control";
this.mylabel.TextAlign = System.Drawing.ContentAlignment.MiddleCenter;

// form properties...
}
```

8.3. Creating a Button and Handling Events

You want to create a button and perform an action when the user clicks the button.

Technique

Drag and drop a button control onto your Windows Form within the Windows Forms designer. Alter the appearance of the button as necessary by changing the button's properties. There are two options available when creating an event handler for the Click event. Because the Click event is the most commonly used event that is handled for a button, you can double-click on the button itself and the form designer generates the necessary event-handling method within your class and opens the source code file, placing the cursor at the Click event-handler method body. The second option available when creating an event handler is to select the button within the form designer and click on the lightning bolt toolbar icon within the property browser. The property browser then lists all the possible events that the Button control can fire. Double-click the field next to the name of the event to create an event handler for that event, or type in the name of the event handler in that same field and press the Enter key.

Comments

Just as there are numerous properties for each Windows Form control, there are almost an equal number of events that you can create event handlers for. Furthermore, in addition to visually changing a control's property using the property browser, you can also create an event handler using that same tool window.

Because there are so many events associated with any given control, keeping track of what each event does is obviously a nontrivial task. Thankfully, when you single-click on an event name within the property browser, a small help string appears at the bottom of the property browser, giving you information on when that event will be fired. For obvious tasks such as adding the Click event to a button control, there is little value in that small help string, but you'll soon find yourself referring to it for the more obscure events such as the ChangeUICues event.

Windows Forms controls event handlers use two parameters. The first parameter, which is the same regardless of the control, is a System.Object parameter named sender that allows you to access the control that fired the event. In most cases, you don't need to use that parameter because you already know what control fired the event and more than likely already have a private member variable associated with the control. The next parameter is a collection of event-handler arguments, which are different based on the control and the event being handled. The rule of thumb for this parameter is that if the parameter data type is System.EventArgs, then there is no additional information available for that event. For instance, if you create an event handler for the MouseHover event, you might expect the event arguments to give you the current location of the mouse cursor relative to that control. Unfortunately, because the second parameter of that MouseHover event handler is System.EventArgs, there is no such information available. In such cases, you have to either call any necessary methods to determine that information or use other event handlers for events which do provide that information. In the case of the MouseHover event, you can also create an event handler for the MouseMove event, saving the mouse coordinates specified in the MouseEventArgs parameter of that event handler.

If you look under the hood at the code that is generated when creating an event handler, you'll see that control events (as well as events for the form itself) use multicast delegates as the main event-handling mechanism. Listing 8.3 creates a form with two buttons. Each button's Click event is associated with an event handler. You make this association using the addition assignment (+=) operator on the Click property of each button. You can in fact programmatically associate multiple event handlers for a single event using this method as well as dynamically add or remove event handlers during application runtime.

Listing 8.3 **Associating Events with an Event Handler Using the Multicast Delegate Syntax**

```
private void InitializeComponent()
{
    this.sayHello = new System.Windows.Forms.Button();
    this.closeForm = new System.Windows.Forms.Button();
    this.SuspendLayout();
    //
    // sayHello
    //
```

Listing 8.3 **Continued**

```
    this.sayHello.Location = new System.Drawing.Point(98, 16);
    this.sayHello.Name = "sayHello";
    this.sayHello.Size = new System.Drawing.Size(96, 23);
    this.sayHello.TabIndex = 0;
    this.sayHello.Text = "Say Hello";

    // event handler association for the Click event
    this.sayHello.Click += new System.EventHandler(this.sayHello_Click);

    //
    // closeForm
    //
    this.closeForm.Location = new System.Drawing.Point(98, 64);
    this.closeForm.Name = "closeForm";
    this.closeForm.Size = new System.Drawing.Size(96, 23);
    this.closeForm.TabIndex = 1;
    this.closeForm.Text = "Close Form";
    this.closeForm.Click += new System.EventHandler(this.closeForm_Click);
    //
    // Form1
    //
    this.AutoScaleBaseSize = new System.Drawing.Size(5, 13);
    this.ClientSize = new System.Drawing.Size(292, 118);
    this.Controls.Add(this.closeForm);
    this.Controls.Add(this.sayHello);
    this.Name = "Form1";
    this.Text = "Form1";
    this.ResumeLayout(false);
}
```

8.4. Displaying an Open File Dialog Box

You want to allow the user to browse for a file using the standard Windows open file dialog box.

Technique

You can create an open file dialog box using the forms designer. Open the form in the forms designer that will need to have access to an open file dialog box, and drag and drop the OpenFileDialog control from the toolbox onto the form. The OpenFileDialog is a nonvisual control, so it is displayed at the bottom of the form designer. Select the control and change any properties appropriate to your application.

The most common properties associated with an `OpenFileDialog` include the `Filter`, `Title`, and `Multiselect` properties.

To display the open file dialog to the user, call the `ShowDialog` method from the object that was generated when you created the control. This method returns a `DialogResult` enumerated data type. If the user clicks the `Open` button, then it returns the value `DialogResult.OK`.

Comments

In addition to common visual controls, the forms designer also lets you create instances of nonvisual controls using the same drag and drop methods. To distinguish visual and nonvisual controls from each other, the nonvisual controls appear at the bottom of the forms designer within a list view. This view displays the toolbox icon of the control as well as the generated private member variable that was created within the form class.

You will undoubtedly have to change the value of three properties. The `Title`, as you have probably guessed, changes the caption of the open file dialog when it appears. The `Filter` property controls the file type drop-down box on the open file dialog. The `Filter` property is a string that uses a pipe (|) separated list of values for its display. These values are grouped using a friendly name for the file type separated by the file extension of that file type using a wildcard specification. For instance, to specify two items in the drop-down box where the first item displays all text (`.txt`) files and the second item displays all files regardless of file type, you use the following to specify the `Filter` property:

```
this.openFileDialog1.Filter = "Text Files|*.txt|All Files|*.*";
```

The `Multiselect` property allows a user to select multiple files at one time. With a single-selection open file dialog box, you can access the path of the file the user selected through the `FileName` property of the `OpenFileDialog` object. If `Multiselect` is `True`, however, you have to access each file using the `FileNames` collection. It is a collection of strings containing the path of the files that you can use in a `foreach` loop or other enumeration process.

8.5. Creating and Attaching Menus to a Windows Form

You want to create a main menu for your Windows Form.

Technique

You can create a menu and its associated menu items by dragging and dropping a `MainMenu` control from the form designer toolbox onto the form that uses the menu. The menu editor appears directly in your form, allowing you to perform an in-place edit of the menu. To create a menu item, type text in the Type Here locations of the menu editor. You can create pop-up menus by editing the menu items that pop up in the editor to the left or right side of an already existing menu item. To insert a new menu item between two existing menu items, press the Insert key on the keyboard. You can also insert a menu separator by right-clicking on the menu and selecting the Insert Separator menu option.

As a shortcut, you can directly edit the menu item variable names within the menu editor by right-clicking on the menu and selecting the Edit Names menu item. The variables that represent the generated private member variables for each menu item then appear, allowing you to change those values, as shown in Figure 8.1.

Figure 8.1   Edit the associated menu item variable names by entering the Edit Names mode of the menu editor.

Comments

Menus allow you to place a large amount of application functionality using a minimal amount of screen real estate. Creating a menu within the forms designer is unique because rather than use the property browser as is custom with most other controls, you alter the appearance of the menu using a WYSIWYG menu editor. Using the form designer menu editor, you can create any number of top-level menu items, each with their own associated submenu items and separators. Each one of those submenu items can also contain any number of pop-up cascading menu items themselves.

To create an event handler for a specific menu item, select the menu item in the menu editor and double-click it to add the Click event handler. Another event that you can handle which might prove useful is the Popup event. By creating an event handler for this event, you can dynamically alter the contents of the menu before it appears to the user. For instance, the Popup handler can check whether any text is selected within a TextBox control. If no text is selected, you can disable any text operations such as Cut, Copy, or Paste.

8.6. Creating Context Menus

You want a context menu to display whenever a user right-clicks on a control or on your Windows Form.

Technique

To create a context menu, drag a ContextMenu control from the form designer toolbox and drop it on your form. Design the menu using the menu editor as described in the previous recipe. To associate a context menu with a control, select the control that you want to attach the context menu to in the form designer and change the ContextMenu property of that control. The property browser enumerates any available context menus that you have created and lists them in the ContextMenu property drop-down selection box.

Comments

In addition to a main menu, you can also create smaller control-specific context menus that appear whenever a user right-clicks on a control or your form. Using the same menu editor as the MainMenu control, you can create a small or extremely sophisticated context menu. Furthermore, you can also associate the context menu with any number of your controls on your form.

A major difference within the form designer between a MainMenu control and a ContextMenu control is that a ContextMenu control isn't always displayed within the editor. Because both types of menus occupy the same space within the form designer, one of them has to remain hidden while the other is being edited. When no menus are selected, the MainMenu control is visible within the forms designer. To edit an existing ContextMenu control, select its nonvisual representation at the bottom of the form designer. This action replaces the MainMenu within the form with the ContextMenu and opens the in-place menu editor, allowing you to add or delete menu items.

8.7. Displaying System Tray Icons

You want your application to display a system tray icon as another means to access its functionality.

Technique

The forms designer toolbox contains a NotifyIcon control that allows you to place an icon in the system tray in Windows, as shown in Figure 8.2. To associate a NotifyIcon with your Windows Form, drag a NotifyIcon control from the form designer toolbox and drop it on the form. In most instances, a NotifyIcon has an associated context menu. The procedure to create a ContextMenu object and associate it with the NotifyIcon is the same as shown in the previous recipe.

Figure 8.2   Use the `NotifyIcon` control to display a system tray icon for applications that run in the background.

Comments

If you want your application's main form to remain invisible when the application starts and only to show when the user selects a context menu item from the `NotifyIcon`, you have to perform a few additional steps in addition to setting the `Visible` property of your Windows Form. The generated code that was created when you initially created your application calls the `Application.Run` method, passing an instance of your form as the parameter of the method. Even if you set the `Visible` property of your form to `false`, the form still shows because the overloaded `Application.Run` method that accepts a `Form` object in turn sets the `Visible` property to `true`. Therefore, modify the application entry point method, `Main`, by creating an instance of your form before `Application.Run` is called, and then call `Application.Run` without any parameters, as shown in the following code:

```
[STAThread]
static void Main()
{
    Form1 mainForm = new Form1();
    Application.Run();
}
```

If you want to add the ability to exit your application using the context menu of the notify icon, you must explicitly remove the icon from the tray before exiting your application. If you do not, the tray icon remains in the tray even when your application has exited, and it does not disappear until the mouse hovers over it. Therefore, set the `Visible` property of your `NotifyIcon` property to `false` when your application exits.

8.8. Opening Web Pages with a `LinkLabel` Control

You want to open the default system Web browser when a user clicks a link associated with a `LinkLabel` control.

Technique

A `LinkLabel` control simply serves as a label whose text and cursor is formatted to appear like a Web hyperlink. You must handle the `LinkClicked` event to create any additional functionality with the control.

When the `LinkClicked` event is fired, you can open the default Web browser by calling the `System.Diagnostics.Process.Start` method, passing a URL string to navigate to as the parameter. After the `LinkClicked` event handler is invoked, you can optionally set the `LinkVisited` property of the `LinkLabel` control to `true` to change the color of the text. This color is specified in the `VisitedLinkColor` property:

```
private void linkLabel1_LinkClicked(object sender,
    System.Windows.Forms.LinkLabelLinkClickedEventArgs e)
{
    System.Diagnostics.Process.Start( linkLabel1.Text );
    linkLabel1.LinkVisited = true;
}
```

Comments

The `LinkLabel` is derived from the `Label` control, which is why there are so many similarities between the two. Although you might assume a `LinkLabel` opens a Web browser to a specified page, that is simply just one of any number of possibilities. There is no "default" behavior associated with a `LinkLabel`, which means it is up to you to define that behavior.

The `System.Diagnostics.Process.Start` is a powerful method that contains several overloads. These overloads use system interoperability to call a number of different system-defined methods. For instance, passing a `ProcessInfo` object or two strings (application name and command-line arguments), the `Start` method calls the `CreateProcess` method in the `kernel32.dll` file. In the example shown earlier, which accepts a single string parameter, the `Start` method eventually uses the `ShellExecuteEx` method in the `shell32.dll` library. These methods allow you to pass a string that represents a moniker. A moniker is a system-defined object that is associated with a certain task or object. For example, a URL moniker in this example is associated with an object that can launch the default system browser. Fortunately, all this complicated material is transparent to the developer using the `Start` method. In addition to a URL moniker, if you pass a string representing a path to a file, the file moniker associated with that file extension is called, which results in the file being opened in its associated application. In other words, passing the path to a text file in turn causes your default text editor to open and display that text file.

8.9. Determining Check Box State

You want to determine whether a check box is checked and also be notified when the state of a check box changes.

Technique

The `Checked` property of a `CheckBox` control lets you know whether a check box is checked. To perform an action when the check box is clicked, you can handle the `CheckedChanged` event. A check box can also have three states if the `ThreeState` property is set to `true`. In addition to the checked and unchecked states, a three state check box also has an indeterminate state. For these check boxes, you can view the state using the `CheckState` property. This property contains a value in the `CheckState` enumerated data type. Additionally, when a three-state check box's state changes to the `CheckState.Indeterminate` state, which visually appears as a gray check box that is checked, the `CheckedChanged` event is not thrown. However, you can create an event handler for the `CheckStateChanged` event.

Comments

Check box controls are inclusive controls used to control the value of a Boolean variable. In most cases, the check box is either checked (`true`) or unchecked (`false`). However, a check box can also have an indeterminate state, which is shown as a grayed-out check in the check box, as shown in Figure 8.3. In this figure, the application allows you to change the appearance of a label by checking a series of check boxes. The last check box in the group labeled `Color` is a three-state check box. When the check box is in the `CheckState.Indeterminate` state, the user wants to change the color of the label but has not checked the `Red` check box. If this were a real application, then the color choice would obviously have more selections. Once the user checks the `Red` check box, the state of the `Color` check box can change to `Checked`.

Figure 8.3   Check boxes can be in a checked, unchecked, or indeterminate state.

8.10. Creating Grouped Radio Buttons

You want to create several groups of radio buttons.

Technique

Because radio button groups are mutually exclusive, you need to separate each group using a control container. Some of the possible control containers include the `GroupBox`, `Panel`, and a Windows Form itself. Determine which container you want to use and perform a drag and drop operation from the toolbox onto your Windows Form. To create a group of radio buttons within the control container you just created, drag each individual radio button in the group and drop it on the control container that you just created.

Comments

Radio buttons are similar to check boxes in that a radio button can either be checked or unchecked. The differences lie in the relationship between other like controls. Check boxes are inclusive, meaning that the state of one check box does not directly affect the state of another check box unless you programmatically make it so. In other words, two check boxes can be checked at the same time. Radio buttons, on the other hand, are mutually exclusive. Given a group of radio buttons, only one of them can be checked at one time. When a user clicks on a single radio button from a group of radio buttons, the state of that radio button changes to checked and any other radio buttons are set to unchecked.

To create separate groups of radio buttons, you have to place each group within different control containers. Control containers act to logically group controls to delineate them from any other controls on a form. GroupBox controls have been used since the beginning of Windows and are still valuable to this day. A GroupBox control uses a label and border around the controls it contains. A Panel control is a new control designed for the .NET Framework. By default, a Panel control is invisible during runtime and is simply a control container. You can, however, change a Panel control's properties such as its BackColor to give a visual indication to the user that a group of controls is related.

8.11. Determining the Selected Radio Button

You want to determine the currently selected radio button in a group of radio buttons as well as be notified when the state of a radio button changes.

Technique

The RadioButton control is similar to the CheckBox control because both contain a Checked property that can translate into an internal Boolean variable for your form. Radio buttons do not have the option to display three states so there is no ThreeState property. The events that allow you to perform an action when the radio button is manipulated include the CheckedChanged and Click events. It's recommended that you handle the CheckedChanged event because the event is fired whenever the Checked property changes, which is either a result of the user clicking the radio button or through programmatic means by changing the Checked property.

Comments

Radio buttons and check boxes are similar controls. Each of these controls can be in an on or off state. Even though the visual appearance of a radio button is either an empty or filled circle, it still uses the idea of being in a checked state similar to a check box.

You use the CheckedChanged event to perform an action when the state of a single radio button changes. If you use a group of radio buttons, this event can fire twice. When a user clicks a radio button in a group, the radio button that is currently checked is set to the unchecked state. This move causes the CheckedChanged event for that radio button to be called, and subsequently, the Checked property for that button is set to false. Next, the CheckedChanged event is fired for the radio button that was clicked because its Checked property has changed to true.

If you need to enumerate the radio buttons within a radio button group, you can access the Controls collection of the control container the radio buttons are located on. You should, however, ensure that you perform a type check on each element because the control container might also contain nonradio buttons. The following code enumerates two groups of radio buttons. Each group is naturally contained within its own control container. As each control is accessed in the Controls collection, its type is checked using the GetType method defined in the Control class, which all .NET controls derive from, and compares the result of that method call using the typeof operator on the RadioButton class. If the logical statement is true, then a radio button is found and can therefore be cast accordingly, as shown in Listing 8.4.

Listing 8.4   **Examining Radio Button Checked State**

```
private void UpdateLabels()
{
    // enumerate each control in the control container (GroupBox)
    foreach( Control ctrl in groupColor.Controls )
    {
        // determine if radio button
        if( ctrl.GetType() == typeof(RadioButton) )
        {
            // cast control to RadioButton object
            RadioButton radio = (RadioButton) ctrl;
            if( radio.Checked == true )
            {
                labelColor.Text = "Color: " + radio.Text;
                break;
            }
        }
    }

    foreach( Control ctrl in groupSize.Controls )
    {
        if( ctrl.GetType() == typeof(RadioButton) )
        {
            RadioButton radio = (RadioButton) ctrl;
            if( radio.Checked == true )
            {
```

Listing 8.4   **Continued**

```
            labelSize.Text = "Size: " + radio.Text;
            break;
        }
    }
  }
}
```

8.12. Adding and Removing Items in a `ListBox` Control

You want to create a list of items and programmatically add and remove items from the list.

Technique

Use the `ListBox` control if you want to display a simple list. To add a list of items using the form designer, select the `ListBox` control and click the browse button, which you see when you select the `Items` property. This move displays the string collection editor. Add new items to the `ListBox` by inserting strings individually on separate lines.

You can also programmatically add items by calling the `Add` method defined in the `Items` collection of an existing `ListBox` object. This method accepts a `System.Object` parameter, which means you are free to add any type of object to the collection. When the object appears in the `ListBox`, its `ToString` representation appears:

```
foreach( string selectedName in lbContacts.SelectedItems )
{
    lbRecip.Items.Add( selectedName );
}
```

You can also add an array of objects to the `ListBox` by calling the `AddRange` method on the `Items` collection. The following code copies all the items from one `ListBox` control to another:

```
lbRecip.Items.AddRange( lbContacts.Items );
```

To remove an item from a `ListBox`, call the `Remove` method defined in the `Items` collection. The `Remove` method uses the properties of object equality to find the object within the collection. For instance, using string objects, it looks for the item with the same string value:

```
lbContacts.Items.Remove( "Doug Deprenger" );
```

You can also remove an item by its position by calling the RemoveAt method. This method uses the zero-based index of the item in the collection as its parameter. To remove all items in a ListBox, call the Clear method:

```
lbContacts.Items.RemoveAt( 0 );
lbContacts.Items.Clear();
```

Comments

A ListBox is useful if you want to display a list of strings to the user and give the user the ability to select the strings to perform some action. This list, for instance, could be a list of contact names or items on a shopping list. The items in a ListBox are contained within the Items collection, which contains the necessary methods to add and remove items. When you add a string to the Items collection, the ListBox is updated and the new item string representation appears.

A ListBox supports a few different selection methods. To specify the allowable selection a user can make, change the SelectionMode property using a value from the SelectionMode enumerated data type. If the selection mode is None, then the user will be unable to select an item in the list. When you set SelectionMode to single, then the list items are mutually exclusive, which means that when one item is selected, the previous item is unselected. You can also use a multiple-selection list box by specifying a selection mode of MultiSimple or MultiExtended. The difference between the two involves the use of the Ctrl key on the keyboard. With a MultiExtended style, the user must hold down the Ctrl key to select multiple items. The MultiSimple does not require the use of the Ctrl key, and the user selects or deselects items simply by clicking on them. In a multiple-selection list box, you can determine which items are selected by accessing the SelectedItems or SelectedIndices collection. In a single-selection list box, you can reference the SelectedItem or SelectedIndex properties.

In Listing 8.5, you can see event handlers for the five buttons shown in Figure 8.4. In this application, you can move names between the two list boxes. The methods btnSingleAdd_Click and btnSingleRemove_Click enumerate the selected items and move them to the corresponding list box. The event handlers btnAddAll_Click and btnRemoveAll_Click use the ListBox methods AddRange and Clear to add or remove an entire group of items from one list box to the other.

Listing 8.5   Moving Items Between Two Multiple-Selection ListBox Objects

```
private void btnSingleAdd_Click(object sender, System.EventArgs e)
{
    // enumerate selected items
    foreach( string selectedName in lbContacts.SelectedItems )
    {
        // add item to other list box
        lbRecip.Items.Add( selectedName );
    }
}
```

Listing 8.5   **Continued**

```
    // create a copy of all contacts items
    // this is done since an exception is thrown if you
    // add items to a collection while that
    //     collection is being enumerated within a foreach loop
    ListBox.ObjectCollection newContacts =
        new ListBox.ObjectCollection( lbContacts, lbContacts.Items );

    foreach( string selectedName in lbContacts.SelectedItems )
    {
        // remove the item from the temporary collection
        newContacts.Remove( selectedName );
    }
    // clear all items and insert items from temporary collection
    lbContacts.Items.Clear();
    lbContacts.Items.AddRange( newContacts );
}

private void btnAllAdd_Click(object sender, System.EventArgs e)
{
    // add all items from contacts to recipient's listbox
    lbRecip.Items.AddRange( lbContacts.Items );

    // clear contacts list box
    lbContacts.Items.Clear();
}

private void btnSingleRemove_Click(object sender, System.EventArgs e)
{
    foreach( string selectedName in lbRecip.SelectedItems )
    {
        lbContacts.Items.Add( selectedName );
    }

    ListBox.ObjectCollection newRecip =
        new ListBox.ObjectCollection( lbRecip, lbRecip.Items );

    foreach( string selectedName in lbRecip.SelectedItems )
    {
        newRecip.Remove( selectedName );
    }

    lbRecip.Items.Clear();
    lbRecip.Items.AddRange( newRecip );
}
```

Listing 8.5   **Continued**

```
private void btnAllRemove_Click(object sender, System.EventArgs e)
{
    lbContacts.Items.AddRange( lbRecip.Items );
    lbRecip.Items.Clear();
}

private void btnNew_Click(object sender, System.EventArgs e)
{
    // Note: NewContact class not shown
    NewContact contactForm = new NewContact();
    contactForm.ShowDialog();

    // add new contact to contact list
    lbContacts.Items.Add( contactForm.ContactName );
}
```

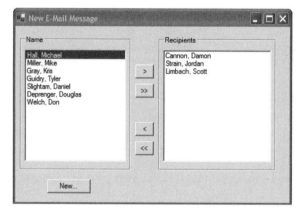

Figure 8.4   You can move multiple items from one ListBox to the other.

8.13. Using a `ListView` Control

You want to add and remove items from a `ListView` control.

Technique

As with the `ListBox` control, you manipulate a `ListView`'s items using the `Items` collection. The `Add` method of the `Items` collection contains three overloaded methods. You can add an item just by passing a string object:

```
lvAvailable.Items.Add( "Normal" );
```

To allow more customizability of a `ListView` item, create a `ListViewItem` object and set its properties accordingly. Some of the properties include color properties and check states:

```
ListViewItem listViewItem1 = new ListViewItem( "Happy" );
listViewItem1.ForeColor = Color.Red;
lvAvailable.Items.Add( listViewItem1 );
```

You can also add a range of `ListViewItem` objects by creating an array and calling the `AddRange` method of the `Items` collection:

```
// adding an array of ListViewItems
ListViewItem[] lvItems = new ListViewItem[]{ new ListViewItem("Sad"),
                                             new ListViewItem("Angry"),
                                             new ListViewItem("Surprised"),
                                             new ListViewItem("Bashful")};

lvAvailable.Items.AddRange( lvItems );
```

Removing `ListView` items is similar to removing items from a `ListBox` control, which is demonstrated in the previous recipe. However, the `Remove` method only allows removal using a `ListViewItem` object. To retrieve `ListViewItem` objects, you can access the `SelectedItems` collection or use the `Items` indexer:

```
private void btnSingleRemove_Click(object sender, System.EventArgs e)
{
    foreach( ListViewItem selectedEmoticon in lvChosen.SelectedItems )
    {
        lvAvailable.Items.Add( (ListViewItem) selectedEmoticon.Clone() );
    }
    foreach( ListViewItem lvItem in lvChosen.SelectedItems )
        lvChosen.Items.Remove( lvItem );
}
```

Comments

A `ListView` control is similar to a `ListBox`, but it allows you to display items in a variety of different view modes. The `ListView` works with a specially designed data type rather than a generic `object` used by a `ListBox`. The `ListViewItem` class contains several properties, allowing you to individually alter the appearance of individual items within a `ListView`. Adding new items, however, is still similar to that of a `ListBox` because both controls contain an `Items` collection with the main difference being the data type stored in that collection. The `ListViewItems` editor, which is invoked through the `Items` property in the property browser, contains more information and available properties for each item than the simple string collection editor used by the `ListBox` control. The next few recipes go into detail about manipulating the `ListView` control and its individual items.

8.14. Using `ImageList`s in a `ListView` Control

You want to assign different images to the items in a `ListView` control.

Technique

The first step to assign an image list to a `ListView` control is to create an `ImageList` control. Drag and drop an `ImageList` control from the form designer toolbox onto your Windows Form. To add images to the `ImageList`, invoke the `ImageList` editor by accessing the edit button within the `Images` collection. To add an image within the editor, click on the `Add` button and browse to an image file.

When you finish adding images to the `ImageList`, associate the `ImageList` with the `ListView` by selecting a value from the drop-down lists in the `SmallImageList` and `LargeImageList` properties. You use the `SmallImageList` property when the `ListView` is in the `SmallIcon`, `List`, and `Detail` view modes, and you use the `LargeImageList` property with the `LargeIcon` view mode. The next recipe fully explains these modes. You can also specify a `StateImageList`, which is used when an application-defined state changes on an item. For instance, if the `CheckBoxes` property is `true` and a `StateImageList` is specified, the check boxes that normally appear are replaced by the images contained within the `StateImageList`.

Comments

A `ListView` control has the ability to display items as text, as an image, or both. An `ImageList` control is a nonvisual control used to hold information about a collection of images. Methods are available in the `Images` collection of the `ImageList` to add or remove individual images as well as obtain information about each image.

Because a `ListView` contains four separate view modes, it needs to be able to display both small and large images. Although the documentation mentions no defined image size, it is best to use images that are 16 x 16 for small images and 32 x 32 for large images. When creating images for a `ListView`, you should strive to create images that provide some sort of additional information about the item type the image represents. For instance, when viewing a list of files in Windows Explorer, you see icons that provide additional information about a file type that a filename cannot provide, assuming, of course, that you are not a walking encyclopedia of file extensions. If you are using a `ListView` and associated images for the control simply for aesthetic reasons, then you might want to rethink the design or at least limit the different views that the `ListView` displays.

8.15. Changing a `ListView` Mode

You want to programmatically change the mode of a `ListView` control.

Technique

You can view a `ListView` in one of four different modes. The `View` property controls the mode and you can set it using a value defined in the `View` enumerated data type. In the `SmallIcon` mode, the items are arranged in rows using small icons as specified in the `SmallImageList` property. An example of a `ListView` in small icon mode appears in Figure 8.5.

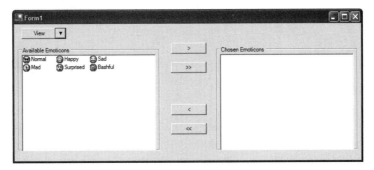

Figure 8.5   `ListView` control whose `View` property is set to `SmallIcon`.

The `LargeIcon` view is similar to the `SmallIcon` view with the main obvious difference being the size of the icons that appear. It should be noted that you can use the same `ImageList` used in the `SmallImageList`. The `ListView` simply expands each item's draw rectangle to accommodate larger images, as shown in Figure 8.6.

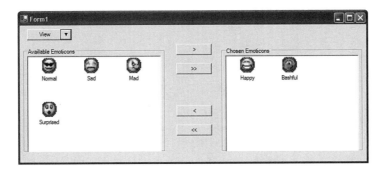

Figure 8.6   `ListView` control using the `LargeIcon` mode.

The `List` mode is similar to the `SmallIcon` mode except the items are arranged within a single column rather than the matrix style used in the small icon mode. Finally, the `Details` mode allows you to create additional columns containing extra information. Each column also contains a column header displaying a string denoting what the string in each column for each item represents. The next recipe demonstrates creating columns for a `ListView`.

Comments

One of the obvious powerful features of the `ListView` control is its ability to change the way items are visually represented to a user. In the `List` view, items appear in a single column similar to that of a `ListBox`. However, the `ListView` is able to alter the appearance of each individual item within this mode using different color combinations or by utilizing an `ImageList`.

Icon views in a `ListView` are similar to the default view method you see when browsing files in Windows Explorer. The items are arranged in a matrix-like fashion using a number of columns and rows. An advantage of using these modes is that you are able to display more items in a smaller space than is possible with either the `List` or `Details` view.

The `Details` view is the only view that takes advantage of the `SubItems` collection of each `ListViewItem`. The `Details` view is similar to the `List` view, but it allows you to create additional columns to display extra information about each item. For instance, in Windows Explorer, the `Details` view allows you to inspect additional file attributes such as the file's size; creation date; last modified date; and, in some instances, file-specific information, such as picture sizes for bitmaps. The next recipe demonstrates how to add columns and assign data to the subitems of each `ListViewItem` so that this information appears in each column.

8.16. Creating `ListView` Columns

You want to add columns that are displayed in the `Details ListView` mode.

Technique

Using the form designer, select the `ListView` whose columns you want to edit and invoke the `ColumnHeader` collection editor using the `Columns` property in the property browser. Click the Add button in the editor to add new columns. You can change the order of the columns using the up and down arrows. You can also programmatically add columns by creating new `ColumnHeader` objects and calling the `Add` method of the `Columns` collection defined in the `ListView`. Each column indexes a list view item's `SubItems` collection for its display.

Comments

The `Details` view is for users who want a little more information about the items they are working with. Unlike the other views, which simply display an item label and optional icon, the `Details` view allows you to create any number of additional columns of information.

You add new columns by accessing the `Columns` collection of a `ListView`. Like most other control collections, it contains methods that allow you to add or remove objects programmatically and also contains its own visual collection editor accessed from the property browser. You use `ColumnHeader` objects as the collections object type, although the `Add` method of the collection is overloaded to also accept a simple string.

Each `ListViewItem` object added to the `ListView` contains a corresponding `SubItems` collection whose indices coincide with the columns of the list view. The first item within the `SubItems` collection is the label of the item that is shown regardless of the mode the `ListView` is in. In other words, even if the `ListView` does not contain extra column information, the `SubItems` collection of each `ListViewItem` still contains at least one object. Also, just as you're able to programmatically or visually add a `ListViewItem` and `ColumnHeader` object to their corresponding collections, you can also programmatically or visually add a `ListViewSubItem` object to the `SubItems` collection.

8.17. Using the `TreeNode` Editor

You want to use the `TreeNode` editor in the forms designer to add items to a `TreeView` control.

Technique

You display the `TreeNode` editor by selecting the `Nodes` property of a `TreeView` control in the property browser and clicking the edit button. Because a `TreeView` displays data hierarchically, you can choose to add a new root item or add a child to the currently selected node, as shown in Figure 8.7.

Comments

The `TreeView` control displays data using a right-handed tree display scheme, which models hierarchical data through the notion of parent and child relationships. A good example of a tree control you've undoubtedly used is the folder tree within Windows Explorer. The roots of the tree contain the many different shell namespace objects such as "My Computer" or "My Documents." These root objects contain child items consisting of folders and files. Each folder is a child of one item and a parent of another, assuming, of course, the folder itself isn't empty.

Figure 8.7   Use the `TreeNode` editor to populate your `TreeView` control with an initial set of `TreeNode` items.

When you launch the `TreeNode` editor from the `Nodes` property within the property browser, you see a dialog box like Figure 8.7. You use the editor to initially populate the tree control with static data items. As you add new root and child items, the forms designer modifies the `InitializeComponent` method within your form class by generating code that creates new `TreeNode` objects within the `TreeView` internal member object. To add new items using the `TreeNode` editor, you must first create a root item. As its name implies, the root item is the top-level item within the tree. However, the `TreeView` control is not singly rooted, which means you are free to create as many root items as necessary. A root item can be a parent or a sibling item but never a child, which means that any attempt to access a root item's `Parent` property results in a thrown exception. To add a child to an existing item, you must first select the parent item within the TreeNode editor and then click on the Add Child button.

8.18. Programmatically Adding Items to a `TreeView` Control

You want to dynamically add hierarchical items to a `TreeView` control using the `TreeView` control's methods.

Technique

The data type for a single node in a tree is named `TreeNode`. To add a new root node to a `TreeView`, call the `Add` method defined in the `Nodes` collection passing a `TreeNode` object:

```
TreeNode[] roots = new TreeNode[2];
for( int i = 0; i < 2; i++ )
{
    roots[i] = new TreeNode( "Root " + i.ToString() );
    treeView1.Nodes.Add( roots[i] );
}
```

To add a child item, call the Add method defined in the Nodes collection of the parent
TreeNode object:

```
private void BuildChildren( int count, TreeNode parent )
{
    for( int i = 0; i < count; i++ )
    {
        parent.Nodes.Add("Child " + (i+1).ToString() );
    }
}
```

Comments

Although the TreeNode editor is a quick way of creating an initial set of TreeView
items, your application is more likely going to be dynamic in nature, thus facilitating the
need to dynamically add TreeNode items during application runtime. Unlike most other
collection-based controls, the TreeView control needs to maintain a couple of object-
accessor properties for each item within the control to allow hierarchical navigation.
These properties within each TreeNode object consist of the Nodes collection, which
contains all child items of the node, and a Parent object, which allows you to navigate
up one level in the tree. Furthermore, because each tree view item contains a Nodes collection, you add new items to the TreeView control using methods defined within the
TreeNode objects themselves rather than the TreeView control as is the case with most
other collection-based controls. The only exception is with root items.

Because the root item within the tree does not have a parent, you create a root item
using the Nodes property of the TreeView control. Any time you add an item to this
collection, a new tree root is created. To add a child item using an already created root
item as the parent, use an indexer of the tree view's Nodes collection and call the appropriate addition method on the object that is returned from the indexer.

One thing you need to keep in mind when dynamically building a tree is performance issues. Although it might seem easy to simply search for the corresponding location
to place a new child item each time you need to add an item, the time spent searching
can dramatically grow as more items are added. You should therefore create internal
TreeNode member variables within your form class that allow you to perform an immediate addition to the tree at a specified location rather than continuously search each
time. If the data you receive is random and periodic, then this procedure might not be
feasible, but if, for instance, you are populating a tree control using a directory traversal
routine, you should maintain some sort of state so you know that the next file should be

inserted underneath the last folder that was added. In other words, if you find yourself enumerating through several `Nodes` collections to insert a single item each time, look for ways to decrease the amount of time searching to increase runtime performance.

8.19. Using Images in a `TreeView`

You want to create and display images in a `TreeView` control for each item.

Technique

Create an `ImageList` object as explained in Recipe 8.14, "Using `ImageLists` in a `ListView` Control." Associate the `ImageList` object with a `TreeView` control by setting the `TreeView` control's `ImageList` property. To assign images to the individual `TreeNode` objects, set the `Image` property of the `TreeNode` equal to the index of the image in the `ImageList` you want to use. You can also use the `TreeNode` editor by selecting the image from the `Image` drop-down list. A `TreeNode` can also display a state image that is displayed when the user selects the tree node. You specify this image using the index of an `ImageList` and assigning that index to the tree node's `SelectedImage` property.

If you want all the tree nodes to share the same image, you can specify default images. The `ImageIndex` property specifies the index of an `ImageList` object to use as the default image for tree nodes. The `SelectedImageIndex` property is the default for all tree nodes when the user selects a tree node.

Comments

Recipe 8.14 demonstrates how to add images to a `ListView` control. The process for a `TreeView` control is strikingly similar, which is not surprising given the object-oriented nature of .NET. The underlying feature that allows you to create images within .NET controls is another control itself named the `ImageList`. An `ImageList` contains a collection of `Image` objects as well as methods to manipulate the collection and properties used to access information about the images or `ImageList` itself. Once you add images to the `ImageList`, you can then assign images to a `TreeView` control using the index of an image within the `ImageList`, as described in the "Technique" section.

8.20. Selecting Items Using the `PathSeparator` Property

You want to programmatically select an item in the `TreeView` by passing an item path whose items are delineated by the current `PathSeparator` property of the `TreeView` control.

Technique

Because a `TreeView` displays information in a hierarchical fashion, you can use a path-based syntax to manipulate the individual tree nodes. The `PathSeparator` property is a string value that separates root nodes and the corresponding child nodes. By default, the `PathSeparator` is set to the character '\'.

To programmatically select an item using path-based syntax, create a method that parses the path using the `PathSeparator` property to access individual nodes. If the `PathSeparator` is a single character, you can use the `String.Split` method, which conveniently places each node's string value into a string array. Enumerate this array and for each string select the corresponding `TreeNode` object, as shown in Listing 8.6.

Listing 8.6   **Selecting a `TreeNode` Programmatically**

```
private void SelectTreeNode( TreeView tv, string path )
{
    string[] nodes = path.Split( new char[]{tv.PathSeparator[0]} );
    TreeNodeCollection curNodes = tv.Nodes;

    foreach( string curNode in nodes )
    {
        foreach( TreeNode child in curNodes )
        {
            if( child.Text == curNode )
            {
                child.EnsureVisible();
                tv.SelectedNode = child;
                curNodes = child.Nodes;
                break;
            }
        }
    }
}
```

Comments

Data that is arranged hierarchically carries with it the distinct advantage of being able to reference individual items using path-based syntax. The Windows file system uses paths to access individual files and folders. The Registry uses a path to access individual keys, and Extensible Markup Language (XML) and Extensible Stylesheet Language Transformations (XSLT) can use XPath to access a single node, group of nodes, or attributes, for example. You divide individual items within a path-based syntax string using a path separator. In most cases, it is a single character such as '\'. The `TreeView` control utilizes the `PathSeparator` property exactly for this purpose.

Each item within a `TreeView` control contains a property named `FullPath`, which, when called, returns a string containing a list of ordered items beginning with the root object of the tree, all separated using the currently defined `PathSeparator`. Unfortunately, no other method or property defined in the `TreeView` class takes advantage of an items path, which leaves any implementation details up to you. In the code shown in the "Technique" section, you can see a method that uses a string path to programmatically select an item within a tree view. It first splits the path into several individual strings and places them into an array by calling the `Split` method defined in the `string` class. Doing so creates an array of items that corresponds to the order or navigation of a tree control, where the first item in the array corresponds to the root item of a tree, the second item in the array corresponds to a child of the previous root, and so on. When the method returns, the tree control is expanded and the last item in the string path is the currently selected `TreeNode` object.

8.21. Creating `ToolBar`s

You want to create a `ToolBar` control for your application and add buttons to the toolbar.

Technique

Drag and drop a `ToolBar` control from the form designer toolbox onto your Windows Form. To add buttons to the `ToolBar`, invoke the `ToolBarButton` collection editor by accessing the `Buttons` property in the `ToolBar` properties. A toolbar's buttons can contain a combination of text and images. The `ImageIndex` property of a toolbar button is an index value into the `ImageList` object associated with the `ToolBar` control. Recipe 8.14 demonstrates how to create an `ImageList` and associate it with a control.

Comments

So far in this chapter, you have seen both command-based and data-based controls. A command-based control is designed to run some sort of logic within your application when the user interacts with the control, whereas a data-based control provides a visual representation of the data your application maintains. The `ToolBar`, just like the `MainMenu` and `ContextMenu` controls, is command based. A `ToolBar` is a collection of buttons arranged in a vertical or horizontal containing bar. You can visually represent the buttons themselves using text, images, or a combination of both. Most document-centric applications use a toolbar as a shortcut to run commonly used commands.

You can add new buttons to a `ToolBar` by accessing the `ToolBarButton` editor through the `Buttons` collection in the property browser for the control. As with other collection editors, you can add a new button by clicking the Add button and setting the appropriate properties for the button. Furthermore, if your `ToolBar` control has an associated `ImageList`, you can set the image for the button using the `ImageIndex` property of the `ToolBarButton` object. The `Style` property of each toolbar button also controls how the button appears. For instance, if the `Style` is `Separator`, a button does not appear, but in its place is a slight blank space used to separate the buttons to its left and right. Other possible button styles include the `ToggleButton` style, which remains in the pressed state when it is clicked, and the `DropDownButton` style, which, when an associated context menu is defined in the button's `DropDownMenu` property, displays a menu when clicked.

If you want to dynamically create new buttons, you can call the `Add` method defined in the `Buttons` collection. This method contains two overloads, allowing you to specify either a regular string for the text of the button or a new `ToolBarButton` object. Furthermore, the order of the toolbar button objects within the `Buttons` collection corresponds to the order in which the buttons appear on the toolbar from left to right.

8.22. Capturing `ToolBar` **Button Clicks**

You need to determine which button on a `ToolBar` control was clicked by the user.

Technique

You cannot create individual event handlers for each toolbar button. Therefore, create an event handler for the `ToolBar` object's `ButtonClick` method. There are two options you can use to determine which button was clicked. Each `ToolBarButton` object has an associated `Tag` property whose data type is `System.Object`. You can use this user-defined object however you see fit. For instance, by placing a string in the `Tag` property, you can create a switch statement that compares the `Button.Tag` property of the `ToolBarButtonClickEventArgs` object with the strings in the `Tag` property, as shown in Listing 8.7.

Listing 8.7   **Using** `Tag` **for Custom Data**

```
private void toolBar1_ButtonClick(object sender,
    System.Windows.Forms.ToolBarButtonClickEventArgs e)
```

Listing 8.7   **Continued**

```
{
    switch( e.Button.Tag.ToString() )
    {
        case( "New" ):
        {
            richTextBox1.Clear();
            break;
        }
        case( "Open" ):
        {
            if( openFileDialog1.ShowDialog() == DialogResult.Cancel )
                return;

            richTextBox1.Clear();
            richTextBox1.LoadFile( openFileDialog1.FileName );

            break;
        }
        case( "Cut" ):
        {
            richTextBox1.Cut();
            break;
        }
        case( "Copy" ):
        {
            richTextBox1.Copy();
            break;
        }
        case( "Paste" ):
        {
            richTextBox1.Paste();
            break;
        }
        default:
        {
            break;
        }
    }
}
```

Another option is to use the IndexOf method of the Buttons collection of the ToolBar object, passing it the Button property of the event argument's object. This returns an index value that you can use to determine which button was clicked, as shown in Listing 8.8.

Listing 8.8   **Determining the Clicked** `ToolBar` **Button**

```
private void toolBar1_ButtonClick(object sender,
    System.Windows.Forms.ToolBarButtonClickEventArgs e)
{
    switch( toolBar1.Buttons.IndexOf(e.Button) )
    {
        case( 0 ):
        {
            richTextBox1.Clear();
            break;
        }
        case( 1 ):
        {
            if( openFileDialog1.ShowDialog() == DialogResult.Cancel )
                return;

            richTextBox1.Clear();
            richTextBox1.LoadFile( openFileDialog1.FileName );

            break;
        }
        case( 2 ):
        {
            richTextBox1.Cut();
            break;
        }
        case( 3 ):
        {
            richTextBox1.Copy();
            break;
        }
        case( 4 ):
        {
            richTextBox1.Paste();
            break;
        }
        default:
        {
            break;
        }
    }
}
```

Comments

`ToolBar` events are fired from the toolbar itself and not any of its individual buttons. Any event handlers you create that are fired as a result of a toolbar button interaction must use logic to determine which button was manipulated. The `ButtonClick` event defined in the `ToolBar` control contains an event argument parameter that you can use for this determination.

The code in the "Technique" section shows two ways you can determine whether a toolbar button was clicked. One technique takes advantage of the `Tag` property of each toolbar button, and the other uses information about the index into the `Button` collection to make the determination. Although both are valid methods of doing the same thing, the `Tag` method has a distinct advantage. If you are creating an application that models the toolbar behavior of some other application in which buttons can dynamically be added or removed by a user during runtime for customization purposes, you are not always guaranteed that a toolbar button will have the same index value in the `Buttons` collection. The second method then associates the wrong commands with the wrong toolbar buttons. By using the `Tag` method, you are guaranteed that the logic for a single button is always called, regardless of where on the toolbar the button resides. Also, ensure that you create an event handler for the `ButtonClick` event to capture toolbar button clicks rather than the `Click` event, which fires when any portion of the `ToolBar` control is clicked.

8.23. Adding `StatusBar` Panels to Display Application State

You want to create various status bar panels at the bottom of your application's form to display application information.

Technique

Using the form designer toolbox, drag a `StatusBar` control and drop it onto your Windows Form. A `StatusBar` can contain zero or more panels, each of which contain a `Text` property to display text in the panel. The following code uses a `StatusBar` object with a single panel to display information to the user when the mouse moves over a toolbar button. Using the `MouseMove` event, you find the corresponding toolbar button by computing the index of the toolbar button using the current location of the mouse cursor. If the mouse cursor is over a toolbar button, the button's tooltip property is accessed and its text is used as the value to the `StatusBar` control's `Text` property:

```
private void toolBar1_MouseMove(object sender,
    System.Windows.Forms.MouseEventArgs e)
{
    // determine button based on mouse coords and width of buttons
```

```
int buttonIndex = e.X/toolBar1.ButtonSize.Width;
if( buttonIndex > toolBar1.Buttons.Count - 1 )
{
    statusMessage.Text = "";
}
else
{
    statusMessage.Text = toolBar1.Buttons[buttonIndex].ToolTipText;
}
}
```

Comments

A status bar is a useful control that allows a user to quickly retrieve information about the state of the application without any form of interaction necessary. For instance, while working with code in the Visual Studio .NET IDE, you always know the row, column, and character where the text cursor is currently located by looking at the corresponding information in the status bar at the bottom of the IDE window.

The status bar can contain any number of panels used to separate the information it displays. Some of the common groupings include cursor location information, document information such as number of pages, and key state information such as the state of the CapsLock or Insert keys.

The StatusBar control uses the Panel collection to create additional panels for display. Each of these panels contains a Text property to display an informational message and an optional icon on the left of the message defined in the StatusBarPanel Icon property, as shown in Figure 8.8.

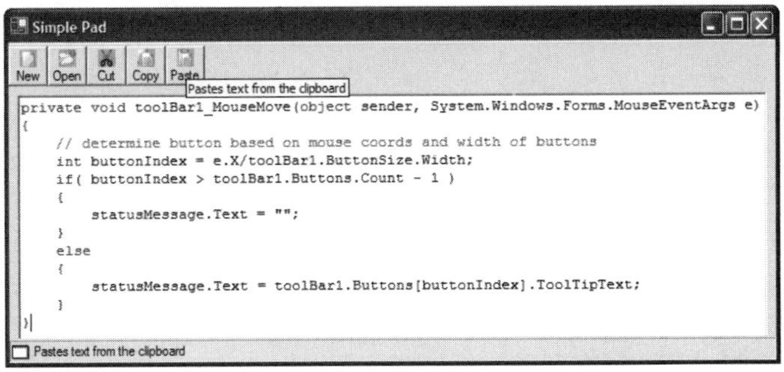

Figure 8.8   The StatusBar control can contain a text message with an optional leading icon.

8.24. Adding Tooltips to Controls

You want to create tooltips and assign them to individual controls on your Windows Form.

Technique

To display a tooltip for a control, use the `ToolTip` control by dragging it from the form designer toolbox. Although the `ToolTip` control is a visual control during runtime, it appears in the form designer control tray at the bottom of the designer window. The `ToolTip` control has properties that allow you to specify how long the delay is in milliseconds for the tooltip to display, how long the tooltip appears, and the text for the tooltip. Once you create a `ToolTip` control in the form designer, each control on a form adds a `ToolTip` property in its corresponding property list displayed in the property browser. Associate a tooltip with a control by accessing the `ToolTip` drop-down list for each individual control. Also note that you can use the same `ToolTip` for multiple controls.

Comments

Sometimes a control containing a text label and associated image just isn't enough information for a user. Rather than force a user to launch your help system and spend precious moments searching for a help topic, you can use tooltips to give them that extra bit of information they're looking for.

The `ToolTip` control remains invisible to the user until a certain event occurs. This event is generally a mouse hover action in which the mouse cursor remains motionless over a control for a short period of time. Once that time period elapses, a small text message appears, giving additional information about the control the mouse is hovering over. By default, most Windows Forms do not implement their own tooltip behavior. Rather, they rely on the `ToolTip` class to do it for them. Once you add a `ToolTip` control to a Windows Form, you can associate it with each control that uses the tooltip using the `ToolTip` property, which is available within the control's properties in the property browser. Without a defined `ToolTip` control in the form, these properties are hidden within the property browser.

8.25. Anchoring Controls

You want your controls to automatically size as the size of your main Windows Form changes.

Technique

Select the control within the forms designer that you want to anchor and click on the anchor editor accessible through the `Anchor` property. You see a small UI Type Editor, as shown in Figure 8.9. There are four possible anchor points for a control, corresponding to the top, left, bottom, and right sides of the Windows Form. When the anchor point is dark, the control is anchored to the corresponding anchor point on the form. By default, all controls are anchored to the top and left sides of a form.

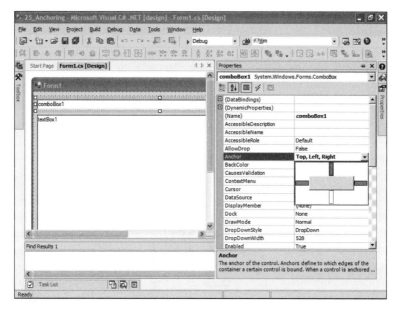

Figure 8.9   The anchor editor allows you to select the edges of a form to anchor the edges of a control to.

Comments

The `Anchor` property is defined in the base class `System.Windows.Forms.Control`, which means it is accessible in Windows Forms controls. By setting this property, you can be sure that when the user resizes the Windows Form, the controls also resize in response to maintain a consistent user interface. Based on which side or sides a control is anchored to, it does one of two things in response to a form resize. If only a single side of opposite sides is anchored—the left but not right side, for example—then the control's position changes in the Windows Form. However, if both competing sides are anchored, then the control resizes itself but stays in the same location. Therefore, if you want a control to cover the entire width of a form, you want to specify a left- and right-side anchor. If instead you would rather have a control stay the same size but remain pinned to the right side of a form, then only specify a right-side anchor. Furthermore, if you have a control that should cover the entire form, which is the case for many document-based interfaces such as Notepad, then you should anchor all sides of the control. This step ensures that the control is properly resized when the user increases both the width and height of a Windows Form.

8.26. Docking Controls

> You want a control or a group of controls to dock to the edge of a Windows Form.

Technique

Select the control or control container to dock within the forms designer and access the docking UI Type Editor using the `Dock` property. Because the `Dock` property is exclusive, select one of the buttons within the editor. The available options include one of the four edges of the Windows Form or all the edges, which is known as a fill dock.

Comments

Docking is similar to that of anchoring in that it allows you to easily associate the edges of a control with the edges of the form so that any resizing of the form translates into a resizing of the control. However, the `Anchor` property can accept any combination of anchor values, whereas the `Dock` property can use only a single value.

Docking, as its name implies, allows you to force a control to always remain on the edge of the Windows Form without any visible separation between the forms border and the control edge. The Visual Studio .NET IDE uses a special form of docking for the various tool windows. Although it is off by default, you can collapse a docked tool window so that it only shows a tab on the edge of the IDE by clicking the push-pin icon on the top right of the tool window. When the mouse cursor hovers over the tab, the tool window expands back to full size, allowing you to work with it. By using the `Dock` property and handling certain mouse events, you can imitate this same behavior.

To create a collapsible docked control, change the `Dock` property so that the control docks to the edge of the Windows Form. Within the forms designer, resize the docked control to the maximum size you want when it is in its expanded form. In Figure 8.10, you can see a Windows Form with two control containers docked to the left and right edges of the form. The left side of the form contains a docked `Panel` control and the right side contains a docked `TabControl`, both of which hold a collection of controls themselves.

The next step is to create a few mouse event handlers. For each docked control on the form, add an event handler for the `MouseEnter` event and add an event for the form's `MouseMove` event. Switch to code view within the IDE after you create the event handlers.

At this point, you have visually created two docked controls and added three mouse event handlers. You can now add the code necessary to expand and collapse the docked controls. We chose to create a simple class that holds information about the maximum and minimum size of each control as well as the state of its expansion. Therefore, create a class named `ToolDockInfo`, as shown in Listing 8.9.

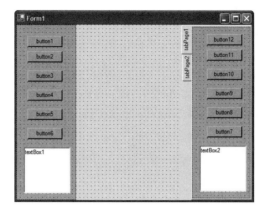

Figure 8.10   Create collapsible groups of controls by docking control containers and changing their corresponding `Size` property.

Listing 8.9   **Docking Information for Tool Windows**

```
public class ToolDockInfo
{
    public System.Drawing.Size Min;
    public System.Drawing.Size Max;
    public bool Expanded;

    public ToolDockInfo( System.Drawing.Size Min, System.Drawing.Size Max )
    {
        this.Min = Min;
        this.Max = Max;
        Expanded = false;
    }
}
```

As you can see, the class contains two `Size` variables that will hold the maximum and minimum size of the control corresponding to the expanded and collapsed size of the control, respectively. There is a reason why we chose a class over a struct even though it is a likely candidate to be a value type. An instance of the class will be placed in each docked control's `Tag` property, which is a `System.Object` data type. If `ToolDockInfo` were a struct, there would be extra steps involved to box the struct when assigning it to the `Tag` property.

Now that you have created the docking information class, you can create new instances of this type and assign them to each docked control container's `Tag` property. Within the form class constructor, create an instance of the `ToolDockInfo` class for each docked control and assign it to the `Tag` property of each control. The constructor is also a good place to initially collapse each docked control, which you can do by changing the Size property using the Min variable in the ToolDockInfo object for that control:

```
public Form1()
{
    InitializeComponent();

    panelLeft.Tag = new ToolDockInfo( new Size( 10, panelLeft.Size.Height),
        panelLeft.Size );

    panelLeft.Size = ((ToolDockInfo) panelLeft.Tag).Min;

    tabControl1.Tag = new ToolDockInfo( new Size( 19, tabControl1.Size.Height),
        tabControl1.Size );

    tabControl1.Size = ((ToolDockInfo) tabControl1.Tag).Min;
}
```

The final step involves filling in the definition for the three mouse event handlers. The MouseEnter event handler for each docked control simply changes the Size property of each control based on the ToolDockInfo.Max information defined within the control's Tag property that you created earlier:

```
private void panelLeft_MouseEnter(object sender, System.EventArgs e)
{
    panelLeft.Size = ((ToolDockInfo) panelLeft.Tag).Max;
    ((ToolDockInfo)panelLeft.Tag).Expanded = true;
}

private void tabControl1_MouseEnter(object sender, System.EventArgs e)
{
    tabControl1.Size = ((ToolDockInfo) tabControl1.Tag).Max;
    ((ToolDockInfo)tabControl1.Tag).Expanded = true;
}
```

You might be wondering why you didn't create MouseLeave event handlers for the controls to control the subsequent collapse of the control when the mouse leaves the control's area. The reason is due to the controls within the control containers. In Figure 8.10, you can see that each control container contains a series of buttons and a text box. Once the mouse cursor moves over one of those controls, the control container receives the MouseLeave event, which subsequently collapses the control container. Within the MouseMove event handler for the main form, check each docked control's Expanded property defined in the ToolDockInfo class. If the control container is in an expanded state, also check to see whether the mouse cursor is outside of that control container's area. If it is, then collapse the control by setting the Size property to the Min value specified in its corresponding ToolDockInfo object.

Listing 8.10 **Expanding Docked Windows**

```
private void Form1_MouseMove(object sender,
    System.Windows.Forms.MouseEventArgs e)
{
    if( (((ToolDockInfo)panelLeft.Tag).Expanded == true) &&
        e.X >= (((ToolDockInfo)panelLeft.Tag).Max.Width) )
    {
        ((ToolDockInfo)panelLeft.Tag).Expanded = false;
        panelLeft.Size = ((ToolDockInfo) panelLeft.Tag).Min;
    }
    if( (((ToolDockInfo)tabControl1.Tag).Expanded == true)
        && e.X <= (this.Size.Width-((ToolDockInfo)tabControl1.Tag).Max.Width) )
    {
        ((ToolDockInfo)tabControl1.Tag).Expanded = false;
        tabControl1.Size = ((ToolDockInfo) tabControl1.Tag).Min;
    }
}
```

When you build and run the application, you see that both control containers are collapsed to the edges of the form. The only visible portions of the TabControl are the tabs themselves. When the mouse cursor moves over one of the tabs, the TabControl expands to show the internal controls it contains.

8.27. Implementing Control Validation

You want to validate user input within a control or group of controls and display an error next to the controls that failed the validation.

Technique

Control validation uses a combination of the ErrorProvider control and control events. After designing the form, drag and drop an ErrorProvider control from the toolbox onto the form. To validate a control, create an event handler for the Validating and Validated events.

Within the Validating event handler, perform any necessary validation for the control, such as empty string checks or regular expression matches. If the control data is not valid, call the SetError method defined in the ErrorProvider object instance, passing it the instance of the control that failed validation and a string message used as the tooltip of the error control.

If you want to force a user to enter valid data before interacting with any other part of the form, set the Cancel property of the CancelEventArgs parameter passed in the Validating event handler. Any attempt to interact with another control or to close the form before valid data is entered, however, will fail, which might or might not be in line with your customer-experience design goals.

Listing 8.11   **Validating Form Input**

```
private void tbLastName_Validating(object sender,
    System.ComponentModel.CancelEventArgs e)
{
    if( tbLastName.Text == "" )
    {
        // setting e.Cancel to true requires user to
        // fill in field before continuing
        e.Cancel = true;
        errorProvider1.SetError( tbLastName, "Please enter a last name" );
    }
}

private void tbFirstName_Validating(object sender,
    System.ComponentModel.CancelEventArgs e)
{
    if( tbFirstName.Text == "" )
    {
        // set error field but allow user to set focus to other controls
        errorProvider1.SetError( tbFirstName, "Please enter a first name" );
    }
}
```

If the Cancel property is not set to true, then the Validated event handler is called next. You should therefore perform the same validation step and set the ErrorProvider object accordingly. If Cancel is set to true, however, then you are assured that the Validated event is only fired when the control contains valid data. You should clear the error within the ErrorProvider for the valid control by calling the SetError method as before, passing an empty string as the string parameter.

Listing 8.12   **Displaying Errors with** ErrorProvider

```
private void tbPhone_Validated(object sender, System.EventArgs e)
{
    Regex phoneExp = new Regex( @"^\(\d{3}\)\s\d{3}-\d{4}$" );

    if( tbPhone.Text == "" )
    {
        errorProvider1.SetError( tbPhone, "Please enter a phone number" );
    }
    else if( phoneExp.Match( tbPhone.Text ).Success == false )
    {
```

Listing 8.12   **Continued**

```
        errorProvider1.SetError( tbPhone, "Invalid Phone Number" );
    }
    else
    {
        errorProvider1.SetError( tbPhone, "" );
    }
}

private void tbFirstName_Validated(object sender, System.EventArgs e)
{
    // clear error if they filled in first name
    if( tbFirstName.Text != "" )
        errorProvider1.SetError( tbFirstName, "" );
}

private void tbLastName_Validated(object sender, System.EventArgs e)
{
    // clear error since control is validated
    errorProvider1.SetError( tbLastName, "" );
}
```

You can also force form validation to occur at any time, such as at a button click, by calling the `Validate` method, which is defined in the `System.Windows.Forms` base class of your form.

Comments

A large issue with allowing users to enter data manually into a control is that you aren't guaranteed that the data they enter is in the format your application can use. For instance, if you create a `TextBox` control and ask the user to enter his phone number, he might inadvertently insert a letter or skip a few digits. It is imperative that you utilize control validation to ensure this mistake doesn't happen.

The `ErrorProvider` control within .NET is a control designed to automatically alert the user when a control fails validation. The `ErrorProvider` doesn't perform any validation itself, which means it's still up to you to write the validation code. However, it does free you from having to write any necessary custom code to display an error.

When a validation error does occur, as shown in the "Technique" section, the `SetError` method of the `ErrorProvider` is called. The control that failed validation is then flagged with an icon, which by default is located to the right side of the control and which blinks on and off for a small period of time to alert the user. When the user hovers the mouse cursor over the icon, a tooltip explains the error. Just as every other control, the `ErrorProvider` contains several different properties that allow you to customize its display. For instance, you can display a custom icon by changing the `Icon` parameter or change the speed at which the icon blinks by changing the `BlinkRate` property.

8.28. Visual Inheritance

You want to create a base Windows Form that is used as a template for other Windows Forms.

Technique

Create the base Windows Form and its associated controls within the forms designer. If you want to give derived forms the ability to change the properties of a control within the base form, change that control's Modifiers property. The available modifiers are the same as the access control modifiers explained in Chapter 2, "Objects and Components."

To create a new Windows Form using a base form as a template, click on Project, Add Inherited Windows Form from the main menu. When the Inheritance Picker dialog box appears, select the form to use as the base class. If the base Windows Form is contained within a separate assembly, you can click the Browse button to locate it.

Comments

Visual inheritance is a good time-saving method that allows you to define a common set of controls on a form that you can then customize among a set of derived forms. For instance, you might create a base Windows Form that simply contains a private Label control whose Image property is set to your company's logo. With the requirement that any new Windows Forms should derive from this common form, you can enforce that your logo is always displayed throughout the application. Another advantage is that a change to the base form is propagated to every derived form within the hierarchy. If instead you copied the necessary form code for each form, the amount of changes required to do something as simple as changing the location of a control would be daunting.

User Controls

9.0. Introduction

The .NET Framework contains several well-developed controls that are ready for use on a Windows Form. Some of these controls are making their first appearance within a Microsoft technology base, whereas others have been around since the advent of Windows itself. Even with a large constituent of common controls that have gone through iterative changes for technological adaptability, sometimes a control still just doesn't do what you need it to do.

This chapter details various situations that might arise when you create new controls to use within a Windows Form application. It shows the differences between the different control types from controls based on an already defined control to a user control that performs custom rendering.

9.1. Extending Common Controls

You want to create a new control that is similar to a control that is already defined.

Technique

To create a custom control derived from an existing Windows Form control, click on Project, Add User Control from the main menu or Alt+P, U on the keyboard. After Visual Studio creates the control file, open it in Code View by right-clicking on the file in Solution Explorer and selecting View Code from the Context menu.

By default, a user control derives from `System.Windows.Forms.UserControl`. You can change it to any of the defined Windows Forms controls or to a control already created within a Windows Control Library. To alter the behavior or appearance of the control, override any properties or methods defined in the base class. In Listing 9.1, you can see a control that is derived from the `Panel` Windows Form control. When placed on a Windows Form, the control shows a preview of the screensaver, which you set using the custom `ScreenSaverPath` property.

To render the screensaver, you override the base class method `OnPaint`. This method is called whenever the control needs to render itself and is called as a result of the `Paint` event. `OnPaint` checks whether it needs to launch the screensaver, and if so, it uses the `Process.Start` method, passing the appropriate command-line arguments to the screensaver so that it renders within the control's window.

Listing 9.1 `ScreenSaverPreview` **Control Based on the** `Panel` **Control**

```
using System;
using System.Collections;
using System.ComponentModel;
using System.Drawing;
using System.Data;
using System.Windows.Forms;
using System.IO;
using System.Diagnostics;

namespace _1_ComCtrlExtension
{
    public class ScreenSaverPreviewPanel : System.Windows.Forms.Panel
    {
        private System.ComponentModel.IContainer components;
        private string screenSaver = "";
        private Process saverProcess = null;

        private bool launched = false;

        public ScreenSaverPreviewPanel()
        {
            InitializeComponent();
        }

        protected override void OnPaint(PaintEventArgs e)
        {
            if( launched == false )
            {
                try
                {
                    if( saverProcess != null )
                    {
                        saverProcess.Kill();
                        saverProcess = null;
                    }
```

Listing 9.1   **Continued**

```
            if( this.Visible == true && screenSaver != "")
            {
                ProcessStartInfo startInfo = new ProcessStartInfo(
                    screenSaver + " \"/p " + this.Handle.ToString() +
                    "\"", "" );
                startInfo.UseShellExecute = false;
                saverProcess = Process.Start( startInfo );
                launched = true;
            }
            else
            {
                this.Visible = false;
            }
        }
        catch( Exception ex )
        {
            throw new Exception( "Could not launch screensaver", ex );
        }
    }
    base.OnPaint (e);
}

protected override void Dispose( bool disposing )
{
    if( disposing )
    {
        if( components != null )
            components.Dispose();
    }
    base.Dispose( disposing );
}

#region Component Designer generated code>
private void InitializeComponent()
{
    this.components = new System.ComponentModel.Container();

}
#endregion

public string ScreenSaverPath
{
    get
    {
        return screenSaver;
```

Listing 9.1   **Continued**

```
            }
            set
            {
                this.Visible = true;
                screenSaver = value;
                launched = false;
                Invalidate();
            }
        }
    }
}
```

Comments

A powerful feature of object-oriented programming is the ability to slightly alter the behavior of a class so that it better suits the problem you are trying to solve. Although there are several available controls for you to use, sometimes a certain control just doesn't do what you want it to do. If you come from a WIN32 background, the thought of creating a control that is based on an existing common control might conjure up fears of subclassing or performing various conniving tricks, such as writing to process memory. Although people like us find joy in such methods, it is still complicated and error-prone. With C# and the .NET Framework, creating a new control that is similar to an existing control simply entails defining a class that is derived from one of the many .NET Windows Forms controls.

When you derive a class from an existing Windows Form control, you inherit all the base functionality of the control you are deriving from. The control functions within the designer as a user sets properties and manipulates its positions. It properly interacts with its parent form when docking or anchoring, and it contains full functionality when a user is using it during runtime. All that you need is to override or create any properties or methods needed for the customization.

Listing 9.1 created a new control by deriving from the System.Windows.Forms.Panel control. If no properties or methods were overridden in the derived class, the control would behave exactly like any other Panel control. Although the thought of creating a new control that allows you to preview a screensaver, as shown in Figure 9.1, sounds like a complicated task, the process to do so is relatively trivial. You create a custom property so the control knows which screensaver to preview and override the OnPaint method so the screensaver successfully attaches to your control's window.

Figure 9.1   Windows Form application using the
`ScreenSaverPreviewPanel` control.

In the code that accompanies this recipe, the custom control was created within the
same executable assembly as the Windows Form that uses the control to reduce the
amount of projects contained within this chapter's solution. In most cases, however, you
want to create a Windows Control Library that creates a dynamic link library (DLL)
assembly. Creating a control library is discussed in Recipe 2.13, "Creating and Using
Class Libraries." When you create a control within a executable-based assembly, you can
only use it on Windows Forms objects within the same assembly. By placing the control
within a Windows Control Library, you can use it in any Windows Form application.

To place a control onto a Windows Form, you must first add it to the toolbox.
Recipe 9.6, "Programmatically Adding Controls to the Toolbox," demonstrates how you
do so programmatically during the installation of your control, but for testing, it is easier
to manually perform the necessary steps. Right-click on the toolbox window and select
Add/Remove Items. In the Customize Toolbox dialog, click on the Browse button and
select the assembly that contains your control. An icon appears within the toolbox corresponding to your control. You can then drag and drop the icon onto a Windows Form
just as you would with any other .NET control.

9.2. Creating Composite Controls

You want to create a control that is a combination of several controls that interact with each other to implement certain functionality.

Technique

To create a composite control, choose Project, Add User Control (Alt+P, U). When the Visual Studio .NET Integrated Development Environment (IDE) creates the control, you can use the forms designer to visually lay out your control, as shown in Figure 9.2. You can set properties and create event handlers using the same procedures as in a regular Windows Form application. Furthermore, you can create additional custom properties and methods to customize the behavior of the composite control.

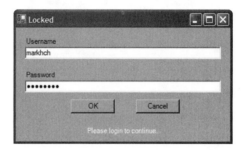

Figure 9.2   A composite control within the Forms Designer and the result of running it within an application.

Comments

Creating composite controls is similar to creating a regular Windows Form application. When the control code is generated by Visual Studio, the forms designer opens, allowing you to visually design the control. Design the control just as you would any other Windows Form by setting properties and creating any necessary event handlers. When you look at the code that is generated, you'll even see that the only noticeable difference between the control and a Windows Form is the base class that your class derives from. In fact, in most cases you can easily convert a Windows Form to a composite control by changing the base class to System.Windows.Forms.UserControl and removing AutoScaleBaseSize, which is not defined within the UserControl class.

Composite controls are best when you need to encapsulate functionality within a single module that you can then use within several forms and applications. In Figure 9.2, you can see a composite control used to perform some sort of application login. Although you could leverage the code using classic copy and paste methods for each Windows Form that uses it, the ramifications of doing so are quite apparent because a change in the original code is multiplied by the projects that use that code. In fact, you might not identify all the places within the forms that you create across multiple projects as prime candidates for a composite control. For instance, if the applications that you create use a company logo, create a composite control that contains a `PictureBox` control that displays the company logo. You can then change every logo in all applications that use that composite control simply by changing the control's source code rather than individually edit each project's source code.

9.3. Creating Custom Controls

You want to create a control that needs to perform custom rendering because it is not similar to an already existing control.

Technique

Create a new custom control by clicking on Project, Add Class from the main menu. Select the Custom Control item in the list of Item Templates. Because the control is an owner-drawn control, you are unable to visually design the control using the forms designer. The `OnPaint` virtual method is automatically overridden in the control's class definition. Use this method to perform the rendering of your control, as shown in Listing 9.2.

Listing 9.2   **The `TemperatureGauge` Control Using the `OnPaint` Method to Render a Thermometer**

```
using System;
using System.Collections;
using System.ComponentModel;
using System.Drawing;
using System.Data;
using System.Windows.Forms;

namespace _3_CustomControl
{
    public class TemperatureGauge : System.Windows.Forms.Control
    {
        private System.ComponentModel.Container components = null;
        private int percent = 50;

        public TemperatureGauge()
        {
            // This call is required by the Windows.Forms Form Designer.
            InitializeComponent();
        }

        protected override void Dispose( bool disposing )
```

Listing 9.2   **Continued**

```
    {
        if( disposing )
        {
            if( components != null )
                components.Dispose();
        }
        base.Dispose( disposing );
    }

    private void InitializeComponent()
    {
    }

    protected override void OnPaint(PaintEventArgs pe)
    {
        // compute rects
        Rectangle gaugeRect = new Rectangle( this.Width/6, 0,
            this.Width-(2*this.Width/6), this.Height-(this.Height/10) );

        Rectangle bulbRect = new Rectangle(0, this.Height-(this.Height/5),
            this.Width-2, this.Height/5-2);

        Rectangle emptyRect = new Rectangle( gaugeRect.X, gaugeRect.Y,
            gaugeRect.Width, (gaugeRect.Height/100)*(100-percent));

        Rectangle filledRect = new Rectangle( gaugeRect.X,
            emptyRect.Y+emptyRect.Height, gaugeRect.Width,
            gaugeRect.Height-emptyRect.Height );

        // draw gauge
        pe.Graphics.FillEllipse( new SolidBrush( Color.Red ), bulbRect );
        pe.Graphics.DrawRectangle( new Pen(new SolidBrush( Color.Red )),
            emptyRect );

        pe.Graphics.FillRectangle( new SolidBrush( Color.Red ), filledRect );

        // draw ticks
        for( int i = 1; i < 10; i ++ )
        {
            pe.Graphics.FillEllipse( new SolidBrush( Color.Black ),
                gaugeRect.X, (gaugeRect.Height/100)*(10*i),
                gaugeRect.Width/3, 3 );
        }

        base.OnPaint(pe);
```

Listing 9.2 **Continued**

```
        }

        protected override void OnSizeChanged(EventArgs e)
        {
            base.OnSizeChanged (e);
            Invalidate();
        }

        public int Percentage
        {
            get
            {
                return percent;
            }
            set
            {
                if( value < 0 || value > 100 )
                    return;
                percent = value;

                Invalidate();
            }
        }
    }
}
```

Comments

The previous two recipes relied on existing controls to perform any of the necessary logic required for rendering the control onto the Windows Form. In a majority of the controls created using those methods, you create custom code to alter the behavior rather than the underlying appearance of the control or controls that it relies on. When you create a custom control, however, the work of providing the code that renders the control onto a Windows Form is up to you.

A custom control is derived from the `System.Windows.Forms.Control` class. This class provides several properties and methods to aid in the construction of your control. When you first begin implementation, your control is already able to perform actions, such as resizing or docking, and fire events, including mouse and keyboard events. If you've created controls using other technologies before, you'll immediately see gains not only in simplicity but also in the time saved from not having to add additional stock functionality to your control.

When you first create your control, you are placed into a designer. However, it isn't the forms designer, as shown in the previous two recipes. Rather, this designer allows you to add any components that you need to aid in the functionality of your control, which can include timers, performance counters, or database objects. You can switch out of the designer and view the code for your control by selecting the hyperlink displayed in the designer or by right-clicking the filename of your control within Solution Explorer and selecting the View Code menu item.

Rendering a control occurs within the `OnPaint` method. This method uses a single parameter named `PaintEventArgs`. One interesting aspect to point out is that the `OnPaint` method uses the same methodology as a delegate, but there is no associated code within your class that associates this delegate with the `Paint` event. This functionality is contained within the `Control` base class. In that class, delegates are associated with events, and those delegates are also made virtual, thereby allowing you to override them without having to create the necessary event-handling plumbing code. In fact, in the code listed earlier, you can also see that the `OnSizeChanged` method is overridden, and it is called whenever your control receives the `SizeChanged` event. You can capture a large portion of the events that your control receives within your class by overriding its associated delegate defined in the `Control` base class.

The `PaintEventArgs` object contains a `Graphics` object that you can use to render your control. The `Graphics` class encapsulates a specific type of drawing surface, which is created using the newest version of the Graphics Device Interface known as GDI+. In the code for this recipe, you can see how the `Graphics` object is used in conjunction with the various properties of the control to render shapes using brushes and pens of a specified color, as shown in Figure 9.3. Chapter 10, "Programming Graphics with GDI+," provides a thorough examination of GDI+.

Figure 9.3   The `TemperatureGauge` control uses the `OnPaint` method to render itself using a `Graphics` object.

9.4. Using Design-Time Attributes

You want to control various design-time behaviors of your control to aid users who use your control within their Windows Forms.

Technique

Use attributes on your control's class declaration and any properties or events it contains to insert additional information about your control that can be read by the Visual Studio .NET property browser. You apply attributes to a class, property, or method by placing the attributes and their associated parameters within brackets immediately preceding the type declaration. These attributes only add information to the property browser during design time, and they have no effect on the control at runtime. Listing 9.3 shows design-time attributes used on the control class to set the default property of the control, which is the initial property that a user edits when the control is first created within the forms designer. The `Percentage` property in Listing 9.3 contains several design-time attributes that control the category of the property within the property browser, the description that appears when the user selects the property, parentheses that are used on the property name, and a default value that is initially filled in property browser. The `LogFile` property also uses the `EditorAttribute` attribute to assign the editor used to edit the property's value, which in this case is a open file dialog editor.

Listing 9.3   **Properties of a Control with Design-Time Attributes**

```
[Description("Percentage of gauge that is filled."),Category("Data"),
ParenthesizePropertyNameAttribute(true), DefaultValue(100)]
public int Percentage
{
    get
    {
        return percent;
    }
    set
    {
        if( value < 0 || value > 100 )
            return;
        percent = value;

        Invalidate();
    }
}

[Category("Appearance"), Description("Color of filled gauge."),
ParenthesizePropertyNameAttribute(true), DefaultValue(typeof(Color), "Red")]
public Color GaugeColor
```

Listing 9.3   **Continued**

```
{
    get
    {
        return gaugeColor;
    }
    set
    {
        gaugeColor = value;
        Invalidate();
    }
}

[Description("Filename to log runtime data to."),
Category("Behavior"),
ParenthesizePropertyNameAttribute(true),
EditorAttribute(typeof(System.Windows.Forms.Design.FileNameEditor),
    typeof(System.Drawing.Design.UITypeEditor))
]
public string LogFile
{
    get
    {
        return fileName;
    }
    set
    {
        fileName = value;
    }
}
```

Comments

Attributes provide a way to associate additional information for a class, method, or property. When an attribute is encountered during compilation, it is placed within the metadata accompanying the type to which it is bound. An attribute itself is nothing more than an instance of a .NET class derived from System.Attribute. In fact, the syntax when applying an attribute to a type translates to the code used for the constructor of the object that is created for that attribute. In Listing 9.3, you can see a Description attribute for the Percentage property.

When you place the control onto a Windows Form and select a property within the property browser, the property browser queries the property using Reflection to retrieve the DescriptionAttribute by accessing the property's Attributes collection. This is just one example of how an attribute is used within the context of a property.

Other attributes are used in different ways, either as information to the CLR or some custom consumer of that information. You can easily create your own custom attributes by deriving a class from the `System.Attribute` class and then access that information in a manner similar to the way the property browser accesses attributes for a control. Chapter 23, "Reflection," contains a more extensive examination of custom attributes.

9.5. Changing a Control's Toolbox Icon

> You want to create a custom icon that is shown for your control within the Visual Studio .NET IDE toolbox.

Technique

Create a bitmap file that is 16 x 16. You can embed this bitmap within the assembly to free you from having to deploy it by choosing Project, Add Existing Item and selecting the bitmap file. To associate the bitmap file with your control, apply the `ToolboxBitmap` attribute to your control's class declaration. The first parameter to this attribute is a reference to the type of your control, which you can retrieve by using the `typeof` keyword. The second parameter is the name of the bitmap file:

```
[
    DefaultProperty("Percentage"),
    ToolboxBitmap(typeof(TemperatureGauge3), "ToolboxIcon.bmp")
]
public class TemperatureGauge3 : System.Windows.Forms.Control
{ ... }
```

Comments

As a control author, you should strive to make your control look as professional as possible if you plan to allow other developers to use it. By default, when you create a control within Visual Studio, it receives a default icon.

Changing that icon is a trivial matter, as demonstrated earlier, but doing so allows you to distinguish it from other controls as well as give users a quick visual indication of what the control is. This step is especially important for users who turn off the text labels in the toolbox by right-clicking and unselecting the List View menu item. In that case, all that appears is an icon for each control, which is all the more reason to create an effective and informative toolbox bitmap for your control.

9.6. Programmatically Adding Controls to the Toolbox

During the installation of your control, you want to automatically add the control's icon to the Visual Studio .NET IDE toolbox.

Technique

To add your control to the list of controls that is displayed within the Customize Toolbox without initially adding the control to the toolbox, you can create a Registry value during installation. The Registry key is

```
HKEY_LOCAL_MACHINE\SOFTWARE\Microsoft\VisualStudio\7.1\AssemblyFolders\control_name
```

Create a default value for this key that is the path to the folder which contains the assembly housing your control.

To programmatically add the control icon to the toolbox, use the extensibility features of Visual Studio .NET. After obtaining the main Visual Studio .NET object, retrieve the `Toolbox` interface from that object, as shown in Listing 9.4. To add a new tab to the toolbox, call the `Add` method defined in the `ToolboxTabs` collection of the `Toolbox` interface. This step returns a `ToolboxTab` interface. To add the icon to that tab, call the `Activate` method, which selects the newly created tab, and then call the `Add` method defined in the `ToolBoxItems` collection. This method has three parameters denoting the name of the control to add, the path to the assembly that contains the control, and a value from the `vsToolBoxItemFormat` enumerated data type, which specifies what type of object you are adding to the toolbox. In this case, the object is a .NET control, so use the `vsToolBoxItemFormatDotNETComponent` value for this parameter.

Listing 9.4 Programmatically Adding an Icon to the Visual Studio .NET Toolbox

```csharp
private void btnInstall_Click(object sender, System.EventArgs e)
{
    if( openFileDialog1.ShowDialog(this) == DialogResult.Cancel )
        return;

    try
    {
        EnvDTE.DTE dte;
        dte = (EnvDTE.DTE)System.Runtime.InteropServices.Marshal.GetActiveObject
                ("VisualStudio.DTE.7.1");

        EnvDTE.ToolBox tb = (EnvDTE.ToolBox)
            dte.Windows.Item(EnvDTE.Constants.vsWindowKindToolbox).Object;

        EnvDTE.ToolBoxTab tbTab = tb.ToolBoxTabs.Add( "My Custom Controls" );
```

Listing 9.4   **Continued**

```
        tbTab.Activate();
        tbTab.ToolBoxItems.Add( "6_AutoCustomToolbox Control",
            openFileDialog1.FileName,
            EnvDTE.vsToolBoxItemFormat.vsToolBoxItemFormatDotNETComponent );
    }
    catch( Exception ex )
    {
        MessageBox.Show( ex.Message );
    }
}
```

Comments

Deployment strategy is as important if not more important than the actual solution implementation itself. After all, if your application or control doesn't install onto a user's system properly, then you encounter extra costs in the way of support. When implementing a control to be used by other developers, you might want to consider installing the control into the toolbox within Visual Studio .NET.

Visual Studio .NET contains substantial extensibility support, allowing you to programmatically interact and manipulate the environment using an COM-enabled language such as JavaScript, VBScript, C++, and C#. The object model, which details the hierarchical relationship of individual objects within the IDE, allows you to access almost any area imaginable related to Visual Studio. Some of these areas include supporting windows, menus, project and solution settings, and, of course, the toolbox.

To obtain a reference to the toolbox, you must first obtain a reference to the main Visual Studio .NET object. In Listing 9.4, you can see that the GetActiveObject method passes the programmatic identifier (progid) of the Visual Studio .NET Extensibility object. Once you do this step, you then have access to the methods, properties, and any subobjects contained within the main object. One of these objects is the ToolBox object. Because the design of Visual Studio .NET extensibility is COM-based, you'll notice that you will work with interfaces instead of .NET objects. The remainder of the code in Listing 9.4 creates a new tab within the toolbox, activates that tab so that the control icon is placed correctly, and then inserts the control.

The last parameter of the Add method is a value from the EnvDTE. vsToolBoxItemFormat enumerated data type. The value is vsToolBoxItemFormatDotNETComponent, signifying that the item being added is a .NET object. One thing to note is that you are not limited to just inserting .NET components into the toolbox. If you look at the toolbox within the IDE, you'll notice a tab named Clipboard Ring. It is a collection of toolbox items containing text that represents a history of items copied onto the Clipboard. By using the value vsToolBoxItemFormatText you can insert text, or by using vsToolBoxItemFormatHTML you can insert HTML.

9.7. Creating Extender Provider Controls

You want to create a control that works with several controls on a Windows Form similar to the `ToolTip` control.

Technique

Create a new class derived from `System.ComponentModel.Component` and `System.ComponentModel.IExtenderProvider`. Because `IExtenderProvider` is an interface, you must implement its sole method named `CanExtend`. This method is called whenever a control on the form is selected in the forms designer. Within the method definition, check the type of the object passed as the parameter. If it is a control type that your extender provider supports, return a `true` value from the method:

```
bool IExtenderProvider.CanExtend(object target)
{
    if (target is Control && !(target is BalloonTip))
    {
        return true;
    }
    else
    {
        return false;
    }
}
```

An extender provider inserts additional properties into each control that it extends. For each property that you want to add to a control, apply the `ProvideProperty` attribute to the class declaration. The first parameter is a string specifying the name of the property, and the second parameter is the type of the objects that receive the property, which in most cases is `System.Windows.Forms.Control`:

```
[
    ProvideProperty("BalloonText",typeof(Control))
]
public class BalloonTip : Component, System.ComponentModel.IExtenderProvider
{
...
}
```

The implementation for each extended property uses methods with a defined syntactical name rather than a property-based syntax. You construct the getter method for an extended property by using the word `Get` followed by the name of the property. For the `BalloonText` property shown earlier, the getter method would be named

GetBalloonText. Likewise, the setter method uses the Set word, which translates into SetBalloonText:

```
private Hashtable balloonTexts;


[DefaultValue("")]
public string GetBalloonText(Control control)
{
    string balloonText = (string)balloonTexts[control];
    if (balloonText == null)
    {
        balloonText = string.Empty;
    }
    return balloonText;
}

public void SetBalloonText(Control control, string balloonText)
{
    if (balloonText == null)
    {
        balloonText = string.Empty;
    }

    if (balloonText.Length == 0)
    {
        balloonTexts.Remove(control);

        control.MouseHover -= new EventHandler(OnControlMouseHover);
        control.MouseMove -= new MouseEventHandler(OnControlMouseMove);
    }
    else
    {
        balloonTexts[control] = balloonText;

        control.MouseHover += new EventHandler(OnControlMouseHover);
        control.MouseMove += new MouseEventHandler(OnControlMouseMove);
    }
}
```

Comments

An extender provider control generally provides additional information about another control on a Windows Form. For example, the ToolTip control displays help information in a small window whenever the mouse cursor hovers over a control for a specified amount of time. You insert the additional information for a control by using properties. Once you place the extender provider using the forms designer, any controls on the

Windows Form that are supported by the extender provider have additional properties that are implemented by the extender provider control. The name of the property is the name used within the extender provider, specified using the `ProvideProperty` attribute followed by the word on and the variable name of the extender provider object. For instance, if you create a `BalloonTip` object within a Windows Form named `balloonTip1`, then each control on the Windows Form has an additional property named `BalloonText on ballonTip1`.

We mentioned that an extender provider works with several controls at once on a single Windows Form. This implies that you'll need a collection object to save the values that your extender provider adds to each control it supports. In most instances, you'll find that the best collection type for this need is a `Hashtable`, where each key within the collection represents a control and each associated value is the corresponding property value. If your extender provider control utilizes only a single property, then the `Hashtable` collection can store values using the data type of that property. However, if your extender provider supports several properties per control it supports, then use a second `Hashtable` object, where the key for each element represents the property name and the value is that property's value.

9.8. Creating a UI Type Editor

You want to create a custom editor for a control's property.

Technique

You construct a type editor with a class separate from the control that uses the editor. Create a new class derived from `System.Drawing.Design.UITypeEditor`. You need to add a reference to the `System.Design.dll` to your project by choosing Project, Add Reference and selecting the `System.Design` assembly.

The `UITypeEditor` contains a virtual method named `EditValue`, which is called when a property using the type editor is being edited. To capture this event, override the `EditValue` in your derived class. The three parameters passed into the method allow you to access the control the property is associated with, obtain a reference to the Windows Forms editor service, and obtain a reference to the value itself. After ensuring that the necessary parameters are not null, create a new instance of the editor control that you want to use, initialize it with the value passed into the `EditValue` method for consistency, and call the `DropDownControl` method defined in the editor service object, as shown in Listing 9.5. The object value that is returned from the method is the value that is placed in the property field.

Listing 9.5   **The UI Type Editor for the** Percentage **Property Displaying a** TrackBar
Control to Change the Property's Value

```csharp
using System;
using System.Collections;
using System.ComponentModel;
using System.Drawing;
using System.Data;
using System.Windows.Forms;
using System.Windows.Forms.Design;
using System.Drawing.Design;

namespace _8_UITypeEditor
{
    public class TemperatureGaugeDesigner : UITypeEditor
    {
        private IWindowsFormsEditorService editorService = null;
        private TemperatureGauge5 tempGauge = null;

        public override object EditValue(ITypeDescriptorContext context,
                                    IServiceProvider provider, object value)
        {
            if (context != null && context.Instance != null && provider != null)
            {
                // save the editor service object for later
                editorService = (IWindowsFormsEditorService)provider.GetService
                    (typeof(IWindowsFormsEditorService));

                // save the control instance associated with this editor
                this.tempGauge = (TemperatureGauge5) context.Instance;

            if (editorService != null)
            {
                // create trackbar control
                TrackBar tb = new TrackBar();
                tb.Minimum = 0;
                tb.Maximum = 100;
                tb.Orientation = System.Windows.Forms.Orientation.Vertical;
                tb.TickFrequency = 5;
                tb.Size = new System.Drawing.Size(75, 160);
                tb.ValueChanged += new EventHandler(this.ValueChanged);

                // init with current property value
                tb.Value = (int)value;

                editorService.DropDownControl(tb);
```

Listing 9.5 **Continued**

```
                            value = tb.Value;
                        }
                }
                return value;
        }

        public override UITypeEditorEditStyle GetEditStyle(
            ITypeDescriptorContext context)
        {
            if (context != null && context.Instance != null)
            {
                return UITypeEditorEditStyle.DropDown;
            }

            return base.GetEditStyle(context);
        }

        private void ValueChanged(object sender, EventArgs e)
        {
            // update the associated control on the Windows Form
            this.tempGauge.Percentage = ((TrackBar)sender).Value;
        }
    }
}
```

To associate a UI type editor with a property in a control, apply the `Editor` attribute to the property declaration. This attribute accepts two parameters denoting the type of the editor, which you can find by using the `typeof` keyword, and the type of the base class of the editor:

```
[
Editor(typeof(TemperatureGaugeDesigner), typeof(UITypeEditor)),
Description("Percentage of gauge that is filled."),Category("Data"),
ParenthesizePropertyNameAttribute(true), DefaultValue(100)]
public int Percentage
{
    get
    {
        return percent;
    }
    set
    {
        if( value < 0 || value > 100 )
            return;
```

Listing 9.5   **Continued**

```
        percent = value;

        Invalidate();
    }
}
```

Comments

The property browser is an extensible container allowing you to customize how properties are edited by creating your own property editor. In some cases, creating a property is useful if the property value can benefit from a different editor from the default editor for that value type. For instance, the `Percentage` property defined earlier is an integer type. The default editor is a `TextBox` control that allows a user to type in the value for the property. However, it would seem beneficial to allow the user to use a different control that both constrains the range of values for the property and provides a visual indication of the changes that are occurring as the value of the property is incremented or decremented. The `TrackBar` control is well suited for this type of functionality, but a `NumericUpDown` control would also work well.

In Listing 9.5, you can see that an event handler for the `ValueChanged` event fires when the `TrackBar` control is created. Although this step isn't required, it does allow you to perform real-time feedback as a user changes the value of the property. When the trackbar changes, the `TemperatureGauge` control within the forms designer automatically updates. Because of this feature, the developer using the control does not have to guess the effect that the value change has on the control because she receives a visual indication as the property value runs the full gamut of its available range. Granted, not all controls benefit from this type of functionality, but for those that do, it can be a tremendous help and alleviate some of the frustration of property value editing that might occur during design time.

9.9. Utilizing Custom Designers

You want to change the design-time behavior of a control without affecting the runtime functionality.

Technique

To create a custom designer for a control, define a new class derived from `System.Windows.Forms.Design.ControlDesigner`. To change the behavior of a form while it is being moved or sized within the forms designer, override the `SelectionRules` property. This property returns a `SelectionRules` value, which is a bit array of `SelectionRules` values defined in the `System.Windows.Forms.Design`.

`SelectionRules` enumerated data type. In other words, perform a logic OR (|) for each selection rule. To turn off horizontal sizing while still allowing vertical sizing, moving, and visibility, use the following selection rules:

```
public override SelectionRules SelectionRules
{
    get
    {
        return System.Windows.Forms.Design.SelectionRules.TopSizeable |
            System.Windows.Forms.Design.SelectionRules.BottomSizeable |
            System.Windows.Forms.Design.SelectionRules.Moveable |
            System.Windows.Forms.Design.SelectionRules.Visible;
    }
}
```

If you want to add visual cues to a control during design time, override the `OnPaintAdornments` method. This method is called after the `Paint` handler for the control and allows you to use the `Graphics` object within the `PaintEventArgs` parameter to add any additional visual adornments to the currently selected control:

```
protected override void OnPaintAdornments(PaintEventArgs pe)
{
    pe.Graphics.DrawRectangle(new Pen( Color.Black ), 0, 0,
        this.Control.Width-1, this.Control.Height-1);
}
```

The `ControlDesigner` contains several methods that allow you to hook into the design process based on a variety of different events. For instance, you can override the event handler for various mouse events such as `MouseEnter` to perform a custom action.

To associate a control designer with a control, apply the `Designer` attribute to the class declaration of the control. This attribute takes a type reference to the control designer you want to use, which you can find by using the `typeof` keyword:

```
[Designer(typeof(RandomShapeDesigner))]
public class RandomShape : System.Windows.Forms.Control
{
...
}
```

Comments

A control designer is a useful construct that allows you to alter the design-time behavior of a control to aid the developer who is designing a Windows Form that uses the control. A control designer can either alter the default behavior of the forms designer or enhance its functionality. One way of altering the way the forms designer manipulates a control is to change the selection rules of a control. Selection rules determine whether a control can be resized or moved in addition to locking or changing the visibility attribute of the control.

The `ControlDesigner` class contains several virtual methods representing event delegates that you can override to alter how the forms designer responds to events fired as a result of user interaction. For instance, when the user moves a control on the Windows Forms, the default control designer captures this event and subsequently updates the `Location` property of the control. Similarly, if you override the `OnMouseDragBegin` *method*, your control designer can perform a custom action whenever this event occurs. Other event handlers also allow you to play an active role in the design of the control such as the `OnPaintAdornments` method, which is called when a control finishes painting, thereby allowing you to draw additional objects at design time.

It should be noted that a custom designer is only used during the design-time phase of a control. During runtime, the custom designer is out of the picture, so to speak. In other words, if you perform any custom painting through the `OnPaintAdornments` method, that code is not called when the application housing the Windows Form runs. The remaining two recipes of this chapter finish the discussion of control designers by looking at how to extend the design-time context menu of a control and how to add and remove additional properties of a control.

9.10. Extending the Design Time Context Menu

You want to add a new item to the context menu of a control during design time.

Technique

The context menu is built from a collection of objects known as *verbs*. These verbs are defined in the `DesignerVerbCollection` of a control designer. Create a class derived from `System.Windows.Forms.Design.ControlDesigner` and override the `Verbs` property. The getter method of the `Verbs` property returns a `DesignerVerbCollection` object. Within the implementation of the `Verbs` getter method, create a new `DesignerVerbCollection` object and call its `Add` method for each verb you want to add. The `Add` method accepts two parameters: a string parameter used as the display string for the menu item and an `EventHandler` delegate, which is called when the verb is selected by the user:

```
public override System.ComponentModel.Design.DesignerVerbCollection Verbs
{
    get
    {
        DesignerVerbCollection v = new DesignerVerbCollection();

        v.Add(new DesignerVerb("Randomize", new
```

```
EventHandler(RandomizeVerbHandler)));
        return v;
    }
}

private void RandomizeVerbHandler(object sender, System.EventArgs e)
{
    ((RandomShape)this.Control).Randomize();
}
```

Comments

The last recipe showed how to act in concert with the forms designer to alter the behavior of a control during design time. The code associated with the last recipe, which you can download from the publisher's Web site http://www.samspublishing.com, created a custom control that simply draws a specified number of random shapes of differing colors. The drawing area of the control is used as a rough indication for each shape's location. In other words, a shape is always guaranteed to draw mainly on the control. However, if the control is resized in any direction, the locations and sizes of each drawn shape are not recalculated. This anomaly fits well into the discussion of extending the design-time context menu using verbs.

A verb is an action associated with a display string. Even though we mentioned that you can extend the context menu using verbs, each verb is also placed into the property browser of a control as a blue hyperlink, as shown in Figure 9.4. When a user selects the context menu item associated with a verb or clicks on the hyperlink within the property browser, the verb's associated event handler method is called. In the case of the RandomShapeControl, the Randomize event is called. Before this verb was used, the user would have to force the randomize method by either rebuilding the project or forcing the form to repaint somehow during design time. By adding the Randomize verb, you let the user change the size of the control and then select the verb without having to force the shape randomization.

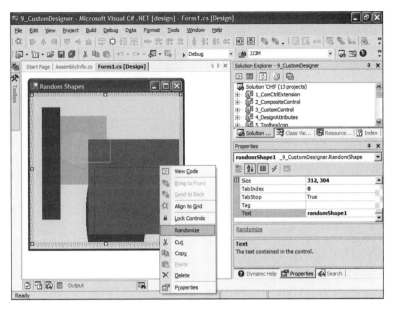

Figure 9.4   Adding items to the designer context menu.

9.11. Removing Control Properties Using Metadata Filtering

You want to add a property to a control for use by a custom control designer, or you want to remove a control property from the property browser.

Technique

The `ControlDesigner` class allows you to add property filters to add or remove properties from the property browser when a control is selected in the forms designer. In either case, create a new class derived from `System.Windows.Forms.Design.` `ControlDesigner`. To add a new property, override the `PreFilterProperties` method. The `properties` parameter is a `IDictionary` collection whose keys represent the names of the properties and whose associated values are instances of the corresponding properties values. Before adding to the collection, you must call the base class `PreFilterProperties` method to initialize the property's collection. You can then call the static method `CreateProperty` defined in the `TypeDescriptor` class to add the property to the property browser. The first parameter is a type reference to the class that defines the property, which in most cases is the result from calling `GetType()` in your control designer. The remaining parameters include a string value representing the name of the new property, the data type of the property, and any attributes that apply to the property. You can apply attributes by creating an array of `Attribute` values:

```
protected override void PreFilterProperties(IDictionary properties)
{
    // call base first
    base.PreFilterProperties (properties);
    properties["DrawDesignBorder"] = TypeDescriptor.CreateProperty(
        this.GetType(), "DrawDesignBorder", typeof(bool),
        new Attribute[] {CategoryAttribute.Design});
}
```

To remove properties from the property browser, override the `PostFilterProperties` method. Just like the `PreFilterProperties`, this method accepts an `IDictionary`-based collection representing the collection of control properties. To remove a property, simply call the `Remove` method defined in the collection, passing the name of the property to remove. You must then call the base class version of `PostFilterProperties` to make the change within the property browser:

```
protected override void PostFilterProperties(IDictionary properties)
{
    // remove the Visible property
    properties.Remove("Visible");

    // call base last
    base.PostFilterProperties (properties);
}
```

Comments

In Recipe 9.9, "Utilizing Custom Designers," the `OnPaintAdornments` method was overridden to display a border around the `RandomShapeControl` during design time. One caveat with this method is that the border is always drawn even if the user didn't want this behavior to appear. However, by filtering a control's properties, you can add a design-time property to enable this functionality. In the `PreFilterProperties` method shown earlier, a `DrawDesignBorder` property is added to the property browser whenever the control is selected by the user in the forms designer. Setting this value to `false` updates the corresponding property defined in the custom control designer, thereby allowing you to turn off the drawing of the design border. However, one side effect of doing so is the code generation that occurs by the forms designer.

When a property is added to the properties collection and is subsequently changed by the user when designing the control, the added property is added to the `InitializeComponent` method defined in the original control's class definition. However, this step generates a compiler error because the `DrawDesignBorder` property is defined in the control designer and not the control itself. To prevent this behavior, create an additional method to turn off serialization for this property. When a property value is changed within the property browser, the forms designer checks whether the property should be serialized. By default, every property is serialized, which means the code to change the property is inserted into the control's class. To turn off serialization for a property, create a method in the control designer class named ShouldSerialize*PropertyName*, where *PropertyName* is the name of the property for which you want to turn off serialization. To turn off serialization for the DrawDesignBorder property, for instance, create a ShouldSerializeDrawDesignBorder method and return false:

```
public bool ShouldSerializeDrawDesignBorder()
{
    return false;
}
```

You can also remove properties from the property browser at design time by implementing the PostFilterProperties method and calling the Remove method defined in the IDictionary collection passed in as the parameter. Doing so removes the associated property from the property browser but does not remove the property from the control itself. In other words, you are still able to access the property within source code, but a user designing a Windows Form that contains the control will not be able to change the property visually. This method is yet another way to control the behavior of a control during design time.

10

Programming Graphics with GDI+

10.0. Introduction

The Graphics Device Interface (GDI) is a system library designed to allow device-independent access to a system's hardware. At the heart of GDI is the device context that contains information about a hardware device and renders data to the device. Regardless of the device context and which device it refers to, the underlying rendering API for GDI is similar for most devices. In other words, you can render a string to two devices using the same API calls even if one device is the main computer display or an attached printer. However, using GDI within the confines of a WIN32-based application can be cumbersome and difficult to master for even the most basic rendering tasks.

GDI+ is the logical evolution of GDI designed to address the degree of difficulty that accompanies GDI as well as add new features that either were nonexistent with GDI or required extensive algorithms to implement. Whereas the heart of GDI is the device context, GDI+ uses a `Graphics` object to encapsulate the bookkeeping necessary for interacting with devices through the device context. This process allows you to spend more time working on rendering algorithms rather than making sure you have correct device context handles. This chapter explores some of the many features of GDI+ from the basics of working with a `Graphics` object to some advanced features such as animated GIF's and print preview support.

10.1. Obtaining a Graphics Object

You want to render objects to a Windows Form or an individual control.

Technique

There are several ways to obtain a `Graphics` object. If you override the `OnPaint` method in your form or control, the `PaintEventArgs` contains a `Graphics` object. You can also retrieve a `Graphics` object at any time by calling the `CreateGraphics` method. This method is defined in the `System.Windows.Forms.Form` class as well as the classes used for Windows Form controls. When finished with the `Graphics` object created using the `CreateGraphics` method, you must destroy the object using the `Dispose` method. To render onto a `Label` control, for instance, call the `CreateGraphics` defined in the `Label` object instance:

```
Label lbl = new Label();
Graphics g = lbl.CreateGraphics();
// do some rendering here
g.Dispose();
```

You can also obtain a `Graphics` object from a window handle or a device context handle. This step is necessary if your code utilizes WIN32 API functions. A window handle is a unique systemwide identifier that is created for each window on the system. Likewise, a handle to a device context (HDC) is a unique identifier for a device information structure. If you obtain a `Graphics` object using these methods, you must destroy them when finished by calling the `Dispose` method:

```
Graphics g1 = Graphics.FromHwnd( this.Handle );
Graphics g2 = Graphics.FromHdc( g1.GetHdc() );
g1.Dispose();
g2.Dispose();
```

Comments

Rendering using a `Graphics` object is a lot like painting on a canvas. In fact, this similarity is so innate that you'll see various artistic references to painting when working with GDI+. Drawing lines, for instance, uses a `Pen` object and you fill areas with colors and patterns by using a `Brush`. In fact, the event handler that is called when a form is about to be rendered is `OnPaint`.

A `Graphics` object hides the details of working with a device context. In GDI, you had to first retrieve a handle to the device context of the particular device you wanted to render to. The device context is a structure within system-allocated memory used by your application, the operating system, and the hardware driver for the associated device. Add to the mix the fact that you can create memory-based device contexts not particularly associated with a hardware device, and you can begin to see why the learning curve is a little high. The GDI+ `Graphics` object removes a large portion of the complexities inherent with WIN32-based GDI programming and also adds several features absent in GDI. That's not saying that there are portions of GDI+ that are impossible to accomplish with GDI; it's just that GDI+ contains several features that would require extensive algorithms to achieve the same results in GDI.

10.2. Drawing a Rectangle

You want to draw a rectangle on a Windows Form and optionally fill it with a defined color.

Technique

After obtaining a `Graphics` object, call the `DrawRectangle` or `FillRectangle`. The `DrawRectangle` method uses a `Pen` object to draw a rectangle. Create a `Pen` object passing a `SolidBrush` object to draw a solid border. The `SolidBrush` object uses a `Color` value that you can specify using a predefined static value defined in the `Color` structure, such as `Color.Black` or a custom color created with a call to the static method `FromArgb` defined in the `Color` structure. This method uses three parameters denoting the red, blue, and green mixtures to use. Each parameter must be a value in the 0–255 range. You can optionally use a predefined brush by calling one of the static methods defined in the `System.Drawing.Brushes` class, as shown in the following code:

```
Brush myBrush = System.Drawing.Brushes.DeepSkyBlue;
```

The `FillRectangle` is similar to the `DrawRectangle` method, but it only needs a `Brush` object instead of a `Pen`. Both methods also need X, Y, width, and height values. The X and Y values are relative to the container the rendering is occurring on. In other words, if rendering is occurring on a Windows Form, then the X and Y values are relative to the upper-left corner of the form. The upper-left corner coordinates are (0,0) with subsequent viewable coordinates increasing in the positive direction, as shown in Listing 10.1.

Listing 10.1   **Drawing Randomly Sized Rectangles with Random Colors**

```
private void Form1_Click(object sender, System.EventArgs e)
{
    Random randNum = new Random( DateTime.Now.Millisecond );

    int width = randNum.Next( this.Width-mouseHit.X );
    int height = randNum.Next( this.Height-mouseHit.Y );
    int r = randNum.Next(255);
    int g = randNum.Next(255);
    int b = randNum.Next(255);
```

Listing 10.1   **Continued**

```
    Graphics surface = this.CreateGraphics();

    if( randNum.Next(2) == 0 )
    {
        surface.FillRectangle( new SolidBrush(Color.FromArgb(r,g,b)),
            mouseHit.X, mouseHit.Y, width, height );
    }
    else
    {
        surface.DrawRectangle( new Pen( new SolidBrush(Color.FromArgb(r,g,b))),
            mouseHit.X, mouseHit.Y, width, height );
    }
    surface.Dispose();
}

private void Form1_MouseDown(object sender,
    System.Windows.Forms.MouseEventArgs e)
{
    mouseHit = new Point( e.X, e.Y );
}
```

Comments

When creating custom rendering algorithms, you might find it beneficial to visualize a piece of paper sitting on a desk. The top-left corner of the paper has a X coordinate of 0 and a Y coordinate of 0. As you move to the right across the paper, the X coordinate increases. If you move to the left, which is off the paper and onto the desk, the X coordinate is a negative number. The same can be said with the Y coordinate; the down direction is positive and the up direction is negative. If you were to take a pen and begin drawing a line going to the right of the paper, you would eventually reach the end. What would happen if you then continued drawing in the same direction? You would begin drawing on the desk itself, and in GDI+, this type of behavior is completely legal. You won't see the rendered output, but the rendering surface itself is there. In fact, if you were to move the actual piece of paper to the right—the rendering surface, in the case of GDI+—you would eventually see the output drawn beyond the initial position of the surface. This method of moving is known as *translation* and is covered in Recipe 10.8.

Once you decide on the location to render a shape, you need to create a Pen or Brush object. A Brush object is for shapes whose interiors are filled. In the following recipes, you'll see how you can use different types of brushes to perform the filling method. To fill the interior of a shape with a solid color, create a SolidBrush object and specify a predefined color from the static values defined in the Color class, or define your own color using three values representing the red, green, and blue components of the color.

For shapes whose interiors are not filled, you need to use a `Pen` object. You create a `Pen` by associating it with a `Brush` object or `Color` value and an optional width. For instance, to create a `Pen` that renders a 2 pixel wide solid magenta color, you can use the following three methods:

```
Pen p = new Pen( new SolidBrush( Color.Magenta ), 2.0f );
Pen p = new Pen( Color.Magenta, 2.0f );
Pen p = new Pen( Color.FromArgb( 255, 0, 255 ), 2.0f );
```

10.3. Drawing a Rectangle with a Hatch Brush

You want to draw a rectangle and fill its interior with a certain pattern.

Technique

The `DrawRectangle` and `FillRectangle` method both use a `Brush` object. The previous recipe used a `SolidBrush` to fill the border or interior of a rectangle with a single solid color. To draw the border or fill the interior with a specified color and a pattern, use a `HatchBrush` object. In addition to a background `Color` value and foreground `Color` value, the `HatchBrush` constructor also requires a value from the `HatchStyle` enumerated data type.

Listing 10.2   **Drawing Rectangles with a** `HatchBrush`

```
private void Form1_Click(object sender, System.EventArgs e)
{
    Random randNum = new Random( DateTime.Now.Millisecond );

    int width = randNum.Next( this.Width-mouseHit.X );
    int height = randNum.Next( this.Height-mouseHit.Y );
    int fr = randNum.Next(255);
    int fg = randNum.Next(255);
    int fb = randNum.Next(255);
    int br = randNum.Next(255);
    int bg = randNum.Next(255);
    int bb = randNum.Next(255);

    Graphics surface = Graphics.FromHwnd(this.Handle);
    surface.FillRectangle( new HatchBrush((HatchStyle)Enum.Parse(
        typeof(HatchStyle), comboBox1.SelectedItem.ToString()),
        Color.FromArgb(fr,fg,fb), Color.FromArgb(br,bg,bb)),
        mouseHit.X, mouseHit.Y, width, height );
}

private void Form1_MouseDown(object sender,
```

Listing 10.2   **Continued**

```
    System.Windows.Forms.MouseEventArgs e)
{
    mouseHit = new Point( e.X, e.Y );
}

private void comboBox1_SelectedIndexChanged(object sender, System.EventArgs e)
{
    Invalidate();
}
```

Comments

In the last recipe, you saw how to create a `SolidBrush` object representing a solid color. You could then use this brush to fill the interior of a shape or use it as the ink for a `Pen` object. Every shape-rendering method within the `Graphics` class uses a generic `Brush` object, but through object-oriented programming principles, you can pass any object that is derived from the `Brush` class. One of these is the `HatchBrush`, which renders a solid color that is then overlaid with a pattern rendered in a different color.

There are three main components to a `HatchBrush`. The `BackgroundColor` property is the solid color that is displayed in the areas not filled with the pattern. The pattern itself is rendered using the color specified in the `ForegroundColor` property. Finally, the `HatchStyle` property defines the pattern and is set to one of the several different values defined in the `HatchStyle` enumerated data type. In Figure 10.1, you can see different rectangles rendered with different hash styles.

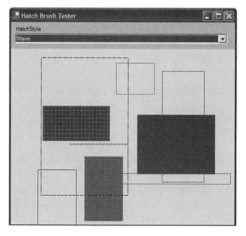

Figure 10.1   You can use a `HatchBrush` to render patterns within the interior of a shape or as the ink for a `Pen` that draws an unfilled shape.

10.4. Filling a Rectangle with a Texture Brush

You want to create a rectangle that uses an image to fill its interior.

Technique

The process of drawing a rectangle, or any other shape, using a texture-based brush is similar to those of the last two recipes. Call the `DrawRectangle` or `FillRectangle` method using a `TextureBrush` object as the brush. The `TextureBrush` constructor uses a single parameter, which is an `Image` object. Recipe 10.15 details different ways to load an image. The easiest way is to call the static method `FromFile` defined in the `Image` class passing the path to an image file on the file system:

```
Graphics g = panel1.CreateGraphics();
Image img = Image.FromFile( "myimage.jpg" );
g.FillRectangle( new TextureBrush(img), e.X, e.Y, img.Width, img.Height );
g.Dispose();
```

Comments

You can use a `HatchBrush` to fill a shape with a specified pattern. However, the `HatchBrush` class doesn't allow a developer to define his own pattern. You can use the `TextureBrush` class to create your own pattern, although you lose the benefit of being able to specify a background and foreground color. A `TextureBrush` uses an `Image` as its rendering output.

When rendering a shape using a `TextureBrush`, the image is not aligned with the X and Y coordinate of the shape being drawn. For instance, the top-left corner of the image associated with a `TextureBrush` is not aligned with the top-left corner of the shape being drawn. In fact, the image is aligned with the corner of the visible surface being rendered to, and if the image is smaller than the width and height of the surface, it is tiled. With that little bit of information, you can see how easy it is to create a Windows Form whose background contains a tiled image:

```
protected override void OnPaint(PaintEventArgs e)
{
    e.Graphics.FillRectangle( new TextureBrush( myImage ),
        0, 0, this.Width, this.Height );
}
```

10.5. Using Gradient Fills

You want to create a shape that uses a gradient fill.

Technique

Create a `LinearGradientBrush` using two `Point` objects or a single `Rectangle` object, a starting and ending `Color` value, and an optional orientation angle.

```
brush = new LinearGradientBrush(new Rectangle(new Point(0,0), new
Size(panel1.Width, panel1.Height)),
                Color.White, Color.Black, LinearGradientMode.ForwardDiagonal );
```

You can also control how the color blend is performed by setting the `Blend` property of the `LinearGradientBrush` object. A `Blend` object contains a `Positions` array and a `Factors` array, both of which are `float` arrays. Each value in the `Positions` array defines a percentage of the gradient fill area. Each value in the `Factors` array represents the percentage up to the point of the corresponding position value that consists of the starting color:

```
gradientBlend = new Blend(3);
gradientBlend.Positions[0] = gradientBlend.Factors[0] = 0.0f;
gradientBlend.Positions[1] = gradientBlend.Factors[1] = 0.4f;
gradientBlend.Positions[2] = gradientBlend.Factors[2] = 1.0f;
brush.Blend = gradientBlend;
```

Comments

To fill a shape using a gradient fill method, use a `LinearGradientBrush` object. There are several constructors available to use when creating the brush. You can specify two `Point` structures or a single `Rectangle` that corresponds to the starting and ending points of the area to fill with the gradient. Any other area outside of those areas is filled using a solid brush. Each gradient brush also uses two `Color` values corresponding to the starting and ending color. The brush interpolates the colors in between those two values to create the gradient fill. Finally, you can specify the orientation of the gradient fill either by passing a value from the `LinearGradientMode` enumerated data type or by passing a `float` value denoting the orientation angle. When you specify an orientation angle, the gradient brush draws each line of the fill perpendicular to the orientation angle. For instance, if the angle is 0, then the gradient fill is horizontal across the drawing area, as shown in Figure 10.2.

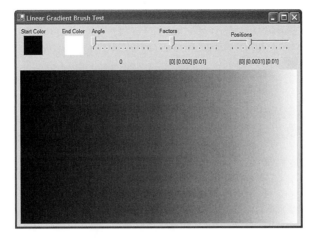

Figure 10.2   A `LinearGradientBrush` with an orientation angle of 0
degrees renders itself horizontally across the rendering surface.

10.6. Drawing Connected Lines and Polygons

You want to plot a series of points and connect the points using lines and
optionally close the endpoints to create a polygon.

Technique

To draw a single line, use the `DrawLine` method. This method contains three parameters
corresponding to the `Pen`, the starting `Point` value, and the ending `Point` value. You can
optionally use four individual `int` or `float` values to specify the starting and ending
coordinates.

A polygon is a series of connected lines whose starting and ending points are automatically connected. To create a polygon, call the `DrawPolygon` method, passing a `Pen`
and an array of `Point` values. To create a filled polygon, call the `FillPolygon` method.

Listing 10.3   **Drawing Lines and Polygons in Response to Clicking on a `Panel` Control**

```
using System.ComponentModel;
using System.Windows.Forms;
using System.Data;

namespace _6_LinesAndPolygons
{
    public class Form1 : System.Windows.Forms.Form
    {
        private System.Windows.Forms.Label label1;
```

Listing 10.3 **Continued**

```
private System.Windows.Forms.Panel panel1;
private Point lastPoint = new Point(-1,-1);
private ArrayList alPoints;
private System.ComponentModel.Container components = null;

public Form1()
{
    InitializeComponent();

    alPoints = new ArrayList();
}

protected override void Dispose( bool disposing )
{
    if( disposing )
    {
        if (components != null)
        {
            components.Dispose();
        }
    }
    base.Dispose( disposing );
}

// Windows Form Designer generated code

[STAThread]
static void Main()
{
    Application.Run(new Form1());
}

private void panel1_MouseDown(object sender,
    System.Windows.Forms.MouseEventArgs e)
{
    Graphics g = panel1.CreateGraphics();
    Random rand = new Random( DateTime.Now.Millisecond );

    int rc = rand.Next(255);
    int gc = rand.Next(255);
    int bc = rand.Next(255);

    if( e.Button == MouseButtons.Left )
    {
        g.FillRectangle( new SolidBrush(Color.Black), e.X, e.Y, 5, 5 );
```

Listing 10.3 **Continued**

```
            if( lastPoint.X != -1 && lastPoint.Y != -1 )
            {
                g.DrawLine( new Pen(new SolidBrush(Color.Black)),
                    lastPoint, new Point(e.X, e.Y ) );
            }

            lastPoint.X = e.X;
            lastPoint.Y = e.Y;

            alPoints.Add( lastPoint );
        }
        else if( e.Button == MouseButtons.Right )
        {
            Point[] points = (Point[]) alPoints.ToArray( typeof(Point));

            if( rand.Next(2) == 0 )
            {
                g.DrawPolygon( new Pen( new SolidBrush(
                    Color.FromArgb(rc,gc,bc ))), points );
            }
            else
            {
                g.FillPolygon( new SolidBrush( Color.FromArgb(rc,gc,bc )),
                    points );
            }
            alPoints.Clear();
            lastPoint.X = -1;
            lastPoint.Y = -1;
        }
        g.Dispose();
    }
  }
}
```

Comments

When it comes to actually drawing on a piece of paper, we find it extremely difficult to draw even a straight line. Any graphics work we do is on computers because we can draw extremely straight lines on it, provided we have the right tools to do the job. A line is a connection between any two given points. It comes as no surprise then that to draw a line in GDI+, you must specify two points. If you continue drawing lines starting from the last point and continuing to a new point, not only would you have a facsimile of a dot-to-dot puzzle, but you would also be one step closer to creating a polygon. By simply closing the first point with the last point in a series of connected lines, you create a polygon.

10.7. Drawing Arc and Pie Shapes

You want to create an arc or pie shape.

Technique

Creating an arc or a pie is analogous to the method used for drawing lines and polygons in the last recipe. An arc uses a `Pen` object to draw an arc shape starting at a specified point. The arc is drawn by projecting a line from the start point using a specified start angle. Rendering the arc begins at the endpoint of the line and continues by creating an elliptical path ending at the endpoint, which is based on a sweep angle. Figure 10.3 shows the result of creating an arc from the following code. One point of confusion is that the start angle is measured clockwise from the X axis rather than the counterclockwise method defined within a regular Cartesian coordinate system:

```
graphics.DrawArc( new Pen( new SolidBrush(Color.Black)), 200, 200,
    200, 200, 45.0f, 180.0f );
```

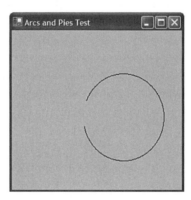

Figure 10.3   The `DrawArc` method draws a semicircular shape.

Comments

One of the many uses of the shape-drawing methods of GDI+ is charting data. The `DrawRectangle` or `FillRectangle` methods are well suited for bar charts. The `DrawLine` method is perfect for creating line charts, and the `DrawPolygon` method makes creating area charts simple. Throw in a few `HatchBrush` objects with different hatch styles to differentiate data points, and you can see how you can use all these objects to create the next charting application or control. Arcs and pies are naturally suited for pie and doughnut charts.

Creating an arc and creating a pie are virtually identical because the only difference is that a pie is simply an arc whose endpoints join together at the center of the partial ellipse. Each method uses a start and ending point as well as a width and height. When rendering begins with a call to DrawArc, DrawPie, or FillPie, GDI+ starts at the initial X and Y coordinates and moves in the direction specified as the start angle to a distance that is half of the width and height set in the method parameters. The actual rendering of the arc or pie then begins by drawing an elliptical shape that stops when the sweep angle is reached. A clockwise direction means a sweep angle of 90 degrees with a start angle of 0 would be a U shaped semicircle. If you are rendering a pie, then two lines are drawn from the two endpoints and meet in the center point of the shape, as shown in Figure 10.3.

10.8. Using Rotation and Translation Transformations

You want to render a shape that is rotated or translated from a base coordinate.

Technique

Rotation and translation is accomplished by manipulating the transformation matrix of a Graphics object. To rotate the rendering surface, call the RotateTransform method. This method uses a single float value representing the angle of rotation in the clockwise direction:

```
// rotate clockwise 45 degrees
e.Graphics.RotateTransform( 45.0f );
```

To move or translate the drawing surface, use the TranslateTransform method, passing an X and Y value. The rendering origin moves to the right for positive X values and down for positive Y values:

```
// moves origin 100 pixels to the right and 50 pixels down
e.Graphics.TranslateTransform( 100.0f, 50.0f );
```

Comments

Drawing a rectangle using GDI+ is a trivial task. Simply by knowing the location on the form and the width and the height of the rectangle you want to draw, you can render a rectangle with a single function call. What would happen if you wanted to rotate that rectangle 1 degree to the right? The DrawRectangle method would be utterly useless. Instead, you would have to resort to tricky rotational mathematics combined with four separate DrawLine calls. The trivial problem transforms into a complicated algorithm even though you are still in essence drawing a rectangle. The transformation matrix defined in the Graphics class was designed to handle these situations.

10.9. Using Graphics Containers

You want to manipulate the drawing of a shape without affecting any other shapes that are drawn concurrently.

Technique

When you rotate or translate the origin of the rendering surface, you affect any subsequent drawing operations. To save the transformation matrix and restore it when finished, use a GraphicsContainer object. Assign the result of calling the BeginContainer method defined in the Graphics class to a GraphicsContainer variable. Call the EndContainer method, passing the GraphicsContainer object as the parameter when you are finished rendering:

```
private void DrawStar( Graphics g )
{
    GraphicsContainer container = g.BeginContainer();

    Point[] starPoints = { new Point(-20,0), new Point(20,0),
        new Point(0,40), new Point(-20,0)};

    for( int i = 0; i < 8; i++ )
    {
        g.FillPolygon( new SolidBrush(Color.Red), starPoints );
        g.DrawPolygon( new Pen(new SolidBrush(Color.Black)), starPoints );

        g.RotateTransform( 45.0f );
    }

    g.EndContainer( container );
}
```

Comments

In the previous recipe, you used rotation and translation of the transformation matrix defined within the Graphics class to simplify the drawing of arbitrary shapes. A side effect of doing so, however, is that subsequent rendering happens on the rotated and translated matrix. To change this behavior, you have to save the current transformation matrix, perform any necessary rendering, and restore the original matrix when you are finished.

You use a GraphicsContainer object to change rendering options temporarily without affecting any subsequent operations. It might seem logical to just save the transformation matrix into a Matrix variable and use that matrix to restore the transformation matrix to its original state when finished. So you might be wondering why you should want to use a `GraphicsContainer` instead of a `Matrix` object. The `GraphicsContainer` also saves different graphics states that are currently in use. The current transformation matrix is one of those states, but others include any clipping regions, text rendering options, and the current composition mode. In other words, a `GraphicsContainer` is useful for saving and restoring a transformation matrix, but you should also use it if you need to temporarily change any rendering options without affecting the current state of the `Graphics` object for future rendering tasks.

10.10. Forcing a Repaint

> You want to force a repaint of a control or Windows Form to call your rendering code.

Technique

Sometimes, you need to force a form or control to repaint, as is the case with animations. To perform an asynchronous repaint, call the `Invalidate` or `Refresh` method. There are several overloaded versions. If you specify no parameters, the entire form repaints. You can also pass a `Rectangle` or `Region` object to repaint only a specified area of the form:

```
private void timer1_Tick(object sender, System.EventArgs e)
{
    curRotation += 30;
    if( curRotation > 360 )
        curRotation = 0;

    this.Invalidate();
}
```

Comments

In most cases, controls automatically update themselves whenever one of their properties changes. Setting the `Text` property of a `TextBox` control, for instance, automatically causes the `TextBox` to update itself. However, when you are working within the realm of GDI+ and custom rendering algorithms, you might have to manually cause a repaint event to occur. This case is especially true when you are performing some type of animation.

10.11. Performing Flicker-Free Animation

You want to remove the flicker that occurs as a result of continuously repainting during animation sequences.

Technique

When performing animation, you might find that the rendered objects flash slightly. To remove this anomaly, call the `SetStyle` method, passing three values from the `ControlStyles` enumerated data type. These three values appear in the following code and are turned on and off with the last parameter:

```
private void menuFlickerFree_Click(object sender, System.EventArgs e)
{
    if( menuFlickerFree.Checked == true )
    {
        menuFlickerFree.Checked = false;
        SetStyle(ControlStyles.AllPaintingInWmPaint, false);
        SetStyle(ControlStyles.DoubleBuffer, false);
    }
    else
    {
        menuFlickerFree.Checked = true;
        SetStyle(ControlStyles.UserPaint, true );
        SetStyle(ControlStyles.AllPaintingInWmPaint, true);
        SetStyle(ControlStyles.DoubleBuffer, true);
    }
}
```

Comments

The code in the technique portion of this recipe, which comes from the demonstration application created for Recipe 10.8, "Using Rotation and Translation Transformations," allows you to specify whether rendering should use double buffering to eliminate flickering based on the current state of a menu item. This code appears in the downloadable code for this book. When you run the application and double buffering is not enabled, you see brief flickers of white as a new frame in the animation renders. Double buffering works by creating a separate area of video memory identical to the rendering surface. GDI+ therefore works with two different surfaces, sometimes referred to as *pages*. When you make rendering calls such as `DrawRectangle`, GDI+ renders the output to the currently hidden buffer. Using synchronization with the horizontal scan lines of the display adapter, GDI+ performs a page flip so that the surface that is being rendered to is shown while the other page is hidden and used for subsequent operations. This method ensures that a rendered surface always displays rather than a surface that is continuously erased and redrawn, which in turn causes the flickering.

One thing to note is that you should always enable or disable the `ControlStyles.DoubleBuffer` style in conjunction with the `ControlStyle.UserPaint` and `ControlStyle.AllPaintingInWmPaint` styles. This step allows GDI+ to perform its double-buffering technique. The `UserPaint` style transfers rendering control from the operating system to GDI+. Forgetting to set that style would restrain GDI+ from performing its double-buffering technique. The `AllPaintingInWmPaint` rendering style refers to how painting should occur in response to the `WM_PAINT` window message. Windows within the operating system are controlled and manipulated by messages that are dispatched by the operating system. The `WM_PAINT` message is sent to your form whenever the operating system determines a repaint of the window should occur. Another message, `WM_ERASEBKGND`, also arrives before the `WM_PAINT` message to erase the current contents of the window. `AllPaintingInWmPaint` notifies the form that the contents of the form should not be erased in response to a `WM_ERASEBKGND` message, thereby allowing GDI+ to render using double buffering.

10.12. Enumerating System Fonts

You want to retrieve a list of the fonts installed on a user's system.

Technique

You can get the list of fonts on a user's system by using an `InstalledFontCollection` object. After creating this object, enumerate the `Families` array to access each `FontFamily` object. The name of the font is contained within the `GetName` method:

```
public Form1()
{
    //
    // Required for Windows Form Designer support
    //
    InitializeComponent();

    // enumerate system fonts and add to combobox
    InstalledFontCollection installedFonts = new InstalledFontCollection();

    foreach(FontFamily family in installedFonts.Families)
    {
        cbFonts.Items.Add( family.GetName(0) );
    }

    cbFonts.SelectedIndex = 0;
}
```

Comments

If your application is document centric, meaning the user manipulates a document containing some sort of textual information, you should allow the user to change the font to better suit her preferences. Due to the rich collections support built into the .NET Framework, enumerating the list of installed fonts on a user's system is the same as enumerating any list-based collection that you've seen so far. You use the `InstalledFontCollection` to enumerate each `FontFamily` object in the collection. Each `FontFamily` object contains a method named `GetName` that you use to retrieve the name associated with that family.

You might be wondering why the term *family* refers to fonts. A *font family* is a group of fonts that share the same basic rendering characteristics. Let's use `Arial` as an example. `Arial` by itself is considered a font family. Once you start adding characteristics, such as a bold style or character size, you then have a font. When you create a new `Font` object, the first parameter to the constructor is the font family, followed by any additional characteristics needed for the final font.

10.13. Displaying Text

> You want to display a string of text using a specified font.

Technique

To render text, you must first create a `Font` object. The `Font` class contains several different constructors, allowing you to control precisely how the font should appear. You can also use the different member methods within the `Font` class to manipulate the font after it is created. In most cases, you want to specify a `FontFamily`, which can be found within the `InstalledFontCollection` object described in the last recipe, or an equivalent string value representing the name of the font. You may also specify the size of the `Font` using a float value, which by default is specified in points. You can change the unit of measurement from points to a different unit by specifying a `GraphicsUnit` value. To add bold, italic, underline, or other style, use a logical OR of the values defined in the `FontStyle` enumeration:

```
FontStyle fs = 0;
if( menuBold.Enabled == true && bold == true )
    fs |= FontStyle.Bold;
if( menuItalic.Enabled == true && italic == true )
    fs |= FontStyle.Italic;
if( menuUnderline.Enabled == true && underline == true )
    fs |= FontStyle.Underline;

Font f = new Font( cbFonts.SelectedItem.ToString(), 12.0f, fs );
```

To render a string to the current drawing surface, call the `DrawString` method defined in the `Graphics` class. The first parameter is the string you want to render. The second parameter to the method is the `Font` object created earlier. The additional parameters are the type of `Brush` to use and the bounding rectangle to render the text to.

```
e.Graphics.DrawString( "C# Font Test", f,
    new SolidBrush( Color.Black ), panel1.DisplayRectangle);
```

Comments

The previous recipe noted that you create a `Font` object by specifying a font family name, font styles, and the point size of the font. Once this object is created, you can call the `DrawString` method to render a string to the associated rendering surface. You can additionally associate a `StringFormat` object with the `DrawString` method to support such things as right-to-left rendering using the `Alignment` property; vertical text, which you do by adding the `DirectionVertical` flag to the `FormatFlags` property; and the hotkey prefix, which creates an underlined character indicating a keyboard shortcut. You make a hotkey by setting the `HotKeyPrefix` property to either `Hide`, `None`, or `Show`.

10.14. Enabling Antialiasing

You want to remove the jagged appearance that appears when you render text.

Technique

A `Graphics` object uses a `TextRenderingHint` value to determine how text should be rendered with a call to the `DrawText` method. To render antialiased text, set the `TextRenderingHint` property to one of the six values specified in the `TextRenderingHint` enumerated data type. For normal-sized fonts, use the `ClearTypeGridFit` value if the system supports it. For large point fonts or for systems that don't support ClearType, use the `AntiAlias` or `AntiAliasGridFit` values:

```
e.Graphics.TextRenderingHint = TextRenderingHint.AntiAlias;
```

Comments

Windows XP took a leap forward in its user interface by incorporating ClearType technology for text rendering. The pixilated text displayed in previous version of Windows was supplanted by smooth text that is visually more appealing. It comes as no surprise that this technology is carried over and made available within the .NET Framework.

A standard display consists of several thousand small areas known as *pixels* that emit light from the visible color spectrum. Even though these pixels are small, the human eye is still able to detect discontinuity between pixels that are drawn in anything but the horizontal or vertical plane. When a line is drawn without antialiasing, you notice a stair-stepping effect in the line, as shown in Figure 10.4. Antialiasing works by using color averages for neighboring pixels and the background color. In the antialiased portion of Figure 10.4, you see text being drawn with a blend starting from black to grey and moving finally to white to give the rendered text a smooth appearance.

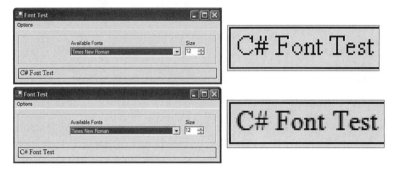

Figure 10.4 Without antialiasing, rendered text has a noticeable stair-step effect.

10.15. Loading and Displaying Images

You want to load an image on the file system and display it on a Windows Form.

Technique

To load an image, use the `FromFile` static method defined in the `Image` class, passing a filename as the parameter. You can also obtain an `Image` object by using the `FromHbitmap` method, passing a handle to an existing bitmap. This method primarily applies when you directly access GDI+ in an interoperability scenario. Chapter 12, "File I/O and Serialization," details stream-based data access, which you can use with the `FromStream` method to read image data directly from a stream object:

```
private void menuOpen_Click(object sender, System.EventArgs e)
{
    if( openFileDialog1.ShowDialog() == DialogResult.OK )
    {
        image = Image.FromFile( openFileDialog1.FileName );
        this.Text = "Image Test - " + openFileDialog1.FileName;
        Invalidate();
    }
}
```

```
protected override void OnPaint(PaintEventArgs e)
{
    if( animating == true )
        ImageAnimator.UpdateFrames();

    e.Graphics.DrawImage( image, 0, 0 );
}
```

Comments

To say that GDI+ along with the .NET Framework makes loading and displaying images simple is an understatement. Not only is bitmap display much simpler with GDI+ than previous technologies, but you also get the added benefit of a slew of other image types to work with. Furthermore, your code doesn't even have to change to work with different file formats. As far as you are concerned, you have an `Image` object. It's up to GDI+ to make sure the file is parsed and rendered correctly based on its file format.

The `Image` class itself loads and displays images, but support for any type of image manipulation is sparse. For instance, if you want to rotate the image, you can call the `RotateFlip` method, passing a value from the `RotateFlipType` enumerated data type. However, if you want to scale the image, there is no corresponding method to easily perform this operation. To perform this type of operation, you can use a technique that creates a new image object whose size is the final size of the scaled image and then use the `DrawImage` method to copy the old image to the newer scaled image, as in the following code:

```
private void menuScale_Click(object sender, System.EventArgs e)
{
    if( image == null )
        return;

    ScaleImageForm scale = new ScaleImageForm();
    if( scale.ShowDialog(this) == DialogResult.OK )
    {
        int newHeight = (int)(image.Height * (scale.ScaleHeight/100.0f));
        int newWidth = (int)(image.Width * (scale.ScaleWidth/100.0f));

        Image oldImage = (Image) image.Clone();
        image = new Bitmap( newWidth, newHeight );
        Graphics g = Graphics.FromImage( image );
        g.DrawImage( oldImage, new Rectangle(0,0,image.Width, image.Height), 0, 0,
                    oldImage.Width, oldImage.Height, GraphicsUnit.Pixel );
        Invalidate();
    }
}
```

Likewise, if you want to crop out parts of an image, you must follow the same procedure. Listing 10.4 demonstrates how to crop an image. Whenever you select the Crop menu item, the application is placed into cropping mode, indicated by changing the current Cursor. Event handlers are created to handle mouse events. When a user initially clicks a mouse button, the location of that click is saved into a cropping rectangle variable. As the mouse moves, the Form1_MouseMove method updates the cropping rectangle's Width and Height properties. Once the user releases the mouse button, a new Image object is created whose size is the same as the cropping rectangle that was constructed. The corresponding area of the main image is then placed into that new Image, and the form is updated to reflect the new cropped image.

Listing 10.4   **Cropping Images**

```
private void menuCrop_Click(object sender, System.EventArgs e)
{
    if( image != null )
    {
        this.Cursor = Cursors.Cross;
        cropping = true;
    }
}


private void Form1_MouseDown(object sender,
    System.Windows.Forms.MouseEventArgs e)
{
    if( cropping == true )
    {
        cropRect.X = e.X;
        cropRect.Y = e.Y;
    }
}


private void Form1_MouseMove(object sender,
    System.Windows.Forms.MouseEventArgs e)
{
    if( cropping == true )
    {
        cropRect.Width = e.X - cropRect.X;
        cropRect.Height = e.Y - cropRect.Y;
        Invalidate();
    }
}


private void Form1_MouseUp(object sender,System.Windows.Forms.MouseEventArgs e)
{
    if( cropping == true )
```

Listing 10.4 **Continued**

```
    {
        cropping = false;

        // move old picture
        Image oldImage = (Image) image.Clone();

        // create new image object
        image = new Bitmap( cropRect.Width, cropRect.Height );

        // get graphics object from new image
        Graphics g = Graphics.FromImage( image );

        // draw old image into new image using crop rect
        g.DrawImage( oldImage, new Rectangle(0,0,image.Width, image.Height),
            cropRect.X, cropRect.Y, cropRect.Width,
            cropRect.Height, GraphicsUnit.Pixel );

        // reset
        cropRect.X = cropRect.Y = -1;
        this.Cursor = Cursors.Default;
        Invalidate();
    }
}
```

10.16. Loading and Displaying Animated GIF's

You want to determine whether a GIF contains animation frames and display it on a Windows Form.

Technique

The `ImageAnimator` class determines whether an image contains animation frames as well as controls when the image should be updated to display the next frame. To determine whether an image is animated, use the static method `CanAnimate` defined in the `ImageAnimator` class, passing an `Image` object instance. To start the animation, call the static method `Animate`, passing the `Image` object in the first parameter and an `EventHandler` delegate as the second parameter:

```
private void menuOpen_Click(object sender, System.EventArgs e)
{
    if( openFileDialog1.ShowDialog() == DialogResult.OK )
    {
        image = Image.FromFile( openFileDialog1.FileName );
```

```
        this.Text = "Image Test - " + openFileDialog1.FileName;

        // check if animated image
        if( ImageAnimator.CanAnimate( image ) == true )
        {
            animating = true;
            ImageAnimator.Animate(image, new EventHandler(this.OnImageAnimate));
        }
        else
        {
            animating = false;
        }
        Invalidate();
    }
}

private void OnImageAnimate(object o, EventArgs e)
{
    //Force a call to the Paint event handler.
    this.Invalidate();
}
```

The ImageAnimator is responsible for ensuring that each frame within an animated image is selected as the current frame. To move to the next frame and render an image, call the UpdateFrames static method, passing the Image object to update. Rendering the image itself is similar to rendering other Image objects, which you accomplish by calling the Graphics method DrawImage:

```
protected override void OnPaint(PaintEventArgs e)
{
    if( image == null )
    {
        return;
    }

    if( animating == true )
        ImageAnimator.UpdateFrames();

    e.Graphics.DrawImage( image, new Rectangle(0,0,image.Width, image.Height),
➥0, 0,
                          image.Width, image.Height, GraphicsUnit.Pixel );
}
```

Comments

GDI+ supports several different file formats, including animated GIF's. An animated GIF contains several frames within a single file that you can enumerate on a time interval to render the animation. However, simply calling the `DrawImage` method does not cause an animated GIF to render on a frame-by-frame basis. In this case, only the first frame is rendered. In the code for this recipe, you can see how the `ImageAnimator` class updates the current frame pointer within an animated GIF. When the image is rendered using `DrawImage`, GDI+ looks to see what frame is currently selected and renders just that frame. You perform subsequent frame updates by calling the `UpdateFrames` method defined in the `ImageAnimator` class.

Just as simply calling `DrawImage` is not enough to render each frame within an animated GIF, calling the `Save` method defined in the `Image` class does not save all the frames within the image. It simply saves the first frame and ignores any subsequent frames. To save an animated GIF so that all its frames are preserved, you must follow the `Save` method call with a `SaveAdd` call for each frame within the image.

10.17. Converting Image File Formats

You want to convert an image from one file format to a different file format.

Technique

To convert a file format, you need to save it to the file system, specifying which format you want to save the image to. Call the `Save` method from an `Image` instance, passing a filename to save the image to and a value from the `ImageFormat` enumerated data type:

```
private void menuSave_Click(object sender, System.EventArgs e)
{
    if( image == null )
        return;

    if( saveFileDialog1.ShowDialog(this) == DialogResult.OK )
    {
        ImageFormat format = ImageFormat.Bmp;

        if( saveFileDialog1.FileName.EndsWith("bmp"))
        {
            format = ImageFormat.Bmp;
        }
        else if( saveFileDialog1.FileName.EndsWith("gif"))
        {
            format = ImageFormat.Gif;
        }
        else if( saveFileDialog1.FileName.EndsWith("jpg"))
        {
            format = ImageFormat.Jpeg;
        }
```

```
        else if( saveFileDialog1.FileName.EndsWith("png"))
        {
            format = ImageFormat.Png;
        }
        // other file formats ...

        image.Save( saveFileDialog1.FileName, format );
        image = Image.FromFile( saveFileDialog1.FileName );
        this.Text = "Image Test - " + saveFileDialog1.FileName;
    }
}
```

Comments

The code allows a user to save an image in one of four different file formats, but GDI+ allows you to save an image using 10 different formats. The code to support all different file formats therefore appears redundant for illustration purposes. It makes sense for the Save method to simply determine the file format to save the image to based on the file extension, as shown in the code earlier, and at one point in the development of the Image class, this was the case. For unknown reasons, however, this design was changed in favor of the ImageFormat enumerated data type.

10.18. Printing Documents

You want to print the contents of your current document with an attached printer.

Technique

Printing a document requires the use of a helper class that is associated with a print dialog implemented by the .NET Framework. Create a new class derived from the PrintDocument class in the System.Drawing.Printing namespace. In most cases, you just need to override the OnPrintPage method and allow the base class to handle the remaining printing tasks. The OnPrintPage virtual method has a single PrintPageEventArgs parameter containing several properties that allow you to cancel the print job, query for the page and margin boundaries, and perform rendering using the printer's associated Graphics object.

The actual act of printing is the same as it is for rendering to the display. Use the methods defined in the Graphics class for rendering using the MarginBounds and PageBounds to stay within the confines of the printed page. The OnPrintPage method is called only once per page, so if you need more pages for rendering, set the HasMorePages property in the PrintPageEventArgs to true to force another PrintPage event.

Listing 10.5 is the printing code for the image editor application whose source code accompanies this book. The OnPrintPage method first determines the size of the header that will be printed, which consists of a string followed by a horizontal line. After the header is rendered, a Rectangle is computed so that an image is drawn underneath the header. Furthermore, if the image is too large to fit on a single printed page, its height and width are scaled down, and the resulting rectangle is centered on the page using information from the MarginBounds property.

Listing 10.5   **Printing Documents**

```
public class ImagePrintDocument : PrintDocument
{
    private Image document;

    public ImagePrintDocument( Image doc )
    {
        this.document = doc;
    }

    protected override void OnPrintPage(PrintPageEventArgs e)
    {
        // calculate information string and update header height
        int headerHeight = e.MarginBounds.Y;
        SizeF strSize = e.Graphics.MeasureString(
            "Visual C# .Net Developer's Cookbook Chapter 10",
            new Font("Times New Roman", 12), e.MarginBounds.Width);

        headerHeight += (int) strSize.Height;

        // draw the header string
        e.Graphics.DrawString( "Visual C# .Net Developer's Cookbook Chapter 10",
                        new Font("Times New Roman", 12),
                        new SolidBrush(Color.Blue ),
                        new RectangleF(e.MarginBounds.X,
                        e.MarginBounds.Y,
                        strSize.Width, strSize.Height));

        // draw a line under the string
        e.Graphics.DrawLine( new Pen( new SolidBrush(Color.Black)),
                        e.MarginBounds.X, headerHeight+5,
                        e.MarginBounds.Width+e.MarginBounds.X,
                        headerHeight+5 );

        headerHeight += 10;

        // computer rectangle for image so it's centered on
```

Listing 10.5 **Continued**

```
        // page and scaled down if too large
        Rectangle rcImage = new Rectangle(0,0,0,0);

        if( document.Width >= e.MarginBounds.Width )
        {
            rcImage.X = e.MarginBounds.X;
            rcImage.Width = e.MarginBounds.Width;
        }
        else
        {
            // image width is smaller than printed page so center it
            rcImage.X = (int)((e.MarginBounds.Width/2)-(document.Width/2) +
                e.MarginBounds.X);

            rcImage.Width = document.Width;
        }
        if( document.Height >= e.MarginBounds.Height-headerHeight)
        {
            rcImage.Y = (int)(e.MarginBounds.Y + strSize.Height+20);
            rcImage.Height = (int)(e.MarginBounds.Height)-headerHeight;
        }
        else
        {
            // image width is smaller than printed page so center it
            rcImage.Y = (int)((e.MarginBounds.Height/2)-(document.Height/2));
            rcImage.Height = document.Height;
        }

        // print the image
        e.Graphics.DrawImage( document, rcImage, 0, 0, document.Width,
            document.Height, GraphicsUnit.Pixel );

        e.HasMorePages = false;
    }
}
```

To start the printing process, create a `PrintDialog` object and set any necessary properties to control its behavior. Next, create an instance of the `PrintDocument` class created earlier and assign it to the `Document` property of the `PrintDialog` object. Finally, call the `ShowDialog` method of the `PrintDialog` object, and if the result is `DialogResult.OK`, transfer the `PrinterSettings` property of the `PrintDialog` object to the `PrinterSettings` property of the `PrintDocument` object and call `Print` from the `PrintDocument` instance:

```
private void menuPrint_Click(object sender, System.EventArgs e)
{
```

```
if( image == null )
    return;

PrintDialog dlg = new PrintDialog();
dlg.AllowSelection = false;
dlg.AllowSomePages = false;

ImagePrintDocument doc = new ImagePrintDocument( image );
dlg.Document = doc;

if( dlg.ShowDialog() == DialogResult.OK )
{
    doc.PrinterSettings = dlg.PrinterSettings;
    doc.Print();
}
}
```

Comments

A printer is similar to a display adapter in that both are rendering devices. Whereas a display adapter renders output to a monitor, a printer renders its output to a page. However, due to their similarities, the rendering code for both can be the same. The differences lie in the fact that printer output can span multiple pages and a page has a defined margin that you cannot render to.

The `PrintDocument` class is the base class for a helper class that you create to print the contents of your application's current document. As mentioned earlier, in most cases you might just need to override the `OnPrintPage` method, which in the `PrintDocument` base class is the event handler delegate for the `PrintPage` event. In the code listing for this recipe, you might notice that the code to render the `Image` object is considerably longer than the code used to render the `Image` to the display. This was merely a design choice on our part. Our goal when printing was to scale the image to fit on a single printed page, center the image on the page, and add a header to the top of the document. This design choice therefore led to some basic math to ensure those design choices applied.

10.19. Displaying a Print Preview Dialog

You want to add the ability for a user to see what the printed output will look like before he prints.

Technique

Displaying a preview of printed output is similar to the method used to show the print dialog. Create a `PrintPreviewDialog` object and the helper class derived from the `PrintDocument` class created in the previous recipe. Associate the `PrintDocument` object with the print preview dialog by setting the `Document` property of the

`PrintPreviewDialog` to the `PrintDocument` instance. To display the print preview window, call the `ShowDialog` method of the `PrintPreviewDialog` object:

```
private void menuPrintPreview_Click(object sender, System.EventArgs e)
{
    if( image == null )
        return;

    PrintPreviewDialog dlg = new PrintPreviewDialog() ;
    ImagePrintDocument doc = new ImagePrintDocument( image );
    dlg.Document = doc;
    dlg.ShowDialog(this);
}
```

Comments

Creating a print preview dialog for your application can almost be considered a freebie when using the .NET Framework. If you created the `PrintDocument` derived class for your application for printing, you can associate that class with a `PrintPreviewDialog` object. The .NET Framework displays a Windows Form containing the common features associated with most print preview dialogs within Windows. This class also provides the functionality necessary to preview multiple pages at once, zoom the document within the window, and automatically print the document when the user clicks on the print button within the print preview dialog. Figure 10.5 shows a print preview dialog for the image editor application created for this chapter.

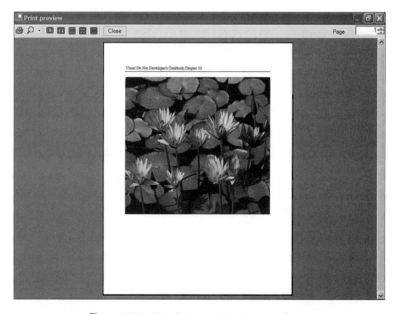

Figure 10.5 Displaying a Print Preview form.

11

Localization and Resources

11.0. Introduction

This chapter looks at two related concepts, localization and resources. The relationship between these two items is purely hierarchical rather than symbiotic. The resource classes form a foundation to store static data that can be embedded within an assembly or loaded dynamically at runtime. Localization sits on top of that foundation and utilizes those classes to dynamically display the correct user-interface elements based on a certain culture. In other words, you can use resources without needing localization, but you can't perform localization without the rich support of the resource classes. The first part of this chapter demonstrates various techniques to localize and globalize your application. The latter part focuses on creating and using resources as an application design decision without regard for localization or globalization.

11.1. Determining a User's Culture Information

You want to determine culture information based on the current settings of the user's operating system.

Technique

You use the `CultureInfo` class to retrieve and set the currently executing thread's culture information. The static method `CurrentCulture` defined within the `CultureInfo` class creates a `CultureInfo` object that you can use to retrieve various cultural properties. Some of these properties include the locale Id (`LCID`), calendars used in that culture, International Organization for Standardization (ISO) identifiers, and the name of the culture as displayed in the language of that culture. Figure 11.1 shows the CultureInfo Browser application created as a supplement for this recipe. The property grid within the application contains the various `CultureInfo` properties for the Farsi culture.

Figure 11.1   The `CultureInfo` class is the primary class used to retrieve information about a user's current culture settings.

Comments

The `CultureInfo` class is the first stepping stone into the globalization realm. Whenever your application executes, the Windows API function `GetUserDefaultLCID` retrieves the locale identifier for the current user. This identifier is then used to create the `CultureInfo` object that you can retrieve with a call to the static `CurrentCulture` method. You are then free to access the various properties within this `CultureInfo` object to effectively display correct information for that culture. Some of the properties that you will most likely access include the `NumberFormatInfo` object used to correctly display culturally aware numbers and the `DateTimeFormat` object used for the correct date and time display or manipulation. Recipes later in this chapter demonstrate how to use these objects.

11.2. Localizing Windows Forms Controls

You want to localize the text displayed on controls and display the correct language based on a user's culture information.

Technique

After creating your Windows Forms application, select the form in the form designer and set the `Localizable` property to `true`. Use the form designer to add controls and set the text using the language you want to use as the default. To add text for a different language, select the form and set the `Language` property to the language you want to localize to. Change the `Text` property for each control to the correct string for that language. You can continue adding new languages by changing the `Language` property of your Windows Form.

Comments

Setting actual translation issues aside, localizing a Windows Form is a rather trivial process. Simply set the `Localizable` property to `true` and then change the `Text` property for each control as you change the `Language` property of the form. However, even though the process is relatively simple, it can be tedious, especially if your application is large and supports many languages. Fortunately, there is a way to speed up this process. Whenever you change the `Language` property of your Windows Form, a new file is created within your project's source directory whose filename is a concatenation of your form's implementation class name and the culture ISO identifier followed by a `.resx` extension. This `.resx` file is an Extensible Markup Language (XML) file used to store that culture's language information. In other words, by simply editing the correct data/value pairs within the `.resx` file, you can localize a language without having to use the forms designer.

Directly editing the generated `.resx` files can be a real time-saver, but you should ensure that the controls display the strings correctly by verifying them within the forms designer. A small string in one language can be a very large string in a different language, and the control that uses that string might not be large enough. Fortunately, you don't have to change the size for that control in every language to accommodate the larger string for that single language. You can also use resource files, `.resx` files, to store object data, which in this case would be the `Size` object defined within a Windows Form control. To resize the control for that single language, set the `Language` property to the correct language and resize the control. The control is then resized only for that language. Recipe 11.5, "Using Fallback Resource for Unsupported Regions," discusses how the .NET Framework uses resource files to load the correct resources at runtime.

11.3. Programmatically Changing the Current Culture

You want to change an application's current culture during runtime.

Technique

The `CurrentCulture` property defined within the `CultureInfo` class allows you to retrieve the currently set culture but doesn't allow you to set it. To specify a new culture for a running application, use the `CurrentUICulture` property defined in the `Thread.CurrentThread` object. Create a `CultureInfo` object by using the new keyword and passing the ISO identifier of the culture and optional country/region identifier or by passing the LCID of the culture:

```
CultureInfo ci1 = new CultureInfo("en-US");
CultureInfo ci2 = new CultureInfo("de");
CultureInfo ci3 = new CultureInfo( 0x0409 );
CultureInfo ci4 = new CultureInfo( 0x0407 );
```

Change the current culture by setting the CurrentUICulture property defined in the currently executing thread object:

```
CultureInfo newci = new CultureInfo("de");
Thread.CurrentThread.CurrentUICulture = newci;
```

Comments

We wish we could tell you that simply changing the current culture of an application during runtime automatically updates the user interface with the new localized strings for that culture's language. Unfortunately, it doesn't, but there is a way to add that functionality to your application as was done for the application that accompanies this recipe, shown in Figure 11.2.

Figure 11.2   You can change the language of the user interface at runtime by setting the CurrentUICulture property and retrieving control text using the ResourceManager class.

As you are well aware, the InitializeComponent method that the Integrated Development Environment (IDE) generates automatically for a Windows Form application is hidden from view by using a code region. When you set the Localizable property to true within the forms designer, the code for the InitializeComponent method changes drastically. Rather than explicitly setting control properties, the method utilizes the ResourceManager class to look up data within resource files to set the various properties for a Windows Form and its associated controls. Using that method as a guide, you can therefore create the code necessary to reload the user interface for the new culture by creating a ResourceManager object and setting the necessary properties using that object. For instance, when a user clicks on the German radio button on the application shown in Figure 11.2, a new `ResourceManager` class is created, and the `TextBox` objects' `Text` properties are set by looking up the corresponding resource string:

```
private void rbGerman_CheckedChanged(object sender, System.EventArgs e)
{
    Thread.CurrentThread.CurrentUICulture = new CultureInfo("de");
    ReloadControlText();
}

private void ReloadControlText()
{
    System.Resources.ResourceManager resources =
        new System.Resources.ResourceManager(typeof(Form1));

    label1.Text = resources.GetString( "label1.Text" );
    label2.Text =  resources.GetString("label2.Text" );
    label3.Text = resources.GetString( "label3.Text" );
}
```

11.4. Enumerating Culture Types

You want to access all the cultures of a given culture type.

Technique

Use the `GetCultures` static method defined in the `CultureInfo` class. This method requires a value from the `CultureTypes` enumerated data type. The four possible values include `CultureTypes.AllCultures`, which retrieves every culture defined in the .NET Framework; the `CultureTypes.InstalledWin32Cultures` value, which returns only the cultures that have been installed on the current system; the `CultureTypes.NeutralCultures` used for cultures that do not have an associated country or region; and the `CultureTypes.SpecificCultures`, which returns cultures that are specific to a certain country or region:

```
public Form1()
{
    InitializeComponent();

    // adds list of cultures to 4 different combo boxes
    foreach( CultureInfo curCI in
        CultureInfo.GetCultures( CultureTypes.AllCultures ))
    {
        cbAll.Items.Add( curCI.DisplayName );
```

```
    }
    foreach( CultureInfo curCI in
        CultureInfo.GetCultures( CultureTypes.InstalledWin32Cultures ))
    {
        cbWin32.Items.Add( curCI.DisplayName );
    }
    foreach( CultureInfo curCI in
        CultureInfo.GetCultures( CultureTypes.NeutralCultures ))
    {
        cbNeutral.Items.Add( curCI.DisplayName );
    }
    foreach( CultureInfo curCI in
        CultureInfo.GetCultures( CultureTypes.SpecificCultures ))
    {
        cbSpecific.Items.Add( curCI.DisplayName );
    }
}
```

Comments

Code reuse is a valuable asset. Almost as valuable is the concept of data reuse. The .NET Framework supports a vast array of cultures and their different country and regions. If you run the application created for this recipe and look at the values returned from the GetCultures method with the CultureTypes.AllCultures parameter, you'll see what we mean. We couldn't even begin to fathom having to manually enter that information in our code. Thankfully, we don't have to because it's already been done within the CultureInfo class.

Cultures work with two key pieces of information. The first is what is known as a *neutral* culture. A neutral culture is one that is not associated with a country or region. For instance, English is spoken in many different places around the world. Therefore, English by itself is a neutral culture. The other key piece is any associated countries or regions that use that cultural information. Continuing with the English example, there are specific cultures for the United States, Great Britain, and Zimbabwe, to name a few.

11.5. Using Fallback Resource for Unsupported Regions

You want cultures that are not supported by your application to use neutral culture resources.

Technique

The `ResourceManager` class uses a hierarchical searching algorithm based on the `CurrentUICulture` of the executing thread to find the correct resources for that culture. To ensure that unsupported specific cultures still receive the correct language strings for their culture, set the `Language` property to a neutral culture when localizing the application.

Comments

Localized resources are created in a hierarchical fashion. When the `ResourceManager` class begins a data lookup for the correct resources to use within an application, it first looks for the resources of the specific culture defined in the `CurrentUICulture` property of the executing thread. For instance, if we were using an English system whose country code was set to Canada, the `ResourceManager` would look for a corresponding `en-CA` resource assembly. Because the application being run doesn't use the word *color* (*colour* in Canada), it doesn't have an `en-CA` resource assembly. The `ResourceManager` then moves up the hierarchy and checks for a neutral resource assembly. In this case, it checks whether an `en` resource is present. If that also fails, it uses the default values embedded within the main assembly.

You might be wondering why we keep referring to the resources as assemblies. Recipe 11.2, "Localizing Windows Forms Controls," showed that a `.resx` file is created whenever you change the `Language` property of a form within the forms designer. This `.resx` filename is a combination of the class name of the Windows Form followed by the culture identifier. If you select a neutral culture, the two-letter ISO identifier is used, and if you select a specific culture, an additional two-letter country/region code is used. You can view the list of `.resx` files within the Solution Explorer by clicking on the Show All Files toolbar button at the top of the Solution Explorer and then expanding the associated Windows Form class. When you select a `.resx` file and view its properties within the Property Browser, you see that the `Build Action` property is set to `Embedded Resource`, as shown in Figure 11.3. This setting tells the compiler to generate a satellite assembly within a subdirectory of the output folder corresponding to the ISO identifier of the culture specified. The `ResourceManager`, using the ISO information within the `CurrentUICulture` object, searches the subdirectories of the executing assembly, and if it finds the correct satellite assembly, it loads it and extracts the correct string information being requested for that culture. All of this functionality happens behind the scenes without any extra work needed on your part. However, being able to perform this method using ordinary resources is a valuable technique to learn and is discussed in Recipe 11.9, "Creating and Using Satellite Assemblies."

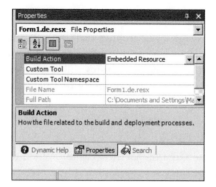

Figure 11.3 When Build Action is set to Embedded Resource, the
compiler automatically generates satellite assemblies.

11.6. Formatting Numbers Correctly Based on Culture

You want to ensure that you correctly format any numbers that are displayed
to a user based on her culture.

Technique

Numbers can be formatted by objects that support the IFormatProvider interface. For
applications that need to display numbers in different cultures other than the current
culture, create a new CultureInfo object and pass the NumberFormatInfo property as
the IFormatProvider parameter. For instance, to display a number with thousands and
decimal separators based on a given culture, the code appears as follows:

```
private void numericUpDown1_ValueChanged(object sender, System.EventArgs e)
{
    // demonstrates formatting a value using correct
    // culture number format cbLanguage is a combobox
    // containing specific cultures using ISO identifiers
    NumberFormatInfo currentNFI = new
        CultureInfo( cbLanguage.SelectedItem.ToString(), false ).NumberFormat;

    lblUpDown.Text = numericUpDown1.Value.ToString("N", currentNFI);
}
```

Comments

Various methods within the .NET Framework such as ToString and Parse allow you to specify how formatting should be performed by using an object that implements the IFormatProvider interface. For numerical data, the NumberFormatInfo object defined within a CultureInfo object allows you to format a number correctly for a given culture.

By default, you might find that you really never need to pass an IFormatProvider to these methods. If you do not specify a format provider, the default provider for the CurrentCulture is used. For instance, if you remove the currentNFI parameter in the ToString method shown earlier, the number is formatted correctly on a German system and likewise for a user running on an English install.

11.7. Displaying Culture Aware Date and Time

You want to ensure that you format any date and time information so that it appears correctly within a specific culture.

Technique

The CultureInfo class contains a DateTimeFormatInfo object used to format date and time information for a specific culture. Create a new CultureInfo object and use the DateTimeFormatInfo property of that object in any methods that utilize an IFormatProvider parameter. Also, just as you can use a format specifier to control how a number is displayed, various date and time format specifiers control how the date and time appears within that given culture. The following code shows how to display different date formats within a given culture using a CultureInfo's DateTimeFormatInfo property and various format specifiers:

```
currentDTFI = new CultureInfo("de-DE", false ).DateTimeFormat;
Console.WriteLine(DateTime.Today.ToString("d", currentDTFI ));
Console.WriteLine(DateTime.Today.ToString("D", currentDTFI ));
Console.WriteLine(DateTime.Today.ToString("f", currentDTFI ));
Console.WriteLine(DateTime.Today.ToString("F", currentDTFI ));
```

Comments

Again, just as it isn't necessary to specify a NumberFormatInfo object to format a number using a user's default culture, there is no need to specify a DateTimeFormatInfo object either. However, when you in fact need to display date and time information for a culture that is different from the CurrentCulture object within the CultureInfo class, the code in the "Technique" section allows you to do so.

11.8. Formatting Currency for a Specific Culture

> You want to format a number so that it is displayed as a currency for a given culture.

Technique

Displaying currency information is similar to displaying culturally aware numerical data. Because currency itself is a number, you can use the same technique of passing a `NumberFormatInfo` object into a method that utilizes an `IFormatProvider` parameter. To change a number so it is formatted as currency, use the currency format specifier within the method:

```
private void numericUpDown1_ValueChanged(object sender, System.EventArgs e)
{
    // demonstrates formatting a value using correct culture number format
    NumberFormatInfo currentNFI =
        new CultureInfo(cbLanguage.SelectedItem.ToString(),false).NumberFormat;

    // C is the currency format specifier
    lblCurrency.Text = numericUpDown1.Value.ToString( "C", currentNFI );
}
```

Comments

Currency itself is simply a number, and which is why there is no need for a `CurrencyFormatInfo` object. The `NumberFormatInfo` class contains several currency-related properties that it uses within its `GetFormat` method to correctly format a number as a currency value. Also, you only need to specify a `NumberFormatInfo` object if you want to display a currency value in a culture different from that of the user's current culture. One thing you should know is that the formatting does not take current exchange rates into consideration.

11.9. Creating and Using Satellite Assemblies

> You want to create resource libraries that you can load at runtime based on the current culture of the executing thread. You also want to include images as well as strings within the resource assembly.

Technique

The first step to create a satellite assembly is to create a resource file. There are two main ways to do so, and each method depends on the design of your application. To create a satellite assembly that simply houses localized strings, create a text file containing key/value pairs on separate lines:

```
myString1=This is a string.
myString2=This is another string.
```

To create a resource file that uses images in addition to strings, you can use the `ResEditor` tool. Before you can use the tool however, you must compile it. By default, the source is located in the following folder:

```
C:\Program Files\Microsoft Visual Studio .NET
2003\SDK\v1.1\Samples\Tutorials\resourcesandlocalization\reseditor
```

Build the application by running the supplied `build.bat` file. After launching the tool, add new resources by selecting the type of the resource from the Add drop-down box, giving the resource an identifying string, and clicking the Add button. The resource appears within the property grid, and you can then edit it by either entering the string value for a string object or browsing to an image file for a `Bitmap` object. When you are finished, save the resource file, ensuring that you choose the `.resx` file format from the file type drop-down box in the Save File dialog.

Once you create the necessary text or `.resx` files, add them to your solution by selecting Project, Add Existing Item. If you are adding text files, you have to perform one additional step. Select the text file within the Solution Explorer and change the Build Action property from `Content` to `Embedded Resource`, as shown in Figure 11.4.

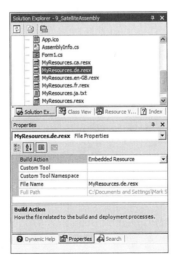

Figure 11.4   When adding localized strings in a text file to a project, you have to change the `Build Action` to `Embedded Resource` to build satellite assemblies.

If you want to create satellite assemblies for different cultures, add the ISO identifier for the culture and an optional dash (-) and country/region identifier in the filename. For instance, a default resource can be named `MyResources.resx`, but that same resource with localized content for different cultures would be named `MyResources.en.resx` or `MyResource.en-GB.resx`.

Comments

Recipe 11.2 demonstrates a technique you can use to localize the text for each control on a Windows Form using the forms designer. What you don't see, however, is what is going on underneath the virtual IDE hood. Whenever the `Language` property of the Windows Form changes, a new resource file with a `.resx` file extension is created. `.resx` files are XML-based files containing a group of key and value elements. These `.resx` files are automatically added to the project as embedded resources. When the application is built, separate resource-only assemblies, known as *satellite assemblies*, are created. Based on the culture and optional country/region of that resource file, the compiler places these assemblies in a subdirectory underneath your main executing assembly. During runtime, the `ResourceManager` class created within the `InitializeComponent` method searches the correct subdirectory based on the `CurrentUICulture` to locate the correct resource assembly.

This nice feature adds value to you as a developer, so you should use it to your advantage. The "Technique" portion of this recipe demonstrates how to manually perform the same steps the compiler uses to create satellite assemblies for localized Windows Forms data. The process itself might seem a little obscure, however, because it revolves around a tool shipped as a sample within the .NET Framework software development kit (SDK). The reason, which is clearer in Recipe 11.11, "Saving Resource Information Using the `ResourceWriter` Class," is that resources are simply objects and creating a tool that can embed all possible objects within a resource file would be a cumbersome task. One could argue, however, that most satellite assemblies usually only contain string and image resources, which would necessitate a built-in IDE tool, but we leave politics for the politicians and concentrate on the technique instead.

If you choose to use the `ResEditor` tool to create your resource files, you might have noticed that you have the option of saving the final file as a `.resx` or `.resources` file. A `.resources` file is the binary form of a resource file. We encourage you to refrain from initially saving your resources in this file format. Because a `.resx` file is a simple text file, you are free to edit any values using a simple text editor. Also, once you add the `.resx` file to the project, the compiler converts it to a `.resources` file before it creates the satellite assembly. If you choose to save your resource file in the `.resources` binary format, realize that to edit it, you have to use a custom tool such as `ResEditor`.

11.10. Using `ResourceReader` to Display an Image Resource

You want to load an `Image` from a satellite assembly to display it on a Windows Form.

Technique

To load an image within a satellite assembly, create an instance of the `ResourceManager` class passing the root name of the resources and a reference to the `Assembly` object where the resources are defined. In most cases, you can simply use the `GetExecutingAssembly` static method defined in the `Assembly` class if you are retrieving resources within the same application:

```
// create a resourcemanager to load satellite assembly
ResourceManager resMan = new ResourceManager(
    "_9_SatelliteAssemblyClient.MyResources",
    Assembly.GetExecutingAssembly() );
```

Once you create the `ResourceManager`, you can use its various methods to extract resources using the name of the resource given when you created the resource file. To extract a string, use the `GetString` method, passing the string identifier as the parameter. To extract any other data type within the resource file, use the `GetObject` method. It returns a `System.Object`, which you can then cast to the appropriate data type such as `Image` for images:

```
// set picture box
pbFlag.Image = (Image) resMan.GetObject( "flag" );


// set label
lblHello.Text = resMan.GetString( "Hello" );
```

Comments

One common pitfall with creating resource files using the methods demonstrated in this and the last recipe is filenames. When you create a `ResourceManager` object, you need to pass the root name of the resource file to use. The confusion arises from the name given to the `.resx` file that was added to the project and the name of the `.resources` file that the compiler automatically generates. When the embedded resource is built into a satellite assembly, a `.resources` file is created whose filename is a combination of the project name and the original name given to the `.resx` file. In other words, if you create a resource file named `MyResources.en-GB.resx` within a project named `MyProject`, the generated `.resources` file is `MyProject.MyResources.en-GB.resources`. The base name for this resource is everything in the filename except for the ISO culture identifiers and file extension, which for this example would be `MyProject.MyResources`.

Once you create the `ResourceManager` object, retrieving objects from the resource file is trivial. Based on the `CurrentUICulture`, the `ResourceManager` handles the job of finding the correct satellite assembly and retrieving the requested resource. All that you need is the associated `GetString` and `GetObject` method calls to retrieve those resources. In the code associated with this recipe, you can see how different culture-based resources are used at runtime to extract a given country's animated flag and a localized `Hello` string.

11.11. Saving Resource Information Using the `ResourceWriter` Class

You want to create a custom resource that you can use within a satellite assembly.

Technique

Create the object definition of the resource you want to store in a satellite assembly, making sure that you place the `Serializable` attribute before the class declaration:

```
using System;
using System.Drawing;

namespace _11_ResourceObjects
{
    [Serializable]
    public class ImageWithCaption
    {
        public string caption;
        public Image image;

        public ImageWithCaption( string caption, Image image )
        {
            this.caption = caption;
            this.image = image;
        }

        public string Caption
        {
            get
            {
                return this.caption;
            }
            set
            {
                this.caption = value;
```

```
            }
        }

        public Image Picture
        {
            get
            {
                return this.image;
            }
            set
            {
                this.image = value;
            }
        }
    }
}
```

After creating an instance of the resource object, or any other object, you can save it to a
.resources file by using the ResourceWriter class or a .resx file using a
ResXResourceWriter instance. Using either one of these classes is similar, with the difference being the file format output. Each constructor expects a Stream to write data to
or a string value denoting the filename. After you create the appropriate object, use the
AddResource method, passing an object to save to the resource file. After you add all the
necessary resources, call the Generate method to create the resource file. Keep in mind
that any attempts to add resources after the Generate method has been called result in
an exception.

The following function uses the list view data in Figure 11.5 to write several
ImageWithCaption objects, which were shown earlier:

```
private void btnSave_Click(object sender, System.EventArgs e)
{
    if( saveFileDialog1.ShowDialog() == DialogResult.OK )
    {
        ResourceWriter rw = new ResourceWriter( saveFileDialog1.FileName );

        foreach( ListViewItem lvItem in lvItems.Items )
        {
            _11_ResourceObjects.ImageWithCaption obj =
                new _11_ResourceObjects.ImageWithCaption(
                    lvItem.SubItems[0].Text,
                    Image.FromFile( lvItem.SubItems[1].Text ));
            rw.AddResource( lvItem.SubItems[0].Text, obj );
        }

        rw.Generate();
    }
}
```

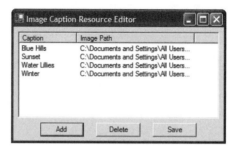

Figure 11.5 The Image Caption Resource Editor saves custom resource objects into a resource file that is later compiled into satellite assemblies.

Comments

We admit that when we first started looking at programmatically creating resources, we thought that we would never need to use that capability. However, after creating the code that accompanies this recipe, you could say that our eyes were opened. When you get across the hurdle of thinking that resources consist only of string or image data, you might be able to think of creative ways to use custom resources. The code that accompanies this recipe is separated into three different projects. The first project is a simple class library used to define a custom resource object named ImageWithCaption. By itself, it isn't some elaborate object that will win any awards. It's just a simple class containing a string and Image object without appropriate accessor properties.

Another project created the resource files themselves using a custom resource editor that, as you guessed, creates ImageWithCaption resource files. You can see the application running in Figure 11.5. Some of the code for this application uses the ResourceWriter class to generate .resources files. These files can then be embedded into an assembly by creating satellite assemblies or can be read at runtime, which is what the third and final application does.

You do not have to use the resource classes within the .NET Framework solely for satellite assembly resource access. You are free to use .resources directly at runtime, although we don't recommend doing so. The last project associated with this recipe reads the .resources file created by the resource editor and displays an image with its associated caption, as shown in Figure 11.6.

Figure 11.6   This application reads `ImageWithCaption` resource objects
created with the editor in Figure 11.5.

Data Access

12

File I/O and Serialization

12.0. Introduction

This chapter shows the necessary steps to read and write to a file, use the local file system, and create persistent objects through a process known as *serialization*. This chapter really serves as the foundation for some of the data access chapters in the remainder of this section. For instance, in the next chapter, you'll see how to read and write XML files. The methods for doing so tie into the information in this chapter.

12.1. Creating a New File

You want to programmatically create a new file on the local file system.

Technique

One of the first things you have to consider before you start writing the code to write data to a file is the file format. When we say file format, however, we don't mean how the data itself is logically organized within the file but instead the type of data that will eventually be written. A file is either text-based or binary, although the differences between the two are fuzzy because files by nature are always binary. However, text-based file formats write data out according to its string representation. For instance, if you want to write integer values to a text file, the ASCII values of the integers rather than the integers themselves are written. In other words, if you write the integer 42 to a text file, you actually write the ASCII equivalent of 0x34 and 0x32, representing each digit. A binary formatting scheme uses the actual value of 42.

To create new file in preparation for writing text, use the `StreamWriter` class in conjunction with the `File.CreateText` method. The `CreateText` method has a single parameter, which is the path of the file to create:

```
private void SaveText( string text, string file )
{
    StreamWriter sw = null;

    try
    {
        // 1. Creating a new file for text output
        sw = File.CreateText( file );
    }
    catch( Exception e )
    {
        MessageBox.Show( e.Message );
    }
    finally
    {
        if( sw != null )
            sw.Close();
    }
}
```

Whenever data is written using the method just mentioned, data is converted to its ASCII equivalent. Whenever you open the file in a simple text editor, the data is readable. The converse is writing binary data. There are a myriad different ways to create a file for binary output. One of these, similar to the method shown earlier, is to call the Create method defined in the File class. This method returns a FileStream object:

```
private void SaveBinary( byte[] bytes, string file )
{
    FileStream fs = null;

    try
    {
        if( File.Exists( file ) )
        {
            File.Delete(file);
        }

        //1. Creating a new file for binary output
        fs = File.Create( file );
        fs.Write( bytes, 0, bytes.Length );
    }
    catch( Exception e )
    {
        MessageBox.Show( e.Message );
    }
    finally
    {
```

```
        if( fs != null )
            fs.Close();
    }
}
```

Comments

The concept of text- and binary-based file formats is an important one. Each one has its advantages and disadvantages. In some cases, however, the answer on which format to support is pretty clear cut. Text-based formats have the distinct advantage of human readability. If your application uses a text-based file formats, you have a large assortment of external text-editing tools at your disposal. Sure, you can edit binary files using a hex editor, but the possibility of entering bad data is extremely high in those circumstances. One disadvantage of text that is an advantage for binary files is size. If you recall, the integer 42 actually translates into 2 bytes in a text file, one for each digit. In a binary file, you can write that same data in only 1 byte. When the data is of considerable size, the resultant file size is orders of magnitude bigger in a text-based format than in a binary format.

The `StreamWriter` and `FileStream` classes are both specializations of certain .NET base classes. The `StreamWriter` is a `TextWriter` object, which makes sense because its purpose is to write textual data to a file. Some of the other derived classes include the `HtmlTextWriter`, which contains methods to output HTML tags and attributes; the `StringWriter`, which performs writing on a string object rather than an actual file; and the `HttpWriter` class, which sends data to a remote client application.

The `FileStream` is one class in a group of `Stream`-based classes. Some of these classes are designed to work with binary values in memory, networking, and cryptography. Each one of these classes simply represents a specialized way to write out a sequence of bytes to their applicable destinations.

12.2. Verifying the Existence of a File

You want to verify that a file exists given the path to that file.

Technique

The `File` class contains a method named `Exists`, which returns a Boolean value:

```
if( File.Exists( file ) )
{
    File.Delete( file );
}
```

Comments

The `Exists` method returns `true` if a file exists at a specified location or `false` if it doesn't. However, if the current security permissions on the file don't allow the user to access it, the `Exists` method returns `false` even though the file does exist.

The path to the file can be either a relative or absolute path. An *absolute* path is the full path of the file starting from the drive letter. A file named `file.txt` located in the `temp` directory of the hard drive therefore has an absolute path of

```
c:\temp\file.txt
```

A *relative* path means the file is relative to a certain location. This location is the current directory of the operating system. Take note that it isn't always the directory your application is running in. To determine the current directory, call the static method `Directory.GetCurrentDirectory`. If you do in fact want to retrieve the directory that your application is running from, call the static method `Application.StartupPath`. An example of an app trying to discover the existence of itself includes code such as the following:

```
Directory.SetCurrentDirectory( Application.StartupPath );
if( File.Exists("1_FileView.exe ") )
{
    MessageBox.Show( "I Am" );
}
```

12.3. Opening a File for Reading Using the File Class

You want to open a file for reading either text or binary data.

Technique

The technique for opening a file is similar to the techniques in Section 12.1, "Creating a New File." However, instead of two methods based on either text or binary formats, opening a file actually has three. The comments section explains why a third method exists.

To open a file for text-based reading, call the `OpenText` method defined in the `File` class. Like all methods in the `File` class, it is static, so you don't need a `File` object instance. `OpenText` returns a `StreamReader` object used to eventually read the textual data from the file:

```
private string OpenText( string file )
{
    StreamReader sr = null;

    try
```

```
    {
        // open the file
        sr = File.OpenText( file );
    }
    catch( Exception e )
    {
        MessageBox.Show( e.Message );
    }
    finally
    {
        // close the StreamReader
        if( sr != null )
            sr.Close();
    }

    // placeholder
    return "";
}
```

To open a file so that its individual byte data can be read, call the OpenRead method. This method returns a FileStream object, which you recall is the same object type used when creating a new binary file:

```
private byte[] OpenBinary( string file )
{
    FileStream fs = null;
    try
    {
        // open the file
        fs = File.OpenRead( file );
    }
    catch( Exception e )
    {
        MessageBox.Show( e.Message );
    }
    finally
    {
        // close the FileStream
        if( fs != null )
            fs.Close();
    }

    // placeholder
    return null;
}
```

Comments

Opening a file using the `File` class is quite similar to the methods for creating a new file. Each method, regardless of the eventual data format, takes a single string parameter denoting the location of the file that you want to work with. A third open method takes additional parameters.

The `Open` method is a method that combines the ability to open an existing file and create a new file if so desired. In other words, you can use this method in place of any of the methods discussed so far (including the `Exists` method from Section 12.2, "Verifying the Existence of a File"). Depending on the level of control that you want, there are four overloaded versions of this method with each version allowing more control. The first parameter for these methods is a string representing the filename. If that is the only parameter to the method, then it is equivalent to calling the `OpenRead` method. The second parameter is a value from the `FileMode` enumerated data type. This value allows you to control how the file should be accessed in a variety of circumstances. If you specify `FileMode.Append`, the file is opened and its file pointer set to the end of the file so that any subsequent read or write method calls begin at the end of the file. Of course, calling a read operation at the end of the file results in an exception being thrown. If a file is not found, then a new one is created.

`FileMode.Create` creates a new file. If the file exists, it is overwritten. `FileMode.CreateNew` is similar to the previous value, but if the value already exists, an exception is thrown. You can therefore use this value to check for the existence of a file, but rather than take a performance hit to handle the exception, you are better off simply calling the `Exists` method. You use `FileMode.Truncate` when a file already exists and you want its contents to be overwritten. If you just want to create a file and have it work regardless of whether the file exists, use the `FileMode.Create` value.

`FileMode.Open` and `FileMode.OpenOrCreate` are similar to the create values just mentioned. The `Open` value throws an exception if the file does not exist, whereas the `OpenOrCreate` value does not.

The third optional parameter to the `Open` method is a flag telling the method what you plan to do with the file. The value is from the `FileAccess` enumerated data type and can be set to read the file, write to the file, or do both operations. This setting corresponds to the values `Read`, `Write`, and `ReadWrite`, respectively.

Finally, the last parameter is a value used to specify the level of file access for any external threads that want to use the file. You can allow threads to access for reading, writing, doing a combination of the two, or doing nothing at all. If you have the file open for reading, for instance, you want to use `FileShare.Read` or `FileShare.None` to prevent external threads from writing to the file as you're trying to read. Very rarely will you want to set the parameter to `FileShare.Write`. Doing so entails proper synchronization code to ensure data integrity.

12.4. Using the `FileInfo` Class to Display File Information

You want to determine various attributes of an existing file.

Technique

The `FileInfo` class contains properties that allow you to retrieve information about an existing file. One of them is the attributes of a file. The `Attributes` property returns a `FileAttributes` enumerated data type specifying whether the file is read only, archived, hidden, and many others. To determine whether a file is read only, bitwise AND (&) the result of calling `GetAttributes` with the `FileAttributes.ReadOnly` value. If the result is greater than 0, the file is read only:

```
FileInfo fileInfo = new FileInfo( filePath );
if( (fileInfo.Attributes & FileAttributes.ReadOnly) > 0 )
    MessageBox.Show( "File is read only" );
```

You can also retrieve file access times. They include the properties `CreationTime`, which is a `DateTime` object corresponding to the time the file was created; `LastAccessTime`, corresponding to the last time the file was accessed either for reading or writing; and `LastWriteTime`, which represents the last time data was written to the file.

A few path-location properties let you retrieve information about the file as it relates to the local file system. For instance, to retrieve the current directory name of the file, access the `DirectoryName` property. If you want to actually manipulate that directory, then retrieve the corresponding `Directory` object by accessing the `Directory` property. Finally, to retrieve the filename of the file, you can use the `Name` property, which returns the name of the file; the `FullName` property, which returns the full path and filename of the file; or the `Extension` property, which retrieves the file's extension.

Comments

The `FileInfo` class shares a lot of similarities with the `File` class, but the differences are enough to warrant a section of its own. The major difference between the two classes is that `FileInfo` methods are all instance methods, whereas the `File` class methods are all static. Having all instance methods can be beneficial if you plan to reuse the same object over and over within your class. For instance, if you were using a `File` class to work with a file, you would have to keep a copy of the file path around to access such things as file attributes. Once you create the `FileInfo` object, however, all the relevant information is contained within the object and can be retrieved at any time. If your application only occasionally needs to perform file I/O, then using either one of these classes isn't any better than the other. In most instances, the method signatures and functionality are the same, although the `FileInfo` methods don't need the mandatory string value denoting the location of the file you want to operate on, as is the case with the `File` class.

12.5. Copying and Moving a File

You want to copy or move a file from one location on the local file system to a different location.

Technique

The `FileInfo` and `File` classes both contain methods to manipulate files without having to perform any type of I/O methods on them beforehand. This section looks at the `File` methods, but the methods work with the `FileInfo` class as well. The previous section discusses some of the differences between the two.

To copy a file to a different location, call the static `Copy` method. This method accepts two strings denoting the full path of the source and the destination to copy the file to. Note that the filenames themselves don't have to be the same. If the filenames are the same, an optional Boolean value tells the method what to do. If you set this value to `true`, the destination file is overwritten. Setting the value to `false` causes the method to throw an exception if the final destination file already exists. If no value is specified, then the method throws an exception if the file exists. In other words, the default overwrite method is set to `false`:

```
private void mnuSaveAs_Click(object sender, System.EventArgs e)
{
    if( saveFileDialog1.ShowDialog(this) == DialogResult.OK )
    {
        // back up the file first by copying it a new file
        File.Copy( curFilePath, "bkup.bak", true );

        // save to new file
        SaveText( tbView.Text, saveFileDialog1.FileName );

        // update new filename
        curFilePath = saveFileDialog1.FileName;

        // reset dirty flag
        bDirty = false;

        // update window title to remove dirty indicator
        this.Text = "Simple Pad - " + curFilePath;
    }
}
```

Moving a file utilizes the same methodology. The method to move a file is called `Move`, and it accepts the same type of parameters as the `Copy` method. One thing that you must ensure is that you don't have a stream open on the source file. If the file is open and inaccessible to outside processes, an exception is thrown and the method fails. One notable difference between `Move` and `Copy`, other than the fact that the source file is removed when calling `Move`, is the absence of the overwrite flag. Because the method is designed to move the file from one location to another, the destination file cannot exist. The workaround is to call the `File.Exists` method on the destination file, and if it returns `true`, call `File.DeleteFile` before moving:

```
try
{
    if( File.Exists( destPath ) )
        File.Delete( destPath );
    File.Move( srcPath, destPath );
}
catch( Exception e )
{
    MessageBox( e.Message );
}
```

Comments

Moving and copying files from one location to another is pretty straightforward when using the `File` or `FileInfo` class. One thing that you have to be wary of, however, is the time it takes to move or copy a file. Both of these methods are synchronous, which means they do not return until the operation finishes. If the file you are copying or moving is large, then your application appears as if it has hung. To combat this issue, you have to use the threading techniques discussed in Chapter 22, "Threading and Synchronization," to keep the Windows messages flowing on your main UI thread.

Additionally, there is no default user interface showing the progress of the file-copy operation. Whenever you copy or move a file within Windows Explorer, you'll notice a small window with an animation denoting what Explorer is currently doing. For large files, this window stays up for a considerably longer amount of time—as compared to smaller files in which you see just a quick flash as the window quickly opens and closes. You can, however, use one of the shell functions in `shell32.dll` named `SHFileOperation` to perform a copy or move and display the animation window. To do so, you utilize something called `PInvoke`, which is discussed in Chapter 21, "Securing Your Code."

12.6. Making a File Read Only

You want to change the read-only attribute on a file.

Technique

You can use the `SetAttributes` method defined in the `File` class or the `Attributes` property defined in the `FileInfo` class to change various attributes of a file, one of which is the read-only attribute. To change just the read-only attribute without affecting any other attributes, use bitwise operators on the current attributes of the file with the attribute you want to change. For instance, to make a file read only, use the logical OR (|) operator:

```
File.SetAttributes( fileName, File.GetAttributes(fileName) |
FileAttributes.ReadOnly );
```

To remove the read-only attribute from a file, perform a logical AND (&) with the current file attributes and the bitwise complement of the `FileAttributes.ReadOnly` value. The bitwise complement operator is the tilde (~) character:

```
File.SetAttributes( fileName, File.GetAttributes(fileName) &
(~FileAttributes.ReadOnly) );
```

Comments

The technique just discussed uses a well-known method for manipulating bit fields. The `FileAttributes` enumerated data type contains values corresponding to a single bit of an integer. In other words, the value 1 corresponds to the value `ReadOnly`, 2 is for the `Hidden` attribute, 4 denotes a `System` file, and so on. If you want to set a certain attribute on a file without affecting any other attributes that are set or cleared, you can simply logically OR the attribute you want to set with the current attribute list. For example, if a file has its hidden attribute set and you also want to set it to read only, you use the code shown earlier. If you look at the values as bits, you see the following:

0 0 1 0 = current attributes

0 0 0 1 = `FileAttributes.ReadOnly`

0 0 1 1 = current | `ReadOnly`

Note that if the `Hidden` attribute is cleared to begin with, it remains clear because 0 | 0 = 0. If you then want to turn the `FileAttributes.Hidden` value off, you must first take the bitwise complement of the `FileAttributes.Hidden` value and logically AND (&) it with the current attribute list. The bitwise complement is the result of changing any 1s to 0s and any 0s to 1s:

0 0 1 1 = current attributes

1 1 0 1 = bitwise complement of `FileAttribute.Hidden`

0 0 0 1 = current and `Hidden` complement

Although you can use this technique with many other enumerated data types within the .NET framework, you must ensure that the values in the enumeration follow a bit-flag pattern. If the values are anything other than a 2^n domain you have to utilize a different method.

12.7. Writing to a File

You want to write data to a text-based or binary file.

Technique

Section 12.1 explained how to create a new file in preparation for writing text or bytes to it. When you create a new text file, you receive a `StreamWriter` object. The `Write` method defined in this object is able to take most .NET data types and write their values to the file. One particular note, which has been mentioned before, is that the data is written according to its ASCII equivalent. If you call the `Write` method and pass a `float` data type, each digit is converted to its actual ASCII table value. Because the `Write` method contains several overloaded versions, each accepting a different .NET data type, you should have no problem sending it data as you see fit:

```
private void SaveText( string text, string file )
{
    StreamWriter sw = null;

    try
    {
        // Check if file exists
        if( File.Exists( file ) )
        {
            File.Delete( file );
        }

        // Create a new file for text output
        sw = File.CreateText( file );
        sw.Write( text );
    }
    catch( Exception e )
    {
        MessageBox.Show( e.Message );
    }
    finally
    {
        if( sw != null )
            sw.Close();
    }
}
```

If you want to write your data to a binary files:format of, use the `BinaryWriter` class by creating an instance and passing the `FileStream` object returned from the `Open` method of the `File` class to the constructor. To write to the file, call the `Write` method from the

`BinaryWriter` object. This method is one of those methods that contain a lot of over-loaded versions, and each version allows you to write out a certain data type. For instance, to write an integer, call the `Write` method passing an integer, but to write a string, call the `Write` method with a string:

```
private void TestBinaryWrite( string file )
{
    FileStream fs = null;
    BinaryWriter bw;

    try
    {
        // open the file
        fs = File.Open( file, FileMode.Create );
        bw = new BinaryWriter( fs );

        // write 5 integers
        for( int i = 0; i < 5; ++i )
        {
            bw.Write(i);
        }

        // write 5 strings
        for( int i = 0; i < 5; ++i )
        {
            bw.Write( "string" + i.ToString() );
        }
    }
    catch( Exception e )
    {
        MessageBox.Show( e.Message );
    }
    finally
    {
        // close the FileStream
        if( fs != null )
            fs.Close();
    }

    return;
}
```

Comments

As you can see from the two different techniques just shown, writing to either a text-based file or in binary really isn't that much different. The differences lie in how that data is finally translated internally within the classes and written to the file. The

`BinaryWriter` actually performs some additional work to ensure data integrity when the data is finally read by the corresponding `BinaryReader` mentioned in the next section. When a certain data type is written to the file, the `BinaryWriter` writes out a number of bytes equivalent to the size of the data type. For instance, if you pass an integer to the `Write` method that is less than 255, you could actually utilize a single byte of data. However, the `BinaryWriter` writes 4 bytes of data regardless of how small the actual value is. The remaining bytes in this case are all 0s. If size constraints are within the design constraints of your application, then you need to take this fact into account.

If a binary file contains string data, how does the `BinaryReader` know how many bytes to read of that string unless you specifically tell it the amount (which in and of itself would be difficult)? Whenever these situations occur, the data is prefaced with the size of the corresponding data. With strings, the length of the string is written, followed by the string itself.

12.8. Reading from a File

You want to read the text from a text-based file, make changes, and write the result back out to the file.

Technique

Section 12.1 used the `File.OpenText` method to open an existing text file from the local file system. This method returns a `StreamReader` object that you can use to read text into a string. You can choose to read a single character at a time, a single line at a time, a block of characters, or the entire file at once. To read a single character, use the method `Read` with no parameters. This method returns an integer value representing the ASCII code of the character, which you can cast to its `char` equivalent. This method differs with respect to the return value from the other read methods because it returns a `-1` if the end of file was reached. The other methods return the integer `0` at the end of a file:

```
private string OpenText( string file )
{
    string result = "";
    int curChar = 0;

    // open file
    StreamReader sr = File.OpenText( file );

    // read each character and place in string
    while((curChar = sr.Read()) != -1 )
        result += (char)curChar;

    // close streamreader
    sr.Close();
```

```
    // return result
    return result;
}
```

Instead of reading a file character by character, you can break the reading into blocks by reading a certain number of characters during each read operation. You can use the `Read` method in this instance as well as the `ReadBlock` method. Both of these methods use the same number and types of parameters, so either one works the same. To read blocks of character data, create a character array and pass it as the first parameter to the method, followed by the starting index to place the characters at in the array and the number of characters to read. Note that if the number of characters that you request to read is larger than the size of the character array being passed in, an `ArgumentException` is thrown:

```
private string OpenText( string file )
{
    StreamReader sr = null;
    char[] tempBuffer = new char[10];
    StringBuilder result = new StringBuilder("");

    try
    {
        sr = File.OpenText( file );
        while( sr.Read( tempBuffer, 0, 10 ) != 0 )
        {
            result.Append(tempBuffer);
        }
    }
    catch( Exception e )
    {
        MessageBox.Show( e.Message );
    }
    finally
    {
        // close streamreader
        if( sr != null )
            sr.Close();
    }

    // return result
    return result.ToString();
}
```

If you want to read the entire file all at once into a `string` object, call the `ReadToEnd` method defined in the `StreamReader` class. It reads the remainder of the file based on the current location of the internal file pointer of the `StreamReader` class. In other words, if you initially read characters by calling the `Read` method, calling `ReadToEnd` would continue where the last `Read` took place:

```
private string OpenText( string file )
{
    StreamReader sr = null;
    string contents = "";

    try
    {
        // open the file
        sr = File.OpenText( file );
        contents = sr.ReadToEnd();

    }
    catch( Exception e )
    {
        MessageBox.Show( e.Message );
    }
    finally
    {
        // close the StreamReader
        if( sr != null )
            sr.Close();
    }

    // placeholder
    return contents;
}
```

If you are reading binary files, then use a `BinaryReader` class to effectively parse the binary data as it comes in. To create a `BinaryReader` object, pass the `FileStream` object that was created when the file was opened into the `BinaryReader` constructor. Several methods within the `BinaryReader` class read a given .NET data type. For instance, to read an integer, call the `ReadInt32` method, and to read a string, call the `ReadString` method:

```
private void TestBinaryRead( string file )
{
    FileStream fs = null;
    BinaryReader br;
    int[] intData = new int[5];
    string[] strData = new string[5];

    try
    {
        // open the file
        fs = File.OpenRead( file );
        br = new BinaryReader( fs );
```

```
        // read 5 integers
        for( int i = 0; i < 5; ++i )
        {
            intData[i] = br.ReadInt32();
        }

        // read 5 string
        for( int i = 0; i < 5; ++i )
        {
            strData[i] = br.ReadString();
        }
    }
    catch( Exception e )
    {
        MessageBox.Show( e.Message );
    }
    finally
    {
        // close the FileStream
        if( fs != null )
            fs.Close();
    }

    // display data
    StringBuilder sb = new StringBuilder();

    sb.Append( "Int Data: " );
    for( int i = 0; i < 5; ++i ) sb.Append( intData[i].ToString() + " " );

    sb.Append( "\nString Data: " );
    for( int i = 0; i < 5; ++i ) sb.Append( strData[i] + " " );

    MessageBox.Show( sb.ToString() );
    return;
}
```

Comments

Reading a file character-by-character has performance issues associated with it for large files. If you don't need character-by-character processing, then the remaining methods are faster. That being said, even if you are doing character-by-character processing, reading larger chunks of data and then parsing the in-memory representation would eliminate any performance issues. In any case, if your application is designed to work with large files, Chapter 22 demonstrates how to use threading to create worker threads while leaving the user-interface thread free to process incoming events.

In the previous section, you saw how to write binary data by utilizing the `Write` method defined in the `BinaryWriter` class. When using the `BinaryReader` and `BinaryWriter` classes together, you can easily start to formulate custom file formats merely by keeping the reading and writing in synch. For instance, if your application consists of a series of records, each of which contains four integer values followed by two strings and then five `bool` values, you can easily begin to create your own parser to write that data in the format one record at a time and subsequently read any file using that format with the `BinaryReader` class.

12.9. Appending Data to an Existing File

You want to append data to a file.

Technique

The `File` class contains a method named `AppendText` that opens a file and sets the current starting point at the end. Any subsequent calls to `Write` will result in data being written to the end of the file. Additionally, if the file does not exist when `AppendText` is called, a new file is created:

```
using System;
using System.IO;

namespace _9_AppendText
{
    class Class1
    {
        [STAThread]
        static void Main(string[] args)
        {
            if( args.Length <= 0 || args.Length > 2 )
            {
                DisplayUsage();
                return;
            }

            if( File.Exists( args[0] ) == false )
            {
                DisplayUsage();
                return;
            }

            StreamWriter sw = File.AppendText( args[0] );
            sw.Write( args[1] );
```

```
        sw.Close();
        return;
    }

    static void DisplayUsage()
    {
        Console.WriteLine( "Usage: append <filename> \"<text>\"\n" );
    }
  }
}
```

Comments

Appending text is useful for applications that use some sort of logging mechanism for debugging purposes or those that utilize persistent data in some way. When using this method of file I/O, you should ensure that the application doesn't get carried away by writing too much data to a file without ever resetting the file so that the file size doesn't become too large. A popular technique for doing so is to create a circular logging file. Any time you write to the file, you should check the current file size. If the file size plus the size of the data you are planning to write is larger than a predetermined threshold value, then you must eliminate the data from the top of the file equal to the number of bytes you are adding to the bottom of the file. This move ensures that you always have the most recent data while still maintaining a suitable file size. Of course, if all the data is necessary and cannot be thrown out, then this point becomes unnecessary.

12.10. Improving Performance with a
MemoryStream

> You want to eliminate the performance bottleneck that occurs when continuously writing large amounts of data to a file by working with a memory-based stream.

Technique

The memory stream is a specialized stream class that allows you to work with an in-memory representation of a file. The MemoryStream class contains the usual methods to read and write different data types but also contains several methods that allow you to set the current position of the stream anywhere within the defined memory block. You can create a MemoryStream object by passing in a prebuilt array of bytes, an integer value, or no parameters. When you pass in an array of bytes, the MemoryStream is limited to working with that array only. Any attempts to write past the bounds of the array result in an exception being thrown. If you pass an integer or no parameters into the MemoryStream constructor instead, the internal memory buffer expands as necessary to accommodate extra data. You can pass in an integer value specifying the initial size of the internal buffer.

The MemoryStream class also contains an internal position representing the current location where reading and writing takes place. By using the Seek method, you can move that position relative to the beginning, end, or current position. For instance, to move the current stream location 1KB from the beginning of the memory stream, call Seek passing the integer 1024 and the SeekOrigin value of SeekOrigin.Begin. The other SeekOrigin values are SeekOrigin.End and SeekOrigin.Current. The code in Listing 12.1 shows how to use a MemoryStream class to quickly manipulate the contents of a file. The application itself reads in a file specified on the command line, places the file's data into a MemoryStream object, and then proceeds to swap the beginning bytes with the ending bytes, which has the effect of reversing the bytes in the file. When the reverse is finished, the MemoryStream is written to a new file using a BinaryWriter.

Listing 12.1   **Reversing a File with a** MemoryStream

```
using System;
using System.IO;

namespace _10_MemoryStream
{
    class Class1
    {
        [STAThread]
        static void Main(string[] args)
        {
            if( args.Length <= 0 || args.Length > 2 )
            {
                DisplayUsage();
                return;
            }

            if( File.Exists( args[0] ) == false )
            {
                DisplayUsage();
                return;
            }

            ReverseFile( args[0], args[1] );

            return;
        }

        static void ReverseFile( string src, string dest )
        {
            // open src
```

Listing 12.1   **Continued**

```
FileStream fsSrc = File.OpenRead( src );
BinaryReader rdr = new BinaryReader( fsSrc );

// create dest
FileStream fsDest = File.Open( dest, FileMode.Create );

// create memory stream
MemoryStream memStream = new MemoryStream();

int curChar = 0;

// read source into memory stream
while( (curChar = rdr.Read()) != -1 )
{
    memStream.WriteByte( Convert.ToByte(curChar) );
}

for( int i = 0; i < memStream.Length/2; ++i )
{
    byte tempTop, tempBottom;

    // get top byte
    memStream.Seek( i, SeekOrigin.Begin );
    tempTop = (byte) memStream.ReadByte();

    // get bottom byte
    memStream.Seek( -i-1, SeekOrigin.End );
    tempBottom = (byte) memStream.ReadByte();

    // set new bottom byte
    memStream.Seek( -1, SeekOrigin.Current );
    memStream.WriteByte( tempTop );

    // set new top byte
    memStream.Seek( i, SeekOrigin.Begin );
    memStream.WriteByte( tempBottom );
}

// write memory stream to disk
memStream.Seek( 0, SeekOrigin.Begin );

byte[] memBytes = memStream.ToArray();
```

Listing 12.1   **Continued**

```
        BinaryWriter bw = new BinaryWriter( fsDest );
        bw.Write( memBytes );

        // clean up (note: closing BinaryReader and
        // BinaryWriter closes streams also)
        bw.Close();
        rdr.Close();
    }
    static void DisplayUsage()
    {
        Console.WriteLine( "Usage: reverse <source filename> " +
            "<destination filename>\n" );
    }
  }
}
```

Comments

Memory files, as they are most commonly referred to, are very powerful constructs that eliminate one of the biggest bottlenecks of computers today, file I/O. Once data has to move along the computer bus from the registers and RAM to a fixed disk, the performance of an application can come to a grinding halt. Naturally, if your application only periodically writes files to disk, then regular writing using a `FileStream` or `TextWriter` is perfectly fine.

We should mention a few caveats about using a `MemoryStream` that are readily apparent. The first concerns tradeoffs. Using a `MemoryStream` means you have to trade off system memory. If your `MemoryStream` object becomes quite large, then you might get to a point where the virtual-memory system of the operating system begins thrashing. In other words, once your memory becomes full and the operating system has to temporarily free some of that memory by writing it to disk, the file I/O bottleneck really comes into play, and it slows down not only your application but the entire system as well. However, with memory sizes in today's computers, it would take a very large `MemoryStream` to get the virtual-memory system to start thrashing.

One other caveat concerns volatility. The `MemoryStream` object that you are using exists purely in memory. We shouldn't have to tell what would happen if the power to your computer all of a sudden shut off. If the `MemoryStream` were somehow linked to the document a user was working on, then all his information would be lost. Sure, it's a regular occurrence anyway, but you still should think about utilizing an auto-save system whereby the `MemoryStream` object is flushed after a certain period of time to a temporary location on the hard disk.

12.11. Monitoring File and Directory Changes

You want to be notified whenever a file, directory, or collection of files and directories change.

Technique

The `FileSystemWatcher` class is designed to watch a group of files and directories and fire appropriate events based on the actions currently occurring to those groups. Using a `FileSystemWatcher` object is a four-step process. The first step is to create an instance of the `FileSystemWatcher`. You can use a default constructor when you create it, a single string denoting the directory path to watch, or an additional string beyond that specifying a filter, which is used to monitor individual file changes within a directory.

You can configure the `FileSystemWatcher` by setting certain properties. The first and most important is the `Path` property. Without this value, the `FileSystemWatcher` does not know the location to begin monitoring. Note also that it should be a path to a directory and not a path to a file. If you want to watch an individual file, then you want to set the `Filter` property. You use the `Filter` property to narrow down the list of files to watch and you can specify it using wildcards. For example, if you just want notification on changes occurring to text files, then the filter property is `*.txt`.

The `IncludeSubdirectories` property does just as its name implies. If any of the files change in the directory being monitored, or in any subdirectory underneath that directory, then the appropriate event is fired. If `IncludeSubdirectories` is `false`, then only the directory specified in the `Path` property is monitored.

Last but definitely not least is the event-handling mechanism. `FileSystemWatcher` fires off four different events based on the changes occurring to the monitored directory. One of these events is the `Changed` event. This event uses information in the `NotifyFilters` property to fire events whenever a certain change to a file or directory occurs. These changes can include attribute changes, last write time changes, and size changes, among others. To specify multiple `NotifyFilters`, logically OR (|) each value from the `NotifyFilters` enumeration that you want to include:

```
fileWatcher.NotifyFilter = NotifyFilters.LastAccess | NotifyFilters.LastWrite |
    NotifyFilters.FileName | NotifyFilters.DirectoryName;
```

The other available events that are fired from a `FileSystemWatcher` object include `Deleted`, `Renamed`, and `Created`. The delegates for each of these events contain the obligatory `object` representing the sender and a `FileSystemEventArgs`. However, the `Renamed` event uses a `RenamedEventArgs`, which adds information about what the file was named before the renaming took place. In Listing 12.2, you can see a Windows Form application that allows you to specify a path, pattern, and whether to include subdirectories. When the `Go` button is clicked, the `FileSystemWatcher` is called into action by setting its `EnableRaisingEvents` property to `true`. Then, the appropriate events are fired and handled within their corresponding delegates. Take note that the wizard-generated code for the Windows Forms controls is left out for brevity, but the important `FileSystemWatcher` code is there.

Listing 12.2   **The `FileSystemWatcher` Application**

```
using System;
using System.Drawing;
using System.Collections;
using System.ComponentModel;
using System.Windows.Forms;
using System.Data;
using System.IO;

namespace _11_FileWatcher
{
    public class Form1 : System.Windows.Forms.Form
    {
        private System.Windows.Forms.GroupBox groupBox1;
        private System.Windows.Forms.TextBox tbPath;
        private System.Windows.Forms.Button btnBrowse;
        private System.Windows.Forms.TextBox tbActivity;
        private System.Windows.Forms.GroupBox Activity;
        private System.Windows.Forms.Button btnGo;
        private System.Windows.Forms.FolderBrowserDialog folderBrowserDialog1;
        private System.IO.FileSystemWatcher fileSystemWatcher1;
        private System.Windows.Forms.CheckBox cbIncludeSubdirs;
        private System.Windows.Forms.TextBox tbPattern;
        private System.Windows.Forms.Label label1;

        private System.ComponentModel.Container components = null;

        public Form1()
        {
            InitializeComponent();
        }

        protected override void Dispose( bool disposing )
        {
            if( disposing )
            {
                if (components != null)
                {
                    components.Dispose();
                }
            }
            base.Dispose( disposing );
```

Listing 12.2 **Continued**

```
    }

    private void InitializeComponent()
    {
        // fileSystemWatcher1
        this.fileSystemWatcher1 = new System.IO.FileSystemWatcher();

        this.fileSystemWatcher1.Deleted += new
            System.IO.FileSystemEventHandler(
            this.fileSystemWatcher1_Deleted);

        this.fileSystemWatcher1.Renamed += new
            System.IO.RenamedEventHandler(
            this.fileSystemWatcher1_Renamed);

        this.fileSystemWatcher1.Changed += new
            System.IO.FileSystemEventHandler(
            this.fileSystemWatcher1_Changed);

        this.fileSystemWatcher1.Created += new
            System.IO.FileSystemEventHandler(
            this.fileSystemWatcher1_Created);

        // remaining windows forms control code removed
    }

    [STAThread]
    static void Main()
    {
        Application.Run(new Form1());
    }

    private void btnBrowse_Click(object sender, System.EventArgs e)
    {
        // choose which folder to monitor
        if( folderBrowserDialog1.ShowDialog() == DialogResult.OK )
            tbPath.Text = folderBrowserDialog1.SelectedPath;
    }

    private void btnGo_Click(object sender, System.EventArgs e)
    {
        if( btnGo.Text == "Stop" )
        {
            // stop monitoring
            fileSystemWatcher1.EnableRaisingEvents = false;
```

Listing 12.2   **Continued**

```
                // change button text back to Go
                btnGo.Text = "Go";
        }
        else
        {
                // make sure path exists
                if( Directory.Exists( tbPath.Text ) == false )
                {
                        tbActivity.Text = "Directory \"" + tbPath.Text +
                            "\" does not exist.";

                        return;
                }

                // set filesystemwatcher properties
                fileSystemWatcher1.Path = tbPath.Text;
                fileSystemWatcher1.Filter = tbPattern.Text;
                fileSystemWatcher1.IncludeSubdirectories =
                        cbIncludeSubdirs.Checked;

                // start monitoring
                fileSystemWatcher1.EnableRaisingEvents = true;

                btnGo.Text = "Stop";
        }
}

private void fileSystemWatcher1_Changed(object sender,
        System.IO.FileSystemEventArgs e)
{
        tbActivity.Text += "\r\nChanged: " + e.FullPath;
}

private void fileSystemWatcher1_Created(object sender,
        System.IO.FileSystemEventArgs e)
{
        tbActivity.Text += "\r\nCreated: " + e.FullPath;
}

private void fileSystemWatcher1_Deleted(object sender,
        System.IO.FileSystemEventArgs e)
{
        tbActivity.Text += "\r\nDeleted: " + e.FullPath;
}
```

Listing 12.2 **Continued**

```
        private void fileSystemWatcher1_Renamed(object sender,
            System.IO.RenamedEventArgs e)
        {
            tbActivity.Text += "\r\nRenamed from " + e.OldFullPath +
                " to " + e.FullPath;
        }
    }
}
```

Comments

File-change notification is nothing new to the Windows world. The `FileSystemWatcher` component is a wrapper around the WIN32 API methods `FindFirstChangeNotification` and `FindNextChangeNotification`. If you read the documentation on these methods, you will note many similarities between them and the equivalent `FileSystemWatcher` class in the .NET framework.

The `FileSystemWatcher` class uses an internal buffer to store the various notifications as they are received from the operating system. When the operating system begins any type of serious thrashing on the hard disk, the internal buffer within the `FileSystemWatcher` class will undoubtedly fill up. When an overflow of that buffer is finally reached, the `FileSystemWatcher` class throws an `Error` event that you can handle within your own class. If you find this event occurring often, you might want to take some of the following steps. First, setting the `IncludeSubdirectories` property to `true` can have a large effect on the buffer size if the initial directory to monitor contains several files and subdirectories. If one of these subdirectories is the main Windows folder, that is definitely the case. Second, you might not need to monitor all the `NotifyFilter` types. For instance, if you simply want to know when a file is changed, then you can specify `NotifyFilter.LastWrite`. There should be no need to specify any additional filters because they will more than likely result in more than one notification being sent. Finally, you can change the internal buffer size of a `FileSystemWatcher` by setting the `InternalBufferSize` property. The default value is 8192, so you should set it to something larger. Additionally, the documentation also mentions that for best performance, the buffer size should be in multiples of 4KB. This suggestion means that you use values of 12288, 16384, and so on.

12.12. Creating a Directory

You want to create a new directory on the file system.

Technique

To create a new directory, call the static method `CreateDirectory` defined in the `Directory` class. This method uses a single string denoting the full path of the directory to create. The path itself must be absolute, which means you cannot specify a new directory relative to the currently selected directory. To simulate a relative path, concatenate the results of calling `Directory.GetCurrentDirectory` with the relative path of the new directory to create. Additionally, the path itself can contain several subdirectories, which you specify by using the forward slash character (\) to separate the values, as shown in the following code:

```
private string CreateTempDirectory( string logFile )
{
    DirectoryInfo di = Directory.CreateDirectory(
        Directory.GetCurrentDirectory() + @"\temp\log" );

    Directory.SetCurrentDirectory( di.FullName );
    return Directory.GetCurrentDirectory();
}
```

One thing you'll notice is that the `CreateDirectory` method returns a `DirectoryInfo` object. This object is explained in greater detail in Recipe 12.13, "Retrieving Directory Information." The `DirectoryInfo` class contains a method named `CreateSubdirectory`, allowing you to specify a relative path to create additional subdirectories.

Comments

A hard-coded path is a string within code that refers to a directory on your own system. Usually, this directory isn't on anyone else's machine because computers support multiple users and keep user directories to enforce data separation. The `Directory` class makes working with directories virtually trivial.

Even though directories are easy to work with, they can spell disaster at the touch of a button. When you are performing file operations, you should always be wary of the current directory, making sure that you add necessary error handling in case something were to go wrong. We could tell the anecdote of a colleague who wrote a recursive file-deletion algorithm and accidentally wiped out a couple of team member's hard drives, but we've already said enough. In short, don't take directories for granted, and always ensure that your code is accessing the proper locations at all times.

12.13. Retrieving Directory Information

You want to query various attributes for a given directory.

Technique

Whenever you create a new directory, a `DirectoryInfo` object is returned from the `CreateDirectory` method. This class contains several properties that allow you to obtain various bits of information about a certain directory. To create a new `DirectoryInfo` object on an existing directory, pass the existing path name as a string into the `DirectoryInfo` constructor:

```
DirectoryInfo dirInfo = new DirectoryInfo( @"C:\" );
```

Once you obtain a `DirectoryInfo` object, you can access several properties to obtain information similar to the procedure in Section 12.4, "Using the `FileInfo` Class to Display File Information." In addition to standard time-based properties, such as `CreationTime` and `LastAccessTime`, and the `Attributes` property, you can also retrieve information about directories relative to the `DirectoryInfo` object. For instance, the `Parent` property returns a `DirectoryInfo` object pointing to the parent directory. The `Root` points to the root folder of the hard drive:

```
public void ShowDirInfo()
{
    Console.WriteLine( "Path: {0}", dirInfo.FullName );
    Console.WriteLine( "Root: {0}", dirInfo.Root.ToString() );

    if( dirInfo.Parent != null ) Console.WriteLine( "Parent Dir: {0}",
        dirInfo.Parent.FullName );
    else Console.WriteLine( "Parent Dir: None" );

    Console.WriteLine( "Attributes: {0}", dirInfo.Attributes.ToString() );

    Console.WriteLine( "Creation Time: {0}", dirInfo.CreationTime.ToString() );

    Console.WriteLine( "Last Access Time: {0}",
        dirInfo.LastAccessTime.ToString() );

    Console.WriteLine( "Last Write Time: {0}",
        dirInfo.LastWriteTime.ToString() );
}
```

A directory naturally holds a collection of files and additional subdirectories. The `GetFiles` and `GetDirectories` methods return a collection of `FileInfo` and `DirectoryInfo` objects, respectively. Each of these methods contains an overloaded version that lets you specify a wildcard pattern to narrow the search of files or directories to return. For instance, to return a collection of `FileInfo` objects for all text files (`.txt`) in a directory, you specify the `*.txt` wildcard pattern:

```
Console.WriteLine( "Num Files: {0}", dirInfo.GetFiles("*.txt").Length );
foreach( FileInfo file in dirInfo.GetFiles("*.txt") )
    Console.WriteLine( "\t{0}", file.Name );
```

Comments

The `FileInfo` and `DirectoryInfo` classes both derive from the `FileSystemInfo` class, which is why you see a lot of similarities in property and method names. Additionally, both use a caching scheme to improve performance. Whenever an instance of one of those objects is created, it retrieves the current information about a file or directory at the time of creation. If you create a `DirectoryInfo` object, for example, and don't use it until later in your application, the data at that point might be old because the contents or attributes of the directory might have changed. To update a `FileInfo` or `DirectoryInfo` object, call the `Refresh` method.

12.14. Enumerating Files and Subdirectories in a Directory

You want to list every subdirectory and file within a directory.

Technique

Using the `GetDirectories` and `GetFiles` methods is fine if you want to get the directory and filenames that are direct descendants of a directory. However, sometimes you might want to get all the descendants. To do so, you can employ a common programming technique known as *recursion*. In the next code listing, the `Enumerate` method enumerates each `FileSystemInfo` object within a certain directory. If the `FileSystemInfo` is a `DirectoryInfo` type, then the method calls itself passing in the new starting location:

```
private void Enumerate( DirectoryInfo diStart, int indent )
{
    try
    {
        // for each subdirectory and file
        foreach (FileSystemInfo diNext in diStart.GetFileSystemInfos())
        {
            // indent the output
            for( int i = 0; i < indent; ++i )
            {
                swLogFile.Write( "\t" );
            }
```

```
                // check if object is a subdirectory
                if( diNext.GetType() == typeof( DirectoryInfo ))
                {
                    // write out subdirectory name surrounded by brackets
                    swLogFile.WriteLine( "< " + diNext.Name + ">");

                    // recursive function call with new starting location
                    Enumerate( (DirectoryInfo) diNext, ++indent );
                }
                else
                {
                    // write out name of file
                    swLogFile.WriteLine( diNext.Name );
                }
            }
        }

        catch (Exception e)
        {
            Console.WriteLine("The process failed: {0}", e.ToString());

        }
    }
}
```

Comments

The preceding code might take a while to run if you point the starting location to the root folder of a large hard drive. The indenting was placed in the file for readability purposes, but it also demonstrates how the runtime stack is used within the Common Language Runtime (CLR). Without knowing anything about recursion or call stacks, one might assume that each time the indent parameter is incremented, the output just keeps indenting and never reverts back to a lower value. Whenever parameters are used within a method, they are placed on the stack by the caller. Therefore, when you see the Enumerate method call itself in response to finding a new subdirectory, the new subdirectory contained within the DirectoryInfo object and a new incremented indent value is placed onto the call stack and the call is made. When the second Enumerate method returns, the old indent value is restored because value types are popped off the stack when the callee begins execution. However, if the parameter being passed in was by reference, then the new value would remain and the indentation would be incorrect. If you have run into recursion before, then the procedure more than likely isn't anything new to you. If you have never seen recursive procedures before, then don't feel bad if you don't understand it conceptually.

12.15. Saving Object State with Serialization

You want to save the current state of an object to disk using serialization techniques.

Technique

Serialization is the term used for the process that creates a snapshot of a current object's state and writes that information to a stream, which in most cases means to a file. The .NET Framework contains three main serialization schemes: binary, XML, and Simple Object Access Protocol (SOAP) serialization.

The first step in serializing an object is to apply the `Serializable` attribute to it, as shown in the following code. Without this attribute, the object cannot be serialized. However, even if the attribute is applied to a class, you might not be able to serialize it if any base classes do not have the attribute applied either. In other words, if you want to serialize a class derived from `System.Windows.Forms.Form`, the serialization process will throw an exception because the `Form` class cannot be serialized:

```
[
Serializable
]
public class SerializedObject
{
    public string stringVariable = "This is a public string variable";
    public int intVariable = 42;

    private int[] intArray;

    public SerializedObject()
    {
        intArray = new int[]{1,2,3,4,5,6,7,8,9,10};
    }

    public int[] Integers
    {
        get
        {
            return intArray;
        }
        set
        {
            intArray = value;
        }
    }
}
```

The code listing is enough to make an object serializable using any of the serialization techniques available. Later sections build upon this simple example to control the serialization process, but this code will never have to change. Once you create a serializable object, you have to write the code to perform the serialization. Before you do so, you have to add one of three namespaces to your project, depending on the serialization technique you use.

Binary serialization, as its name implies, converts an object into a stream of bytes that can then be written to a fixed disk. You use the `BinaryFormatter` object defined in the `System.Runtime.Serialization.Formatters.Binary` namespace. The actual act of serialization needs a stream object and the object being serialized. To serialize an object using a `BinaryFormatter`, call the `Serialize` method, passing a stream object and the object to serialize, as shown in the following code:

```
private void mnuSaveBinary_Click(object sender, System.EventArgs e)
{
    saveFileDialog1.FilterIndex = 1;
    if( saveFileDialog1.ShowDialog() != DialogResult.OK )
        return;

    // create the serialization formatter
    IFormatter formatter = new BinaryFormatter();

    // open a file stream
    Stream stream = new FileStream(saveFileDialog1.FileName, FileMode.Create,
        FileAccess.Write, FileShare.None);

    // serialize the object using the formatter
    formatter.Serialize(stream, mObject);

    // close the file stream
    stream.Close();
}
```

The `SoapFormatter` is similar, with the major difference being the output of the serialization process. In keeping with well-defined naming standards, the `SoapFormatter` serializes objects using the SOAP format, which you will see more of in Chapter 17, "Web Services." At the most basic level, SOAP is an XML file format. In addition to adding the namespace declaration, `System.Runtime.Serialization.Formatters.Soap` also must add an assembly reference to the assembly of the same name. To serialize an object using a `SoapFormatter`, simply change the code shown earlier by creating a `SoapFormatter` object instead of a `BinaryFormatter`.

XML serialization is one of the most customizable of the all serialization techniques. However, the actual serialization process is virtually identical to the previous two techniques. The main serialization class used for XML serialization is the `XmlSerializer` class. At a minimum, the constructor for an `XmlSerializer` object needs a type reference to the object being serialized. You can either use the `typeof` keyword or call the `GetType` method on the object being serialized. The other optional constructor parameters give you the ability to map internal variables or properties within the class being serialized into different attribute names as well as the ability to change the root element of the final XML document. Once the `XmlSerializer` object is created, you once again create a new stream and call the `Serialize` method to complete serialization:

```
private void mnuSaveXML_Click(object sender, System.EventArgs e)
{
    saveFileDialog1.FilterIndex = 2;
    if ( saveFileDialog1.ShowDialog() != DialogResult.OK )
        return;

    // create the XML serializer. mObject is the object being serialized
    XmlSerializer formatter = new XmlSerializer( mObject.GetType() );

    // open a new file stream
    Stream stream = new FileStream(saveFileDialog1.FileName, FileMode.Create,
        FileAccess.Write, FileShare.None);

    // serialize the object
    formatter.Serialize( stream, mObject );

    // close the file stream
    stream.Close();
}
```

Comments

Serialization is a powerful tool when used correctly. Once you become familiar with how to create serialized objects within your applications, you'll start to see little areas where the techniques would fit in well. One particular application of this method could be configuration. You could create a class that holds configuration information for your application. As the user changes properties within your application, the configuration object can be serialized to the hard disk. Then, whenever your application loads, the configuration object can be deserialized (explained in the next section) and the user settings are restored. If you compare this method to other configuration methods such as reading XML or INI files, you will see the advantage. In those methods, the process generally entails reading a value from the file, setting a certain member variable, and repeating that process for each member. As new member variables are added, you have to also add the code to read in the configuration settings for that variable. With serialization, however, all you have to worry about is the initial code to enable serialization, and then you add new member variables and properties without having to revisit the configuration code.

Serialization wasn't created just so you could save and later restore an object from disk, although that is a pretty handy feature to have. One of the biggest advantages lies within distributed computing. For instance, if one computer has an assembly containing a certain data type and another remote computer does also, you can create an application that utilizes one of the serialization techniques to send an object snapshot to the remote computer so that it can be recreated in its exact state on a different machine.

This section looked at two types of serialization, binary and XML. Each method has its distinct advantages and disadvantages, which you should weigh when formulating your application's design. Binary serialization's strongest advantage is the accurate representation of type data. Because binary serialization serializes both public and private members of an object, the state of that object can be faithfully recreated during deserialization. You should not use XML serialization, on the other hand, if you need to save the exact state of an object because only public properties and fields are serialized. Any instance data contained within private fields is lost during the serialization process. However, XML serialization's greatest strength is its portability. Because XML and SOAP are both open standards, any XML-aware application or technology can consume the final output of the serialization process.

12.16. Recreating Objects with Deserialization

You want to construct a new object that has been previously serialized to a file.

Technique

The technique for deserialization is generally much easier than the initial steps for serialization because most of the steps are already finished. To deserialize an object, create the appropriate serialization formatter as discussed in the previous section. Note that you must use the same serialization object for deserialization, meaning you can't serialize an object with a `BinaryFormatter` and deserialize it with an `XmlSerializer`. Once the object is created, open a file stream for reading and call the `Deserialize` method, passing the stream object as the only parameter. This method returns an `Object` type that you must cast to the data type of the object being deserialized. The following code shows the deserialization of an object using each serialization method:

```
private void mnuLoadBinary_Click(object sender, System.EventArgs e)
{
    openFileDialog1.FilterIndex = 1;
    if( openFileDialog1.ShowDialog() != DialogResult.OK )
        return;

    IFormatter formatter = new BinaryFormatter();
    Stream stream = new FileStream(openFileDialog1.FileName, FileMode.Open,
FileAccess.Read, FileShare.None);
```

```
        mObject = (SerializedObject) formatter.Deserialize(stream);
        stream.Close();

        pgObject.SelectedObject = mObject;
}

private void mnuLoadXML_Click(object sender, System.EventArgs e)
{
        openFileDialog1.FilterIndex = 2;
        if( openFileDialog1.ShowDialog() != DialogResult.OK )
            return;

        XmlSerializer formatter = new XmlSerializer( mObject.GetType() );
        Stream stream = new FileStream(openFileDialog1.FileName, FileMode.Open,
            FileAccess.Read, FileShare.None);

        mObject = (SerializedObject) formatter.Deserialize( stream );
        stream.Close();

        pgObject.SelectedObject = mObject;
}

private void mnuLoadSoap_Click(object sender, System.EventArgs e)
{
        openFileDialog1.FilterIndex = 3;
        if( openFileDialog1.ShowDialog() != DialogResult.OK )
            return;

        IFormatter formatter = new SoapFormatter();
        Stream stream = new FileStream(openFileDialog1.FileName, FileMode.Open,
            FileAccess.Read, FileShare.None);

        mObject = (SerializedObject) formatter.Deserialize(stream);
        stream.Close();

        pgObject.SelectedObject = mObject;
}
```

Comments

One thing you must take into consideration when deserializing an object is that no initialization code is run when an object is successfully created through the deserialization
process. In other words, the constructor for an object is not called, which means you
might have to perform additional initialization for internal data that might need initialization. Although the data members might be successfully recreated, some data might rely
on external factors to be valid. Take, for example, a private member variable that contains

the name of the machine the application is being run on. If the object is serialized on one machine and then deserialized on another, then the internal data member becomes invalid and must be reinitialized somehow.

12.17. Preventing Object Items from Being Serialized

You want to prevent the serialization of a data member within an object.

Technique

To prevent serialization on a member variable from occurring within a class, apply the NonSerialized attribute. When the serialization process occurs, the formatter checks each data item being serialized for that attribute. If it is present, the item is skipped and not serialized to the data stream:

```
[
Serializable,
]
public class SerializedObject
{
    public string stringVariable = "This is a public string variable";
    public int intVariable = 42;

    // this var is non-serialized
    [NonSerialized]
    private int nonInt = 42;

    [XmlIgnore]
    public int NonSerializedInteger
    {
        get
        {
            return nonInt;
        }
        set
        {
            nonInt = value;
        }
    }
}
```

The XmlSerializer class is the only serialization object that serializes object properties. You might want to prevent serialization of properties as well. However, the XmlSerializer utilizes a different attribute, named XmlIgnore. If you place this attribute on any public member variables or properties, the `XmlSerializer` skips that item during serialization.

Comments

Section 12.16, "Recreating Objects with Deserialization," mentioned that when an object is deserialized, no initialization code, such as the constructor, is called. If you know that a certain data item within your class will be invalid upon deserialization, or it at least has the potential to become invalid, then you should consider applying the `NonSerialized` attribute if using binary or SOAP serialization or the `XmlIgnore` attribute if using XML serialization. Additionally, you should also check whether any data items contain sensitive information. For instance, if a private member variable was a string containing credit card information, then serializing that string presents a large security and privacy risk. Therefore, you should either consider not serializing that data item or at least applying some type of encoding or cryptography to prevent the unintentional security risk.

12.18. Customizing the Serialization Process

> You want to take control over the serialization process by creating your own custom serialization scheme.

Technique

Even though the binary, XML, and SOAP serializers do a good job of serialization, you might need more control over the items that get serialized. You have to implement the `ISerializable` interface. This interface contains a single method that you must implement: `GetObjectData`, which is used during the serialization process, and an additional constructor for deserialization, which is discussed shortly.

The `GetObjectData` method has two parameters. The first parameter is a `SerializationInfo` object used to hold all the necessary serialization data. Data is stored using a key/value pair method in which the key is a string object and the value can be any .NET object type. To add a new value to the collection, call the `AddValue` method, passing a string and the object to add. The second parameter is a `StreamingContext` object used to describe both the source and destination streams:

```
[Serializable]
public class CustomSerializedObject : ISerializable
{
    private int data = 42;

    public CustomSerializedObject()
    {
    }
```

```
    public CustomSerializedObject( SerializationInfo info, StreamingContext
➥context )
    {
        data = info.GetInt32( "data" );
    }
    #region ISerializable Members

    public void GetObjectData(SerializationInfo info, StreamingContext context)
    {
        info.AddValue( "data", data );
    }

    #endregion
}
```

During the deserialization of an object that utilizes a custom serialization scheme, a special object constructor is called. Because there is no way to enforce the creation of this constructor, the only error that you will receive for a custom serialized object is an exception being thrown during the deserialization process. In other words, forgetting the custom constructor appears during runtime and not during compile time. The overloaded constructor uses the same parameters as the GetObjectData method. However, within the body of the constructors, you will want to call the various Get methods to retrieve data. Again, because the data is stored using key/value pairs, the methods themselves accept a string denoting a key and return the corresponding data type.

Comments

Once you implement the ISerializable interface in a class, the serialization process immediately becomes a hands-on process. Any of the attributes that you have applied to prevent data items from being serialized are no longer valid. Even more so, data items that are normally automatically serialized will not be. Implementing a custom serializer entails having to create all the necessary AddValue calls for the serialization process.

The last section mentioned that some data members within a class open up a potential security risk if the corresponding data were to be serialized. One solution was to simply prevent the data from being written to disk, but in some situations, this step might not be desirable. Another solution is to use a custom serializer. When the GetObjectData method is called, you have the opportunity to change the actual data before it is serialized to eliminate these unnecessary risks. A field containing credit card information, for instance, could be encrypted during serialization and subsequently unencrypted when deserialized.

13

XML in .NET

13.0. Introduction

Every once in a while, a seemingly simple concept turns into a revolutionary idea. When you take a step back and look at it, you feel like hitting yourself for not thinking of it first. In its simplest form, the Extensible Markup Language (XML) is just a text file following a specific format consisting of tagged elements and their associated attributes. However, it is this flexible file format that allows efficient hierarchical data organization and has lead to its wide adoption in everything from configuration files to database implementation.

In this chapter, you'll see how to use the .NET Framework to create, parse, analyze, and manipulate XML documents. Because XML is used in several areas within the framework, this chapter is really just a stepping-stone to help you become familiar with XML before applying that knowledge to other areas within .NET. As soon as you become proficient in reading, writing, and manipulating XML programmatically, you'll have the necessary toolset available to utilize, enhance, and extend several key technologies later.

13.1. Reading XML Documents with `XmlTextReader`

You want to open an XML file and parse its contents using an `XmlTextReader` object.

Technique

Just like many other classes within the .NET Framework, the `XmlTextReader` class contains several different constructors you can use to create and initialize an object. If you group the constructors based on the way the `XmlTextReader` retrieves the XML data, you can see three main groupings. You can pass a string specifying the file path or URL of the XML file, a `Stream` object that you created using one of the many classes derived from `Stream` or a `TextReader` object. The previous chapter demonstrates how to utilize `Stream` and `TextReader` objects. Some constructors optionally allow you to pass an `XmlNameTable` or an `XmlNodeType` with an associated `XmlParserContext` object.

An `XmlNameTable` is an object designed to optimize string comparisons for element and attribute names within an XML document. When the document is parsed, each unique element and attribute name is added to the table as an object. You can then use this information to your advantage by performing object comparisons rather than using the more expensive string comparison methods. Let's assume, for example, that you had an XML file containing a list of names and phone numbers for the city that you live in. If your city is large, then the file itself would also be large. If you want to extract just the last names from the XML file as it's read, you can just do a string comparison on each element. However, this process will eat up clock cycles more than using the `XmlNameTable` method would. An example of using an `XmlNameTable` for this problem might be the following:

```
XmlTextReader rdr = new XmlTextReader( "cityphone.xml" );

NameTable names = new NameTable();
string lastName = names.Add( "last_name" );

while( rdr.Read() )
{
    if( rdr.NameTable.Get( "last_name" ) == lastName )
        Console.WriteLine( "Found last name of {0}", rdr.Value );
}
```

You use the `XmlNodeType` and its associated `XmlParserContext` object to specify the type of XML document you are parsing. You use it when you want to parse a small part of XML rather than an entire document. For instance, if you just want to parse a single element rather than all the required parts of an XML document, such as the XML declaration, you pass a value of `XmlNodeType.Element`. However, the XML data that you pass might still contain entity or namespace references that the parser might not know about. You use the `XmlParserContext` object to resolve the cases in which these situations occur. For example, if the XML fragment you are using is an `XmlNodeType.Element` and one of the inner elements contains a reference to a namespace named `phone`, you have to create an `XmlParserContext` object and insert the namespace into the object so that it is properly resolved during parsing:

```
string name = "<person> " +
    "<first_name>Scott</first_name>" +
    "<last_name>Limbach</last_name>" +
    "<phone:area_code>360</phone:area_code>" +
    "<phone:main>555-5555</phone:main>";
```

```
NameTable nt = new NameTable();
XmlNamespaceManager nsmgr = new XmlNamespaceManager(nt);
nsmgr.AddNamespace("phone", "urn:cityphonedb");

//Create the XmlParserContext.
XmlParserContext context = new XmlParserContext(null, nsmgr, null, XmlSpace.None);

//Create the reader.
XmlTextReader reader = new XmlTextReader(xmlFrag, XmlNodeType.Element, context);
```

Once you create an instance of an `XmlTextReader` object, you are ready to begin parsing the XML file. Reading XML data is performed by calling the `Read` method defined in the `XmlTextReader` class. This method reads the next node type in the document from its current position. To determine the type of the node that was just read in, you can use a switch statement on the `XmlNodeType` property of the `XmlTextReader` object using the values from the `XmlNodeType` enumerated data type. Depending on the type of the node just read, you can access the associated data either through the `Name` or `Value` property. Listing 13.1 shows how to populate a `TreeView` control on a Windows Form. The parsing occurs in the `PopulateTreeView` method. When the `XmlTextReader` begins parsing the document and an `element` is encountered, a new `TreeNode` is created. Any associated `attributes` for the element are placed in a `Hashtable`, which is then assigned to the `Tag` property of the `TreeNode` object. When the attributes have all been read using the `MoveToNextAttribute` method in the `XmlTextReader` class, the `TreeNode` is added to the tree. One thing to note is the `Stack` object that is being used. Because XML is hierarchical, the `TreeView` must display that hierarchy by creating `TreeNode` objects as children of other `TreeNode` objects. When a new element is found by the `XmlTextReader`, the last `TreeNode` that was created is pushed onto the stack. When an `EndElement` is encountered, then that parent node is "popped" off and made current. You can also use recursion, but a nonrecursive stack-based mechanism is better for performance and simplicity.

Listing 13.1   Populating a `TreeView` Using XML

```
using System;
using System.Drawing;
using System.Collections;
using System.ComponentModel;
using System.Windows.Forms;
using System.Data;
using System.Xml;

namespace _1_XmlTextReader
{
    public class Form1 : System.Windows.Forms.Form
    {
        private System.Windows.Forms.MainMenu mainMenu1;
        private System.Windows.Forms.MenuItem menuItem1;
```

Listing 13.1 **Continued**

```
private System.Windows.Forms.MenuItem mnuOpen;
private System.Windows.Forms.MenuItem menuItem3;
private System.Windows.Forms.TreeView tvXML;
private System.Windows.Forms.OpenFileDialog openFileDialog1;
private System.Windows.Forms.ListView lvAttributes;
private System.Windows.Forms.ColumnHeader columnHeader1;
private System.Windows.Forms.ColumnHeader columnHeader2;
private System.Windows.Forms.Label label1;
private System.Windows.Forms.Label lblTextNode;

private System.ComponentModel.Container components = null;

public Form1()
{
    InitializeComponent();
}

protected override void Dispose( bool disposing )
{
    if( disposing )
    {
        if (components != null)
        {
            components.Dispose();
        }
    }
    base.Dispose( disposing );
}

#region Windows Form Designer generated code
#endregion

[STAThread]
static void Main()
{
    Application.Run(new Form1());
}

private void mnuOpen_Click(object sender, System.EventArgs e)
{
    if( openFileDialog1.ShowDialog(this) == DialogResult.OK )
    {
        PopulateTreeView( openFileDialog1.FileName );
    }
}
```

Listing 13.1   **Continued**

```csharp
private void PopulateTreeView( string fileName )
{
    XmlTextReader rdr = new XmlTextReader( fileName );

    Stack nodeStack = new Stack();
    TreeNode curTreeNode = null;

    // clear tree view
    tvXML.Nodes.Clear();

    while( rdr.Read() )
    {
        switch (rdr.NodeType)
        {
                // new start element found
            case XmlNodeType.Element:
            {
                // push last element onto stack
                if( curTreeNode != null )
                    nodeStack.Push( curTreeNode );

                // create new element
                curTreeNode = new TreeNode( rdr.Name );
                curTreeNode.Tag = new Hashtable();

                // populate attribute hashtable for element
                if( rdr.HasAttributes == true )
                {
                    curTreeNode.ForeColor = Color.Red;
                    while( rdr.MoveToNextAttribute() )
                    {
                        ((Hashtable) curTreeNode.Tag).Add(
                            rdr.Name, rdr.Value );
                    }
                }

                // add element to proper place in tree.
                // Parent node is on top of stack
                if( nodeStack.Count > 0 )
                    ((TreeNode)nodeStack.Peek()).Nodes.Add(curTreeNode);
                else
                    tvXML.Nodes.Add( curTreeNode );

                if( rdr.Name.EndsWith( "/>" ))
                {
```

Listing 13.1 **Continued**

```
                                if( nodeStack.Count > 0 )
                                    curTreeNode = (TreeNode) nodeStack.Pop();
                            }
                            break;
                    }
                    case XmlNodeType.Text:
                    {
                        ((Hashtable) curTreeNode.Tag).Add("Text", rdr.Value);
                        break;
                    }
                    case XmlNodeType.EndElement:
                    {
                        // pop the last parent node off the stack
                        if( nodeStack.Count > 0 )
                            curTreeNode = (TreeNode) nodeStack.Pop();

                        break;
                    }
                    default:
                    {
                        break;
                    }
                }
            }
        rdr.Close();
    }

    private void tvXML_AfterSelect(
        object sender,
        System.Windows.Forms.TreeViewEventArgs e )
    {
        // clear attribute list view
        lvAttributes.Items.Clear();

        Hashtable atts = (Hashtable )tvXML.SelectedNode.Tag;
        IDictionaryEnumerator attsEnum = atts.GetEnumerator();

        // enumerate tree node attribute hashtable and add to listview
        while( attsEnum.MoveNext() )
        {
            if( attsEnum.Key.ToString() != "Text" )
                lvAttributes.Items.Add(new ListViewItem(
                    new string[]{attsEnum.Key.ToString(),
                    attsEnum.Value.ToString()} ));
        }
```

Listing 13.1   **Continued**

```
        if( ((Hashtable) tvXML.SelectedNode.Tag).ContainsKey( "Text" ))
        {
            lblTextNode.Text = ( ((Hashtable)
                tvXML.SelectedNode.Tag)["Text"].ToString());
        }
        else
        {
            lblTextNode.Text = "";
        }
    }
  }
}
```

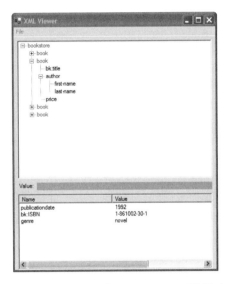

Figure 13.1   The XML Viewer application parses an XML document using
`XmlTextReader` and displays the information in a `TreeView`.

Comments

The `XmlTextReader` is one of three different readers that parse XML data. Each one of
these classes parses XML data, allowing you to place the data in a data structure more
appropriate to your application. The other two classes, `XmlNodeReader` and
`XmlValidatingReader`, are covered in the next two sections.

`XmlTextReader` is forward only, noncached, and nonvalidating. As the XML parser
encounters a new element, that element is not validated against a Document Type
Definition (DTD) or XML schema, and the parser does not allow you to reverse the

parsing process to revisit a node because the nodes are not saved in memory by the parser after having been read. If you used the Simple API for XML (SAX) model of reading XML in the past, these terms might seem familiar. However, XmlTextReader uses a pull model to control the reader, whereas SAX utilized a push model. One of the advantages of using an XmlTextReader is performance. If you aren't concerned with validating XML against a schema or Document Type Definition (DTD), then XmlTextReader should be high on your list of design decisions. Additionally, even though validation does not occur, the XML file or fragments must still be well formed. If the file is not well formed, then the Read method throws an exception, which you must handle. Sections 13.2, "Reading DOM Tree with XmlNodeReader," and 13.5, "Validating XML Documents with Schemas," look at the remaining two XML readers that inherit from the XmlReader class. The XmlValidatingReader allows you to perform validation against a schema or DTD, and you use an XmlNodeReader object when you want to parse XML data from an existing XmlNode object.

13.2. Reading with XmlNodeReader

You want to parse only a given portion of an XML document by using an XmlNodeReader to process nodes from an XmlDocument object.

Technique

Unlike the XmlTextReader discussed in the previous section, the XmlNodeReader class only has a single constructor. Because the sole functionality of an XmlNodeReader is to read XML data contained within an XmlNode object, the constructor only requires a single XmlNode object as a parameter. You can create this parameter by creating an XmlDocument object, loading an XML file, and passing the XmlDocument object as the constructor parameter. This process causes the XmlNodeReader to parse the entire contents of the XML document:

```
XmlDocument xmlDoc = new XmlDocument();
xmlDoc.Load( "file.xml" );
XmlNodeReader rdr = new XmlNodeReader( xmlDoc );
```

To only parse a small fragment of the document, load the XML file using an XmlDocument object, but instead of passing the XmlDocument instance to the constructor, you can do one of two things. First, several XML objects, such as XmlAttribute, derive from the XmlNode class, which means you can pass an instance of one of these objects to the XmlDocument constructor. Second, you can use the result that is returned from calling the SelectSingleNode method defined in the XmlDocument class or any other method that returns an instance to an XmlNode object:

```
XmlDocument xmlDoc = new XmlDocument();
xmlDoc.Load("books.xml");
```

```
XmlNodeReader rdr = new XmlNodeReader( xmlDoc.SelectSingleNode
  ( "/bookstore/book/bk:title" ));
```

Once you have an `XmlNodeReader` associated with an `XmlNode` object, you can begin reading the XML data. Reading with an `XmlNodeReader` is similar to the method employed in the previous section. Call the `Read` method and then check to see the `NodeType` of the data that was read. Checking the `NodeType` property in the `XmlNodeReader` instance lets you know what type of XML data was just read in, such as an element, attribute, comment, processing instruction, and so on.

Comments

The `XmlNodeReader` and `XmlTextReader` classes are strikingly similar. Other than the obvious difference that one works with `XmlNode` objects and the other with XML files or strings, `XmlTextReader` is the only reader capable of decoding Base-64 and bin-hex strings within an XML document. Therefore, if you know that your XML file will contain any of these encodings, you have to use an `XmlTextReader` to do so.

One other key difference, and one you'll probably see more frequently than the previous difference, is entity resolution. Each class contains a method named `ResolveEntity`. However, calling that method with an `XmlTextReader` object throws an `InvalidOperationException` because the `XmlTextReader` class, by design, does not allow entity resolution. The `XmlNodeReader` is capable of resolving the entities. If you are unfamiliar with entities, the best way to think of them are as string-substitution constructs within an XML file. Entity declarations are created at the beginning of the XML file and utilize a key value pairing scheme. Within the body of the XML document, preface the key name with an ampersand (&), which tells the XML parser to replace the key with its associated value when the `ResolveEntity` method is called. For example, given the following XML document, use this code:

```
<?xml version="1.0"?>
<!-- A fragment of a book store inventory database -->
<!DOCTYPE book [<!ENTITY hc 'hardcover'>
                        <!ENTITY sc 'softcover'>]>
<bookstore xmlns:bk="urn:sampls">
    <book genre="novel" publicationdate="1997" bk:ISBN="1-861001-57-8">
        <bk:title>Pride And Prejudice</bk:title>
        <author>
         <first-name>Jane</first-name>
         <last-name>Austen</last-name>
        </author>
        <binding>&sc;</binding>
        <price>24.95</price>
    </book>
    <book genre="novel" publicationdate="1992" bk:ISBN="1-861002-30-1">
        <bk:title>The Handmaid's Tale</bk:title>
        <author>
```

```
          <first-name>Margaret</first-name>
          <last-name>Atwood</last-name>
      </author>
      <binding>&hc;</binding>
      <price>29.95</price>
  </book>
</bookstore>
```

The following code resolves any entity references and displays the result of the resolution in the output window:

```
private void btnResolve_Click(object sender, System.EventArgs e)
{
    XmlNodeReader reader = null;

    try
    {
        //Create and load an XML document.
        XmlDocument doc = new XmlDocument();
        doc.LoadXml( tbXML.Text );

        //Create the reader.
        reader = new XmlNodeReader(doc);

        tbXML.Clear();

        while( reader.Read() )
        {
            switch (reader.NodeType)
            {
                case XmlNodeType.EntityReference:
                {
                    tbXML.Text += "Entity " + reader.Name + " resolved to ";
                    reader.ResolveEntity();
                    reader.Read();
                    tbXML.Text += reader.Value + "\r\n";
                    break;
                }
            }
        }
    }
    finally
    {
        if (reader != null)
            reader.Close();
    }
}
```

When choosing between an `XmlTextReader` and `XmlNodeReader`, you have to look at the differences and similarities between the two and find the best match based on your current application design. Because of the flexibility of the two different classes, you are even able to combine the two as you see fit. For instance, if you want to use an `XmlNodeReader` but still want to decode bin-hex or base-64 data, simply create an `XmlTextReader` object and pass it the short XML fragment to decode while still leaving the majority of the processing up to the `XmlNodeReader` object.

13.3. Navigating XML Documents with XPath

You want to select a single node or a group of nodes using an expression.

Technique

XPath is an expression-based language that uses path syntax to select nodes within an XML document. XPath itself is too large to explain in this section (let alone this book), so further reading might be required if you are unfamiliar with how to construct an XPath statement.

XPath expressions are used in the methods `SelectSingleNode` and `SelectNodes` defined within the `XmlDocument` class. These methods, when given an XPath expression, return a single `XmlNode` or `XmlNodeList` object, respectively. They allow you to navigate through an XML document in a random fashion rather than use forward-only techniques employed by the `XmlReader`-based classes.

The following code sets the `Text` property of a `Label` control based on a treeview item selected by the user. Because the `TreeView` control is hierarchically organized, you can programmatically generate an XPath expression from any node as shown in Figure 13.2, assuming the TreeView models the XML data contained within an `XmlDocument` object:

```
private void tvXML_AfterSelect(object sender, System.Windows.Forms.
  TreeViewEventArgs e)
{
    // clear attribute list view
    lvAttributes.Items.Clear();

    // query using XPath
    XmlNode selNode = xmlDoc.SelectSingleNode(
        tvXML.SelectedNode.FullPath, nsmanager );

    // enumerate attributes in returned node and add to list view
    foreach( XmlAttribute att in selNode.Attributes )
    {
```

```
        lvAttributes.Items.Add(new ListViewItem(
            new string[]{att.Name, att.Value} ));
    }


    // set Label control Text to XPath expression
    lblElementXPath.Text = tvXML.SelectedNode.FullPath;
    lblAttXPath.Text = "";
}
```

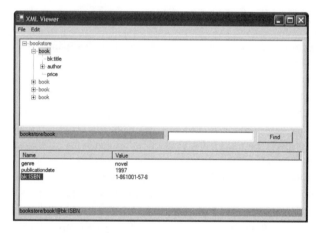

Figure 13.2 Using the `FullPath` property as XPath expressions.

Comments

Because XML is a hierarchical text-based file format, it seems natural to represent individual nodes within XML using path-based expressions. However, a simple path is only a portion of what XPath is capable of. In Figure 13.2, you can see the XPath expression that selects an attribute on an element on the bottom label. Although this list is by no means exhaustive, the following examples show different ways of selecting a node or nodes using XPath expressions. Let's assume that we have an XML document that looks like the following:

```
<?xml version="1.0" encoding="ISO-8859-1"?>
<catalog>
  <cd id='0'>
    <title>Blue Light, Red Light</title>
    <artist>Harry Connick, Jr.</artist>
    <country>USA</country>
    <company>Sony/Columbia</company>
    <price>14.99</price>
    <year>1991</year>
  </cd>
```

```
<cd id='1'>
  <title>The Matrix</title>
  <artist>Various</artist>
  <price>14.99</price>
  <year>1999</year>
</cd>
</catalog>
```

To select all the CD nodes in the XML document, use an XPath expression as a parameter to the `SelectNodes` method defined in the `XmlDocument` class:

```
XmlNodeList cdNodes = xmlDoc.SelectNodes( "/catalog/cd" );
```

You can also use an indexer to retrieve just a single CD node. The following example uses the `SelectSingleNode` method to retrieve the first CD node in the XML document:

```
XmlNode cdNode = xmlDoc.SelectSingleNode( "/catalog/cd[0]" );
```

In addition to selecting a group of nodes or a single node, you can also specify specific portions of a node. For instance, to select the text node of an element, you can use the XPath function `text()`. The following line only selects the text within the `title` node of the first CD:

```
XmlNode textNode = xmlDoc.SelectSingleNode( "/catalog/cd[0]/title/text()" );
```

You can select attributes, as shown in Figure 13.2, by prefacing the attribute name with the @ symbol. Doing so selects the value for the attribute:

```
XmlNode idNode = xmlDoc.SelectSingleNode( "/catalog/cd[0]/@id" );
```

XPath expressions can also use conditional statements for node selection. For example, if you want to select the CD whose `id` attribute is equal to 1 and the CDs whose price is greater than $10.00, you use the following expressions:

```
XmlNode cdNode = xmlDoc.SelectSingleNode( "/catalog/cd[@id=='1']" );
XmlNodeList cdList = xmlDoc.SelectNodes( "/catalog/cd[price>'10.00']" );
```

Finally, XPath also allows you to select nodes using relative positioning. Whenever you construct an XPath expression, you can visualize a pointer into the document pointing to a node. That node then becomes your current axes point, which you can use as a basis for any relative node tests. For instance, if you want to find the CD that immediately followed the CD whose `id` attribute is 0, you use the following:

```
XmlNode nextNode = xmlDoc.SelectSingleNode( "/catalog/cd[@id='0']/
  following-sibling::*" );
```

Other types of node tests involve selecting a single child node, all descendants of a node, or all ancestors of a node, to name a few.

13.4. Using `XmlConvert` to Convert XML Data Types

You want to ensure that XML elements and attributes do not contain invalid characters. You additionally want to convert XML strings into different Common Language Runtime (CLR) data types.

Technique

You use the `XmlConvert` class to manipulate and translate the strings contained within elements and attributes of an XML file. To ensure a string does not contain invalid characters, pass the original string into the static method `EncodeName` defined in the `XmlConvert` class. It returns a valid XML-equivalent string. To convert the string back to its original form, use the `DecodeName` method in the same manner:

```
private void tvXML_AfterLabelEdit(object sender, NodeLabelEditEventArgs e)
{
    string newName = XmlConvert.EncodeName( e.Label );
    string originalName = XmlConvert.DecodeName( newName );
}
```

You can also use the `XmlConvert` class to convert XML strings into .NET data types and vice versa. The conversion methods are modeled closely after the methods defined in the `Convert` class. For instance, to convert a string extracted from an XML document into a `DateTime` equivalent, call the static method `ToDateTime` defined in the `XmlConvert` class, passing in the string to convert. If the conversion cannot occur due to formatting issues, you have to catch the `FormatException` exception:

```
public void ConvertXMLString( string xmlString )
{
    DateTime dt;
    try
    {
        dt = XmlConvert.ToDateTime( xmlString );
        Console.WriteLine( "Converted string = {0}", dt.ToString() );
    }
    catch( FormatException e )
    {
        Console.WriteLine( "Cannot convert \"{0}\" to DateTime", xmlString );
    }
}
```

Comments

XML has a certain range of valid characters that it can use, as defined in the XML 1.0 (Second Edition) recommendation. Some of the invalid characters, for instance, are spaces, the ampersand (&), and the asterisk (*). Because of this limitation, the `XmlConvert` class was created to allow you to convert arbitrary strings into well-formed and valid XML string equivalents. In most cases, the hexadecimal value of each invalid character is inserted into the string. For instance, if you call the `EncodeName` method using the string `"An Element"`, the resultant string is `"An_x0020_Element"`. As you can see, the space character was replaced by its Unicode-based hexadecimal value, surrounded by two underscore characters.

In the application that was created for this chapter, a simple XML editor, XML elements are placed within an editable `TreeView` control. The user is able to click on a tree node's label and change its value, which internally changes the element value within the XML document. However, without any sort of checking or conversion, you have the potential for the user to input an invalid string. Therefore, the `XmlConvert` class is used whenever an `AfterLabelEdit` event is thrown. Within the event handler, the new text is converted using `EncodeName` to ensure the XML document remains valid.

The other function provided by the `XmlConvert` class, as mentioned earlier, is to convert XML strings to .NET data types or the other way around. If you recall from earlier chapters, you use the `Convert` class to convert data types. So you might be wondering why you even have to bother with the `XmlConvert` class because the `Convert` class already provides this functionality. In most cases, you are probably safe using the `Convert` methods. However, the `XmlConvert` class was designed to work with data types specified in XML schemas. In other words, the `date` data type in the XML schema might not necessarily be the same as the `DateTime` data type in the .NET framework. Therefore, if you pass an XML schema–based string representing a date time value into the `Convert` method `ToDateTime`, you might receive a `FormatException`. Again, for simple data types like integers, you might be safe. However, when working with XML string conversions, you might as well use the `XmlConvert` as an extra layer of protection.

13.5. Validating XML Documents with Schemas

> You want to ensure an XML file is valid by testing it against a defined schema.

Technique

You validate an XML document by using the `XmlValidatingReader` class instead of `XmlTextReader` or `XmlNodeReader`. However, the `XmlValidatingReader` only validates the data that is being read and delegates the actual loading and parsing of the XML file to one of the other classes. To create an `XmlValidatingReader` object that will read from an XML file, create an `XmlTextReader` or `XmlNodeReader` object and pass it into the `XmlValidatingReader` constructor:

```
XmlTextReader xmlTR = new XmlTextReader( currentDoc );
XmlValidatingReader xmlVR = new XmlValidatingReader( xmlTR );
```

Validation utilizes events rather than exceptions to report any validation errors. It allows you to continue parsing the document even if a portion of it is invalid, thereby allowing you to notify the user of all validation errors that were encountered. The event that is fired is named appropriately enough `ValidationEventHandler`, and the delegate accepts a `ValidationEventArgs` object in addition to the standard `System.Object` representing the sender of the event. Combining these facts with the code shown earlier, setting up validation appears as follows:

```
private void mnuValidate_Click(object sender, System.EventArgs e)
{
    ValidateOpen vo = new ValidateOpen();
    if( vo.ShowDialog(this) == DialogResult.OK )
    {
        // load document
        XmlTextReader xmlTR = new XmlTextReader( currentDoc );
        XmlValidatingReader xmlVR = new XmlValidatingReader( xmlTR );
        xmlVR.ValidationEventHandler +=
            new ValidationEventHandler (SchemaValidationHandler);

        while( xmlVR.Read() )
        {
            // process XML
        }

        xmlVR.Close();
    }
}

public void SchemaValidationHandler(object sender, ValidationEventArgs args)
{
    string error = "*** Validation Failed ***\n";
    error += args.Message;

    MessageBox.Show( this, error, "XML Viewer",
        MessageBoxButtons.OK, MessageBoxIcon.Error );
}
```

Comments

Because XML files can come in all shapes and sizes, schemas define a certain XML file format that you can validate generated XML files against. The XML schema language itself can be difficult to understand, which is why several books exist just on that single topic. In most cases, however, you can utilize one of the many XML tools and even Visual Studio .NET to automatically generate a schema based on an existing XML file.

To do so using Visual Studio .NET, open an XML file and click on XML, Create Schema from the main menu. Although this method works for most XML files that you deal with, sometimes you will have to hand-edit the schema so that it better fits your XML file format.

Once you define an XML schema for your XML file format, you can use it to validate XML files that are created off that schema. When you use the `XmlValidatingReader` class in the .NET Framework, you have two options available to associate a schema with an XML document. There is no clear-cut best practice with using any option, so you should therefore pick the option that more closely fits with your project's design objectives.

One of these options is to simply place a reference to the schema file within the XML file itself. For instance, to associate a schema file named `XMLSchema.xsd` located in the same file directory as an XML file that uses that schema, the XML file makes a reference at the root element as follows:

```
<?xml version="1.0" encoding="utf-8"?>
<root xmlns:xsi="http://www.w3.org/2001/XMLSchema-instance"
    xsi:noNamespaceSchemaLocation="XMLSchema.xsd"/>
```

When you use the `XmlValidatingReader` class to parse the XML file, the `ValidationEventHandler` fires whenever the XML file doesn't conform to the schema it references.

One other option is to programmatically add a schema reference before parsing begins. You do so by accessing the `Schemas` collection defined in the `XmlValidatingReader`. The `Schemas` collection contains an `Add` method that allows you to either add an entire prebuilt collection or specify a filename to the `xsd` file. Once you do so, validation occurs even if there is no schema referenced within the original XML file:

```
xmlVR.Schemas.Add( null, vo.Path );
while( xmlVR.Read() ){}

xmlVR.Close();
```

13.6. Programmatically Generating XML Documents

> You want to programmatically add or remove elements and attributes from an XML document.

Technique

The `XmlDocument` class contains several methods that allow you to generate various nodes within an XML document. The first step is to find the node that you will append the new node to. For instance, if you create a new attribute using the `CreateAttribute` method, you need a corresponding element node to append it to. For new elements, you need to know the node that you will use as the axes for node insertion depends on which insertion method you call.

To create new attribute for an existing element, call the `CreateAttribute` method, passing a string for the attribute name. It returns an `XmlAttribute` object whose `Value` property is used for the attribute value. To add the new attribute to an existing element, call the `SetNamedItem` method defined in the `Attributes` collection of the selected `XmlNode` object:

```
// get selected node
XmlNode selNode = xmlDoc.SelectSingleNode( tvXML.SelectedNode.FullPath );

// add attribute
XmlAttribute newAtt = xmlDoc.CreateAttribute( newAttributeName );
newAtt.Value = newAttributeValue;
selNode.Attributes.SetNamedItem( newAtt );
```

You can optionally use some of the insertion methods to the attribute in a certain position in the attribute list. Some of these methods, defined in the `Attributes` collection of the `XmlNode` class, include `Prepend` and `Append`, which add the attribute to the beginning or end of the attribute list, respectively, and `InsertAfter` and `InsertBefore`, which place the node in the corresponding position of an attribute retrieved using the `Item` property:

```
// add to beginning of attribute list
selNode.Attributes.Prepend( newAtt );

// add to end of attribute list
selNode.Attributes.Append( newAtt );

// insert before middle element
selNode.Attributes.InsertBefore(
    newAtt,selNode.Attributes[selNode.Attributes.Count/2]);

// insert after middle element
selNode.Attributes.InsertAfter(
    newAtt,selNode.Attributes[selNode.Attributes.Count/2]);
```

Creating new elements or any of the other XML constructs is similar to attribute creation, but there is no need to add the newly created item to a collection. Instead, you simply select the node that will be used as the reference and call one of the insert methods that allows you to place the newly created element at a position relative to the reference node.

Comments

If you use XML extensively in your application or at least plan to, you'll eventually need to programmatically add new data into the XML document. XML files contain several individual "pieces" to them, and each one has a corresponding creation method defined in the `XmlDocument` class. These methods generally use string parameters for any pertinent data corresponding to the node being created. As an example, the `CreateComment` method uses a single string that, as you might have guessed, is the text of the comment to insert. The `CreateXmlDeclaration` method uses three strings, corresponding to the version, the encoding, and the value of the standalone attribute, which is generally set to `null`.

Each one of these methods returns a custom data type. However, these data types are ultimately derived from `XmlNode` so they can be used in the insertion functions defined in `XmlDocument`, as explained earlier.

13.7. Controlling `XmlTextWriter` **Formatting**

You want to alter the way an XML document is saved with the `XmlTextWriter` class.

Technique

An `XmlTextWriter` object is used in conjunction with the `Save` method of an `XmlDocument` object to write XML to a file. After you create an `XmlTextWriter` object, you control the formatting by changing the `Formatting`, `IndentChar`, `Indentation`, and `QuoteChar` properties.

You use the `Formatting` property to control indentation. If it is not set to `Formatting.Indented`, then indentation does not occur when the file is written. If indentation is enabled, you can set the `IndentChar` property. It allows you to change the default character used for indention. The default value is a space character, but you can change it to any character you desire. Note, however, that any nonwhitespace character causes extra text nodes to be created in the final document, which can cause side effects if you read it in later. You generally want to set this value to the tab character (`'\t'`) or leave the default.

`Indentation` is also coupled with the `Formatting` property as well as the `IndentChar` property. `Indentation` refers to the number of `IndentChar` characters to insert whenever indentation is output to the final XML file. In other words, if this value is set to 2 and the `IndentChar` is the space character, then two spaces are inserted for each indentation level.

You use the `QuoteChar` property to set the character used for attribute values. Each attribute value within an XML document must be surrounded by either single or double quotation marks. Changing the `QuoteChar` property allows you to choose which punctuation symbol to use:

```
XmlTextWriter writer = new XmlTextWriter( filename, NULL );
writer.Formatting = Formatting.Indented;
writer.IndentChar = '\t';
writer.Indentation = 2;
```

```
writer.QuoteChar = '\'';
xmlDoc.Save( writer );
writer.Close();
```

Comments

`XmlTextWriter` is a class designed to write well-formed XML data to a file or stream. It can be used by the `XmlDocument` class to save the XML document to a file, but you are also free to use the `XmlTextWriter` methods themselves. There are, of course, advantages and disadvantages to doing so. First of all, being able to write the XML yourself using this class gives you a little bit of flexibility in APIs to use. In other words, you might prefer the `XmlTextWriter` methods for XML node creation over the corresponding methods defined in the `XmlDocument` class. However, this flexibility carries with it the disadvantage of utilizing file I/O, which for large files can be slow. Furthermore, the XML document is not retained in memory, which means that any changes require you to read the file into an `XmlDocument` object and use the node creation methods in that object anyway. If these disadvantages don't apply to you, then the `XmlTextWriter` class might be the best match for your application.

13.8. Working with XML Namespaces

> The XML document that your application is parsing contains namespaces that you must resolve.

Technique

When you load an XML file containing namespace declarations and references using the `XmlDocument` class, you'll notice something peculiar: nothing. Everything is working just as you want with no exceptions or errors being returned—that is, until you decide to call the `SelectSingleNode` method to retrieve an `XmlNode` object. If it occurs and the node you are attempting to retrieve contains a namespace prefix, an exception is thrown. This exception occurs because the XML readers do not automatically resolve namespaces for you. It's something you have to do yourself.

The `SelectSingleNode` contains an additional overload that uses an `XmlNamespaceManager` object. This object is used by the `XmlDocument` class to resolve any namespace prefixes it encounters when asked to navigate the document using XPath expressions. Within this class is a table called the `NameTable`. Its purpose is to simply associate a namespace prefix with its corresponding URI. The table itself, however, isn't created by simply parsing an XML document. You have to manually add the namespace prefixes and URIs when the document is being parsed.

If you are already familiar with the namespaces that will be used within an XML document and you don't expect the prefixes for those namespaces to change, you can just call the `AddNamespace` method defined in the `XmlNamespaceManager` class. For instance, after you load an XML file into an XmlDocument object, create an XmlNamespaceManager object, associate it with the XmlDocument, and then call the AddNamespace method:

```
XmlDocument xmlDoc = new XmlDocument();
xmlDoc.Load( "books.xml" );
XmlNamespaceManager xmlNS = new XmlNamespaceManager( xmlDoc.NameTable );
xmlNS.AddNamespace( "book", "urn:test" );
XmlNode node = xmlDoc.SelectSingleNode( "//book:info[@title='A Book Title']" );
```

Whenever an XML node is queried for using SelectSingleNode and it contains the "book" namespace prefix, the XmlDocument object is able to successfully resolve the URI of the namespace prefix by accessing the NameTable in the XmlNamespaceManager.

There might be instances where your application isn't tied to a specific schema but instead works with any XML documents, as is the case with XML editors. In these instances, you have to build the NameTable as the file is being parsed. One possible solution is to do a substring check on any attributes of elements that are encountered. The substring to check for is "xmlns:", which indicates that the attribute is a namespace declaration. The following code is a fragment of code from the project accompanying this chapter:

```
while( rdr.Read() )
{
    switch (xmlVR.NodeType)
    {
        // new start element found
        case XmlNodeType.Element:
        {
            // populate attribute hashtable for element
            if( xmlVR.HasAttributes == true )
            {
                while( xmlVR.MoveToNextAttribute() )
                {
                    if( xmlVR.Name.StartsWith( "xmlns:" ))
                    {
                        namespaceTable.AddNamespace(
                            xmlVR.Name.Substring( 6 ), xmlVR.Value );
                    }
                }
            }
        }
        break;
        }
    }
}
```

Another possible solution, which doesn't require parsing the entire file, is to use an XPathNavigator to enumerate the namespaces contained within an XmlDocument. The

XPathNavigator contains two enumeration methods named MoveToFirstNamespace and MoveToNextNamespace, allowing you to quickly jump to each namespace without having to parse through the individual elements and determine whether they contain a namespace prefix or not. You can easily place the following code into an application and return an XmlNamespaceManager that you can use in XPath query methods:

```
private XmlNamespaceManager FillNamespaceTable( XmlDocument xmlDoc )
{
    XmlNamespaceManager xmlNS = new XmlNamespaceManager(xmlDoc.NameTable);
    XPathNavigator xPath = xmlDoc.DocumentElement.CreateNavigator();
    if (xPath.MoveToFirstNamespace())
    {
        do
        {
            if ( xPath.Name.StartsWith("xml") == false )
            {
                xmlNS.AddNamespace(xPath.Name, xPath.Value);
            }
        } while (xPath.MoveToNextNamespace());
    }
    return xmlNS;
}
```

Comments

Namespaces were created to avoid ambiguity. If two different developers are writing an application for a pet store, and both applications use a data layer consisting of XML files, the possibility that they will create the same element names is quite high. Furthermore, even if the elements do refer to the same physical entity, the semantics might still differ. In other words, if both developers used an element named "price" referring to the price of an object, one might use retail while the other is referring to wholesale price. This little scenario, of course, doesn't mention the probability that one developer's XML file will be sent to the other developer's application, but if they use namespaces, it wouldn't matter.

You might find it surprising that you have to put so much work into supporting XML namespaces into your application. You might even believe the assumption that the .NET classes should contain that functionality, freeing you from the hassle (albeit small hassle) of working with namespaces. The reasoning behind this assumption take us to the W3C recommendation.

XML namespaces are not identifiers for elements. They are merely placed for the convenience of the developer parsing the data to disambiguate element names. In fact, it's entirely legal to declare a namespace prefix twice in the same document but give them different URIs, as shown in the following example:

```
<item:book xmlns:prefix="http://www.samspublishing.com"/>
<item:book xmlns:prefix="http://www.anotherpublisher.com"/>
```

When an XPath expression is created to select an `item:book` node, the XPath processor will be unable to determine which element it refers to. However, because you are more intimately familiar with the file format that your application consumes, you can use the `XmlNamespaceManager` to resolve the ambiguities at runtime for the benefit of the XPath processor. In this case, one solution is to change the prefix of one of the namespaces so a collision doesn't occur by specifying a different key in the call to `AddNamespace`:

```
xmlNS.AddNamespace( "samsitem:book", "http://www.samspublishing.com" );
```

13.9. Transforming XML Documents with XSLT

You want to use Extensible Stylesheet Transformations (XSLT) to transform an XML document into a different format.

Technique

The `XslTransform` class implements XSLT 1.0 and allows you to transform the contents of an XML file into a different file format. This different file format itself doesn't have to be XML but can be any other text-based file format, such as HTML or XHTML. If you use the `XslTransform` class in version 1.0 of the .NET Framework, then you'll notice that it has undergone several design changes with regards to its API in version 1.1.

The main workhorse of this class is the `Transform` method. Most of the version 1.0 overloaded methods of this class have been marked as obsolete and replaced with new methods, each one differing in how the data is read and the object to use to write the resultant output.

One of these methods is a special case, which is discussed later in this section, so we look at the remaining eight methods first. Each `Transform` method requires either an `XPathNavigator` or an object that implements the `IXPathNavigable` interface. You can retrieve an `XPathNavigator` object by calling the `CreateNavigator` method defined in the `XmlDocument` class. However, the `XmlDocument` class also implements the `IXPathNavigable` interface, which means you are free to simply pass the `XmlDocument` object itself into the method.

The second parameter to the `Transform` method, which is the same in all overloaded versions, is an argument list whose data type is `XsltArgumentList`. XSLT can access arguments passed into it similar to the way an application is able to access command-line arguments. To add a new parameter to the argument list, call the `AddParam` method, passing the name of the parameter, an optional namespace URI or empty string, and the value of the parameter.

The third parameter is the object used to handle the resultant output from the XSLT processor. As with many file output scenarios, and as mentioned in the previous chapter, it can be a stream-based or file-based object.

Finally, the final parameter shared among the six overloaded methods is an `XmlResolver` object. You use this object whenever you make a resolution of a DTD, schema, or entity declaration. In most cases, you can simply pass `null` for this parameter. However, if the references are not local to the file being parsed (they exist on a secure server, for instance), then you need to create an `XmlResolver` object to supply the proper credentials to resolve the reference. The following code shows how to load an XML document, create an output file, and perform the XSLT transformation using the parameters explained so far:

```
XmlDocument xmlDoc = new XmlDocument();
xmlDoc.Load("some.xml");

XslTransform xslt = new XslTransform();
xslt.Load("stylesheet.xsl");

XsltArgumentList args = new XsltArgumentList();
args.AddParam( "param", "", "paramValue" );

XmlTextWriter writer = new XmlTextWriter("output.html", null );
xslt.Transform(xmlDoc.CreateNavigator(), args, writer, null);
```

The following code contains a lot of setup to finally get to the point of transformation. Fortunately, the `Transform` method also contains an overloaded version, the special case mentioned earlier, that simply expects two filenames passed as string objects and an `XmlResolver` object, which can be null:

```
XslTransform xsl = new XslTransform();
xsl.Load( "stylesheet.xsl" );
xsl.Transform( xmlDoc, "output.html", null );
```

Comments

We are big fans of XSLT. Anytime we even start to think that we need to transform an XML document in an application, we immediately start thinking of XSLT templates. Sure, you could write a class that would take an XML document and transform it into something else, but you lose one of the major advantages that XSLT provides, simplicity. That's not saying, of course, that the XSLT language is something you can pick up in a day. It's merely stating that once you are familiar with what XSLT can do, you'll see that it can provide tremendous cost savings due to the quick turnaround time of creating an XSLT stylesheet.

We wish we could really get into some of the intricacies of XSLT and how to utilize the templates to do some amazing things, but just like most other XML-based technologies, it warrants an entire book of its own.

14

Database Programming with ADO.NET

14.0. Introduction

At the heart of every application, information provides the fuel that logic uses to drive a presentation. Whether it's individual bits in an image file or large tables from a large database server, almost every application utilizes data and presents it to a user for display and manipulation. This chapter is going to look at one of the cornerstones of the .NET framework, ADO.NET.

ADO.NET is the successor to the Active Data Objects (ADO) used in years past. Although some similarities exist, the fundamental design changed to keep pace with the data-centric world we live in. No doubt the majority of these changes were a result of the rising popularity of Web applications and their interaction with database servers. ADO.NET introduces a new way to think about database connectivity by using a disconnected client scenario. In short, applications no longer have to maintain a constant connection with a database, instead relying on a special object to cache the data and make updates when necessary. This chapter discusses more of how ADO.NET operates and how to use the new objects introduced with its arrival.

14.1. Creating a Database Connection

You want to open a connection to a database.

Technique

You make a database connection within .NET by first creating a database connection string. This semicolon-delimited list of values contains various connection parameters to control how a connection is made. ADO.NET contains a couple of connection classes based on the type of database you are utilizing. For instance, a connection to an SQL Server uses the `SqlConnection` class, whereas Object Linking and Embedding (OLEDB)-supported databases use the `OleDBConnection` class. Most of the connection objects support a subset of connection string parameters but are not required to support all. You must investigate the possible connection-string parameters for your type of connection.

This chapter utilizes SQL Server for its discussions. However, you don't need the full version of SQL Server to use it. A copy of the Microsoft SQL Server 2000 Desktop Engine is included with Visual Studio .NET 2003 and the .NET Framework software development kit (SDK) but is not installed by default. Once installed, it allows you to use SQL databases within your application.

To create a connection to an SQL Server database, pass a connection string to the `SqlConnection` constructor when instantiating an `SqlConection` object. To open the connection, call the `Open` method, and likewise, to close the connection, call the `Close` method defined within the `SqlConnection` class. The application in this chapter uses a connection string containing three parameters. The first is `Integrated Security`, which is set to `SSPI` and tells SQL Server that you want to enable Windows-based authentication. The `Data Source` parameter is set to your machine name, which is obviously different from the machine name we are using. Finally, the `Initial Catalog` parameter is set to `Northwind` because the examples in this chapter use the Northwind database.

```
[STAThread]
static void Main(string[] args)
{
    SqlConnection connection;
    string connectionString = "Integrated Security=SSPI;" +
        "Data Source=VCSMARKHSCH6;Initial Catalog=Northwind;";

    // create new SqlConnection specifying the connection string
    connection = new SqlConnection( connectionString );

    // open the connection
    connection.Open();

    // get the data

    // close the connection
    connection.Close();
}
```

Comments

The major hurdle to overcome when creating a database connection is figuring out the correct connection string to use. Using an Access database with the `OleDBConnection` class uses the same Open and Close methods; the only difference between it and SqlConnection lies within the connection string.

As mentioned in the introduction, you can use ADO.NET in a disconnected state. In other words, you can open an initial database connection, transfer data to a cache object, and then close the connection. However, you are still free to manipulate the data, only reconnecting when you want to apply those changes. The objects involved in this scenario include a data adapter such as SqlDataAdapter, which you use to manage the transfer of data between a database and the in-memory data-representation object called the DataSet. Each of these objects is explained in the following sections.

14.2. Creating and Filling DataSets

> You want to transfer information from a database into a DataSet object.

Technique

You use a DataSet object to store information retrieved from a database. Filling a DataSet refers to transferring information from the database using a data adapter as the managing agent. The first step is to generate the SELECT SQL statement, which the command sent to the server through the data provider to extract the appropriate information. In the following example, an SQL statement extracts all the rows from the Products table within the Northwind database. You can use the SELECT string in one or two ways. The example that follows creates an SqlCommand object using the SELECT string as a parameter along with the SqlConnection object. This SqlCommand object is then used to construct an SqlDataAdapter object. The second option, which doesn't appear here, is to simply pass the SELECT string to the SqlDataAdapter along with the connection object. Both methods give you the same result.

After you create the SqlDataAdapter, you are ready to transfer the information from the database to the DataSet object. You do so by using the Fill method. The method uses the DataSet object as the first parameter and an optional table name as the second. This table name gives a name to the table that is generated within the DataSet and should not be confused with the name of the tables from the database. If you do not specify a table name, a default table named "Table" is used. Once the Fill method returns, you can close the connection and begin working with the DataSet object:

```
[STAThread]
static void Main(string[] args)
{
    SqlConnection connection;
    SqlDataAdapter dataAdapter;
    DataSet productsDS;
    SqlCommand selectCommand;
```

```
    string connectionString = "Integrated Security=SSPI; " +
        "Data Source=VCSMARKHSCH6;Initial Catalog=Northwind;";

    string selectCmd = "SELECT * From Products";

    // create new SqlConnection specifying the connection string
    connection = new SqlConnection( connectionString );

    // create new dataset object and data adapter used to fill it
    productsDS = new DataSet();
    selectCommand = new SqlCommand( selectCmd, connection );
    dataAdapter = new SqlDataAdapter( selectCommand );

    // open the connection
    connection.Open();

    // fill the dataset from products table
    dataAdapter.Fill(productsDS, "Products" );

    // close the connection
    connection.Close();
}
```

Comments

The actual transfer of data from a database to your application uses three objects. The first was explained in the previous section outlining how to create a connection to a database. The second object is the data adapter, which controls the flow of information between a database connection and the third object, the DataSet. A DataSet is an object that contains a memory-based representation of a database, exposing a hierarchical object model consisting of tables, columns, and rows as well as constraints and table relationships. Because of this hierarchical nature, you can easily serialize a DataSet using XML or automatically generate a schema based on the database representation it contains.

DataSet objects can be either typed or untyped. An untyped DataSet is similar to the example shown earlier. At the point when the fill occurs, no predefined XML schema was generated for the DataSet. A typed DataSet, on the other hand, is a specially designed class derived from the DataSet class built to take advantage of the database representation contained within an XML schema. In other words, a typed DataSet is one in which the database format is known beforehand and uses properties and methods specifically designed for that format. Furthermore, you can construct typed DataSets by using some tools that ship with Visual Studio .NET. Recipe 14.7, "Displaying a DataGrid," demonstrates using a typed DataSet in conjunction with Windows Forms controls and Recipe 16.9, "Using the DataGrid Web Form Control," shows how to use a typed DataSet in Web Form applications.

14.3. Generating an XML Schema for an Untyped `DataSet`

> You want to generate a schema for an untyped `DataSet` that can then be used to create a typed `DataSet`.

Technique

A typed `DataSet` is a class derived from a `DataSet` containing specific methods and properties designed to work with certain tables in a database. Creating a typed `DataSet` involves creating an XML schema for an untyped `DataSet` by using the tools within Visual Studio .NET. This example creates a typed `DataSet` from the Products table in the Northwind database.

Assuming you have a project created, choose Project, Add New Item. Select the Data Set template and give it a name. The name that you place within the Name field will be the name of the generated class. When the item is created, you will be placed in a design view. Open Server Explorer and locate the data connection you want to use. For this example, use the `MachineName.Northwind.dbo` data connection. Expand the data connection until you locate the Products table within the Tables node, and drag and drop the table onto the designer. When you save the XML schema file, Visual Studio .NET will generate the underlying `DataSet` class. By default, the C# source file is hidden from view within Solution Explorer. To view the generated class, either click on the Show All Files toolbar button located at the top of Solution Explorer or view the class using Class View.

Comments

A `DataSet` presents data hierarchically by utilizing properties and collections extensively, each returning other ADO.NET objects. For instance, accessing the `Tables` property of the `DataSet` class returns a `DataTable` object, and using the `Relations` collection returns a `DataRelation` object. Within the `DataTable` is a collection of `DataColumn` and `DataRow` objects as well as any relational links using the `ParentRelations` and `ChildRelations` collection, each of which is implemented as a `DataRelation` collection. When using an untyped `DataSet`, you work directly with these classes to access the data contained within the `DataSet`. However, the APIs for these classes are generic in that no custom methods and properties can be created and added to these objects at compile or runtime. A typed `DataSet` solves this problem.

The "Technique" section demonstrated a method to create a typed `DataSet`. The result of this procedure generated an XML schema representing the data format and a generated C# class containing custom classes, methods, and properties specifically designed for the table or tables it represents. The example generated four classes. The first is the typed `DataSet`, which in our project is named `ProductsDS`. This class is derived from the `DataSet` class, allowing you to use it wherever a `DataSet` class is used to represent the Products table. Within the class is a single property named `Products`, which you might have guessed represents the Products table for the database whose data type is a class derived from `DataTable` named `ProductsDataTable`. Once you start investigating this class, you can start to see where the customized methods and properties come into play. Some of the methods within the `ProductsDataTable` include `AddProductsRow`; `NewProductsRow`; `FindByProductID`, which was created because the `ProductID` field in the database is a primary key; and `RemoveProductsRow`. The rows themselves are another custom class derived from the `DataRow` class, which is named `ProductsRow`. The `ProductsRow` class contains several methods to check whether a certain field is `null` and a property that you can access corresponding to each field within the row. Furthermore, because the XML schema that was generated contained type information gathered from the SQL database, each property has a related .NET data type. The last class that is created is an `EventArg` derived class used as arguments passed to a delegate in response to a row within the `Products` table being changed.

14.4. Reading Database Records Using SqlDataReader

> You want to read each record within a certain table in an SQL database.

Technique

The `SqlDataReader` class provides a quick forward-only reader that streams data from a database. Using an `SqlDataReader` does not utilize a data adapter or a `DataSet`, leaving the in-memory data-storage details up to the developer.

Two objects are used in conjunction with the `SqlDataReader`. The first is an `SqlConnection`, and the second is an `SqlCommand` used to perform the database query. After the `SqlConnection` is created, create a new `SqlCommand` object passing a string used for the `SELECT` command and the `SqlConnection` object. Next, open the database connection by calling the `Open` method from the `SqlConnection` object. You create an `SqlDataReader` by calling the `ExecuteReader` method from the `SqlCommand` object, which returns an `SqlDataReader` ready for use.

The `SqlDataReader` reads a record from the database each time its `Read` method is called. If no more records are left to read, the method returns `false`. Furthermore, calling `Read` reads the record into the object and you must then extract any fields using one of several reading methods defined in the `SqlDataReader` class corresponding to the data type of the column. Each of these methods uses an integer denoting the column index of the data you want to read. For instance, if a cell contains integer data in the fourth column, you call the `GetInt32` method passing the integer 4 as a parameter. The following code makes a connection to the Northwind database and creates an `SqlCommand` object that returns all the records from the Products table. After the `ExecuteReader` method is called from the `SqlCommand` object, a `while` loop is created to read all the records from the table. Within the loop, the code writes each cell within the current record to the console using the GetValue method. This method simply returns the corresponding cell data in a System.Object:

```
using System;
using System.Data;
using System.Data.SqlClient;

namespace _4_SqlReader
{
    class Class1
    {
        [STAThread]
        static void Main(string[] args)
        {
            string connectionString = "Integrated Security=SSPI; " +
                "Data Source=VCSMARKHSCH6;Initial Catalog=Northwind;";
            SqlConnection connection = new SqlConnection( connectionString );
            SqlCommand select =
                new SqlCommand("SELECT * From PRODUCTS", connection );
            SqlDataReader rdr;

            connection.Open();
            rdr = select.ExecuteReader();
            bool writeColumns = true;

            while (rdr.Read())
            {
                if( writeColumns == true )
                {
                    for( int i = 0; i < rdr.FieldCount; i++ )
                    {
                        Console.Write(rdr.GetName(i) + "\t" );
                    }
                    Console.WriteLine();
                    writeColumns = false;
                }
                for( int i = 0; i < rdr.FieldCount; i++ )
                {
                    Console.Write( "\"{0}\" ", rdr.GetValue(i).ToString() );
                }
                Console.WriteLine();
            }

            rdr.Close();
            connection.Close();
```

```
            }
        }
    }
}
```

Comments

The previous recipes within this chapter demonstrated how to set up data adapters to fill a `DataSet` object as well as the method to create a typed `DataSet`. All these operations created several objects in the process to contain the data, and once the data was read, it was cached in a `DataSet` object to support random access. The `SqlDataReader` class takes an opposite approach to data access. Instead of creating several different objects to create an in-memory representation of the data, it leaves that functionality up to you. In other words, an `SqlDataReader` simply reads data and discards it with each subsequent `Read` method call. Additionally, because this data is discarded, you cannot make random access, which is why an `SqlDataReader` is known as a forward-only reader.

The two methods shown so far in this chapter both support the access of data but use different methodologies. Choosing one depends on the type of functionality you need. If your goal is to use the data throughout the lifetime of an application, with the ability to update the database periodically, then using a data adapter coupled with a `DataSet` is the best method. If you need to simply read data using the most efficient way possible, with regards to performance, then consider using an `SqlDataReader` or other suitable data reader.

14.5. Creating Forms with the Data Form Wizard

You want to quickly create a Windows Form application that allows you to edit tables within a database.

Technique

The Data Form Wizard is a special component within Visual Studio .NET that quickly sets up a database-editing application by asking you a series of questions using a wizard. To use the wizard, create a new Windows Form application and add a new item with Project, Add New Item. Select the Data Form Wizard template. This example uses the Northwind database to show a list of customers and the orders that each customer has placed. The first question asks for a name used for the `DataSet` object that is created, which for this example can be something like `CustomerOrdersDS`. Next, select the data connection to use by using the drop-down list or creating a new connection to the Northwind database, if one hasn't been created already. The next step allows you to select the data that the controls on the form will display. Controls can display data from tables or views. Select Customers, Orders, and Order Details from the list of tables.

You need to specify how the tables you selected are related. The Customers and the Orders tables are related because they both share a `CustomerID` key field. Therefore, enter a name of `CustomerOrders` in the name field, and select Customers as the parent table and Orders as the child table. The key field for both of these tables is `CustomerID`. The next relationship binds the Orders table with the Order Details table. The parent table is the Orders table, and the child is the Order Details table, each sharing a key field named `OrderID`.

You can further customize the amount of data that is shown by selecting the columns that are displayed. To hide a column from view, uncheck the check box next to the column name. Finally, you can control how the data controls are created. The two choices are to use `DataGrid` controls or to create an individual control for each data column. The `DataGrid` column, explained further in the next section, presents data within a spreadsheet-like view. Choosing to utilize individual controls creates separate controls for each column in the master table and a `DataGrid` for the detail views. This arrangement closely resembles the forms generated using Microsoft Access. You can run the generated Windows Form within your application, knowing that any record additions, deletions, and updates are automatically handled for you. Also, if you want to use the generated form as the startup form, open your project properties and specify it as the startup object within the General properties tab.

Comments

If you told us a couple of years ago that we could take a database and automatically create a full custom Windows application that edited the database tables, all without writing a single line of code, we would have thought you were crazy. Visual Studio .NET, through its extensibility model, allows you to create custom wizards and item templates for coding processes you use frequently. The Data Form Wizard is one example.

Although the Data Form Wizard does a pretty good job of creating the necessary data access code, you still want to edit it to make it a little more visually appealing. If you use the `DataGrid` display method, you can choose one of the predefined formats by right-clicking on the `DataGrid` within the Windows Form designer and selecting AutoFormat. Likewise, you can rearrange and add styles to any of the individual controls if you chose the individual control method.

14.6. Using Commands and Stored Procedures

You want to use stored procedures defined in SQL Server to retrieve data.

Technique

SQL stored procedures allow you to manipulate data using procedures created and stored within the database. These stored procedures can then be called by your application to return the data the stored procedures represent.

The following example demonstrates how to call the `CustOrderHist` stored procedure within the Northwind SQL database. The first steps within the code that follows open a data connection using an `SqlConnection` object and ask the user for a customer ID. To call a stored procedure, you need an `SqlCommand` object. This object was used in previous sections but represented SQL commands rather than stored procedures. The constructor for the `SqlCommand` object uses the name of the stored procedure as specified in the database and a reference to the `SqlConnection` object:

```
static void ViewCustomerOrderHistory()
{
    string connectionString = "Integrated Security=SSPI; " +
        "Data Source=VCSMARKHSCH6;Initial Catalog=Northwind;";
    SqlConnection connection = new SqlConnection( connectionString );
    string customerID;

    connection.Open();

    // get customer ID from user
    Console.Write( "Enter a customer ID: " );
    customerID = Console.ReadLine();

    // create new command using SQL stored procedure name
    SqlCommand myCommand = new SqlCommand("CustOrderHist", connection);
```

Next, to specify that you will be calling a stored procedure instead of sending an SQL statement, change the `CommandType` property of the `SqlCommand` object to `CommandType.StoredProcedure`. Add any parameters that the stored procedure uses. You do so by creating a series of `SqlParameter` objects and adding them to the `Parameters` collection of the `SqlCommand` class. When creating a new `SqlParameter` object, pass the name of the parameter as the first parameter of the constructor. The next parameter is the SQL data type followed by the size of the parameter. In the following example, the `CustomerID` parameter is an `SqlDbType.NChar` data type with a string length of 5. Next, you set the value of the parameter using the `Value` property, which in this case is the customer ID string entered by a user from the application:

```
    // Mark the Command as a stored procedure
    myCommand.CommandType = CommandType.StoredProcedure;

    // Add Parameter to SPROC
    SqlParameter param1 = new SqlParameter("@CustomerID", SqlDbType.NChar, 5);
    param1.Value = customerID;
    myCommand.Parameters.Add(param1);
```

After you add the `SqlParameter` to the `Parameters` collection using the `Add` method defined in the `SqlCommand` class, you create an `SqlDataReader` to read the results. Once the `ExecuteReader` method is called, the stored procedure runs and you can read its results from the `SqlDataReader` object using the same technique described in the previous section:

```
SqlDataReader rdr = myCommand.ExecuteReader();
if( rdr.FieldCount == 0 )
    Console.WriteLine( "No orders found for customer" );

while( rdr.Read() )
{
    for( int i = 0; i < rdr.FieldCount; i++ )
        Console.Write( "{0} ", rdr.GetValue(i) );
    Console.WriteLine();
}
rdr.Close();
connection.Close();
}
```

You can optionally use a stored procedure to fill a `DataSet`. You use an `SqlDataAdapter` instead of an `SqlCommand` object. The procedure is quite similar up to the point where the data is returned from the stored procedure. Rather than call the `ExecuteReader` command to begin reading with an `SqlDataReader`, you call the `SqlDataAdapter`'s `Fill` method to place the results within a `DataSet`. If you know the format of the data being returned and can generate an XML schema for it, you can optionally use a typed `DataSet` for the results. The following example uses the same stored procedure shown earlier but utilizes an `SqlDataAdapter` and `DataSet` object to retrieve the data:

```
public DataSet GetCustomerHistory(string customerID)
{
    string connectionString = "Integrated Security=SSPI; " +
        "Data Source=VCSMARKHSCH6;Initial Catalog=Northwind;";
    SqlConnection connection = new SqlConnection( connectionString );

    SqlDataAdapter adapter = new SqlDataAdapter("CustOrdersHist", connection);

    // Mark the Command as a SPROC
    adapter.SelectCommand.CommandType = CommandType.StoredProcedure;

    // Add Parameters to SPROC
    SqlParameter parameterCustomerId = new SqlParameter("@CustomerID",
SqlDbType.NChar, 5);
    parameterCustomerId.Value = customerID;
    adapter.SelectCommand.Parameters.Add(parameterCustomerId);

    // Create and Fill the DataSet
    DataSet myDataSet = new DataSet();
    adapter.Fill(myDataSet);
```

```
    // Return the DataSet
    return myDataSet;
}
```

Comments

One of the primary tenants of model-view-controller or n-tier application designs is to ensure you create a clear separation between the various pieces of your application. Data access code should be as loosely coupled as possible from the code that is used to access a database. Furthermore, the logic code that accesses a database should be independent from the code that retrieves the data. Although there will be overlap in some areas, you want to strive as much as possible to keep that overlap to a minimum.

The technique in this recipe is one that we use. By keeping data access code within SQL stored procedures, you are free to change the logic code as you see fit to another language, for instance, knowing that the stored procedures still give you the necessary data. Furthermore, if you decide to create a different methodology within your logic layer to better support a presentation layer, you know that you don't have to touch the data layer—whereas a complete rewrite is necessary if the logic module also contains the commands to interact with the underlying data.

14.7. Displaying a `DataGrid`

You want to use a `DataGrid` to display information from a database table.

Technique

The `DataGrid`, as its name implies, displays information from a database using an interface similar to a spreadsheet. Data is bound to the `DataGrid` using any of the methods discussed in this chapter. To create a `DataGrid`, create a new Windows Forms application and drag and drop the `DataGrid` control from the toolbox onto the Windows Form designer. All that is required to display data within the `DataGrid` is to set the `DataSource` property using a `DataSet` object, which can be either typed or untyped. Although you are certainly free to create the necessary code for the `DataSet` within your source file, the following method uses the Windows Form designer to generate the data access objects.

With the Windows Form designer open, open the Server Explorer tool window and locate the database table that you want to bind to the `DataGrid`. Once you find the table, simply drag and drop it onto the designer. This move automatically creates an `SqlConnection` and `SqlDataAdapter` object for you (`OleDbConnection` and `OleDbDataAdapter` if you are using an Access database). Next, select the `SqlDataAdapter` from the component list within the designer, and click on the Generate Dataset Property Browser verb. After giving your `DataSet` object a name, select the `DataGrid` and set the `DataSource` property to the `DataSet` you just created.

The last step is to ensure the `DataSet` is filled when your application begins. Open the form's source code and locate the form constructor. Use the `Fill` method from the `SqlDataAdapter` object, passing the typed `DataSet` object that was created when you generated the `DataSet`. At this point, you can run the application and the `DataGrid` displays the values:

```
public Form1()
{
    InitializeComponent();
    sqlDataAdapter1.Fill( productsDS1 );
}
```

While the user manipulates the data within the `DataGrid`, the underlying `DataSet` is also updated. However, because ADO.NET is working in a disconnected environment, those changes are not replicated back to the database. If you want to save any of the changes that are made to the `DataSet`, call the `Update` method defined in the `SqlDataAdapter` class, passing the `DataSet` object as a parameter. Listing 14.1 demonstrates how to detect whether any changes have been made to the `DataSet` object during the course of the session. If so, the user is prompted to save the database, and if the user chooses to save, the `Update` method is called. To determine whether a `DataSet` has been modified, check the `HasChanges` property:

Listing 14.1   Detecting `DataSet` Changes

```
private void dgProduct_CurrentCellChanged(object sender, System.EventArgs e)
{
    if( productsDS1.HasChanges() )
    {
        statusBar1.Text = "Modified";
    }
}


private void Form1_Closing(object sender, System.ComponentModel.CancelEventArgs e)
{
    if( productsDS1.HasChanges() )
    {
        DialogResult result;
        result = MessageBox.Show( this, "Would you like to save your changes?",
            "Northwind Products", MessageBoxButtons.YesNoCancel,
            MessageBoxIcon.Question );

        if( result == DialogResult.Cancel )
        {
            e.Cancel = true;
            return;
        }
        else if( result == DialogResult.No )
```

Listing 14.1   Continues

```
        {
            return;
        }
        else
        {
            sqlDataAdapter1.Update( productsDS1 );
        }
    }
}
```

Comments

The `DataGrid` control is a powerful control that allows you to create a database application in mere minutes. The features it supports would probably be enough to fill a book in itself. The technique in this section demonstrates the minimum essentials to create and use a `DataGrid` control within your application.

One thing you might have noticed when running an application with a `DataGrid` is the lack of any visual appeal. By default, the `DataGrid` simply renders a grid in white and black with a blue header. You can either change the several different properties that relate to the `DataGrid`'s style or choose one of several different canned formats by right-clicking on the `DataGrid` and selecting AutoFormat.

One interesting item to note is that a `DataGrid` doesn't have to be bound to a certain table within a `DataSet`. If you recall, a `DataSet` object can contain several tables of information, although this chapter has used the Products table for most examples. You can in fact set the `DataSource` property of the `DataGrid` to the `DataSet` itself rather than an individual table. When you do so, the `DataGrid` displays a tree control along the left side that, when expanded, contains links to each table within the `DataSet`. When you click a table link, the `DataGrid` expands and shows each cell within that table. Additionally, a back button within the `DataGrid`'s header allows you to go back to the list of tables.

14.8. Databinding Windows Form Controls

You want to use values from a database as values for certain properties of Windows Form controls.

Technique

Databinding a Windows Form control utilizes a separate approach than that taken by a `DataGrid` and ASP.NET controls. Rather than use a `DataSource` property and set a specific property for the display value, you create a data binding, which establishes a connection between the control and the underlying data source using a `BindingContext`.

The following example demonstrates creating a Windows Form application that creates a data binding between the text within a `TextBox` and the `ProductName` field within the Products table in the Northwind database. Furthermore, it demonstrates how to use the `BindingContext` object to easily navigate the records of the table to update the text displayed in the `TextBox`, as shown in Figure 14.1.

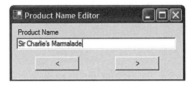

Figure 14.1   Navigating records using a `BindingContext`.

The application contains a single `TextBox` named `tbName` and two buttons named `btnPrev` and `btnNext`, which you use to select the previous or next record in the table, respectively. To databind a control, expand the `DataBindings` property item within the control's properties list. You see a list of possible properties that can be bound to. This example uses the `Text` property. Assuming you created the `SqlConnection`, `SqlDataAdapter`, and a typed `DataSet`, set the `Text` data-binding property to the `ProductName` field of the Products table defined in the `DataSet`. To display the text when the application starts, ensure that you call the `Fill` method defined in the `SqlDataAdapter` class, passing the `DataSet` as a parameter to that method. When your application runs at this point, the `TextBox` displays the name of the first product in the table. The next step is to create the navigation controls.

For the two buttons on the Windows Form, create event handlers for the `Click` event. Each `BindingContext` that is automatically created within your class for a data source contains a current position value indicating the current record it is pointing to in a specified table. Because a Windows Form can have more than one data source, the `BindingContext` is implemented as a collection of `BindingManagerBase` objects. To get the correct `BindingManagerBase` associated with the `TextBox` control, you use the `BindingContext` indexer passing the `DataSet` object and the table within the `DataSet` as the parameters. It returns the corresponding `BindingManagerBase`, which contains a property named `Position`. By incrementing or decrementing that property, you change the record that is currently in view and thus change the text within the `TextBox` control (and any other controls that are bound to that data source). Listing 14.2 shows the entirety of the application. Also, just as in the last section, as the text is edited within the `TextBox`, the underlying `DataSet` field is changed. To replicate the changes back to the database, call the `Update` method defined in the `SqlDataAdapter` class using the `DataSet` as a parameter.

Listing 14.2 **Performing Database Updates**

```
using System;
using System.Drawing;
using System.Collections;
using System.ComponentModel;
using System.Windows.Forms;
using System.Data;

namespace _8_DataBoundControls
{
    public class Form1 : System.Windows.Forms.Form
    {
        private System.Windows.Forms.TextBox tbName;
        private System.Windows.Forms.Button btnPrev;
        private System.Windows.Forms.Button btnNext;
        private System.Windows.Forms.Label label1;
        private System.Data.SqlClient.SqlCommand sqlSelectCommand1;
        private System.Data.SqlClient.SqlCommand sqlInsertCommand1;
        private System.Data.SqlClient.SqlCommand sqlUpdateCommand1;
        private System.Data.SqlClient.SqlCommand sqlDeleteCommand1;
        private System.Data.SqlClient.SqlConnection sqlConnection1;
        private System.Data.SqlClient.SqlDataAdapter sqlDataAdapter1;
        private _8_DataBoundControls.ProductDS productDS1;

        private System.ComponentModel.Container components = null;

        public Form1()
        {
            InitializeComponent();
            sqlDataAdapter1.Fill( productDS1 );
        }

        protected override void Dispose( bool disposing )
        {
            if( disposing )
            {
                if (components != null)
                {
                    components.Dispose();
                }
            }
            base.Dispose( disposing );
        }

        // Windows Form Designer Generated Code
```

Listing 14.2   **Continues**

```
[STAThread]
static void Main()
{
    Application.Run(new Form1());
}

private void btnPrev_Click(object sender, System.EventArgs e)
{
    tbName.BindingContext[productDS1, "Products"].Position -= 1;
}

private void btnNext_Click(object sender, System.EventArgs e)
{
    this.BindingContext[productDS1, "Products"].Position += 1;
}

private void Form1_Closing(object sender,
    System.ComponentModel.CancelEventArgs e)
{
    if( productDS1.HasChanges() )
    {
        DialogResult result;
        result = MessageBox.Show( this,
            "Would you like to save your changes?",
            "Northwind Products", MessageBoxButtons.YesNoCancel,
            MessageBoxIcon.Question );

        if( result == DialogResult.Cancel )
        {
            e.Cancel = true;
            return;
        }
        else if( result == DialogResult.No )
        {
            return;
        }
        else
        {
            sqlDataAdapter1.Update( productDS1 );
        }
    }
}
```

Comments

A `BindingContext` collection is created for any object that inherits from the `Control` class. This collection contains each `BindingManagerBase` object that is used by that control and every contained control. In the code just shown, you can see that changing the `Position` property of a `BindingManagerBase` was done from the `BindingContext` of the form itself and not the `TextBox` control. You do so knowing that the change will propagate itself down the hierarchy of contained controls, of which the `TextBox` is one. If you create several container controls such as a `GroupBox` or `Panel` control, you can use the `BindingContext` for those groups to affect their contained controls, allowing you to control which controls see which current record's position of a `DataSet` object. While one group of controls is currently viewing one record, another group is viewing a completely different record.

When you add a `DataGrid` onto a Windows Form in addition to other Windows Form controls, each control has a `DataSource` and `DisplayMember` property added to its list of properties. These two properties behave similarly to the corresponding properties of the `DataGrid`, which means you can forego the use of the `DataBinding` properties. Believe it or not, even though you aren't specifically creating a data binding using the technique discussed in this section, the controls still get updated if the data source used is the same as that of the `DataGrid`. If you set the same data source for the `DataGrid` and another control, that control uses the same `BindingManagerBase` as the `DataGrid`. Therefore, when the `DataGrid` automatically sets the `Position` property as the user clicks within a new cell, the other Windows Form control is also automatically updated. You can see an example of this feature in the downloadable code available on the Sams Web site (`http://www.samspublishing.com`) within the `7_DataGrid` project.

14.9. Using `CommandBuilder` to Automatically Generate Commands

> You want to create an `SqlDataAdapter` that automatically creates the correct INSERT, DELETE, and UPDATE commands.

Technique

The `SqlCommandBuilder` class is designed to work in conjunction with an `SqlDataAdapter` to automatically create SQL statements to manipulate a database. Before you create an `SqlCommandBuilder`, create an `SqlDataAdapter` and ensure that you set the `SelectCommand` property. Once you do so, create a new `SqlCommandBuilder` instance, passing the `SqlDataAdapter` as a parameter to the constructor. The following code demonstrates how:

```
[STAThread]
static void Main(string[] args)
```

```
{
    SqlConnection connection;
    SqlDataAdapter dataAdapter;
    DataSet productsDS;
    SqlCommandBuilder commandBuilder;
    SqlCommand selectCommand;

    string connectionString = "Integrated Security=SSPI; " +
        Data Source=VCSMARKHSCH6;Initial Catalog=Northwind;";
    string selectCmd = "SELECT * From Products";

    // create new SqlConnection specifying the connection string
    connection = new SqlConnection( connectionString );

    // create new dataset object and data adapter used to fill it
    productsDS = new DataSet();
    selectCommand = new SqlCommand( selectCmd, connection );
    dataAdapter = new SqlDataAdapter( selectCommand );

    // create command builder
    commandBuilder = new SqlCommandBuilder( dataAdapter );

    // open the connection
    connection.Open();

    // fill the dataset from products table
    dataAdapter.Fill(productsDS, "Products" );

    // manipulate the database here

    // update the database.  The SqlCommandBuilder will be used
    // to create the UPDATE SQL command
    dataAdapter.Update( productsDS );

    // close the connection
    connection.Close();
}
```

Comments

When you create an SqlDataAdapter, you specify an initial SelectCommand using either its constructor or an SqlCommand object. To insert, update, or delete records from a database, you also have to create commands for the InsertCommand, UpdateCommand, and DeleteCommand properties. You can use the SqlCommandBuilder as a quick way of automatically generating these commands. It does so by looking at the SelectCommand that you specified to create a schema that is used to generate each command. Once a

RowUpdating command is triggered, the SqlCommandBuilder generates the necessary statements. To view the generated commands from a console window, you can access the various commands, as shown in the following code:

```
Console.WriteLine( "INSERT command: {0}\n",
commandBuilder.GetInsertCommand().CommandText );
Console.WriteLine( "UPDATE command: {0}\n",
commandBuilder.GetUpdateCommand().CommandText );
Console.WriteLine( "DELETE command: {0}\n",
commandBuilder.GetDeleteCommand().CommandText );
```

When using an SqlCommandBuilder, you have to be aware of a few limitations that can cause it to fail and throw an exception in certain instances. First of all, the SelectCommand must return at least one column that is a primary key within the database. If it does not, an InvalidOperation exception is thrown and the command generation fails. Second, commands can only be generated for single table updates. Therefore, for any updates that utilize relationships or constraints such as a foreign-key constraint, the SqlCommandBuilder will be unable to generate the necessary commands. Finally, if at any time the SqlDataAdapter changes its SelectCommand, Connection, CommandTimeout, or Transaction properties, the generated commands become invalid. To recreate the SqlCommandBuilder commands for these cases, call the RefreshSchema method defined in the SqlCommandBuilder class.

14.10. Creating Different DataViews of a Table

You want to create different views of a table to enable sorting and filtering.

Technique

A DataSet object stores data just as it is received from the database. It doesn't allow you to perform custom sorting nor does it allow you to apply a filter to create a subset of data to bind to a control. The DataView class allows you to create custom views of a single table residing in a DataSet. By using a separate DataView, you are able to apply sorting, column-based filtering, and row-state filtering. Row-state filtering filters rows based on states such as rows that have been added, removed, and modified, to name a few.

To create a DataView object, you can programmatically create one of the supplied constructors or drag and drop it from the Windows Form designer toolbox within the Data tab onto your form. To associate the DataView with a table, set the Table property equal to a DataTable object. If you are using a typed DataSet, each table within the DataSet is a property, whereas tables within an untyped DataSet are located in the Tables collection.

After the DataSet object is filled from a data adapter, you can apply sorting and filtering to the DataView. To sort the table, pass a comma-delimited string of column names with an optional ASC or DESC modifier for each column to specify ascending or descending order for the `Sort` property of the `DataView` object. For instance, to sort the `Products` table of the Northwind database by `CategoryID` followed by `ProductName` in descending order, the `Sort` property appears as follows:

```
dataView1.Sort = "CategoryID, ProductName DESC";
```

You use the `RowFilter` property to display a subset of data within the table. The property is also a string value and uses logical expressions using the same syntax as SQL queries. If the expression returns `false` for a given row, that row is not displayed in any controls that are bound to the `DataView`. A filter that only displays products within a certain `CategoryID` looks like this:

```
dataView1.RowFilter = "CategoryID=3";
```

The `RowStateFilter` allows you to filter the rows of a table based on the current status in the `DataSet`. The possible values are contained within the `DataViewRowState` enumerated type and include such values as `None`, in which no rows are displayed; `Unchanged`, specifying rows that have not been modified; `Added`; and `Deleted`. You can also use values that let you filter using data before it was modified such as `Original` and `ModifiedOriginal`, as well as their current values using `Current` and `ModifiedCurrent`. The following example is a culmination of all the `DataView` techniques described in this section. The application itself contains a `DataGrid` that is bound to the `DataView` itself rather than a `DataSet`. Because the `DataView` uses the `DataSet` as its source, any changes within the `DataGrid` get automatically propagated to the `DataSet` as before. Additionally, you use two `ComboBox` controls to modify the `RowFilter` and `RowStateFilter` properties of the `DataView` object. The `RowFilter` allows you to filter the list of products within the `DataGrid` by only including those products within a certain category as shown in Listing 14.3.

Listing 14.3   **Controlling Views with Row Filters**

```
using System;
using System.Drawing;
using System.Collections;
using System.ComponentModel;
using System.Windows.Forms;
using System.Data;

namespace _10_DataViews
{
    /// <summary>
    /// Summary description for Form1.
    /// </summary>
    public class Form1 : System.Windows.Forms.Form
    {
        private System.Windows.Forms.DataGrid dgProducts;
        private System.Data.SqlClient.SqlCommand sqlSelectCommand1;
```

Listing 14.3 **Continued**

```csharp
private System.Data.SqlClient.SqlCommand sqlInsertCommand1;
private System.Data.SqlClient.SqlCommand sqlUpdateCommand1;
private System.Data.SqlClient.SqlCommand sqlDeleteCommand1;
private System.Data.SqlClient.SqlConnection sqlConnection1;
private System.Data.SqlClient.SqlDataAdapter sqlDataAdapter1;
private System.Data.SqlClient.SqlCommand sqlSelectCommand2;
private System.Data.SqlClient.SqlCommand sqlInsertCommand2;
private System.Data.SqlClient.SqlCommand sqlUpdateCommand2;
private System.Data.SqlClient.SqlCommand sqlDeleteCommand2;
private System.Data.SqlClient.SqlDataAdapter sqlDataAdapter2;
private _10_DataViews.ProductCategoriesDS productCategoriesDS1;
private System.Windows.Forms.Label label1;
private System.Data.DataView dataView1;
private System.Windows.Forms.ComboBox cbCategories;
private System.Windows.Forms.Label label2;
private System.Windows.Forms.ComboBox cbRowState;
private System.ComponentModel.Container components = null;

public Form1()
{
    InitializeComponent();

    // fill rowstate combo box items
    foreach( string state in Enum.GetNames( typeof(DataViewRowState) ))
    {
        cbRowState.Items.Add( state );
    }

    sqlDataAdapter1.Fill( productCategoriesDS1, "Products" );
    sqlDataAdapter2.Fill( productCategoriesDS1, "Categories" );

    // sort by prodcut name
    dataView1.Sort = "ProductName ASC";
}

private void SetFilters()
{
    int curCatID = Convert.ToInt32(cbCategories.SelectedValue);
    dataView1.RowFilter = "CategoryID=" + curCatID;

    if( cbRowState.SelectedIndex != -1 )
        dataView1.RowStateFilter = (DataViewRowState)
            Enum.Parse( typeof(DataViewRowState),
                cbRowState.SelectedItem.ToString(), true );
```

Listing 14.3   **Continued**

```
        dgProducts.DataSource = dataView1;
}


/// <summary>
/// Clean up any resources being used.
/// </summary>
protected override void Dispose( bool disposing )
{
    if( disposing )
    {
        if (components != null)
        {
            components.Dispose();
        }
    }
    base.Dispose( disposing );
}


#region Windows Form Designer generated code
// …
#endregion

/// <summary>
/// The main entry point for the application.
/// </summary>
[STAThread]
static void Main()
{
    Application.Run(new Form1());
}


private void cbCDategories_SelectedIndexChanged(
    object sender,
    System.EventArgs e)
{
    SetFilters();
}


private void Form1_Closing(
    object sender,
    System.ComponentModel.CancelEventArgs e)
{
    if( productCategoriesDS1.HasChanges() )
    {
        DialogResult result;
```

Listing 14.3   **Continued**

```
                    result = MessageBox.Show( this,
                        "Would you like to save your changes?",
                        "Northwind Products", MessageBoxButtons.YesNoCancel,
                        MessageBoxIcon.Question );
                    if( result == DialogResult.Cancel )
                    {
                        e.Cancel = true;
                        return;
                    }
                    else if( result == DialogResult.No )
                    {
                        return;
                    }
                    else
                    {
                        sqlDataAdapter1.Update( productCategoriesDS1 );
                    }
                }
            }

        private void cbRowState_SelectedIndexChanged(
            object sender,
            System.EventArgs e)
        {
            SetFilters();
        }
    }
}
```

Comments

You can probably just as easily perform this technique by using an SqlCommand or
SELECT statement provided to the SqlDataAdapter object to perform sorting and filtering. For instance, if you want to create a DataTable within a DataSet that returns all the
products sorted by name, you can use the following SELECT statement:

```
"SELECT * From Products Order By ProductName ASC"
```

The data is returned. However, what if in the same session, you want to view the products in descending order or to sort by a different column. You then have to recreate the
DataSet and create another connection and subsequent data transfer to the server. The
DataView class was designed to eliminate this type of data-transfer paradigm, allowing
you to continue working in the disconnected scenario. Furthermore, in addition to sorting by multiple columns and filtering rows based on the result of an expression, you can

also filter the rows based on the current status. If you only want to display the rows that have changed so you can, for instance, generate a change report, you can simply set the RowStateFilter property of the DataView object to ModifiedCurrent. You can then use the methods defined in the DataView class to extract the current data view. The following code demonstrates how to set the RowStateFilter to only return modified rows and how to read the DataView contents to display those rows:

```
private void DisplayModifiedRows()
{
    dataView1.RowStateFilter = DataViewRowState.ModifiedCurrent;

    foreach( DataRowView curRow in dataView1 )
    {
        for( int i = 0; i < dataView1.Table.Columns.Count; i++ )
        {
            Console.Write( curRow[i].ToString() + " " );
        }
        Console.WriteLine();
    }
}
```

14.11. Adding New Tables to a DataSet

You want to dynamically add a new table to an existing DataSet.

Technique

A DataSet contains a property named Tables, which is a dictionary-based collection containing DataTable objects. To add a new DataTable, call the Add method from the Tables collection, passing a string denoting the name of a table, an existing DataTable object, or no parameters if you want the name to be generated for you automatically. The name that is generated uses the syntax TableN where N denotes the next number in a sequence for multiple tables. The following example creates a new table within a DataSet and binds a DataGrid on a Windows Form to that DataSet:

```
public Form1()
{
    InitializeComponent();
    ds = new DataSet();
    ds.Tables.Add("ParentTable");
    dataGrid1.SetDataBinding( ds, "ParentTable" );

}
```

Each table contains a collection of DataColumn objects accessed through its Columns property. A DataColumn contains at least a string denoting its name and the data type for values within the column. You can optionally specify an Expression to create a data column that calculates a value using the values in other columns. The following example creates a DataTable that is used like a spreadsheet to calculate the y coordinate of a line using the equation y=mx+b. Within the code, you can also see how to create a column that increments the previous row's value and forces a user to keep the number unique. You do so by setting the AutoIncrement and Unique properties of a DataColumn object to true:

```
public Form1()
{
    InitializeComponent();

    ds = new DataSet();
    DataTable table = ds.Tables.Add("MyTable");

    DataColumn keyCol = new DataColumn();
    keyCol.ColumnName = "ID";
    keyCol.DataType = typeof( int );
    keyCol.AutoIncrement = true;
    keyCol.Unique = true;
    table.Columns.Add( keyCol );

    table.Columns.Add( "M", typeof(int) ).DefaultValue = 0;
    table.Columns.Add( "X", typeof(int) ).DefaultValue = 0;
    table.Columns.Add( "B", typeof(int) ).DefaultValue = 0;
    table.Columns.Add( "Y", typeof(int), "M*X+B" ).DefaultValue = 0;
    dataGrid1.SetDataBinding( ds, "MyTable" );
}
```

Comments

Earlier in this chapter, it was mentioned that a DataGrid behaves similarly to that of a spreadsheet application. Until this point, the similarity was the visual appearance of the DataGrid. In this section, you get a first glimpse of how to use a DataTable and its associated DataColumns to mimic the functionality of a spreadsheet. Although the expression support available for the DataColumn falls quite short of the functionality of an Excel column, it does allow you to perform several common calculations, including standard deviations, variance, and substring determination.

14.12. Creating Unique Constraints

You want to ensure that certain columns within a `DataTable` are unique.

Technique

Some columns within a `DataTable` must be unique to provide a way to uniquely identify a record. Furthermore, columns might need to be unique to prevent duplicate data entry. If your `DataTable` only needs to force a unique constraint on a small amount of columns, you can set the `Unique` property to `true` for that `DataColumn`, as shown in the following code:

```
public Form1()
{
    InitializeComponent();

    ds = new DataSet();
    DataTable table = ds.Tables.Add("MyTable");

    DataColumn keyCol = new DataColumn();
    keyCol.ColumnName = "ID";
    keyCol.DataType = typeof( int );
    keyCol.AutoIncrement = true;
    keyCol.Unique = true;
    table.Columns.Add( keyCol );
}
```

If you have several columns that need to be unique, you can use a `UniqueConstraint` collection. It allows you to create a group of unique columns by passing the collection to the `Constraints` property defined in the `DataTable` class. The `UniqueConstraint` class contains nine overloaded constructors, allowing for several options. In most cases, you can pass a collection of `DataColumn` objects or a string collection whose items represent the names of each column, which is shown in the following example:

```
public Form1()
{
    InitializeComponent();

    ds = new DataSet();
    DataTable table = ds.Tables.Add("MyTable");

    DataColumn keyCol = new DataColumn();
    keyCol.ColumnName = "WinnerID";
    keyCol.DataType = typeof( int );
    keyCol.AutoIncrement = true;
    table.Columns.Add( keyCol );
```

```
    table.Columns.Add( "PrizeID", typeof(int) );
    table.Columns.Add( "EMail", typeof(string) );
    table.Constraints.Add(new UniqueConstraint(
        "Constraints",
        new string[]{"WinnerID", "PrizeID"},
        false));
}
```

Comments

The last example in this section used a group of columns to create unique constraints. Entering a value into the column that already exists in a different row causes an error. One of the nice things about the `DataGrid` is that it is designed to do the "right" thing when a user does something unexpected. Rather than deal with exceptions or event handlers to display a message that a unique constraint was violated, the `DataGrid` just displays the message itself without any extra work on your part.

In many cases, the data you display to a user is placed into a `DataSet` that is bound to a control. Before the data is displayed, you have the option of creating additional unique constraints by accessing the `Columns` property from a `DataTable` within the `DataSet`.

14.13. Creating `ForeignKey` Constraints

You want to link a column from one table to a column from another and control the behavior when the values are updated or deleted.

Technique

A *foreign key* denotes a relationship between two columns within two separate tables in a database. You use a foreign-key constraint to create special rules that specify the action to take for the value in the child table should the value in the parent table change. To create a foreign-key constraint, pass two `DataColumn` objects, one of which is from the parent `DataTable` and the other from the child `DataTable`, to the constructor of the `ForeignKeyConstraint` class. Add the resulting `ForeignKeyConstraint` object to the `Constraints` collection of the child `DataTable`.

A foreign key constraint can use one of four different rules that specify the action to take when a parent column value changes. The values are defined in the `System.Data.Rule` enumerated data type. `Rule.None` simply ignores the constraint. `Rule.Cascade` propagates the change from the parent to the child value. `Rule.SetNull` changes the child column's value to `null`, and `Rule.SetDefault` sets the value to the default value specified when the column was created. If a default value wasn't specified using the `DefaultValue` property defined in the `DataColumn` class, the value is set to `null`. These rules are applied to the `UpdateRule` and `DeleteRule` of the `ForeignKeyConstraint` object. The `UpdateRule` action runs whenever an existing value within the parent column changes. The `DeleteRule` runs whenever the parent value is removed. Listing 14.4 demonstrates a Windows Form application containing two `DataGrid` objects that display a parent table and a child table. A `ComboBox` control sets the current `Rule` used for both the `UpdateRule` and `DeleteRule` of the `ForeignKeyConstraint`. Changing this value allows you to see the relationship between the two columns of data as the parent value is updated or removed.

Listing 14.4   **Foreign-Key Constraints**

```
using System;
using System.Drawing;
using System.Collections;
using System.ComponentModel;
using System.Windows.Forms;
using System.Data;

namespace _13_ForeignKeyConstraints
{
    public class Form1 : System.Windows.Forms.Form
    {
        private System.Windows.Forms.DataGrid dgParent;
        private System.Windows.Forms.DataGrid dgChild;
        private System.Windows.Forms.ComboBox cbConstraints;
        private System.Windows.Forms.Label label1;
        private System.Windows.Forms.Button btnSet;
        private DataSet ds;
        private ForeignKeyConstraint fkConstraint;

        private System.ComponentModel.Container components = null;

        public Form1()
        {
            InitializeComponent();

            // fill constraint combo
            cbConstraints.Items.Add("Cascade");
            cbConstraints.Items.Add("SetNull");
            cbConstraints.Items.Add("SetDefault");
            cbConstraints.Items.Add("None");
            cbConstraints.SelectedIndex = 3;

            // create tables
            ds = new DataSet();
            DataTable parentTable = ds.Tables.Add( "ParentTable" );
            DataTable childTable = ds.Tables.Add( "ChildTable" );
```

Listing 14.4   **Continued**

```
        // create columns
        parentTable.Columns.Add( "ID", typeof(int) );
        DataColumn linkedParent = parentTable.Columns.Add(
            "LinkedID", typeof(int) );

        childTable.Columns.Add( "ID", typeof(int) );
        DataColumn linkedChild = childTable.Columns.Add(
            "LinkedID", typeof(int) );

        // create the foreign key constraint and set to None
        fkConstraint = new ForeignKeyConstraint( "LinkedIDFK",
            linkedParent, linkedChild );
        fkConstraint.UpdateRule = Rule.None;
        fkConstraint.DeleteRule = Rule.None;

        // add constraint to child column
        childTable.Constraints.Add( fkConstraint );

        // data bind the 2 DataGrids
        dgParent.SetDataBinding( ds, "ParentTable" );
        dgChild.SetDataBinding( ds, "ChildTable" );
    }

    protected override void Dispose( bool disposing )
    {
        if( disposing )
        {
            if (components != null)
            {
                components.Dispose();
            }
        }
        base.Dispose( disposing );
    }

    private void InitializeComponent()
    {
        // wizard generated code removed
    }

    [STAThread]
    static void Main()
    {
        Application.Run(new Form1());
    }
```

Listing 14.4   **Continued**

```csharp
        private void btnSet_Click(object sender, System.EventArgs e)
        {
            // change the constraint based on ComboBox value
            if( cbConstraints.SelectedItem == null )
                return;

            string constraintName = cbConstraints.Text;
            if( constraintName == "None" )
            {
                fkConstraint.DeleteRule = Rule.None;
                fkConstraint.UpdateRule = Rule.None;
            }
            else if( constraintName == "Cascade" )
            {
                fkConstraint.DeleteRule = Rule.Cascade;
                fkConstraint.UpdateRule = Rule.Cascade;
            }
            else if( constraintName == "SetNull" )
            {
                fkConstraint.DeleteRule = Rule.SetNull;
                fkConstraint.UpdateRule = Rule.SetNull;
            }
            else if (constraintName == "SetDefault" )
            {
                fkConstraint.DeleteRule = Rule.SetDefault;
                fkConstraint.UpdateRule = Rule.SetDefault;
            }
        }
    }
}
```

Comments

You use a foreign-key constraint to map a column from one table to another. A common use for foreign keys is to create a link between the two tables so that as one record is updated, the corresponding linked table is also updated. For instance, in the Northwind Products table, you can see a column named CategoryID. This value is linked to the Categories table, which allows you to look up additional information about the product's category. A question arises when you delete a category. Because the category no longer exists, do you also delete any products from the linked Products table as well by creating a foreign-key constraint and setting the DeleteRule to Rule.Cascade? More than likely, you would want to instead use a DeleteRule or Rule.SetNull.

14.14. Inserting New Rows into a `DataTable`

You want to add data to a `DataTable` by inserting new rows.

Technique

A `DataTable` contains a collection of `DataColumn` objects representing each column as well as a `Rows` property, which you use to access a collection of `DataRow` objects. Creating a new row differs from creating a new column: You create the `DataRow` by calling the `NewRow` method defined in the `DataTable` class rather than create an instance and add it to a collection, which is the procedure for columns. After calling `NewRow` from a `DataTable` object, you can set individual column values by using the `DataRow` indexer. Each column name within the row is specified as a string parameter to the `DataRow` indexer, although you can optionally use an integer specifying the zero-based column index. Listing 14.5 demonstrates adding a new row to the `DataTable` and setting its initial values. Note that calling `NewRow` does not add the row to the `DataTable`. Once the column values are created, add it to the `DataTable` by calling the `Add` method defined in the `Rows` collection of the `DataTable`.

Listing 14.5   **Adding New** `DataRows`

```
using System;
using System.Data;

namespace _14_DataRows
{
    class Class1
    {
        [STAThread]
        static void Main(string[] args)
        {
            char input;

            // create inventory table
            DataTable table = new DataTable("Inventory");

            // add primary key column
            DataColumn col = new DataColumn( "ID", typeof(int) );
            col.AutoIncrement = true;
            col.Unique = true;
            table.Columns.Add( col );
            table.PrimaryKey = new DataColumn[]{col};

            // create item and count columns
            table.Columns.Add( new DataColumn("Item", typeof(string) ));
```

Listing 14.5   **Continued**

```
table.Columns.Add( new DataColumn("Count", typeof(int) ));

do
{
    Console.WriteLine();
    Console.WriteLine( "A)dd new record" );
    Console.WriteLine( "M)odify record" );
    Console.WriteLine( "D)elete record" );
    Console.WriteLine( "V)iew records" );
    Console.WriteLine( "Q)uit" );
    Console.Write( "Enter command: " );
    input = Char.ToUpper(Console.ReadLine()[0]);

    switch( input )
    {
        case( 'A' ):
        {
            DataRow row = table.NewRow();
            Console.Write( "Enter item name: " );
            row["Item"] = Console.ReadLine();
            Console.Write( "Enter item count: " );
            row["Count"] = Int32.Parse( Console.ReadLine() );
            table.Rows.Add( row );

            break;
        }
        case( 'M' ):
        {
            break;
        }
        case( 'D' ):
        {
            break;
        }
        case( 'V' ):
        {
            DataRow[] currRows = table.Select(null,
                null, DataViewRowState.CurrentRows);

            if (currRows.Length < 1 )
                Console.WriteLine("No Current Rows Found");
            else
            {
                foreach (DataColumn myCol in table.Columns)
                    Console.Write("\t{0}", myCol.ColumnName);
```

Listing 14.5 **Continued**

```
                       Console.WriteLine("\tRowState");

                       foreach (DataRow myRow in currRows)
                       {
                           foreach (DataColumn myCol in table.Columns)
                               Console.Write("\t{0}", myRow[myCol]);

                           Console.WriteLine("\t" + myRow.RowState);
                       }
                   }

               break;
           }
           case( 'Q' ):
           {
               break;
           }
           default:
           {
               Console.WriteLine( "Invalid command" );
               break;
           }
       }
   } while( input != 'Q' );
   }
  }
}
```

Comments

In the sample code for this recipe, viewing the DataTable also outputs the RowState value for each row. This RowState value specifies whether the row has been added, modified, unchanged, or deleted. In this application, all rows have a RowState of Added. To change this value from Added to Unchanged, you must call the AcceptChanges method from the DataTable object. You can, however, discard any newly added rows to a DataTable by calling the RejectChanges method. When working in a disconnected state, it is common to perform batch updates to a data source using only the rows that have changed within a table. In other words, by calling the GetChanges method of the DataTable, you receive a subset of values within another DataTable corresponding to the rows that have a RowState value other than Unchanged. Once this batch update occurs, you call the AcceptChanges or RejectChanges method so that the same rows are not repeated in the next batch update.

14.15. Modifying Rows in a `DataTable`

You want to change column values in an existing row within a `DataTable`.

Technique

Once you add a row to a `DataTable`, you can use the `Find` method defined in the `Rows` collection of the `DataTable` to find a row by passing a value for the primary key. You can optionally use the indexer of the `Rows` collection, passing a zero-based index for the desired row to modify. Both of these techniques return a `DataRow` object, and any edits made to that `DataRow` automatically cause the updates to occur within the `DataTable`, as shown in the following code, which is continued from the previous section:

```
case( 'M' ):
{
    Console.Write( "Enter an item ID: " );
    int id = Int32.Parse( Console.ReadLine() );

    DataRow modRow = table.Rows.Find( id );
    Console.Write( "Enter item name: " );
    modRow["Item"] = Console.ReadLine();
    Console.Write( "Enter item count: " );
    modRow["Count"] = Int32.Parse( Console.ReadLine() );

    break;
}
case( 'D' ):
{
    Console.Write( "Enter an item ID: " );
    int id = Int32.Parse( Console.ReadLine() );

    DataRow delRow = table.Rows.Find( id );
    table.Rows.Remove( delRow );
    break;
}
```

If you are allowing users to enter data for a specific `DataRow`, you can create a custom event handler that cancels the change if the data they enter is not valid for a specific column. You add an event handler for the `ColumnChanged` event fired from the `DataTable` class. Before the value for a specific column is changed, call the `BeginEdit` method, and after the value is changed, call the `EndEdit` method. Doing so calls the `ColumnChanged` event handler, allowing you to ensure the entered value is valid. If it isn't, call `CancelEdit` on the `DataRow` object so the row isn't updated, as shown in the following code:

```
public void ModifyRow()
{
    if( handlerAdded == false )
        table.ColumnChanged+=new DataColumnChangeEventHandler(OnColumnChanged);

    Console.Write( "Enter an item ID: " );
    int id = Int32.Parse( Console.ReadLine() );

    DataRow modRow = table.Rows.Find( id );

    modRow.BeginEdit();

    Console.Write( "Enter item name: " );
    modRow["Item"] = Console.ReadLine();
    Console.Write( "Enter item count: " );
    modRow["Count"] = Int32.Parse( Console.ReadLine() );

    modRow.EndEdit();
}

private void OnColumnChanged(Object sender, DataColumnChangeEventArgs args)
{
  if (args.Column.ColumnName == "Count")
    if (Convert.ToInt32(args.ProposedValue) < 0)
    {
      Console.WriteLine("Count cannot be less than 0");
      args.Row.CancelEdit();
    }
}
```

Comments

The example for this recipe uses an event handler to check the proposed value for a row that is being edited. The DataTable class actually contains several other events that might prove useful when manipulating data within the table. These events include the RowChanging and RowChanged events, which are called when the BeginEdit and EndEdit methods of a DataRow are called. Both of these methods use a DataRowChangeEventArgs object, which contains the current action being done to the data row accessed through the Action property. This property tells you whether the row is being added, changed, committed, deleted, or rolled back in the case of a change cancel. The other possible events include RowDeleting and RowDeleted as well as ColumnChanging and ColumnChanged.

14.16. Navigating Tables Using `DataRelations`

You want to access tables that are joined with a `DataRelation`.

Technique

To create a relationship between two tables, pass to the `DataRelation` constructor the two columns between which you want to create a relationship, as shown in the following code:

```
DataColumn parentCustID;
DataColumn childCustID;

// get the DataColumn objects
dcCustomerCustID = ds.Tables["Customers"].Columns["CustID"];
dcOrdersCustID = ds.Tables["Orders"].Columns["CustID"];

// Define the relationship
DataRelation drCustID;
drCustID = new DataRelation("CustomerOrders", parentCustID, childCustID);
```

The example creates a relationship between the two columns but does not create a foreign-key constraint. Any time the column in the parent table changes, an exception will be thrown. Therefore, you want to use the technique discussed in Recipe 14.13, "Creating `ForeignKey` Constraints," to set the foreign-key constraint rule.

Now that a relationship exists between two different tables, you can navigate from one to the other using the various properties and methods defined in the `DataTable` and `DataRow` classes. To access all the child relationships that a table contains, enumerate the `ChildRelations` collections, which will return a `DataRelation` object for each defined relationship of that table. You can then use each of these `DataRelation` objects as a parameter to the `GetChildRows` method of the `DataRow` class. In other words, enumerate each `DataRelation` class; for each `DataRelation` encountered, enumerate each row within the `DataTable` and call the `GetChildRows` method, passing the `DataRelation` object, as shown in the following code:

```
private static void PrintChildRowValues()
{
    DataTable parentTable = ds.Tables[ "Customers" ];
    DataRow[] childRows;
    foreach(DataRelation curRelation in parentTable.ChildRelations)
    {
        foreach(DataRow curRow in parentTable.Rows)
        {
            PrintRow (curRow, "Parent Row Values" );
            childRows = curRow.GetChildRows(curRelation);
```

```
        // Print values of rows.
        PrintRow ( childRows, "Child Row Value" );
    }
  }
}
```

Comments

Recipe 14.13 demonstrated how to create foreign-key constraints, which you use for columns that are common between two different tables. Without a mechanism to maintain these relationships, you would have to write a lot of custom code to ensure tables are updated correctly. The DataRelation class allows you to define a relationship between two different tables. Creating a ForeignKeyConstraint between similar columns of two different tables creates a relationship but does not allow you to easily navigate between those relationships. Likewise, creating a DataRelation between two tables doesn't allow you to define a rule for the foreign-key constraint, which is why you want to use both techniques to ensure a robust solution.

14.17. Saving DataSet Information to an XML File

You want to save the current state of a DataSet object to an XML file.

Technique

A DataSet maintains internal data using a hierarchical organization scheme that lends itself well to creating an XML representation. To save a DataSet to an XML file, call the WriteXml method, passing a string in the first parameter designating the filename and a value from the XmlWriteMode enumerated data type. The possible values for this parameter include XmlWriteMode.WriteSchema, which includes the schema inline with the document; XmlWriteMode.IgnoreSchema, which simply writes the XML data only; and XmlWriteMode.DiffGram. A DiffGram not only contains the current state of each record in the DataSet but also contains the original values of each modified record. Listing 14.6 demonstrates a database-editing application that lets you save the current state of a DataSet to an XML file without updating the underlying data source. The next section expands on this example, further showing how to reload the DataSet from the XML file.

Listing 14.6   **Saving a DataSet to XML**

```
using System;
using System.Drawing;
using System.Collections;
```

Listing 14.6   **Continued**

```csharp
using System.ComponentModel;
using System.Windows.Forms;
using System.Data;

namespace _14_DataSetToXml
{
    /// <summary>
    /// Summary description for Form1.
    /// </summary>
    public class Form1 : System.Windows.Forms.Form
    {
        private System.Windows.Forms.MainMenu mainMenu1;
        private System.Windows.Forms.MenuItem menuItem1;
        private System.Windows.Forms.MenuItem mnuOpen;
        private System.Windows.Forms.MenuItem mnuSave;
        private System.Windows.Forms.MenuItem mnuExit;
        private System.Windows.Forms.MenuItem menuItem5;
        private System.Windows.Forms.MenuItem mnuLoad;
        private System.Windows.Forms.MenuItem mnuUpdate;
        private System.Windows.Forms.DataGrid dataGrid1;
        private System.Data.SqlClient.SqlCommand sqlSelectCommand1;
        private System.Data.SqlClient.SqlCommand sqlInsertCommand1;
        private System.Data.SqlClient.SqlCommand sqlUpdateCommand1;
        private System.Data.SqlClient.SqlCommand sqlDeleteCommand1;
        private System.Data.SqlClient.SqlConnection sqlConnection1;
        private System.Data.SqlClient.SqlDataAdapter sqlDataAdapter1;
        private _14_DataSetToXml.ProductsDS productsDS1;
        private System.Windows.Forms.SaveFileDialog saveFileDialog1;
        private System.Windows.Forms.OpenFileDialog openFileDialog1;
        /// <summary>
        /// Required designer variable.
        /// </summary>
        private System.ComponentModel.Container components = null;

        public Form1()
        {
            InitializeComponent();

            // fill the dataset and bind to datagrid
            sqlDataAdapter1.Fill( productsDS1 );
            dataGrid1.SetDataBinding( productsDS1, "Products" );
        }

        protected override void Dispose( bool disposing )
        {
```

Listing 14.6   **Continued**

```
        if( disposing )
        {
            if (components != null)
            {
                components.Dispose();
            }
        }
        base.Dispose( disposing );
    }

    /* Windows Forms Designer Generated Code */

    [STAThread]
    static void Main()
    {
        Application.Run(new Form1());
    }

    private void mnuLoad_Click(object sender, System.EventArgs e)
    {
        if( productsDS1.HasChanges() )
        {
            if( AskUser("The Dataset has changed. " +
                " Are you sure you want to continue? ")==DialogResult.No )
            {
                return;
            }

        }
        // clear dataset and get data from database
        productsDS1.Clear();
        sqlDataAdapter1.Fill( productsDS1 );
        dataGrid1.SetDataBinding( productsDS1, "Products" );
    }

    private DialogResult AskUser(string question)
    {
        return MessageBox.Show( question, "DatasetToXml",
            MessageBoxButtons.YesNo, MessageBoxIcon.Question );
    }

    private void mnuSave_Click(object sender, System.EventArgs e)
    {
        if( saveFileDialog1.ShowDialog() == DialogResult.OK )
        {
```

Listing 14.6   **Continued**

```
                productsDS1.WriteXml( saveFileDialog1.FileName,
                    XmlWriteMode.DiffGram);
        }
    }

    private void mnuUpdate_Click(object sender, System.EventArgs e)
    {
        if( productsDS1.HasChanges() )
        {
            // update the database
            sqlDataAdapter1.Update( productsDS1, "Products" );
        }
    }

    private void mnuOpen_Click(object sender, System.EventArgs e)
    {
        // implemented in next section
    }

    private void mnuExit_Click(object sender, System.EventArgs e)
    {
        this.Close();
    }
    }
}
```

Comments

Being able to save an entire DataSet to an XML file has advantages, especially when transferring the DataSet across machine boundaries. Additionally, you can take advantage of DataSet-generated XML files within ASP.NET. Although not covered until Chapter 16, "ASP.NET," the following technique is worth mentioning here. When an ASP.NET page that utilizes a database connection loads, you need to fill a DataSet. However, once the final response is sent back to the client, the DataSet is lost because you cannot have instance data within an ASP.NET application persist across subsequent page loads. You can utilize a special dictionary-based collection called Session. However, placing a DataSet object into the collection for each connected user can very well fill up entire amounts of memory on your server. To combat this issue, use the technique described in this section by writing the XML representation of the DataSet object and read it using the technique in the next section each time your page loads. Not only does it allow you to persist the changed data across subsequent page loads, but it also gives a slight performance increase because you don't need to constantly connect and transfer data from the database server.

14.18. Restoring a `DataSet` from an XML File

You want to restore the data within an XML file previously generated by a `DataSet` back into another `DataSet` object.

Technique

In the previous recipe, the `WriteXml` method defined in the `DataSet` class generated an XML file containing the current state of the data within the `DataSet`. This XML file also supported the generation of an inline schema as well as a special file format called a `DiffGram` containing the original values of any modified records. To restore the `DataSet` using the data within that generated XML file, call the `ReadXml` method. The parameters to this method are similar to the `WriteXml` method. The first parameter is a string denoting the file path of the XML file to load. The second parameter is a value from the `XmlReadMode` enumerated data type. This enumeration contains a few more values than the `XmlWriteMode` enumeration. The similar values include `XmlReadMode.DiffGram`, which reads in the current values as well as the values of any records that were modified. It allows you to then accept or reject the changes within the new `DataSet` by calling the `AcceptChanges` or `RejectChanges` methods. The `XmlReadMode.ReadSchema` reads the inline schema contained within the XML file. You can optionally allow the method to infer the organization of data by using `XmlReadMode.InferSchema`. If you use this value, the inline schema, if present, is ignored. The `XmlReadMode.IgnoreSchema` also ignores the schema, but if the `DataSet` already contains a schema from a `ReadSchema` method call, the XML file is validated using that schema and throws an exception if the file is invalid. Finally, `XmlReadMode.Auto` automatically selects the best `XmlReadMode` based on the format of the XML file. The following example continues the application created in the last section:

```
private void mnuOpen_Click(object sender, System.EventArgs e)
{
    if( productsDS1.HasChanges() )
    {
        if( AskUser("The Dataset has changed. Continue?") == DialogResult.No )
        {
            return;
        }
    }

    if( openFileDialog1.ShowDialog() == DialogResult.OK )
    {
        productsDS1.Clear();
        productsDS1.ReadXml( openFileDialog1.FileName, XmlReadMode.Auto );
        dataGrid1.SetDataBinding( productsDS1, "Products" );
    }
}
```

Comments

The `ReadXml` method presents an interesting twist on using a `DataSet` object. If you were to take an informal poll and ask people to define a `DataSet`, most would probably say that it is used in a disconnected environment to store tables and data extracted from a database. Although it is certainly true, it doesn't fully list all the possible scenarios for the different uses a `DataSet` has. A `DataSet` can read an XML file, logically deduce how to best organize that data, and even automatically generate a schema from that data. There is in fact no requirement that you have to use a `DataSet` to store data that comes from a database. By using `WriteXml` and `ReadXml`, you can create a data-storage mechanism for your application that works solely with XML files, rather than make trips to a database server. By pondering the possibilities of the different ways to exploit the `DataSet` class, you'll undoubtedly come up with some interesting uses if you realize a database doesn't always have to be in the equation.

14.19. Merging `DataSets`

You want to merge the data from one `DataSet` object with information from another `DataSet`.

Technique

You merge two `DataSets` by calling the `Merge` method from the target `DataSet`. The target in this case is the `DataSet` that will contain the final merged data. You can merge data into a `DataSet` by using another `DataSet`, a `DataTable`, a collection of `DataRow` objects, or a single `DataRow`. You can specify a Boolean value to control whether current changes within the target `DataSet` are preserved. For instance, if the target `DataSet` contains a row that has been modified, and a source `DataSet` contains a row with the same primary key with different values, specifying `true` preserves the target `DataRow` and `false` overwrites that row with data from the source `DataSet`. Finally, the last optional parameter you can specify is a value from the `MissingSchemaAction` enumerated data type. This parameter controls the action to take should the schemas of the two `DataSets` differ. A value of `MissingSchemaAction.Add`, for instance, adds a new column to the target `DataSet` if it does not exist. `MissingSchemaAction.AddWithKey` also adds the new column to the target `DataSet` and additionally creates primary keys if any columns are marked as such within the source `DataSet`. A value of `MissingSchemaAction.Error` throws an `InvalidOperationException` if a column exists in the source `DataSet` but not in the target `DataSet`, whereas the value `MissingSchemaAction.Ignore` simply discards the data from the source `DataSet`.

The following source-code example is a continuation of the sample application created in the last couple sections. The method shown here is an event handler for a menu item that will merge a `DataSet` created from an XML file to the `DataSet` currently used as a data source for a `DataGrid` control:

```
private void mnuMerge_Click(object sender, System.EventArgs e)
{
    DataSet mergeData = new DataSet();
    if( openFileDialog1.ShowDialog() == DialogResult.OK )
    {
        try
        {
            mergeData.ReadXml( openFileDialog1.FileName, XmlReadMode.Auto );
            productsDS1.Merge( mergeData, true, MissingSchemaAction.Error );
            dataGrid1.SetDataBinding( productsDS1, "Products" );
        }
        catch( Exception ex )
        {
            MessageBox.Show( ex.Message );
        }
    }
}
```

Comments

Passing around `DataSet` objects that contain large amounts of data might not be the best solution for objects that communicate with one another, especially if that communication occurs remotely. For instance, a `DataSet` object is initially filled from a middle-tier component and sent to a receiving object. The `DataSet` itself might be quite large, so continually passing it back and forth between the two objects could take a performance hit. Instead, you should use merging to your benefit. After you send the initial `DataSet` to the receiving object, you should handle the rest of the communication by only sending and receiving any changes to the `DataSet`, which you find by calling the `GetChanges` method defined in the `DataSet` class. It only returns the subset of records that have changed and places them into a new `DataSet` object. You can then send and merge this object using the techniques described in this section to the original `DataSet`.

14.20. Modifying Pooling Behavior for SQL Server Connections

You want to examine the current behavior of a .NET data provider's connection pooling behavior.

Technique

Connection pooling is a caching mechanism used by the SQL Server .NET Data Provider to increase the performance of multiple connections created from a process. You control how the data provider uses connection pooling by setting parameters within the connection string. As new connections are made using the same connection string, the connection is placed within the same pool. Table 14.1 lists the available connection string parameters to control connection pooling.

Table 14.1   **Connection Pooling Connection String Parameters**

Parameter	Default	Behavior
Connection Lifetime	0	Controls how long a connection remains within a connection pool even after the process ends. A value of 0 specifies the maximum lifetime.
Connection Reset	true	Resets the connection when it is removed from the pool, which causes an additional round-trip to the server.
Enlist	true	Enlists the connection into the current transaction context if one exists.
Max Pool Size	100	Total number of connections that can exist in a single pool.
Min Pool Size	0	Minimum number of connections that must be in a pool.
Pooling	true	Controls whether to use pooling for this connection.

Comments

Connection pooling is the process of returning a connection that is already open, triggered by a different connection attempt. Rather than create another connection to the same database, the process shares the connection among two objects. For instance, suppose you made an SqlConnection to the Northwind database using the code:

```
SqlConnection conn = new SqlConnection();
conn.ConnectionString = "Integrated Security=SSPI;Initial Catalog=northwind";
conn.Open();
```

While this connection is open, let's say that another thread opens another connection using the same connection string, and within a certain time period, eight more connections are made within a single connection pool. As the application continues, a few connections close. However, because connection pooling is enabled, the connections actually remain open within the connection pool and remain open for the amount of time specified in the Connection Lifetime parameter. Suppose then that the application creates yet another connection to the database. The .NET data provider realizes that three connections are open but are not active because the application requested that they get closed. Therefore, the active connections that weren't being used can now be passed back to the application, avoiding a trip to the database server for another connection attempt.

If you place this concept within the realm of an ASP.NET application, you can see why pooling can give your application a performance advantage. By configuring the connection string for connection pooling, you can use the performance monitor to ensure that your application is getting the best possible performance when creating and closing connections repeatedly. One particular connection string parameter worth mentioning is `Min Pool Size`. It specifies how many connections should remain in the connection pool during an application's lifetime. For instance, if your Web application is a high-traffic application, meaning several clients are always on at any point in time, you should consider setting the `Min Pool Size` parameter to a higher number. When your application runs for the first time and makes a single database connection, setting `Min Pool Size` to 10, for instance, automatically creates and places 10 connections in the pool, only 1 of which is currently active. This means that the next nine clients that use your application do not have to make a trip to the database server to create a connection. Rather, the connection is just handed to your application right out of the pool and ready to go.

14.21. Ensuring Data Integrity Using Transactions

> You want to use a transaction when performing a database update.

Technique

You use a transaction when you must make a series of updates to a data source. You want to ensure that, as the updates are made, the changes are not committed unless all the commands sent to the database server are successful. To implement transactions, the .NET framework defines a class named `SqlTransaction` that works in conjunction with an `SqlCommand` object. You create an `SqlTransaction` object by assigning it to the return value of the `BeginTransaction` method defined in the `SqlConnection` class. This `SqlTransaction` object is then assigned to the `Transaction` property of the `SqlCommand` object. As the updates occur, the transaction object keeps track of the changes being made and retains the original state of the data source should an update fail. If all the commands are successful, you call the `Commit` method from the `SqlTransaction` object to finish the transaction. If an exception is thrown while you are performing updates, then an update did not work, and any data changes must revert back to their old state. You do so with the exception `catch` block by calling the `Rollback` method defined in the `SqlTransaction` class. Listing 14.7 demonstrates how to use the `SqlTransaction` class in conjunction with an `SqlConnection` and an `SqlCommand` object. Within the `try` block, you can see two attempts to create new products within the Products table of the Northwind database. The second `INSERT` statement is intentionally wrong because the `ProductName` field in the table cannot be `null`. Because of this statement, the updates fail and the transaction rolls the data back to its previous state, which means the changes made from the first INSERT statement are not committed.

Listing 14.7   **Supporting Transactions**

```
using System;
using System.Data;
using System.Data.SqlClient;

namespace _21_Transaction
{
    class Class1
    {
        [STAThread]
        static void Main(string[] args)
        {
            SqlConnection connection = new SqlConnection("Integrated
Security=SSPI;Data
[ic:ccc]Source=VCSMARKHSCH6;Initial Catalog=Northwind;");
            connection.Open();

            SqlCommand insertCommand = connection.CreateCommand();
            SqlTransaction transaction;

            // Start a local transaction
            transaction = connection.BeginTransaction();

            // assign connection and transaction to command
            insertCommand.Connection = connection;
            insertCommand.Transaction = transaction;

            try
            {
                // this command will succeed
                insertCommand.CommandText =
                  "Insert into Products (ProductName ) VALUES ('New Product')";
                insertCommand.ExecuteNonQuery();

                // this command intentionally fails
                // since ProductName cannot be null
                insertCommand.CommandText =
                  "Insert into Products (ProductName) VALUES (null)";
                insertCommand.ExecuteNonQuery();

                transaction.Commit();
                Console.WriteLine("Database Updated Successfully");
            }
```

Listing 14.7 **Continued**

```
        catch(Exception e)
        {
            transaction.Rollback();
            Console.WriteLine( e.Message );
        }
        finally
        {
            connection.Close();
        }
    }
  }
}
```

Comments

Transactions play a vital role for applications that work with critical data. If a single command fails during a sequence of updates to a database, then to ensure data integrity, the changes do not happen because any updates might have adverse side effects. Suppose an application that performs money transfers for stocks first removes the money from your bank account—and just before it uses the money to buy shares, the power goes out. Without transaction support, you would lose that money or at least go through a couple miles of red tape to get it back.

IV

Internet and Networking

15

Network Programming
with Sockets

15.0. Introduction

In Chapter 12, "File I/O and Serialization," it was shown that in many cases, local data access ultimately found its way into the basic layers of the file classes. Whether you are creating an advanced Extensible Markup Language (XML) processing application, working with the latest database technology, or using a simple configuration scheme, the probability is high that the file classes will soon come into play whether you realize it or not. This chapter also serves as a starting point with a key difference. This time, you'll work with remote data.

The socket library is a low-level API designed to do one thing, communicate with a remote computer. How the communication is performed is left up to the server. Any clients that want to connect to the server must follow a set of rules to successfully interact. These sets of rules are generally standardized and published as *protocols*. Some of the better known protocols include the Hypertext Transfer Protocol (HTTP), File Transfer Protocol (FTP), Network News Transfer Protocol (NNTP), and the Simple Object Access Protocol (SOAP). This chapter looks at the underlying mechanics that each of these protocols utilize. Additionally, you'll see how you can easily create your own protocol as you work through the sample code to create a client- and server-based number-guessing game.

15.1. Creating a Stream-Based Server

You want to create a server application that connects and communicates with client applications using a defined protocol.

Technique

A stream-based server is one in which the connection between a client and server remains open until you close the socket itself. The data at both endpoints travels using a stream-based method that is similar to the methodology employed by the various file-based streaming methods.

Creating a stream-based server generally involves two main steps, listening for incoming connections and communicating with connected clients. To listen for incoming connections, use the `TcpListener` class. The constructor for this class uses a `IPAddress` object for the first parameter and an integer value specifying the port number you want to listen on. You can, however, combine the two parameters into a single `IPEndPoint` object. A computer might have several network interfaces, so to simplify the process of finding the most appropriate interface, you can pass `IPAddress.Any` as the first parameter. For the port number, the normal range of values is between 1024 and 5000 because others are standardized to specific protocols. Therefore, to create a `TcpListener` object on port 2003 using a default network interface, the code would appear like the following:

```
TcpListener listener = new TcpListener( IPAddress.Any, 2003 );
```

Once you create the listener, you are ready to begin listening for incoming connections. This is accomplished by calling the `Start` method defined in the `TcpListener` class. Your application can then do one of two things. If you are not worried about making a blocking call to a function, then call the `AcceptSocket` method. This method does not return until a client connects to your server. For console applications, this choice is generally fine, but for Windows Forms applications, you run the risk of starving your user-interface thread. To prevent this problem, you should periodically, through either a `Timer` or a `Thread` object, call the `Pending` method defined in the `TcpListener` class. This method returns a Boolean value denoting whether a client is attempting a connection. If this value is `true`, then you can call the `AcceptSocket` method mentioned earlier. Listing 15.1 demonstrates the process of creating a `TcpListener` object that listens on port 2003.

Listing 15.1   **Creating a** `TcpListener`

```
static void Main(string[] args)
{
    Random rand = new Random( DateTime.Now.Millisecond );
    int curRandom;
    try
    {
        // listen on port 2003
```

Listing 15.1   **Continued**

```
            TcpListener tcpl = new TcpListener(IPAddress.Any, 2003);
            tcpl.Start();

            Console.WriteLine("Number Guess Server Started");

            while (true)
            {
                string cmd = "";
                bool bCloseConnection = false;

                // Accept will block until someone connects
                Socket s = tcpl.AcceptSocket();
```

It is at this point where a connection is made to a client and communication can begin. It is also at this point where a well-defined protocol comes into being. The data being sent and received is pointless without some sort of contract between the client and server specifying how to interpret the data. In keeping with the standard numerical code followed by the descriptive message scheme used in many protocols, this protocol uses three sets of numbers. The 300-level messages are commands sent from the client to the server. The 400-level messages are sent from the server to the client, and the number 200 is a generic message for sending an OK status, which appears in the following code:

```
            Console.WriteLine( "Incoming client connected: IP={0}",
            s.RemoteEndPoint.ToString() );

            // send the OK status message
            SendData( s, "200\r\nOK\r\n\r\n" );

            // generate new random number
            curRandom = rand.Next( 1, 100 );
```

In the main body of the do/while loop in Listing 15.2, after the connection is made, the server receives data by calling the helper method ReceiveData and then parses the received message to determine the action to take based on what the client has sent.

Listing 15.2   **Establishing a Defined Protocol**

```
            do
            {
                cmd = ReceiveData( s );

                // determine which action to take based on response
                switch( GetResponseCode( cmd ))
                {
                    case( 300 ):
```

Listing 15.2 **Continued**

```
        {
            // client wants instructions on how to play
            SendData( s, "200\r\nPick a number " +
                "between 1 and 100 and the server will " +
                "return if it's too high, too low or " +
                "correct\r\n\r\n" );
            break;
        }
        case( 301 ):
        {
            // client is guessing number
            try
            {
                int guess = Int32.Parse(
                    GetResponseData( cmd ));

                if( guess < curRandom )
                {
                    SendData( s,
                        "401\r\nNumber is too low\r\n\r\n");
                }
                else if( guess > curRandom )
                {
                    SendData( s,
                        "401\r\nNumber is too high\r\n\r\n");
                }
                else
                {
                    SendData( s, "400\r\nCorrect! The " +
                        "number is " + curRandom +
                        "\r\n\r\n" );

                    bCloseConnection = true;
                }
            }
            catch
            {
                SendData(s,"404\r\nInvalid guess!\r\n\r\n");
            }

            break;
        }
        case( 302 ):
        {
            // client is quitting
```

Listing 15.2   **Continued**

```
                                    bCloseConnection = true;
                                    break;
                            }
                            default:
                            {
                                    break;
                            }
                    }
            } while( GetResponseCode( cmd ) !=
                    302 && bCloseConnection == false );
```

In the `ReceiveData` method, a `do/while` loop reads incoming data from the client using a packet size of 1024 bytes. Due to the nature of this application, 1KB is a liberal packet size because the data being received will never be that large. The point is that as you develop your application, you might want to experiment with that number to see what value gives optimal performance. Additionally, the `Receive` method expects a byte array to place data in, which means you might have to convert it as is the case with the `GetString` method defined in the `Encoding.ASCII` class. Listing 15.3 shows how to read incoming data from a client and also contains the methods used to parse the incoming data to extract the protocol codes.

Listing 15.3   **Receiving Client Data**

```
public static string ReceiveData( Socket client )
{
    string data = "";
    int bytesRecvd = 0;
    int totalBytes = 0;

    byte[] recvData = new byte[1024];   // 1k packet size

    do
    {
        bytesRecvd = client.Receive( recvData, 0,
            1024, SocketFlags.None );

        if( bytesRecvd > 0 )
        {
            data += Encoding.ASCII.GetString( recvData );
            totalBytes += bytesRecvd;
        }
    } while( bytesRecvd == 1024 );

    return data;
}
```

Listing 15.3   **Continued**

```
// methods to break apart protocol messages
// extracts the numerical identifier at beginning of message
public static int GetResponseCode( string response )
{
    string code = response.Substring( 0, response.IndexOf( '\r' ));
    return Int32.Parse( code );
}

// extracts extra message data
public static string GetResponseData( string response )
{
    return response.Substring( response.IndexOf('\n')+1,
        response.LastIndexOf("\r\n\r\n")-response.IndexOf('\n')+1 );
}
```

In Listing 15.2, once a valid command is received, an appropriate return message is sent with corresponding data using the `SendData` method. The act of sending the data is a lot less involved than receiving because you are able to send the entire buffer without worrying about chunking data. Recipe 15.6, "Creating a Connectionless UDP–Based Client," creates a client that interacts with this server:

```
public static void SendData( Socket client, string response )
{
    // Convert the string to a Byte Array and send it
    Byte[] data = Encoding.ASCII.GetBytes(response.ToCharArray());
    client.Send(data, data.Length, SocketFlags.None);
}
```

Comments

A majority of Internet technologies in use today utilize the same methods shown in this section. Specifically, the Transmission Control Protocol (TCP) is the underlying protocol that enforces how the transfer of data flows from one remote computer to another. A server and client using TCP remain in a connected state throughout the duration of the session as data is streamed between the two.

The listings in this section show how to implement a simple server that uses TCP to connect to and communicate with remote computers. As you read the code, you'll see the steps outlined earlier. The server first creates a new `TcpListener` object that sits and waits for incoming connections. Once a connection is detected, which occurs whenever the blocking method `AcceptSocket` returns, the main server/client communication loop begins. This communication uses the `Socket` class to both receive and send data to the client computer. The steps and type of data that is sent and received is termed the *protocol*, and it is necessary to ensure data integrity and consistent communication between server and client.

One thing to note is the number of, or lack of, simultaneous connections that this server can handle. Once the `AcceptSocket` method returns and the communication loop begins, the server is unable to service any other connection attempts made by any other client. This limit means that only one client can use the server's information at one time, leaving a large queue of other clients waiting for their turn. Solving this problem requires the use of *threading*. Threading is discussed in detail in Chapter 22, "Threading and Synchronization." Any time a blocking method is called, it should signal to you that your application might need threading. Threading is especially important when using Windows Forms applications so the user-interface thread can continue uninterrupted and with networking applications where the potential for multiple simultaneous connections exists.

To make the server in Listing 15.1 able to support multiple connections, move the communication loop into the thread procedure. Create a new `Thread` object that can utilize the created `Socket` object representing the new client object after the `AcceptSocket` method returns. After the new thread starts, the server can then call the `AcceptSocket` method again and wait for another connection while currently connected clients are being serviced within the thread.

15.2. Determining Connection Client Information

> You want to determine information about a connecting client within a server application.

Technique

The `Socket` class contains several useful properties that allow you to determine information about a connecting client. One of the key pieces of information is the `RemoteEndPoint` property that returns an `EndPoint` object. The `EndPoint` class itself is abstract, so to glean useful information, cast the `EndPoint` to an `IPEndPoint` object. The `IPEndPoint` class contains the IP address and port number of the remote client. You can also use the `LocalEndPoint` property defined in the `Socket` class to access information regarding the server:

```
Console.WriteLine( "Client End Point: IP: {0} Port: {1}",
    ((IPEndPoint)s.RemoteEndPoint).Address.ToString(),
    ((IPEndPoint)s.RemoteEndPoint).Port.ToString() );
```

```
Console.WriteLine( "Server End Point: IP: {0} Port: {1}",
    ((IPEndPoint)s.LocalEndPoint).Address.ToString(),
    ((IPEndPoint)s.LocalEndPoint).Port.ToString() );
```

The `Socket` class is designed to work with all types of network addressing schemes known as *address families*. The `AddressFamily` property returns a value specifying the addressing mode being used by the socket. In most cases, and because the Internet Protocol (IP) is the most widely used addressing method, the `AddressFamily` is `AddressFamily.InterNetwork`.

Listing 15.1 created a server using TCP as the communication protocol. Data is passed back and forth between the client and server in a streaming fashion. You can verify this information by accessing the `ProtocolType` and `SocketType` properties, which return `TCP` and `stream` values, respectively.

The last significant property is `Connected`. This Boolean value represents the state of the connection during the last data transmission. You should not use this property, however, as a method to detect whether the client computer is still connected because it's unreliable. Each time data is sent and received, the `Connected` property can be updated, but during the time in between, the property cannot be updated because there is no reliable method to make this determination.

Comments

The `Socket` class is an extremely versatile class that can support a wide variety of underlying protocols. One thing to note to avoid confusion is that even though the `Socket` class is able to support these different protocols, the protocols themselves must be installed and available on the operating system. The `Socket` class simply provides an abstracted API to those protocols.

You'll see properties being used throughout the .NET Framework simply for informational purposes. It's up to the developer to determine whether to use that information and, if so, in what way. The `EndPoint` information contained within the `LocalEndPoint` and `RemoteEndPoint` properties is a good example. While used within the `Socket` class itself, these properties can also serve certain purposes within your application. The `RemoteEndPoint` is a good example. This property contains the IP address and port of the connecting client. With this information, your server can create a configurable filtering mechanism to prevent any inherent security risks. One of the most popular server exploits is the denial-of-service (DoS) hack. It occurs when a group of remote computers repeatedly connects and sends data to a server in the hopes of overloading it so incoming connections cannot be made. Of course, this type of attack is usually limited to Web servers, but it is something you should keep in mind.

15.3. Resolving an IP Address or Hostname Using DNS

> You want to resolve a hostname or an IP address using the Domain Name System (DNS).

Technique

The DNS class contains a collection of static methods designed to resolve an IP address or a hostname using DNS. Each of the methods returns an IPHostEntry object containing the IP address of the host computer being searched for. The DNS.GetHostByName method searches for the given host given the friendly string name of an IP address such as www.samspublishing.com. DNS.GetHostByAddress uses a string or an IPAddress object to perform a lookup. This method and GetHostByName return a null value if the specified host is not found, which makes them a good candidate to ensure the server you want to connect to is operational before you connect to it.

The last method is a combination of the two methods just mentioned. The DNS.Resolve method accepts a string parameter that can denote either a hostname or an IP address. The Resolve method determines which scheme is being specified and resolves the hostname accordingly. The following code first checks for any command-line arguments specifying the server to connect to, and if none are present, it uses the localhost IP address. The DNS.Resolve method creates an IPHostEntry object that will be used to connect to the remote computer, as shown in Listing 15.4.

Listing 15.4   **Performing DNS Lookup**

```
[STAThread]
static void Main(string[] args)
{
    TcpClient client = new TcpClient();
    Byte[] read = new Byte[1024];

    string gameServer = "";

    if (args.Length != 1)
    {
        gameServer = "127.0.0.1";
    }
    else
    {
        gameServer = args[0];
    }

    // Verify that the server exists
```

Listing 15.4 **Continued**

```
    IPHostEntry serverIP = Dns.Resolve( gameServer );
    if( serverIP == null )
    {
        Console.WriteLine("Cannot find server: {0}", gameServer);
        return;
    }
    else
    {
        Console.WriteLine( "Found server. {0}", serverIP.HostName );
    }
}
```

Comments

DNS was designed to associate a friendly string value with a numerical IP address. For
instance, whenever you navigate to a Web address within a Web browser, the browser
itself contacts a DNS server to translate the Web address to the numerical IP address
before it makes a connection to that address.

You can also use the DNS class itself and its static methods to effectively detect whether
an active Internet connection has already been established. You do so simply by resolving a
well-known hostname. If the DNS method is able to successfully resolve that hostname,
then the machine currently has an active Internet connection. However, you must ensure
that you don't inadvertently receive a false negative, which can occur if the hostname that
you are trying to resolve is currently disconnected. Therefore, attempt to resolve a group of
different hostnames because the probability that all of them would be down at the same
time is pretty low. If you are able to resolve at least one of them, then an Internet connection is active. Also, note that there are many different ways to determine an active Internet
connection. The DNS lookup method is a reliable method, but you can also use the
Internet Control Message Protocol (ICMP) to perform server pings or use PInvoke,
shown in Recipe 21.11, "Calling Native Unmanaged Code Using PInvoke," to call the
InternetGetConnectedState method defined in the wininet.dll library.

15.4. Creating a Stream-Based Client

> You want to create a stream-based client to communicate with a server using a
> specified protocol.

Technique

To connect to a server using TCP, create a TcpClient object and call the Connect
method, passing the remote server's IP address and port number as parameters into the

method. The method will return, but you are not guaranteed that the connection has been made. In Listing 15.5, the Connect method is contained within a try block that will catch an error if the connection attempt fails.

Listing 15.5   **Connecting to a Remote Server**

```csharp
[STAThread]
static void Main(string[] args)
{
    TcpClient client = new TcpClient();
    Byte[] read = new Byte[1024];

    string gameServer = "";

    if (args.Length != 1)
    {
        gameServer = "127.0.0.1";
    }
    else
    {
        gameServer = args[0];
    }

    // Verify that the server exists
    IPHostEntry serverIP = Dns.Resolve( gameServer );
    if( serverIP == null )
    {
        Console.WriteLine("Cannot find server: {0}", gameServer);
        return;
    }
    else
    {
        Console.WriteLine( "Found server. {0}", serverIP.HostName );
    }

    // Try to connect to the game server on port 2003
    try
    {
        client.Connect(gameServer, 2003);
    }
    catch (SocketException e)
    {
        Console.WriteLine("Cannot connect to {0}: {1}",
          gameServer, e.Message);
        return;
    }
```

Once you successfully make a connection using the `Connect` method, you are ready to begin communicating with the server. Create a new `Stream` object and assign it using the return value of the `GetStream` method defined in the `TcpClient` class. You will use this `Stream` object to both send and receive data to the server. The `Read` and `Write` methods of the `Stream` class both accept a byte array, an offset to where you want the method to read or write to in the array, and the total number of bytes to read or write. If you recall, these are the same methods employed when reading from a file stream, and the code is similar to the server-based code in Listing 15.2 for the `Socket` object.

Listing 15.6 is the remaining client portion of the number-guessing game server shown in Recipe 15.1, "Creating a Stream-Based Server." The main communication loop occurs in the `StartGame` method and uses the same protocol defined in that section. The code for this method is available for download on this book's Web site at `http://www.samspublishing.com`.

Listing 15.6 **Communicating with a Remote Server**

```
            // Get the stream
            Stream s;
            try
            {
                s = client.GetStream();
            }
            catch (InvalidOperationException exc)
            {
                Console.WriteLine("Cannot connect to {0}: {1}",
gameServer, exc.Message);
                return;
            }

            Console.WriteLine( "Connected to game server" );
            string response = GetResponse(s);
            Console.WriteLine( "Response\r\n--------\r\nCode: {0} Message: {1} ",
                GetResponseCode(response), GetResponseData(response));

            // connected begin game
            StartGame( s );

            client.Close();

            // Wait for user response to exit
            Console.WriteLine("Press Return to exit");
            Console.Read();

            client.Close();
        }
```

Comments

This recipe and Recipe 15.1 complete the necessary pieces to create a server and a client that can connect using a protocol that was designed to play a number-guessing game. Utilizing other protocols such as HTTP, FTP, and NNTP follows a similar pattern of commands being sent to a server, which in turn returns the requested information. The code uses numerical status messages and commands, which is consistent with other protocols, to alleviate any issues such as case consistency.

Creating a client for a specific server is similar to creating the actual server itself. In fact, a lot of the objects that are in use are mirrored on both ends. For instance, a TcpListener class is used to listen for incoming connections on a server, and a TcpClient is used to make those connections. Furthermore, the server uses a Socket object and its associated Send and Receive methods to stream data back to the client, and the client utilizes a Stream object and the methods Read and Write, whose parameters are almost identical to the Send and Receive Socket methods.

15.5. Creating a Connectionless UDP-Based Server

You want to create a server that uses the User Datagram Protocol (UDP) for connectionless communication to client systems.

Technique

UDP is a connectionless protocol because communication between a server and a client happens using packets of information called *datagrams* rather than a continuous stream of data. In other words, a stream-based protocol creates a connection and streams data until the session ends. UDP, however, sends packets of information to a specified IP address and port without keeping a continuous connection open.

You use the UdpClient class to facilitate UDP-based communication. This section looks at creating a centralized server to broadcast information to a known group of IP addresses on specific ports. The first step to create the server is to instantiate a UdpClient object on a known port. You can use a default port by not specifying port information within the constructor, but server applications are generally designed to work on a specific port. Therefore, create a new UdpClient and specify the port you want to use, as shown in the constructor of the UDPServer class in Listing 15.7.

Listing 15.7   **Creating a UDP Server**

```
using System;
using System.Net;
using System.Net.Sockets;
using System.Text;
```

Listing 15.7   **Continued**

```
using System.Collections;

namespace _5_UDPServer
{
    class Class1
    {
        [STAThread]
        static void Main(string[] args)
        {
            UDPServer server = new UDPServer();
            server.Run();
        }
    }

    struct ConnectedClient
    {
        public IPEndPoint ip;
        public string name;
    }

    class UDPServer
    {
        private UdpClient udp;
        private IPEndPoint remoteEndPoint;
        private ArrayList clients;

        public UDPServer()
        {
            clients = new ArrayList();
            udp = new UdpClient( 2003 );
        }
    }
}
```

Once you create the UdpClient, you are ready to begin receiving data. The UdpClient class contains a method named Receive, which accepts a reference to an IPEndPoint object. When the method returns, the IPEndPoint object contains the relevant data concerning the client that sent the data:

```
public void Run()
{
    while( true )
    {
        remoteEndPoint = new IPEndPoint( new IPAddress(0), 0 );
```

```
        byte[] data = udp.Receive( ref remoteEndPoint );

        Console.WriteLine( "Received data: {0}",
➡Encoding.ASCII.GetString( data ));

        ProcessMessage( Encoding.ASCII.GetString( data ));
    }
}
```

You can then use this IPEndPoint object as a parameter to the Send method defined in the UdpClient class to reply to the client. This back and forth communication utilizes byte arrays whose data depends on the communication protocol used by the server and client. Listing 15.8 contains the remaining significant methods of the UDPServer class started earlier. The protocol is similar to the TCP server created in Recipe 15.1 in that numeric commands followed by relevant data constitute a command to the server. The server itself implements a chat server that broadcasts chat messages to each client that requests to be added. Each client's information is contained within the private ArrayList collection contained within the server.

Listing 15.8   **UDP Chat Server**

```
        private void ProcessMessage( string message )
        {
            switch( GetResponseCode( message ) )
            {
                case (300): // add new user
                {
                    ConnectedClient newClient;
                    newClient.ip = remoteEndPoint;
                    newClient.name = GetResponseData( message );

                    clients.Add( newClient );
                    BroadcastMessage( newClient.name +
                        " has entered the conversation." );
                    break;
                }
                case (301): // remove user
                {
                    BroadcastMessage( FindName( remoteEndPoint) +
                        " has left the conversation." );
                    RemoveClient( remoteEndPoint );
                    break;
                }
                case( 400 ): // chat message
                {
                    BroadcastMessage( FindName( remoteEndPoint ) + ": " +
                        GetResponseData( message ) );
```

Listing 15.8   **Continued**

```
                break;
            }
        }
    }


    private void BroadcastMessage( string message )
    {
        foreach( object obj in clients )
        {
            try
            {
                ConnectedClient client = (ConnectedClient) obj;
                udp.Send( Encoding.ASCII.GetBytes( message.ToCharArray ()),
                    message.Length, client.ip );
            }
            catch( Exception e )
            {
                Console.WriteLine( e.Message );
            }
        }
    }
}
```

Comments

Now that you've seen two different technologies, TCP and UDP, that essentially perform the same function, you'll have to determine which one to use in certain instances. The deciding factor is the communication protocol you use. A stream-based server maintains a connection with each client it is servicing, which therefore allows it to maintain some sort of state information for each client. To put it into a physical metaphor, a stream-based server is a lot like a conversation that you are holding with someone. You make the initial connection, begin communicating, and build up a session history until the conversation is over. A UDP-based server, on the other hand, does not follow this convention. You are never guaranteed that a client will keep communicating with you after an initial connection because that connection is immediately dropped after the datagram arrives, thereby making it difficult to maintain state information for each client connecting to the server.

The UdpClient itself uses the methods of the Socket class for communication. As mentioned earlier, UDP uses packets of information known as datagrams to transfer data. However, unlike a stream-based connection where data arrives in sequential order, datagrams not only can arrive out of order but can also be duplicated. It is up to the receiver to place the datagrams back in order. Fortunately, this task is already done for you within the UdpClient class. All that your application has to deal with is the final transferred data.

15.6. Creating a Connectionless UDP-Based Client

You want to create a client application that can communicate with other computers using UDP.

Technique

UDP is merely a protocol that enables the exchange of datagrams between two computers. You can use the `UdpClient` class in both server and client applications. It means that sending and receiving data for a client application is the same process. All that you need is an IP address and port to send data to and a subsequent call to the `Receive` method, which fills in the details of the connecting application in the `IPHostEntry` object when the method returns. In Listing 15.9, you can see the code for a client application designed to work with the server from Listing 15.7. It is a Windows Forms application, which means that any blocking calls on the `UdpClient` class happen within a thread so that the user interface remains responsive.

When the application initializes, it creates an `IPEndPoint` object to contain the IP address and port of the server application. Next, it creates a `UdpClient` object by specifying an `IPEndPoint` whose IP address and port number are generated automatically to avoid any collisions with clients that might already be running on the same machine. After the `UdpClient` is created, the application creates the thread that listens for incoming data, whose functionality is contained within the thread procedure `ReceiveBroadcast`. If you compare this method with the `Run` method from the server, you'll see that the actual process of receiving data using a `UdpClient` is the same, regardless of whether the application is a server or a client. Likewise, sending data is also the same. The client application only has to deal with sending and receiving data with a single IP address, the server.

Listing 15.9   **The UDP Chat Client Application**

```
using System;
using System.Drawing;
using System.Collections;
using System.ComponentModel;
using System.Windows.Forms;
using System.Data;
using System.Threading;
using System.Net;
using System.Net.Sockets;
using System.Text;

namespace _5_UDPFormClient
{
```

Listing 15.9 **Continued**

```
public class Form1 : System.Windows.Forms.Form
{
    private System.Windows.Forms.TextBox tbTranscript;
    private System.Windows.Forms.TextBox tbMessage;
    private System.Windows.Forms.Button btnSend;
    private Thread chatThread;
    private System.ComponentModel.Container components = null;
    private string name;

    UdpClient client;
    private System.Windows.Forms.TextBox tbName;
    private System.Windows.Forms.Label label1;
    private System.Windows.Forms.Button btnSetName;
    IPEndPoint serverIP;

    public Form1()
    {
        InitializeComponent();

        serverIP = new IPEndPoint( IPAddress.Parse( "127.0.0.1" ), 2003 );
        client = new UdpClient( new IPEndPoint( IPAddress.Any, 0 ));

        name = tbName.Text;

        // create a thread to start receiving broadcast messages
        chatThread = new Thread( new ThreadStart( ReceiveBroadcast ));
        chatThread.Start();

        SendCommand( "300 " + name );
    }

    public void ReceiveBroadcast()
    {
        IPEndPoint receiveIP = new IPEndPoint(IPAddress.Any, 0);

        while( true )
        {
            byte[] data = client.Receive( ref receiveIP );
            tbTranscript.Text += Encoding.ASCII.GetString( data,
                0, data.Length ) + "\r\n";
        }
    }

    protected override void Dispose( bool disposing )
    {
```

Listing 15.9 **Continued**

```
        if ( disposing )
        {
            if (components != null)
            {
                components.Dispose();
            }
        }
        base.Dispose( disposing );
    }

    private void InitializeComponent()
    {
        this.tbTranscript = new System.Windows.Forms.TextBox();
        this.tbMessage = new System.Windows.Forms.TextBox();
        this.btnSend = new System.Windows.Forms.Button();
        this.tbName = new System.Windows.Forms.TextBox();
        this.label1 = new System.Windows.Forms.Label();
        this.btnSetName = new System.Windows.Forms.Button();
        this.SuspendLayout();

        // Windows Form initialization code removed

        this.ResumeLayout(false);

    }
    [STAThread]
    static void Main()
    {
        Application.Run(new Form1());
    }

    private void SendCommand( string command )
    {
        byte[] bytes = Encoding.ASCII.GetBytes(command);
        int ret = client.Send(bytes, bytes.Length, serverIP );
    }

    private void btnSend_Click(object sender, System.EventArgs e)
    {
        SendCommand( "400 " + tbMessage.Text );
    }

    private void btnSetName_Click(object sender, System.EventArgs e)
    {
        SendCommand( "301 " + name );
```

Listing 15.9 **Continued**

```
            SendCommand( "300 " + tbName.Text );
            name = tbName.Text;
        }

        private void Form1_Closed(object sender, System.EventArgs e)
        {
            SendCommand( "301 " + name );
        }
    }
}
```

Comments

The previous section used the `UdpClient` class to perform the functions of a server. Because UDP is a connectionless protocol, the line between server and client becomes a little fuzzy. Because the whole purpose of UDP is to send a message from one computer to the other, a client/server architecture doesn't necessarily have to be your design. Some applications might only use a server as an intermediary to introduce two clients to each other. Once it makes this connection, the two clients can simply send and receive datagram messages back and forth with each other.

The client application in Listing 15.9 performs its interaction with the server from Listing 15.7. The only messages the client sends and receives are from the server itself. It is up to the server to properly broadcast messages from a client to all the other clients. Again, this arrangement is purely a design decision based on the fact that the chat application should act more like a chat room rather than an instant messenger, which performs one-on-one communication between two clients.

15.7. Controlling Socket Lingering Behavior

You want to cause a socket to finish sending unsent data after its `Close` method is called.

Technique

Once a socket connection is closed, any data that has not been sent is lost, even if the data transmission is in midstream. You can change this default behavior by changing the *linger time* of the socket. The linger time is the amount of seconds a socket remains open after its `Close` method is called so it can finish sending any remaining data. If the time-out occurs or the remaining data has finished transmitting, the socket closes the connection. To set the linger time, call the `SetSocketOption` method. The first parameter is a value from the `SocketOptionLevel` enumerated data type and corresponds to the set of options for a given socket type. Some of these values include `Tcp` for TCP-based sockets, `Udp` for UDP sockets, or `Socket`, which applies to all socket types. The value for the second parameter depends on the value specified in the first parameter. The `SocketOptionName` enumerated data type contains a list of options corresponding to groups of options for a given `SocketOptionLevel`. To specify the linger option, use the value `SocketOptionName.Linger`. The last parameter for `SetSocketOption` is the corresponding value to set the option to. This parameter can be a byte array, integer, or custom object depending on the option being set. For the `Linger` option, create a new `LingerOption` object, passing a `true` value and the number of seconds to set the linger time in the `LingerOption`:

```
// set a linger time of 1 minute
LingerOption lingerOption = new LingerOption(true, 60);
socket.SetSocketOption(SocketOptionLevel.Socket,
    SocketOptionName.Linger, lingerOption);
```

Comments

The `SetSocketOption` method allows you to set several different options on a socket to control its behavior. Once a socket is created, it operates in differing ways, depending on the type of protocol. Not all options are valid for any socket type. The amount of possible options can seem overwhelming, and you can't know how each one affects the socket without investigating further. Luckily, the `Socket` class is built upon the Berkeley Sockets Interface developed in 1978, which means finding information on a certain options should be no trouble.

The linger option is useful if you want to ensure that any remaining data is sent before the socket is closed. Some other options that might prove useful include the `KeepAlive` option, which tells the socket to periodically send keepalive packets to the connected computer in between sending and receiving periods when the connection becomes latent. The `ReceiveTimeOut` and `SendTimeOut` options control the amount of time the socket remains blocked in a call to `Receive` or `Send` before returning due to an unsuccessful transfer of data.

15.8. Using the `WebRequest` Class for HTTP Communication

You want to download an Internet resource using a `WebRequest` object using HTTP.

Technique

You can use the `WebRequest` class to perform communication using HTTP without having to implement the protocol at a lower level using sockets. To download an

Internet resource using the `WebRequest` class, create a new `WebRequest` object by using the static method `Create`. Once you make the request, you can start streaming in the data. However, to avoid latency issues, you might want to specify a timeout period for unresponsive servers. To do so, set the `Timeout` method to a value in milliseconds:

```
// create a web request using web address in text box
WebRequest request = WebRequest.Create( tbWebAddress.Text );

// set timeout to 10 seconds
request.Timeout = 10000;
```

After you make an initial request, you must then create a `WebResponse` object to handle the data that is sent by the server. Calling the `GetResponse` method from the request object created earlier:

```
WebResponse response = request.GetResponse();
```

The `WebResponse` class contains a stream object that you can use to stream the data from the server to your application. You use the stream object just like the stream classes discussed in Chapter 12. To access the `WebResponse` stream, call the `GetResponseStream` method, passing the returned `Stream` object to a `StreamReader` that can be used to read the data into a buffer. Finally, close the stream object after the data stream is read:

```
// get response stream and create a stream reader
Stream responseStream = response.GetResponseStream();
StreamReader reader = new StreamReader(responseStream, Encoding.ASCII);

// read in data and set as textbox text
String content = reader.ReadToEnd();
tbContent.Text = content;
responseStream.Close();
```

Comments

The `WebRequest` class is abstract, which means you are unable to directly instantiate it using the new keyword. The preceding example creates a `WebRequest` object by calling the static `Create` method in the `WebRequest` class to create a new request. The parameter to this method is a Uniform Resource Identifier (URI). Depending on the protocol specified in the URI, the `WebRequest` class creates an appropriate object for that protocol. This example creates an `HttpWebRequest` object, which means you can cast the `WebRequest` object to `HttpWebRequest` to gain access to more specific HTTP properties.

HTTP headers accompany both a request and response object. Headers are a part of the HTTP protocol that facilitate communication between a server and a connected client application. The headers themselves are nothing more than key/value pairs, but you can change their values to change the way the server interacts with your application. You can retrieve HTTP headers by directly accessing the `Headers` collection defined in the `WebResponse` class:

```
StringBuilder headerValues = new StringBuilder();

foreach( string key in response.Headers.AllKeys )
{
    headerValues.Append( "Key: " + key + " Value: " + headers.Get(key) + "\n" );
}

MessageBox.Show( headerValues.ToString(), "Header Collection" );
```

This headers collection, because it's a dictionary-based collection, contains an indexer that accepts a string object representing the header key. To alleviate any case issues or to avoid incorrectly specifying a header key, you can also cast the WebResponse object to an HttpWebResponse object and use the several different properties the HttpWebResponse class exposes to view header values:

```
MessageBox.Show(((HttpWebRequest)wReq).UserAgent);
```

15.9. Requesting Web Documents Through a Proxy Server

You want to read a Web document but must go through a proxy server to do so.

Technique

You manage proxies by creating a WebProxy object and setting it as the default proxy that is used by all Web requests within your application. When creating a WebProxy object, pass the proxy server address and port number to the constructor. You can then set the default proxy server for all Web requests by calling the static method Select defined in the GlobalProxySelection class:

```
void SetProxy( string address, int port )
{
    WebProxy proxyObject = new WebProxy( address, port );

    // don't use proxy for local addresses
    proxyObject.BypassProxyOnLocal = true;

    // make change global
    GlobalProxySelection.Select = proxyObject;
}
```

Comments

Most businesses use firewalls as a way to prevent external machines from accessing an internal network. An external computer attempting to access a machine in the internal network is denied access by the firewall. This arrangement, of course, presents a dilemma for two-way communication protocols such as HTTP. Because HTTP is a connection-oriented protocol, it requires a client to send data to the server and vice versa. If a firewall exists at the client site, the server cannot service the client request. To solve this problem, you can use a proxy server. This server acts as a liaison between the server and client, whereby all communication between the two first goes through the proxy server.

Using a proxy server within the .NET Framework is a trivial matter. In fact, in most cases, you might not need to ask the user to specify the proxy address to use. The `GlobalProxySelection` by default uses the proxy returned by the `WebProxy.GetDefaultProxy`, which itself appears within the Internet Explorer settings.

15.10. Creating Asynchronous Web Requests

You want to read a Web document asynchronously to avoid making blocking calls.

Technique

Creating an asynchronous Web request requires the use of two callback methods and an object that holds the current state of the read operation. If you recall from Section 15.8, "Using the `WebRequest` Class for HTTP Communication," the order of steps for a Web request began with creating a request, retrieving a response, and then reading the data contained within the response. The procedure is similar here, but you use callback methods to process the response from the initial request.

Before we look at the necessary callbacks, you need to create a state object to hold intermediary and final results. Although you are more than welcome to use member variables within a class, you must ensure proper synchronization to ensure data integrity. This example creates a state object for each Web request so that the state of the request is tracked from the beginning of the operation to the end. The following code shows the class used to hold the current state of a Web request. The class itself contains just a few member variables, which include a `StringBuilder` to hold the final results, a byte array to hold intermediary results after each read operation, the initial request object, and the subsequent stream for reading operations:

```
public class RequestState
{
    public StringBuilder Content;
    public byte[] BufferRead;

    public HttpWebRequest Request = null;
    public Stream ResponseStream = null;

    public RequestState()
```

```
    {
        BufferRead = new byte[1024];
        Content = new StringBuilder("");
    }
}
```

The first callback method handles the actual Web response that is called from the `WebRequest` object. It is within this method that you want to begin reading the associated data. In the following code, you can see that the state object can be acquired from the `IAsyncResult` parameter. After this step, you create the stream object from the response object similar to the way you did in Recipe 15.8. Finally, you perform an asynchronous call to the `BeginRead` method defined in the response object. It eventually calls the second callback method when the reading of the data is finished:

```
private void ResponseCallback(IAsyncResult result)
{
    // get state object attached to final result
    RequestState state = (RequestState) result.AsyncState;

    // Get the request and response objects
    HttpWebRequest request = state.Request;
    HttpWebResponse response = (HttpWebResponse) request.EndGetResponse(result);

    // place response stream into state
    state.ResponseStream = response.GetResponseStream();

    // start reading asynchronously
    IAsyncResult iarRead = state.ResponseStream.BeginRead(state.BufferRead,
        0, 1024, new AsyncCallback(ReadCallBack), state);
}
```

The last callback method you have to define is the method used to notify your application that the reading is finished or the supplied buffer is filled. The first step within the method in the following code is to extract the state object from the `IAsyncResult`, as was done earlier. Next is the call to `EndRead`, which returns the number of bytes filled into the buffer within the state object. When no more data is available, this method returns a value of `0`, but as long as the number is greater than `0`, you have to repeatedly call the `BeginRead` method and repeat the process, as shown in the following code:

```
private void ReadCallBack(IAsyncResult asyncResult)
{
    // get state and response objects
    RequestState state = (RequestState)asyncResult.AsyncState;

    // end the reading and get bytes available
    int read = state.ResponseStream.EndRead( asyncResult );
```

```
      if (read > 0)
      {
          // get buffer data and append to state content result
          state.Content.Append( Encoding.ASCII.GetString(state.BufferRead,
    ➡0, read ));

          // continue with data read
          IAsyncResult ar = state.ResponseStream.BeginRead( state.BufferRead,
              0, 1024, new AsyncCallback(ReadCallBack), state);
      }
      else
      {
          if(state.Content.Length > 1)
          {
              tbContent.Text = state.Content.ToString();
          }

          // Close down the response stream
          state.ResponseStream.Close();
      }
      return;
}
```

The final step is to actually start the process by creating the request. The actual method itself, shown in the following code, does nothing more than create the initial Web request with the URI of the document to receive followed by the creation of the state object that is passed through the different asynchronous callback methods. You then start the whole process by calling the `BeginGetResponse` method, passing the callback method that will be used and the state object that is then placed in the `IAsyncResult` parameter of the callback method:

```
private void btnGo_Click(object sender, System.EventArgs e)
{
    // create the request and state objects
    HttpWebRequest request = (HttpWebRequest)
        WebRequest.Create(tbAddress.Text);

    RequestState state = new RequestState();

    // place request into state object
    state.Request = request;

    // start the asynchronous call
    IAsyncResult res = (IAsyncResult) request.BeginGetResponse(
        new AsyncCallback(ResponseCallback), state);
}
```

Comments

Recipe 15.8 created a WebRequest object to read a document from the Web. The code itself assumed that the data coming in would always come quickly and without interruptions of any kind. In fact, the reading of the data itself isn't even placed within a thread. This type of design, although fine for examples, might lead to problems later. The problem lies in the creation of the request and the subsequent reading of the data within the response object. The methods are all blocking, which means they will not return until the methods have either timed out or have received all the data. If the server that the application is connecting and reading from is slow, or the data itself is fairly large, then the application will appear as if it has hung. Making asynchronous calls to the request and response objects will solve this dilemma, as shown in the technique earlier. By doing so, you are freeing your application to respond to other events that might occur, such as user-interface events on your main thread.

16

Building ASP.NET Applications

16.0. Introduction

ASP.NET represents a significant leap forward for the Web because it transforms the simple Web page into a Web application. ASP.NET's predecessor, Active Server Pages (ASP), could process a Web page server side using a special tag-based notation to interact with a database without having to push this database across the wire to a connected client. ASP.NET still follows this convention, but its roots within ASP stop there because radical changes have occurred with the availability of the .NET Framework. The most notable addition is the ability to place a Web application's logic into the main unit of the .NET deployment model, an assembly. Whereas ASP used an interjected script within a Web page to manipulate the Web document, ASP.NET offers a tremendous advantage in performance and flexibility because the Web page, with help from the .NET Framework, accesses code within compiled binaries written in any .NET language the developer chooses. Additionally, creating a Web application is significantly easier than with ASP because it allows for better separation of the presentation from the logic designed to control the presentation.

This chapter looks at various facets of ASP.NET. You start by creating a simple Web application and learn how to use the various controls for presentation. The methods are so strikingly similar to those in the construction of Windows Forms that ASP.NET pages are also known as Web Forms. Later in the chapter, you'll see how to integrate the concepts discussed in Chapter 14, "ADO.NET," to bind data to certain Web Forms controls as well as how to create your own controls. The chapter ends by looking at how to increase performance through caching and how to create your own Web server to host ASP.NET Web pages.

16.1. Creating a Simple Web Form

You want to create a new ASP.NET Web application.

Technique

To create a new Web application, use the New Project dialog box and use the ASP.NET Web Application project template. The location box displays a different path from what you have used so far. Instead of an absolute path to the project's source code, a virtual directory is created within Internet Information Server (IIS). After you create the project, the Web Forms designer opens to allow you to design the initial Web Form. The next recipe explains how to use the Web Forms designer to add server-side controls to the page.

Comments

Working with a Web Form is similar to working with a Windows Form in that you use a designer to design the form and a source file to control the behavior of the form at runtime. However, Windows Forms information is contained within a single source file, whereas a Web Form contains both an HTML-based file for presentation and a corresponding C# file for the Web Form logic. To view the HTML associated with the ASP.NET page, open the default WebForm1.aspx file and click on the bottom-left button labeled HTML. To switch back to design view, click the design button.

The first thing you'll notice in the HTML for the .aspx page is the @Page directive. ASP.NET uses this directive during runtime to determine the correct assembly to use when the page is requested as well as certain attributes that control how the page is processed by ASP.NET. The rest of the page is regular HTML because nothing has been added for server-side processing.

The C# file that is generated is known as the code-behind file because it is literally the code that is behind the main page controlling the behavior of server-side controls as they are processed by ASP.NET. To open the source file, right-click on the WebForm1.aspx file within Solution Explorer and select View Code. Within the generated code is the Page_Load method. As its name implies, this method is called each time a page is loaded by ASP.NET. This loading occurs on the server before the final HTML is generated, and it is where initialization code is placed. If you expand the source code region named Web Form Designer generated code, you'll see that the Page_Load is actually an event handler for the Load event defined in the System.Web.Page class, which your Web Form class derives from. Event handlers are discussed in detail in Recipe 16.3, "Handling Web Control Events."

16.2. Displaying Server-Side Controls

You want to place server-side controls on a Web Form for an ASP.NET page.

Technique

The first thing you have to choose before placing Web Form controls is the type of page layout scheme to use by changing the pageLayout property. The two choices include FlowLayout and GridLayout. FlowLayout uses relative positioning for each control, which doesn't use traditional x and y coordinates for each control but instead positions each control relative to the control just placed. This type of layout follows the more traditional layout method used within HTML. GridLayout, on the other hand, uses absolute positioning, which follows the method used in Windows Forms. In this layout scheme, you can position controls anywhere on the Web Form and have an associated coordinate pair denoting the position of the control relative to the top-left coordinate of the form.

To create a server-side control, drag and drop a control from the Web Form Designer toolbox. The designer places the control relative to the last control placed on the page if in FlowLayout mode or places it at its drop location if using GridLayout. Once the control is placed, you can access and change any properties by using the Property Browser window. In most cases, you'll see that working with a Web Form control uses the same methods employed by Windows Forms controls. For instance, if you create a server-side button, change the text on the face of the button by changing the Text property. You can change the text color by specifying a value for the ForeColor property.

Comments

The ultimate goal of an ASP.NET page is to produce an HTML page that can be sent and rendered to the computer connected to the Web application. Each ASP.NET control must eventually produce an HTML representation of itself. The properties of an ASP.NET control translate to attributes on the corresponding HTML control that is produced. For instance, the ASP.NET code for a button containing a tooltip and a specified ForeColor appears as follows:

```
<asp:Button id="Button1" runat="server" Text="This is a button"
ForeColor="#0000C0" ToolTip="This is the tooltip"></asp:Button>
```

When ASP.NET generates the final HTML page, the ForeColor property translates to a value within the style attribute and the Tooltip property is used for the title attribute:

```
<input type="submit" name="Button1" value="This is a button"
id="Button1" title="This is the tooltip" style="color:#0000C0;" />
```

The generated HTML page contains an HTML form to contain the controls as it's displayed to the user. As a user manipulates the control, certain controls might automatically cause the page to perform a post back. A *post back* is a round-trip operation in which the properties of each control are placed into a dictionary-based collection known as the ViewState and submitted as form data back to the Web application. Some controls such as buttons automatically generate a post-back event, although others don't because of the frequency with which a post back would occur. However, by changing the AutoPostBack property to true, you can cause a post back to occur. For example, the TextBox control does not generate a post back to occur whenever the text within the control changes. In this next recipe, you'll see how to create event handlers to respond to the events generated as the user interacts with the form.

16.3. Handling Web Control Events

You want to create an event handler to respond to an event fired from a Web Form control.

Technique

To create an event handler for a Web Form control, select the control within the designer and click the Events toolbar button located in the Property Browser. The Property Browser displays a list of valid events for a control. To create an event handler for a specific event, either double-click the event field to create a handler with a default name or enter a different name for the event handler. In Listing 16.1, you can see the code-behind file for a Web application created for this recipe called Web Shell. In the code listing, you can see how a delegate is created for an ImageButton control and associated with the Click event. The code for the event handler simply toggles the value of a Boolean variable and sets the visibility of TextBox control accordingly. A few things in this code are worth noting.

In the ImageButton.Click event handler, you can see a Boolean member variable being used. The member itself is declared static. If it weren't, then its value would not persist each time the page loads, which happens whenever a post back occurs. In other words, if the variable were not static, then even after it was changed within the event handler, it would be reset to its initialization value. Recipe 16.12, "Managing Application and Session State," demonstrates how to persist objects using the ViewState collection, and Recipe 16.13, "Creating Custom Web Controls," shows how to use session tracking.

Listing 16.1 **Web Shell Code-Behind File**

```
using System;
using System.Collections;
using System.ComponentModel;
using System.Data;
using System.Drawing;
using System.Web;
```

Listing 16.1   **Continued**

```
using System.Web.SessionState;
using System.Web.UI;
using System.Web.UI.WebControls;
using System.Web.UI.HtmlControls;
using System.IO;

namespace _3_EventHandling
{
    public class WebForm1 : System.Web.UI.Page
    {
        protected System.Web.UI.WebControls.TextBox ShellBox;
        protected System.Web.UI.WebControls.Label Label1;
        protected System.Web.UI.WebControls.ImageButton btnMinimize;
        static private string curDir;
        static protected bool bIsMinimized;

        private void Page_Load(object sender, System.EventArgs e)
        {
            if( !Page.IsPostBack )
            {
                curDir = Server.MapPath( "." );
                ShellBox.Text = "Welcome to WebShell\n";
                DisplayPrompt();
            }
            else
            {
                // get command
                string cmd = ShellBox.Text.Substring(
                    ShellBox.Text.LastIndexOf( '>' )+1);
                if( cmd != null && cmd != "" )
                {
                    string ret = ProcessCommand( cmd );
                    ShellBox.Text = ShellBox.Text + "\n" + ret + "\n";
                    DisplayPrompt();
                }

                if( bIsMinimized == true )
                    ShellBox.Visible = false;
                else
                    ShellBox.Visible = true;
            }
        }

        private string ProcessCommand( string cmd )
        {
```

Listing 16.1 **Continued**

```
          string ret = "";

          switch( cmd )
          {
              case( "ver" ):
              {
                  ret =  "WebShell Version 1.0";
                  break;
              }
              case ("cls"):
              {
                  ShellBox.Text = "";
                  ret = "";
                  break;
              }
              case ( "dir" ):
              {
                  DirectoryInfo di = new DirectoryInfo(curDir);
                  FileInfo[] fi = di.GetFiles();

                  foreach (FileInfo fiTemp in fi)
                      ret = ret + fiTemp.Name + "\n";

                  break;
              }
              default:
              {
                  ret = cmd + "' is not recognized as an internal or " +
                          "external command, operable program or batch file.";
                  break;
              }
          }

          return ret;
      }

      private void DisplayPrompt()
      {
          ShellBox.Text = ShellBox.Text + curDir + ">";
      }

      #region Web Form Designer generated code
      override protected void OnInit(EventArgs e)
      {
          InitializeComponent();
```

Listing 16.1   **Continued**

```
        base.OnInit(e);
    }

    private void InitializeComponent()
    {
        this.btnMinimize.Click += new
            System.Web.UI.ImageClickEventHandler(this.btnMinimize_Click);
        this.Load += new System.EventHandler(this.Page_Load);

    }
    #endregion

    private void btnMinimize_Click(object sender,
        System.Web.UI.ImageClickEventArgs e)
    {
        if( bIsMinimized == true )
        {
            ShellBox.Visible = true;
            bIsMinimized = false;
        }
        else
        {
            ShellBox.Visible = false;
            bIsMinimized = true;
        }
    }
}
}
```

When using event handlers, you must be cognizant of the order of method calls for each load of an ASP.NET page. Because each post back requires your class to be reconstructed using the information in the ViewState collection, the class initialization functions are called again. This process occurs before the actual event handler is called. In the Page_Load method in Listing 16.1, you can see how to check whether the page is being loaded in response to a post back by checking the IsPostBack property. If the page is a post back, you can also see that the TextBox.Visible property is changed. It might seem logical to simply change the controlling Boolean variable within the event handler, thinking that the Page_Load method controls the TextBox properly. However, the event handler for the ImageButton is called after the Page_Load method, which means the Boolean value is wrong at the time of Page_Load. You should ensure that control properties that rely on member variables which themselves might change within an event handler are set within the event handler as well as within the proper initialization methods.

Comments

The event-handler code is created within the code-behind file for the ASP.NET page. ASP.NET event handlers are created and associated with events in the same way as their Windows Forms counterparts and all other classes within the .NET Framework, by using delegates. Furthermore, each event-handler delegate remains consistent in its use of parameters. The first parameter to every delegate is always a System.Object representing the sender of the event. The second and last parameter is either an EventArgs object or a class derived from EventArgs to supply additional information. In other words, a large part of the discussion in Chapter 8, "Windows Forms Controls," regarding the creation of event handlers applies equally to Web Form controls as they do to Windows Forms controls.

The previous recipe noted that ASP.NET controls are translated into HTML for rendering in a user's browser. This process means that you can also create client-side events in order to prevent making a trip back to the server to update the form accordingly. Listing 16.2 shows the .aspx file that accompanies the code-behind file in Listing 16.1. In this listing, you can see several JavaScript methods that are processed within the user's browser as they manipulate the controls. These methods are attached to various events of the HTML form object that is created when the project is initially created. Within the body of the ASP.NET page, you can see a few server-side controls. One of them is a label control named Titlebar. One of the attributes is named onclick and contains a call to the JavaScript alert method. Within the Integrated Development Environment (IDE), a small red wavy line appears underneath this attribute because onclick is not defined for a label control. Rather than disregard the attribute, however, ASP.NET simply passes the attribute to the HTML page, which in turn creates a JavaScript event handler. You can optionally add the onclick attribute to your code-behind file. Each control contains an Attributes collection, which translates into the attributes of the final HTML code.

Listing 16.2   **Web Shell ASP.NET Page**

```
<%@ Page language="c#" Codebehind="WebForm1.aspx.cs" AutoEventWireup="false"
Inherits="_3_EventHandling.WebForm1" %>
<!DOCTYPE HTML PUBLIC "-//W3C//DTD HTML 4.0 Transitional//EN" >
<HTML>
    <HEAD>
        <title>WebShell 1.0</title>
        <meta name="vs_snapToGrid" content="False">
        <meta content="Microsoft Visual Studio .NET 7.1" name="GENERATOR">
        <meta content="C#" name="CODE_LANGUAGE">
        <meta content="JavaScript" name="vs_defaultClientScript">
        <meta content="http://schemas.microsoft.com/intellisense/ie5"
            name="vs_targetSchema">
        <script language="javascript" id="clientEventHandlersJS">
<!--
```

Listing 16.2   **Continued**

```
function getkey(e)
{
    if (window.event)
        return window.event.keyCode;
    else if (e)
        return e.which;
    else
        return null;
}

function Form1_onkeypress()
{
    if( getkey(event) == 13 )
    {
        Form1.submit();
    }
    else
    {
        window.status = "Key Pressed: " + getkey(event);
        setShellBoxFocus();
    }
}

function setShellBoxFocus()
{
    if( document.Form1.ShellBox != null )
    {
        document.Form1.ShellBox.focus();
        var oRng = document.Form1.ShellBox.createTextRange();
        oRng.collapse(false);
        oRng.select();
    }
}
function window_onload()
{
    setShellBoxFocus();
}

function Form1_onmouseup()
{
    setShellBoxFocus();
}

//-->
    </script>
```

Listing 16.2   **Continued**

```
        </HEAD>
        <body language="javascript" onload="return window_onload()"
            ms_positioning="GridLayout">

            <form language="javascript" onkeypress="return Form1_onkeypress()"
                id="Form1" method="post" runat="server"
                onmouseup="return Form1_onmouseup()">

                <P align="center">
                    <asp:textbox id="ShellBox" runat="server" Width="759px"
                        Height="488px" TextMode="MultiLine" BackColor="Black"
                        ForeColor="White" AutoPostBack="True"
                        style="Z-INDEX: 101; LEFT: 256px; POSITION:
                        absolute; TOP: 56px"></asp:textbox>
                </P>
                <DIV style="Z-INDEX: 102; LEFT: 256px; WIDTH: 765px;
                    POSITION: absolute; TOP: 24px; HEIGHT: 43px"
                    ms_positioning="GridLayout">

                    <asp:Label onclick="alert('Web Shell 1.0');" id="Titlebar"
                        style="Z-INDEX: 101; LEFT: 0px; POSITION: absolute;
                        TOP: 11px" runat="server" Width="760px" Height="24px"
                        ForeColor="White" BackColor="Blue">Web Shell 1.0</asp:Label>

                    <asp:ImageButton id="btnMinimize" style="Z-INDEX: 102;
                        LEFT: 731px; POSITION: absolute; TOP: 12px"
                        runat="server" ImageUrl="minimize.jpg"></asp:ImageButton>
                </DIV>
                <P align="center"> </P>
            </form>
        </body>
</HTML>
```

16.4. Forcing a Post Back from a Web Control Event

> You want to force a post back to occur when a Web control event fires.

Technique

Only a certain number of ASP.NET controls cause a post back to occur when the user manipulates them. One of these controls is the Button control because a user expects something to occur when he or she clicks the button. Some controls do not automatically perform a post back when they change. An example is the `RadioButton` control. By default, the `RadioButton` control does not cause a post back to occur when it's clicked. To cause a post back to occur in response to a change in a server control, set the `AutoPostBack` property of the control to `true`.

Comments

A trip from the client to the server is a lengthy process. Of course in this day and age, it's not as bad as it used to be, but then again, not everyone is using a broadband Internet connection yet. To reduce the trips an ASP.NET page might take in response to interaction from the user with a control, post backs do not occur for every control. The control's event handler is not called until some other control causes the form to be submitted. Internally, the `ViewState` of the page is written in HTML as a hidden control. This `ViewState` value is an encrypted string containing the current properties of each control. ASP.NET examines the `ViewState` when a form is submitted and compares each control's value to the current value within the posted data. If the `ViewState` value is different from the value in the post data, then an event has occurred and ASP.NET calls the corresponding event handler. If you set `AutoPostBack` to `true`, then any change within the control causes a post back to occur.

16.5. Redirecting Users to a Different Web Page

You want to redirect users to a different Web page or Web site using server-side code.

Technique

The class that is created for each ASP.NET page is derived from the `System.Web.UI.Page` class within the .NET Framework. Within this class is a `Response` object that is used to send data constituting a response from the client's initial request. To cause a page redirection to occur, call the `Response.Redirect` method, passing the URL of the page to redirect the user to. You can optionally pass a Boolean value for the second parameter. If this value is `true`, then execution of the current page stops. In the following example, an event handler for a `Button` control redirects a user to a different site:

```
private void btnGo_Click(object sender, System.EventArgs e)
{
    Response.Redirect( "http://www.samspublishing.com" );
}
```

Comments

The Response object is created as a result of an initial request by a remote user for a Web page. The request itself is packaged and placed within a HttpRequest object. The page being requested is loaded by ASP.NET, which subsequently creates a Page object, and a response is formulated to send back to the client by creating a HttpResponse object. Both the HttpRequest and the HttpResponse are managed by the Page object, which means that because your class derives from the Page class, you have full access to those objects via the Request and Response properties.

The HttpResponse class contains several properties and methods that allow you to alter or add data to the outgoing response stream sent back to a client. For instance, if you want to create a custom header value, call the AddHeader method passing a key/value pair. It is then added to the header collection sent to the client. ASP also used the Response object extensively to add HTML data to the output stream by calling the Response.Write method. The same applies to ASP.NET, although the line becomes a little fuzzy about where to call Response.Write because of the separation of presentation and logic using code-behind files. For more information on writing to the output stream, see Recipe 16.14, "Using Page Output Caching."

16.6. Validating Input Data and Displaying Errors

You want to perform validation on a form and display an error if validation fails for certain fields.

Technique

A validator within the .NET Framework works to notify a user that a value within a control in a Web Form is invalid and must be changed before the form can be submitted successfully. You can apply five possible validators to controls on a Web Form.

The RequiredFieldValidator causes validation to fail if the user leaves the value of a control blank. To create a RequiredFieldValidator, drag the RequiredFieldValidator control from the toolbox and drop it next to the control to validate. Next, change the Text and ErrorMessage properties that appear when validation fails. You can optionally create a ValidationSummary control, which lists all error messages for controls that have failed validation. If you use a summary, the ErrorMessage property appears in the summary, and the Text property appears at the location of the validation control:

```
<asp:ValidationSummary id="ValidationSummary1" runat="server"
  Width="619px" HeaderText="The following errors occurred."/>
```

Finally, change the ControlToValidate property of the RequiredFieldValidator by selecting the Web Form control that you are validating. The following example creates a

TextBox control that displays an error message from a `RequiredFieldValidator` control if the `TextBox` is left blank:

```
<asp:TextBox id="tbName" runat="server" Width="392"></asp:TextBox>
<asp:RequiredFieldValidator id="RequiredFieldValidator1" runat="server"
ErrorMessage=
  "Name is required" ControlToValidate="tbName">*</asp:RequiredFieldValidator>
```

Another validation control you can use is the `RangeValidator`. This validator checks the value of the input field and determines whether it falls within a specific range of values. Creating a `RangeValidator` follows the same method as the `RequiredFieldValidator`. After you drag and drop the validator and set the `ErrorMessage`, `Text`, and `ControlToValidate` properties, you can set the range of possible values. The `MinimumValue` and `MaximumValue` values denote the range of possible values the input field can have. However, this range of values does not automatically assume that the values are integers. To create an integer range, change the `Type` property to `Integer`. Other possible types include `double`, `currency`, `date`, and `string` values. The `RangeValidator` converts the input field to the type specified in the `Type` property before making the range check. The following example uses a `TextBox` with a valid range of values from 1 to 100:

```
<asp:textbox id="tbNumber" runat="server" Width="392px"></asp:textbox>
<asp:rangevalidator id="RangeValidator1" runat="server"
 ErrorMessage="Number must be between 1 and 100"
ControlToValidate="tbNumber" MinimumValue="1" MaximumValue="100"
 Type="Integer">*</asp:rangevalidator>
```

The `CompareValidator` performs a comparison on the values of two controls. It too contains `ErrorMessage`, `Text`, and `ControlToValidate` properties as do the other validator controls. To compare the control being validated against the value of another control, set the `ControlToCompare` property. Just like the `RangeValidator`, the `CompareValidator` converts the values of each control to a specified type before performing the comparison. To control the type conversion, change the `Type` property of the validator. Finally, you use the `Operator` property to control the logical operation to perform. For instance, to compare the control values to see whether they are equal, set the `Operator` property to `Equal`. Other possible values include `NotEqual`, `GreaterThan`, and `GreaterThanEqual` to name a few. The following example shows two `TextBox` controls with a `CompareValidator` attached to the `tbConfirmPassword` control. Whenever the user submits the form, a comparison happens to ensure that the confirmation password is equal to the password entered in the first `TextBox`:

```
<asp:textbox id="tbPassword" runat="server" Width="392px"
 TextMode="Password"></asp:textbox>

<asp:textbox id="tbConfirm" runat="server" Width="392px"
 TextMode="Password"></asp:textbox>
```

```
<asp:comparevalidator id="CompareValidator1" runat="server"
    ErrorMessage="Confirmation password does not match Password field"
    ControlToValidate="tbConfirm" Display="Dynamic"
    ControlToCompare="tbPassword">*
</asp:comparevalidator>
```

The RegularExpressionValidator matches the input field of the control with a regular expression that you supply. In addition to the normal error message strings and the ControlToValidate properties that are present on all validator controls, set the ValidationExpression property to a string representing the regular expression. To validate a phone number contained within a TextBox, attach a RegularExpressionValidator, as shown in the following code:

```
<asp:textbox id="tbPhone" runat="server" Width="392px"></asp:textbox>
<asp:regularexpressionvalidator id="RegularExpressionValidator1" runat="server"
    ErrorMessage="Phone number must be in the form XXX-XXX-XXXX"
    ControlToValidate="tbPhone" ValidationExpression="^\d{3}-\d{3}-\d{4}$">*
</asp:regularexpressionvalidator>
```

Sometimes, none of the validation controls are sufficient to perform validation on a control. For these cases, you can use a CustomValidator control. The only properties to set for this validation control are the ErrorMessage, Text, and ControlToValidate properties, just as you do with the other validation controls. To validate the control, create an event handler for the ServerValidate event. The second parameter for the event handler is a ServerValidateEventArgs object that contains a property named Value which contains the value of the control being validated. To specify that the control value is invalid, set the IsValid property defined in the event arguments object to false, which causes the validation to fail and a subsequent error message to display. For instance, to validate a TextBox value against a list of colors, the code would look like Listing 16.3.

Listing 16.3   **Validating a** TextBox **Control**

```
private void ColorValidator_ServerValidate(object source,
    System.Web.UI.WebControls.ServerValidateEventArgs args)
{
    string[] colorArray = new string[]{"red", "orange", "yellow",
        "green", "blue", "indigo", "violet"};
    ArrayList colorList = new ArrayList( colorArray );

    if( colorList.Contains( args.Value.ToLower() ))
    {
        args.IsValid = true;
    }
    else
    {
        args.IsValid = false;
    }
}
```

Comments

The first time we saw .NET in action was at a developer conference. Two things stood out as truly remarkable. The first was the `Anchor` property for Windows Forms, and the other was form validation within ASP.NET. If you've ever had to write dynamically resizing control code or validate input fields for an HTML form, then you'll probably agree.

As mentioned earlier, the .NET Framework contains five controls that allow you to seamlessly add form validation to your Web application. In the examples shown earlier for each of the validation controls, it was assumed that a `ValidationSummary` control accompanied the page. This `ValidationSummary` extracts the `ErrorMessage` field of each control that fails validation and places those messages within a HTML list. Once you add a `ValidationSummary` control to a form, the semantics of each validation control change with respect to the `ErrorMessage` and `Text` properties. The `ErrorMessage` appears in the `ValidationSummary`, and the `Text` value appears within the validation control. If either property value is blank, then the remaining value is used in both places. If instead there is no `ValidationSummary`, the validation control first checks the `Text` property and uses it. If the `Text` property is an empty string, then the `ErrorMessage` property is used.

One thing you have to watch when using validators is the possibility of empty fields within the form. If a user leaves a field blank and that field uses a validator, the field actually passes validation. In other words, if a `RangeValidator` validates the value in a `TextBox` and the user leaves that `TextBox` blank, the validation actually passes and no error message appears. To fix this problem, create a `RequiredFieldValidator` to prevent the user from leaving the field blank.

16.7. Databinding Web Controls

You want to extract the values for a server-side control from a database.

Technique

The ultimate goal of databinding an ASP.NET control is to get to the point where you can associate a `DataSet` with the control itself. How you ultimately do it is up to you because you can take several different avenues to wind up with this goal. Chapter 14 demonstrated how to work with databases to create `DataSet` objects and fill them by using a `DataAdapter`. This recipe presents two techniques for databinding a Web control. Each method results in the same solution but goes about it using two different methods.

The first method for databinding a Web control uses the techniques explained in Chapter 14. In other words, you write code to create a database connection, construct an adapter, and finally fill a `DataSet` that will be bound to the control. This example and the examples later in this chapter regarding data-bound controls use the Northwind database through a `SqlConnection` object.

To bind a control, create a data connection to the database you plan to use. This example creates a `SqlConnection` object by passing the connection string to the `SqlConnection` constructor to connect to the Northwind database:

```
private void Page_Load(object sender, System.EventArgs e)
{
    string connectionString = "Data Source=localhost;Integrated
     Security=SSPI;Initial Catalog=northwind";

    // create database connection
    SqlConnection sqlConn = new SqlConnection( connectionString );
```

The next step is to create a `DataAdapter`, which in this case is a `SqlDataAdapter`. The first parameter of the constructor is the SELECT command specifying the rows to extract from a table. In the following example, the SELECT command returns all rows from the table named `Products`. The second parameter to the constructor is the database connection object created earlier:

```
    // create a data adapter passing the SELECT statement
    SqlDataAdapter nwDA = new SqlDataAdapter( "SELECT * FROM PRODUCTS", sqlConn );
```

After you create the database connection and data adapter, you are ready to extract the data into a `DataSet`. To do so, create a new `DataSet` and call the `Fill` method defined in the `DataAdapter`, passing the `DataSet` to fill as the parameter:

```
    // create dataset to fill
    DataSet nwDS = new DataSet();

    // fill dataset
    nwDA.Fill( nwDS );
```

At this point, the `DataSet` contains the data that you want to bind to the control. In the examples shown, the `DataSet` contains each row from the `Products` table of the Northwind database. To bind this data to a control, set the `DataSource` equal to the `DataSet` object that you created. To specify the text to use for each option within the control, set the `DataTextField` property equal to the column name of the data table. You can also specify a `DataValueField` that represents the actual value of each option of a control (each item in a drop-down list, for example). You would also use a column name from the data table. In the following code, a drop-down list is bound to the `DataSet` created in this recipe. The text for each item in the list represents the values from the `ProductName` column, and each item value is the corresponding `ProductID`. Finally, to populate the drop-down list, call the `DataBind` method defined in the `Page` class:

```
    // bind control
    ddlCode.DataSource = nwDS;
    ddlCode.DataTextField = "ProductName";
```

```
    ddlCode.DataValueField = "ProductID";

    // databind will populate both controls
    DataBind();
}
```

The method just shown demonstrates how to databind a control programmatically. Another method is to let the Web Form designer generate the code for you. Just as with the previous data-binding method, there are advantages and disadvantages, which are explained in the corresponding comments for this recipe.

Assuming that you have created the necessary controls for the Web Form, you are now ready to bind the necessary controls. Within the designer, open the Server Explorer, which by default is docked to the left side of the IDE. Expand the Servers tree and select the Products table from the Northwind SQL database, as shown in Figure 16.1. To create the `SqlConnection` and `SqlDataAdapter` objects, drag and drop the Products table from Server Explorer onto the Web Form. To create the `DataSet` object, select the `SqlDataAdapter` that was created within the form and click on the Generate Dataset verb located at the bottom of the Property Browser. When the Generate Dataset dialog appears, you can accept the defaults or change the name of the `DataSet` to something more meaningful.

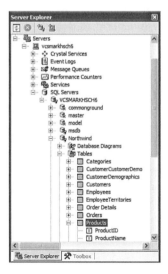

Figure 16.1   The Northwind database in Server Explorer.

At this point, the database connection object has been created as well as the data adapter and a specialized `DataSet` object. To bind the data to a control, select the control within the Web Form designer and set the `DataSource` property to the `DataSet`. The Property Browser can determine the available data sets, which means you can simply select the correct object from a drop-down list. Next, select the column name that will be used for each item's text by accessing the `DataTextField` property. Likewise, set the column name that is used for each item's value by selecting the correct column name in the `DataValueField` property.

Although the Web Form designer generates a lot of code for databinding controls, you still have to add the code to fill the `DataSet` and bind the resultant data to a control. Open the code-behind file. In the `Page_Load` method, fill the `DataSet` by calling the `Fill` method defined in the generated `SqlDataAdapter` object. Finally, call the `DataBind` method to populate the data-bound controls:

```
private void Page_Load(object sender, System.EventArgs e)
{
    // fill dataset for designer bound control
    sqlDataAdapter1.Fill( productsDS1 );

    // databind controls
    DataBind();
}
```

Comments

What was just shown represents two different ways of binding data from a database to a Web Form control. Neither one is better than the other, but each has its advantages and disadvantages that you must consider. You can programmatically databind a control with just a few lines of code to create the database connection, create an adapter, and fill a `DataSet` with the adapter. As you can see from the example, the code is easily manageable because it all resides within the same method. This method is well suited for read-only controls that simply display data from a database. However, once you start adding the necessary code to insert, delete, and update tables within the database while still maintaining the databinding code, the complexity begins to rise.

Using the designer to databind a control is also a fairly trivial matter once you understand the necessary steps. However, for controls that simply serve to display data, the amount of generated code that the designer provides might be overkill. After creating the necessary data binding with a control, expand the hidden region within the code-behind code, and assuming you accepted the defaults when generating the `DataSet`, you see a lot of lines of code related to such things as the insert, delete, update, and select commands as well as the code that associates the necessary data objects with each other. For anything but the simplest control, however, the generated code saves a lot of time and possibly eliminates simple mistakes that can occur if you write the code yourself. Additionally, the customized `DataSet` object that is created also contains helper methods that allow you to easily perform various operations on the data without having to use SQL commands because they have also been automatically generated. For example, to insert a new row into the Products table of the Northwind database using the objects that were created by the designer, the code appears as follows:

```
productsDS1.Products.AddProductsRow( "New Product", 1, 1, "1", 1.00m, 0,
  10, 1, false );
sqlDataAdapter1.Update( productsDS1 );
```

16.8. Using the `DataList` Web Control

> You want to display a formatted repeating list of data that is extracted from a database.

Technique

You use the `DataList` control to display data from a database using a series of templates that control how each item should be displayed. You can define styles to delineate individual items. The `DataList` also supports the ability for a user to select an item in the list as well as the ability to edit the item. This functionality, however, does not come for free and must be enabled by the developer. To begin creating a `DataList` control that is data-bound to values from a SQL database table, drag and drop a `DataList` control onto the Web Form and create the `SqlConnection`, an `SqlDataAdapter`, and a `DataSet`. Within the `Page_Load` event, add the code to fill the `DataSet` and databind the page controls if the loading is not the result of a post-back event:

```
private void Page_Load(object sender, System.EventArgs e)
{
    if( !Page.IsPostBack )
    {
        sqlDataAdapter1.Fill( productsDS1 );
        DataBind();
    }
}
```

There are three item templates for a `DataList` control. These templates appear based on the current state of each individual item that is placed into the `DataList`. The `ItemTemplate` and `AlternatingItemTemplate` display each item in succession for items that are not selected or not currently being edited. If no `AlternatingItemTemplate` is specified, the `SelectedItemTemplate` is used instead. The `SelectedItemTemplate` formats the item that the user has selected. The `EditItemTemplate` formats an item that is being edited.

To specify the format of any of the templates, right-click on the `DataList` control and select Edit Templates, Item Templates. Drag and drop controls from the toolbox into the template recipe being edited. The `DataList` control itself is bound to a `DataSet`, but no data from the `DataSet` is displayed unless a control within the template is bound to the data. To do this step, select the control that you want to databind from within the template and open the `DataBindings` property. In the `DataBindings` dialog, select the

Text property as the property to bind and then expand the Container tree within the available bindings. Select the appropriate column name from the DataItem collection.

You can associate commands within the DataList to control selection and the ability to edit and update an individual item. These commands associate server-side controls with special keywords indicating the DataList command to take. For instance, within an ItemTemplate, you can create a LinkButton whose CommandText property is set to select. Once the user clicks this link button, a corresponding ItemCommand event is fired. Within the event handler for this method, set the SelectedItemIndex property of the DataList to the item that was clicked on and rebind the DataList to make the formatting changes. In the following example, a DataList control displays the name of each product in the Northwind database Products table. The name of each product is also a LinkButton whose CommandText property is set to select. When the user clicks on the name of the product, the selected index changes and the SelectedItemTemplate for that item is used. In the same manner, the SelectedItemTemplate contains a LinkButton that will place the item into edit mode by setting the CommandText property of the LinkButton to edit and changing the EditItemIndex of the DataList within the event handler for the EditItem event, as shown in Listing 16.4.

Listing 16.4   **Creating** DataList **Commands**

```
<asp:DataList id="DataList1" runat="server" BorderColor="#999999"
    BorderStyle="None" BackColor="White" CellPadding="3" GridLines="Vertical"
    BorderWidth="1px" DataSource="<%# productsDS1 %>" DataKeyField="ProductID"
    DataMember="Products" Width="648px" CellSpacing="5">

    <!-- DataList Styles -->
    <ItemStyle ForeColor="Black" BackColor="#EEEEEE"></ItemStyle>
    <SelectedItemStyle Font-Bold="True" ForeColor="White" BackColor="#CCCCFF"/>
    <AlternatingItemStyle BackColor="Gainsboro"></AlternatingItemStyle>
    <SeparatorStyle BorderStyle="Solid"></SeparatorStyle>
    <FooterStyle ForeColor="Black" BackColor="#CCCCCC"></FooterStyle>
    <HeaderStyle Font-Bold="True" HorizontalAlign="Center" ForeColor="White"
BackColor="#000084"></HeaderStyle>

    <!-- DataList Templates -->
    <HeaderTemplate>Products</HeaderTemplate>

    <SelectedItemTemplate>
    <P><FONT color="#000000">
        <%# DataBinder.Eval(Container.DataItem, "ProductName") %>
        <asp:LinkButton id="btnRename" Runat="server"
            CommandName="edit" Text="Rename"/>
        <BR>
        ID: <%# DataBinder.Eval(Container.DataItem, "UnitPrice") %> <BR>
        Price: <%# DataBinder.Eval(Container.DataItem, "UnitPrice") %> <BR>
    </FONT></P>
```

Listing 16.4   **Continued**

```
        </SelectedItemTemplate>

        <ItemTemplate>
            <asp:LinkButton id=LinkButton1 Runat="server" CommandName="select"
                Text='<%# DataBinder.Eval(Container.DataItem, "ProductName") %>'/>
        </ItemTemplate>

        <EditItemTemplate>
            <asp:TextBox id="tbRename" runat="server" Width="294px"
                Text='<%# DataBinder.Eval(Container.DataItem, "ProductName") %>'/>
            <asp:LinkButton id="btnUpdate" Runat="server" CommandName="update"
                Text="Update"></asp:LinkButton><BR>
        </EditItemTemplate>

</asp:DataList>
```

Listing 16.5 shows the relevant code from the code-behind file for Listing 16.4.

Listing 16.5   **Handling** DataList **Command Events**

```
// event handler when an item is selected
private void DataList1_ItemCommand_1(object source,
    System.Web.UI.WebControls.DataListCommandEventArgs e)
{
    DataList1.SelectedIndex = e.Item.ItemIndex;
    sqlDataAdapter1.Fill( productsDS1 );
    DataBind();
}

// event handler when user wants to edit an item
private void DataList1_EditCommand(object source,
    System.Web.UI.WebControls.DataListCommandEventArgs e)
{
    DataList1.EditItemIndex = e.Item.ItemIndex;
    sqlDataAdapter1.Fill( productsDS1 );
    DataBind();
}
```

The EditItemTemplate in the Web Form code just shown contains a LinkButton for the update command. Just as the other commands do, clicking this button fires an event, which in this case is named UpdateCommand. It is within this event handler that you update the database and return the DataList item being edited into selection mode. The update event handler for the DataList shown earlier performs the steps just mentioned. One thing to note is the use of the DataKeys property defined in the DataList. You initially set this property by specifying the column name within the database table that is used as a key value for each row. For the Products table, the column name is the `ProductID`. When the list is data-bound, each item within the `DataList` has a corresponding key within the `DataKeys` collection, enabling you to make a two-way association between the `DataList` and database table.

Listing 16.6 **Updating a Database Using** `DataList` **Commands**

```
private void DataList1_UpdateCommand(object source,
    System.Web.UI.WebControls.DataListCommandEventArgs e)
{
    // stop editing and select item
    DataList1.EditItemIndex = -1;
    DataList1.SelectedIndex = e.Item.ItemIndex;

    // update database
    ProductsDS.ProductsRow row =
        productsDS1.Products.FindByProductID(
            (int)DataList1.DataKeys[e.Item.ItemIndex]);
    row["ProductName"] = ((TextBox)e.Item.FindControl("tbRename")).Text;

    sqlDataAdapter1.Update( productsDS1 );
    DataBind();
}
```

Comments

The `DataList` control is one of the functionally richest controls in ASP.NET. By utilizing a template approach to render data based on the state of each individual item, you can really begin to see why the Web page of yesterday is being called the Web application of today. For most intents and purposes, the example shown earlier really is an application presented within a Web browser because it allows full editing and interaction by a user.

Although the `DataList` control is a full-featured control allowing great flexibility, it is missing a few features that another control, the `DataGrid`, addresses. The most prominent feature is pagination, which is covered in the next recipe. The `DataList` renders all data from a table, and if the table itself is large, the data consumes a lot of virtual real estate within the browser. In other words, a table with a lot of rows generates a large `DataList`, which might be confusing to a user. Pagination allows you to render a set number of items with links to subsequent pages for the rest of the data. For large data sets, the `DataGrid` might be better suited to display the data, but if your goal is to simply render small datasets, then the `DataList` might be a better fit.

16.9. Using the `DataGrid` Control

You want to use a data-bound list that renders items in a pageable grid.

Technique

The `DataGrid` control displays data in a similar fashion to a spreadsheet. Rows within a data table appear as individual rows in the `DataGrid` using a template-based rendering method similar to the `DataList` discussed in the previous recipe. However, the `DataGrid` control adds pagination, sorting, and more advanced rendering techniques using a columnar layout.

Creating the initial `DataGrid` is similar to using the methods to initially databind a control. After you create the data connection, adapter, and dataset, select the `DataSet` object as the `DataSource` of the control; select the table within the `DataSet`, which for the example in this recipe is the Products table in the Northwind database; and finally, set the `DataKeyField` equal to the column used to uniquely identify each item within the data table. For the Products table, this column is the `ProductID`. Finally, within the `Page_Load` event handler, fill the dataset using the data adapter and call the `DataBind` method.

When you view the Web page, you'll see that by default every column within the data table is rendered as a column within the `DataGrid`. Unlike the `DataList` control, the `DataGrid` automatically generates the proper ASP.NET controls for each value within a column without even needing to edit the templates. Of course, you'll also notice that from a visual standpoint, the default style of the `DataGrid` is less than stunning. The next recipe looks into the different ways you can improve the visual appeal of a `DataGrid` by changing style information.

By default, the `DataGrid` renders every column within a database table. Sometimes, however, you will want to display only a few columns. Set the `AutoGenerateColumns` property to `false`. At this point, the `DataGrid` does not render any columns and you see a blank page when you run it. To add the columns within a database table to the `DataGrid`, right-click on the `DataGrid` and select Property Builder. Next, select the Columns tab and move the columns you want rendered from the Available Columns list to the Selected Columns list. Within the properties for each column, you can also change the text for the header. The header appears at the top of each column, specifying what each value within the column represents.

At this point, the `DataGrid` displays only the columns that you selected. However, the default control to use for each column is the `Literal` control, which displays the values using a label. For most items, this control is satisfactory, but other values don't fit well. For instance, the Discontinued column within the Products table is a Boolean value. If it were an editable `DataGrid`, then a user would have to type either `true` or `false`, which just leads to the possibility of error. You can make the column a template-based column and specify the exact control to use, which in this case should be a `CheckBox`. To make a template-based column, open the Property Builder form and select the corresponding column from the list of selected columns. Within the properties recipe for the column, click on the link to make the column template-based. Next, right-click on the `DataGrid` control and select the template to edit from the Edit Template menu. The designer opens the available templates for the item. Editing each template for an item is the same as it was for the `DataList`. Drag and drop controls from the `ToolBox` onto a template and bind the appropriate data column using the `DataBindings` form. For the `Discontinued` column, place a `CheckBox` control in the `ItemTemplate` and `EditItemTemplate` templates. Because you use the `ItemTemplate` only when viewing and not editing data, set the `Enabled` property of the `CheckBox` control to `false`. When you view the `DataGrid`, you now see check boxes for the Discontinued column.

Comments

The `DataGrid` is the most advanced ASP.NET control within the .NET Framework. A major difference between the `DataList` and `DataGrid` control is the actual rendering of the data. If you recall from the last recipe, templates controlled the rendering of each item within a `DataList`. The layout of each item was your responsibility because no default is provided. A `DataGrid`, on the other hand, although still using template-based rendering, begins with a set of default templates, making the initial control creation more versatile. Furthermore, a `DataGrid` works with data on a columnar level, whereas a `DataList` uses a template for each item. Using columns, you can focus on a single column for a data item rather than the entire data item itself.

A `DataGrid` supports the ability to render the data using a series of linked pages, called *pagination*. To enable pagination, you have to go through a few steps because simply changing a property is not enough. To start, change the `AllowPaging` property to `true`. Next, set the number of rows per page you want displayed by changing the `PageSize` property. When the `DataGrid` is rendered, you see a series of links at the bottom of the grid denoting each page. You can change the default rendering of the pages by accessing the `Pages` tab within the Property Builder. When you click on a page number at this point, the `DataGrid` does not go to the next page. Create an event handler for the `PageIndexChanged` event, and within that handler, set the `CurrentPageIndex` property of the `DataGrid` control, as shown in the following code:

```
private void DataGrid1_PageIndexChanged(object source,
    DataGridPageChangedEventArgs e)
{
    DataGrid1.CurrentPageIndex = e.NewPageIndex;

    // rebind data
    sqlDataAdapter1.Fill( productsDS1 );
    DataBind();
}
```

This recipe looked at the `DataGrid` control as a way to display columns of data from a database table. You also saw how to change the default columns that are displayed to choose which columns to display and which ones to hide. Furthermore, you saw how to edit an individual columns template to use a different control instead of the default label control. The next two recipes continue with this discussion by examining how to change the style of the `DataGrid` for a better visual appearance and how to make items within the `DataGrid` editable.

16.10. Changing `DataGrid` Style Information

You want to change the visual styles of a `DataGrid` control.

Technique

The Web Forms designer contains several different automatic styles that you can apply to a `DataGrid` control. If you've used the AutoFormat function within some Microsoft Office applications, then this procedure should look familiar. To apply an automatic formatting style to a `DataGrid`, right-click on the `DataGrid` within the Web Forms designer and select Auto Format. Select a format from the list of available formats and apply it to the `DataGrid`.

Comments

Applying an automatic format is the easiest way to begin editing the style of a `DataGrid` because it fills in a lot of the initial values for you. However, our recommendation is to avoid something we call the FrontPage template syndrome. Microsoft FrontPage contains a lot of Web templates that you can use to quickly get a site up and running. As far as functionality, it serves its purpose and it does it quite well. When viewing a Web site that uses a FrontPage template, however, we recognize the template, which makes the site lose the small amount of professionalism it has. Of course, choosing a canned `DataGrid` format is far less noticeable, but you still need to know how to change the visual style without using the automatic format feature.

To change the visual style of a `DataGrid`, right-click on the control, open the Property Builder, and select the Format tab. You see a tree control listing the various pieces of a `DataGrid`, including the header, footer, pager, and individual item template styles. Clicking one of these items displays the available style properties that you can change for the item. You can additionally access the Borders tab to change border styles for the `DataGrid` as well.

16.11. Creating an Editable DataGrid

You want to give users the ability to edit individual items within a DataGrid.

Technique

Just as with the DataList, you can allow users to edit individual items within a DataGrid. However, the DataGrid automatically generates the edit template used for each column, so you don't have to manually edit the template yourself. To create an editable DataGrid, open the Property Builder dialog for the control. Click on the Columns tab because you will be adding a new column for the user to select a row for editing. In the list of available columns, select Edit, Update, Cancel within the Button Column tree node. When you add the new column, it appears in the last column of the DataGrid. You can move the column by using the up and down arrows next to the list of selected columns.

The DataGrid now displays a LinkButton that fires an EditCommand event. Create an event handler, and within the handler, set the EditItemIndex property as shown in the following code:

```
private void DataGrid1_EditCommand(object source,
    System.Web.UI.WebControls.DataGridCommandEventArgs e)
{
    DataGrid1.EditItemIndex = e.Item.ItemIndex;
    sqlDataAdapter1.Fill( productsDS1 );
    DataBind();
}
```

When the user clicks the edit link button and places an item into edit mode, the labels within each column appears as text boxes, allowing the user to edit the values. You can change the control used in an individual column, converting the column to a template-based column and editing the EditItemTemplate as discussed in the previous recipe.

Once the user selects the edit link button, the link button changes to an update and cancel link button. Both of these buttons correspond to the UpdateCommand and CancelCommand events, respectively. The event handler for the CancelCommand simply sets the EditItemIndex to -1 causing any editable items to be placed back into a noneditable state. The UpdateCommand event handler is called when the user clicks the update link button, and it updates a row in the database with the new values the user entered. In the previous recipe, you were able to simply get the value of the controls within the template by using the FindControl method and passing the ID of the control. However, because the controls for the DataGrid are automatically generated, there is no way of knowing the identifiers of the controls. The DataGridCommandEventArgs parameter in the event handler contains a Cells collection representing each column within the row being edited. Furthermore, because each column can potentially contain several controls, use the Controls collection to find the correct control containing the updated data. Listing 16.7 updates a `DataGrid` row for the Products table by accessing the individual cells and their corresponding `Controls` collection. Also note that each control must be cast to its correct control type.

Listing 16.7   **Handling the** `DataGrid` `Update` **Command**

```
private void DataGrid1_UpdateCommand(object source,
    System.Web.UI.WebControls.DataGridCommandEventArgs e)
{
    // stop editing and select item
    DataGrid1.EditItemIndex = -1;
    DataGrid1.SelectedIndex = e.Item.ItemIndex;

    sqlDataAdapter1.Fill( productsDS1 );

    // get the row from the database
    ProductsDS.ProductsRow row = productsDS1.Products.FindByProductID (
        (int)DataGrid1.DataKeys[e.Item.DataSetIndex]);

    // set corresponding values from datagrid
    row["ProductName"] =       ((TextBox) e.Item.Cells[2].Controls[0]).Text;
    row["QuantityPerUnit"] = ((TextBox) e.Item.Cells[3].Controls[0]).Text;
    row["UnitPrice"] =         ((TextBox) e.Item.Cells[4].Controls[0]).Text;
    row["UnitsInStock"]=       ((TextBox) e.Item.Cells[5].Controls[0]).Text;
    row["UnitsOnOrder"]=       ((TextBox) e.Item.Cells[6].Controls[0]).Text;
    row["Discontinued"]=       ((CheckBox) e.Item.Cells[7].Controls[1]).Checked;

    // update database and rebind
    sqlDataAdapter1.Update( productsDS1 );
    DataBind();
}
```

Comments

By adding editing capabilities to the `DataGrid` control, you are able to create a full-fledged database-editing application that can be used over the Web. The final output of the `DataGrid` is a simple HTML table with HTML controls interspersed within each cell. All the functionality that the `DataGrid` represents can be used on any platform supporting the latest HTML standards, which in turn makes a `DataGrid` in a Web application extremely versatile.

This recipe and the last two recipes covered a lot of ground explaining the various facets of the `DataGrid` control. The `DataGrid` control was designed to take away a lot of the burden in creating and adding functionality to the control, allowing you to focus on visual appearance and database interaction. So far in this chapter, you might have noticed that the data adapter fills the dataset with most operations. For a large data table, this constant database interaction can be time-consuming, especially if the Web page is serving multiple clients at the same time. The next few recipes demonstrate how to persist objects during the timeframe of a single user session to prevent a constant data flow that rarely changes.

16.12. Managing Application and Session State

You want to persist data across an entire user's session or across all users currently using the ASP.NET application.

Technique

Whenever a user connects to an ASP.NET application, an `HttpSessionState` object is created to serve as a repository of data that should persist as the user navigates through pages of the application. Previous recipes showed that each time a page is loaded due to a post-back event, data connections are reestablished and the data adapter is created to extract data from a database table into a `DataSet` object. In other words, the data from these data objects was not persisted across each page-load event. The `HttpSessionState` object is designed to handle such situations as well as serve as a collection of data that needs to persist across the session but can be thrown out when the session has ended.

You can access the `HttpSessionState` object through the `Session` property of the `System.Web.UI.Page` class that your class inherits from. In addition to being able to store data in a dictionary-based collection, the `Session` object also contains statistical information that you can access. For instance, the `SessionID` property is a unique value that is created when a new session starts, and it is guaranteed to be unique for each user accessing the site. The `Timeout` property determines when a session should end. Because you are not guaranteed to be notified that a user has finished interacting with your site, you use a timeout value, and when that time period elapses, the session has ended. By changing the `Timeout` property, you control the amount of time that can elapse between the last communication from the client and the end of the session. In the following example for a `Page_Load` event, a `DataSet` object is filled with data from a `SqlDataAdapter` and placed within the `Session` collection. Additionally, the `Timeout` property is changed to shorten the time it takes for a session to end:

```
private void Page_Load(object sender, System.EventArgs e)
{
    if( !Page.IsPostBack )
    {
        sqlDataAdapter1.Fill( productsDS1 );
        Session["DataSet"] = productsDS1;
        Session.Timeout = 5;
        DataBind();
    }
}
```

The Session is an object that is unique for each user who is accessing the Web application. Another object that serves the same purpose, temporary object storage, but is designed to work across all users currently engaged in using the application is the Application object. It too should only be used for temporary in-memory storage because it is destroyed whenever the last user session ends. Listing 16.8 uses the Application object to create an ASP.NET chat application. The actual ASP.NET code itself simply consists of a large read-only TextBox named tbTranscript used to display the chat messages; a TextBox named tbMessage used by a user to enter a message; and a simple Button named Send, which causes the form post back to occur. Individual messages are placed into the Application collection using an incrementing ID, which itself is placed into the collection as well.

Listing 16.8   **Persisting Data with the** Application **Object**

```
using System;
using System.Collections;
using System.ComponentModel;
using System.Data;
using System.Drawing;
using System.Web;
using System.Web.SessionState;
using System.Web.UI;
using System.Web.UI.WebControls;
using System.Web.UI.HtmlControls;


namespace _12_ApplicationState
{
    public class WebForm1 : System.Web.UI.Page
    {
        protected System.Web.UI.WebControls.TextBox tbTranscript;
        protected System.Web.UI.WebControls.TextBox tbMessage;
        protected System.Web.UI.WebControls.Button btnSend;

        private void Page_Load(object sender, System.EventArgs e)
        {
            RefreshTranscript();
        }

        override protected void OnInit(EventArgs e)
        {
            InitializeComponent();
            base.OnInit(e);
        }

        private void InitializeComponent()
        {
```

Listing 16.8 **Continued**

```csharp
            this.btnSend.Click += new System.EventHandler(this.btnSend_Click);
            this.Load += new System.EventHandler(this.Page_Load);

        }

        public void RefreshTranscript()
        {
            int msgID = 0;
            string transcript = "";

            // enumerate through application collection
            while( Application[msgID.ToString()] != null )
            {
                transcript += Application[msgID.ToString()].ToString()+"\r\n";
                msgID++;
            }

            tbTranscript.Text = transcript;
        }

        private void btnSend_Click(object sender, System.EventArgs e)
        {
            int lastMsgID;

            if( Application["lastMsgID"] == null )
            {
                lastMsgID = 0;
            }
            else
            {
                lastMsgID = Int32.Parse(
                    Application["lastMsgID"].ToString() ) + 1;
            }

            // save data in application collection
            Application[lastMsgID.ToString()] = Session.SessionID.ToString() +
                ": " + tbMessage.Text;
            Application["lastMsgID"] = lastMsgID.ToString();

            RefreshTranscript();
        }
    }
}
```

Comments

Software development contains a lot of opposites. A bit is on or it's off. A value can be either `true` or `false`. You either save time or you save money. If you want performance, you must sacrifice memory. This last truth corresponds to this recipe. It was mentioned that the `Session` and `Application` collections can hold any .NET object. This feature has tremendous advantages and opens a lot of possibilities that otherwise weren't available. Using these collections also boosts performance because objects don't have to be constructed and destroyed over and over again, spending clock cycles doing so. You can place a `DataSet` object, which normally is filled with data during each post-back event, within the `Session` object to limit the number of database accesses. As far as performance goes, this step has tremendous advantages if you want your site to run quickly. (Of course, we assume that your server contains enough memory.) Without using any type of storage mechanism for a `DataSet`, the object is destroyed once the data is sent to the client's browser for rendering. Once you add the `DataSet` to the `Session` object, it stays around for the lifetime of the session. Multiply a single `DataSet` by the number of users currently interacting with your application, and you'll see that the memory grows tremendously.

One possible solution to the situation is to move the `DataSet` into the `Application` object. Once you do so, however, you must ensure proper synchronization, which itself is no easy task. If the `DataSet` is merely a read-only entity, then the problem is solved. If, on the other hand, the application updates the `DataSet`, you run the risk of data stagnation—when data becomes out of date because one user updates the data while multiple users still retain the older data—and synchronous data writing, in which multiple users update the database at the same time. In short, if you place data within the `Application` object, you should look for any place where a data update can occur and make sure the proper synchronization is in place.

16.13. Creating Custom Web Controls

You want to create a custom Web control that ASP.NET pages can use.

Technique

Just as Windows Forms allows you to create custom controls for use on a form, ASP.NET contains a similar mechanism. To create a new custom control, select the `Web Control Library` from the project templates in the New Project dialog. When the project is created, the main C# file opens, allowing you to add any necessary properties and methods. The properties appear within the Property Browser when a user uses the custom control on his or her Web Form. To maintain consistency, the attributes that can be placed on each property are the same as those used by Windows Forms controls. For instance, to change the category for a property, use the `Category` attribute, passing the name of the category for the property within the Property Browser.

Because the final output of any Web control is HTML, you perform rendering by
using an HtmlTextWriter object within the Render method. The HtmlTextWriter
allows you to write regular HTML using the Write method or to use a hierarchical
approach—by using the WriteBeginTag followed by any attributes using the
WriteAttribute method and finally closing the tag using WriteEndTag. Listing 16.9
shows how to create a custom gauge control. Although far from being perfect, it does
demonstrate the principle just explained. Once the control is created, add it to the toolbox by right-clicking on the toolbox and selecting Add Item. Click the Browse button
and locate your control's assembly. You can then create a new ASP.NET Web application
and place your custom control on the new page.

Listing 16.9   **Gauge Custom Web Control**

```
using System;
using System.Web.UI;
using System.Web.UI.WebControls;
using System.ComponentModel;
using System.Drawing.Drawing2D;
using System.Drawing;

namespace _14_CustomWebControl
{
    [DefaultProperty("Text"),
    ToolboxData("<{0}:WebCustomControl1 runat=server></{0}:WebCustomControl1>")]
    public class WebCustomControl1 : System.Web.UI.WebControls.WebControl
    {
        private string text;
        private int level = 50;
        private Color gaugeColor = Color.Red;

        public WebCustomControl1()
        {
            this.Height = 100;
            this.Width = 50;
        }

        [Bindable(true),
        Category("Appearance"),
        DefaultValue("")]
        public string Text
        {
            get
            {
                return text;
            }
```

Listing 16.9   **Continued**

```
        set
        {
            text = value;
        }
    }

    public int Percentage
    {
        get
        {
            return this.level;
        }
        set
        {
            if( value < 0 )
                this.level = 0;
            else if( value > 100 )
                this.level = 100;
            else
                this.level = value;
        }
    }

    public Color GaugeColor
    {
        get
        {
            return gaugeColor;
        }
        set
        {
            gaugeColor = value;
        }
    }

    protected override void Render(HtmlTextWriter output)
    {
        output.Write( "<TABLE cellspacing='0' cellpadding='0' height='" +
            Height + "' width='" + Width + "'>" );

        output.Write( "<TR height='" + (100-level).ToString() +
            "' bgcolor='" + ColorTranslator.ToHtml( Color.LightGray ) +
            "'><TD/></TR>" );

        output.Write( "<TR height='" + level + "' bgcolor='"
```

Listing 16.9   **Continued**

```
            + ColorTranslator.ToHtml( gaugeColor ) + "'><TD/></TR>" );

        output.Write( "</TABLE>" );

        output.Write( text );
        }
    }
}
```

Comments

All of the ASP.NET controls that you have used so far use the same methods shown here. The ultimate goal of any Web control is to create an HTML-based representation of itself. The HTML equivalent of the Button control, for instance, is an HTML Input control with a type attribute of button. When creating the Render method, you can do a few things to help the design of your control.

You might find it easier to use the Web Form designer to visually create how you want your final control to appear. Doing so lets you see the resultant HTML code that you can then simply place within the Write method of the HtmlTextWriter. You naturally want to replace any HTML control attributes with the properties defined in your class, as shown in Listing 16.9.

Your control might be a composite of different HTML controls. The HtmlTextWriter is designed to write the final output, but that doesn't mean your code has to be the one that utilizes that object. In other words, you can create an instance of an ASP.NET control, set any necessary properties, and then call the RenderControl method of that control passing the HtmlTextWriter as the parameter. The following example shows how to use an ASP.NET TextBox and Label control to render a custom Web control:

```
protected override void Render(HtmlTextWriter output)
{
    Label lbl = new Label();
    TextBox tb = new TextBox();

    lbl.Text = "Please enter your name: ";
    lbl.RenderControl( output );
    tb.RenderControl( output );
}
```

16.14. Using Page Output Caching

You want to cache the final output of an ASP.NET page to improve performance.

Technique

Page output caching in ASP.NET allows you to cache the response content from a page to speed retrieval of content that is updated periodically. To enable page output caching, place a @OutputCache directive at the top of the .aspx file. This directive has three possible attributes of which only two are required. The two required attributes include Duration and VaryByParam. The Duration attribute denotes the time in seconds before the cached response is invalid and a new response stream should be generated. The VaryByParam attribute caches different copies of the result. For instance, an ASP.NET page can produce output denoting weather patterns for a certain country but produce different results for different countries. The VaryByParam attribute allows you to control how ASP.NET should determine the correct result to extract from the cache. The attribute that is not required is Location. The caching that occurs is based on HTML 1.1 standards and is not an ASP.NET-only concept. Caching can occur on the server hosting the application, on a proxy server, or on the client's machine itself, and you send it within the header value Cache-Control. The possible values for the Location attribute include Any, Client, Downstream, Server, or None. An example of a page with caching enabled would appear like the following:

```
<%@ OutputCache Duration="100" VaryByParam="none" Location="Server"%>
```

Comments

Page output caching can provide noticeable performance improvements to high traffic Web sites. For instance, let's assume a page is accessed 100 times by multiple users in 1 minute. With no caching enabled on the ASP.NET page, the database will be accessed 100 times, resulting in a large data transfer. With caching enabled, the database is accessed only once and the processing of the ASP.NET page happens only once, with the resultant cached output sent to each client.

Instead of using the OutputCache directive, you can also do so programmatically. You access the Cache property through the Response object. To set the cache duration, call the SetExpires method, passing the number of seconds for the duration. To set the cache location, call the SetCacheability method, passing a value from the HttpCacheability enumerated data type. For example, to cache a document on both the client and proxy server for a duration of 60 seconds, the code would appear as follows:

```
Response.Cache.SetExpires(DateTime.Now.AddSeconds(60));
Response.Cache.SetCacheability(HttpCacheability.Public);
Response.Cache.SetValidUntilExpires(true);
```

16.15. Writing and Reading Cookies

You want to store data locally on a connecting client's machine.

Technique

You write and read cookies within the .NET Framework by using the `HttpCookie` class. Cookies are stored in a `HttpCookieCollection` object accessed by the `Cookies` property in either the `Request` or `Response` object. When reading cookies, use the collection defined in the `Request` object, and when writing, use the `Response` object. To write a new cookie to a user's system, create a new `HttpCookie` object, passing two strings denoting the key and value of each cookie. If you don't set an expiration date, the cookie is removed after the user's session ends. To create an expiration date, set the `Expires` property equal to a `DateTime` object, specifying the date when the cookie is invalid, as shown in the following code:

```
private void btnSubmit_Click(object sender, System.EventArgs e)
{
    HttpCookie cookie = new HttpCookie( "Name", tbName.Text );

    // cookie expires 1 year from now
    DateTime dt = DateTime.Now;
    TimeSpan ts = new TimeSpan( 365, 0, 0, 0, 0 );

    cookie.Expires = dt.Add(ts);

    Response.Cookies.Add(cookie);

    lblHello.Text = "Hello " + tbName.Text + "! Welcome back!";
    tbName.Visible = false;
    btnSubmit.Visible = false;
}
```

Reading a cookie from a `Request` object is simply a matter of accessing a dictionary-based collection. The `Cookies` property contains an indexer, allowing you to pass the name of the cookie to retrieve the value. An `HttpCookie` object is returned, allowing you to view the expiration date as well as the value, which you access via the `Value` property:

```
private void Page_Load(object sender, System.EventArgs e)
{
    if( Request.Cookies["Name"] != null )
    {
        lblHello.Text = "Hello " + Request.Cookies["Name"].Value + "! Welcome
back!";
        tbName.Visible = false;
```

```
        btnSubmit.Visible = false;
    }
    else
    {
        lblHello.Text = "Please enter your name: ";
    }
}
```

Comments

Cookies are yet another way to persist data, but rather than stored in memory on the server like the Application and Session objects, the data is stored on the local file system of a connecting user. You shouldn't rely on cookies for vast amounts of data storage. Because cookies are viewed by some users as an invasion of privacy, they might have turned off the ability for the browser to accept cookies. In other words, if your page will not function without the use of data contained within a cookie, then you should find a different method of data storage.

17

ASP.NET Web Services

17.0. Introduction

When the World Wide Web was first created, the goal was to get hyperlinked textual data from a server to any connecting computers. The discovery that static Web pages required continuous updating and maintenance to keep up with the fast-paced world brought about the advent of dynamic server-side pages using the Common Gateway Interface (CGI). An explosion in server-side technologies led to such programs as PHP: Hypertext Preprocessor (PHP), ColdFusion, and, of course, Active Server Pages (ASP). However, the original equation of a single server communicating with multiple clients still existed. Web Services bridge the communication barrier between servers by using open standards to facilitate definition, discovery, and a communication protocol of data methods between remote computers. This chapter looks at how to create, implement, and publish ASP.NET Web Services and how to use a Web Service with a Windows Form and Web Form application.

17.1. Creating an ASP.NET Web Service

You want to create an ASP.NET Web Service.

Technique

Web Services are represented as a set of standards specifying everything from the actual definition of a Web Service to the protocol used between two machines when exchanging information. The amount of information that you must have to create a simple Web Service is not something you can pick up in a day. However, Visual Studio .NET has created a rich Web Services infrastructure, so someone new to the topic can quickly create and use a Web Service, assuming knowledge in a .NET language, of course.

To create a new Web Service, select the ASP.NET Web Service template from the New Project dialog. The project is created within a virtual directory in Internet Information Server (IIS), just like an ASP.NET Web Application, and also contains several defaults that you want to change before publishing the Web Service.

When the project opens, you see a special design view that you can use to drag and drop any necessary components your Web Service might need. Because a Web Service isn't a visual entity, only toolbox items on the Components tab are available. The next recipe describes how to add methods to your Web Service to expose its functionality. To open the code-behind file for a Web Service, click on the corresponding link in design view or right-click on the .asmx file in Solution Explorer and select the View Code menu item.

An ASP.NET Web Service itself appears as an ordinary class library. The New Project Wizard has already created a default class whose name you will want to change to better fit the description of your Web Service. Each Web Service contains an associated Web Service Description Language (WSDL) document describing various facets of the service, including the methods it supports. This WSDL file is handled by the ASP.NET runtime, which means you can only view it. However, you are able to inject additional information by applying the WebService attribute to your Web Service class.

The WebService attribute contains a few parameters that add information to the generated WSDL file. The Description parameter, as its name implies, allows you to enter a descriptive statement explaining what the Web Service does. The Name parameter is the actual name of the Web Service. If you omit this parameter, the name of the class is the name of the Web Service. Finally, the Namespace class serves the same purpose here as it does in XML documents, which is to uniquely identify your Web Service to alleviate any ambiguities that might arise if someone else were to create a Web Service of the same name. This chapter demonstrates a random-number generator Web Service called the Lottery Web Service. The service itself allows a connecting client to request a specified series of numbers within a certain range that might or might not include duplicate numbers. Listing 17.1 shows the WebService attribute for this Web Service.

Listing 17.1   Attributes Help Describe Web Services

```
using System;
using System.Collections;
using System.ComponentModel;
using System.Data;
using System.Diagnostics;
using System.Web;
using System.Web.Services;

namespace _1_LotteryService
{
    [ WebService( Namespace="http://samspublishing/1_LotteryService",
    Description="Provides the ability to generate a set of random numbers",
    Name="Lottery Web Service")]
```

Listing 17.1   **Continued**

```
public class LotteryNumberGenerator : System.Web.Services.WebService
{
    public LotteryNumberGenerator()
    {
        InitializeComponent();
    }

    private IContainer components = null;

    private void InitializeComponent()
    {
    }

    protected override void Dispose( bool disposing )
    {
        if(disposing && components != null)
        {
            components.Dispose();
        }
        base.Dispose(disposing);
    }
}
}
```

Comments

Once you create the initial project for the ASP.NET Web Service, you can view its output using your browser because of the internal framework that is automatically provided by ASP.NET. After you run the application, the browser is open, displaying your Web Service's .asmx file. The .asmx file is initially opened in design view and by default does not contain a lot of information. In fact, if you open the .asmx file in a text header, all you see is the ASP.NET Web Service directive:

```
<%@ WebService Language="c#" Codebehind="LotteryService.asmx.cs"
Class="_1_LotteryService.LotteryNumberGenerator" %>
```

This header is similar to that of an ASP.NET application that uses the @Page directive in that it specifies the language of the service along with the filename of the code-behind file and the class that implements the Web Service. With just this information, ASP.NET can automatically generate the WSDL file using the Reflection methods discussed in Chapter 23, "Reflection." To view the current WSDL file for the Web Service, click on the Service Description link in the .asmx file within the browser. As you might have guessed, WSDL, like all other Web Service technologies, is XML based. Listing 17.2 provides the generated WSDL file for the Lottery Web Service.

Listing 17.2 **Lottery Web Service WSDL File**

```
<?xml version="1.0" encoding="utf-8" ?>
<definitions xmlns:soap="http://schemas.xmlsoap.org/wsdl/soap/"
    xmlns:tns="http://samspublishing/1_LotteryService"
    xmlns:s="http://www.w3.org/2001/XMLSchema"
    xmlns:http="http://schemas.xmlsoap.org/wsdl/http/"
    xmlns:tm="http://microsoft.com/wsdl/mime/textMatching/"
    xmlns:mime="http://schemas.xmlsoap.org/wsdl/mime/"
    xmlns:soapenc="http://schemas.xmlsoap.org/soap/encoding/"
    targetNamespace="http://samspublishing/1_LotteryService"
    xmlns="http://schemas.xmlsoap.org/wsdl/">
    <types/>
    <service name="Lottery_x0020_Web_x0020_Service">
        <documentation>Provides the ability to generate a set
            of random numbers</documentation>
    </service>
</definitions>
```

The first thing you see in a WSDL file is all the namespace declarations. The `targetNamespace` attribute is the namespace that was added in the `Namespace` parameter of the `WebService` attribute. After the namespace declarations is the `types` element, which will be filled in with the schema definitions for the Web Service method names and their associated parameter names and types. Finally, the `service` element holds general information about the Web Service, and it is here where you see the `Name` of the Web service along with its `Description`, which were both supplied as parameters to the `WebService` attribute.

17.2. Adding Web Service Methods

You want to add methods that clients can use to access the Web Service.

Technique

Adding a new method to a Web Service uses the same procedures that adding a method to a class uses. In other words, you can use the Add Method Wizard to add new methods or use the code view to manually add each method to the class. The difference is that a `WebMethod` attribute is applied to the method for ASP.NET to delineate between regular class methods and those exposed by the Web Service. Some of the parameters for this attribute are discussed in following recipes. The Lottery Web Service creates a Web Service method that returns an array of random integers. The parameters let you specify how many numbers to generate, the minimum and maximum values, and whether or not to include duplicates, as shown in Listing 17.3.

Listing 17.3 **Creating a Web Service Method**

```
[WebMethod( Description="Generates a list of numbers between
                        Min and Max with or without duplicates" )]
public int[] GenerateNumbers(int Count, int Min, int Max, bool AllowDuplicates)
{
    Random rand = new Random( DateTime.Now.Millisecond );
    ArrayList numbers = new ArrayList( Count );

    for( int i = 0; i < Count; i++ )
    {
        int newNum = rand.Next( Min, Max );
        if( AllowDuplicates == false )
        {
            while( numbers.Contains( newNum ) == true )
            {
                newNum = rand.Next( Min, Max );
            }
        }

        numbers.Add( newNum );
    }

    return (int[]) numbers.ToArray(typeof(int));
}
```

Comments

After you add a new method to a Web Service, you have the ability to test it immediately without having to write any code that accesses the Web Service. The .asmx file in the last recipe simply contained a link to the WSDL file, but when you run a Web Service with a defined Web, an additional link is created to test the functionality of that method.

Once you click on the method name, you see the method name as well as TextBox controls for each parameter, allowing you to enter parameters to test the method. After you enter the necessary parameters, click the Invoke button to see the response. Assuming everything worked correctly, you see an XML document containing the response from your Web Service. If instead you see a file-not-found or other, similar error, then the method invocation failed within the method itself.

Web Service methods, unlike regular class methods, are limited to the types they can use for return values and parameters. Because Web Services are a multiplatform open standard, data types had to be standardized to accommodate all platforms. Most value types within the .NET framework are supported. You aren't, however, limited to just these types because composites of these types are also permitted. The example shown earlier returned an integer array, which is supported by Web Services. Also permitted are classes or structs that expose properties which also conform to these data types, allowing you to create custom Web Service data types without the risk of breaking any clients consuming the Web Service.

17.3. Providing Web Method Descriptions

You want to add a descriptive statement to a method defined in a Web Service.

Technique

The `WebMethod` attribute contains several different parameters, allowing you to specify additional information about the method as well as control how memory buffers and caching is utilized. To add a statement reflecting the functionality of a Web method, add the `Description` parameter to the `WebMethod` attribute:

```
[WebMethod( Description="Generates a random number within a range",
  MessageName="GenerateNumberInRange" )]
public int GenerateNumber( int Min, int Max )
{
    Random rand = new Random( DateTime.Now.Millisecond );
    return rand.Next( Min, Max );
}
```

Comments

One of the nice things about using Web Services within Visual Studio .NET is the hands-off approach, freeing you from burying yourself in all the different XML file formats. Purists say that you'll never learn how things work, but even if you're not sure how a car engine works, you can still start one to get from point A to point B. Of course, we're not saying that you shouldn't learn how Web Services work because eventually you'll get to the point where something doesn't quite perform as expected and you must investigate the data that is generated for you.

If you look at the generated WSDL file, which is available by clicking on the Service Description link, you see that a lot more data is being generated now that a Web method is added. When the Web Service was initially created with no methods, the `types` element in the WSDL document was empty. Now you can see type information for both the inputs to the Web method as well as the type for the output specified using XML schema definitions. Each `message` element contains information about each message, broken into its constituent request and response parts with a link to the schema definition of each message's parameters. The `portType` element starts to make the bridge from concrete to abstract as it combines the request and response portions of a method into an abstract entity. It is within this element that you see the description of the method that was generated when you applied the `Description` parameter to the `WebMethod` attribute. The last element to discuss, because the previous recipe discussed the `service` element recipe, is the `binding` element. This node describes the document format and the protocols that the Web Service utilizes in its exchange with a client. In the WSDL document in Listing 17.4, you can see that the Web service uses Simple Object Access Protocol (SOAP) over HTTP.

Listing 17.4   **Lottery Web Service WSDL File**

```xml
<?xml version="1.0" encoding="utf-8"?>
<definitions xmlns:http="http://schemas.xmlsoap.org/wsdl/http/"
   xmlns:soap="http://schemas.xmlsoap.org/wsdl/soap/"
   xmlns:s="http://www.w3.org/2001/XMLSchema"
   xmlns:s0="http://samspublishing/1_LotteryService"
   xmlns:soapenc="http://schemas.xmlsoap.org/soap/encoding/"
   xmlns:tm="http://microsoft.com/wsdl/mime/textMatching/"
   xmlns:mime="http://schemas.xmlsoap.org/wsdl/mime/"
   targetNamespace="http://samspublishing/1_LotteryService"
   xmlns="http://schemas.xmlsoap.org/wsdl/">
  <types>
    <s:schema elementFormDefault="qualified"
        targetNamespace="http://samspublishing/1_LotteryService">
      <s:element name="GenerateNumberInRange">
        <s:complexType>
          <s:sequence>
            <s:element minOccurs="1" maxOccurs="1" name="Min" type="s:int" />
            <s:element minOccurs="1" maxOccurs="1" name="Max" type="s:int" />
          </s:sequence>
        </s:complexType>
      </s:element>
      <s:element name="GenerateNumberInRangeResponse">
        <s:complexType>
          <s:sequence>
            <s:element minOccurs="1" maxOccurs="1"
                name="GenerateNumberInRangeResult" type="s:int" />
          </s:sequence>
        </s:complexType>
      </s:element>
    </s:schema>
  </types>
  <message name="GenerateNumberInRangeSoapIn">
    <part name="parameters" element="s0:GenerateNumberInRange" />
  </message>
  <message name="GenerateNumberInRangeSoapOut">
    <part name="parameters" element="s0:GenerateNumberInRangeResponse" />
  </message>
  <portType name="Lottery_x0020_Web_x0020_ServiceSoap">
```

Listing 17.4 **Continued**

```
    <operation name="GenerateNumber">
     <documentation>Generates a random number within a range</documentation>
     <input name="GenerateNumberInRange"
       message="s0:GenerateNumberInRangeSoapIn" />
     <output name="GenerateNumberInRange"
       message="s0:GenerateNumberInRangeSoapOut" />
    </operation>
  </portType>
  <binding name="Lottery_x0020_Web_x0020_ServiceSoap"
      type="s0:Lottery_x0020_Web_x0020_ServiceSoap">
    <soap:binding transport="http://schemas.xmlsoap.org/soap/http"
      style="document" />
    <operation name="GenerateNumber">
     <soap:operation
soapAction="http://samspublishing/1_LotteryService/GenerateNumberInRange"
       style="document" />
     <input name="GenerateNumberInRange">
       <soap:body use="literal" />
     </input>
     <output name="GenerateNumberInRange">
       <soap:body use="literal" />
     </output>
    </operation>
  </binding>
  <service name="Lottery_x0020_Web_x0020_Service">
    <documentation>Provides the ability to generate a set of
       random numbers</documentation>
    <port name="Lottery_x0020_Web_x0020_ServiceSoap"
       binding="s0:Lottery_x0020_Web_x0020_ServiceSoap">
      <soap:address location="http://localhost/TestService/Service1.asmx" />
    </port>
  </service>
</definitions>
```

17.4. Aliasing Web Method Names

You want to create an alias for a Web method to avoid naming collisions.

Technique

If two methods within a class that implements a Web Service use the same method name, add the MessageName parameter to the WebMethod attribute:

```
[WebMethod( Description="Generates a random number within a range",
    MessageName="GenerateNumberInRange" )]
public int GenerateNumber( int Min, int Max )
{
    Random rand = new Random( DateTime.Now.Millisecond );
    return rand.Next( Min, Max );
}


[WebMethod( Description="Generates a random number",
    MessageName="GenerateNumber" )]
public int GenerateNumber()
{
    Random rand = new Random( DateTime.Now.Millisecond );
    return rand.Next();
}
```

Comments

It was mentioned that ASP.NET generates the .asmx file at runtime as well as the WSDL file when requested. It does so by using reflection, which allows you to inspect type information of an object within a .NET assembly as well as extract any attributes applied to that data type. One side effect of this method, which works well, is the inability to detect errors at compile time. For example, if you create a Web method for a Web Service that returns a Hashtable object, your assembly will compile just fine. However, once you run the .asmx file within the browser, an exception is thrown, indicating that the Hashtable is an IDictionary-based collection, which is not a supported XML schema type. Likewise, if you create two Web methods whose name is the same and they differ only in their parameters or return types, compilation will be successful. When you run the .asmx file, an exception is thrown, indicating that two messages have the same name. If you recall from the last recipe, WSDL documents have a series of message elements for each request and response, which means having two methods with the same name invalidates that portion of the WSDL XML document. Method overloading is fine as long as you ensure that you change the message name if you are going to use those methods within a Web Service.

17.5. Managing Web Service State

You want to save state information during a session between your Web Service and a connecting client.

Technique

By default, the Session object that is used in ASP.NET applications is not created when a client calls a method contained within a Web Service. You can, however, enable the

Session object for use by adding the EnableSession parameter to the WebMethod attribute. Once you do so, the Session object is created, if it hasn't already been created by a subsequent Web method call, and it is available for use until the session between your Web Service and a connecting client has finished. Listing 17.5 continues the Lottery Web Service example by creating three methods that hold state information. These methods allow a connecting client to specify an initial minimum and maximum value as well as whether to allow duplicates via the BeginNumberList method. Once this method is called, the client can repeatedly call the NextNumber method, which returns a new randomly generated number within the parameters contained in the Session object.

Listing 17.5   Maintaining State Information in Web Services

```
[WebMethod( Description="Begins state enabled random number generation",
    EnableSession=true)]
public void BeginNumberList( int Min, int Max, bool AllowDuplicates )
{
    Session["Min"] = Min;
    Session["Max"] = Max;
    Session["Duplicates"] = AllowDuplicates;
    Session["NumberList"] = new ArrayList();
}


[WebMethod( Description="Gets next number for state enabled number generation",
    EnableSession=true)]
public int NextNumber()
{
    if( Session["Min"] == null || Session["Max"] == null ||
        Session["Duplicates"] == null || Session["NumberList"] == null )
        return -1;

    // generate random number
    Random rand = new Random( DateTime.Now.Millisecond );
    int newNum = rand.Next( (int) Session["Min"], (int) Session["Max"] );

    // check if duplicates are allowed
    if( ((bool)Session["Duplicates"]) == false )
    {
        // get current list and check if any numbers still available
        ArrayList list = (ArrayList) Session["NumberList"];;
        if( list.Count >= (int)Session["Max"]-(int)Session["Min"] ) return -1;

        // generate a non-duplicate random number
        while( list.Contains( newNum ) == true ) newNum = rand.Next(
            (int)Session["Min"], Session["Max"] );

        // save in list
        list.Add( newNum );
```

Listing 17.5   **Continued**

```
    }

    return newNum;
}

[WebMethod( Description="Ends state enabled random number generation",
    EnableSession=true)]
public void EndNumberList()
{
    Session.Remove( "Min" );
    Session.Remove( "Max" );
    Session.Remove( "Duplicates" );
    Session.Remove( "NumberList" );
}
```

Comments

An ASP.NET Web Service behaves similarly to an ASP.NET Web application in that the class is not guaranteed to be loaded at all times. You cannot add instance data that will be preserved across repeated method invocations. By setting the `EnableSession` parameter in the `WebMethod` attribute to `true`, you in effect are turning on the ability to save state information using the `HttpSessionState` object defined in the `WebService` class, which your class derives from. You are can access the `Application` object at any time without using any attributes or attribute parameters. The `Application` object is a singleton, which means that one instance is used across all sessions. In other words, placing a value in the `Application` collection while in the space of one user session makes that value available to all other user sessions. Chapter 16, "ASP.NET," demonstrated this process when the `Application` collection was used to create an ASP.NET chat room.

17.6. Publishing and Registering an ASP.NET Web Service

You want to publish your Web Service and allow others to use it.

Technique

Publishing a Web Service uses the same procedure as publishing an ASP.NET application. To deploy the Web Service to another server, click on Project, Copy Project from the main menu. Specify the name of the server by using a Uniform Resource Identifier (URI), which contains the address of the Web server and the application virtual directory on the server. This method assumes that the FrontPage server extensions are installed within IIS on the remote server.

Registering a Web Service so that others can easily locate it involves accessing a Universal Description, Discovery, and Integration (UDDI) server and registering for an account. Microsoft runs a UDDI server at `http://uddi.microsoft.com/visualstudio`, but you should use it only for Web Services that have been fully tested. If you want to test your Web Service using a UDDI registry, you can go to `http://test.uddi.microsoft.com/visualstudio`. After you register yourself or your company—which is free, by the way—you can add your Web Service. Registering a new Web Service simply requires telling the UDDI registry where your WSDL file is located. However, the registry calls a WSDL file a tModel, which stands for *type model*. These two terms are synonymous. When registering a new tModel, you can give the name, description, and location of the WSDL file. ASP.NET automatically generates the WSDL file for you, which means there is no associated path for it. To specify the WSDL file, enter the location of the `.asmx` file followed by a WSDL query argument with no associated value. For instance, if you publish the Lottery Web Service on this book's Web site, you could find the WSDL file at `http://www.csharpcookbook.com/LotteryService/LotteryService.asmx?WSDL`.

Comments

UDDI is an open standard that serves as a registry for Web Services. Started by Microsoft, it has since become an open standard that gives interested parties the ability to search for a Web Service that their applications can consume. If there is one way to really come up to speed on Web Services, it's by playing with the UDDI registry. From simple Hello World Web Services to stock-ticker services, the UDDI registry is growing as more developers see the advantage of using Web Services. You can find additional information at the main UDDI page by visiting `http://www.uddi.org`.

17.7. Consuming Web Services with a Windows Form Application

You want to call methods defined in a Web Service from a Windows Form application.

Technique

To use a Web service, you have to add a reference to it, similar to adding a reference to a .NET assembly. After you create your Windows Form application, click on Project, Add Web Reference from the main menu. This example uses a Web Service on the local machine, but you can also access the Microsoft UDDI registry to search for the Web Service you want to use.

Within the Add Web Reference dialog, click on the link to browse Web Services on the local machine. Visual Studio .NET searches within IIS for available Web Services.

After clicking on the Web Service you want to use, click on the Add Reference button to add it to your project.

Using the Web Service within your Windows Form code is a matter of simply instantiating an object and calling the methods. You use a class called the *proxy class* to interact with the Web Service, and it is created within a defined namespace. Use Class View to determine the namespace and class name of the proxy class. Listing 17.6 shows how to use the Lottery Web Service with a Windows Form control. The form itself contains five labels that display five unique random numbers from the Web Service when the user clicks a button on the form.

Listing 17.6   **Consuming Web Services with Windows Forms**

```
using System;
using System.Drawing;
using System.Collections;
using System.ComponentModel;
using System.Windows.Forms;
using System.Data;

namespace _7_LotteryClient
{
    public class Form1 : System.Windows.Forms.Form
    {
        private System.Windows.Forms.GroupBox groupBox1;
        private System.Windows.Forms.Label lbl1;
        private System.Windows.Forms.Label lbl3;
        private System.Windows.Forms.Label lbl4;
        private System.Windows.Forms.Label lbl5;
        private System.Windows.Forms.Label lbl2;
        private System.Windows.Forms.Button btnGo;

        private System.ComponentModel.Container components = null;

        public Form1()
        {
            InitializeComponent();
        }

        protected override void Dispose( bool disposing )
        {
            if( disposing )
            {
                if (components != null)
                {
                    components.Dispose();
                }
```

Listing 17.6 **Continued**

```
            }
            base.Dispose( disposing );
        }

        private void InitializeComponent()
        {
            this.groupBox1 = new System.Windows.Forms.GroupBox();
            this.lbl1 = new System.Windows.Forms.Label();
            this.lbl3 = new System.Windows.Forms.Label();
            this.lbl4 = new System.Windows.Forms.Label();
            this.lbl5 = new System.Windows.Forms.Label();
            this.lbl2 = new System.Windows.Forms.Label();
            this.btnGo = new System.Windows.Forms.Button();
            this.groupBox1.SuspendLayout();
            this.SuspendLayout();

        // forms designer generated code removed
        }

        [STAThread]
        static void Main()
        {
            Application.Run(new Form1());
        }

        private void btnGo_Click(object sender, System.EventArgs e)
        {
            localhost.LotteryWebService gen=new localhost.LotteryWebService();
            int[] result = gen.GenerateNumbers( 5, 0, 100, false );

            lbl1.Text = result[0].ToString();
            lbl2.Text = result[1].ToString();
            lbl3.Text = result[2].ToString();
            lbl4.Text = result[3].ToString();
            lbl5.Text = result[4].ToString();
        }
    }
}
```

Comments

The recurring pattern throughout this chapter is that Web Services within Visual Studio
.NET are handled by Visual Studio with a minimal amount of intervention on your part.
Adding a Web reference to your project launches a few steps to integrate the necessary

code into your project. When the reference is made, the WSDL document of the Web Service is read in and subsequently added to your project. Additionally, a static discovery file is added to the project. A discovery file, which has a `disco` extension, contains all the information needed to find the location of the Web Service, entries for the location of the WSDL document and `.asmx` file, and binding information that is used for SOAP.

The largest function that adding a reference performs is the generation of a proxy class. This proxy class is generated by translating the messages within the WSDL file into corresponding class methods that your client application uses as a proxy to the Web Service. This proxy class is derived from the `SoapHttpClientProtocol` class defined within the .NET framework, which performs the main communications between your client and the associated Web Service. Furthermore, the proxy class also adds methods that allow you to call Web Service methods asynchronously, which is a topic covered in Recipe 17.9, "Calling Web Methods Asynchronously."

17.8. Consuming Web Services with ASP.NET Applications

You want to consume a Web Service with an ASP.NET application.

Technique

Consuming a Web Service from an ASP.NET application uses the same methods shown in the previous recipe. After you add a Web reference, you can access a proxy class within the code-behind file of your Web application.

Comments

Recipe 17.2, "Adding Web Service Methods," said that Web Service methods are only able to use a subset of the data types within the .NET framework. They are usually limited to the normal value types such as strings and integers as well as arrays of value types, but you can also return a `DataSet` object, which makes Web Services suitable as a data source for ASP.NET applications. For example, a Web Service that returns a `DataSet` representing the Products table from the Northwind SQL database could be consumed by an ASP.NET `DataGrid` control, as shown in the following code:

```
private void Page_Load(object sender, System.EventArgs e)
{
    if( !Page.IsPostBack )
    {
        localhost.ProductsService northwind = new localhost.ProductsService();
        DataGrid1.DataSource = northwind.GetProducts();
        DataBind();
    }
}
```

17.9. Calling Web Methods Asynchronously

You want to call a method implemented in a Web Service asynchronously.

Technique

In addition to containing methods for each method defined in a Web Service, the generated proxy class also contains the methods needed to call Web Service methods asynchronously. Each method within the proxy class has an additional two methods used for asynchronous invocation, corresponding to the beginning of the asynchronous call and the asynchronous method call results.

The following example uses the GenerateNumbers method defined in the Lottery Web Service created earlier in this chapter. To begin the method call, call the Begin version of the method, which for the lottery service is called BeginGenerateNumbers. All the parameters are the same as those in the GenerateNumbers method except for two additional parameters specifying the callback method and an object to use for the final result. The callback method is called when the Web Service method returns. The return type is void, and the parameter is an object implementing the IAsyncResult interface. Within the callback method, call the EndGenerateNumbers method, passing the IAsyncResult object to obtain the results.

Listing 17.7   **Making Asynchronous Web Method Calls**

```
private void btnGo_Click(object sender, System.EventArgs e)
{
    localhost.LotteryNumberGenerator gen = new
        localhost.LotteryNumberGenerator();
    gen.BeginGenerateNumbers( 20000, 0, 100000, true,
        new AsyncCallback(GenerateNumbersCallback), gen );

    startTime = DateTime.Now;
    pbWait.Value = 0;
    timer1.Enabled = true;
}


public void GenerateNumbersCallback(IAsyncResult ar)
{
    DateTime endTime = DateTime.Now;

    // get result
    localhost.LotteryNumberGenerator gen =
        (localhost.LotteryNumberGenerator) ar.AsyncState;
    string result = gen.EndGenerateNumbers( ar );
```

Listing 17.7   **Continued**

```
    // stop timer and computer total time
    timer1.Enabled = false;

    TimeSpan span = new TimeSpan( endTime.Ticks - startTime.Ticks );
    MessageBox.Show( "Call time = "+span.ToString()+"\nResult: "+result );
}

private void timer1_Elapsed(object sender, System.Timers.ElapsedEventArgs e)
{
    pbWait.PerformStep();
    if( pbWait.Value >= pbWait.Maximum )
        pbWait.Value = 0;
}
```

Comments

If you read Chapter 15, "Sockets," then this process of making an asynchronous call should seem familiar. In Chapter 15, a series of asynchronous calls were made to request a Web document. The proxy class acts as a dual proxy of sorts. When you call one of the asynchronous methods, the actual call doesn't occur within the proxy class but rather a generic base class asynchronous method named `BeginInvoke`. The same method of passing the actual method invocation to `SoapHttpClientProtocol` also occurs when calling a method synchronously in that the actual method call is through the `Invoke` method defined in the base class of the proxy class.

17.10. Using Transactions in Web Services

You want to roll back any database commands that have executed if a subsequent command fails.

Technique

A *transaction* comes from the concept of creating a safe method of updating data to ensure data integrity. For instance, if a Web Service implements a method that updates several tables within a database, the possibility for data corruption is high should one of the updates fail. In this case, the Web Service should use a transaction to ensure that any database changes are rolled back to their initial state if any update fails.

To make database updates occur within a transaction in a Web Service method, add the `TransactionOption` parameter to the `WebMethod` attribute. Listing 17.8 shows an example of updating two tables within a database in which one table does not exist, thereby throwing an exception. Once the second database update occurs, the database is automatically rolled back. In other words, the change that took place before the second update executed is reversed.

Listing 17.8   **Using** `TransactionOption` **for Transactions**

```
[WebMethod(Description="This is a transaction sample.",
    TransactionOption=TransactionOption.RequiresNew)]
public void DeleteValueByID( int ID )
{
    string firstCmdString = "DELETE FROM TestTable WHERE ID='" + ID + "'" ;
    string secondCmdString = "DELETE FROM NonExistentTable WHERE ID='" + ID + "'";

    SqlCommand firstCmd = new SqlCommand(firstCmdString, sqlConnection1);
    SqlCommand secondCmd = new SqlCommand(secondCmdString, sqlConnection1);

    // execute first product deletion
    firstCmd.Connection.Open();
    firstCmd.ExecuteNonQuery();

    // execute second command. When this throws an exception then the
    // first command is automatically rolled back since we're
    // participating in a transaction
    secondCmd.ExecuteNonQuery();
    sqlConnection1.Close();
}
```

Comments

Transactions are implemented within the `System.EnterpriseServices` namespace. The `EnterpriseServices` namespace contains several classes that interact with COM+ services, in which transactions play a role. The `TransactionOption` enumerated data type does a lot of behind-the-scenes work to enable transactions. Rather than require you to write all the necessary code to commit or roll back a transaction, the `TransactionOption` attribute automatically creates a transaction object that is accessed by the .NET data provider. If the provider finds this transaction object within your object's context, it participates by enlisting with the COM+ Distributed Transaction Coordinator. One thing to note is that using this attribute assumes the Web Service is being accessed remotely by a connecting client. If instead a client adds a normal assembly reference to your Web Service and calls the method directly, the transactional behavior does not occur.

18

.NET Remoting

18.0. Introduction

This chapter examines how to perform common tasks related to .NET Remoting. .NET Remoting is the .NET technology to access objects from different application domains.

Application domains are boundaries of applications that isolate applications from each other, where these applications can also run within a single process. You can use .NET Remoting to access objects in other application domains that are running within the same process, in a different process, or across the network.

Unlike ASP.NET Web Services, with .NET Remoting both the client and the server application have to use .NET technologies. With .NET Remoting, the assemblies of objects that are passed across the network must be available on both the client and the server. XML Web Services uses a schema to describe the objects, so the objects used on the client and the server are different types. XML Web Services also let you use different technologies on the client and the server.

In this chapter, you'll see how to create remote objects, clients, and servers using code and configuration files, and stateless and stateful objects, as well as how to create a sink that makes it possible to intercept method calls.

18.1. Creating a Remotable Object

You want to create an object that is called across different application domains, such as across the network.

Technique

The only requirement to create an object that is accessed across the network is to derive it from the base class `System.MarshalByRefObject`:

```
public class RemoteObject : MarshalByRefObject
{
    public void RemoteObject()
    {
        Console.WriteLine("Constructor RemoteObject");
    }
    public string Greeting(string name)
    {
        Console.WriteLine("Greeting");
        return "Hello, " + name;
    }
}
```

Comments

When you derive the remotable object from the class `MarshalByRefObject`, the object is bound to the application domain, and a client accessing the object from a different application domain has to use a proxy. All public methods and properties of this class are accessed by using a proxy. Static methods are not accessed across the network.

Figure 18.1 shows a client calling methods of the proxy. The proxy passes the method call into a channel that is responsible for sending the call across the network. On the server side, a dispatcher invokes the method in the remote object.

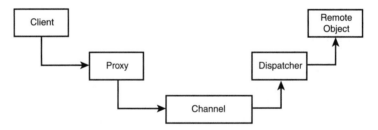

Figure 18.1   A client calling methods of the proxy.

What's important with a remote object is that you have to be aware of state management. Remotable objects can be stateless or stateful—depending on how the objects are configured with the server. You just have to be aware because it influences the implementation of the remote object class.

With stateless objects, you can only use a default constructor. With client-activated stateful objects, you can use specialized constructors. Client-activated objects are discussed in Recipe 18.4, "Performing Client-Side Activation of Remotable Objects."

For parameters of remote methods, if you want to serialize an object across the network, from the server to the client or the client to the server, the class must be marked with the attribute class `SerializableAttribute`. Classes that derive from `MarshalByRefObject` are passed by reference, and the object stays in the application domain where it was created. You use a proxy from the other side of the network to access the object. If a class is not marked `Serializable` or derived from `MarshalByRefObject`, it cannot be used as a parameter of a remote method.

18.2. Creating Host Applications for Remotable Types

You want to host the remotable object in a custom application to make it available to client applications.

Technique

To offer an object by .NET Remoting, you have to create a network channel and register the object with the remoting runtime. When you register the channel, a port is opened, and the server listens for requests.

You create a network channel by instantiating an object of a channel class, such as `TcpChannel`, as in the code here. With the server, you also have to specify a port number where the server is listening. Next, you must register the channel with the .NET Remoting runtime using `ChannelServices.RegisterChannel`:

```
TcpChannel channel = new TcpChannel(8088);
ChannelServices.RegisterChannel(channel);
```

After the channel is registered, you can register the remote object class with the runtime. You do so by using the `RemotingConfiguration` class. The method `RegisterWellKnownServiceType` registers the object as a well-known object, which means that in cooperation with the parameter `WellKnownObjectMode.SingleCall`, the object will be created anew with every method call. This way is a scalable way of dealing with resources on the server because no server resources are kept with the server after method calls. However, with .NET Remoting, you can also create singletons and stateful objects. Client-activated stateful objects are covered in Recipe 18.4; singletons are covered in Recipe 18.5, "Creating Server-Activated Singleton Objects."

```
RemotingConfiguration.RegisterWellKnownServiceType(
                typeof(_1_RemoteObject.RemoteObject),
                "Demo", WellKnownObjectMode.SingleCall);
```

After registering the object, you just have to ensure that the server doesn't get stopped; the server keeps running to listen for requests.

Comments

Remote objects can be hosted in any application type. You can create a Windows Forms application where multiple users can use peer-to-peer communication. You can create a Windows service that hosts remoting objects. .NET enterprise services have a built-in functionality for .NET Remoting, and it is also possible to host remoting objects within Internet Information Server (IIS). All you have to do is create a channel and register the remote object.

With the .NET Framework 1.1, you get channels for two different protocols: TCP and HTTP. The HttpChannel class communicates using the HTTP protocol, and the TcpChannel class uses a faster transport mechanism by using the TCP protocol directly.

With both the HTTP and TCP channels, you get server-side and client-side channels. TcpServerChannel and HttpServerChannel are the classes that offer server-side functionality, and TcpClientChannel and HttpClientChannel offer client-side functionality.

The classes TcpChannel and HttpChannel have the functionality of both a client and a server channel. You need them on the client and on the server if you do callbacks from the server to the client.

With all the channel classes, you have different constructors to instantiate the channels. You can set a port number, which is a requirement with the server, but you can also specify a priority that is used if multiple channels are offered. You can specify a sink provider that should be used with the channel. Sink providers are discussed later in this chapter.

18.3. Calling Remote Objects from Client Applications

After you create a remoting object and a server, you want to use a client application to call methods of the remote object.

Technique

Similar to the server, with the client you also have to register a channel using ChannelServices.RegisterChannel. The channel to be registered must use the same protocol that is offered by a server channel:

```
ChannelServices.RegisterChannel(new TcpChannel());
```

To get an instance of a proxy that is needed to invoke methods in the remote object, you can use the Activator class. Activator.GetObject returns a proxy to a well-known remote object. For the proxy, you need the type of the remote object class, here RemoteObject, and the URL to the remote object. The URL consists of the protocol (tcp), the server and port number, and the name of the remote object (Demo):

```
_1_RemoteObject.RemoteObject obj =
        (_1_RemoteObject.RemoteObject)Activator.GetObject(
                typeof(_1_RemoteObject.RemoteObject),
                "tcp://localhost:8088/Demo");
obj.Method();
```

Instead of using the `Activator` class, you can also register the remoting object with the runtime, as you did on the server side earlier. The difference with the server side is that with the client you must call the method `RegisterWellKnownClientType`. After the remote object class is registered, you can use the `new` operator to instantiate the remote object:

```
RemotingConfiguration.RegisterWellKnownClientType(typeof(RemoteObject),
                                             "tcp://localhost:8088/Demo");

RemoteObject obj = new RemoteObject();
obj.Method();
```

18.4. Performing Client-Side Activation of Remotable Objects

You want to use stateful remoting objects with .NET Remoting.

Technique

To keep state in the remote object, it is just necessary to register the remote object as a client-activated object with the method `RegisterActivatedServiceType` after the channel is registered:

```
RemotingConfiguration.RegisterActivatedServiceType(
        typeof(_1_RemoteObject.RemoteObject));
```

With the client application, you can use the `CreateInstance` method of the `Activator` class with client-activated objects.

With the client application, you can use either the `Activator` class or the class `RemotingConfiguration` to configure the client-activated object type. With the `Activator` class, you use the method `GetObject` with well-known objects, but with client-activated objects, you need the method `CreateInstance`. With this method, you can pass arguments to a nondefault constructor (`null` in this example) and attributes. With the attributes, you have to set the URL to the remote object:

```
object[] attrs = { new UrlAttribute("tcp://localhost:8088/Demo") };
_1_RemoteObject.RemoteObject obj =
        (_1_RemoteObject.RemoteObject)Activator.CreateInstance(
                typeof(_1_RemoteObject.RemoteObject), null, attrs);
```

A second way to instantiate client-activated objects is to use the `RemotingConfiguration` class with the method `RegisterActivatedClientType`. This way, you can use the `new` operator to instantiate the remote object, as discussed before:

```
RemotingConfiguration.RegisterActivatedClientType(
        typeof(_1_RemoteObject.RemoteObject),
        "tcp://localhost:8088/Demo");
```

Comments

Using stateless objects is the preferred programming model with distributed solutions. With stateful objects, the server has allocated resources for a client.

With stateful objects, be aware that the objects are destroyed on the server after a timeout of a leasing time. The leasing mechanism is discussed in Recipe 18.9, "Controlling Lifetime Leases."

18.5. Creating Server-Activated Singleton Objects

You want to share state between multiple clients by using a single object on the server.

Technique

To configure a remoting object as a singleton object, all you have to do is call the method `RegisterWellKnownServiceType` with the option `WellKnownObjectMode.Singleton`:

```
RemotingConfiguration.RegisterWellKnownServiceType(
        typeof(_1_RemoteObject.RemoteObject), "Demo",
        WellKnownObjectMode.Singleton);
```

Comments

Configuring the object as a singleton object has the effect that only one object is created, and every client gets a reference to the same object. With such a behavior, you have to pay attention to threading issues. With multiple clients, the same object might be accessed from multiple threads simultaneously, and you have to pay attention to locking issues.

Singleton objects do have a timeout with the leasing mechanism similar to client-activated objects. Recipe 18.9 discusses how you configure the timeout values.

18.6. Using Remoting Configuration Files

You want to use configuration files to define the channel and remote object instead of defining this information in the code.

Technique

Instead of creating channels and registering the remote object in the code, you can replace the entire channel and object registration with a single line of code. The method

`RemotingConfiguration.Configure` reads a configuration file and creates and registers all channels and objects accordingly:

```
RemotingConfiguration.Configure("6_Server.exe.config");
```

To define the configuration of a well-known object with the HTTP channel, the configuration file for the server is shown in Listing 18.1. The `<wellknown>` element specifies a well-known object. You can specify the `SingleCall` or `Singleton` object type with the mode attribute. The `type` attribute defines the type and the assembly of the remote object. `objectUri` specifies the name of the object that the client will use. With the `<channels>` element, the remoting channels are specified.

Listing 18.1   **A Server Configuration File to Define a Well-Known Object with the HTTP Channel**

```xml
<?xml version="1.0" encoding="utf-8" ?>
<configuration>
    <system.runtime.remoting>
        <application>
            <service>
                <wellknown mode="SingleCall"
                        type="_1_RemotingObject.RemoteObject, 1_RemoteObject"
                        objectUri="Demo" />
            </service>
            <channels>
                <channel port="8088" ref="http" />
            </channels>
        </application>
    </system.runtime.remoting>
</configuration>
```

Listing 18.2 shows the configuration file for the client. With the client, you need only the `url` and the `type` attributes with the `<wellknown>` element. With the client configuration file, you must specify the protocol, server name, port number, and object name with the `url`. The `<channel>` configuration of the server defined the port number of the server because the client application must know this port number. With the client application, there is no need to define a fixed port number. If you set the port number to `0`, any free port number is selected automatically.

Listing 18.2   **A Client Configuration File to Define a Well-Known Object with the HTTP Channel**

```xml
<?xml version="1.0" encoding="utf-8" ?>
<configuration>
    <system.runtime.remoting>
        <application>
            <client>
```

Listing 18.2   **Continued**

```
                <wellknown url="http://localhost:8088/Demo"
                    type="_1_RemoteObject.RemoteObject, 1_RemoteObject" />
            </client>
            <channels>
                <channel port="0" ref="http" />
            </channels>
        </application>
    </system.runtime.remoting>
</configuration>
```

To define client-activated objects, you can specify the `<activated>` element in the configuration file.

Comments

Using configuration files for .NET Remoting makes it easy to change the configuration without the need to change the code.

18.7. Hosting Remotable Types with IIS

You want to use IIS as a hosting server for the remoting objects.

Technique

Hosting the remote object in IIS, you just have to write code for the remote object, but you don't have to write a custom server. All that you need is to copy the assembly of the remote object class to the `bin` directory of the Web application and add the remoting configuration to the ASP.NET configuration file `web.config` to specify the `<wellknown>` element within the `<service>` element. Listing 18.3 shows a configuration file that you can use with IIS.

Listing 18.3   `web.config` **to Specify a Remoting Object with IIS**

```
<?xml version="1.0" encoding="utf-8" ?>
<configuration>
    <system.runtime.remoting>
        <application>
            <service>
                <wellknown mode="SingleCall"
                    type="_1_RemoteObject.RemoteObject, 1_RemoteObject"
                    objectUri="Demo.soap" />
            </service>
        </application>
    </system.runtime.remoting>
</configuration>
```

Comments

If you use the facility to host remote objects with IIS, you can only use well-known single-call objects. Because the ASP.NET worker process is recycled, you cannot use a stateful client-activated or a stateful singleton object.

The channel that is offered automatically is the HTTP channel with the port that is defined with the IIS configuration. The default port number is port 80. You can change the port number with the IIS configuration.

The name of the object must use the extension soap or bin, depending on whether you use the SOAP or binary formatters. These extensions are defined with the ASP.NET configurations.

18.8. Using Channels and Formatters

You want to specify what channels and formatters are used.

Technique

The .NET Framework 1.1 offers two channels with two formatters. The channel is responsible for transferring the method call in a form of a message from the client to the server and from the server to the client. The formatter is responsible for converting the method call and parameters to pass it across the network.

The HTTP channel by default uses the SOAP formatter, but the TCP channel by default uses the binary formatter. The binary formatter is more efficient compared to the SOAP formatter.

The server example uses both available channels, so the server is available both by TCP and HTTP channels. After that, the formatter of the HTTP channel is changed to a binary formatter.

You can add the channel to be used to the <channels> recipe in the remoting configuration file:

```
<channels>
    <channel port="8088" ref="http" />
    <channel port="8989" ref="tcp" />
</channels>
```

To change the default formatter of a channel, you can set the <serverProviders> element with the child element <formatter> to specify a different formatter—in this example, a binary formatter with the HTTP channel:

```
<channels>
    <channel port="8088" ref="http">
        <serverProviders>
            <formatter ref="binary" />
        </serverProviders>
```

```
        </channel>
        <channel port="8989" ref="tcp" />
    </channels>
```

Comments

In the configuration file, you can define what channel to use. The configuration of the channel can be very simple, using a reference (with the `ref` attribute) to a channel that is already configured in the file `machine.config`.

With SOAP, you have to be aware that multiple SOAP styles do exist. The default SOAP style used by ASP.NET Web Services is the document style, which is the newer style. The .NET Remoting SOAP formatter just supports the older RPC style.

18.9. Controlling Lifetime Leases

You want to change the default values that specify the lease times for a remote object on the server.

Technique

You can change the default values for the lease time configurations by setting the `<lifetime>` element in the .NET Remoting configuration file, as shown here. Setting the `leaseTime` attribute to `15M` defines a lease time of 15 minutes instead of the default 300 seconds. The value defined with `renewOnCallTime` specifies the time that the lease time is incremented with every method call:

```
<?xml version="1.0" encoding="utf-8" ?>
<configuration>
    <system.runtime.remoting>
        <application>
            <lifetime leaseTime="15M" renewOnCallTime="3M" />
        </application>
    </system.runtime.remoting>
</configuration>
```

You can also specify lease-time values with the remoting object instead. You have to override the method `InitializeLifetimeService` of the base class `MarshalByRefObject`, where you can change the lease values using the `ILease` interface:

```
public class RemoteObject : MarshalByRefObject
{
    public string Greeting(string name)
    {
        return "Hello " + name;
    }
```

```
    public override object InitializeLifetimeService()
    {
        ILease lease = (ILease)base.InitializeLifetimeService();
        lease.InitialLeaseTime = TimeSpan.FromMinutes(20);
        lease.RenewOnCallTime = TimeSpan.FromSeconds(50);
        return lease;
    }
}
```

Comments

For the lease time, you use four configuration values. The lease time has a default initial value of 300 seconds that is also the maximum value. Every time a method is called, the lease time is incremented by 120 seconds up to the maximum lease time.

You can change these values by setting new values in the configuration file or by overriding the method InitializeLifetimeService. The values set directly in the object class override the values in the configuration file.

Leasing applies only to stateful objects. Well-known single-call objects are created with every method call, so leasing does not apply here.

18.10. Performing Asynchronous Remoting Calls

You want to invoke the remoting calls asynchronously. Calling methods across the network can take a while. So that the client doesn't have to wait until a method finishes, the method can be called asynchronously.

Technique

To invoke a method of a remoting object asynchronously, you can create a delegate with the same signature and return type as the method of the remote object:

```
public delegate string GreetingDelegate(string s);
```

Creating a delegate instance, you can pass the method of the remote object to the constructor of the delegate. The sample code passes the method Greeting. Then, you can start the method Greeting by invoking the method BeginInvoke using the delegate instance. BeginInvoke accepts the same parameters as the input parameters of the method Greeting and two parameters more. The first additional parameter is of type AsyncCallback, which lets you specify a method that should be called when the Greeting method is finished. The second additional parameter lets you pass any object that can be accessed again when the method completes:

```
GreetingDelegate del1 = new GreetingDelegate(obj.Greeting);
// start the method call
```

```
IAsyncResult ar = del1.BeginInvoke("Simon", null, null);
// do something else
```

After the method starts, you can check whether the asynchronous method is already completed with the `IAsyncResult` object that is returned from `BeginInvoke`. Calling `EndInvoke` waits until the asynchronous method is completed:

```
string greeting = del1.EndInvoke(ar);
```

Comments

Using delegates, you can invoke any method in an asynchronous way. There's no difference whether you are calling .NET Remoting objects or not.

Delegates allow different ways to get the return values from the asynchronous method: you can pass an `AsyncCallback` delegate that specifies the method which should be called when the asynchronous method completes, you can check with the `IAsyncResult` object whether the method is finished, and you can wait until the method is completed with `EndInvoke`.

18.11. Creating Proxies for Message Interception

You want to create a custom proxy to intercept method calls before they are passed to a sink.

Technique

As you already have seen in Recipe 18.1, "Creating a Remotable Object," the client application does not invoke the remote object directly, but it uses a proxy instead. .NET Remoting uses two kinds of proxies: a transparent and a real proxy. The transparent proxy looks like the remote object with the same methods as the remote object. However, the transparent proxy does nothing more than forward the method calls to the real proxy by calling the method `Invoke`. The responsibility of the real proxy is to create a message from the method and to pass the message to the message sinks and into the channel.

Figure 18.2 shows the transparent proxy and the real proxy that are called by the client. In the example, the client invokes the `Greeting` method of the transparent proxy. The method `Greeting` is also available with the remote object. The transparent proxy in turn invokes the `Invoke` method of the real proxy.

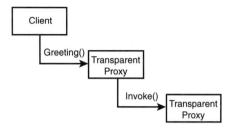

Figure 18.2 A client invoking the Greeting method
of the transparent proxy.

To create a custom proxy, you have to create a class that derives from RealProxy; in the
example, the class is named CustomProxy. The constructor of the class CustomProxy calls
the constructor of the RealProxy, where it creates a transparent proxy of the type that is
passed. The second argument of the CustomProxy constructor defines the URL to the
remote object. This URL is used to create a message sink with the help of a channel.
ChannelServices.RegisteredChannels returns an array of all channels that are registered with the remoting runtime:

```
public CustomProxy(Type type, string url)
    : base(type)
{
    this.url = url;

    foreach (IChannel channel in ChannelServices.RegisteredChannels)
    {
        IChannelSender channelSender = channel as IChannelSender;
        if (channelSender != null)
        {
            string uri;
            sink = channelSender.CreateMessageSink(url, null,
                                                    out uri);
            if (sink != null)
                break;
        }
    }

    if (sink == null)
    {
        throw new Exception("A channel supporting the URL "
                            + couldn't be found!");
    }
}
```

With the custom proxy class, you have to override the method `Invoke`. This method is called for any method that is invoked with the transparent proxy. In the implementation, the message representing the method call is passed to the `sink` object created earlier with the method `SyncProcessMessage` to process the method call with the remote object. `SyncProcessMessage` returns a return message that is returned from the `Invoke` method:

```
public override IMessage Invoke(IMessage msg)
{
    //...
    IMessage returnMessage = sink.SyncProcessMessage(msg);
    //...
    return returnMessage;
}
```

In Listing 18.4, you can see the complete implementation of the `Invoke` method that displays information about the message that represents the method call.

Listing 18.4 **A Custom Proxy Implementation**

```
public override IMessage Invoke(IMessage msg)
{
    Console.WriteLine("proxy started");

    if (msg is IMethodCallMessage)
        Console.WriteLine("IMethodCallMessage");

    if (msg is IMethodReturnMessage)
        Console.WriteLine("IMethodReturnMessage");

    Type msgType = msg.GetType();
    Console.WriteLine("Message Type: {0}", msgType.ToString());
    Console.WriteLine("Message Properties");
    IDictionary dict = msg.Properties;
    // Set the '__Uri' property of 'IMessage' to 'URI' property of 'ObjRef'.
    dict["__Uri"] = this.url;
    IDictionaryEnumerator dictEnum =
            (IDictionaryEnumerator)dict.GetEnumerator();

    while (dictEnum.MoveNext())
    {
        object key = dictEnum.Key;
        string keyName = key.ToString();
        object val = dictEnum.Value;
        Console.WriteLine("\t{0} : {1}", keyName, dictEnum.Value);
        if (keyName == "__Args")
        {
```

Listing 18.4   **Continued**

```
            object[] args = (object[])val;
            for (int i = 0; i < args.Length; i++)
            {
                Console.WriteLine("\t\targ: {0} value: {1}", i, args[i]);
            }
        }

        if ((keyName == "__MethodSignature") && (val != null))
        {
            object[] args = (object[])val;
            for (int i = 0; i < args.Length; i++)
            {
                Console.WriteLine("\t\targ: {0} value: {1}", i, args[i]);
            }
        }
    }

    IMessage returnMessage = sink.SyncProcessMessage(msg);

    IMethodReturnMessage methodReturnMessage =
            (IMethodReturnMessage)returnMessage;
    Console.WriteLine("IMethodReturnMessage.ReturnValue: {0}",
                        methodReturnMessage.ReturnValue);

    Console.WriteLine("proxy finished");

    return returnMessage;
}
```

For the custom proxy, you have to create an instance of the `CustomProxy` class in the client application and get the transparent proxy with a method of the base class `RealProxy`. `GetTransparentProxy` returns the transparent proxy that can be used by the client to invoke the methods of the remote object:

```
RemotingConfiguration.Configure("11_client.exe.config");
_11_CustomProxy.CustomProxy proxy =
        new _11_CustomProxy.CustomProxy(typeof(_1_RemoteObject.RemoteObject),
                                        "http://localhost:8088/Demo");
_1_RemoteObject.RemoteObject obj =
        (_1_RemoteObject.RemoteObject)proxy.GetTransparentProxy();
string s = obj.Greeting("Christian");
```

Figure 18.3 shows the output of the client application that displays the information about the message inside the custom proxy.

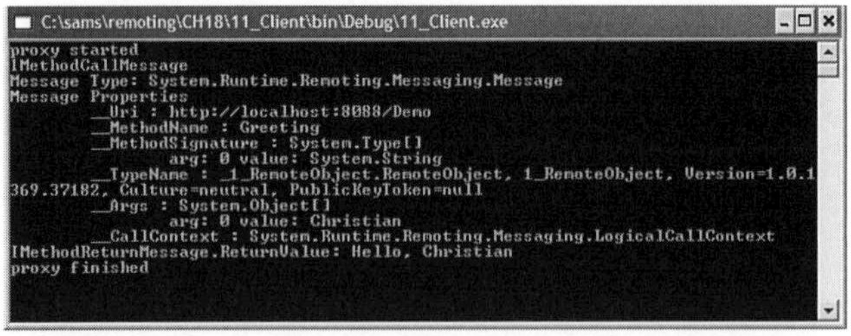

Figure 18.3 Console output using the custom proxy.

Comments

With a custom proxy, you create a class that derives from the `RealProxy` class, and you have to override the method `Invoke`. In the `Invoke` method, you have full access to the message, so you can change it accordingly or select different servers, depending on their load.

Using a custom proxy, you lose the configurability of the remote object with the client. In the client, you have to create an instance of the custom proxy and ask for the transparent proxy. You can make a different approach to intercepting methods by creating channel sinks. Using proxies just has an advantage if you don't want to use channels and if you want to intercept calls to local objects.

18.12. Creating Custom Channel Sinks for Logging

> You want to create a custom channel sink to intercept the method call to the remote object on the client.

Technique

Sink objects can intercept the method calls both on the client and on the server. The formatters discussed in Recipe 18.8, "Using Channels and Formatters," are such sink objects, too.

Such sinks are connected in a chain of multiple sink objects, where one sink hands over the message to the next sink. With the client, every sink object implements the interface `IClientChannelSink`, whereas on the server, the interface `IServerChannelSink` must be implemented.

A sink provider class implements a factory pattern to create sink objects. Sink providers are assigned to the channel. You can assign the sink provider by using a configuration file or by setting parameters in the constructor of a channel class.

Figure 18.4 shows how sink objects are mapped into a message chain.

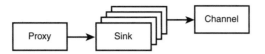

Figure 18.4   Sink objects.

To create a custom channel sink, you must create two classes: a sink and a sink provider. The sink must implement interface `IClientChannelSink`, and the sink provider that is responsible for creating a sink object must implement the interface `IClientChannelSinkProvider`. For using the sink with the client, you can define the sink provider with the .NET Remoting configuration file.

In the example, the class `LoggingSink` is an implementation of a sink class that writes remoting requests to a log file before the request is passed to the next sink. `LoggingSink` derives from the base class `BaseChannelSinkWithProperties` that provides a common implementation for sinks that are configurable with properties and implements the interface `IChannelSinkBase`. `IClientChannelSink` derives from `IChannelSinkBase`. So by using the base class `BaseChannelSinkWithProperties`, it is not necessary to implement the methods of the base interface yourself:

```
public class LoggingSink : BaseChannelSinkWithProperties, IClientChannelSink
{
```

In the constructor of a sink class, you have to remember the next sink to pass the request to this sink after the message was processed. With the `LoggingSink` class, you also need a filename in the constructor to define where the log information should be stored:

```
public LoggingSink(IClientChannelSink sink, string logFilename)
{
    nextSink = sink;
    this.logFilename = logFilename;
}
```

If you do not need asynchronous requests with your sink, you can throw an exception of type `NotImplementedException` with the methods `AsyncProcessRequest` and `AsyncProcessResponse`. However, because these methods are defined with the interface `IClientChannelSink`, it is necessary to write an implementation:

```
public void AsyncProcessRequest(IClientChannelSinkStack sinkStack,
                                IMessage msg,
                                ITransportHeaders headers, Stream stream)
{
    throw new NotImplementedException();
}

public void AsyncProcessResponse(
            IClientResponseChannelSinkStack sinkStack, object state,
            ITransportHeaders headers, Stream stream)
```

```
    {
        throw new NotImplementedException();
    }
```

The read-only property `NextChannelSink` must return the next sink object. The next sink object was assigned in the constructor of the class `LoggingSink`:

```
public IClientChannelSink NextChannelSink
{
    get
    {
        return nextSink;
    }
}
```

The method `GetRequestStream` must return a stream object where the message is to be serialized:

```
public Stream GetRequestStream(IMessage msg, ITransportHeaders headers)
{
    return(nextSink.GetRequestStream(msg, headers));
}
```

The heart of the sink class is in the method `ProcessMessage`. With this method, the request from the client is received, and the response must be returned. In this method, you can access the properties and methods of the message, the request headers, and the request stream itself to write some information to a log file. To build up the response, you just have to call the next sink to process the message:

```
public void ProcessMessage(IMessage msg,
                           ITransportHeaders requestHeaders,
                           Stream requestStream,
                           out ITransportHeaders responseHeaders,
                           out Stream responseStream)
{
    StreamWriter writer = new StreamWriter(logFilename, true);
    writer.WriteLine("---- Message from the client ({0:T}) ----",
                DateTime.Now);

    //...
    // Hand off to the next sink in the chain.
    nextSink.ProcessMessage(msg, requestHeaders, requestStream,
                        out responseHeaders,
                        out responseStream);
}
```

Listing 18.5 shows the complete implementation of the method `ProcessMessage`, where information about the message is written to the console.

Listing 18.5   **A Sink Class Implementation to Log Remoting Requests to a File**

```
public void ProcessMessage(IMessage msg, ITransportHeaders requestHeaders,
                           Stream requestStream,
                           out ITransportHeaders responseHeaders,
                           out Stream responseStream)
{
    StreamWriter writer = new StreamWriter(logFilename, true);
    writer.WriteLine("---- Message from the client ({0:T})----", DateTime.Now);
    writer.WriteLine("...Request Headers...");
    foreach (DictionaryEntry header in requestHeaders)
    {
        writer.WriteLine("header - {0} = {1}", header.Key, header.Value);
    }
    writer.WriteLine();

    IDictionary dict = msg.Properties;
    foreach (object key in dict.Keys)
    {
        writer.WriteLine("{0} = {1}", key, dict[key]);
    }

    long pos = requestStream.Position;
    byte[] buffer = new byte[requestStream.Length];
    requestStream.Read(buffer, 0, (int)requestStream.Length);

    System.Text.ASCIIEncoding enc = new System.Text.ASCIIEncoding();
    string request = enc.GetString(buffer, 0, buffer.Length);
    writer.WriteLine("...Request...");
    writer.WriteLine(request);
    Console.WriteLine();

    // set stream to previous position for message processing
    requestStream.Seek(pos, SeekOrigin.Begin);

    writer.WriteLine("---------------------------------------------");
    writer.Close();

    // Hand off to the next sink in the chain.
    nextSink.ProcessMessage(msg, requestHeaders, requestStream,
                            out responseHeaders,
                            out responseStream);
}
```

In addition to the sink class, you need a sink provider. The sink provider is responsible for creating the sink class.

The client sink provider has to implement the interface IClientChannelSinkProvider.

In the constructor of the sink provider, you pass the properties that are configured with the sink provider as the first argument. In the LoggingSinkProvider example, the property file defines the filename for the log file:

```
private string logFilename = "c:\remotingdemo.log";

public LoggingSinkProvider(IDictionary properties,
                           ICollection providerData)
{
    channelSinkProperties = properties;
    if (properties["file"] != null)
    {
        logFilename = properties["file"].ToString();
    }
    //...
}
```

The sink provider interface defines the property Next. This property is called to set the next provider:

```
public IClientChannelSinkProvider Next
{
    get
    {
        return nextProvider;
    }
    set
    {
        nextProvider = value;
    }
}
```

The method CreateSink creates a sink object of type LoggingSink. You perform this step by using the CreateSink method of the next provider and passing this sink to the LoggingSink constructor as well as the name of the log file:

```
public IClientChannelSink CreateSink(IChannelSender channel,
                                     string url,
                                     object remoteChannelData)
{
    //...
    IClientChannelSink nextSink = null;

    if (nextProvider != null)
    {
        nextSink = nextProvider.CreateSink(channel, url,
                                           remoteChannelData);
        //...
```

```
                return new LoggingSink(nextSink, logFilename);
        }
        return nextSink;
    }
```

You can assign the sink provider to the channel by changing the configuration file (see Listing 18.6). The sink provider is defined with the `<provider>` element. You just have to set the `type` attribute that consists of the class name as well as the name of the assembly. `<provider>` is a child element of `<clientProviders>` that itself is a child element of `<channelSinkProviders>`. You assign the provider to the channel by setting the child element `<clientProviders>` of the `<channel>` element.

Listing 18.6 **Remoting Configuration File with a Sink Provider**

```xml
<?xml version="1.0" encoding="utf-8" ?>
<configuration>
    <system.runtime.remoting>
        <channelSinkProviders>
            <clientProviders>
                <provider id="logger"
                        type="_12_LoggingSink.LoggingSinkProvider,
12_LoggingSink" />
            </clientProviders>
        </channelSinkProviders>
        <application>
            <client>
                <wellknown url="http://localhost:8088/Demo"
                        type="_1_RemoteObject.RemoteObject, 1_RemoteObject" />
            </client>
            <channels>
                <channel port="0" ref="http">
                    <clientProviders>
                        <formatter ref="soap" />
                        <provider ref="logger" file="c:/log.txt" />
                    </clientProviders>
                </channel>
            </channels>
        </application>
    </system.runtime.remoting>
</configuration>
```

Comments

Sinks make it possible to intercept method calls. With this interception, you can read message information before it is passed to the server, change it, encrypt or decrypt messages, or perform any other technique you can imagine.

Figure 18.5 shows the output of the client application that displays the information about the message inside the custom channel sink.

Figure 18.5   Log file output using the channel sink.

V

Deployment and Security

19

Assemblies

19.0. Introduction

Assemblies are the basic units into which managed code is packaged. An assembly can contain one or more files of executable code or resources (modules), and additionally can be associated with one or more satellite assemblies, which contain culture-specific resources. In this chapter, we cover common tasks involving the creation of assemblies and the extraction of information from them.

19.1. Setting Informational Assembly Attributes

You want to have the compiler embed in an assembly attributes that identify the software product and provide other useful information about the origin of the assembly.

Technique

If you have a project created with VS.NET, then navigate to the `AssemblyInfo.cs` file that VS.NET created for you. Identify the lines in this code that look something like this:

```
[assembly: AssemblyTitle("")]
[assembly: AssemblyDescription("")]
[assembly: AssemblyConfiguration("")]
[assembly: AssemblyCompany("")]
[assembly: AssemblyProduct("")]
[assembly: AssemblyCopyright("")]
[assembly: AssemblyTrademark("")]
[assembly: AssemblyCulture("")]
```

Simply add the information to be placed in the assembly inside the quotes. For example, to change the company name to Sams Publishing and the product name to C# Cookbook Sample, amend those lines to

```
[assembly: AssemblyCompany("Sams Publishing")]
[assembly: AssemblyProduct("C# Cookbook Sample")]
```

Then simply rebuild the project.

If your project was not created with VS.NET, then you most likely won't have an `AssemblyInfo.cs` file. In that case, simply add the required attribute definitions to any file in the project. Note that there is no special significance in the `AssemblyInfo.cs` file; VS.NET creates this file and places assembly attributes in it so all the assembly attributes for a project are in one place. You can declare the assembly attributes in any file in your code (although each one should be declared only once in the project).

Comments

The preceding code uses standard C# syntax for declaring custom attributes. Note that as part of the process of compiling the project, the compiler actually instantiates the attributes you declare and executes the appropriate constructors. Any errors in the data you supply for an attribute that would prevent that attribute from being constructed are therefore picked up at compile time.

Also bear in mind that executable assemblies cannot be localized. Hence, you'll get a compilation error if you supply any culture information for a project that will be compiled into an `.exe` assembly.

19.2. Setting the Assembly Version

You want to have the compiler set the version of an emitted assembly.

Technique

The technique here is almost identical to that for setting the informational assembly attributes because the assembly version is controlled by an attribute, `AssemblyVersionAttribute`. You can find this attribute in the `AssemblyInfo.cs` file of VS.NET-generated projects or which you can add yourself:

```
[assembly: AssemblyVersion("1.0.1.12")]
```

This line causes the compiled assembly to have version `1.0.1.12.` (major version 1, minor version 0, build 1, revision 12).

If you omit this attribute entirely, the C# compiler gives the assembly the version `0.0.0.0`.

One useful point about this particular attribute is that the compiler accepts wildcards in the version number. Wildcards cause the compiler to automatically generate part of the version for you. The possible forms you can supply are

```
<n>
<n>.<n>
<n>.<n>.*
<n>.<n>.<n>
<n>.<n>.<n>.*
<n>.<n>.<n>.<n>
```

Here, `<n>` indicates any positive integer. If you omit part of the version, the compiler sets the relevant version numbers to zero, but `*` asks the compiler to generate the rest of the version automatically. For example, the following line results in an assembly version of `3.5.0.0`:

```
[assembly: AssemblyVersion("3.5")]
```

The following line results in the build and revision numbers being generated automatically:

```
[assembly: AssemblyVersion("3.5.*")]
```

For example, we compiled a program with that setting and got an assembly version of `3.5.1281.31179`. According to the documentation, the compiler calculates the build number as the number of days since 1 January 2000 and the revision number as half of the number of seconds since yesterday at midnight. However, there's little point ascribing any significance to the actual number. (Besides, our own tests appear to show a bug in the revision number that ignores Daylight Savings Time.) The real significance is that every time you do a new build of your project, the build and revision numbers increase—which can be useful if it's important that successive builds don't have the same version.

Comments

You need to supply the assembly version in the correct format: the different parts of the version number are separated by dots, in contrast to the ILDasm format, which separates them with colons (as in `1:0:1:12`). Fortunately, if you use the wrong format in your C# code, you get a compilation error, which makes the problem easy to correct.

19.3. Viewing Assembly Contents with ILDasm

You want to examine the metadata and intermediate language (IL) code in an assembly.

Technique

Type in the command `ILDasm` from the VS.NET command prompt. (Note that this command is case-insensitive; typing in `ildasm` works too. But we use the usual case convention for the name of the IL disassembler utility here.)

A new `ILDasm` window opens. Click on the File menu and navigate to the assembly you want to examine. To illustrate what happens, we created a small Windows Forms application called `HelloWorldDlg`. Other than the default code added by VS.NET, this sample contains a button with a click-event handler that displays a message box:

```
private void btnHelloWorld_Click(object sender, System.EventArgs e)
{
    MessageBox.Show("Hello, World!", "Hello World Message Box");
}
```

Now, running `ILDasm.exe` and opening the release build of the compiled `.exe` file from this project results in Figure 19.1, which lists the types and assembly attributes in the assembly in a treeview.

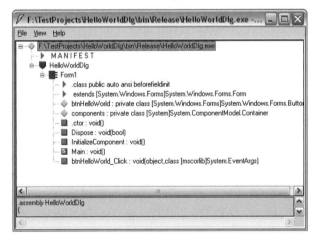

Figure 19.1   Viewing an assembly with ILDasm.

If you want to examine the IL code for a function, double-click on that function in the tree control. For example, Figure 19.2 shows what you get if you click on the `Form1.btnHelloWorld_Click()` method.

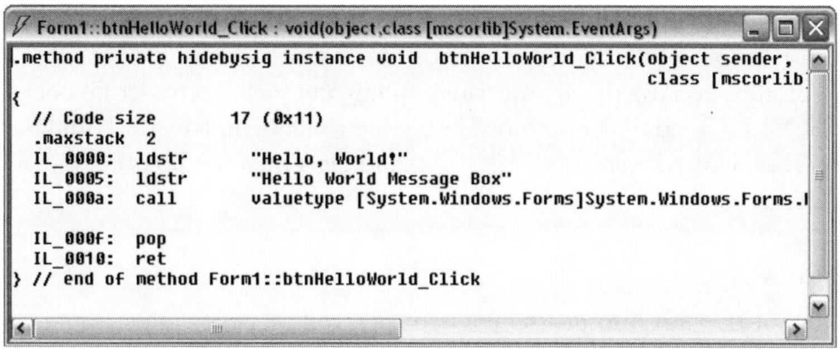

Figure 19.2   Viewing the code for a method with ILDasm.

The IL shown in Figure 19.2 is what the C# code for the method compiles to, in a textual format.

To examine the manifest, which includes details of any referenced assemblies and any assembly-level attributes, double-click on the MANIFEST node in ILDasm's main treeview, as shown in Figure 19.3.

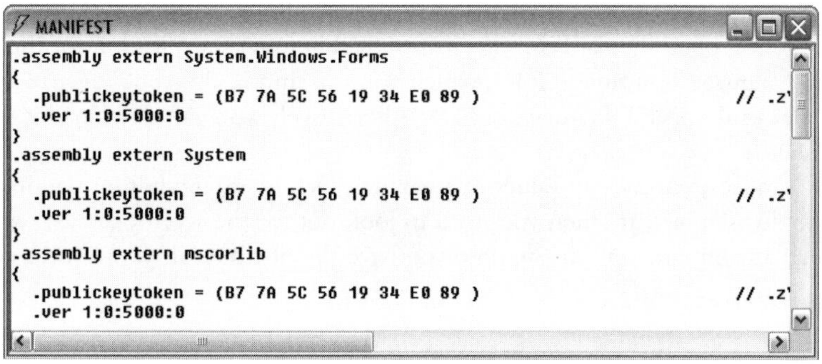

Figure 19.3   Viewing an assembly manifest with ILDasm.

If, instead of using the ILDasm Windows Forms-based user interface, you prefer to store the textual representation of the IL code and metadata in a text file for later viewing or editing, you can use the following command-line syntax:

```
ILDasm AssemblyFile /out:OutputFile
```

For example, the command you use for this project is

```
ILDasm HelloWorldDlg.exe /out:HelloWorldDlg.il
```

This command causes ILDasm to dump a complete textual representation of the IL code and metadata into a text file. Note that although this file is a plain-text file, it's customary to give it the extension .il.

In most cases, you need to use the VS.NET command prompt to run `ILDasm.exe`. On most installations of VS.NET, you cannot run `ILDasm.exe` from the default Windows command prompt because the appropriate symbols and paths aren't set up correctly. You can find the VS.NET command prompt in the Start menu, under Visual Studio.NET 2003, Visual Studio.NET (or for VS.NET 2002, under Visual Studio.NET, Visual Studio.NET Tools).

Comments

The purpose of ILDasm is to disassemble the code and metadata in an assembly into a textual form. The actual code and metadata is, of course, stored in a binary format, but ILDasm provides a convenient textual representation, with much the same relationship to IL as assembly language has to native executable code. In general, you will rarely need to disassemble assemblies that you have compiled. However, doing so can be useful to better understand how the C# code that you write gets translated into IL. It might assist in your understanding subtle nuances of C#, or it might help you to optimize code. In addition, if you lose the source code for some compiled project, it might be the only way available to understand how the code was supposed to work! To read the IL code, you need some familiarity with IL. The various IL commands are defined in Partition III of the European Computer Manufacturers Association (ECMA, an organization dedicated to promoting open standards in information technology) specification for the Common Language Runtime (CLR), which you can find in the `Tool Developers Guide` folder of the .NET Framework SDK. Alternatively, you can download it from `http://msdn.microsoft.com/net/ecma`.

If you want to examine the values of attributes, such as assembly informational attributes in the disassembled IL, then you need to look out for the word `.custom`, which indicates an attribute definition. Suppose you have this attribute in your source code:

```
[assembly: AssemblyProduct("C# Cookbook Sample ")]
```

ILDasm disassembles the attribute in the compiled assembly to the following:

```
.custom instance void
[mscorlib]System.Reflection.AssemblyProductAttribute::.ctor(string) =
( 01 00 12 43 23 20 43 6F 6F 6B 62 6F 6F 6B 20 53 61 6D 70 6C 65 00 00 )
   // ...C# Cookbook Sample..
```

The binary representation of the text is a consequence of the fact that attributes can have any binary value, depending on what data type the constructor of each attribute expects; their values are not confined to text.

Although using ILDasm to disassemble your own code can be useful, you should bear in mind that license agreements might prohibit you from disassembling code that you have purchased from other organizations. Check individual license agreements before you proceed.

19.4. Creating a Multifile Assembly

You want to create an assembly in which the IL code is spread across a number of files.

Technique

Visual Studio.NET does not support the ability to generate multifile assemblies, so you need to compile from the command line. You must first compile the files that will form the additional modules using the `csc` command and the `/target:module` flag:

```
csc /reference:Assemblies referenced /target:module source files
```

Finally, you compile the prime module (that is to say, the main assembly file, which contains the manifest), in the normal way, but using the `/addmodule` flag to inform the compiler about the additional modules in the assembly. You can specify multiple modules, separated by a semicolon: `/addmodule:file1.netmodule;file2.netmodule`. Note that `.netmodule` is the conventional extension for assembly module files. The actual effect of `/addmodule` is to cause the compiler to add the metadata (but not the IL code) from the specified modules to the generated assembly.

For example, suppose you have three source files, `Main.cs`, `Rare1.cs`, and `Rare2.cs`. `Rare1.cs` and `Rare2.cs` contain the source code for some rarely used types that will go into a separate module, whereas `Main.cs` contains the code that will go into the prime module. Suppose also that the code references `System.dll` and `System.Windows.Forms.dll` from both modules. You should in this case compile the complete assembly using these commands:

```
csc /target:module /reference:system.dll;system.windows.forms.dll
/out:rare.netmodule rare1.cs rare2.cs
csc /target:winexe /reference:system.dll;system.windows.forms.dll

/addmodule:rare.netmodule /out:main.exe main.cs
```

Recall that the `/out` flag indicates the name of the file containing the assembly or module generated, and `/target:winexe` indicates that a `.exe` file containing a Windows Forms application should be generated. The full set of options are

- `/target:exe` generates a console application.
- `/target:library` generates a DLL assembly that contains no start method, so you cannot start it directly.
- `/target:winexe` generates a Windows application.
- `/target:module` generates a module, which must be included in an assembly before you can execute it.

After you execute these commands, the files `main.exe` and `rare.netmodule` are created, which between them contain the entire assembly.

Comments

As you might have guessed from the names used in the preceding example, the main purpose of creating multifile assemblies is to be able to separate rarely used code or resources. The idea is that if some code or resources are large but rarely used, then most of the time it is better for that code or resources not to be loaded at all when the assembly is loaded; in most cases, it just causes an unnecessary performance hit. By separating those parts of the assembly into one or more individual files, you ensure that they are only loaded on demand.

19.5. Creating a Strong Name Assembly

You want to create an assembly that has a strong name.

Technique

You first need to create a key file that contains the public and private keys that make up the strong name. You can do so from the command line using the strong name utility, `sn`:

```
sn -k KeyFile.snk
```

This line creates a key file called `KeyFile.snk`, which contains a new randomly generated strong name. The name of the file is entirely your choice, but key files often have the extension `.snk`.

You can now ensure that an assembly will be signed with this strong name by placing the following line in your C# source code:

```
[assembly: AssemblyKeyFile(@"C:\Keys\KeyFile.snk")]
```

Note that this code presumes that you placed the key file in a folder, `C:\Keys`.

If you are working with a project created with VS.NET, then you'll find an empty `AssemblyKeyFile` attribute declared in the `AssemblyInfo.cs` file, so you should modify this existing attribute instead. (You'll get a compilation error if `AssemblyKeyFile` is declared more than once.) When a project is first created, VS.NET by default generates this code in `AssemblyInfo.cs`:

```
[assembly: AssemblyDelaySign(false)]
[assembly: AssemblyKeyFile("")]
[assembly: AssemblyKeyName("")]
```

This code indicates no key name or key file, so it causes the compiler to generate an assembly without a strong name.

Unless you intend to use delay signing, you should leave `AssemblyDelaySign` as `false`, and if you are using a key file, you should leave the `AssemblyKeyName` attribute blank:

```
[assembly: AssemblyDelaySign(false)]
[assembly: AssemblyKeyFile(@"C:\Keys\KeyFile.snk")]
[assembly: AssemblyKeyName("")]
```

An alternative technique is to actually install the key into the list of digital signatures maintained in the background by the Windows operating system's security services (more correctly, the cryptography service provider, or CSP). To do so, you can use the sn command with the /i flag once you create the key:

```
sn -k KeyFile.snk
sn -i KeyFile.snk MySampleKey
```

With these commands, you first create a key file containing the strong name, then you install the strong name in the Windows CSP, giving it the name MySampleKey. Now you can have the assembly signed by amending the VS.NET-generated source code to read as follows:

```
[assembly: AssemblyDelaySign(false)]
[assembly: AssemblyKeyFile("")]
[assembly: AssemblyKeyName("MySampleKey")]
```

You have a clear choice here: You can either set the AssemblyKeyName attribute to indicate that you want the compiler to ask the CSP for the key, or you can indicate a file containing the key using the AssemblyKeyFile attribute. Setting both attributes works, but it can be a bad idea because it could be confusing to developers. (With both attributes set, the compiler asks the CSP for a key with the given name first. If that fails, it looks for the specified key file.)

Comments

A *strong name* is a digital signature embedded in the assembly, in a format specific to managed code and recognized by the CLR. It is a security precaution that guarantees the integrity of an assembly. Having a strong name ensures that, if any unauthorized persons who do not have access to the key file tamper with the file, it is detected by the CLR, resulting in the CLR refusing to load the file.

Giving an assembly a strong name is an essential prerequisite for installing that assembly in the global assembly cache (GAC). The CLR does not let you install an assembly into the GAC unless it has a strong name. Bear in mind, however, that simply adding a strong name does not by itself create a shared assembly. At this stage, if you follow the preceding procedure, you have a private strong-named assembly—in other words, an assembly that happens to have a strong name but which is nevertheless a private application-specific assembly that is not installed in the GAC.

19.6. Delay Signing an Assembly

You want to use delay signing to create a strong-named assembly.

Technique

To use delay signing, you must first create a key file that contains only the public key. There are several stages. To start, you must create a full key file containing both a public and private key. (Of course, you can skip this step if you already have such a key file.) Then, you create the public key file from this key file.

At the command prompt, you type something like the following:

```
sn -k KeyFile.snk
sn -p KeyFile.snk PublicKey.snk
```

The p flag instructs the sn utility to extract just the public key from a key file and install it in the named file—so the preceding commands result in the file PublicKey.snk containing just the public key created by the first sn command. To compile the assembly from the C# source code, you need to ensure that the assembly attributes in your source code are set as follows:

```
[assembly: AssemblyDelaySign(true)]
[assembly: AssemblyKeyFile(@"C:\Keys\PublicKey.snk")]
[assembly: AssemblyKeyName("")]
```

As before in this code, you assume that the file PublicKey.snk is in the folder C:\Keys. Notice that the AssemblyDelaySign attribute is set to true, indicating that the compiler will add the public key to the file but will not sign the assembly with the private key.

Before actually running the assembly, there is one further step you must take: You must run sn again on the assembly, this time specifying the option -Vr:

```
sn -Vr MyDelaySignedLibrary.dll
```

sn -Vr marks the assembly for verification skipping. This means that the CLR will not attempt to verify that the assembly has been signed with a private key. If you don't mark the assembly for verification skipping, then it will not be possible to ever load it. This is because the CLR would see a public key in the assembly and would try to use that public key to check the assembly had been signed with the corresponding private key. Of course, a delay-signed assembly will not have been signed, so this check would fail—which would cause the CLR to throw a security exception and refuse to load the assembly.

Prior to shipping, you need to get the final release build of the assembly signed properly. You do so with the -R flag of the strong-name utility, which actually adds the digital signature encrypted with the private key to the specified delay-signed assembly:

```
sn -R MyAssembly.exe KeyFile.snk
```

Obviously, there is no need to mark this build for verification skipping.

Comments

Delay signing means that the public key is stored in the assembly as if it has been signed, but no corresponding digital signature (the part of the strong name that requires the private key) is placed in the assembly.

The purpose of delay signing is to shield the developer from any requirement to have access to an organization's private key. Private keys must by their very nature be kept as secure as possible. If the private key leaks out to any unauthorized person, the whole point of using it—to guarantee the authenticity of the code—is lost. Hence, it is desirable for only one or two highly trusted people in an organization to have access to the private key. With delay signing, the developer who builds the code needs access only to the file that contains the public key. She requires no access to the private key, so the procedure allows an organization to protect the private key far more effectively than if assemblies had to be signed with the private key every time they were built. With delay signing, the trusted person takes responsibility for extracting the public key from the key file using the `sn -p` command and distributing the public key file to the developers. Then, once the software is complete and ready to ship, he also needs to re-sign the generated assemblies. The trusted person needs to be comfortable with using the command prompt but does not need to be a skilled programmer.

19.7. Creating a Shared Assembly

You want to create a shared assembly.

Technique

To convert a private assembly into a shared assembly, you need to install it into the GAC. Note that the private assembly must already have a strong name.

You install an assembly into the GAC using another command-line tool, `gacutil`. The purpose of `gacutil` is quite simply to manage the placement and removal of assemblies in the GAC. To install an assembly into the cache, you should run `gacutil` with the `-i` flag. For example, to install an assembly, `MyLibrary.dll`, you use the following:

```
gacutil -i MyLibrary.dll
```

Notice we assume the assembly in question is a DLL assembly. The whole point of getting an assembly in the GAC is so other applications can use its types. Almost invariably, the only assemblies you normally want to install as shared assemblies are DLL assemblies.

If an assembly has been delay-signed, you must mark it for verification skipping before attempting to install it in the GAC:

```
sn -Vr MyDelaySignedLibrary.dll
gacutil -I MyDelaySignedLibrary.dll
```

Of course, once you re-sign a delay-signed assembly with `sn -R`, you can install it directly into the GAC, with no need for the additional `sn -Vr` step.

Comments

On occasions, you might want to uninstall an assembly from the GAC. To do that, you should run `gacutil` with the -u flag:

```
gacutil -u MyDelaySignedLibrary
```

Note, however, there is a subtle difference in syntax between installing and uninstalling: When you install an assembly, you need to provide only the filename, because `gacutil` can read the full identity of the assembly from the file. Recall that the assembly identity includes the name, version, strong name, and culture of that assembly, and all this information is required to place the assembly in the cache. However, when you remove an assembly from the cache, you cannot specify a filename, so you need to specify instead the identity of the assembly. That's why the preceding code omitted the `.dll` extension from the name: We were specifying the assembly name, not the filename. Because this code indicates only the name of the assembly, the result is that all assemblies that have this name are removed from the GAC. If you know that there are multiple assemblies with a given name in the cache—such as multiple versions of an assembly or copies of a satellite assembly with different cultures—and you only want one of them removed, then you need to be more specific:

```
gacutil -u MyDelaySignedLibrary Version=3.1.0.0
```

This line uninstalls any assemblies that have the name `MyDelaySignedLibrary` and the version number `3.1.0.0`, whereas the following line is even more specific:

```
gacutil -u MyDelaySignedLibrary Version=3.1.0.0 Culture=en-GB
```

It uninstalls only the `en-GB` (that is, UK English) culture version of this assembly.

19.8. Securing Satellite Assemblies

You want to secure an assembly that contains satellite assemblies.

Technique

If you want to give a strong name to an assembly that has associated satellite assemblies, you need to separately ensure that all the satellite assemblies are also signed with the same strong name as the main assembly. For satellite assemblies that VS.NET knows about as part of the project, VS.NET should do this step automatically. If you are using delay signing, you have to manually re-sign all satellite assemblies with the private key prior to shipping, just as with the main assembly. For example, to re-sign the `en-GB` and `en-US` satellites of an assembly called `MyAssembly`, use the following:

```
sn -R /en-GB/MyAssembly.resources.dll KeyFile.snk
sn -R /en-US/MyAssembly.resources.dll KeyFile.snk
```

You can write a batch script if you have a large number of files.

If you are not using VS.NET to generate your satellite assemblies but are doing so manually, then you need to sign the assembly at the point at which you compile each resources file into the assembly. In this situation, you have most likely used the `resgen` command at the command prompt to produce a compiled resources file for each culture, and you intend to use the `al` assembly linker utility to convert each resources file into a satellite assembly. At this point, you should the `/keyfile` flag to indicate to `al` that the assembly should be signed with a key:

```
al /embed:MyResources.en-US.resources /c:en-US /keyfile:/MyKey.snk
/out:MySample.resources.dll
```

This command compiles the resource file `MyResources.en-US.resources` into the `en-US`-cultured satellite assembly `MySample.resources.dll`, signing it with the key read in from the file `MyKey.snk`. If `MyKey.snk` contains only a public key and you are using delay signing, then the equivalent command is

```
al /embed:MyResources.en-US.resources /c:en-US /keyfile:/MyKey.snk /delay+
    /out:MySample.resources.dll
```

If you are using a key container from the CSP rather than a key file, then you replace the `/keyfile` flag with `/keyname` (whether or not delay signing is used):

```
al /embed:MyResources.en-US.resources /c:en-US /keyname:/MyKey /delay+
    /out:MySample.resources.dll
```

Comments

For the most part, the techniques for signing satellite assemblies are no different in either concept or command-line syntax from the equivalent techniques for signing the main assembly. The main difference is that, because satellites have no C# source code, it is not possible to indicate to the compiler via attributes in the source code that the assembly is to be signed. Hence, you need to use flags passed to the `al` utility to indicate that resource files should be signed.

19.9. Explicitly Loading an Assembly Programmatically

> You want to explicitly load an assembly from another running application. You might want to manipulate the assembly programmatically (for example, to query the information in the manifest or to use reflection to run code in the assembly).

Technique

You explicitly load an assembly using the static `Assembly.Load()` and `Assembly.LoadFrom()` methods. These methods load the indicated assembly and return an `Assembly` reference to that assembly. If the assembly is already loaded, then they simply return the `Assembly` reference to the preloaded assembly.

Note that the `Assembly` class is defined in the `System.Reflection` namespace:

```
using System.Reflection;
```

If you want to load an assembly where you know the name or identity of that assembly, then you should use `Assembly.Load()`. For example, if you have an assembly with the name `MyAssembly`, you use the following:

```
Assembly loadedAssembly = Assembly.Load("MyAssembly");
```

However, supplying merely the name of an assembly is only sufficient if the assembly you are trying to load is located in the same folder as the executing assembly (or, depending on the probing rules for that assembly, in a subfolder). If you want to load a shared assembly from the GAC, you need to supply the full identity of that assembly. For example, to load `System.Drawing.dll`, you use

```
Assembly loadedAssembly = Assembly.Load("System.Drawing, Version=1.0.5000.0,

Culture=neutral, PublicKeyToken=b03f5f7f11d50a3a");
```

You use `Assembly.LoadFrom()` instead if you want to load an assembly where you know the name and location of the file that contains the manifest:

```
Assembly loadedAssembly = Assembly.LoadFrom(@"C:\MyAssemblies\MyAssembly.exe ");
```

If you want to explicitly load one of the assemblies supplied in the .NET Framework class library, then on developer machines that have VS.NET installed, you can supply a path that leads to copies of these assemblies that are installed outside the assembly cache in a subfolder of `%WINDIR%\Microsoft.NET\Framework` for the benefit of VS.NET. For example, to load the .NET 1.1 version of `System.Drawing.dll`, you use the following:

```
Assembly loadedAssembly = Assembly.LoadFrom
    (@"C:\WINDOWS\Microsoft.NET\Framework\v1.1.4322\System.Drawing.dll");
```

This technique has the advantage that you don't need to know the full identity of the assembly, but it might not work on user machines on which only the .NET runtime is installed. However, there is a workaround: You can use `Assembly.LoadFrom()` to load the assembly on your developer machine and then use the `Assembly.FullName` property to obtain the identity of the assembly:

```
Assembly loadedAssembly =
 Assembly.LoadFrom
    (@"C:\WINDOWS\Microsoft.NET\Framework\v1.1.4322\System.Drawing.dll");
Console.WriteLine(loadedAssembly.FullName);
```

The `FullName` property returns a string representation of the assembly identity in exactly the format required by `Assembly.Load()`—so you can cut and paste this string into the code that is to be compiled and shipped.

Note that we present here the simplest overloads of `Assembly.Load()` and `Assembly.LoadFrom()`. Other overloads of these methods allow you to supply evidence that determines the security permissions for the assembly or to supply the name in different formats (such as an instance of the `System.Reflection.AssemblyName` class). In addition, version 1.1 of the .NET Framework brings a new method, `Assembly.LoadFile()`, which is similar in its effect to `Assembly.LoadFrom()`:

```
Assembly loadedAssembly = Assembly.LoadFile(@"C:\MyAssemblies\MyAssembly.exe ");
```

Comments

In general, assemblies are loaded automatically as they are needed. For example, the `Color` struct is contained in `System.Drawing.dll`. Suppose your code tries to instantiate a `Color` instance directly (that is, without using reflection):

```
Color color = Color.Red;
```

The compiler of course refuses to compile this code unless your project references `System.Drawing.dll`, in which case the emitted assembly will contain a reference to `System.Drawing.dll` in the manifest. The CLR will, on executing the preceding code that instantiates the `color` variable, automatically load `System.Drawing.dll` if that assembly hasn't previously been loaded. However, when assemblies are automatically loaded on demand in this way, your code doesn't get any explicit access to the assembly. The advantage of using `Assembly.LoadFrom()` or `Assembly.Load()` is that these methods give you a `System.Reflection.Assembly` reference. The `Assembly` class provides access to explicitly manipulate an assembly and also provides the gateway to the part of .NET's reflection technology that deals with assemblies. We don't demonstrate many applications of the `Assembly` reference in this chapter because that's really the topic of reflection, so it is discussed in Chapter 23, "Reflection."

In general, it is not possible to obtain an `Assembly` reference without loading the assembly—because it's not possible to manipulate an assembly without loading it first.

However, it's worth pointing out that there are simpler ways of obtaining this `Assembly` reference if the assembly in question is already loaded.

If you want to obtain a reference to the assembly which contains the code that is currently executing, you can use the static `Assembly.GetExecutingAssembly()` method:

```
Assembly execAssembly = Assembly.GetExecutingAssembly();
```

You can also use the static method, `Assembly.GetEntryAssembly()` to get an assembly reference to the `.exe` assembly that the current process started off executing. With this technique, code in a library can obtain a reference to the ultimate caller:

```
Assembly entryAssembly = Assembly.GetEntryAssembly();
```

If you want to access the assembly that defines a particular type which is already loaded, then you can use the `Type.Assembly` property. For example, to obtain an assembly reference to the assembly that defines the `SortedList` type (this assembly happens to be `mscorlib.dll`), you use

```
Assembly assblyForSortedList = typeof(System.Collections.SortedList).Assembly;
```

Alternatively, if you have some object reference, you use the following:

```
// assume myObj is a variable which can be declared to be of any type
Type objType = myObj.GetType();
Assembly assblyForSortedList = objType.Assembly;
```

19.10. Reading Assembly Identity Programmatically

> You want to obtain information related to an assembly's identity, including its name, version, culture, and public key.

Technique

Identity information is available via the `System.Reflection.AssemblyName` class. Hence, you need to obtain an `AssemblyName` instance that represents the required assembly and then use various properties on this class to obtain the details of the assembly.

If an assembly is loaded and you have an `Assembly` reference, then you can use the `Assembly.GetName()` method to retrieve an `AssemblyName` instance:

```
// assume someAssembly is an Assembly reference
AssemblyName name = someAssembly.GetName();
```

However, the neat thing about `AssemblyName` is that you can get an `AssemblyName` object without having to load the assembly concerned: There is a static method, `AssemblyName.GetAssemblyName()`, which opens an assembly file, reads the manifest from that file, extracts the identity information about the assembly, and then closes the file. This method avoids the memory overhead of having that assembly loaded permanently into the application domain, which is always a consequence of obtaining an `Assembly` reference:

```
AssemblyName name =

    AssemblyName.GetAssemblyName(@"c:\CookbookSamples\MyAssembly.exe ");
```

Once you have the `AssemblyName` reference, you can use various properties and methods to extract specific aspects of the fully qualified name. Listing 19.1 shows how to do so for the currently executing assembly.

Listing 19.1 **Displaying Information About Assembly Identity**

```
// get the AssemblyName reference for the required assembly -
// in this case the currently executing assembly
Assembly execAssembly = Assembly.GetExecutingAssembly();
AssemblyName name = execAssembly.GetName();

// now extract various bits of information
Console.WriteLine("Name: " + name.Name);
Console.WriteLine("Culture: " + name.CultureInfo.Name);
Console.WriteLine("Version: " + name.Version.ToString());
byte [] publicKeyToken = name.GetPublicKeyToken();
if (publicKeyToken == null)
    Console.WriteLine("This assembly does not have a strong name");
else
{
    Console.Write("Public Key Token: ");
    foreach (byte b in publicKeyToken)
        Console.Write(b.ToString() + "  ");
    Console.WriteLine();
}
```

There are several classes at work here, which between them allow a very fine degree of control over the information you can obtain:

- `AssemblyName.Name` returns a string containing the name of the assembly.
- `AssemblyName.CultureInfo` returns a `System.Globalization.CultureInfo` instance, which implements various properties to obtain, for example, the LCID (locale ID), calendar, date-time format, or the language name corresponding to that culture.
- `AssemblyName.Version` returns a `System.Version` instance, which contains properties to return the major, minor, build, and revision numbers of the version and methods to compare versions to see which one has the higher version number.

- The public-key token is returned as a `Byte[]` array because it is the appropriate format. This array is returned via a method, `AssemblyName.GetPublicKeyToken()`, rather than a property. .NET class design guidelines indicate that you should not normally use properties to return arrays. Note that another method, `AssemblyName.GetPublicKey()`, can return the full public key, also as a byte array.

If you simply want the fully qualified name of an assembly as a string, and you already have the appropriate `Assembly` reference, then there is no need to use an `AssemblyName` class. There's a shortcut via the `Assembly.FullName` property:

```
Assembly execAssembly = Assembly.Load("mscorlib");
Console.WriteLine(execAssembly.CodeBase);
```

This code, for version 1.1 of the .NET framework, generates the following output:

```
mscorlib, Version=1.0.5000.0, Culture=neutral, PublicKeyToken=b77a5c561934e089
```

Comments

Note that the assembly identity is sometimes referred to as its fully qualified name.

If you want to read the informational attributes of an assembly, or any other information stored in the form of custom attributes, you need to use the `System.Attribute` class and techniques from reflection. Details of how to do so appear in Chapter 23.

19.11. Identifying the File or URL from Which an Assembly Was Loaded

You want to find out programmatically where an assembly was loaded from.

Technique

The technique depends on whether you explicitly want the file path on the local computer or you need to know the original source of the assembly.

If you need the exact file path to the file where the assembly was directly loaded, you should use the `Assembly.Location` property:

```
Assembly execAssembly = Assembly.GetExecutingAssembly();
Console.WriteLine(execAssembly.Location);
```

The `Location` property returns a string giving the exact file path in a format such as `C:\CookbookSamples\MyLibrary.dll`. In some cases, this format is what you want, but in other cases, it might be misleading. For example, if an assembly was downloaded from the Internet, it is first copied to the local machine and stored in a special download section of the assembly cache before being executed. The `Assembly.Location` property in this case returns the exact path of the local copy inside the assembly cache. If what you really need to know is the URL where the assembly was originally downloaded, you should use the `Assembly.CodeBase` property. For example, to display the original location of the currently executing assembly, you use the following:

```
Assembly execAssembly = Assembly.GetExecutingAssembly();
Console.WriteLine(execAssembly.CodeBase);
```

For assemblies whose origin is the local machine, `CodeBase` returns a URL of the form `file:///C:/CookbookSamples/MyLibrary.dll`, but for assemblies downloaded over the Internet, `CodeBase` returns a URL of the form `http://www.SomeDomain.com/FileWasHere/MyLibrary.dll`.

Comments

One useful point is that `AssemblyName` also exposes a property, `CodeBase`, which normally returns the same string as `Assembly.CodeBase`, but without the need to have the assembly loaded into the current application domain.

19.12. Loading an Assembly into a New Application Domain

You want to load an assembly but at the same time confine the assembly to some application domain other than the one currently executing.

Technique

The `Assembly` class is not remotable. In general, it is not possible to manipulate an assembly in a remote application domain. Loading an assembly with some method such as `Assembly.Load()` generally loads that assembly into the domain that is currently executing. If you want an assembly loaded into a new application domain, you need to explicitly create that domain and then have that domain itself execute the code that loads the assembly.

Listing 19.2 illustrates a `Main()` method that loads an assembly with the path specified by the first argument so you can examine that assembly's fully qualified name.

Listing 19.2   `Main()` **Method That Loads Another Assembly**

```
static void Main(string[] args)
{
    Console.WriteLine(AppDomain.CurrentDomain.FriendlyName + ":  " + args[0]);
    Assembly assembly = Assembly.LoadFrom(args[0]);
    Console.WriteLine(assembly.FullName);
}
```

This code loads the assembly onto the current application domain. To execute this code in a separate domain, let's assume the assembly containing this code is stored in the file `C:\CookbookSamples\AssemblyLoader.exe`. Listing 19.3 shows how you would execute Listing 19.2 in a new application domain to examine `System.Windows.Forms.dll`.

Listing 19.3   Executing Code in a New Application Domain

```
string path =
    @"C:\WINDOWS\Microsoft.NET\Framework\v1.1.4322\System.Windows.Forms.dll";
AppDomain childDomain = AppDomain.CreateDomain("child domain");
childDomain.ExecuteAssembly(@"C:\CookbookSamples\AssemblyLoader.exe ",
    null, new string[]{path} );
AppDomain.Unload(childDomain);
```

This code shows three steps:

1. You create the new application domain using the static `AppDomain.CreateDomain()` method. The string passed to `AppDomain.CreateDomain()` is the user-friendly name of the new application domain and has no significance here.

2. You execute the `AssemblyLoader.exe` assembly in the new domain by calling `AppDomain.ExecuteAssembly()`. Note that no new thread is created here: When `AppDomain.ExecuteAssembly()` is invoked, the current thread simply swaps domains into the specified application domain and starts executing the given assembly, just as if you'd just started running that assembly as a new process. Once execution finishes, the thread reverts to the current application domain. The overload of `AppDomain.ExecuteAssembly()` used here takes three parameters: the path of the assembly to be executed, any evidence used to set security for the new assembly (you are not using this parameter here so you pass `null`), and a `string[]` array containing the arguments to be passed to the entry method of the new assembly.

3. Finally, you unload the new application domain. This step removes the application domain from memory and also removes from memory any assemblies that were loaded into that application domain (provided those assemblies are not also being used by another application domain).

Comments

One reason for loading an assembly into a separate application domain is to allow for unloading: The CLR does not at present supply any means to unload an individual assembly, but it is possible to unload an application domain. This step might be important, for example, if your application needs to load a large number of assemblies—perhaps to examine information about those assemblies. Once it does so, it no longer needs each assembly. If those assemblies remain loaded, it could impact performance by increasing the application's virtual-memory requirements.

20

Setup and Deployment Projects

20.0. Introduction

Although theoretically the .NET framework can reduce deployment to a simple matter of copying files, in practice for commercial applications things usually aren't that simple. For example, you probably want the appropriate Registry entries made so that your software can be uninstalled through the standard Control Panel Add or Remove Programs dialog. You might also want user-specific configurations files installed, and you certainly want to offer the user a setup program that allows him to choose such things as where in the file system he wants your software installed. Fortunately, Visual Studio.NET makes these goals relatively easy to achieve with a *setup project*. Depending on the type of setup project you ask VS.NET to create, this project, when built, will generate all the files you need to distribute to the end user to install and deploy the application on her computer. The capabilities of VS.NET with setup projects are somewhat limited, especially in the appearance of the user interface, and you might find that you need to purchase a dedicated setup package instead. However, for most applications, VS.NET can provide a basic ability to deploy applications simply.

  This chapter covers common tasks associated with creating and coding setup projects in VS.NET.

20.1. Creating `setup.exe`-Based Installations

> You have an application coded as a VS.NET solution, and you want to create a basic setup program that will install the application to a target computer.

Technique

The usual technique involves adding a deployment project to the VS.NET solution that contains the projects to be deployed. Use the VS.NET menus in the usual way to add a new project, and select Setup Wizard as the type of project to create.

The wizard guides you through a couple of steps, including asking what type of application you want to create a setup project for. In this chapter, we work with a Windows application.

The wizard then asks what parts of the solution need to be deployed. To illustrate this, we created a solution that contained two projects called `MyApplication` and `MyLibrary` and added a setup project to this solution. Figure 20.1 shows how we indicate that both of these generated assemblies must be deployed. In general, to deploy the assemblies that are built from your solution, you select Primary Output for each of the projects in the solution (in other words, the emitted assembly for each project), as well as any localized resources associated with each project.

Figure 20.1   Choosing the files to be deployed.

Depending on the nature of the application you need to redistribute, you might also want the setup program to install documentation files (autogenerated documentation), as well as the source files, content files, and debug symbols. In an additional step, the wizard asks you to specify any files that are not part of the solution but need to be installed.

The basic setup project is now complete, although you might want to change the product name as well as other basic information about the setup. You can do so by selecting the project in the VS.NET solution explorer. You then find that the Properties Window allows you to modify various information properties of the setup project, such as `ProductName`, `Manufacturer`, and `ManufacturerUrl`.

Note that building the solution normally builds all the projects *except* the setup project. To build the setup project, you need to specifically tell VS.NET to build that project. If you select the setup project in the solution explorer, you then see a separate Build *Setup Project Name* menu item under the Build menu in VS.NET. When the setup project is selected in the VS.NET solution explorer, you also see that the VS.NET main Project menu contains Install and Uninstall menu items, which run the setup program on the developer machine; selecting these items will cause the setup program to run, either installing or uninstalling the other projects in the same way that they would be on the end user's machine.

Comments

For a Windows application, building the setup project generates three files, called `setup.exe`, `setup.ini`, and *Setup Project Name*`.msi`:

- `setup.exe` is the file that is actually executed to perform an install or uninstall.

- `setup.ini` contains some additional configuration information used by `setup.exe` in XML format.

- *Setup Project Name*`.msi` is a Windows Installer database file that contains all the information required for the setup process. Embedded in this file are all the individual files that might need to be installed.

To redistribute your project, all that is required is to redistribute these three files (possibly on redistributable media such as CD-ROM) and instruct the end user to execute the `setup.exe` file.

In this chapter, although we work with Windows setup projects, most of the techniques are unchanged for the other types of setup projects. The other types of project you can create are

- *Web setup project*—Similar to a Windows setup project but aimed at installing ASP.NET code on a Web site. Running this project installs the files and also sets up IIS correctly to run the project.

- *Merge module*—Again similar to a Windows setup project, but this type produces a Windows installer file with the extension `.msm`, which you can include in other setup projects. You can almost think of it as the setup project's equivalent of a dynamic link library (DLL). Use a merge module to write an install program for components that need to be installed by many other setup programs.

- *Cab project*—This type is aimed at deploying files that are intended to be downloaded over the Internet or a network connection. The project produces a cabinet file with the extension `.cab`, which contains a number of other files packaged into one unit. Note that most of the techniques discussed in this chapter cannot be applied to Cab projects: Essentially, all you can do with a Cab project is select files to be installed and set some properties. This type of project does not generate any setup program—merely a single cabinet file.

To create any of these projects, select the appropriate project type in the Setup Wizard.

The default project Windows Forms setup project generated by VS.NET presents a standard user interface. Running the compiled `setup.exe` from this project results in the user seeing the following dialog boxes:

- A welcome dialog (see Figure 20.2). Note that the text in the title bar comes from the setup project `name`.

Figure 20.2 The default setup project Welcome dialog.

- A dialog asking which folder the user wants the project installed to (see Figure 20.3).

Figure 20.3 The Installation Folder dialog.

- A confirmation dialog to give the user a final chance to cancel before the installation actually happens (see Figure 20.4).

Figure 20.4   The Confirm Installation dialog.

- A progress dialog with a standard progress-bar control showing the installation progress (see Figure 20.5).

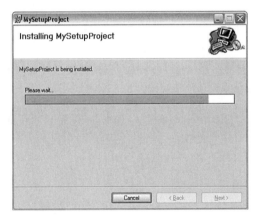

Figure 20.5   The installation-progress dialog.

- A final dialog to indicate install is complete (see Figure 20.6).

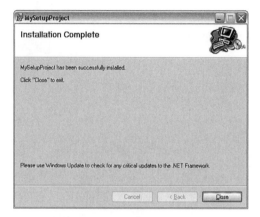

Figure 20.6   The Finished dialog.

The setup program places all the assemblies and other files to be installed in the folder chosen by the user and adds the application to the list of installed applications so that it appears in the Control Panel's `Add or Remove Programs` dialog. Also, because the installation is controlled by Windows installer, Windows installer automatically repairs the application if, for example, someone accidentally removes installed files later.

20.2. Creating a Windows Setup Project Without Using the Wizard

You want to create a setup project for a Windows application, and you cannot or don't want to use the wizard.

Technique

Create a setup project, but choose Setup Project (or whichever type of project you need) instead of Setup Wizard as the project type. VS.NET generates an install project that has all the features required of that type of install project, but that has no files in its list of files to install. For a Cab project, you need to add files by right-clicking on the project in solution explorer and selecting Add from the context menu. For all other install projects, you can use this technique, but for other project types, VS.NET offers a range of editors to specify the tasks to be performed by the setup project, and you'll find that using these editors gives you greater flexibility. These editors are all available under the VS.NET View, Editor menu whenever you select the setup project in solution explorer.

To add files, you need to use the File System Editor. (You might find that VS.NET opens this editor automatically when you create the setup project, but if not, it's under the `View, Editor` menu along with all the other setup project editors.) The File System

Editor has a classic Windows Explorer-style treeview and listview. The treeview for a Windows setup project by default contains three items: Application Folder, User's Desktop, and User's Program Menu, as shown in Figure 20.7.

Figure 20.7   The File System editor treeview.

These are so-called virtual folders, conceptual folders that represent locations to which files and shortcuts might be installed by the setup program:

- `Application Folder` is the folder that the user specifies in the Installation Folder dialog when installing the application.
- `User's Desktop` is the desktop on the installation machine.
- `User's Programs Menu` represents the `All Programs` menu of the desktop Start menu.

To add files to the folder to which the software will be installed, simply right-click on `Application Folder` in the tree view and select `Add` from the context menu. You see the option to create a subfolder under `Application Folder`, to add the project output from the project, and to add a specific file or shared assembly from the developer machine. To add the generated files from a project in the solution, select `Project Output`, and then select the appropriate project and type of output from the dialog that appears.

Figure 20.8 shows the File System Editor after project output consisting of the primary output and localized resources from two projects has been added. Note that this same situation was the example shown earlier of creating a setup project using the wizard.

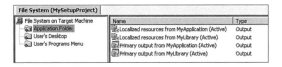

Figure 20.8   The File System Editor after adding project outputs.

Comments

The File System Editor is of course available whether or not you use the wizard to create the project. The wizard simply provides a quick way of initially choosing the project output to add to the setup project. The File System Editor is slightly harder to use but offers more flexibility, including the ability to create subfolders under Application Folder and add files to those subfolders. In many cases, you use the wizard to create a project roughly along the lines you need and then use the File System Editor to fine-tune the files to be deployed.

You can also add project output to the User's Desktop and User's Programs Menu items in the File System Editor, but in practice, you are more likely to add shortcuts to these folders.(You'll see how to do so in the next recipe.)

Note that the three virtual folders listed by default in the File System Editor constitute only a small number of the virtual folders available. To see the complete list, just right-click on the root File System node in the treeview, and select Add Special Folder from the context menu. Other locations on the target computer to which you can add files include the Program Files folder, the Windows System folder, the Start menu, and the User's Favorites folder.

20.3. Adding a Shortcut on the User's Desktop

> You want the setup program to place a shortcut to the application on the user's desktop.

Technique

In the File System Editor, navigate to the file that you want the shortcut to lead to. In most cases, it is the primary output from the main executable project in the solution, which you added to the Application Folder virtual folder. Right-click on this item in the listview, and select the Create Shortcut menu option from the context menu. This action adds a shortcut to the file in the same virtual folder, as shown in Figure 20.9.

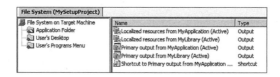

Figure 20.9   Adding a shortcut to a project output item.

Now you can simply use the mouse to move this shortcut into the User's Desktop virtual folder by dragging and dropping.

Comments

Although we explained this technique for placing a shortcut on the user's desktop, the technique is the same for placing a shortcut anywhere: Find the item you want a shortcut created to, right-click on it, and select Create Shortcut from the context menu; then, move the new shortcut to the desired virtual folder.

Note that it's very tempting, but wrong, to right-click on the location where you want the shortcut to go and then select Create Shortcut from the context menu. For example, if you right-click on the User's Desktop in the treeview, you see a Create

Shortcut context menu item. However, selecting it doesn't give you the results you want because it creates a shortcut *to* the desktop, whereas what you need is a shortcut to a file that is located *in* the desktop.

20.4. Customizing the Appearance of the Setup Dialogs

You want to change aspects of the appearance of the dialogs displayed by the setup program, such as replacing the icon or changing the text.

Technique

To change the appearance of dialog boxes, you need to navigate to the User Interface Editor in VS.NET. (You can find it along with all the other setup project editors under the `View`, Editors menu when you select the setup project in the solution explorer.) Figure 20.10 shows the default appearance of the User Interface Editor.

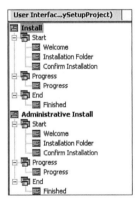

Figure 20.10 The User Interface Editor.

The editor shows two different installations: Install, which is the default user installation, and Administrative Install, which is intended for administrators and which is what executes if the setup program is passed the /a flag. If you are planning to allow administrative installations, then you need to edit both installation routines separately. Here we concentrate on the normal install because the technique is the same for both.

Click on the appropriate dialog box node in the User Interface Editor and modify the properties in the Properties Window. The properties available depend on the dialog in question, and the ability to customize the dialog is quite restricted: You can change the banner bitmap (that is, the bitmap displayed in the top-right corner of the dialog) and you can change the contents of the text blocks displayed. However, you cannot change the size of the dialog or add any other text or images, for example.

20.5. Adding User-Interface Dialogs

You want to add dialogs to the setup user interface, for example, to display additional information or to ask the user questions about installation preferences.

Technique

In the User Interface Editor, select the point in the setup process at which you want your dialog to appear. As shown in Figure 20.10, the options are Start (before installation commences), Progress (during the installation) and End (after the installation is complete), although, in practice Start and End are normally the only sensible points at which to add new dialogs. Right-click on the appropriate section and select Add Dialog from the context menu. You see a dialog box inviting you to select from a number of dialog templates.

Figure 20.11 shows the 14 different dialog templates you can choose.

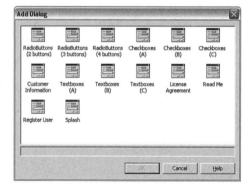

Figure 20.11   Choosing a dialog to add to the setup user interface.

- Three radio button dialogs, from which the user can select between mutually exclusive options using radio buttons
- Three check box dialogs, from which the user can select one or more options using check boxes

- Three text box dialogs, from which the user can supply information using a number of text boxes (up to three per dialog)
- A customer-information dialog
- A license-agreement dialog
- A read-me dialog asking whether the user wants to view a read-me file
- A register-user dialog offering a registration URL
- A splash screen

Just as with the standard dialogs, there is limited support for customization of the additional dialogs using the VS.NET Properties Window. Note, however, that you can customize each additional dialog only once. So it's not possible, for example, to have two different splash screens.

You simply select the required dialog, whereupon it is added to the user interface as the last dialog in the chosen section. For example, if we try to add a License Agreement dialog to the Start section, it will be placed after the Confirm Installation dialog.

Of course, following the Confirm Installation dialog is not the best of places to display a license agreement. You probably want the user to see the license agreement immediately after the Welcome dialog. If you right-click on any of the dialogs in the User Interface Editor treeview, you see Move Up and Move Down menu items in the context menu, which you can use to reorder them, or you can simply drag it to the appropriate location with the mouse.

Having added the required dialog, all you need to do is select it in the User Interface Editor and then use the VS.NET Properties Window to set the customizable aspects of that dialog. In the case of the license agreement, you can change the banner bitmap, whether the text appears sunken, and the text file that contains the license agreement to be displayed. (Note that it must be a file that you have already added to the list of files to be installed using the File System Editor.)

Comments

Although there is support for customizing these dialogs, it is fairly limited.

Several of the additional dialogs require input from the user. VS.NET does provide a means to make user-supplied data available to the installer so you can customize the installation process based on user choices. This aspect is covered in Recipe 20.7, "Conditionally Installing Files."

20.6. Setting Launch Conditions on the Installation

You want to impose launch conditions on the installation; for example, you want to only install the application if some prerequisites are already installed.

Technique

You can set launch conditions—conditions that must be satisfied or the setup program aborts the entire install—using the Launch Conditions Editor (see Figure 20.12), which you can find under View, Editor.

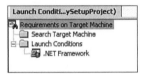

Figure 20.12   The Launch Conditions Editor.

VS.NET automatically adds the condition that the .NET Framework must be installed when it creates the project, and you can add further conditions.

Right-clicking on the Search Target Machine node allows you to add a search of the target computer. You can specify files, Registry keys, or names of applications installed by Windows Installer that must be present on the target machine before the setup program proceeds.

Right-clicking on the Launch Conditions node allows you to add launch conditions that are based on information known to Windows Installer. You can set the details of the conditions by setting values in the Properties Window for each condition. Figure 20.13 shows a launch condition that only allows setup to proceed if the computer is running Windows 2000 or later.

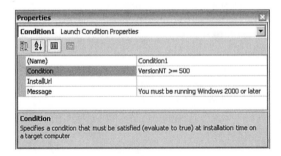

Figure 20.13   Restricting installations to machines running
Windows 2000 or later.

The Message property is the error message that gets displayed if the launch condition fails. The Condition itself comes from a list of properties that are not part of .NET but are defined within the Windows Installer itself. `VersionNT` is a Windows Installer property that has the value `400` on machines running NT4, `500` for Windows 2000, and so on. This property is not available on machines running Windows 9x (which means that any test for this property having any value will fail). The full list of available Windows Installer properties is too long to present here; however, you can find the list at `http://msdn.microsoft.com/library/default.asp?url=/library/en-us/msi/setup/versionnt_property.asp`. Note that as new versions of Windows Installer are released, the list of properties is likely to grow further. Table 20.1 presents a few of the more significant properties.

Table 20.1   **Some Useful Windows Installer Properties**

Property	Values
VersionNT	`400`=NT4, `500`=W2K, `501`=WXP, `502`=W2K3 Server
Version9x	`400`=Win95, `410`=Win98, `490`=Win ME
ServicePackLevel	Number of any installed Windows Service Pack; it has the value `5` if you are running NT4 SP5.
ScreenX	Width of screen in pixels.
ScreenY	Height of screen in pixels.
PhysicalMemory	Size of installed RAM in MB.

20.7. Conditionally Installing Files

You want certain files to only be installed if certain conditions are satisfied.

Technique

Navigate to the files in question in the File System Explorer. Select each file and look at the VS.NET Properties Window. You see a field called Condition. Simply enter the condition in this field using the same format as for a launch condition. For example, to specify that the primary output from a certain project should only be installed on Windows 9x machines, specify the condition `Version9x >= 400`.

A common use for this technique is to install a different set of files according to the operating system on the target machine. For example, you might have one assembly with the condition `Version9x>=400` and an alternate assembly with the condition `VersionNT>=400`. The first assembly is installed on Windows 95/98/XP machines, the second assembly on Windows NT/2000/XP/2003 Server family machines.

Notice that although we worked through the process for files, the procedure for conditionally installing is the same for other items, such as Registry keys. Simply navigate to the item in the appropriate editor and modify its Condition property in the VS.NET Properties Window. (You specify Registry keys to be installed with another of the setup project editors, the Registry Editor, but using a similar procedure to that for adding files.)

Although the syntax of the condition is the same for launch conditions and conditionally installing files, there is an additional flexibility when conditionally installing files: You can impose a condition based on choices selected by the user in a dialog box. This extra flexibility is not available for launch conditions for the simple reason that the launch conditions are evaluated before the setup program solicits any input from the user.

To show how to conditionally install a file based on a user option, we work through the process of putting up a dialog asking the user whether she wants to install diagnostic tools and conditionally install the primary output from a project called Tools only if the user indicates it is required.

First, we add a dialog to the install process as described in recipe 20.5, "Adding User-Interface Dialogs." We use a dialog that displays one check box, so we need to use one of the three check box dialogs.

We want the extra dialog to look like Figure 20.14.

Figure 20.14   Install Diagnostic Tools dialog.

To achieve this we set the properties of the Checkboxes (A) dialog as shown in Figure 20.15.

Figure 20.15 shows we typed in appropriate text for the banner text and body text. We also indicated that the first check box (CheckBox1) is visible, but all other check boxes are not visible. The key point is the value of the CheckBox1Property property, which we set to INSTALLTOOLS. The effect is that after the user exits this dialog, a property of this name is made available to Windows Installer. This property has the value 1 if the user checked the check box and 0 if the user didn't. To conditionally install a file based on this user selection, all that remains is to locate the file in question—with our example, the primary output of the Tools project—in the File System Editor and change its Condition to INSTALLTOOLS=1.

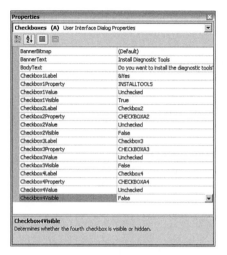

Figure 20.15   Choosing properties to generate the
Add Diagnostic Tools dialog.

20.8. Creating a Custom Executable Action

You want the setup program to execute some custom code that you have written (a custom action).

Technique

For the setup file to execute a custom action, you need to do the following:

- Write the code for the custom action.
- Ensure that the assembly containing the compiled code is one of the items installed on the target machine by the setup project. The easiest way to do so is to have your custom action code as a separate project in the solution and add the primary output from this project to the items installed in the File System Editor.
- Use another of the setup editors, the Custom Actions Editor (available from View, Editors), to add the assembly containing the code to the list of custom actions.

We start by examining how to write code so it can be executed as a custom action. If you intend your custom action to be an executable assembly, you need to have the entry point to the assembly invoke your custom action. To illustrate the code, we continue the example from Recipe 20.7, "Conditionally Installing Files," in which the setup program uses a custom Windows Installer property, INSTALLTOOLS, to indicate whether the user wants some diagnostic tools installed. Suppose now that you want an extra dialog box that you've coded yourself to be displayed when the setup is finished; this dialog box will display a welcome message and confirm whether the diagnostic tools were requested. Listing 20.1 shows the code to achieve this goal.

Listing 20.1   **A Simple Welcome Dialog**

```
class Class1
{
        static void Main(string [] args)
        {
                string message = "Welcome to the C# Cookbook Samples\n";
                if (args.Length > 0 && args[0] == "1")
                        message += "Diagnostic tools have also been installed";
                MessageBox.Show(message, "Welcome");
        }
}
```

The purpose of this code should be obvious, but you might wonder about the `if` statement. The code is based on the assumption that the first element of the `args[]` array passed in as command-line parameters contains the string 1 if the user asked for diagnostic tools to be installed and 0 otherwise. In other words, this string contains the value of our custom INSTALLTOOLS Windows Installer property.

You use the VS.NET Properties Window for the custom action to specify any command-line parameters that Windows Installer should pass to the custom action. You should first build the custom action project and then use the File System Editor to add the primary output for this project to the list of files installed by the setup project. Next, navigate to the setup project's Custom Actions Editor and make the changes shown in Figure 20.16.

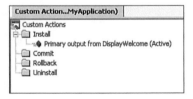

Figure 20.16   The Custom Actions Editor with some custom actions added.

The Custom Actions Editor has four nodes according to the circumstances in which you might want your custom action executed—so you can add custom actions to be executed when the installation is actually performed, committed, rolled back, or uninstalled. Figure 20.16 shows the situation after our custom action was added; for this example, we call the custom action project DisplayWelcome. When you first open the Custom Action Editor, there are no custom actions. To add an action under the Install node, you right-click on the `Install` node and select `Add Custom Action` from the context menu. You then see a dialog box asking you to identify the custom action from the set of files installed. Select the primary output from the required custom action project.

Finally, you need to set the properties for the new custom action using the VS.NET Properties Window. Figure 20.17 shows how to set the properties so our custom action will be executed if the user opts to install the diagnostic tools in our example.

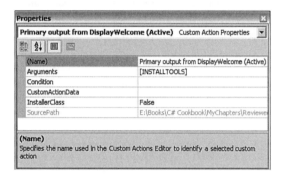

Figure 20.17   Setting the properties for an executable custom action.

Note that the `InstallerClass` property is set to `False` to indicate it is an executable custom action. It is also possible to code custom actions as classes, which is covered in the next recipe. Notice that it is possible to add a Condition governing whether the custom action should be executed. The `Arguments` property indicates the command-line arguments to be passed to the custom action when it is executed. If you want the value of a property passed in, then you must enclose the name of that property in square brackets. (To pass in more than one value, separate the properties by commas, as in `[Version9x]`, `[VersionNT]`). By specifying the `INSTALLTOOLS` property that we created in Recipe 20.7, the result is that the value `1` is passed in if the user opts to install the diagnostic tools.

Comments

Adding a custom action as an executable file is what you need to do if you want the custom action to have a separate user interface. It is easy to code; however, it's not the most flexible means of adding a custom action. For maximum flexibility and power in terms of interaction between your custom action and Windows Installer, you should code the custom action as a class.

20.9. Creating Custom Actions as Classes

You want to write a custom action, implementing it as a class.

Technique

The technique is similar to writing a custom action as an executable project: You write the code, but this time you create it as a DLL project. You add the primary output from this project to the setup project, and then you must use the Custom Actions Editor to add that project as a custom action.

The way you set up the custom action properties for a class is slightly different, as shown in Figure 20.18. You'll also notice that the properties that VS.NET provides are slightly different if VS.NET detects that the custom action project is a DLL; for example, there is no `Arguments` property.

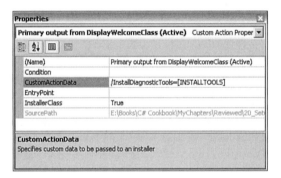

Figure 20.18   Properties for a class custom action.

The properties in Figure 20.18 are intended to have an analogous effect to those of Figure 20.17. You must set the `InstallerClass` property to `True`, and in addition, you specify any custom data using the `CustomActionData` property rather than the (now nonexistent) `Arguments` property. The syntax for `CustomActionData` is slightly different, taking the form `/Key=[Value]`. Any properties passed in to the installer class are passed in via a `StringDictionary` object rather than an array. Recall that each element stored in an `StringDictionary` must be accessed via a key of type `string`.

With the `CustomActionData` property set as shown in Figure 20.18, you can then access the value of the `INSTALLTOOLS` property from your code like this:

```
string installTools = Context.Parameters["InstallDiagnosticTools"];
if (installTools == "1")
        // user did check the INSTALLTOOLS checkbox
```

The `StringDictionary` containing the custom data is accessible via a property of a property, `Context.Parameters`. Your class inherits the `Context` property from a base class, `System.Configuration.Installer.Install`; you need to explicitly derive your class from this class, which is defined in the `System.Configuration.Install.dll` assembly. You should also add the `RunInstaller(true)` attribute to the class. This work all means that your derived class can be recognized by Windows Installer, which can then instantiate the class and call various methods on it. Besides any custom data, `Context` also contains certain data governing the general state of the installation process, including whether the installation is controlled by a transaction, whether you are installing or uninstalling, and the name of any log file being used to record the progress of the setup.

The `Installer` class defines various virtual methods, which you can override to provide custom actions at various points. The main such methods appear in Table 20.2.

Table 20.2   **Some Installer Class Methods That You Can Override**

Method	Purpose
`Install()`	Executed when an installation is required
`Commit()`	Executed when an installation has been successful and the changes to the system can be committed
`Rollback()`	Executed when an installation has been unsuccessful and needs to be rolled back
`Uninstall()`	Executed when an uninstall is required

All these methods return `void` and take one parameter, an `IDictionary` interface called `savedState`. This parameter contains some additional information passed in by Windows Installer, although we don't use that information here. For details, you should look up this class in the MSDN documentation. You need to override whichever of these methods you want to add a custom action for.

To illustrate what all this information means for your code, Listing 20.2 defines a custom action that writes out a file with data about all the values that Windows Installer has passed to the custom action via the `Context` property.

Listing 20.2   **A Custom Action to Write to a File**

```
[RunInstallerAttribute(true)]
public class Class1 : System.Configuration.Install.Installer
{
        public override void Install(System.Collections.IDictionary stateSaver)
        {
                base.Install(stateSaver);
                StringDictionary sd = this.Context.Parameters;
                StreamWriter sr = new StreamWriter(@"c:\SampleInstall.txt");
                sr.WriteLine(sd.Count.ToString() + " parameters");
                if (sd.Count > 0)
                {
```

Listing 20.2   **Continued**

```
                        foreach (string str in sd.Keys)
                        {
                                sr.WriteLine(str + "  :  " + sd[str]);
                        }
                }
                sr.Close();
        }
}
```

Note that for Listing 20.2 to compile, you need the following using statements:

```
using System;
using System.Windows.Forms;
using System.ComponentModel;
using System.Collections.Specialized;
using System.Configuration.Install;
using System.IO;
```

Comments

It's worth pointing out that the technique shown here scarcely touches on the power of the `Installer` class. Although we used a class derived from `Installer` to simply add a custom action, this class is intended to be used by Windows Installer to control many aspects of the install process.

20.10. Installing Assemblies into the Global Assembly Cache

You want to install one or more assemblies as shared assemblies into the global assembly cache (GAC).

Technique

Add the primary output of the relevant projects into the `Application Folder` virtual folder in the File System Editor. Right-click on the root File System on `Target Machine` node in this editor and select `Add Special Folder` from the context menu. You see a list of possible virtual folders, and you should choose `Global Assembly Cache Folder` from this list. You then see the GAC appear as an additional virtual folder in the File System Editor's treeview, as shown in Figure 20.19.

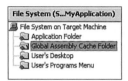

Figure 20.19   File System Editor with the GAC added.

Now simply select the projects whose primary outputs you want to install as shared assemblies under the Application Folder, and use the mouse to drag and drop them into the Global Assembly Cache Folder. Note that each of these assemblies must have been signed with a strong name; otherwise, you get a build error when you next build the setup project.

Comments

One disadvantage of using a setup project here is that it is necessary for the developer to have access to the private key to be able to sign the code. It is possible to work around this requirement, but the workarounds are awkward. Perhaps the easiest way is to code the assemblies that are to be shipped as shared assemblies in one or more completely separate projects and install them as shared assemblies on the developer machine. Then, have the setup project reference these assemblies as prebuilt assemblies rather than as project outputs. When these assemblies are ready to be shipped, they can be signed by the security manager and reinstalled in the developer machine GAC, and the setup project can be rebuilt to reference the signed assemblies.

Also, bear in mind that when you move project outputs in the File System Editor from the Application Folder to the GAC, VS.NET examines the dependencies of the various projects. If it detects that other projects depend on the moved assemblies, it leaves unnecessary copies of them in the Application Folder, which cannot be deleted within the setup project. Having said that, these extra copies are in most cases harmless—other than the waste of disk space on the target machine.

21

Securing Code

21.0. Introduction

In this chapter, we examine how to perform common tasks related to security and securing your code. For the most part, it involves examining how to manipulate security policy and request appropriate security permissions for your code; however, we also cover how to code certain traditionally insecure tasks such as pointers and unsafe code.

21.1. Requesting Permissions for an Assembly Using Declarative Security

You want to use declarative security to indicate the security permissions required by an assembly.

Technique

The technique for requesting assembly permissions using declarative security involves marking assemblies, classes, or methods with attributes. For example, to indicate that an assembly can only reasonably execute if it has read access to the D:\ drive on your computer, you add the following to the source code, usually in the `assemblyinfo.cs` file:

```
using System.Security.Permissions;
[assembly: FileIOPermissionAttribute(SecurityAction.RequestMinimum, Read=@"D:\")]
```

As you can see from the code, the attribute class—in this case, `FileIOPermissionAttribute`—determines the type of permission you are requesting, and the parameters passed to the attribute indicate the precise details of the permission required. Microsoft supplied an individual attribute permission class for each of the permissions defined out of the box with the Common Language Runtime (CLR). For example, you use the `SecurityPermissionAttribute` class to request the Security permission. Table 21.1 shows the main classes.

Table 21.1 **Security Permission Attribute Classes**

Namespace	Class
System.Data.Common	DBDataPermissionAttribute
System.Data.OracleClient	OraclePermissionAttribute
System.Diagnostics	EventLogPermissionAttribute
System.Diagnostics	PerformanceCounterPermissionAttribute
System.DirectoryServices	DirectoryServicesPermissionAttribute
System.Drawing.Printing	PrintingPermissionAttribute
System.Messaging	MessageQueuePermissionAttribute
System.Net	DnsPermissionAttribute
System.Net	SocketPermissionAttribute
System.Net	WebPermissionAttribute
System.Security.Permissions	EnvironmentPermissionAttribute
System.Security.Permissions	FileDialogPermissionAttribute
System.Security.Permissions	FileIOPermissionAttribute
System.Security.Permissions	IsolatedStoragePermissionAttribute
System.Security.Permissions	PrincipalPermissionAttribute
System.Security.Permissions	PublisherIdentityPermissionAttribute
System.Security.Permissions	ReflectionPermissionAttribute
System.Security.Permissions	RegistryPermissionAttribute
System.Security.Permissions	SecurityPermissionAttribute
System.Security.Permissions	SiteIdentityPermissionAttribute
System.Security.Permissions	StrongNameIdentityPermissionAttribute
System.Security.Permissions	UIPermissionAttribute
System.Security.Permissions	UrlIdentityPermissionAttribute
System.Security.Permissions	ZoneIdentityPermissionAttribute
System.ServiceProcess	ServiceControllerPermissionAttribute
System.Web	AspNetHostingPermissionAttribute

The purpose of each class in Table 21.1 should be obvious from the class name, but they are detailed in the MSDN documentation. You need to check the documentation in any case for full details of the parameters that you must pass to each of these attributes. However, in general you will find that the constructors to these classes each take just one parameter, a `SecurityAction` enumeration that indicates how the permission is to be applied. For example, it indicates whether the assembly must have the specified permission, would find it useful to have the specified permission, or must not have the specified permission. You can also pass a number of optional properties to each attribute; for example, in the previous code segment, the `Read` property indicates an area of the file system to which read access is required: `Read=@"D:\"`.

Table 21.2 outlines the actual security actions that are available for assemblies.

Table 21.2   `SecurityAction` **Values**

Value	Meaning
RequestMinimum	The assembly must have these permissions to execute.
RequestOptional	The assembly can execute without these permissions but won't be able to offer full functionality unless it has them.
RequestRefuse	To avoid compromising security, the assembly should always work without these permissions. In particular, if any code called from the assembly requests these permissions, the request should be denied.

With the `RequestMinimum` action, loading the assembly will fail if the relevant permissions cannot be granted. This failure might happen, for example, if another assembly further up the call stack does not have sufficient trust or has specifically requested that certain permissions be denied.

Let's look at two more examples of declarative security requests that are applied to assemblies. The following code ensures that an assembly never directly or indirectly executes unmanaged code or calls into aspects of the .NET infrastructure that are controlled by the Infrastructure permission:

```
[assembly: SecurityPermission(SecurityAction.RequestRefuse, UnmanagedCode=true,
    Infrastructure=true)]
```

The following code indicates that the assembly must have unrestricted access to the `HKLM\SOFTWARE\SamsPublishing` area of the Registry and might in some cases need to read the `HKLM\SOFTWARE\Microsoft` area:

```
[assembly: RegistryPermission(SecurityAction.RequestMinimum,
        All= @"HKEY_LOCAL_MACHINE\SOFTWARE\SamsPublishing")]
[assembly: RegistryPermission(SecurityAction.RequestOptional,
        Read= @"HKEY_LOCAL_MACHINE\SOFTWARE\Microsoft")]
```

It is also possible using the same technique to request a complete permission set. You simply use the `System.Security.Permissions.PermissionSetAttribute` class:

```
[assembly: PermissionSet(SecurityAction.RequestMinimum, Name="LocalIntranet")]
```

Comments

The most significant benefits of declaring assembly permissions using attributes is that the security requirements of an assembly form part of the metadata of that assembly, which makes it possible to examine assemblies and easily determine what permissions they need to run. An administrator can easily decide whether to deploy an assembly or how to configure security policy so that an assembly should be able to execute. In this regard, it's worth noting that a command-line tool called `permview` is designed to display declarative security requests. At the VS.NET command prompt, you simply type `permview` followed by the path to the assembly you want to examine. Listing 21.1 shows `permview` output for an assembly that is marked as requiring access to the `D:\` drive.

Listing 21.1   **Viewing the Permissions Required by an Assembly**

```
C:\>permview testsecurity.exe

Microsoft (R) .NET Framework Permission Request Viewer.  Version 1.1.4322.573
Copyright (C) Microsoft Corporation 1998-2002. All rights reserved.

minimal permission set:
<PermissionSet class="System.Security.PermissionSet"
               version="1">
   <IPermission class="System.Security.Permissions.FileIOPermission, mscorlib, V
ersion=1.0.5000.0, Culture=neutral, PublicKeyToken=b77a5c561934e089"
               version="1"
               Read="D:\"
               Write="D:\"
               Append="D:\"
               PathDiscovery="D:\"/>
</PermissionSet>

optional permission set:
  Not specified

refused permission set:
  Not specified
```

There might also be a performance advantage to using declarative security because if an assembly won't have the required permissions to execute, this fact is detected when the assembly is first loaded. The operation can be aborted rather than continue execution until an exception gets thrown because some method attempts to perform an operation for which it does not have the relevant permissions.

21.2. Requesting Permissions for a Class or Method Using Declarative Security

You want to use declarative security to indicate the security permissions required by a class or a method.

Technique

The technique is similar to that for applying security attributes to an assembly: You simply apply the same attributes to the relevant class or method instead. In this case, the security requests are processed the first time that the class or the method is used. However, the allowed security actions for a class or method are different. For a class or method, you can request the security actions in Table 21.3.

Table 21.3 `SecurityAction` **Values for a Class or Method**

Value	Meaning
LinkDemand	The immediate caller must have been granted the specified permission.
InheritanceDemand	Any class that derives from this class (or any method that overrides this method) must have the specified permission.
Demand	All assemblies in the call stack must have the specified permission. Use this request to indicate when a method or class needs to use a resource protected by a permission.
Assert	This method requires the specified permission and doesn't care whether other assemblies further up the call stack don't have it. Use this request when you know that a method or class has been tested and cannot be used to compromise the resource in question, no matter how its methods are invoked.
Deny	The specified permission should not be granted while executing code in this class or method. Use this request to prevent a method or class from being used by unscrupulous code to damage resources to which it would be allowed access but does not ever actually need to access.
PermitOnly	No permissions other than the specified permission should be granted while executing code in this class or method.

A couple of examples will illustrate this technique. The following code shows a method that needs permission to read the D:\ drive on the file system:

```
[FileIOPermission(SecurityAction.Demand, Read=@"D:\")]
public string [] ListDDriveFolders()
{
```

The next code is a class that often invokes unsafe code but has been thoroughly tested so we are sure it is sufficiently safe to assert this permission:

```
[SecurityPermission(SecurityAction.Assert, UnmanagedCode=true)]
public class SafeClass
{
```

Comments

When applying permissions to methods, you have a choice between using declarative and imperative security. The advantage of using declarative security is that it is often simpler to code and can lead to higher performance because you can perform the security checks when an assembly is loaded.

You also benefit from the extra information because the declarative security is visible through the assembly metadata. Note, however, that this benefit is not that significant for classes and methods because using that information requires an understanding of the classes and methods in an assembly. In addition, permview only displays security attributes applied to the assembly as a whole.

Declarative security does allow a couple of security actions that you cannot accomplish using imperative security. Imperative security does not contain any analogy to the link demand or the inheritance demand, so if you want to enforce those actions, you have no choice but to use declarative security.

21.3. Requesting Permissions Using Imperative Security Requests

You want to request security permissions while a method is executing.

Technique

The technique is to instantiate an instance of the appropriate security class and use methods on that instance to make the security request. For example, suppose a method is about to use isolated storage in a way that you are certain will be safe, no matter how the currently executing method is called, so you want to assert the isolated file storage permission:

```
void AccessIsolatedStorageSafely()
{
        IsolatedStorageFilePermission perm =
            new IsolatedStorageFilePermission(PermissionState.Unrestricted);
        perm.Assert();
        // code to access isolated storage safely goes here
        // etc.
```

On the other hand, suppose you want to prevent a method from being abused by malicious code that uses a file save dialog:

```
void DontWantToUseFileDialogs()
{
        // up to this point we can use save file dialogs
        FileDialogPermission dlgPerm = new FileDialogPermission(
            FileDialogPermissionAccess.Save);
        dlgPerm.Deny();
        // from this point onwards we cannot use save file dialogs

        // when method exits the deny will be cancelled and we can use file
dialogs again
}
```

Table 21.4 lists the four main methods that you can use to control imperative security.

Table 21.4   **Add a Title Here**

Method	Effect
Demand()	Requests the indicated permission.
Assert()	Ensures that until the end of the currently executing method, the indicated permission will always be granted when requested, for example, by a call to Demand(), no matter whether code higher up the call stack has the permission. Note that there is a security permission that controls asserts, and an assembly must have both this permission and the permission you are seeking to assert if this call is to succeed.
Deny()	Ensures that until the end of the currently executing method, any request for the indicated permission will always be denied.
PermitOnly()	Similar to Deny() except that it causes any request for any permission other than the specified permission to be denied.

You'll notice that the Demand() method is somewhat unique because it is the method which is responsible for actually requesting that a permission be given to the executing code. The purpose of the other methods is to influence the result of calling Demand() if it is subsequently called within this method or any method called directly or indirectly from this method. In practice, you will rarely find you need to call Demand() directly because that is almost invariably handled by the classes in the framework class library. For example, if you try to use the System.IO.FileInfo class to open a file, that class "under the hood" demands the appropriate permissions before attempting to open the file.

None of these methods take any parameters. The specified permission is indicated by the object against which the methods are called. As far as the list of security permission classes is concerned, you can simply use Table 21.1 and knock Attribute off the name of each class. For example, corresponding to the attribute EnvironmentPermissionAttribute is a class EnvironmentPermission, which you can instantiate to define an environment permission, and then you call Assert(), Deny(), PermitOnly(), or Demand() against the EnvironmentPermission instance to control the permission. The security permission classes all derive from the class CodeAccessSecurity, which is the class that implements these four methods. Note that you need to check the documentation for details of the parameters to pass to each permission class constructor because it varies according to the nature of each permission.

Comments

Imperative security gives you a much finer degree of control than declarative security: You can place a call to set the security or request a permission at a precise point in a method, which means that, depending on the actual flow of execution, you have the option of not executing that permission if appropriate. For example, you might place the call to `Demand()` inside an `if` block. Alternatively, you can code imperative security so that the details of the permissions demanded are determined at runtime. On the other hand, there is no easy way for outside code to examine an assembly that uses imperative security to find out what security permissions will be required because there is no corresponding metadata to provide this information.

21.4. Viewing Security Policy Information

> You want to view the .NET security policy for your computer or network.

Technique

The usual tool for viewing security policy is in the .NET configuration tool, `mscorcfg.mmc`. This tool is a Microsoft Management Console (MMC) snap-in that you can normally find in the Control Panel, under Administrative Tools. When you launch the configuration tool, you see a series of nodes in the MMC treeview. Click on the runtime security policy node, and you have the choice to view security policy at the enterprise, machine, or user level, as shown in Figure 21.1.

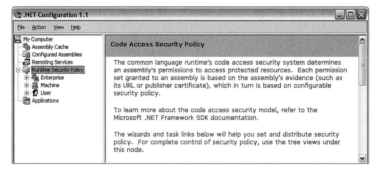

Figure 21.1   The .NET configuration tool.

The .NET Framework lets you set security policy for a Windows domain (Enterprise), for an individual computer (Machine), or for an individual user, with the principle that an action will not be permitted if any one of the security policies does not permit the action. However, when .NET ships out of the box, only the machine level has a substantial security policy set up by default. The other levels are available if you want to use them to add or customize security policy.

Viewing security policy is simply a question of navigating through the treeview in mscorcfg to identify the particular aspects of policy you want to examine. For example, Figure 21.2 shows the configuration tool displaying the permissions set for the LocalIntranet.

Figure 21.2   Viewing the permissions of a permission set.

Continuing this example, you can double-click on one of the permissions in the listview to examine the details of what actions covered by this permission have been granted or denied. Figure 21.3 shows the dialog box that opens if you examine the security permission for the LocalIntranet.

The .NET configuration tool is designed to allow you to manage security policy, which means that you can use it to edit the settings as well as to view them. If your intention is merely to view the current policy, then you should take care not to change anything. In Figure 21.3, the security permission is listed as read only because the LocalIntranet permission set is a system-defined set, which you cannot modify. However, in general you can edit permissions.

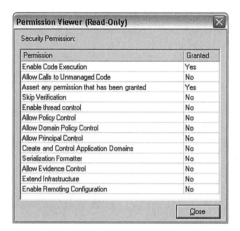

Figure 21.3   The security permission for the `LocalIntranet` permissionset.

You can use the .NET configuration tool to view most aspects of security policy using a friendly dialog-based user interface. However, its user interface very much focuses on drilling down into the details of security policy, which means it is not so good at presenting a broad overview of policy. However, two other options give you this overview. You can use a command-line security tool called `caspol`, or you can view the Extensible Markup Language (XML) files that define the security policy directly. However, both of these options mean you see the policy written out in plaintext format, which might make it harder to understand.

To use `caspol`, simply type `caspol` at the VS.NET command-line prompt. Typing `caspol` without supplying any options lists all the possible options. As far as viewing policy is concerned, the most useful flags are `-lg` (which lists code groups) and `-lp` (which lists permission sets—and generates a *lot* of output). Listing 21.2 shows typical `caspol` output for listing code groups.

Listing 21.2 `caspol` **Output**

```
C:\>caspol -lg
Microsoft (R) .NET Framework CasPol 1.1.4322.573
Copyright (C) Microsoft Corporation 1998-2002. All rights reserved.

Security is ON
Execution checking is ON
Policy change prompt is ON

Level = Machine

Code Groups:
```

Listing 21.2   **Coninued**

```
1.  All code: Nothing
    1.1.   Zone - MyComputer: FullTrust
        1.1.1.   StrongName - 0024000004800000940000000602000000240000525341310004 0
0000100010007D1FA57C4AED9F0A32E84AA0FAEFD0DE9E8FD6AEC8F87FB03766C834C99921EB23BE
79AD9D5DCC1DD9AD236132102900B723CF980957FC4E177108FC607774F29E8320E92EA05ECE4E82
1C0A5EFE8F1645C4C0C93C1AB99285D622CAA652C1DFAD63D745D6F2DE5F17E5EAF0FC4963D261C8
A12436518206DC093344D5AD293: FullTrust
        1.1.2.   StrongName - 00000000000000000400000000000000: FullTrust
    1.2.   Zone - Intranet: LocalIntranet
        1.2.1.   All code: Same site Web.
        1.2.2.   All code: Same directory FileIO - Read, PathDiscovery
    1.3.   Zone - Internet: Internet
        1.3.1.   All code: Same site Web.
    1.4.   Zone - Untrusted: Nothing
    1.5.   Zone - Trusted: Internet
        1.5.1.   All code: Same site Web.
Success
```

Each line of output in Listing 21.2 indicates the name of a code group and names the permission set assigned to that group. For example, the `Intranet` code group is assigned the `LocalIntranet` permission set. You can also use `caspol` to modify policy if you supply the appropriate flags.

The final option, that of directly viewing the configuration files, is the most advanced. It is the only way of viewing the security policy in its entirety, but it isn't for the faint-hearted. The policy files are XML files. The user-level file is located in a user-specific folder, and the machine- and enterprise-level files are named `security.config` and `enterprisesec.config` and are located in the folder `%WINDIR%\Microsoft.NET\ Framework\v1.1.4322\CONFIG`.

Note that you must take special care not to modify these files unless you know what you are doing, because if you introduce a syntax error, for example, you could break the CLR's security policy altogether.

Comments

If you have more than one version of the .NET Framework installed, each version independently maintains its own security policy, so you need to take care that you are viewing the correct policy. The Control Panel, Administrative Tools dialog shows separate .NET configuration tools for each version of the CLR. If using `caspol`, then you need to run `caspol` from the version of the VS.NET command prompt corresponding to the CLR version whose policy you want to view. These same considerations apply when using these tools to modify security policy, as described in the next two recipes.

21.5. Creating Code Groups

You want to create a new code group.

Technique

You use the same tools to create code groups that you do to view security policy: the .NET configuration tool, `caspol`, and editing the XML policy files directly. Modifying the XML files is not recommended, however, because of the risk of corrupting the files, so we consider here only the first two options.

If you are using the .NET Configuration tool, you should navigate to the code group that will be the parent of the new group you want to create. In many cases, it will be the All Code group. Then, you right-click and select New from the context menu that pops up. You see a series of dialog boxes that guide you through the process of creating the new group.

The first dialog, shown in Figure 21.4, offers you the choice between working through the remaining dialogs or simply supplying an XML file that specifies the details of the group. Unless you already have an XML file, it's usually easier to work through the dialogs: The XML file needs to be in a fairly precise format and must specify existing assemblies and managed classes that will implement the code group. You can find documentation on the XML procedure at

`http://msdn.microsoft.com/library/default.asp?url=/library/en-us/cpguide/html/cpconimportingnewsecuritycomponentstosecuritypoli-cyfromxmlfiles.asp.`

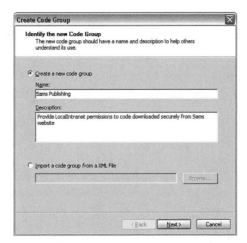

Figure 21.4   Creating a new code group.

Assuming you work through the dialog boxes, a dialog asks you to indicate the membership condition of the group. All the usual choices of membership conditions are possible: You can choose to base the membership condition on the site, the URL, the strong name, the assembly hash, the application directory, or some custom condition for which you separately supply the code to implement the condition.

Figure 21.5 shows the process of creating a code group, which determines permissions granted to code securely downloaded from the Sams publishing site. (Note that we specified a secure HTTPS URL. Using the HTTPS protocol is important when choosing a URL-based membership condition; otherwise, you open a security loophole that is vulnerable to Web site spoofing.) Note that in this dialog, as you choose different permission types in the drop-down list box, the remaining controls change to reflect the different data you need to specify for each condition type.

Figure 21.5   Adding a membership condition to a code group.

The next dialog box (in Figure 21.6, the last one before the final confirmation dialog) asks you to select the permission set that will be given to all code that qualifies for membership in the new code group.

If you prefer to use caspol to create a new code group, then you should specify the addgroup flag and details of the group. The format for the command is

```
caspol -addgroup <parent name> <mship> <pset_name> <flags>
```

<parent_name> is the name of the parent to which the new group will be added, <mship> is the membership condition, <pset_name> is the name of the permission set associated with the group, and <flags> indicates any other flags that you want to specify, supplying more information. (An obvious flag here is the name of the group.) Note that the order of supplying the parent name, membership condition, permission set, and flags is important.

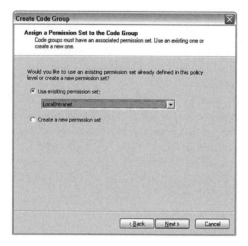

Figure 21.6   Specifying the permission set for a code group.

As an example, Listing 21.3 shows how we use `caspol` to add the same `SamsPublishing` code group, as shown earlier using the .NET Configuration tool.

Listing 21.3   **Adding a Code Group Using** `caspol`

```
C:\>caspol -addgroup All_Code -URL https://www.samspublishing.com/*
    LocalIntranet -name "Sams Publishing"
Microsoft (R) .NET Framework CasPol 1.1.4322.573
Copyright (C) Microsoft Corporation 1998-2002. All rights reserved.

The operation you are performing will alter security policy.
Are you sure you want to perform this operation? (yes/no)
y
Added union code group with "-URL" membership condition to the Machine level.
Success
```

Comments

Adding code groups can be a good way to customize your security policy to provide a framework for code provided in-house—even if the new code group simply uses an existing permission set. The beauty of the system is that if you later decide you need to modify the permissions that code running in this group requires, you can simply change the permission set that this code group uses, and the changes are automatically applied to all code that satisfies the membership condition for this code group. On the other hand, the security policy supplied out of the box by Microsoft is a carefully designed policy that will be useful in many situations, so you might want to think carefully before you fiddle with it. To avoid creating future security loopholes, make sure that you do not give any more permissions than are required for code to run.

21.6. Creating New Permission Sets

You want to create a new permission set.

Technique

Creating a code group is similar in many ways to creating a permission set, and the tools are the same: the .NET Configuration tool, `caspol`, and editing the XML policy files directly. Modifying the XML files is advanced, and usually not recommended, so we do not consider that option here.

If you want to use the .NET Configuration tool, you should use the treeview pane to navigate to the `Permission Sets` node under whichever level you want to set security policy for (enterprise, machine, or user). When you do that, you normally find that the listview contains a `Create New Permission Set` link, but if it's absent, you can just right-click on the `Permission Sets` node in the treeview and select `New` from the context menu. You then walk through a series of dialogs asking you to specify the details of the permission set to be created.

Because we've already discussed the equivalent process for creating a code group, we don't go show the dialogs in detail for a permission set here. The most significant dialog in the chain is arguably the one in Figure 21.7, which asks you to select the permissions to be included in the new permission set.

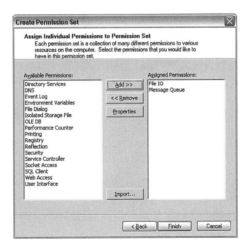

Figure 21.7   Adding permissions to a permission set.

Each time you click on the Add button to add a permission in this dialog, you see a new dialog asking you to specify the details of the access to resources to be granted (such as for the File IO permission, what files or folders the permission set should grant access to).

Just as for adding code groups, you have the option to import the permission set from an XML file. You can find details on the XML file format at the same URL mentioned earlier, `http://msdn.microsoft.com/library/default.asp?url=/library/en-us/cpguide/html/cpconimportingnewsecuritycomponentstosecuritypoli-cyfromxmlfiles.asp`.

If you want to use `caspol`, the required flag is `-addpset` (or `-ap`):

```
c:\> caspol -addpset File.xml
```

However, as the code snippet shows, adding a permission set using `caspol` requires you to have previously defined the permission set in an XML file, in the same format required for the .NET Configuration tool.

Comments

Many of the same precautions apply to adding new permission sets as to adding code groups, and you should think carefully about precisely what permissions you need to include in a permission set. Do not assign more permissions than are going to be required to avoid opening any security loopholes. Be very specific with the permissions you grant; for example, if your organization's code often needs access to certain folders on the C: drive, grant access to those folders, not to the entire C: drive. Be especially careful with permissions that allow the execution of unsafe or unmanaged code and permissions that allow access to the Registry or sensitive or operating-system files. If you find that you need to add a sensitive permission, consider whether this need is caused by poor code design, for example, using the Registry when you could have used isolated storage.

21.7. Determining Whether the Current User Is an Administrator

You want to determine whether the current user is an administrator.

Technique

To determine whether the current user is an administrator, you obtain a `WindowsPrincipal` object that represents the Windows account and group under which the current thread is running and then use the `WindowsPrincipal.IsInRole()` method. The following code shows the technique:

```
WindowsIdentity me = WindowsIdentity.GetCurrent();
WindowsPrincipal principal = new WindowsPrincipal(me);
bool isAdministrator = principal.IsInRole(WindowsBuiltInRole.Administrator);
if (isAdministrator)
        Console.WriteLine("Running under an administrator account ");
```

In this code, we first obtain a `WindowsIdentity` object, which represents the Windows account under which we are running. We easily obtain it using the static `WindowsIdentity.GetCurrent()` method. Given an identity, we can obtain the corresponding principal by passing the identity to the `WindowsPrincipal` constructor. Note that both `WindowsPrincipal` and `WindowsIdentity` are defined in the namespace `System.Security.Principal`:

```
using System.Security.Principal;
```

The previous code is useful for a single use of a principal object. However, if you want to repeatedly access role-based security information, you can gain a cumulative performance benefit by caching the information in the `Thread` object that represents the current thread. The following code illustrates this technique:

```
AppDomain.CurrentDomain.SetPrincipalPolicy(PrincipalPolicy.WindowsPrincipal);
WindowsPrincipal principal = (WindowsPrincipal)Thread.CurrentPrincipal;
bool isAdministrator = principal.IsInRole(WindowsBuiltInRole.Administrator);
if (isAdministrator)
        Console.WriteLine("Running under an administrator account ");
```

The use of the principal here is identical to that in the earlier code. However, you now directly obtain the principal from the `Thread` object, using the static `System.Threading.Thread.CurrentPrincipal` property. The first line of this code, which invokes the `SetPrincipalPolicy()` method of the `AppDomain` instance for the application domain in which the code is executing, is what instructs the current thread to retrieve and cache the current Windows principal. Note that `Thread.CurrentPrincipal` is explicitly cast to a `WindowsPrincipal` object. This property is defined to return an `IPrincipal` interface, reflecting the fact that it is possible to set other principal policies that do not link to Windows accounts.

Comments

You perform the test of whether you are running as an administrator using the `WindowsBuiltInRole` enumeration. You no doubt have guessed that this enumeration contains a value for each of the groups that can come out of the box with Windows. For example, to test whether the account you are running under is a power user, use the following:

```
bool isAdministrator = principal.IsInRole(WindowsBuiltInRole.PowerUser);
```

The possible values of the Windows `BuiltInRole` enum are `AccountOperator`, `Administrator`, `BackupOperator`, `Guest`, `PowerUser`, `PrintOperator`, `Replicator`, `SystemOperator`, and `User`.

21.8. Creating Login Pages with Web Forms Authentication

> You want to create a login page that uses Web Forms authentication and to
> which Web site visitors are always redirected if they access a resource to which
> they do not have permission.

Technique

To create a login page that uses Web Forms authentication, you Create a Web page itself
then modify the Web application's `web.config` file so that it uses forms authentication
and visitors are directed to the login page as appropriate. The design of the login page is
a matter of personal preference, but typically you create a page called `login.aspx`, which
will probably look something like Figure 21.8.

Figure 21.8   A typical Web Forms login page.

Once you create this page, the most significant aspect of the code is what you do in the
event handler to the `Login` button. This event handler needs to check the username and
password and authenticate the user if she is correct. One technique could look like
Listing 21.4.

Listing 21.4   **Handling a Login Event**

```
private void BtnLogin_Click(object sender, System.EventArgs e)
{
        // tbUsername and //tbPassword are the textbox controls,
        // cbRememberMe is the Remember Me checkbox
        if(tbUsername.Text == "simon" && tbPassword.Text == "password")
        {
                bool rememberMe = cbRememberMe.Checked;
                FormsAuthentication.RedirectFromLoginPage(
                                tbUsername.Text, rememberMe);
        }
        else
        {
```

Listing 21.4   **Continued**

```
                //lblError is an (initially blank) label control that
                        //can be used to display an error message
                lblError.Text =
                        "Login failed. Incorrect username or password";

    }
}
```

Here, we hard-coded a specific user and password check, but it's more likely that you will perform the check against some database of registered users. The key part of code is the call to the method, `RedirectFromLoginPage()`. It is a static method defined in the class `System.Web.Security.FormsAuthentication`. Calling this method does two things: It informs the ASP.NET runtime that the user has successfully logged in with the username supplied via the first parameter, and it returns control to the page the user had been trying to access, which prompts the automatic login. The second parameter passed to this method is a `bool` that indicates whether a permanent cookie identifying the user should persist on the browser's machine. As shown in Listing 21.4, this value is typically determined using a Remember Me or similar check box on the login page.

For obvious security reasons, you want to ensure that the login page is accessed over a secure connection. Typically, you can do so by placing it in a directory that is set up in Internet Information Services (IIS) to use the HTTPS protocol.

Next, you need to set up the `web.config` file to enable forms authentication. The relevant part of the file should look like this:

```
<authentication mode="Forms">
        <forms name="TestLoginPage1" path="/" loginUrl =
                "/TestLoginPage/Login.aspx"></forms>
</authentication>
```

The `<authentication>` tag indicates details of how we authenticate users, and setting the mode to `Forms` indicates we will be using a Web Form for this purpose. Then, the `<forms>` tag supplies a number of pieces of information, of which the main ones follow:

- `name` is the name of any cookie that should be stored to identify the user.
- `path` is the path used by the cookie.
- `loginUrl` is the URL of the login page that will be used for authentication.

The documentation details a number of other optional parameters.

Finally, we need to specify which users are allowed to access resources. In the simplest case—in which we don't allow anonymous users to access any page, but we allow authenticated users to access everything—the XML code would look like this:

```
<authorization>
    <deny users="?"></deny>
    <allow users="*" /> <!-- Allow all users -->
</authorization>
```

Note that the string ? indicates any unauthenticated user, whereas * indicates any user.

Comments

The elements inside the `<authorization>` element are processed in order until an element gives a definite result about whether the current user should be authorized to access the current resource—so the first elements always override later ones. You can set different rules for different pages either by putting pages in different directories, each with its own `web.config` file, or by putting the `<authorization>` element inside a `<location>` element to specify individual files.

21.9. Unsafe Code Using Pointers

You want to use unsafe code, such as code that uses pointers, in a C# program.

Technique

Writing unsafe code is relatively simple: You just need to ensure that the relevant code is contained in an `unsafe` block:

```
unsafe
{
    // unsafe code goes here
}
```

If you prefer, you can mark an entire method as unsafe:

```
static unsafe void DoSomethingUnsafe()
{
    // you can put unsafe code in this method without using unsafe blocks
}
```

Or for that matter, you can mark an entire class:

```
unsafe class MyUnsafeClass
{
    // all methods in this class can contain unsafe code
}
```

You also need to ensure that the compiler is set to compile unsafe code. At the command line, you pass the `/unsafe` flag:

```
csc /unsafe MyTest.cs
```

If you are using Visual Studio.NET, you need to set the project properties to allow unsafe code. This setting automatically passes the correct flag to the compiler.

You are now set up to write to whatever unsafe code you want. For example, you can use `sizeof` operator:

```
unsafe
{
        int x = sizeof(double);
        Console.WriteLine("Double occupies {0} bytes ", x);
}
```

As shown in Listing 21.5, you can use a stack-allocated array to circumvent .NET array bounds checking and thereby speed up processing.

Listing 21.5   **Avoiding Array Bounds Checking**

```
unsafe
{
        // allocate an int[10] array
        int *pArray = stackalloc int[10];

        // now do processing with *(pArray+i) to access element i, for example:
        for(int i=0 ; i<10 ; i++)
        {
                *(pArray+i) = 2*i;
        }
        // etc.
}
```

Comments

You should be aware that the usual provisos apply to unsafe code. Assemblies containing unsafe code might not be permitted to execute in partially trusted contexts. And of course, when using unsafe code, you risk corrupting data with pointer arithmetic bugs, so you need to take special care when debugging and checking your program logic.

21.10. Calling Native Unmanaged Code Using `PInvoke`

> You want to call some function that is implemented as unmanaged code in a dynamic link library (DLL), such as a Windows API function.

Technique

To call unmanaged code using the `PInvoke` mechanism, you follow these steps:

1. Identify the unmanaged DLLs that contain the unmanaged functions you want to call.

2. Provide `static extern` definitions for wrapper functions in the C# source code, marking the definitions with the `[DllImport]` attribute and selecting appropriate data types for the parameters and any return values, which are marshaled correctly to the types expected by the unmanaged function.

For example, suppose you are doing some graphics processing and you need to create a memory device context compatible with the screen. You normally use the Windows API function `CreateCompatibleDC()`, defined in the file `gdi32.dll`. This function has the following unmanaged C++ signature:

```
HDC CreateCompatibleDC(HDC hdc);
```

Here, `HDC` is simply a `typedef` for a 32-bit integer used as a handle. Good managed programming practice normally suggests we use a `System.IntPtr` instance to represent 32-bit integers that are intended to be used as Windows handles. Hence, a suitable managed wrapper definition follows:

```
class ClassThatDoesGraphicsProcessing
{
        [DllImport("gdi32.dll")]
        static extern IntPtr CreateCompatibleDC(IntPtr hdc);
```

You can now call the method as if it were a normal static class method. The following code shows this move and also includes the supporting (managed) code to create and release the screen device context to be passed to `CreateCompatibleDC()`:

```
// get a screen device context
// we assume this code is in a Windows.Forms.Control-derived class, hence
// we can call Control.CreateGraphics().
Graphics g = this.CreateGraphics();
IntPtr hdcScreen = g.GetHdc();

// get a memory device context
IntPtr hdcMemory = CreateCompatibleDC(hdcScreen);
// other code to use the device context
g.ReleaseHdc(hdcScreen);
```

Comments

In general, the hardest part of using `PInvoke` to call an unmanaged function is the choice of parameter type. Using an inappropriate type can decrease performance, but in general, you will find that the type you intuitively expect is often the most appropriate type. For example, if an unmanaged function expects a C-style string, then pass in `String`. If it expects a 16-bit integer, then pass in `short` or `ushort`, depending on how the integer is best interpreted in the managed code. For a 32-bit integer, pass in `int`, `uint`, or `IntPtr`, again depending on which one represents the most appropriate usage of the value. Notice that in many cases there is no one correct type: It is a question of what the most appropriate type is depending on the purpose of the parameter. In these cases, choosing an inappropriate type will not cause any bugs but will make your code harder to understand.

Although the security risks are similar for unsafe code and unmanaged code, the two types of code are conceptually very different. There is no need to use the `unsafe` C# statement or `/unsafe` compiler option to invoke unmanaged code. Your code will, however, need the unmanaged code security permission to execute.

The `PInvoke` wrapper functions are always declared as static members of a class. This step is not actually a requirement of the CLR, which simply requires a non-instance function, but is necessary because C# does not support global functions.

VI

Advanced Topics

22

Threading and Synchronization

22.0. Introduction

Using multithreaded techniques in an application can be an important way of improving responsiveness. It means, for example, that the user interface can remain active on one thread while the program is performing a lengthy database access on another thread. It also means that if the processor needs to wait while performing one task (such as retrieving some data over the network), that waiting won't cause the entire application to hang because other threads can still be doing other work. If you have a multiprocessor machine, multithreaded applications are likely to have higher performance because different threads can execute simultaneously on different processors, although you should note that on single-processor machines, this improvement does not apply.

The .NET Framework supports two means of multithreading: You can create your own additional threads explicitly, or you can ask for tasks to be performed on the Common Language Runtime (CLR) thread pool, with the CLR handling many of the details of thread management. In this chapter, we review the main programming details for both techniques. Either way, the additional threads created are normally known as worker threads. Strictly speaking, a thread is known as a worker thread if it is not running a message loop, whereas a thread executing a message loop is known as a user-interface thread, but because in practice additional created threads rarely have a message loop, we informally refer to all created threads in this chapter as worker threads. For Windows Forms applications, the main thread is a UI thread.

When using multithreaded techniques, you need to take care to synchronize access to variables across threads. If an operation to write data takes a number of machine instructions to execute, there is the possibility that the CPU will end a thread's timeslot while it is in the middle of writing data. If that happens and another thread attempts to read the data, then this thread could be reading garbage—which leads to subtle bugs known as thread synchronization bugs. The CLR and the Windows operating system both make available objects known as thread synchronization primitives, which allow you to manage the execution of threads to prevent these bugs occurring. We also examine this topic in this chapter.

Note that to compile the code in this chapter, you need to reference the `System.Threading` namespace:

```
using System.Threading;
```

There is no need to reference any additional assemblies because these classes are defined in `mscorlib.dll`.

22.1. Creating and Starting Threads

> You want to explicitly create and start a new thread to perform some process-ing task.

Technique

There are four things you need to do to explicitly create a thread:

1. First, you need to decide on an entry point method. In a sense, the purpose of the thread is to execute this method. It can be either a static or instance method of a class, but it must have the signature `void SomeMethod()`; that is, it cannot take any parameters nor can it return any value.

2. Next, you need to instantiate a delegate that refers to this method. Microsoft defined a delegate for this purpose, `System.Threading.ThreadStart`.

3. Now you can create the thread, represented by a `System.Threading.Thread` instance. The constructor for this class takes one parameter, a `ThreadStart` dele-gate, which indicates the method to be executed by the thread.

4. Finally, you start the thread using the `Thread.Start()` method.

When you put all these steps together, the code looks like this. First, let us suppose that this is the method you want to be executed on a new thread:

```
class WorkerClass
{
        public void DoSomeWork()
        {
                // code to do the work here
        }
}
```

You can get this method executed on a new thread using this code:

```
WorkerClass worker = new WorkerClass();
ThreadStart workerThreadStart = new ThreadStart(worker.DoSomeWork);
Thread workerThread = new Thread(workerThreadStart);
workerThread.Start();
```

Comments

The advantage of starting a thread this way is that you get a reference to a managed object that encapsulates the new thread. With the preceding code, that reference is stored in the `workerThread` variable. It gives you a fine degree of control over the new thread; if you store this reference, then any other running thread in your application can use the reference to manage the worker thread, for example, by pausing, resuming, or aborting it or by changing its priority.

Provided the new thread is not aborted, it exits normally when its entry method (with the preceding code, the `DoSomeWork()` method) exits. This exit can happen because the flow of execution has reached a `return` statement, or it can be because some unhandled exception has been thrown.

If another thread wants to know whether the worker thread has exited yet, it can use the `Thread.ThreadState` property:

```
if (workerThread.ThreadState == ThreadState.Stopped)
        Console.WriteLine("The worker thread has exited!");
```

The `ThreadState` property returns a `ThreadState` enumeration value: Possible return values appear in Table 22.1.

Table 22.1   `ThreadState` **Enumeration Values**

Value	Meaning
Unstarted	Thread hasn't started yet.
Running	Thread is currently executing.
WaitSleepJoin	Thread is asleep.
SuspendRequested	Thread is about to be suspended.
Suspended	Thread is suspended.
AbortRequested	Thread is in the process of being aborted.
Stopped	Thread has stopped.

The strict requirement that the thread's entry method cannot take any parameters means that you can't use parameters to pass any data to the thread. If you need to supply some initial data to the worker thread, the easiest way is to initialize some member variables of the object containing the thread's entry method before the thread starts. For example, suppose that the worker thread needs to know the name of some file that it is going to process. Modifying our earlier code gives the following, which first includes the `WorkerClass` definition:

```
class WorkerClass
{
        public WorkerClass(string fileName)
        {
                this.fileName = fileName;
```

```
        }
        string fileName;

        public void DoSomeWork()
        {
                // code to do the work here.
        }
}
```

Next is the code to create and start the thread:

```
WorkerClass worker = new WorkerClass(@"C:\ProcessMe.txt");
ThreadStart workerThreadStart = new ThreadStart(worker.DoSomeWork);
Thread workerThread = new Thread(workerThreadStart);
workerThread.Start();
```

Note that once the worker thread starts, you should take care to synchronize access to any of its member fields if those fields can be accessed by other threads. We show the techniques for doing so later in this chapter.

22.2. Pausing and Resuming a Thread

You want to temporarily prevent a thread from running for some period of time.

Technique

The technique depends on whether the thread to be suspended also happens to be the one deciding on the suspension.

If a thread decides that it itself should wait for a set period of time, then it can simply put itself to sleep by calling the static `Thread.Sleep()` method:

```
Thread.Sleep(500);
```

`Sleep()` takes an `int` parameter that indicates the time in milliseconds for which the thread should sleep. The thread simply relinquishes all its timeslots for this length of time, thus consuming virtually no CPU time.

If, on the other hand, one thread decides that another thread should pause, it can call the (instance) method, `Thread.Suspend()`:

```
// assume workerThread is a thread reference.
workerThread.Suspend();
```

When the controlling thread wants to reactivate the suspended thread, it calls `Thread.Resume()`:

```
workerThread.Resume();
```

Comments

Although these techniques represent the simplest ways to suspend a thread, we present them here only for completeness. Sleeping a thread for an arbitrary period of time in the ways shown here is fairly limited in usefulness other than for debugging purposes. Usually, the reason for suspending threads concerns thread or variable access synchronization or the need to call some method regularly at fixed time intervals. For these purposes, there are more powerful thread synchronization and timer classes available, which we discuss later in the chapter.

22.3. Aborting the Execution of a Thread

You want to abort a thread.

Technique

To abort a thread, you need a reference to the `Thread` object for the thread in question. You then simply call `Thread.Abort()`:

```
WorkerClass worker = new WorkerClass("ProcessMe.txt");
ThreadStart workerThreadStart = new ThreadStart(worker.DoSomeWork);
Thread workerThread = new Thread(workerThreadStart);
workerThread.Start();

// later on. . .
workerThread.Abort();
```

It can take a short time for the aborting thread to actually terminate execution. If other threads need to ensure the aborting thread has terminated before they resume execution, then they can call `Thread.Join()`, which simply blocks (that is to say, waits, consuming virtually no CPU time) until the thread in question stops. Thus, to abort a thread, and not carry on processing until the thread termination is complete, use the following:

```
workerThread.Abort();
workerThread.Join();
```

It is perfectly acceptable for a thread to abort itself:

```
Thread.CurrentThread.Abort();
```

However, in most cases, it is more usual for a thread to terminate execution by simply returning from its start method.

Comments

There are a number of reasons why you might want to abort a thread. One common reason is that the user clicked the Cancel button to cancel some lengthy task that was being carried out on a worker thread. Other reasons are that the task was simply taking too long or that some other condition arose which made it preferable to cancel the task.

Aborting a thread works under the hood by causing a `ThreadAbortException` to be thrown on the thread to be aborted. The code to throw this exception is actually injected into the code that the thread in question is running. If this thread is currently asleep or suspended, the CLR resumes it to handle the exception.

`ThreadAbortException` is a special exception supplied by the .NET Framework. It has the unique property that as soon as it is handled, it immediately rethrows itself. It causes all relevant `catch` and `finally` blocks that contain the current execution point to be executed, until the thread exits, which normally guarantees that appropriate cleanup is performed. As a result, aborting a thread is a relatively safe operation, something that was not possible with unmanaged code.

The time taken to abort a thread clearly depends on the code in any `catch` and `finally` blocks that must execute. Also, if the thread is currently executing unmanaged code, the CLR cannot inject the `ThreadAbortException` until it returns to managed code.

One consequence is that you can add your own code to take special action if a thread is aborted by adding suitable `catch` blocks:

```
catch (ThreadAbortException ex)
{
      // code to be executed if thread is to be aborted goes here
}
```

It is even possible for the thread that decided on the abort to supply extra application-specific information to the aborted thread; for example, this information might contain details of the reason for the abort. To do this, you must use a different overload of `Thread.Abort()`, which accepts an object reference as a parameter. For example, to supply a string containing the reason for the abort, use the following:

```
workerThread.Abort("User hit the Cancel button");
```

The supplied object reference is available to the aborting thread as the `ExceptionState` property of the thrown `ThreadAbortException`:

```
catch (ThreadAbortException ex)
{
      if (ex.ExceptionState != null)
            Console.WriteLine("Reason for the exception was: " +
               ex.ExceptionState.ToString());
}
```

There's one additional flexibility: The aborting thread can decide that it doesn't want to abort after all by calling the static `Thread.ResetAbort()` method. This normally happens inside a `catch` handler and prevents the `ThreadAbortException` from auto-rethrowing itself again. One example is if you want a thread to refuse abort requests because it has nearly finished its task:

```
// assume that perCentCompleted is an int that is being used to measure
// how near we are to completing our task.
catch (ThreadAbortException ex)
{
        if (perCentCompleted > 95)
                Thread.ResetAbort();
}
```

Note, however, that this technique cannot prevent the `ThreadAbortException` from being thrown initially—it only prevents it from being rethrown—so you still need to add code to recover the situation once the `catch` block executes if you want the thread to continue executing.

22.4. Changing the Priority of a Running Thread

You want a thread to run at a higher or lower priority, due to the relative urgency of the work it is doing.

Technique

Simply change the priority using the `Thread.Priority` property:

```
Thread.CurrentThread.Priority = ThreadPriority.Highest;
```

To change the priority of another thread (`workerThread` as in the preceding examples), use the following:

```
workerThread.Priority = ThreadPriority.Highest;
```

The choice of priorities comes from the `ThreadPriority` enumeration: possible values are `Highest`, `AboveNormal`, `Normal`, `BelowNormal`, and `Lowest`. If you don't set the priority explicitly, it defaults to `Normal`.

Comments

Be careful of changing thread priorities: in general, it's the kind of thing you should only do if you have a very good reason because of the risk of disrupting other tasks that have a lower priority. For example, a high-priority background thread that is engaged in intensive computations could prevent a user-interface thread from gaining any computer time and so prevent the application from responding to user input.

Setting the priority of a thread essentially provides a hint to the Windows operating system about the relative urgency of the work that thread is performing. Microsoft reserves the right to change the details of precisely how the operating system responds to these hints. However, for current versions of Windows, it is true to say that any thread is only ever given processor time when there are no higher-priority threads demanding that time. If there are any higher-priority threads, then low-priority threads are only able to execute while higher-priority threads are suspended or sleeping (for example, while waiting on thread synchronization primitives).

You should also bear in mind that thread priorities are only set relative to the process that contains those threads. Windows maintains a separate overall process priority for each process—and the process priority takes precedence over thread priorities. In other words, all threads in a high-priority process take precedence over all threads in a lower-priority process, no matter what the individual thread priorities. If you want to change the process priority, you should look up the `PriorityClass` property of the `System.Diagnostics.ProcessClass` class in the MSDN documentation. Bear in mind, however, that changing process priority is potentially even more dangerous than changing thread priority within a process because of the potential to prevent other processes from running. Don't do it unless you know what you're doing and you have an extremely good reason for changing priorities!

22.5. Using the `ThreadPool` to Perform Background Tasks

You want to have some task executed in the background on a thread supplied by the CLR.

Technique

The procedure to have a task executed on a background thread is similar conceptually to the procedure we discussed earlier for explicitly creating a thread to perform some task—except that a different delegate is involved and there is no need to set up the thread explicitly:

1. You must code an entry point method for the task. It can be either a static or an instance method of a class, but it must have the signature `void SomeMethod(object state)`. Note that, unlike the situation for a thread you create explicitly, this entry method accepts a parameter.

2. You instantiate a `System.Threading.WaitCallback` delegate to encapsulate the chosen method.

3. You pass this delegate to the static method `System.Threading.ThreadPool.QueueUserWorkItem()`.

Let's assume this is the method that you want executed on a background thread:

```
class WorkerClass
{
    public void DoSomeWork(object state)
    {
```

```
            // code for the task to be executed here
        }
}
```

You get it executed like this:

```
WorkerClass worker = new WorkerClass();
WaitCallback task = new WaitCallback(worker.DoSomeWork);
ThreadPool.QueueUserWorkItem(task);
```

That's literally all you have to do. Just as for explicitly creating a thread, you can supply data to the DoSomeWork() method by initializing fields in its containing class before you start the task running. However, when queuing a work item, there is an alternative technique: You can supply any additional data by using a two-parameter overload of QueueUserWorkItem():

```
WorkerClass worker = new WorkerClass();
WaitCallback task = new WaitCallback(worker.DoSomeWork);
string taskData = "This is extra data for the task";
ThreadPool.QueueUserWorkItem(task, taskData);
```

Although we used a string here, QueueUserWorkItem() is expecting an object reference for the second parameter, so you can pass in an instance of any class you want. The reference you pass here is available via the state parameter of the method executed—and is indeed the purpose of this parameter:

```
public void DoSomeWork(object state)
{
        if (state == null)
                Console.WriteLine("No initialization data was passed in");
        else
                Console.WriteLine("Data passed in was " + state.ToString());
}
```

Comments

The techniques shown before this recipe in this chapter involve explicitly creating and manipulating dedicated threads for certain tasks. By queuing a user work item, you are still arranging for the task to be performed on a new thread: the crucial difference is that instead of creating the thread in your code, you are asking the CLR to supply a suitable thread and to take control of managing that thread on your behalf. The benefit of doing so is higher performance if you are using multithreading extensively and are likely to have a large number of tasks to execute on different threads. The CLR selects a thread from a thread pool that it maintains. The thread pool consists of a group of threads that are normally asleep: When an item is queued to the pool, the CLR selects a thread from the pool, wakes it, and passes it your task to execute. Once the task finishes, the thread goes back to sleep. Waking the thread involves far less work than creating a brand new thread from scratch, hence the performance improvement. Using the thread pool also guarantees that you don't overload the CPU by creating too many threads because the number of threads in the pool is determined in advance by the CLR, based on what is appropriate to the software and hardware you are running. (Typically, it sets a maximum of 25 worker threads on a single-processor machine.) If all the threads are busy when a new request comes in, the CLR simply holds the request until a thread becomes free.

The disadvantage of using the thread pool is you don't get a great deal of explicit control over the thread. Notice that in the code we presented, at no point does the calling code receive a `Thread` reference that describes the thread on which the task will be performed. Without this reference, the calling thread cannot do tasks such as change the priority of or abort the worker thread. Your code also has no say in which of the thread-pool threads is used for a task; that is entirely at the discretion of the CLR, which in particular means there is no guarantee about whether successive queued tasks will execute on the same thread. There is also a startup cost: The thread pool is created dynamically the first time your code invokes it, but creating a thread pool is obviously more work than merely explicitly creating one thread. If you will be using the thread pool extensively in an application, then this startup cost is far outweighed by the accumulated performance benefits.

It's worth pointing out that when delegates are invoked asynchronously, the actual mechanism used under the hood by the CLR involves the thread pool. Hence, the code we presented here has virtually the same effect as invoking a delegate asynchronously, as discussed in Chapter 5, "Delegates and Events," and to some extent, it's a matter of personal preference which technique you adopt. Asynchronous delegates generally involve more code to set up the asynchronous operation but have the advantage that they feature inbuilt support for allowing the calling thread to monitor the progress of the operation—something that you need to code yourself if you are simply queuing items to the thread pool and you require that feature.

One important point about the thread pool is that thread-pool threads are background threads. They have no power to keep a process alive; a thread that does have that power is known as a foreground thread. Background threads are a concept introduced by the CLR: A process remains running as long as it contains active foreground threads. The CLR terminates a process as soon as all foreground threads finish.

This point means that you should not write code like this:

```
// program entry function
static void main()
{
        WorkerClass worker = new WorkerClass("");
        WaitCallback task = new WaitCallback(worker.DoSomeWork);
        string taskData = "This is extra data for the task";
        ThreadPool.QueueUserWorkItem(task, taskData);
}
```

The problem here is that the main thread queues a task to the thread pool and promptly exits. Because in this code the main thread is the only foreground thread, the CLR removes the entire process when that thread exits the `main()` method, and the queued work item will not have a chance to execute. If you are in a situation where the main thread is ready to exit the application, but there might be thread-pool threads still running, then it's important for the main thread to check whether background threads have finished their tasks. We discuss one technique for doing so using events later in this chapter.

This problem does not occur if you are starting a thread explicitly using `new Thread()` because new non–thread-pool threads are by default foreground threads. You can manually change the status of a thread that you have explicitly created by changing its `IsBackground` property:

```
workerThread.IsBackground = true;
```

This technique is not recommended for thread-pool threads because you are in effect interfering with the CLR's ability to manage these threads. (And if due to a bug in your program, you inadvertently leave a thread-pool thread in a foreground state, then it might become impossible for your application to exit.)

22.6. Creating an Application Timer

You want your application to perform some task on a background thread at regular intervals.

Technique

To have some background task performed at regular intervals, you must first define the method that will be called at the set intervals (the timer callback method). This method must have the signature `void MethodName(object state)`. As usual, this method can be a static or instance member of any class. Then, you should do the following:

1. Wrap this method in a `System.Threading.TimerCallback` delegate.

2. Instantiate a `System.Threading.Timer` object, passing it this delegate as well as information specifying the interval and an object reference containing any additional data you want to pass to the timer callback method.

First, assume that this method needs to be called at regular intervals:

```
class TimerHandler
{
        public void UpdateApp(object state)
        {
                Console.WriteLine("Timer got called again!");
        }
}
```

Now you arrange to have this method called on a timer:

```
TimerHandler timerHandlerObject = new TimerHandler();
TimerCallback timerCallback = new TimerCallback(timerHandlerObject.UpdateApp);
Timer timer = new Timer(timerCallback, null, 2000, 500);
```

This code shows that you must pass several parameters to the timer constructor. The first parameter is the delegate that identifies the timer callback method. The second parameter is passed to the timer callback method as the `state` parameter every time the timer has this method called. A typical use might be to provide information about the source of the timer, although you are free to simply use `null` as we did in this code. The third parameter is the time that the timer will wait until it first calls the timer callback method—known as the due time—and the final parameter is the interval between callbacks thereafter (the period). Both parameters are measured in milliseconds; so with the preceding code, the timer will start callbacks in two seconds and then repeat every half-second.

Note that there are several overloads of the `Timer` constructor, but they differ only in the data type used to specify the due time and period. You can pass the times in milliseconds as `long` or as `uint`, or, more interestingly, you can pass them as `TimeSpan` objects. The preceding code is completely equivalent to this:

```
TimerHandler timerHandlerClass = new TimerHandler();
TimerCallback timerCallback = new TimerCallback(timerHandlerClass.UpdateApp);
TimeSpan dueTime = new TimeSpan(0, 0, 0, 0, 2000);
TimeSpan period = new TimeSpan(0, 0, 0, 0, 500);
Timer timer = new Timer(timerCallback, "Hello", dueTime, period);
```

If you subsequently want to disable the timer, the easiest way is to use its `Change()` method to change the due time and timer interval to infinity:

```
timer.Change(Timeout.Infinite, Timeout.Infinite);
```

`Timeout.Infinite` simply returns the `int` value -1 which the timer interprets as infinite.

Comments

As you might expect from a chapter on multithreading, the `System.Threading.Timer` class uses multiple threads: In fact, the callback method is always executed on a thread-pool thread. Because the thread pool is used, you should be aware that there is no guarantee that the same thread will be used in successive timer callbacks.

Thanks to its use of the thread pool, this timer is, provided there are thread-pool threads free, highly accurate. It is the recommended timer to use if you need an accurate timer interval. However, the CLR does make two other timers available: `System.Windows.Forms.Timer` and `System.Timers.Timer`. The Windows Forms timer is event driven: It works by placing events on the message loop at intervals and therefore does not rely on multiple threads. It is simple to use in a Windows Forms application, but it is not very accurate because if the main thread is engaged in some other task when the timer event is due, the event simply sits on the message loop unprocessed until the main thread becomes free again. The `System.Timers.Timer` class is similarly event-based but is intended for Web server applications. We don't consider either of these timers in this book.

22.7. Synchronizing Variable Access Using the Monitor

You want to prevent multiple threads from accessing the same variable simultaneously.

Technique

If multiple threads might have access to some object, then the easiest way to synchronize access is by locking the object with the C# `lock` statement.

Suppose some variable x contains a reference to the object in question. Then, you simply enclose all code statements that access x in a `lock` block:

```
lock (x)
{
        // code that accesses x here.
}
```

The code enclosed in the `lock` statement is known as a protected block because it is protected against simultaneous variable access by multiple threads.

Bear in mind that x must be a reference type; it is not possible to use this technique on value types. If you need to synchronize access to a value type, the easiest way is to do this:

```
lock (typeof(v))
{
        // code
}
```

We assume v is the variable against which you need to synchronize access. Using `typeof(v)` simultaneously synchronizes access to all instances of v. It can hurt performance because threads might be blocked unnecessarily from simultaneously executing code that actually accesses different instances of the same type, but it is often the simplest solution. In many cases, the only other realistic alternative is to manually hold a boxed copy of v and perform all locks on this boxed copy rather than on v itself—but this alternative requires keeping careful track of boxed instances, so it is potentially difficult to implement without introducing subtle bugs.

You should be aware that when you pass a variable to a `lock` statement, what is important is the object that variable points to, not the variable itself. For example, if x and y both happen to refer to the same object, then the following two code statements are completely equivalent statements that have an identical effect on your program:

```
lock (x)
{
        // code that accesses x here.
}

lock (y)
{
        // code that accesses x here.
}
```

Comments

Although the syntax involved in locking a variable appears quite simple, you need to take considerable care in where you use the `lock` statement because there is a lot of potential for subtle thread synchronization bugs if you do not lock variables correctly. It's therefore worth reviewing precisely what a `lock` statement does.

The CLR internally implements a scheme by which it is able to place markers on objects to indicate that those objects are in use. When the statement `lock(x)` executes, the CLR first checks whether the object referenced by x is already marked as in use. If it is not marked as in use, then the CLR places a marker on the object and continues execution. This marker is removed when execution flow exits the `lock(x)` `{}` block. If, on the other hand, when execution hits the `lock(x)` statement, the CLR finds that the object referred to by x is already marked as in use by a different thread, then it puts the current thread to sleep, automatically wakes it when x becomes free, puts a new marker on x, and allows execution to continue into the protected block. In this way, we can guarantee that no two protected blocks of code that are locked against the same object will ever be simultaneously executed. Note that the locks are thread-specific: If the same thread executes nested `lock(x)` statements, then it will not be blocked because the CLR is only interested in preventing *different* threads from simultaneous access. Also note that locks on different objects are completely independent. Locks placed on any one object have no effect on any `lock` statements that refer to different objects.

With this understanding of how a `lock` statement works, we can now point out what to watch when using locks.

First, locking a variable is only effective if you protect all the blocks of code that might access that variable. Suppose you have a block of code that looks like this:

```
lock (x)
{
        // do something to x
}
```

But somewhere else is some code that can be executed by another thread:

```
// oops! Forgot to put a lock in here
x.DoSomethingToChangeItsValue();
```

x is now effectively unprotected because the second block of code does not check the lock on x. It is perfectly possible for both blocks of code to execute simultaneously, and the possibility of thread synchronization bugs arises.

You should also take care to avoid deadlocks. Deadlocks are situations in which threads are cyclically waiting for each other to exit protected blocks, which means all the threads concerned end up indefinitely blocked. A deadlock can happen if one thread executes code like this:

```
lock(x)
{
        // protected code
        lock (y)
        {
                // protected code
        }
}
```

Another thread executes this code:

```
lock(y)
{
        // protected code
        lock (x)
        {
                // protected code
        }
}
```

With this code is the risk that the first thread will place a lock on x at about the same time that the second thread places a lock on y. When the first thread hits the lock(y) statement, it blocks until the second thread releases its lock on y. However, that will never happen because the second thread is waiting for the first thread to release its lock on x! There are two ways to avoid deadlocks: You can either make sure that you write code that always places nested locks on variables in the same order, or you can use mutexes to obtain locks on multiple objects simultaneously, as discussed later in this chapter.

On the other side are situations in which it is not necessary to lock objects. Most notably, this situation arises with immutable objects. There is no need, for example, to ever protect code against simultaneous access to strings because System.String is immutable. Synchronization bugs can only occur if one thread might actually change the contents of an object while another thread is reading or writing to it. Because the contents of a string can never be changed, strings cannot normally be affected by thread synchronization bugs.

Under the hood, the `lock` statement is converted by the C# compiler into code that uses the class `System.Threading.Monitor`. This class is responsible for handling the thread synchronization. You can invoke `Monitor` methods explicitly if you prefer, but it's almost invariably simpler to use the `lock` statement and let the C# compiler take care of the implementation details. Although `Monitor` is not the only thread synchronization primitive, it is by far the most efficient because it is implemented entirely within the CLR. Some of the other thread synchronization classes that we consider in this chapter, including `ManualResetEvent`, `AutoResetEvent`, and `Mutex`, are in wrappers around Windows kernel thread synchronization primitives—which makes them more powerful in some ways but gives a bigger performance hit.

22.8. Using Events to Synchronize Threads

You want a thread to suspend execution until another thread indicates that it's okay for the first thread to proceed.

Technique

The technique here involves using `System.Threading.ManualResetEvent` or `System.Threading.AutoResetEvent`. For now, we consider `ManualResetEvent`. An event is a thread synchronization object that can be signaled or nonsignaled. The idea is that the thread that needs to suspend execution does so by invoking the method `ManualResetEvent.WaitOne()`. It allows the thread to proceed only if the event is signaled. If the event is not signaled, then the thread blocks until the event becomes signaled. Obviously, some other running thread needs to set the event to signaled when it detects that the first thread can continue.

In terms of code, you first need to instantiate the event. Because this event needs to be accessible to multiple threads, you might want to store it as a field of some class:

```
class ThreadSyncClass
{
        private ManualResetEvent syncEvent = new ManualResetEvent(false);
```

The event constructor takes a Boolean parameter that indicates whether the event should start signaled. The preceding code instantiates an event in the nonsignaled (blocking) state.

To make the executing thread block (wait) until the event is signaled, simply call this code:

```
syncEvent.WaitOne();
```

You can set an event to signaled like this:

```
syncEvent.Set();
```

Note that there is no limit to the number of threads that can call `ManualResetEvent.WaitOne()`. When an event is set to signaled, all threads that are waiting on it are unblocked and can resume.

Because the `ManualResetEvent` class wraps a native object, you should be sure to call `Dispose()` when you finish with it:

```
syncEvent.Dispose();
```

So far the discussion has concerned the `ManualResetEvent` class. All the preceding code would work equally well if `syncEvent` had been defined to be of type `AutoResetEvent`. The only difference between the classes is that if `AutoResetEvent.Set()` is called, then the event becomes signaled only very briefly, allowing any waiting threads to continue, but then immediately reverts to nonsignaled. In contrast, `ManualResetEvent` remains signaled until it is explicitly reset by calling its `Reset()` method:

```
syncEvent.Reset();
```

Comments

One common use for events is for worker threads to let the calling thread know when they finish some task; we indicated earlier that this step can be particularly important when queuing threads to the thread pool. To illustrate the technique in this context, we continue the earlier `QueueUserWorkItem()` example. Let's suppose that the main thread will queue some task and then carry on with some other work but will at some point reach a point where it can't do anything else until the worker thread finishes its task. Perhaps the main thread set the worker thread off retrieving some data from the network, but now the main thread needs to process that data. One possible solution to this problem using events follows.

The main thread executes this code:

```
ManualResetEvent taskFinished = new ManualResetEvent(false);

// assume WorkerClass.DoSomeWork() is the method to be queued
WorkerClass worker = new WorkerClass("");
WaitCallback task = new WaitCallback(worker.DoSomeWork);
ThreadPool.QueueUserWorkItem(task, taskFinished);

Console.WriteLine("background task is running");
// do any work here that can be done while the background task is still running

taskFinished.WaitOne();

Console.WriteLine("background task is done");
// do any work here that must wait until the background task is completed
```

Notice how the event is passed into the background task as the application-specific state data.

The code for the background task, the `DoSomeWork()` method, looks like this:

```
public void DoSomeWork(object state)
{
        ManualResetEvent finished = (ManualResetEvent)state;
        // put code to perform the task here
        finished.Set();
}
```

Notice how in this code the event used to synchronize the threads is passed to the worker thread as the `state` parameter.

In general, events are the simplest of the thread synchronization primitives and are used when you need to explicitly code the logic governing when threads should block. You use other, more sophisticated primitives for more specific scenarios; for example, you use the `Monitor` class behind the C# `lock` statement for synchronizing access to variables.

Other primitives include `Mutex` and `ReaderWriterLock`, both of which you also use for synchronizing access to variables and which we consider next.

`ManualResetEvent` and `AutoResetEvent`, along with `Mutex`, are all inherited from a base class, `WaitHandle`. It is in fact the `WaitHandle` class that provides the implementation of the `WaitOne()` method. In general, `WaitHandle` provides a .NET wrapper around the thread synchronization mechanism supplied by the Windows operating system.

22.9. Using Mutexes to Synchronize Multiple Objects, Avoiding Deadlocks

You want to synchronize access to several variables without using nested `lock` statements so that you avoid the possibility of deadlocks.

Technique

The technique for synchronizing access to multiple variables at the same time involves using a `Mutex`. In general, a `Mutex` provides similar features to the C# `lock` statement, although with a less friendly syntax. To use a mutex, you must instantiate a `Mutex` instance:

```
Mutex mutex = new Mutex();
```

You perform locking against this `Mutex` instance:

```
mutex.WaitOne();
// protected code goes here
mutex.ReleaseMutex();
```

Just as with events, you should make sure you dispose mutexes to free up their associated resources:

```
mutex.Dispose();
```

So far, we have not achieved anything you cannot do with a `lock` statement.

However, one of the benefits of a mutex is that you can set up multiple mutexes and use the static `WaitHandle.WaitAll()` and `WaitHandle.WaitAny()` methods to wait for all of or any of the mutexes simultaneously.

Suppose you have two mutexes, represented by variables `mutex1` and `mutex2`, and you only want to enter a protected block of code if both those mutexes are free. You use the following code.

First come the declarations of the mutexes:

```
Mutex mutex1 = new Mutex();
Mutex mutex2 = new Mutex();
```

Then you have the protected code block:

```
WaitHandle [] mutexArray = new WaitHandle [] {mutex1, mutex2};
WaitHandle.WaitAll(mutexArray);
// protected code
mutex1.ReleaseMutex();
mutex2.ReleaseMutex();
```

`WaitHandle.WaitAll()` takes an array of `WaitHandle` objects and blocks the thread until all those objects are simultaneously free. The method does not lock any of the objects until it is in a position to be able to lock them all simultaneously—thus eliminating the risk of this particular call causing a deadlock involving those objects. Note that, although we used mutexes here, there is no problem with using the `WaitAll()` method to synchronize against an array containing any other objects derived from `WaitHandle`.

Comments

It's worth pointing out the existence of another static method, `WaitHandle.WaitAny()`. This method has exactly the same syntax and effect as `WaitHandle.WaitAll()` except that it unblocks the thread and allows the protected code to execute as soon as any one of the objects in the array it is passed becomes free. It acquires a lock only on this one object. To enter a protected block if any one of two mutexes is free, you use the following:

```
WaitHandle [] mutexArray = new WaitHandle [] {mutex1, mutex2};
WaitHandle.WaitAny(mutexArray);
// protected code
mutex1.ReleaseMutex();
mutex2.ReleaseMutex();
```

Although mutexes are more flexible than the CLR's monitor, they are less efficient because they are not implemented internally within the CLR but instead wrap native Windows kernel objects. You should always use a `lock` statement unless there is some reason why you need the additional flexibility offered by a mutex.

It's worth pointing out one other nice feature of `WaitHandle.WaitOne()`: You can pass a maximum waiting time to it:

```
mutex.WaitOne(500, false);        // wait for 500 ms.
```

The time is measured in milliseconds, or you can pass in a `TimeSpan` object instead. The second parameter is a `bool`, which is only relevant when you are dealing with remoting and contexts, so we ignore it here. The ability to set a maximum waiting time provides another reason why in some circumstances, you might prefer to use a mutex rather than a `lock` statement. If you do set a waiting time, then `WaitOne()` returns `true` if the lock is successfully acquired and `false` if the wait times out. Hence, you should use this overload like this:

```
if (mutex.WaitOne(500, false))
{
        // protected code
}
else
{
        // error-handling code for when lock has not been acquired
}
```

`WaitHandle.WaitAll()` and `WaitHandle.WaitAny()` have similar overloads that work in the same manner.

22.10. Implementing Interprocess Communication Using a Mutex

You want to synchronize execution of some protected blocks of code between threads—but the threads are in different processes.

Technique

The general technique is similar to using a mutex to synchronize threads within one process, except that the mutex must be named and each process must instantiate a mutex object with the same name. For example, suppose we name the mutex `TestMutex`:

```
Mutex mutex = new Mutex(false, "TestMutex");
```

Here we pass two parameters to the `Mutex` constructor. We will examine the first (`bool`) parameter soon. What interests us here is the second parameter, the mutex name. What this constructor does is cause the Windows operating system to examine its internal table of mutexes to see whether a mutex with that name already exists. (Recall that under the hood, mutexes are Windows kernel objects.) If no such mutex exists, then a new one is created. If there is already a mutex of that name, however, the CLR simply attaches the new `Mutex` class instance to the existing mutex. If two applications are running and both execute the preceding line of code, the end result is that they each have a `Mutex` object that wraps the same underlying operating-system mutex.

Now we examine that first parameter to the constructor. This `bool` value indicates whether the mutex should be created in a state in which it is already owned by the current thread. Note the following line:

```
Mutex mutex = new Mutex(true, "TestMutex");
```

It is equivalent to writing the next lines:

```
Mutex mutex = new Mutex(false, "TestMutex");
mutex.WaitOne();
```

From now on, the procedure is the same as before. In each process, you have code like this to synchronize access:

```
mutex.WaitOne();
// protected code here
mutex.ReleaseMutex();
```

Because both processes have access to the same mutex, the fact that two threads might be in different processes is completely irrelevant: The synchronization works just as if the threads were in the same process.

Comments

The ability to synchronize cross-process in this way graphically shows the real underlying power of mutexes. It also provides a useful, albeit limited, means of cross-process communication.

You do need to be careful with the choice of name for the shared mutex because there is the theoretical possibility that an unrelated process might attempt to create a mutex and by coincidence give it the same name and thereby unintentionally end up sharing your mutex. To avoid this problem, make sure that the string you choose for the name is likely to be unique. `TestMutex` is not a good name in production code. Choosing a `Guid`—or for that matter any random string—as a name is quite a good way to ensure uniqueness. You just need to ensure that all processes that intend to share the mutex are aware of the name, which you might choose to do by hard-coding the name.

Note that the underlying mutex kernel object remains alive until all CLR `Mutex` instances that refer to it are disposed or finalized. So take special care with named mutexes to ensure that you call `Dispose()` on them when you have finished with them.

22.11. Synchronizing Resource Access Using Reader/Writer Locks

> You want to synchronize access to some data. The data in question is read more often than it is updated, so the synchronization should be optimized for frequent reads.

Technique

In this situation, the normal technique is to use a `ReaderWriterLock`. As with mutexes, synchronization is performed against the lock itself rather than against the data.

You first need to instantiate the lock:

```
ReaderWriterLock rw = new ReaderWriterLock();
```

If some code needs to read the protected data, the code looks like this:

```
rw.AcquireReaderLock(500);
// protected code here
rw.ReleaseReaderLock();
```

Note that the `AcquireReaderLock()` method takes an `int` parameter which indicates the maximum time in milliseconds that you want to wait for the lock. In this code, we specified half a second. As with other thread synchronization primitives, an `ApplicationException` is thrown if this period times out. You can pass a `TimeSpan` instead of an `int` to this method, but you must pass in a parameter: There is no default no-timeout overload for this method. If you want the thread to wait indefinitely for the lock, then you should pass −1 as an `int`.

If, on the other hand, some code needs to write to the protected data, you code this:

```
rw.AcquireWriterLock(500);
// protected code here
rw.ReleaseWriterLock();
```

`AcquireWriterLock()` has exactly the same semantics as `AcquireReaderLock()`.

Comments

The point of `ReaderWriterLock`, of course, is that you only need to synchronize access to some data if at least one thread is actually writing to the data. It is not possible for thread synchronization bugs to occur if it's simply a case of multiple threads reading data at the same time because the data is always in a consistent state. `ReaderWriterLock` is designed to take account of this optimization: A thread that has a reader lock never blocks any other threads that merely want to acquire reader locks. However, if a thread acquires a writer lock, then it blocks all other threads until the writer lock is released. Note that writer locks also take priority, in the sense that if any thread is even waiting for a writer lock, the CLR does not grant any more threads reader locks: The writer lock gains access first. This process ensures that a writer lock doesn't get blocked out for a long time while reader threads ask for reader locks.

In terms of overhead, a `ReaderWriterLock` is slower than a monitor. However, if many threads are likely to want to read data that is only rarely written to, then you gain performance benefits from using it because in general threads are blocked less often. This point is especially true if the operations that involve reading the data are lengthy operations.

22.12. Getting and Setting Thread Data Using Thread Local Storage

You want to store some data in such a way that each thread keeps its own copy of the data.

Technique

There are two different techniques available for maintaining thread-local storage in .NET: You can use a thread-local static field in a class, or you can use dynamic local data store slots.

To mark a static field as local to a thread, simply mark it with `System.ThreadStaticAttribute`:

```
[ThreadStatic]
static int x;
```

Note that initializing thread-static fields in a static constructor is a bad idea because the static constructor is only executed once, which means only the copy of the field that is used by that thread gets initialized. Any copies associated with other threads that access the class still have their default initial values of zero/null. So you are best off not initializing these variables in any static constructor but assuming that for each thread they start as zeroed-out values.

Thread-local dynamic data store slots are far more versatile. To use them, you first call the static method, `Thread.AllocateDataSlot()` to allocate a slot:

```
LocalDataStoreSlot slot = Thread.AllocateDataSlot();
```

This method returns a `System.LocalDataStoreSlot` reference, which refers to a data slot that you can use to store one object reference. For example, to store a string reference in this slot, use the following code:

```
string s = "Hello";
Thread.SetData(slot, s);
```

You can retrieve the stored data with the static `Thread.GetData()` method, which returns an object reference:

```
string retrievedString = (string)Thread.GetData(slot);
Console.WriteLine(retrievedString);
```

`GetData()` returns `null` if no data is placed in the slot associated with the `LocalDataStoreSlot` parameter that it is passed.

So far, this process simply looks like a roundabout way to store an object reference. The key, however, is that a given `LocalDataStoreSlot` reference always accesses a thread-specific data slot. So with the preceding code snippet, the call to `Thread.GetData()` only retrieves the string `"Hello"` if it is executed on the same thread that executed the previous `SetData()` call. If that same statement with the same slot reference as a parameter is expected on any other thread, then it returns `null` (unless that other thread also previously used that `LocalDataStoreSlot` to store some object reference).

There are no restrictions on how many local data stores a given application, or a given thread, can use:

```
LocalDataStoreSlot slot = Thread.AllocateDataSlot();
LocalDataStoreSlot slot2 = Thread.AllocateDataSlot();
LocalDataStoreSlot slot3 = Thread.AllocateDataSlot();
Thread.SetData(slot, "Hello!");
Thread.SetData(slot2, "Hello again!");
Thread.SetData(slot3, "Bye!");
```

Comments

Which of these two techniques you use depends largely on your situation. In general, using thread-local static fields is only possible if you know at compile time which data you need to store local to threads and whether the data is static. If you need to store instance fields in thread-local storage, or you need to determine dynamically at runtime which data must be stored in thread-local storage, then you need to use the `LocalDataStoreSlot` method.

The simplest way to store instance fields in thread-local storage is to use a field of type `LocalDataStoreSlot` and wrap it with a property. If we assume that thread-local storage is required for a field of type `MyLocalType`, the code would look like this:

```
class MyClass
{
        LocalDataStoreSlot tlsField = Thread.AllocateDataSlot();

        MyLocalType TlsField
        {
                get
                {
```

```
                return (MyLocalType)Thread.GetData(slot);
    }
    set
    {
        Thread.SetData(slot, tlsField);
    }
    }
}
}
```

Bear in mind that in most cases, explicit thread-local storage is only important for fields of types. Variables defined locally to a method are normally available only in that method, and therefore to the thread that is executing that method, unless such variables are explicitly passed to some code being executed by another thread.

23

Reflection

23.0. Introduction

This chapter looks at a powerful feature within the .NET Framework known as *reflection*. Reflection is the ability to programmatically view the contents of an assembly by inspecting its individual modules. The modules in turn contain several different types, which themselves contains several members. This hierarchical structure is implemented within .NET as a series of collections contained within the classes in the `System.Reflection` namespace.

Reflection is a concept that is easy to grasp but difficult to interject into an application design unless you have intimate knowledge of the problem domains that reflection is best suited for. The applicability of reflection within a certain application is called out throughout this chapter as you look into areas such as dynamic code generation, dynamic invocation, and plug-in architectures.

23.1. Viewing Assembly Information

You want to load an assembly and ascertain certain properties about it.

Technique

The first step you must perform before viewing anything about an assembly is to load it. Call the `LoadFile` static method defined in the `Assembly` class within the `System.Reflection` namespace. The following example demonstrates loading an assembly from a open file dialog. The examples in this chapter create an assembly-viewer application:

```
private void mnuOpen_Click(object sender, System.EventArgs e)
{
    if( openFileDialog1.ShowDialog(this) == DialogResult.OK )
```

```
    {
        try
        {
            mAssembly = Assembly.LoadFile( openFileDialog1.FileName );
            PopulateTree();
        }
        catch( Exception ex )
        {
            MessageBox.Show( ex.Message );
        }
    }
}
```

The `CodeBase` and `EscapedCodeBase` properties are Uniform Resource Identifier (URI)–based paths to the location of the assembly, and the `Location` property specifies the location using regular file-system notation. You can determine the Common Language Runtime (CLR) version an assembly needs to run by inspecting the `ImageRuntimeVersion` property.

Even though the `Assembly` class contains only a few properties, you can see more information by calling the `GetName` method. It returns an `AssemblyName` object that you can use to determine information such as the major and minor version as well as the ability to get and set the public key token with strong named assemblies.

Comments

One common theme that you will see as you work with the reflection classes is the use of Get*Xxxx* methods instead of properties. This design choice remains consistent with method names and their associated parameters throughout the `System.Reflection` namespace.

The `AssemblyName` class mentioned earlier plays a vital role within the architecture of the CLR. To avoid file collisions, which occur as a result of installing an older version of a file over a newer version (referred to as *DLL Hell*), the `AssemblyName` class gives identity to the assembly it represents. Rather than use the older methods of simply placing a file in a location, the CLR instead uses the `AssemblyName` class of an assembly to determine whether it's the correct assembly being requested by an application. The name of an assembly consists of a simple name, which is generally the name of the file, the version number, a cryptographic key pair, and a value denoting culture information. This identity, called the `FullName`, is used by any applications that reference the assembly, guaranteeing that an older version, which subsequently will have a different version and cryptographic key pair, is not accessed when a newer version is expected and known to be compatible.

23.2. Examining Module Information

You want to enumerate each module within an assembly and inspect their properties.

Technique

The `GetModules` method of an `Assembly` object returns an array of `Module` objects that you can use to view the properties of each module defined in an assembly. The `Module` class contains fewer properties and methods than the `Assembly` class simply because it's a container of types with no need for identity information such as an assembly. In the following code, which continues from the previous recipe, each module within an assembly is enumerated and placed in a node underneath the assembly name within the `TreeView`:

```
private void PopulateTree()
{
    TreeNode newNode = new TreeNode( mAssembly.GetName().Name );
    newNode.Tag = mAssembly;
    tvAssembly.Nodes.Add( newNode );

    foreach( Module mod in mAssembly.GetModules() )
    {
        AddModule( mod, newNode );
    }
}

private void AddModule( Module mod, TreeNode parent )
{
    TreeNode newNode = new TreeNode( mod.Name );
    newNode.Tag = mod;
    parent.Nodes.Add( newNode );
}
```

Comments

The `Module` class represents the second tier within the assembly hierarchy. Without first going through an assembly, you can't get to a module. Modules themselves are generally just accessed via the CLR when navigating through the hierarchy because most information is contained within the types that it contains. In other words, you work with assemblies and you work with data types, but rarely do you have to work at the module level. Additionally, if you decide to implement a multifile assembly in which code written in one .NET programming language is placed within the same assembly as code written in a different .NET language, then you have to work on the module level (at least during build time).

23.3. Examining Constructor Information

You want to extract information about all constructors within a type defined in a module.

Technique

The previous two recipes looked at assemblies and modules. This recipe is the first of five that looks at the next rung in the ladder, types. If you look within the documentation and compare the number of parameters that the Type class has compared to the Module or Assembly, you'll see why we consider them the main workhorse within an assembly. Consider creating a class that represents declarations for classes, value types, arrays, interfaces, pointers, enumerations, and structs, and you'll know why so many properties exist within the Type class.

Each Type contains a collection of members. In Listing 23.1, you view any members that are marked as constructors by calling the GetConstructors method defined in the Type class. It returns a ConstructorInfo array, allowing you to view detailed properties specific to a constructor. The alternative to this method is to use the GetMembers method to enumerate all the members using a MemberInfo array. Either method works, although using GetMembers requires the extra steps of accessing the MemberType property of each MemberInfo and casting the MemberInfo object to the appropriate member type information class corresponding to the MemberType property. The following example continues the assembly-viewer tool by enumerating each Type object within a Module and proceeds to add any constructors to the TreeView control underneath a Constructors node as shown in Listing 23.1.

Listing 23.1   **Enumerating and Examining Constructors**

```
private void AddModule( Module mod, TreeNode parent )
{
    TreeNode newNode = new TreeNode( mod.Name );
    newNode.Tag = mod;
    parent.Nodes.Add( newNode );

    foreach( Type t in mod.GetTypes() )
    {
        AddType( t, newNode );
    }
}


private void AddType( Type t, TreeNode parent )
{
```

Listing 23.1   **Continued**

```
    TreeNode newNode = new TreeNode( t.Name );
    newNode.Tag = t;
    TreeNode curType;
    TreeNode curMember;

    // note that GetMembers could have been called to enumerate
    // all the members defined in this type.  However, this program
    // will separate them out based on what they are

    // get constructor information
    curType = new TreeNode( "Constructors" );
    foreach( ConstructorInfo constructor in t.GetConstructors() )
    {
        curMember = new TreeNode( constructor.Name );
        curMember.Tag = constructor;
        curType.Nodes.Add( curMember );
    }
    newNode.Nodes.Add( curType );

    // continued...
```

Comments

This recipe and the following four break up the investigation of a `Type` object. `Type` objects are really where the bulk of the functionality for each assembly is contained, with the previous levels of the hierarchy reserved for organizational tasks. This recipe looks at how to enumerate all the available constructors within a given type.

You'll see that a lot of the remaining recipes within this chapter utilize the `Type` class to perform various operations. The introduction for this chapter mentioned that integrating reflection into an application might be difficult because it might be hard to think of how you could use it. You can use the `Type` class and the associated reflection methods for several different things, some of which appear in later recipes. One possible use is automatic documentation generation. The `Type` class contains a `BaseType` property, which contains the inherited `Type` of the current object. Using this information and other methods, you can construct a class hierarchy automatically during runtime. If your application utilizes an object model for any reason, this tool is a valuable debugging tool that you can use.

23.4. Examining Methods Within a Type

You want to view information about all the methods and their associated parameters within a type.

Technique

To enumerate each defined method within a `Type`, call the `GetMethods` method, which returns an array of `MethodInfo` objects. A method can contain 0 or more parameters, which you access through the `GetParameters` method defined in the `MethodInfo` class. Listing 23.2 enumerates all the methods of a given type and in turn enumerates all the parameters of that method by using the techniques just described. The final result for the assembly-viewer application is a list of methods and their parameters, which constitute individual nodes underneath a `Methods` node of the `TreeView` control.

Listing 23.2   **Enumerating Methods and Their Parameters**

```
// get methods
curType = new TreeNode( "Methods" );
foreach( MethodInfo method in t.GetMethods() )
{
    string methodString = method.Name + "( ";
    int count = method.GetParameters().Length;

    foreach( ParameterInfo param in method.GetParameters() )
    {
        methodString += param.ParameterType;
        if( param.Position < count-1 )
            methodString += ", ";
    }
    methodString += " )";
    curMember = new TreeNode( methodString );
    curMember.Tag = method;
    curType.Nodes.Add( curMember );
}
newNode.Nodes.Add( curType );

// continued...
```

Comments

Until this point, you should see a pattern emerging based on the application program interface (API) of the reflection classes. The design of these classes centers on logical method naming. For instance, if you want to get an array of parameters, you logically call the `GetParameters` method, and because parameters are contained within methods, you can deduce that the `GetParameters` method is defined in any member of a `Type` that contains parameters such as the `MethodInfo` and `EventInfo` member types. One thing that wasn't shown is the ability to further investigate a method by accessing various properties. For instance, `IsStatic` lets you know whether the method is a static method, and `IsVirtual` naturally specifies whether a method is virtual. The `MethodInfo` contains several `IsXxxx` methods, allowing you to fully investigate every possible attribute associated with a method.

23.5. Displaying Event Information

You want to determine the events that a type supports within a module.

Technique

To enumerate all the supported events within a `Type`, call the `GetEvents` method, which returns an array of `EventInfo` objects. To determine the data type of the delegate that can bind and listen for this event, use the `EventHandlerType` property, which returns a `Type`. Most events allow an unlimited number of bound listeners. This technique is known as *multicasting*. If an event supports this technique, the `IsMulticast` property returns `true`:

```
// get events
curType = new TreeNode( "Events" );
foreach( EventInfo curEvent in t.GetEvents() )
{
    string eventInfo = curEvent.Name;
    eventInfo += " Delegate Type=" + curEvent.EventHandlerType;
    curMember = new TreeNode( eventInfo );
    curMember.Tag = curEvent;
    curType.Nodes.Add( curMember );
}
newNode.Nodes.Add( curType );

// continued...
```

Comments

Events are specialized methods that invoke bound delegates when they are fired. When you create an event, the event is translated into a class, which contains member methods and overloaded operators to facilitate the addition and removal of event listeners called *delegates*. All this work occurs behind the scenes for the developer creating the event within the class and goes to show how well the event model within the .NET Framework is implemented.

In this recipe and the next, you will see overlap between the member type being discussed and an associated member type. As just mentioned, an event causes additional methods to be added to your class for event-listener addition and removal. If you view the output as a result of calling the `GetMethods` method defined in the `Type` class, you see these `Methods` even though they aren't visible when you create your application. We mention this point solely because if your application utilizes reflection, you realize that extra methods are created, which you might want to ignore based on your application design.

23.6. Displaying Property Information

You want to inspect individual properties in a given type definition.

Technique

The `GetProperties` method defined in the `Type` class returns an array of `PropertyInfo` objects. These objects represent the list of available properties and their associated types that an object supports. Properties can support a `get` or `set` method or both for client access. To determine which methods a given property supports, use the `CanRead` or `CanWrite` properties defined in the `PropertyInfo` class. Based on the values of these properties, you can inspect the corresponding methods using the technique from Recipe 23.4, "Examining Methods Within a Type," to view the property's `get` and `set` methods. To obtain an array of `MethodInfo` objects, call the `GetAccessors` method, or to individually retrieve a single `get` or `set` method, you can call the `GetGetMethod` or `GetSetMethod` methods.

A property can also be defined as an indexer for a class. This indexer contains parameters that a client uses within brackets to retrieve information from the type. Recipe 23.4 demonstrated how to access the `ParameterInfo` object for a given method, and you use the same process for indexer properties. By calling the `GetIndexParameters`, you can enumerate a `ParameterInfo` array to retrieve each parameter declared for an indexer.

The code for this recipe represents the final portion of the assembly-viewer application that was built sequentially in the last recipes. The application uses a `TreeView` control to display assembly information in hierarchical form and a `PropertyGrid` to display individual information for each node as it is clicked. This information is stored within the `Tag` property for each node and is assigned to the `PropertyGrid` whenever you click a new node within the `TreeView`, as shown in the `tvAssembly_AfterSelect` method.

Listing 23.3   **Enumerating Class Properties**

```
// get properties
curType = new TreeNode( "Properties" );
foreach( PropertyInfo property in t.GetProperties() )
{
    curMember = new TreeNode( property.Name );
```

Listing 23.3 **Continued**

```
            curMember.Tag = property;
            curType.Nodes.Add( curMember );
    }
    newNode.Nodes.Add( curType );

    parent.Nodes.Add( newNode );
}

private void tvAssembly_AfterSelect(object sender,
    System.Windows.Forms.TreeViewEventArgs e)
{
    if( e.Node.Tag != null )
    {
        pgObject.SelectedObject = e.Node.Tag;
    }
    else
    {
        pgObject.SelectedObject = null;
    }
}
```

Comments

Properties utilize a special syntax, which is later translated into methods when the Microsoft Intermediate Language (MSIL) code is generated. This method of property implementation is likely a successor to the methods employed in the Active Template Library (ATL) within Visual C++. However, whereas a developer in ATL has to manually create the `get` and `set` methods for property implementation, C# uses a special syntactical construct to mentally distinguish a property from a method. The sample code for this recipe lists properties defined in a specified `Type`. However, if you compare the results with that of the `MethodInfo` enumeration, you see where the two overlap. For instance, a class deriving from `System.Windows.Forms.Form` contains a property named `BackColor`. If you view the list of `MethodInfo` objects, you also see two methods named `get_BackColor` and `set_BackColor`. Depending on your application design, you might not want this duplication, which means you have to filter out all property getter and setter methods, a technique explained in Recipe 23.8, "Searching Assemblies Using Custom Search Techniques."

23.7. Searching Assembly Information Using Filtering

You want to examine specific type data by using a filter.

Technique

The previous recipes used various Get*Xxxx* methods to return an array of methods, parameters, events, and properties. Each one of these cases used an empty parameter list. However, each method also contains another overloaded version, which accepts a number of flags. These flags allow you to filter the returned items based on certain criteria. The BindingFlags enumerated data type contains the FlagsAttribute, allowing you to use it as a bit field to specify several flags at once. Table 23.1 lists the valid values that you can use with reflection. As an example, to return all the methods of a Type that are private static methods, use the Static and NonPublic BindingFlags, as shown in the following code:

```
foreach( MethodInfo method in someType.GetMethods( BindingFlags.Static
  | BindingFlags.NonPublic ) )
{
    MessageBox.Show( method.Name );
}
```

Table 23.1   BindingFlags **Values**

Value	Effect
DeclaredOnly	Only returns members at current hierarchy level. Does not return inherited members.
Instance	Only returns instance members, excluding any static members.
Static	Specifies that static members should be returned.
Public	Returns members with public access permission.
NonPublic	Returns members that are marked as protected or private.
FlattenHierarchy	Returns any static members defined in inherited types.

Comments

The assembly-viewer application up to this point displays a great deal of information about an assembly by enumerating each module, each module's type, and each type's individual members. Additionally, the members are each categorized based on the programmatic construct they define, which includes methods, events, and properties. However, if you compare the member nodes within the tree to the actual member declarations within a specific type, you notice that only public members appear. This behavior is the default behavior of all the GetXxxx reflection methods. To include both public and nonpublic, you have to use the technique discussed in this recipe by utilizing BindingFlags.

All that you need to perform reflection is a Type object. This chapter explicitly loaded an assembly using an OpenFileDialog, which was subsequently enumerated to extract type information. However, you can also use an instantiated object for reflection by calling the GetType method defined for every .NET object. Theoretically, you can call the GetType method of an object and perform a FindMembers call with a BindingFlags.NonPublic to retrieve all the private members within a Type. Furthermore, since the FieldInfo contains a method named GetValue, you'll also be able to get the current value of a private member variable for a Type defined in an assembly that some other developer created. Can you see the problem as it relates to security here? Fortunately, this type of field access is under tight control with .NET security. Without the property ReflectionPermission, you cannot do this move. Any attempt to do so without permission results in a thrown SecurityException. Code access security is discussed in Chapter 21, "Securing Code."

23.8. Searching Assemblies Using Custom Search Techniques

You want more control when searching by using a custom search for assembly type information.

Technique

The last recipe demonstrated how to specify flags to control the information returned when calling various reflection methods. Custom searching allows you to control what gets returned based on a custom criteria algorithm that you define. Custom searching involves the FindMembers method defined within the Type class. In addition to MemberTypes and BindingFlags values used within the first two parameters, a MemberFilter delegate is used as a callback for each found member, allowing you to determine whether it fits your necessary criteria. The MemberFilter delegate uses a MemberInfo object and a second parameter that contains the custom search information you designate. This object is passed into the FindMembers method as the last parameter. Within the delegate, use the MemberInfo object along with the object data you created to determine whether the member fits the specified criteria. Returning true from the delegate means a match was successful.

Listing 23.4 shows an application called asmgrep, although it doesn't purport to achieve the immense functionality of the UNIX grep utility. The object used as filter criteria is obtained on the command line and is placed within an ArrayList. It represents a list of strings to search for. If any Type or any Type's corresponding members are the same as one of the values in the ArrayList, a successful match is made.

Listing 23.4   **Searching for Types Using Custom Searching**

```
using System;
using System.Reflection;
using System.IO;
using System.Collections;

namespace _8_CustomSearch
{
    class Class1
    {
        [STAThread]
        static int Main(string[] args)
        {
            if( args.Length <= 1 )
                return ShowUsage();

            ArrayList filterStrings = new ArrayList();

            // copy search strings to an array
            for( int i = 1; i < args.Length; i++ )
                filterStrings.Add(args[i]);

            // load assembly referenced in first cmd line arg
            Assembly asm = Assembly.LoadFile( args[0] );
            if( asm == null )
            {
                return ShowUsage();
            }

            // create the member filter delegate
            MemberFilter filter = new MemberFilter( OnCustomSearch );

            foreach( Module module in asm.GetModules() )
            {
                // enumerate through all types and search each member
                foreach( Type t in module.GetTypes() )
                {
                    // first check to see if the type name matches
                    if( filterStrings.Contains( t.Name ) )
                        Console.WriteLine( "Found type {0}", t.Name );

                    MemberInfo[] foundMembers = t.FindMembers( MemberTypes.All,
                      BindingFlags.Public | BindingFlags.NonPublic |
                      BindingFlags.Static | BindingFlags.Instance |
                      BindingFlags.DeclaredOnly,
                        filter, filterStrings );
```

Listing 23.4   **Continued**

```
                    foreach( MemberInfo member in foundMembers )
                    {
                        Console.WriteLine( "Found member {0} which is a {1}" +
                        " defined in {2}.", member.Name, member.MemberType,
                        t.Name );
                    }
                }
            }
        return 0;
    }

    public static bool OnCustomSearch( MemberInfo member, object filter )
    {
        // does the member name equal a string in the filter?
        ArrayList al = (ArrayList) filter;
        if( al.Contains( member.Name ))
            return true;

        // check the member type also
        if( al.Contains( member.MemberType ))
            return true;

        return false;
    }
    static int ShowUsage()
    {
        Console.WriteLine( "asmgrep <assemblyname> <string 1 string 2" +
        " ... string n>\n" );
        return -1;
    }
  }
}
```

Comments

Using `BindingFlags` lets you customize a search to a great degree. However, the search only allows you to inspect certain attributes about a member. Custom searching allows you to create a custom search using specific search criteria that can key off any other property information contained in the `MemberInfo` class. In the preceding example, the key was the `Name` property and the `Type` property, with the search criteria being a list of strings that determine equality. Another example could be to key off the `DeclaringType` property to determine the members that are declared as members of a certain type, allowing you to narrow the member information to the members supported by a certain class for instance.

The example for this recipe demonstrates yet another useful application of reflection. Although it doesn't support the advanced feature set of a real grep utility, it does lay the necessary framework to create such an application. To further refine the application, allow it to search all the assemblies contained within the Global Assembly Cache. Additionally, allow regular expressions on the command line as search criteria. If you do these things, you will have an application that lets you quickly determine the appropriate assembly a given type is defined in, which is valuable when adding assembly references to a project. If you are so inclined to follow up and make these additions, send us a copy, will you?

23.9. Creating Dynamic Assemblies

You want to programmatically generate an executable assembly.

Technique

Dynamic assembly generation is the act of programmatically creating a .NET assembly at runtime from within your application. The System.Reflection.Emit namespace contains all the classes you need to create an assembly. This recipe looks at a particular application of dynamic assembly generation called the Animal Builder. In essence, the application asks the user a series of questions about a particular animal she wants to create. Once the questions are finished, the application proceeds to generate a class library containing a new class with two fields, a constructor and a public method that can then be used within another application. The initial steps for the application simply entail getting the answers from the user and setting properties within the AnimalBuilder class.

Listing 23.5   **Programmatically Creating Assemblies**

```
using System;
using System.Reflection;
using System.Reflection.Emit;
using System.Threading;

namespace _9_DynamicAssembly
{
    class Class1
    {
        [STAThread]
        static void Main(string[] args)
        {
            string input;
            AnimalBuilder builder = new AnimalBuilder();

            Console.WriteLine( "Welcome to the .NET Animal Builder!" );
```

Listing 23.5   **Continued**

```
        Console.WriteLine( "This program lets you build an animal and " +
                            " save it as an assembly" );

        input = GetInput( "What type of animal do you want?" );
        builder.AnimalType = input;

        input = GetInput( "What sound does the animal make?" );
        builder.AnimalSound = input;

        input = GetInput( "How many sounds will it make before it gets" +
                            " hoarse (no pun intended)?" );
        builder.SoundsBeforeHoarse = Int32.Parse(input);

        input = GetInput( "Where would you like to save this animal?" );
        builder.BuildAndSaveAnimal( input );
    }

    static string GetInput( string question )
    {
        Console.Write( question + ": " );
        return Console.ReadLine();
    }

    public class AnimalBuilder
    {
        private string animalType;
        private string animalSound;
        private int sounds;

        public string AnimalType
        {
            get
            {
                return animalType;
            }
            set
            {
                animalType = value;
            }
        }

        public string AnimalSound
        {
            get
            {
```

Listing 23.5 **Continued**

```
                return animalSound;
        }
        set
        {
            animalSound = value;
        }
    }

    public int SoundsBeforeHoarse
    {
        get
        {
            return sounds;
        }
        set
        {
            sounds = value;
        }
    }
    public void BuildAndSaveAnimal( string assemblyPath )
    {
    }
        }
    }
}
```

As you can see, the BuildAndSaveAnimal method is blank. It is the dynamic assembly generation method that will take all the property values within the class along with a location to save the final assembly.

The first step in creating an assembly is creating an assembly name by creating an AssemblyName object and setting its Name parameter. Note that it is not the same as the filename used for the assembly. Creating assemblies involves the use of an application domain. Because every .NET assembly runs within the confines of an application domain, you already know that your current application has an application domain that you can use. Calling the Thread.GetDomain method returns the active application domain for your current application, as shown in the following code:

```
public void BuildAndSaveAnimal( string assemblyPath )
{
    // create an assembly name
    AssemblyName asmName = new AssemblyName();
    asmName.Name = animalType;

    // get current appdomain
    AppDomain domain = Thread.GetDomain();
```

Now that you have a name for the assembly and an application domain to create it in, you are ready to generate the assembly in memory. Call the `DefineDynamicAssembly` method. For this example, we are creating a class library, so the second parameter to this method is `AssemblyBuilderAccess.Save`. If it were an executable assembly, you could set the value to `Run` or `SaveAndRun` to utilize the dynamic invocation techniques described in the next recipe. The `DefineDynamicAssembly` method returns an `AssemblyBuilder` object, which is the first stop in the assembly hierarchy.

```
// get an assembly builder from the appdomain
AssemblyBuilder asmBuilder = domain.DefineDynamicAssembly(
   asmName, AssemblyBuilderAccess.Save );
```

Earlier recipes mentioned that assemblies contain a hierarchical organization for constructs defined in them. At the top level is the assembly, followed by one or more modules, each of which defines zero or more types. Each type can also define zero or more members. Therefore, the next step after creating the assembly is to build a module. Call the `DefineDynamicModule` method defined in the `AssemblyBuilder` class created in the previous step:

```
// get a module builder from the assembly builder
ModuleBuilder modBuilder = asmBuilder.DefineDynamicModule(
   animalType, assemblyPath );
```

At this point, you are ready to start defining the types that make up the module. For this application, the only module type defined is a class. To create a new class, call the `DefineType` method from the `ModuleBuilder` object created earlier. The first parameter is the name of the class, and the second parameter is a bit field containing any necessary `TypeAttributes`. For this class, the only necessary attribute is `TypeAttributes.Public`. The method returns a `TypeBuilder` object, which will be used to define two member fields, a constructor and a public method:

```
// create a new public class
TypeBuilder typeBuilder = modBuilder.DefineType( animalType,
  TypeAttributes.Public );
```

The next step is to define the two fields that are used. If you recall from the beginning of this recipe, the `AnimalBuilder` class uses two properties relating to the sound the animal makes and how many times that sound is emitted before the animal's voice becomes hoarse. Therefore, create two fields by using the `DefineField` method of the `TypeBuilder`, specifying the variable name, the variable type, and any necessary `FieldAttributes`, as shown in the following code. These two fields will be referenced later when the constructor body is created, so save each of the returned `FieldBuilder` objects:

```
// add a new field
FieldBuilder soundFld = typeBuilder.DefineField( "Sound", typeof(string),
                     FieldAttributes.Private );
```

```
FieldBuilder countFld = typeBuilder.DefineField( "Count", typeof(int),
                       FieldAttributes.Private );
```

So far, the steps in creating the dynamic assembly haven't been too difficult. Unfortunately, it doesn't stay that way. When you create methods within a dynamic assembly, there is no way to assign C# code to the method bodies. Instead, you have to use an ILGenerator object to emit actual intermediate language (IL) code within the body. Fortunately, the ILDasm tool is able to generate IL code given an assembly. With that knowledge, you can create the code, compile it, and then view the IL to help you with this next step. Before you do so, however, you must first create the constructor. The code that follows creates a constructor using the DefineConstructor method from the TypeBuilder object created earlier. Next, an ILGenerator object is retrieved by using the GetILGenerator method defined in the ConstructorBuilder class. Finally, the IL is emitted using the ILGenerator. If you look at the Emit statements, you can see that the OpCodes class contains several properties corresponding to the available IL opcodes. In most cases, the conversion from IL to an OpCodes property is straightforward. Within the code, also take special note of the load string (ldstr), store field (stfld), and load integer constant (ldc.i4) opcodes. The second parameter for this emitted opcodes references properties within the AnimalBuilder class to retrieve their current values and the FieldBuilder object created earlier with the calls to DefineField:

```
// build the constructor
ConstructorBuilder constructor = typeBuilder.DefineConstructor(
    MethodAttributes.Public, CallingConventions.Standard, null );
ILGenerator gen = constructor.GetILGenerator();

gen.Emit( OpCodes.Ldarg_0 );
gen.Emit( OpCodes.Call, typeof(Object).GetConstructor(new Type[]{}));
gen.Emit( OpCodes.Ldarg_0 );
gen.Emit( OpCodes.Ldstr, animalSound );
gen.Emit( OpCodes.Stfld, soundFld );
gen.Emit( OpCodes.Ldarg_0 );
gen.Emit( OpCodes.Ldc_I4, sounds );
gen.Emit( OpCodes.Stfld, countFld );
gen.Emit( OpCodes.Ret );
```

The constructor method body just shown simply stores the values of the AnimalBuilder class in the dynamically generated class variables of the dynamic assembly using assignment statements. The final step in creating the dynamic assembly is to create the public method of the class. This step unfortunately is a little more involved than the constructor body created earlier. The procedure to actually create the method, however, is similar to the procedure used to create the constructor. To create a new method, call the DefineMethod function defined in the TypeBuilder, passing the name of the method; any MethodAttributes; the CallingConvention, which can simply be set to null if no special convention is needed; and an array of Type object corresponding to the parameter list of the method. Because this method does not use parameters, the array is empty.

After the method is created, the IL code is emitted. The example shown demonstrates how to emit labels within IL code. First, two labels correspond to the branching that occurs as a result of a for loop. Whenever a label needs to be set within IL, call the MarkLabel method defined in the ILGenerator class, passing one of the labels created. One thing to note is that the labels aren't similar to labels used within common programming languages in that no special name is used. The ILGenerator generates the correct label, which incidentally corresponds to the memory location of an instruction, whenever it is used. The branch (br) and branch-if-less-than (blt.s) instructions use the labels created and cause a branch to occur at the point where the MarkLabel method is called. To compare the ILGenerator code with the actual IL code, the IL code is placed within comments following the Emit recipe.

Listing 23.6   **Emitting IL Code**

```
// add the hoarse method
MethodBuilder hoarseMethod = typeBuilder.DefineMethod( "MakeHoarse",
    MethodAttributes.Public, null, new Type[]{} );
ILGenerator gen = hoarseMethod.GetILGenerator();

// create labels for branching
Label endLoop = gen.DefineLabel();
Label beginLoop = gen.DefineLabel();

// create Console.WriteLine MethodInfo
MethodInfo writeLine = typeof(Console).GetMethod( "WriteLine",
                        new Type[]{typeof(string)});

gen.DeclareLocal( typeof(int) );
gen.Emit( OpCodes.Ldc_I4_0 );
gen.Emit( OpCodes.Stloc_0 );
gen.Emit( OpCodes.Br_S, endLoop );
gen.MarkLabel( beginLoop );
gen.Emit( OpCodes.Ldarg_0 );
gen.Emit( OpCodes.Ldfld, soundFld );
gen.EmitCall( OpCodes.Call, writeLine, null );
gen.Emit( OpCodes.Ldloc_0 );
gen.Emit( OpCodes.Ldc_I4_1 );
gen.Emit( OpCodes.Add );
gen.Emit( OpCodes.Stloc_0 );
gen.MarkLabel( endLoop );
gen.Emit( OpCodes.Ldloc_0 );
gen.Emit( OpCodes.Ldarg_0 );
gen.Emit( OpCodes.Ldfld, countFld );
gen.Emit( OpCodes.Blt_S, beginLoop );
gen.EmitWriteLine("...a muffled sound emanates..." );
gen.Emit( OpCodes.Ret );
```

Listing 23.6   **Continued**

```
// MakeHoarse IL Code
/*
    IL_0000:   ldc.i4.0
    IL_0001:   stloc.0
    IL_0002:   br.s        IL_0013
    IL_0004:   ldarg.0
    IL_0005:   ldfld       string ConsoleApplication1.Horse::Sound
    IL_000a:   call        void [mscorlib]System.Console::WriteLine(string)
    IL_000f:   ldloc.0
    IL_0010:   ldc.i4.1
    IL_0011:   add
    IL_0012:   stloc.0
    IL_0013:   ldloc.0
    IL_0014:   ldarg.0
    IL_0015:   ldfld       int32 ConsoleApplication1.Horse::Count
    IL_001a:   blt.s       IL_0004
    IL_001c:   ldstr       "...a muffled sound emanates from the animal."
    IL_0021:   call        void [mscorlib]System.Console::WriteLine(string)
    IL_0026:   ret
*/
```

The `MakeHoarse` method simply uses a `for` loop to output the animal sound the specified number of times. When the count has been exceeded, a message states that the animal can no longer speak and the method exits. At this point, the necessary information
for the assembly has been created, and the final step is to generate it. For each `Type` that
is defined, call the `CreateType` method. This application creates only a single class so
this is done once. Finally, you call the `Save` method defined in the `AssemblyBuilder`
class, which generates and writes the assembly to a file ready to be referenced by an
application:

```
typeBuilder.CreateType();

// save final assembly
asmBuilder.Save( assemblyPath );
}
```

Comments

Dynamic assembly generation might seem odd at first, and like type discovery, using
reflection might be difficult in figuring where an application can use it. However, you
can see evidence of its use within the .NET Framework. For example, the `RegEx` class is
used for regular expressions. One of its methods is named `CompileToAssembly`, which
takes a currently loaded `RegEx` object and compiles its current state to an assembly. This
step allows portability using regular expressions in that a regular expression that matches

URLs, for instance, can be compiled to an assembly for reference in other applications. Therefore, rather than manually add the regular expression for a URL to a project, which is a rather lengthy expression, you can simply add a reference to the generated assembly in your new project.

As another example, you can create an application that utilizes various image resources. Rather than simply store these images within a directory where any user can edit or view them, you can automatically generate an assembly containing the image resources. As resources are added or removed, the assembly is regenerated, providing a single file that dynamically provides data file support. In the future, you will start to see some interesting applications with dynamic assembly generation.

23.10. Performing Dynamic Invocation

You want to call a method using late binding.

Technique

Until this point in the book, your applications always knew the data type of any objects used and their corresponding method names, events, and properties. This concept is known as *early binding* because the object is known to you at compile time. *Late binding* is the term when you create an object and call its methods at runtime without your application knowing its underlying type beforehand.

To dynamically invoke a method within a type, you must first load an assembly and find the appropriate method defined in a certain type you want to call. You use the filtering or custom searching techniques discussed in earlier recipes or enumerate all types within an assembly and search each type's methods. Once you find the appropriate method, you have a `MethodInfo` object, which defines an `Invoke` method used for dynamic invocation. The first parameter to the `Invoke` method is a reference to an object. Call the `CreateInstance` method defined in the `Assembly` class, and pass the name of the `Type` you want to create. The second parameter is an array of objects specifying the parameters to the method. Each element within the array must be the correct data type, and its index must correspond to the index of the parameter within the parameter list. The following example uses the objects created within the dynamic assemblies from the previous recipe. When a directory is specified as a command-line argument, the application enumerates all DLL assemblies and searches for a `MakeHoarse` method within each type defined in each assembly. If the method is found, the object is created using `CreateInstance`, and the `MakeHoarse` method is called using the `Invoke` method.

Listing 23.7   **Loading Assemblies and Invoking Methods**

```
using System;
using System.IO;
using System.Reflection;
```

Listing 23.7 **Continued**

```
namespace _10_DynamicInvocation
{
    class Class1
    {
        [STAThread]
        static void Main(string[] args)
        {
            if( args.Length < 0 )
            {
                ShowUsage();
                return;
            }

            if( Directory.Exists( args[0] ) == false)
            {
                Console.WriteLine( "Cannot find specified directory." );
                return;
            }

            // enumerate all dll files in directory
            foreach (string fileName in Directory.GetFiles( args[0], "*.dll" ))
            {
                // load assembly
                Assembly curAsm = Assembly.LoadFile( fileName );

                // enumerate each type in assembly
                foreach( Type t in curAsm.GetTypes() )
                {
                    // look for MakeHoarse method
                    MethodInfo hoarseMethod = t.GetMethod( "MakeHoarse" );
                    if( hoarseMethod == null )
                        continue;

                    // create object and invoke method
                    object curObj = curAsm.CreateInstance( t.Name );
                    hoarseMethod.Invoke( curObj, null );
                }
            }
        }

        static void ShowUsage()
        {
            Console.WriteLine( "Usage: animalfarm.exe <directory>" );
        }
    }
}
```

Comments

The technique outlined in this recipe is used extensively in typeless languages such as those defined within scripting engines. Because scripting languages are not compiled, there isn't a way to interject objects referenced within class libraries, so you must use late binding to instantiate objects and call their methods. For Component Object Module (COM) objects, this feature was used extensively for scripting through the `ITypeInfo` and `IDispatch` interfaces. Although definitely not for the faint of heart, the solution worked well even though it was somewhat complicated. .NET languages, however, have a plethora of classes and methods within the `Reflection` namespace to enable this functionality, making the procedure much easier and saving a developer time and a little bit of sanity in the process.

The process outlined in the earlier example is just one in myriad different ways to dynamically invoke a member method. In short, all that you need is a reference to a `Type` object or `MethodInfo` object. If you have a `Type` object, you can call the `InvokeMember` method, passing the name of the method and any parameters within an object array. This circumvents any need to create an instance of an object because the method performs that for you and returns the object instance in its return value. You can also use the `Invoke` and `InvokeMember` methods to set properties and even fields within an object.

23.11. Creating a Plug-In Architecture

You want to use reflection to create a plug-in architecture for your application.

Technique

Plug-in architectures are used extensively to add extra functionality to an application after it is built. Because there is no standard way of creating a plug-in architecture, this example merely presents a single way of creating such an architecture using the .NET reflection classes.

The example in this recipe ultimately ends up being a Notepad clone with the ability to extend it using plug-ins. The first step in any plug-in architecture implementation is to define a standard plug-in interface that all plug-ins must implement to successfully integrate with your application. You should create this interface within a class library so the plug-in developer can simply add a reference to the assembly and derive a class from the interface defined within. For the Notepad clone, the plug-in interface is simple enough. The interface contains a single `get` property named `Name` that returns the name of the plug-in, which is used as a menu item in the application's main menu. The interface also contains a method named `Execute`, which accepts a string parameter that contains text from the application. The plug-in method then performs its relevant operation on the text and returns the final result as a string. Here's the interface definition contained within the `NotepadPluginSDK` class library:

```
using System;

namespace _11_NotepadPluginSDK
{
    public interface INotepadPlugin
    {
        string Name
        {
            get;
        }

        string Execute( string selection );
    }
}
```

When a plug-in developer wants to create a new plug-in for the application, all he has to do is add a reference to the plug-in software development kit (SDK) assembly and implement the `INotepadPlugin` interface. The following example shows three different plug-ins contained within the same class library. The implementations aren't anything special because we still aren't dealing with reflection yet. That code is implemented within the Notepad application itself. The three plug-ins are implemented as follows.

Listing 23.8 Implementing Plug-In Interface Methods

```
using System;
using System.Text;
namespace _11_NotepadPlugins
{
    public class Rot13 : INotepadPlugin
    {
        public string Name
        {
            get
            {
                return "Rot13";
            }
        }

        public string Execute(string selection)
        {
            char[] chars = selection.ToCharArray( 0, selection.Length );
            for( int i = 0; i < chars.Length; i++ )
            {
```

Listing 23.8   **Continued**

```
                    if( chars[i] != '\r' && chars[i] != '\n' )
                        chars[i] += (char)13;
            }
            return new StringBuilder().Append(chars).ToString();
        }
    }

    public class UnRot13 : INotepadPlugin
    {
        public string Name
        {
            get
            {
                return "UnRot13";

            }
        }

        public string Execute(string selection)
        {
            char[] chars = selection.ToCharArray( 0, selection.Length );
            for( int i = 0; i < chars.Length; i++ )
            {
                if( chars[i] != '\r' && chars[i] != '\n' )
                    chars[i] -= (char)13;
            }
            return new StringBuilder().Append(chars).ToString();
        }
    }

    public class Reverser : INotepadPlugin
    {
        public string Name
        {
            get
            {
                return "Reverser";

            }
        }

        public string Execute(string selection)
        {
            char[] chars = selection.ToCharArray();
            Array.Reverse(chars);
```

Listing 23.8 **Continued**

```
            // fix \r\n reversal
            for( int i = 0; i < chars.Length; i++ )
            {
                if( chars[i] == '\r' ) chars[i] = '\n';
                else if( chars[i] == '\n' ) chars[i] = '\r';
            }
            return new StringBuilder().Append(chars).ToString();
        }
    }
}
```

The Notepad application itself is a Windows Form–based application containing a main menu and a `TextBox` control for the content. The main menu contains a `File` menu, allowing for such operations as creating a new file, opening an existing file, and saving and exiting the application. The `Plugins` menu is initially empty because we are using late binding to find plug-ins when the application runs.

Within the form constructor, shown in the following code, an `ArrayList` is created to hold all the plug-in instances as they are created. Next, each DLL assembly located within the application's `plugin` subdirectory is loaded. Next, each module in the assembly is enumerated to capture any modules within a multifile assembly. Within each module, every defined `Type` is enumerated using the `GetTypes` reflection method, and a search is performed on each `Type` for the `INotepadPlugin` interface. This step uses the custom searching technique described in Recipe 23.8, "Searching Assemblies Using Custom Search Techniques." If the interface is implemented on a certain `Type`, the corresponding object is created using the `Activator.CreateInstance` method, and the return value is cast to the `INotepadPlugin` interface. At this point, you have an instance of an object that is known to implement the interface, and you are free to call any properties and methods, which is what the next step performs. After the plug-in object instance is added to the `ArrayList` of plug-ins, the `Name` property is accessed and added to the `Plugins` menu item within the main menu. Additionally, an event handler for the menu item is passed in. When the user clicks a certain plug-in menu item, the event handler grabs the corresponding plug-in instance from the `ArrayList` and calls the `Execute` method, passing either the selected text if any exists or the entire text of the `TextBox`.

Listing 23.9 **Creating a Text Editor with Plug-in Support**

```
using System;
using System.Drawing;
using System.Collections;
using System.ComponentModel;
using System.Windows.Forms;
using System.Data;
```

Listing 23.9   **Continued**

```csharp
using System.IO;
using System.Reflection;
using _11_NotepadPluginSDK;

namespace _11_NotepadWithPlugins
{
    public class Form1 : System.Windows.Forms.Form
    {
        private System.Windows.Forms.MainMenu mainMenu1;
        private System.Windows.Forms.MenuItem menuItem1;
        private System.Windows.Forms.MenuItem mnuNew;
        private System.Windows.Forms.MenuItem mnuOpen;
        private System.Windows.Forms.MenuItem mnuSave;
        private System.Windows.Forms.MenuItem mnuSaveAs;
        private System.Windows.Forms.MenuItem mnuExit;
        private System.Windows.Forms.MenuItem mnuPlugins;
        private System.Windows.Forms.MenuItem menuItem8;
        private System.Windows.Forms.TextBox tbContent;
        private System.Windows.Forms.OpenFileDialog openFileDialog1;
        private System.Windows.Forms.SaveFileDialog saveFileDialog1;
        private System.ComponentModel.Container components = null;
        private string fileName = null;
        private ArrayList plugins;

        public Form1()
        {
            InitializeComponent();

            plugins = new ArrayList();

            // enumerate files in plugin directory
            foreach( string fileName in Directory.GetFiles(
                    Environment.CurrentDirectory + @"\plugins", "*.dll" ))
            {
                // load assembly
                Assembly asm = Assembly.LoadFile( fileName );

                // get all modules in assembly
                foreach( Module module in asm.GetModules(false) )
                {
                    // for all types
                    foreach( Type t in module.GetTypes() )
                    {
                        // check to see if it supports the
                        // INotepadPlugin interface
```

Listing 23.9   **Continued**

```
                    foreach (Type iface in t.FindInterfaces(
                            new TypeFilter(PluginInterfaceFilter) ,
                            "INotepadPlugin" ))
                {
                    // create plug-in and add to menu
                    INotepadPlugin plugin = (
                     INotepadPlugin)Activator.CreateInstance(t) ;
                    plugins.Add(plugin) ;
                    mnuPlugins.MenuItems.Add( plugin.Name,
                     new EventHandler(mnuPlugin_Click) ) ;
                }
            }
        }
    }
}


protected override void Dispose( bool disposing )
{
    if( disposing )
    {
        if (components != null)
        {
            components.Dispose() ;
        }
    }
    base.Dispose( disposing ) ;
}

private void InitializeComponent()
{
    this.tbContent = new System.Windows.Forms.TextBox() ;
    this.mainMenu1 = new System.Windows.Forms.MainMenu() ;
    this.menuItem1 = new System.Windows.Forms.MenuItem() ;
    this.mnuNew = new System.Windows.Forms.MenuItem() ;
    this.mnuOpen = new System.Windows.Forms.MenuItem() ;
    this.mnuSave = new System.Windows.Forms.MenuItem() ;
    this.mnuSaveAs = new System.Windows.Forms.MenuItem() ;
    this.menuItem8 = new System.Windows.Forms.MenuItem() ;
    this.mnuExit = new System.Windows.Forms.MenuItem() ;
    this.mnuPlugins = new System.Windows.Forms.MenuItem() ;
    this.openFileDialog1 = new System.Windows.Forms.OpenFileDialog() ;
    this.saveFileDialog1 = new System.Windows.Forms.SaveFileDialog() ;
    this.SuspendLayout() ;

    // NOTE: Form initialization code removed for brevity
```

Listing 23.9   **Continued**

```
        this.ResumeLayout(false);

    }

    [STAThread]
    static void Main()
    {
        Application.Run(new Form1());
    }

    // callback used when searching for implemented interfaces
    public static bool PluginInterfaceFilter( Type typeObj, object criteria )
    {
        if( typeObj.Name == (string) criteria )
            return true;
        return false;
    }

    // Called when user clicks on a plug-in menu item
    private void mnuPlugin_Click(object sender, System.EventArgs e)
    {
        MenuItem item = (MenuItem) sender;
        INotepadPlugin plugin = (INotepadPlugin) plugins[item.Index];

        if( tbContent.SelectionLength > 0 )
            tbContent.SelectedText = plugin.Execute( tbContent.SelectedText );
        else
            tbContent.Text = plugin.Execute( tbContent.Text );
    }

    // the following methods perform normal notepad menu functionality
    private void mnuNew_Click(object sender, System.EventArgs e)
    {
        tbContent.Text = "";
        fileName = null;
    }

    private void mnuOpen_Click(object sender, System.EventArgs e)
    {
        if( openFileDialog1.ShowDialog() == DialogResult.Cancel )
            return;

        tbContent.Text = "";
        fileName = openFileDialog1.FileName;
        OpenText( fileName );
    }
```

Listing 23.9 **Continued**

```
private void mnuSave_Click(object sender, System.EventArgs e)
{
    if( fileName == null )
    {
        mnuSaveAs_Click( sender, e );
        return;
    }

    SaveText( fileName );
}

private void mnuSaveAs_Click(object sender, System.EventArgs e)
{
    if( saveFileDialog1.ShowDialog() == DialogResult.OK )
    {
        SaveText( saveFileDialog1.FileName );
        fileName = saveFileDialog1.FileName;
    }
}

private void mnuExit_Click(object sender, System.EventArgs e)
{
    this.Close();
}

private void OpenText( string fileName )
{
    StreamReader sr = File.OpenText(fileName);
    tbContent.Text = sr.ReadToEnd();
    sr.Close();
}

private void SaveText( string fileName )
{
    StreamWriter sw = File.CreateText(fileName);
    sw.Write( tbContent.Text);
    sw.Close();
}
    }
}
```

Comments

The example in this recipe tied in several techniques described in this chapter. It demonstrated how to load an assembly from the file system, how to enumerate all the modules and types within that assembly, and how to perform custom searching to find the specific item of interest. Furthermore, the example showed how to dynamically create an object at runtime.

In my opinion, plug-in architectures allow you to create an extremely flexible and versatile application. Although most plug-in architectures are designed to allow third parties to extend the functionality of an application, don't pass up using a plug-in architecture if you believe no one will create plug-ins. In some of our past projects, we created plug-in architectures solely for the purpose of allowing us to extend our own applications without messing around with the internals of the main source code.

24

COM Interoperability

24.0. Introduction

The .NET Framework introduced a radically different method of application development and deployment from the methods being used at the time. It was entirely natural
to express interoperability concerns with legacy components because a tremendous
amount of time and money was spent developing them. To alleviate these concerns, the
.NET Framework was designed to integrate with legacy and future Component Object
Model (COM) components with a minimal amount of work. Even though .NET has
been around for a few years, the COM is still being used extensively for component
development and is still supported within Visual Studio .NET 2003 with its additions to
the Active Template Library (ATL) 7.0. This chapter demonstrates how to effectively
integrate objects built using COM with your .NET application and vice versa.

24.1. Creating an ATL-Based COM Component

You want to create a COM object using Visual C++ .NET and ATL.

Technique

To create a simple COM object, select the ATL Project template from the list of Visual
C++ project templates. The object created in this recipe serves as a bridge to the
Windows command interpreter (cmd.exe), allowing a .NET object to send commands as
is done when running within a command console window. Recall that Chapter 16,
"ASP.NET," created an ASP.NET application that provided this functionality, albeit limit-
ed, through a browser interface to a remote server.

　　After the project is created, you have to create the main COM object that will be
used by a .NET application. Select Project, Add Class from the main menu, select the
ATL Simple Object template and give the object a name in the Short Name field. For

this project, we use the name CommandCom. Additionally, click on the Options tab and place a check mark in the Connection Points option. This move allows the COM object to fire events that will be handled within the .NET application created in later recipes.

At this point, you have a fully functional COM object that can be instantiated by a COM-aware language. Its functionality is severely limited, however, without any defined methods or properties. Within the Class View window, right-click on the ICommandCom interface and select the Add Method menu item. You must add this method to the ICommandCom interface rather than the CCommandCom class if you want to ensure that .NET applications can call the method. You'll notice that the return type for the method is disabled. This disabling is by design because all COM methods return a HRESULT data type, which is a 32-bit error code. Recipe 24.6, "Handling HRESULT Errors," provides further explanation of HRESULT return values. After giving the method a name—we use Run—you have to add any necessary parameters. A parameter can be marked as an in, out, or retval parameter type. These types sound just like their names: an in parameter is a value passed in by the callee, and the out and retval parameters are allocated and returned by the COM object. Additionally, retval circumvents the issue with return values because all COM methods (except one, but that's a different story) return HRESULTs.

The first parameter to the Run method is an in parameter whose data type is BSTR. A BSTR is known as a basic string, which internally is a wide character (two bytes per character) with a preceding value denoting its length. The second parameter is a retval parameter whose data type is BSTR*, denoting a pointer to a BSTR. Once the method is created, the Integrated Development Environment (IDE) opens the corresponding .cpp file at the location of the method, allowing you to add its definition, which appears in Listing 24.1.

Listing 24.1 **COM Object Method Implementation**

```
#include "stdafx.h"
#include "CommandCom.h"
#include ".\commandcom.h"
#include <atlfile.h>
#include <atlsafe.h>

void GetResult( LPTSTR fileName, BSTR* Result )
{
    USES_CONVERSION;

    CAtlFile file;
    ULONGLONG len;
    LPBYTE lpBuffer;

    // read file into buffer
    HRESULT hr = file.Create( fileName, FILE_SHARE_READ, 0, OPEN_EXISTING );
    hr = file.GetSize( len );
    lpBuffer = new BYTE[len];
    hr = file.Read( lpBuffer, len );
```

Listing 24.1   **Continued**

```
    file.Close();

    *(lpBuffer+len) = '\0';

    // set return value
    *(Result) = SysAllocString( T2OLE((LPTSTR)lpBuffer) );

    return;
}
STDMETHODIMP CCommandCom::Run(BSTR Cmd, BSTR* Output)
{
    USES_CONVERSION;

    CString finalCmd;
    finalCmd.Format( "%s 1<&2 >\"%s\"", OLE2T(Cmd), mTempFileName );

    system( finalCmd );

    GetResult( mTempFileName, Output );

    return S_OK;
}
```

The Run method definition simply constructs a new command, which does a little stream redirection to place the results into a file. The GetResult method is a class member function that reads the file to get the final result. To keep the C++ code somewhat simple, we used redirection of streams into a file, whereas normally, using named pipes is the better solution. The path of the file is generated within the class constructor and placed into the mTempFileName variable, which is declared in the header file (.h) for the class. Additionally, when you create the .NET application that uses this object, you will see a brief window flash as the cmd.exe process is launched. To combat this flash, you normally want to create the cmd.exe process manually and hide the window using a parameter within the Win32 API function CreateProcess. Doing all of these steps, however, would result in a lot more code, which would complicate things more than they should.

You can now create the COM object and call its Run method. The next step is to add a property. Right-click on the interface again within Class View and select the Add Property menu item. The return type is a BSTR, and the name of the property is CurrentDirectory. The property will supports both a get and set operation, so leave those check boxes checked. The implementation of the methods for the properties are defined as follows:

```
STDMETHODIMP CCommandCom::get_CurrentDirectory(BSTR* pVal)
{
```

```
    USES_CONVERSION;

    TCHAR szBuffer[ MAX_PATH ];

    GetCurrentDirectory( MAX_PATH, szBuffer );

    *(pVal) = SysAllocString( T2OLE(szBuffer) );

    return S_OK;
}

STDMETHODIMP CCommandCom::put_CurrentDirectory(BSTR newVal)
{
    return E_NOTIMPL;
}
```

Now that a method and a property are created, the last step is to give the object the ability to fire an event. Because we can't think of any possible events a command interpreter would fire, the event is used solely for testing. When you created the COM object, you checked the Connection Points check box. It created an additional interface that your class implements. Assuming you named your object `ComClass`, right-click on the interface named `ICommandComEvents` within Class View and add a new method that does not use any parameters. Finally, create a new method on the `ICommandCom` interface that also does not accept any parameters, and within its definition, fire the event that you created earlier using the `raise` keyword, as shown in the following code:

```
STDMETHODIMP CCommandCom::Test()
{
    __raise SomeEvent();

    return S_OK;
}
```

Comments

This recipe serves two purposes. The first is to serve as a reference point for further recipes within this chapter. The second is to familiarize you with COM concepts and ATL so that you understand what we're talking about and to compel you to investigate ATL, a very powerful library.

COM is an interface-based specification that lays a foundation for creating objects with rules governing their activation, use, and lifetime. When objects communicate with each other, they do so on specific interfaces that each one defines. Although .NET objects can also do this, disparate .NET objects have access to public methods and properties that aren't specifically declared as members of a specific interface, instead allowing method and property invocation on a class instance rather than through an interface.

The ATL is a template-based class library that facilitates the creation and use of COM objects. Due to its extensive use of templates and attributes, ATL shields C++ developers from internal COM plumbing code, allowing them to concentrate more on the implementation of their particular component. You can use ATL in a variety of different situations, including Internet Server API (ISAPI) extensions; Object Linking and Embedding Database (OLEDB) providers and consumers; Windows applications; Web services; and ATL Server, which is a tag-based server technology similar to ASP.NET.

24.2. Using COM Objects in .NET

You want to use a COM object within a .NET application.

Technique

Using a COM object within a .NET application is similar to using any other .NET class, with the difference in the initial steps that you need to complete beforehand and the internal mechanics that occur within the Common Language Runtime (CLR). The first step is to create a reference to the COM object within your application. Click on Project, Add Reference from the main menu and select the COM tab within the Add Reference dialog. Assuming you didn't change the COM object name, the object will be named *ProjectName* 1.0 Type Library. For the example created in the previous recipe, the full name is CmdShell 1.0 Type Library.

Once you create a reference to the COM library containing the COM object you created, you can instantiate the object contained within the library, similar to the method used to create a .NET object. The namespace for the COM object is the name of the ATL project and contains interface declarations and class definitions. The following example places two `TextBox` controls on a Windows Form. When the user enters a command in the `tbCommand` text box, it is sent to the `Run` method defined in the COM object created in the last recipe. The result is placed within the `tbTranscript` text box. The following code demonstrates how to do this task. One particular thing to note is the way in which properties on the COM object are accessed. The `CurrentDirectory` property defined in the COM object utilizes the familiar syntax used by C#, even though COM object properties are internally implemented as `get` and `set` methods:

```
private void tbCommand_KeyDown(object sender,
    System.Windows.Forms.KeyEventArgs e)
{
    if( e.KeyCode == Keys.Return )
    {
        tbTranscript.Focus();
        tbTranscript.Text += "\r\n" + commandObj.Run( tbCommand.Text );
        tbTranscript.Text += "\r\n" + commandObj.CurrentDirectory + ">";
        tbTranscript.SelectionStart = tbTranscript.Text.Length;
        tbCommand.Text = "";
    }
}
```

Events that are fired by a COM object use delegates for event handlers within .NET. However, although most delegates use two parameters, indicating the source of the event and any arguments, the delegate for a COM event contains only the event arguments it defines. The `SomeEvent` event created in the previous recipe uses no parameters, which means the delegate will have an empty parameter list. To attach an event handler to the `SomeEvent` event fired from the COM object, create a new delegate instance and assign it to the `SomeEvent` event defined in the COM object:

```
public Form1()
{
    InitializeComponent();
    commandObj = new CmdShell.CCommandComClass();

    commandObj.SomeEvent +=
        new CmdShell._ICommandComEvents_SomeEventEventHandler( OnSomeEvent );
}

private void OnSomeEvent()
{
    MessageBox.Show( "Event handled within .NET object" );
}
```

Comments

As you can see from the discussion, using COM objects within .NET is relatively straightforward, given the interoperability support within the .NET Framework. Adding a reference to a COM library to your .NET project creates a new assembly called the *interop assembly*. This assembly serves as a proxy between the .NET object and the COM object using a specialized .NET object called a *Runtime Callable Wrapper (RCW)*. The wrapper is generated by Visual Studio .NET by reading information from the COM object's type library. Whenever an ATL project is created using the methods described in Recipe 24.1, "Creating an ATL-Based COM Component," a type library is generated each time the project is built. The type library contains all the type information for the library, which includes information about the library itself as well as interfaces and their associated methods, properties, and events, and it is embedded within the library's resource recipe. You can almost consider the type library as the predecessor to the assembly manifest used within .NET assemblies. Whenever the type library for a COM object changes, which occurs as a result of adding or changing interfaces or interface methods, you have to repeat the steps to add the reference to your .NET project. Recipe 24.3, "Automatically Generating an Interop Assembly," describes how to automatically update your .NET project when these changes occur.

In Figure 24.1, you can see how the RCW relates to the COM object and the .NET client that uses it. You can also see the COM Callable Wrapper (CCW), which is discussed in Recipe 24.7, "Using .NET Objects in COM." The RCW lies in between the

COM object and .NET client, facilitating the communication between the two. Furthermore, the RCW is also responsible for type marshalling. *Marshalling* is the process in which data types within one technology are converted to similar objects of the other technology. For instance, COM objects use a SAFEARRAY as a storage mechanism for arrays to support OLE automation clients, which can include scripting clients or Visual Basic 6 applications. The RCW generates a System.Array parameter for the COM method and marshals the data to convert it from a System.Array object to a SAFEARRAY for use within the COM object.

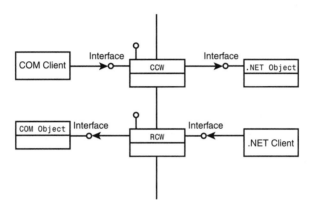

Figure 24.1   Relationship of RCW between a COM object
and a .NET client.

24.3. Automatically Generating an Interop Assembly

You want your .NET application to automatically pick up the changes of a referenced COM object.

Technique

Before we explain the steps to perform this task, note that this method does not apply to ASP.NET-based projects. Instead, you have to manually update your ASP.NET project any time a referenced COM library changes.

To automatically generate an interop assembly, you have to create a custom-build event that calls an interop-assembly–generating tool supplied by Visual Studio .NET. Click on Project, Properties from the main menu and select the Common Properties, Build Events property page. Because you need to generate the assembly before you create your application's assembly, you have to enter a value for a prebuild event. In the Pre-Build Event Command Line, call the tlbimp.exe program, passing the path of the

COM library as the first argument, followed by the name you want for the resulting interop assembly prefaced by the argument switch /out:. The following example uses the full path to the tlbimp.exe file (as it appears on our computer), followed by Visual Studio macros for the two filenames. The $(SolutionDir) is the directory where the main solution is located, which contains both the ATL project and .NET client. The $(ConfigurationName) expands to the values Debug or Release, depending on the build configuration used when building. Finally, the $(TargetDir) is the location where the final .NET assembly for the .NET client is placed:

```
"D:\Program Files\Microsoft Visual Studio .NET 2003\SDK\v1.1\Bin\tlbimp.exe "
"$(SolutionDir)\1_CmdShell\$(ConfigurationName)\1_CmdShell.dll"
    /out:"$(TargetDir)\Interop.CmdShell.dll"
```

Comments

Once you add a reference to a COM library for a .NET project, the interop assembly is generated, but Visual Studio .NET does not continue looking for changes in the main COM library during subsequent builds. If your COM library doesn't change or it only occasionally changes, this setup might be okay. However, if you are developing a COM object concurrently with a .NET client, you might want to consider making the interop assembly generation automatic.

The tlbimp.exe takes as input the resultant binary for a COM project and generates an interop assembly based on the contents of the type library. The tlbimp.exe tool is actually an application built with the .NET Framework. The TypeLibConverter class defined in the System.Runtime.Interop namespace contains methods to convert a type library to an assembly (ConvertTypeLibToAssembly) as well as converting an assembly to a type library (ConvertAsmToTypeLib), which is the process used in Recipe 24.7.

24.4. Using ActiveX Controls in a Windows Form

> You want to use an ActiveX control in a Windows Form application.

Technique

An ActiveX control is COM-based, which means your application makes calls into a RCW to interact with the control. The first step is to add the ActiveX control to the Windows Form designer toolbox. Right-click on the toolbox item and select the Add/Remove Items menu item. Click on the COM tab and locate the COM type library from the list of available libraries. If you don't know the name of the library, you can browse to its associated file using the Browse button.

Once you place the item onto the toolbox, you can use it as you do any other Windows Form control by dragging and dropping it and setting any necessary properties. The downloadable code for this book is available at `http://www.samspublishing.com` and contains a Windows Form media player, which uses the Windows Media Player ActiveX control.

Comments

Keeping with the promise of interoperability, Visual Studio .NET supports most legacy ActiveX controls. Although the term *ActiveX control* became somewhat synonymous with controls that run within Internet Explorer, a wide variety of applications use ActiveX controls, which serve as a successor to the OLE Custom Controls (OCXs) created in years past. If you decide to use an ActiveX control through a third party or through in-house development, you might find that it doesn't show up on the list of available COM controls within the Add/Remove form in the toolbox. COM controls, and all COM binaries for that matter, don't support XCopy deployment as .NET assemblies do. They must be registered on the system before they can be used. Registration of a COM library involves executing a special program called `regsvr32.exe`. This program either calls a COM DLL's `DllRegisterServer` method or passes the `-RegServer` command-line argument with an `.exe` or out-of-proc server. These methods in turn set the necessary Registry keys that all COM components must abide by to be actively used within Windows. Although the ATL library now takes care of this registration and unregistration mechanism, the complexity and maintenance required for COM registration is one of the driving factors behind .NET's use of attributes and XCopy deployment.

24.5. Viewing the RCW Using `ILDasm.exe`

You want to ensure the RCW was created correctly for a type library.

Technique

`ILDasm.exe` is in the Visual Studio .NET 2003 SDK `bin` directory. After running the application, open an interop assembly from the file menu. One thing that will become apparent is the amount of data types that are present compared to what you see in the actual COM object itself. Some of these data types are created during the type-library-to-assembly translation and are used by the CLR to aid in event handling between a COM and .NET object.

As an example, we are going to create a new method within the COM object that will accept an array of commands to send to the command interpreter and then generate an interop assembly to see how the marshalling will occur. Assuming you created the COM object from Recipe 24.1, right-click on the main interface, `ICommandCom` in this example, and select the Add Method menu item. The method name is `ProcessCommands` and the parameters include an in parameter whose data type is SAFEARRAY(BSTR)* with a name of Commands and a second parameter, a pointer to a BSTR (BSTR*) that will hold the resulting output. The implementation of the method is unimportant because we are only interested in viewing the generated intermediate language (IL) for the interop assembly.

After building the project and generating an interop assembly, either by adding a reference to the COM library or using the automatic method explained in Recipe 24.3, open the assembly in ILDasm.exe. Expand the CCommandCom class or ICommandCom interface, and double-click on the ProcessCommands method. A new form appears, showing contents similar to the following Microsoft Intermediate Language (MSIL) code:

```
.method public hidebysig newslot virtual
    instance string  marshal( bstr)  ProcessCommands(
    [in] class [mscorlib]System.Array  marshal( safearray bstr) commands)
    runtime managed internalcall
{
.custom instance void [mscorlib]System.Runtime.InteropServices.DispIdAttribute
::.ctor(int32) = ( 01 00 05 00 00 00 00 00 )

.override CmdShell.ICommandCom::ProcessCommands

} // end of method CCommandComClass::ProcessCommands
```

The portion of this MSIL code that we are interested in is the parameters of the ProcessCommands function. The first parameter of the method takes a System.Array method and marshals it as a SAFEARRAY whose data type is a BSTR. One reason why we chose this example is to show you that you shouldn't believe everything you read and you need to understand the Visual Studio .NET toolset to get the real answer. The MSDN documentation for SAFEARRAY marshalling still uses the documentation for version 1.0 of the .NET Framework. The documentation states that the interop assembly creates a reference to a string array, and you must export the IL code, change it to a System.Array, and then recompile the IL to create the interop assembly. As you can see, however, the behavior of the tlbimp.exe translation has changed, and it now creates the proper .NET data type. By understanding ILDasm, you can easily verify the information before going through the painstaking processes only to find out that it was all for naught.

Comments

ILDasm is an important and extremely helpful tool to use when developing .NET applications. Not only does it aid in understanding how .NET objects interact with the CLR during runtime, but you can also use it to pinpoint performance issues and, in this case, inspect interop assembly marshalling.

24.6. Handling HRESULT Errors

You want to properly handle errors returned from a COM object.

Technique

COM methods always return an HRESULT, which is a 32-bit integer containing bit fields denoting various attributes about the error. However, when you use an interop assembly to call the method within a .NET application, you don't have access to that HRESULT because the parameter marked with retval is the return value. To solve this problem, whenever a COM method returns an HRESULT whose severity bit is set to 1, the runtime throws an exception. The .NET Framework maps most defined HRESULTs to a corresponding exception class.

As an example, create a new method in the COM object that simply returns the value E_NOTIMPL, which is an error specifying that the method is not implemented by the object. This error maps to the NotImplementedException class. Just as there are several different possible exceptions that .NET object can throw, a COM object may return one of several different errors, depending on the situation that caused the error to occur. Some are errors such as E_FAIL, E_POINTER, and E_OUTOFMEMORY. You should ensure that you also create a catch block for any extra exceptions by using the generic Exception class, as shown in the following code:

```
// the following method will generate an exception if not handled
try
{
    commandObj.CurrentDirectory = "C:\\";
}
catch( NotImplementedException ex )
{
    MessageBox.Show( ex.TargetSite.Name + ": " + ex.Message );
}
catch( Exception ex )
{
    MessageBox.Show( ex.Message );
}
```

Comments

HRESULTs were created as a way to perform error handling without requiring the use of exceptions. The reason this method was chosen is that COM is a language-neutral technology and, like .NET, simply provides a specification that all languages, which want to play in the same sandbox, must follow. This being the case, not all languages at that time supported exceptions, and if they did, the exception mechanics were different from those employed within Visual C++.

24.7. Using .NET Objects in COM

You want to expose a .NET object to an unmanaged client that uses COM.

Technique

Creating a .NET object to be used with a COM client is a little more involved than using a COM object within a .NET project. The reasoning is explained later in this recipe. The first step is to create the .NET object. However, the architecture of the .NET object must use interfaces because COM is an interface-based language and expects to interact with other objects through defined interfaces. This example defines three interfaces, which use inheritance to go from a general `IVehicle` interface to the more concrete `IAirplane`. Each interface contains a single property for simplicity. In addition to a class that implements the `IAirplane` interface, create a class that does not implement any interfaces but rather contains a single public method. The final C# code should appear similar to Listing 24.2.

Listing 24.2 **Interface Declarations for a .NET Object**

```csharp
using System;

namespace DotNetObject
{

    public interface IVehicle
    {
        int Wheels
        {
            get;
            set;
        }
    }


    public interface IAirVehicle :  IVehicle
    {
        int Elevation
        {
            get;
            set;
        }
    }


    public interface IAirplane : IAirVehicle
    {
        int Capacity
```

Listing 24.2   **Continued**

```
        {
            get;
            set;
        }
    }

    public class Airplane : IAirplane
    {
        private int capacity, elevation, wheels;

        public Airplane()
        {
            capacity = 200;
            elevation = 0;
            wheels = 4;
        }

        public int Capacity
        {
            get
            {
                return this.capacity;
            }
            set
            {
                this.capacity = value;
            }
        }

        public int Elevation
        {
            get
            {
                return this.elevation;
            }
            set
            {
                this.elevation = value;
            }
        }

        public int Wheels
        {
            get
            {
```

Listing 24.2 **Continued**

```
                return this.wheels;
            }
            set
            {
                this.wheels = value;
            }
        }
    }


    public class NonInterfaceClass
    {
        public void Test()
        {
            Console.WriteLine( "NonInterfaceClass.Test succeeded" );
        }
    }
}
```

The first step to prepare your assembly for COM interop is to generate a *strong key*. COM uses location information within the Registry to locate the library a COM object exists in. However, when you generate the type library shown later, all that is generated is the type library without an associated COM DLL. The COM Callable Wrapper (CCW) that is created when your COM object attempts to instantiate a .NET object is contained within the CLR. Therefore, because the COM object's first line of communication is with the CLR, the location information points to the Microsoft Common Object Runtime Execution Engine (`mscoree.dll`). What you need to do is tell the `mscoree.dll` where your assembly is located, which you do by assigning a strong key to your assembly before you export the type library (which this example demonstrates) or install the assembly into the Global Assembly Cache (GAC).

To generate a strong key name, which you need to do only once, open a command-prompt window and navigate to your .NET project directory. Next, run the strong-key–generation program specifying the name of the key file to create:

```
sn.exe -k strongKey.skn
```

This line assumes that the Visual Studio .NET SDK is in your PATH environment variable. If not, you can open a command prompt using the link in the Tools folder of your Visual Studio .NET 2003 Start menu program group.

Once you generate a strong key, you have to sign your assembly. The C# compiler does this step each time you build. To sign the assembly, open the `AssemblyInfo.cs` file and change the following line:

```
[assembly: AssemblyKeyFile("")]
```

You add the location of the key file. This location is relative to the target directory where your final assembly is placed, so you have to use a relative path if your strong key file is within your main source directory:

```
[assembly: AssemblyKeyFile("../../strongKey.snk")]
```

The last step is similar to the step you used when generating an interop assembly for your .NET object in Recipe 24.2, "Using COM Objects in .NET." Additionally, we make this step automatic so you don't have to repeat the process each time you build your .NET project. Click on Project, Properties from the main menu and select the Common Properties, Build Events property pages. In the post-build event command line, enter RegAsm.exe as the program to execute, passing as arguments the location of your .NET assembly, the location of the resulting type library prefaced with the tlb: switch, and the /codebase switch:

```
"C:\WINDOWS\Microsoft.NET\Framework\v1.1.4322/RegAsm.exe " "$(TargetPath)"
    /tlb:"$(TargetDir)\$(TargetName).tlb" /codebase
```

In this command, $(TargetPath) is the full path to the .NET assembly and $(TargetDir)\$(TargetName).tlb creates a type library in the same location as the assembly and with the same name but using a .tlb file extension. The last argument, /codebase, helps mscoree.dll find your assembly when a COM object requests it. In keeping with COM tradition, the codebase argument places the full path to your assembly within the Windows Registry.

At this point, you now have a .NET assembly containing objects that a COM client can use. The last step to complete this exercise is to create the COM client. Create a new Visual C++ project using the Win32 Console Application template. When the project opens, you see only the required parts for a full C++ application, which isn't much. The first step is to tell the compiler that you are going to use an object contained within another type library. You use the #import keyword. This keyword is somewhat similar to the using keyword in C#, although internally different in many ways. Next, create a method called Test that will be used to test the .NET objects, as shown in the code following this paragraph. The first line is a variable declaration using #import-generated smart pointers. Explaining these smart pointers is well beyond the scope of this book. In general, you are creating an interface pointer whose implementation is contained within the class identified by the CLSID parameter in the constructor. These two objects map to the IAirplane interface and Airplane class, respectively, within your .NET class. At this point, the object is created and ready for use. The last two lines simply set the Capacity property and then print out that property to the console:

```
#include "stdafx.h"

#import "../7_NetClient/bin/Debug/DotNetObject.tlb" named_guids

void Test()
{
```

```
    DotNetObject::IAirplanePtr pAirplane( DotNetObject::CLSID_Airplane );
    pAirplane->Capacity = 500;
    printf( "Airplane Capacity: %d\n", pAirplane->Capacity );
}

int _tmain(int argc, _TCHAR* argv[])
{
    CoInitialize(NULL);
    Test();
    CoUninitialize();

    return 0;
}
```

Comments

As mentioned right at the beginning of this recipe, making a .NET object COM enabled is a lot more involved than the other way around. Even though the process is relatively trivial from the .NET standpoint, you still have to rearchitect your application to make extensive use of interfaces if you haven't already done so. Because COM only uses interface methods when accessing an object, you must implement interfaces on your .NET object if you ever want a COM client to have access. In most cases, you can simply take a .NET class and create interfaces based off existing class members.

When your .NET object is instantiated by a COM object, the CLR creates a CCW, which behaves similarly to the RCW going in the other direction. Calls from the COM client are handled in the proxy object contained within the CLR, and any necessary parameters are marshaled into their equivalent .NET data types before the final call is made on the .NET object.

One of the main reasons that this method is a little more involved than calling a COM object from .NET concerns something known as LocalServer32. When a COM object is registered, its location is placed within a unique identifying number known as a CLSID, which is a globally unique identifier (GUID). Within this key is a subkey called LocalServer32. In most cases, this value is a location to the binary file housing the COM object. However, when using COM interop, the location is pointing to mscoree.dll, thereby losing any information regarding the location of the assembly where the object is located. To solve this problem, you have to tell the CLR where the associated assembly is located, either by using the /codebase argument for the RegAsm tool or by installing the assembly into the GAC.

24.8. Viewing an Exported .NET Type Library

You want to view the resulting type library exported from a .NET assembly.

Technique

Just as you use `ILDasm.exe` to view type information about a .NET assembly, you use the OLE/COM Object Viewer to view information about a type library. You can launch the tool from the Tools menu within Visual Studio .NET.

The tree control on the left side of the tool takes all the information from the Registry concerning registered COM objects and logically groups that information based on its type. For instance, the Type Libraries tree node displays a list of registered type libraries using the friendly name of the type library. The Interfaces tree node displays all the known interfaces within the system. We don't recommend expanding that node on a slow computer. You might have to wait a while. The easiest way to view the contents of a type library without having to search through lists is to use the View Typelib menu item on the File menu. The exported type library created in this chapter for the .NET object uses a `.tlb` extension and is located in the same directory as the .NET assembly.

After you open the type library, another window opens, listing all the available interfaces, dispatch interface, and co-classes. A *dispatch interface* is simply an interface that supports OLE automation and the `IDispatch` interface. Whenever scripting languages are used to call methods on your COM object, they go through the `IDispatch` interface to do so. A *co-class* is the actual COM object itself. You need two pieces to create a COM object instance. The first is the ID of the interface to use and the second is the ID of the co-class to use.

Recipe 24.7 created a .NET object that implemented three interfaces: `IVehicle`, `IAirVehicle`, and `IAirplane`. The class that implemented these interface was named `Airplane`. If you view the type library for this .NET object after it is exported using the RegAsm tool, you can see that there's almost a one-to-one correlation between the .NET interfaces and classes with the generated COM interfaces and co-classes. When you select an interface, the corresponding methods and parameters for the interface are displayed using the Interface Description Language (IDL), which is a language designed to define interfaces and associate them with co-classes. You can almost think of it as a type library in text form.

Comments

In many cases, when working in a COM environment, the most frequent errors occur during runtime. For instance, when you ask a COM object for a certain interface, the actual code compiles just fine because the binding doesn't occur until runtime. By using this tool, you can verify whether a certain COM object supports a specified interface. In other words, to ensure that your .NET object has been exported in the way you think it should have been, verify the resulting type library by opening it in the OLE/COM Object Viewer tool.

24.9. Controlling Managed Thread Apartment States

You want to use a specific threading model in your .NET application when using COM interop.

Technique

COM contains a complex threading model that allows for safe object access in general cases or complete multithreaded access for objects that support direct synchronization. Each thread and object that is created in the COM world is placed into an apartment. An *apartment* is a special threading model explained later. Because a .NET application can create and utilize COM objects, it too must be placed into an apartment. The two possible apartment models available for .NET application include the single-threaded apartment (STA) and the multithreaded apartment (MTA). You can specify the apartment that your application uses by using either the STAThread or the MTAThread attribute on the application's entry point. The other method is to change the Thread.CurrentThread.ApartmentState property by specifying a value from the ApartmentState enumerated data type. Both options appear in Listing 24.3.

Listing 24.3 **Changing .NET Apartment States**

```
using System;
using System.Threading;

namespace _9_ThreadStateMTA
{
    class Class1
    {
        [MTAThread]
        static void Main(string[] args)
        {
        }
    }
}

using System;
using System.Threading;

namespace _9_ThreadStateSTA
{
```

Listing 24.3   **Continued**

```
class Class1
{
    static void Main(string[] args)
    {
        Thread.CurrentThread.ApartmentState = ApartmentState.STA;
    }
}
}
```

Comments

By now you've probably seen the STAThread attribute defined on some of your application's entry points because it is automatically applied during project creation. If you never plan on using COM interop within your application, this attribute becomes unnecessary and you can safely remove it.

An apartment is a conceptual entity designed to control how concurrent access to an object should be handled. The two main apartment models supported by .NET include the STA and the MTA. An STA can contain only one thread but any number of contained objects. If a STA is created and it is the only STA present at that time, it is called the main STA. Any other thread that wants to use the object within the main STA is therefore placed in its own STA, and any calls into the object must be marshaled using a proxy to marshal the data and a stub to unmarshal the data before the call is made on the object. The main benefit of using an STA is that an object must service only a single thread at a time. Because Windows services a single message at a time from its message queue, the STA model uses a hidden window to ensure that object calls are placed within a queue to be serviced one at a time.

An MTA, on the other hand, contains several threads, each interacting with multiple objects. With the STA model, an application contains multiple STAs, each containing a thread, but the MTA model uses only a single apartment. Additionally, the object can service multiple calls at a time coming from different threads, which means the object must ensure proper synchronization to its resources to avoid data corruption.

If the previous discussion left you in the dark (which can happen quite often when talking about apartments), then the following real-world analogy might help. Let's assume that a bank represents a process. Each bank teller within the bank represents a COM object, and each customer represents a calling thread. In an STA model, the customers line up and wait their turn to talk to a bank teller. When a bank teller finishes servicing a request, the serviced customer leaves and the next customer can use the bank teller. With the MTA model, a customer can interrupt the bank teller currently servicing another customer to perform a transaction. At this point, two customers are using the same bank teller, and if the bank teller isn't careful, the transactions can get mixed up.

Based on the analogy, you might automatically assume that using the STA model is more desirable because concurrent access is handled by the unforeseen force that keeps customers in the line and waiting their turn. However, which method do you think would have better performance? Assuming the tellers are good at multitasking and will not mix up concurrent transactions, the line of serviceable customers diminishes more quickly than if a queue were used. As we've said repeatedly throughout this book, the decision must based on the design decisions you make for your application.

Custom Attributes

25.0. Introduction

This chapter covers common tasks related to defining and using your own custom attributes.

25.1. Creating a Custom Attribute Class Definition

You want to define a new custom attribute.

Technique

Defining a custom attribute is simple: You define a class whose name should normally end in the string `Attribute` and which should be derived from the class `System.Attribute`. Listing 25.1 shows an example. For this sample, we assumed that we want to mark any code developed in house with some attribute. (You might perform this task for internal documentation purposes, for example, to distinguish in-house code from code that has been outsourced.)

Listing 25.1 **A Basic Attribute Class**

```
public class InHouseAttribute : Attribute
{
}
```

At the most basic level, that is literally all there is to it: the class defined in Listing 25.1, once compiled, is ready to be used to decorate any other code. Listing 25.2 shows the `InHouse` attribute being used to mark a class definition.

Listing 25.2   **Using the Basic Attribute Class**

```
[InHouse()]
class OurClass
{
        // etc.
```

When you use attributes to decorate other code, it's permissible and customary to omit `Attribute` from the class name in the square brackets, as done here.

More realistically, you might want your attribute to have various values beyond simply being present or absent. Listing 25.3 shows a slightly more sophisticated custom attribute class that you could use to indicate in more detail who wrote some code. This attribute uses a `bool` to indicate whether the code was written in house and a `string` to provide a brief description of where the code originated. Two constructors are supplied, one accepting both parameters and one accepting just the `bool`, which effectively means that the description string is optional.

Listing 25.3   **A More Complex Attribute Class That Takes Parameters**

```
public class ProgrammerTeamAttribute : Attribute
{
        private bool inHouse;
        private string team;

        public ProgrammerTeamAttribute(bool inHouse)
                : this(inHouse, null)
        {
        }
        public ProgrammerTeamAttribute(bool inHouse, string team)
        {
                this.inHouse = inHouse;
                this.team = team;
        }
}
```

This class is also ready to be used, as shown in Listing 25.4.

Listing 25.4   **Using the More Complex Attribute Class**

```
[ProgrammerTeam(true)]
class OurClass
{
        [ProgrammerTeam(false,
"We couldn't figure out how to implement TakeAHoliday so we contracted it out")]
        public void TakeAHoliday()
        {
                // etc.
        }
```

Although the `ProgrammerTeam` attribute defined in Listing 25.3 will work adequately, it does have one problem. There is no way for external code to access the values supplied to the constructor when the attribute is instantiated—as, for example, would happen if some external code uses reflection to search code for attributes. For this reason, you normally add some public properties to allow access to these values, as shown in Listing 25.5.

Listing 25.5   **An Attribute That Exposes its Fields via Public Properties**

```
public class ProgrammerTeamAttribute : Attribute
{
        private bool inHouse;
        private string team;

        public bool InHouse
        {
                get
                {
                        return inHouse;
                }
        }

        public string Team
        {
                get
                {
                        return team;
                }
        }

        public ProgrammerTeamAttribute(bool inHouse)
                : this(inHouse, null)
        {
        }
        public ProgrammerTeamAttribute(bool inHouse, string team)
        {
                this.inHouse = inHouse;
                this.team = team;
        }
}
```

Listing 25.5 ensures that, if some other code uses reflection to examine a class that is decorated with the `ProgrammerTeam` attribute, then it can also retrieve the `inHouse` and `team` values using the corresponding public properties.

Comments

In general, whenever you decorate code with attributes, you must supply parameters that correspond to one of the constructors of the attribute class. Listings 25.3 and 25.5 supplied two constructors, effectively allowing an optional parameter. In general, however, it is conventional to implement optional parameters using properties, as described in Recipe 25.5, "Adding Optional Properties to Custom Attributes." You should also bear in mind that the classes defined in this recipe are minimal classes designed to implement just enough features to qualify as useful attributes. In real-world programming, it would not be considered good programming practice to define an attribute class without also explicitly specifying its usage, as described in the next recipe.

25.2. Declaring Targets for Custom Attributes

You want to declare which portions of code an attribute can be applied to.

Technique

The technique is to apply a Microsoft-defined attribute, `AttributeUsageAttribute`, to your attribute class. For example, suppose you wrote a custom attribute, `InHouseAttribute` (as defined in Recipe 25.1, "Creating a Custom Attribute Class Definition"), and you want to explicitly indicate that it can be applied only to classes. Listing 25.6 shows how you achieve this goal.

Listing 25.6 **Indicating an Attribute Can Only Be Applied to Classes**

```
[AttributeUsage(AttributeTargets.Class)]
public class InHouseAttribute : Attribute
{
        // etc.
```

Of course, you might want an attribute to be applied to any struct, class, or enum, rather than only to classes, as in Listing 25.7.

Listing 25.7 **Indicating an Attribute Can Be Applied to Classes, Structs, or Enums**

```
[AttributeUsage(AttributeTargets.Class | AttributeTargets.Struct |
AttributeClass.Enum)]
public class InHouseAttribute : Attribute
{
        // etc.
```

In general, any attempt to apply an attribute to an item of code that the `AttributeTarget` forbids will result in a compilation error.

As you might guess, `AttributeTargets` is a `[Flags]` enum. (These attributes pop up everywhere!) The full set of possible values of this enumeration follows:

`All`	`Enum`	`Module`
`Assembly`	`Event`	`Parameter`
`Class`	`Field`	`Property`
`Constructor`	`Interface`	`ReturnValue`
`Delegate`	`Method`	`Struct`

The meanings of these values should be self-explanatory. You can combine any of these individual values with a bitwise OR operation. `AttributeTargets.All` is itself a bitwise OR of all the other values. Hence, marking an attribute with `AttributeTargets.All` allows its use anywhere. This behavior is the default if you do not specify `AttributeUsage`. Note the following code:

```
[AttributeUsage(AttributeTargets.All)]
public class InHouseAttribute : Attribute
{
    // etc.
```

It has much the same practical effect as the next code:

```
public class InHouseAttribute : Attribute
{
    // etc.
```

On occasions, you might want to allow an attribute to be applied everywhere except certain places. For example, you might want an attribute to be permissible on any items of source code but not to assemblies or modules. Achieving this goal takes some playing around with logical operations; the correct procedure is to perform a logical AND of `AttributeTargets.All` with the bitwise negation of the attributes you don't want. Listing 25.8 uses this procedure to prevent an attribute from being applied to an assembly or module.

Listing 25.8 Defining an Attribute That Cannot Be Applied at Assembly or Module Scope

```
[AttributeUsage(AttributeTargets.All & (~AttributeTargets.Assembly) &
(~AttributeTargets.Module))]
public class MyAttribute : Attribute
{
    // etc.
```

25.3. Allowing Custom Attributes to Be Applied Multiple Times

> You want to specify that an attribute can be applied more than once to the same item.

Technique

You should specify the `AllowMultiple` property of the `AttributeUsage` attribute, as shown in Listing 25.9.

Listing 25.9   **Add a Title Here**

```
[AttributeUsage(AttributeTargets.All, AllowMultiple=true)]
public class MyMultipleAttribute : Attribute
{
        // etc.
```

With the definition of `MyMultipleAttribute` in Listing 25.9, and with the additional assumption that `MyMultipleAttribute` has a constructor that takes a string, you can use `MyMultipleAttribute` as shown in Listing 25.10.

Listing 25.10   **Using an Attribute More Than Once on the Same Target**

```
[MyMultipleAttribute("This is some text")]
[MyMultipleAttribute("Hey, this is some more text!")]
public override void SomeMethod()
{
        // etc.
```

If we had not specified `AllowMultiple=true` in Listing 25.9, then Listing 25.10 would have resulted in a compilation error, because the default behavior is that a given attribute cannot be applied more than once to the same target.

25.4. Defining the Inheritance Model of Custom Attributes

> You want to specify whether items decorated with some custom attribute can pass the attribute on to inherited items.

Technique

You can control whether decorated items can pass attributes on to derived items with the `AttributeUsage.Inherited` property. By default, this property is set to `true`, mean-

ing that attributes are passed on to inherited items. For example, let's take the
`InHouseAttribute` class presented in Listing 25.1:

```
public class InHouseAttribute : Attribute
{
}
```

Let us assume that it is applied as follows:

```
[InHouse()]
class OurClass
{
        // etc.
```

Suppose also that we have a class defined as follows:

```
class OurDerivedClass : OurClass
{
        // etc.
```

Then, `OurDerivedClass` also has the `InHouse` attribute applied to it, despite the fact that
it is not explicitly indicated as such: it will have inherited the attribute from `OurClass`.
To change this behavior, we must specifically indicate the attribute usage of `InHouse` and
mark its `Inherited` property as `false`. Listing 25.11 shows this process.

Listing 25.11   **Defining an Attribute That Cannot Be Passed on to Inherited Items**

```
[AttributeUsage(AttributeTargets.All, Inherited=false)]
public class InHouseAttribute : Attribute
{
}
```

Now, with `OurDerivedClass` still defined as in Listing 25.11, `OurDerivedClass` will not
be decorated with the `InHouse` attribute.

Comments

The examples shown here illustrate an attribute that has been defined to a type.
However, the same principles apply to any item that can be overridden or inherited
from. It includes classes, methods, or properties. For example, suppose the class `OurClass`
is defined like this:

```
class OurClass
{
        [InHouse()]
        public virtual void DoSomething()
        {
                // etc.
```

Suppose `OurDerivedClass` contained this method:

```
class OurDerivedClass
{
       public override void DoSomething()
       {
                     // etc.
```

By default, the overridden method `OurDerivedClass.DoSomething()` will be marked with the `InHouse` attribute; it will have picked up this attribute with the base class method. However, if `InHouseAttribute` is marked as `Inherited=false`, then `OurDerivedClass.DoSomething()` does not gain this attribute unless explicitly coded.

25.5. Adding Optional Properties to Custom Attributes

You want to allow optional properties to be passed to custom attributes using the `<property>=<value>` syntax in the decoration line.

Technique

The technique is to define a public property in the attribute class with the given name and to ensure that the property has a set accessor. Suppose, for example, that as part of a scheme to link classes to fields in a database, you defined a `Field` attribute, and you want to be able to allow classes that use this attribute to optionally indicate a maximum value. Listing 25.12 shows how you can do so.

Listing 25.12   **An Attribute with an Optional Property**

```
[AttributeUsage(AttributeTargets.Class)]
public class FieldAttribute : Attribute
{
       private int maxValue;
       public int MaxValue
       {
              get
              {
                     return maxValue;
              }
              set
              {
                     maxValue = value;
              }
       }
}
```

The `MaxValue` property in Listing 25.12 is optional only in the sense that when you decorate a class with this attribute, you are free to specify or not specify a value for the property. The property is always present in the attribute but has a default value of zero if not explicitly specified. Listing 25.13 illustrates both possibilities.

Listing 25.13   **Using an Attribute That Has an Optional Property**

```
// this class supplies a MaxValue of 100 with the attribute
[FieldAttribute(MaxValue = 100)]
class PercentSuccessfulSales
{
        // implementation here
}


// this class is also decorated with the attribute, but does not
// specify a value for MaxValue.
// MaxValue in this attribute will retain its default value of zero
[FieldAttribute()]
class NumberOfVisits
{
        // implementation here
}
```

Bear in mind that, despite the suggestive name of the `MaxValue` property, all we are doing in this code is supplying information about the class that is available to be inspected using reflection. This code does not actually enforce any maximum values in any database. If you want to enforce a maximum field value based on this sample, you have to separately write some code that inspects the state of the attribute and that provides appropriate enforcement. Recipe 25.7, "Displaying Assembly Custom Attribute Information Using Reflection," explains how to examine attribute state.

The syntax for decorating a class with a custom attribute is exactly the same as that for an attribute that Microsoft has defined. In particular, when using the attribute, you must declare any optional property values after any values to be passed to a constructor. For example, suppose we modify Listing 25.13 so that the `FieldAttribute` constructor takes one parameter.

Listing 25.14   **An Attribute with a One-Parameter Constructor and an Optional Property**

```
[AttributeUsage(AttributeTargets.Class)]
public class FieldAttribute : Attribute
{
        public FieldAttribute(string tableName)
        {
                this.tableName = tableName;
        }
```

Listing 25.14   **Continued**

```
        string tableName;

        private int maxValue;
        public int MaxValue
        {
                get
                {
                        return maxValue;
                }
                set
                {
                        maxValue = value;
                }
        }
}
```

The possible ways of decorating a class with this attribute appear in Listing 25.15.

Listing 25.15   **Using an Attribute That Has a One-Parameter Constructor and an Optional Property**

```
// this class supplies a MaxValue of 100 with the attribute
[FieldAttribute("Sales", MaxValue = 100)]
class PercentSuccessfulSales
{
        // implementation here
}

// this class is also decorated with the attribute,
// but does not specify a value for MaxValue.
// MaxValue in this attribute will retain its default value of zero
[FieldAttribute("SalespersonVisits")]
class NumberOfVisits
{
        // implementation here
}
```

Comments

The examples in this recipe simply implement the MaxValue property as a wrapper around a field called maxValue. You can, of course, write whatever code you want in the get and set accessors of the property, but for an attribute property, it would be unusual to implement anything substantially different from simply wrapping a field.

You should also bear in mind that the `get` and `set` accessors of an attribute property have slightly different special roles:

- The main purpose of the `set` accessor is to let you specify the property value when an item of code is decorated with the attribute.

- The main purpose of the `get` accessor is to allow the value to be examined if the attribute is examined later on using reflection.

You are free to omit either accessor if you feel it is appropriate. However, if you omit the `set` accessor of an attribute property, then it will not be possible for code to set the property using the syntax style `[MyCustomAttribute(<PropertyName>=<value>)]` when the attribute is used. On the other hand, if you omit the `get` accessor, it will not be possible for code that uses reflection to instantiate the attribute to examine the value of the property.

25.6. Displaying Custom Attribute Information Using Reflection

You want to use reflection to display custom attribute information.

Technique

To access information about custom attributes, follow these steps:

1. Use reflection to obtain a reference to a reflection-based class that describes the item you believe has been decorated with a custom attribute. For example, for a type, it will be a `System.Type` instance; for a method, it will be a `System.Reflection.MethodInfo` instance; and for an assembly, it will be a `System.Reflection.Assembly` instance.

2. Invoke the `ICustomAttributeProvider.GetCustomAttributes()` method on the reflection object. This method actually instantiates all the attributes that are applied to the item and returns them in an `object[]` array. You will find that all the relevant reflection types, including `Type`, `MethodInfo`, `MemberInfo`, `ParameterInfo`, `Assembly`, and so on, implement the `ICustomAttributeProvider` interface and hence implement the `GetCustomAttributes()` method.

3. Cast each attribute to the required type and extract the information you need using the various methods and properties implemented by the attribute class.

It's not really possible to give a specific set of instructions for Step 1 of this procedure because it depends on whether you want to examine the attributes applied to a class, to an assembly, to a method, to a parameter, or to some other item of code. Chapter 23, "Reflection," gave specific instructions for obtaining a reflection-based object in the various different cases. However, we provide a couple of examples to illustrate the general principles here.

We start by considering how to obtain attributes for a type: Let's suppose a type called `MyClass` has been defined somewhere. We want to list the attributes that might have been applied to this type. Listing 25.16 shows how we could do so.

Listing 25.16   **Displaying the Attributes Applied to a Class**

```
Type type = typeof(MyClass);
Console.WriteLine("Attributes defined for MyClass are:");
object [] attribs = type.GetCustomAttributes(true);
foreach (object attrib in attribs)
{
        Console.WriteLine(attrib.ToString());
}
```

Listing 25.16 shows that we first obtain a type reference to the type whose attributes we want to examine. Note that there is no restriction on how we obtain the `Type` reference. For example, if, instead of knowing the name of the type at compile time, you have an object reference, `myObject`, whose type-level attributes you want to examine, then you simply replace the first line of Listing 25.16 with

```
Type type = myObject.GetType();
```

Having obtained a `Type` reference, we invoke the `Type.GetCustomAttributes()` method to get a list of the attributes. This method instantiates all the attributes and returns them as an array. The returned array is of type `object[]` because there is no way to predict in advance what the types of the attributes will be. `GetCustomAttributes()` takes one parameter, which indicates whether the inheritance chain is searched when retrieving attributes. If you pass in the value `false`, then the returned `object[]` array contains only attributes that have been explicitly assigned to this type. If you pass in `true`, then the array also contains any attributes that were applied to base types and for which the `AttributeUsage.Inherited` property was set to `true`.

Next, we simply iterate through the returned array, manipulating the attributes as desired. In Listing 25.16, we display the string representation of each attribute. Suppose, for example, that `MyClass` is defined in the following way:

```
[InHouse()]
[ProgrammerTeam(true)]
class MyClass
{
        // etc.
```

Then, assuming that `ProgrammerTeamAttribute` and `InHouseAttribute` are both defined in a namespace called `TestAttributes`, running Listing 25.16 generates the following results:

```
Attributes defined for MyClass are:
TestAttributes.ProgrammerTeamAttribute
TestAttributes.InHouseAttribute
```

On the other hand, suppose you want to obtain references to the attributes that were applied to a method. For the sake of argument, let's assume you want to examine the attributes applied to a method `MyClass.DoSomething()`. The relevant code appears in Listing 25.17.

Listing 25.17   Obtaining Object References for the Attributes Applied to a Method

```
Type type = typeof(MyClass);
MethodInfo method = type.GetMethod("DoSomething");
object [] attribs = method.GetCustomAttributes(false);
foreach (object attrib in attribs)
{
        // do something with the attribute object reference, for example:
        Console.WriteLine(attrib.ToString());
}
```

This code shows that we simply obtain a `MethodInfo` reference that describes the method we are interested in. Then, the procedure is to call `ICustomAttributeProvider.GetCustomAttributes()`, just as for a class. Similar principles apply for obtaining the attributes of any other code item.

Comments

In this recipe, the emphasis was on displaying information about any custom attributes that you defined. However, you should bear in mind that the Common Language Runtime (CLR) makes no distinction between attributes that you define and custom attributes that Microsoft defines, such as `ObsoleteAttribute` or `BrowsableAttribute`. On the other hand, certain common Microsoft-supplied attributes, such as `DllImportAttribute` and `StructLayoutAttribute`, are not really custom attributes at all but are pseudo attributes. Pseudo attributes are removed by the C# compiler and replaced by various intermediate language (IL) flags, so they are not normally picked up by reflection.

25.7. Displaying Assembly Custom Attribute Information Using Reflection

You want to use reflection to display information about custom attributes that were applied to an assembly.

Technique

The technique is almost identical to that demonstrated in the preceding recipe to obtain custom attributes for a class—except that we need to obtain an `Assembly` reference and call `Assembly.GetCustomAttributes()` instead of `Type.GetCustomAttributes()`. Listing 25.18 demonstrates the technique used to list the attributes that were applied to the currently executing assembly.

Listing 25.18   Listing the Attributes Applied to the Currently Executing Assembly

```
Assembly assbly = Assembly.GetExecutingAssembly();
object [] attribs = assbly.GetCustomAttributes(true);
foreach (object attrib in attribs)
{
        Console.WriteLine(attrib.ToString());
}
```

Just like `Type.GetCustomAttributes()`, `Assembly.GetCustomAttributes()` takes a `bool` parameter. Although in theory, this parameter indicates whether the inheritance chain should be searched for attributes, assemblies don't actually have an inheritance chain. Hence, the parameter is completely ignored: you can set it to either `true` or `false`. The parameter is only present in this case to satisfy the signature requirements of the `ICustomAttributeProvider` interface, which `Assembly` implements.

More realistically, you might want to load an assembly specifically to examine its custom attributes:

```
Assembly assbly = Assembly.LoadFrom(@"c:\My Projects\MyAssembly.dll");
object [] attribs = assbly.GetCustomAttributes(true);
// etc.
```

Chapter 19, "Assemblies," described the main techniques for loading an assembly and acquiring an `Assembly` reference.

25.8. Displaying Properties of an Applied Attribute at Runtime

You want to display the values of specific properties of attributes that were applied to code items.

Technique

To display the values of attribute properties, you clearly need to know the type of the attribute you are expecting. In general, the technique is to simply call `CustomAttributeProvider.GetCustomAttributes()` and then cast the attributes returned to the required type and extract the relevant properties. To make this task easier, you can use an alternative overload of `GetCustomAttributes()`, which takes two parameters and allows you to restrict the returned array to contain only attributes that are castable to a specified type:

```
object [] attribs = type.GetCustomAttributes(typeof(MyCustomAttribute), true);
```

When using this overload, the first parameter is a `Type` reference that indicates the type of the attribute you want to be returned, and the second parameter is the usual `bool` that specifies whether you want to search the attributed item's inheritance chain for attributes. For example, suppose we are searching for occurrences of the `ProgrammerTeam` attribute that was presented in Listing 25.5. Recall that this attribute exposes two properties, `InHouse` (a `bool`) and `Team` (a `string`), and we want to display the values of these properties. Listing 25.19 shows how to do so. This sample assumes that the variable `codeItem` refers to some reflection object that implements `ICustomAttributeProvider`.

Listing 25.19   **Using Reflection to Display Values of Attribute Properties**

```
object [] attribs = codeItem.GetCustomAttributes(typeof(ProgrammerTeamAttribute),
true);
foreach (object attrib in attribs)
{
        ProgrammerTeamAttribute progTeam = (ProgrammerTeamAttribute)attrib;
        Console.WriteLine("Programmer team attribute values:");
        Console.WriteLine("InHouse: " + progTeam.InHouse.ToString());
        Console.WriteLine("Team:    " + progTeam.Team);
}
```

If in Listing 25.19, `codeItem` holds a type reference to a class defined like this:

```
[InHouse()]
[ProgrammerTeam(true, "Dave coded up this class")]
class OurClass
{
```

Then, the result of running Listing 25.19 is this output:

```
Programmer team attribute values:
InHouse: True
Team:    Dave coded up this class
```

Comments

You should be aware that the code listings in this recipe presume that it is safe to cast the attributes returned from `GetCustomAttributes()` to the type we are interested in. If we use the two-parameter overload of `GetCustomAttributes()`, then that is the case because only attributes of the given type are returned. More generally, however, you might have a list of attributes returned from the one-parameter overload of

GetCustomAttributes(), and you cannot be certain of the type of the attributes. In that case, you can use the C# as operator to pick out the attributes you are interested in:

```
object [] attribs = codeItem.GetCustomAttributes(true);
foreach (object attrib in attribs)
{
        // to pick out any instances of MyCustomAttribute
        ProgrammerTeamAttribute myCustomAttrib = attrib as MyCustomAttribute;
        if (myCustomAttrib != null)
                // do something with the attribute
}
```

In the most general case, you might not know at compile time what attributes are going to turn up, and you just want to display all the properties of whatever attributes you find. In this case, you need to use reflection over again to identify the type of each attribute and then iterate over its properties using the techniques described in Chapter 23:

```
object [] attribs = codeItem.GetCustomAttributes(true);
foreach (object attrib in attribs)
{
        Type t = attrib.GetType();
        PropertyInfo [] properties = t.GetProperties();
        foreach (Property property in properties)
        {
                // process this property
        }
}
```

26

Smart Device Extensions

26.0. Introduction

Mobile devices have been experiencing an explosive rise in popularity recently, no doubt because of advances in the mobile technology market. Cell phones are beginning to act more like PDAs and PDAs are beginning to take on the functions of a cell phone. At one time, a mobile device was simply a small palm-sized computer that allowed you to store contact information, keep a calendar, and play a game of solitaire in meetings. Now these devices are used as digital cameras, video phones, multiplayer gaming platforms, and connected appliances because of wireless access points in airports and coffee shops.

The Smart Device Extensions in Visual Studio .NET 2003 represent the first time that mobile-device development is ingrained into the Integrated Development Environment (IDE). When the first mobile platform from Microsoft came out, developers used Visual C++ with a downloadable toolkit. Soon, they used a standalone development environment called Embedded Visual Tools that allowed developers to plug in mobile software development kits (SDKs) for new devices and supported both Visual Basic and Visual C++. The Smart Device Extensions are the largest of mobile development offerings to date with the addition of the .NET Compact Framework, a new language in C#, and the rich design environment of Visual Studio .NET. This chapter looks at various aspects of Smart Device Extensions and the .NET Compact Framework. Because a lot of the material covered in this book translates so well, we focus on mobile-device–specific techniques.

26.1. Understanding the Differences Between the Compact and .NET Frameworks

You want to understand some of the key similarities and differences between the Compact and .NET Frameworks.

Technique

Listing every similarity between the two frameworks would be a tremendous endeavor because they have a lot in common. A lot of the information in this book works within the .NET Compact Framework. For instance, the Common Language Runtime (CLR) still uses the familiar constructs of just in time (JIT), managed code, garbage collection, and a Common Type System (CTS), which contains all the primitive types discussed in this book. The .NET Compact Framework also supports the mixing of multiple languages, although Visual C++ .NET is not included. Visual C++ users must still use the Embedded Visual Tools and unmanaged code for new devices.

Even though the .NET Compact Framework contains several similarities, a few aspects had to be either changed or removed to maintain good performance on devices that are typically slower and memory constrained. Searching in MSDN for the ".NET Compact Framework" presents a list of all the differences. Additionally, any classes, methods, and properties that are not supported in the .NET Compact Framework say so in the corresponding help documentation. Some of the main differences include the following. You cannot create multimodule assemblies in the .NET Compact Framework, but satellite assemblies for resources are still supported. COM interop is not supported. To get around this limitation, you can still use the `PInvoke` methods described in Chapter 21, "Securing Code," to call a DLL written in unmanaged C++ that can act as a proxy to COM objects. ADO.NET has been trimmed substantially. The `System.Data.OleDb` class is not supported, but a .NET Compact Framework Data Provider for SQL Server CE Edition is included.

The .NET Compact Framework supports infrared communication, whereas the .NET Framework does not. In fact, you can use a special listening class that listens for HTTP requests through the infrared port, enabling you to create a Web server for clients that connect via infrared.

Reflection is supported by the Compact Framework, but dynamically creating assemblies is not because the `System.Reflection.Emit` class has been removed. Also, you cannot use the equality operator to compare reflection objects such as `MethodInfo`, `PropertyInfo`, and `ParameterInfo`, to name a few.

Extensible Markup Language (XML) is partly supported within the .NET Framework. Some of the key items left out, however, include schema validation, which means you are unable to check the validity of an XML document and XML serialization. Furthermore, you cannot perform an XPath query on XML documents.

Comments

The differences outlined here are just a few of the many differences you'll encounter when creating a Smart Device Application. However, care was taken to only remove those items that a mobile device developer would rarely use or those items that just aren't feasible given the constraints of mobile devices. This chapter highlights the key differences and ways to address them using the .NET Compact Framework. Before you tackle any sort of large application that targets mobile devices, ensure that the technology is there to support your endeavor.

26.2. Creating a Smart Device Solution

You want to create a new solution that targets mobile devices.

Technique

When you open the New Project dialog in Visual Studio .NET, you see two project templates specifically designed for Smart Device Applications. The one we're interested in for this recipe is the Smart Device Application template. When you create the project, the first screen you see is the Smart Device Application Wizard. This wizard allows you to choose which type of Smart Device Application to create, given four choices. For a graphics Windows-Form–based application, select the Windows Application project type. The Class Library project allows you to create DLL assemblies containing custom data types, and it is similar to the class library project created in the .NET Framework. The next project type is the Nongraphical Application. This type of project is specific to the .NET Framework (although creating a similar type of application in .NET is trivial). Mobile devices do not have a console, as does the Windows operating system, which means EXE-based applications use Windows Forms or run in the background. The last project type is an Empty Project. This type simply creates the necessary project properties for a Smart Device Application, allowing you to add source code as necessary.

Comments

If you're thinking that you will never target a mobile device because you don't have the necessary hardware such as a Pocket PC, you'll find it comforting to know that you don't have to. Ever since the first mobile SDK for Windows CE, Microsoft has shipped with it an emulator that runs within a window on your desktop system. For most applications, ensuring that your application runs within the emulator gets you pretty close to making it work on a real device. We're not saying that you should just create an entire application and ship it once it's finished and working within an emulator. Sometimes, the behavior from the emulator is not quite the same as that from a real device. Additionally, not all devices use the same processor chip, which means you can encounter different behavior when the intermediate language (IL) is generated to machine code. For instance, MIPS processors do not support the full range of values necessary for floating-point precision. While you are running the emulator, the IL is generated to x86 machine code where floating point behaves as expected. Once you place the application on a device with a MIPS processor, you'll find out the floating-point emulation is not a supported feature in the .NET Compact Framework for those devices. So in short, become good friends with that guy holding the iPaq you see on the bus.

26.3. Creating and Displaying Windows Forms

You want to create a Windows-Forms–based Smart Device Application.

Technique

To create a Windows Form application that targets mobile devices, select the Windows Application project type from the Smart Device Application project template. When the project is created, the IDE opens the Windows Form designer, allowing you to drag and drop controls and create event handlers using the same methods you learned for desktop applications.

Although the same procedures and methods apply for using Windows Forms, we need to address a few differences. First, mobile devices by default do not use a mouse. There is no way to get the current location of a mouse unless the user presses the stylus down onto the screen. Your application should not depend on the current position of the mouse unless it's in response to a `MouseDown` event. Furthermore, because there is no mouse, there is no mouse cursor. You can, however, create a wait cursor by setting the static property `Cursor.Current` to `Cursor.Wait`, which displays an animating cursor in the middle of the screen.

Applications that run in the Pocket PC operating system are not supposed to exit when the user presses the close button. Instead, the operating system uses an algorithm that closes applications that are not in use after a certain period of time. You will not receive the `Close` or `Closing` events when the user clicks the close button in the top-right corner of the form. If you ever want to use the "Designed for Pocket PC" logo, then you must allow the operating system to close your form instead of forcing a close from a menu event handler, for instance.

However, you can still allow an application to close while supporting the logo requirements by using a dialog-based approach. Instead of displaying a close (X) button in the upper-right corner of the form, you show an OK button; clicking it causes the `Close` and `Closing` events to fire and subsequently close your application. To support this behavior, set the `MinimizeBox` property of the form to `False`.

Windows Forms generally runs using the entire screen because the screen real estate is small for mobile devices. Even if you decide to set the `Width` and `Height` properties for your form to a small value, the form still expands to fill up the entire screen not covered by the title bar or bottom toolbar. To place your controls for a Pocket PC application, set the `Width` of the form to 240 and the `Height` to 320 while working in the Windows Form designer.

Comments

As you work with Windows Forms in a Smart Device Application, you'll almost forget you're working on a mobile device, at least until you begin to test your code. The .NET Compact Framework was designed to mirror the full .NET Framework as closely as possible, and one of the design decisions was to allow as much Visual Studio .NET designer support as possible.

Because you will do a majority of your initial testing using the emulator, following are a few tips and tricks that might help you if you are new to mobile-device application programming. The first is the default binary location. Even though the IDE communicates with the emulator to allow you to debug or simply launch your application from the IDE, it's still good to know where the final binary is located within the emulator. The default location is the `\Program Files\`*ProjectName* directory. The emulator contains a built-in application called File Explorer, which is the same application that ships with all Pocket PCs. To launch the File Explorer, click the Start button on the top of the toolbar and select the Programs menu item, which brings up a list of programs that are installed (of which File Explorer is one). You might find it easier to move that location to a more accessible area such as the Start menu itself. To do so, open your project property pages and select the Device property page from the Common Properties group. Next, change the Output File Folder to `\Windows\Start Menu`.

When you build your project, you need to deploy it to the emulator before running it. To do so, click on Build from the main menu and select the Deploy *ProjectName* menu item. If you are debugging, deployment occurs automatically. You will eventually run into the problem of not being able to deploy the application because of the Windows closing behavior described in the "Technique" portion of this recipe. Even though the form is gone, the application is still running in the background. There are two ways around this problem. The first is to click on the Start menu within the emulator and select the Settings tab. Next, click on the System tab and open the Memory control panel applet. You then see a tab that says Running Programs, which allows you to stop any applications that are currently running. The second option, which is easier and guarantees that you won't forget to manually stop the process, is to forgo the Pocket PC logo requirements during the implementation phase of your application. You can do so by creating a menu item, a button control, or simply an event handler for the Click event on the form. In any case, when you call the Close method, the application will exit.

26.4. Manipulating the Soft Input Panel

You want to programmatically control the Soft Input Panel (SIP).

Technique

The .NET Compact Framework contains a Windows Form control specifically designed for mobile devices. The control is called InputPanel, and you use it to control when the SIP is shown to the user. The SIP is a special operating system control used to enter data with a small keyboard, by writing letters and numbers with the stylus in designated boxes, or by writing on the screen at any location using the *Transcriber* technology in the Pocket PC operating system.

After creating the project, drag and drop the InputPanel control onto the form. Because it is a nonvisual control, it shows up in the designer tray at the bottom of the designer window. Whenever you want to enable the SIP, set the Enabled property of the InputPanel to true. You want to do so whenever any control that accepts text input receives focus. For instance, you want to create an event handler for the GotFocus event for a TextBox control and set the Enabled property of the InputPanel to true. Likewise, add an event handler for the LostFocus event and set the Enabled property to false, as shown in the following code:

```
private void textBox1_GotFocus(object sender, System.EventArgs e)
{
    inputPanel1.Enabled = true;
}

private void textBox1_LostFocus(object sender, System.EventArgs e)
{
    inputPanel1.Enabled = false;
}
```

Comments

As mentioned earlier, the default SIP for the current version of the Pocket PC operating system allows you enter text using one of three methods. Two of these methods, the keyboard and letter recognizer, display a small window at the bottom of the screen. This window means that the viewable area for your user interface becomes even smaller. While the InputPanel control is enabled, you can retrieve the viewable area by accessing the VisibleDesktop property of the InputPanel. One thing to watch for is controls that are covered once the input panel appears. In other words, if you have a TextBox control at the bottom of your form, users will have a hard time entering text if they cannot see what they are entering.

26.5. Using the `MessageWindow` **Class**

You want to communicate with unmanaged applications by using Window Messages.

Technique

Because COM interop was not included in the .NET Compact Framework, a class was specifically designed for Smart Device Applications for communicating with unmanaged applications rather than relying on `PInvoke`. The result was the creation of two .NET Compact Framework classes called `MessageWindow` and `Message`. These classes allow you to send and receive window messages. A window message consists of a 32-bit value specifying the actual message itself and two values named `WPARAM` and `LPARAM`, which contain extra information about the window message.

The typical use of a `MessageWindow` is to communicate with an unmanaged application by sending and receiving Window messages. If you're new to Win32 API programming, the concepts presented here might seem a little foreign because the .NET Framework kindly shields the developer from working with window handles and messages. This recipe builds an application that displays all the window titles currently active on the system with the option to programmatically close a window by selecting its name in a `ListBox` control and clicking on a `Close` button. You build it by creating an unmanaged C++ application that uses the `EnumWindows` Win32 API method to enumerate all the windows on the system. For each window it finds, it posts a window message back to the managed C# application, which then places the window title into the `ListBox` control.

The first step to create this application is to create the unmanaged C++ application. Recall that you cannot create a Visual C++ Smart Device Application within Visual Studio .NET 2003 but must instead use the Embedded Visual Tools application available as a free download on Microsoft's Web site. If you don't have the application and don't want to download it, the final binary files are included in the code for this book, which is available at `http://www.samspublishing.com`. Also, because this book is written for C# developers, the C++ explanation is rather terse.

For the unmanaged portion, we create a Windows CE (WCE) Dynamic Link Library project with the option to export sample variables, methods, and classes turned on. After the project is created, open the main C++ source file and add an `EnumerateDeviceWindows` method, which accepts a `HWND` parameter but does not return anything. Additionally, wrap the entire method with an `extern "C"` block. This step prevents the compiler from mangling the method name, a concept known as *name decoration*, so that it's easier to use from your C# application. The method body, shown in Listing 26.1, simply starts the window enumeration by calling the Win32 API method `EnumWindows`, passing a pointer to the callback function and the window handle, which is passed from the C# application. Finally, the callback method named `EnumWindowsProc` first checks whether the current window being enumerated is a child and then posts a message to the callback window, which ultimately ends up in the C# application created next. The unmanaged C++ code should appear similar to the code in Listing 26.1.

Listing 26.1   **Enumerating Windows with C++**

```cpp
#include "stdafx.h"
#include "MessageWindowNative.h"

#ifdef MESSAGEWINDOWNATIVE_EXPORTS
#define MESSAGEWINDOWNATIVE_API __declspec(dllexport)
#else
#define MESSAGEWINDOWNATIVE_API __declspec(dllimport)
#endif

// entry point method for DLL's
BOOL APIENTRY DllMain( HANDLE hModule,
                       DWORD  ul_reason_for_call,
                       LPVOID lpReserved )
{
    switch (ul_reason_for_call)
    {
        case DLL_PROCESS_ATTACH:
        case DLL_THREAD_ATTACH:
        case DLL_THREAD_DETACH:
        case DLL_PROCESS_DETACH:
            break;
    }
    return TRUE;
}


// Window message value to send
#define WM_USER_ADDWINDOW WM_USER + 1

BOOL CALLBACK EnumWindowsProc( HWND hwnd, LPARAM lParam )
{
    WPARAM wParam = 0;

    if( GetParent( hwnd ) != NULL )
        wParam = 1;

    // post message to C# application
    PostMessage( (HWND) lParam, WM_USER_ADDWINDOW, wParam, (LPARAM) hwnd );

    return TRUE;
}


extern "C"
```

Listing 26.1   **Continued**

```
{
    MESSAGEWINDOWNATIVE_API void EnumerateDeviceWindows( HWND hCallbackWnd )
    {
        EnumWindows( EnumWindowsProc, (LPARAM) hCallbackWnd );
    }
}
```

The next step is to create a C# Smart Device Application that communicates with the DLL just shown using PInvoke methods and window messages. After creating a Smart Device Windows Application, drag and drop a ListBox control and a Button from the toolbox onto the form and add an event handler for the button. After this step, you add a new class that will perform the communication with the unmanaged DLL.

Create a new class derived from MessageWindow. You have to add a reference to the Microsoft.WindowsCE.Forms assembly in addition to a using declaration to avoid having to namespace-qualify the message classes. To simplify things, this class reports back to the Windows Form by obtaining a reference to it and calling a public method. Therefore, create a field within the class whose data type is the main form type, and assign it by creating a custom constructor that the main form will pass itself as a parameter to. The code for the C# application should appear similar to Listing 26.2.

Listing 26.2   **Communication Using Window Messages**

```
using System;
using System.Drawing;
using System.Collections;
using System.Windows.Forms;
using System.Data;
using Microsoft.WindowsCE.Forms;
using System.Runtime.InteropServices;
using System.Text;

namespace _6_MessageWindow
{
    public class DeviceWindowsForm : System.Windows.Forms.Form
    {
        private System.Windows.Forms.ListBox listBox1;
        private System.Windows.Forms.MainMenu mainMenu1;
        private System.Windows.Forms.Button btnClose;
        private MessageHandler handler;

        public DeviceWindowsForm()
        {
            InitializeComponent();

            handler = new MessageHandler( this );
```

Listing 26.2   **Continued**

```
        }

        protected override void Dispose( bool disposing )
        {
            base.Dispose( disposing );
        }

        private void InitializeComponent()
        {
            this.mainMenu1 = new System.Windows.Forms.MainMenu();
            this.listBox1 = new System.Windows.Forms.ListBox();
            this.btnClose = new System.Windows.Forms.Button();
            //
            // listBox1
            //
            this.listBox1.Size = new System.Drawing.Size(240, 226);
            //
            // btnClose
            //
            this.btnClose.Location = new System.Drawing.Point(80, 232);
            this.btnClose.Text = "Close";
            this.btnClose.Click += new System.EventHandler(this.btnClose_Click);
            //
            // DeviceWindowsForm
            //
            this.Controls.Add(this.btnClose);
            this.Controls.Add(this.listBox1);
            this.Menu = this.mainMenu1;
            this.Text = "Form1";

        }

        static void Main()
        {
            Application.Run(new DeviceWindowsForm());
        }

        private void btnClose_Click(object sender, System.EventArgs e)
        {
        }
    }

    public class MessageHandler : MessageWindow
    {
        // the main application form
```

Listing 26.2   **Continued**

```
        DeviceWindowsForm mainForm;

        public MessageHandler(DeviceWindowsForm mainForm)
        {
            // save the form to post back to
            this.mainForm = mainForm;
        }
    }
}
```

Two lines of communication occur within the application. The first is between the
`MessageWindow` class and the unmanaged DLL, and the second is between the
`MessageWindow` class and the Window Form. We tackle the first technique first. Window
messages are 32-bit integers and can be anything you want to define as long as you don't
use a window message reserved for the system. In the unmanaged C++ code, the window message was named `WM_USER_ADDWINDOW`, which was defined using the `WM_USER`
window message. You can use any value higher than `WM_USER` because it is guaranteed
not to be reserved by the operating system. Therefore, in the `MessageWindow` class, create
a static constant for that value noting that the C++ expression `WM_USER + 1` evaluates to
the number `0x0401`:

```
public const int WM_USER_ADDWINDOW = 0x0401;
```

Next, you need to use the `PInvoke` methods described in Chapter 21 to import the
proper DLL methods from the unmanaged project. Additionally, this application calls the
`GetWindowText` API function to get the window title. The `DllImport` statements should
appear as follow within the `MessageWindow` class:

```
[DllImport(@"\Windows\MessageWindowNative.dll")]
public extern static void EnumerateDeviceWindows(IntPtr hWnd);

[DllImport("coredll.dll")]
static extern int GetWindowText(IntPtr hWnd, StringBuilder text, int count);
```

The line of communication between the `MessageWindow` and unmanaged DLL is almost
complete. The last step is to create the method that listens for the window message posted by the unmanaged method. You override the base class method `WndProc`. A `WndProc`
is the main method the operating system calls in your application when a window message needs to be delivered to you. This method uses the `Message` class as a parameter that
packages up all the necessary components of a Windows message. The actual window
message is accessed using the `Msg` property defined in the `Message` parameter. If this
value is the same as the `WM_USER_ADDWINDOW` constant created earlier, then you know that
the message originated from the unmanaged DLL and you can therefore unpack the rest
of the message to send to the Windows Form for display. Listing 26.3 demonstrates the
`WndProc` method. The `WParam` and `LParam` properties of the `Message` parameter corre-

spond to values passed in the PostMessage method from the unmanaged DLL. Because these values can be anything you want because it is a user defined message, we arbitrarily used the WParam to denote whether the window being enumerated is a child and LParam to be the actual window handle value. This handle is used as a parameter to the GetWindowText API call to get the window's associated title. Additionally, to get the unmanaged DLL to start enumerating windows, create a method named EnumWindows, which will be called by the main Windows Form and will call the unmanaged DLL method using PInvoke.

Listing 26.3   **Overriding WndProc to Handle Window Messages**

```
public void EnumWindows()
{
    // call the native dll function
    EnumerateDeviceWindows( this.Hwnd );
}


// Override the default WndProc behavior to monitor messages.
protected override void WndProc(ref Message msg)
{
    switch(msg.Msg)
    {
        case WM_USER_ADDWINDOW:
        {
            // get the window title using GetWindowText
            StringBuilder windowText = new StringBuilder(1024);
            GetWindowText( msg.LParam.ToInt32(), windowText, 1024 );
            if( windowText.ToString() == "" )
                break;

            // if wParam is 1 then window is a child of someone
            if( msg.WParam.ToInt32() == 1 )
                windowText.Insert( 0, "    " );

            // add it to the listbox of the main form
            mainForm.AddWindow( msg.LParam, windowText.ToString() );
            break;
        }
        default:
        {
            break;
        }
    }

    // Call the base class WndProc for default message handling.
    base.WndProc(ref msg);
}
```

At this point, the `MessageWindow` and unmanaged DLL are able to communicate using window messages. The last step is to simply enable the last line of communication between the `MessageWindow` class and the main Windows form. In the code just shown, you can see a method being called named `AddWindow`. This method is defined in the form class and accepts an `IntPtr` and `string` parameter, denoting the window handle and window title of the window currently being enumerated. A `Hashtable` object stores the window handles with the window title being the `key`. Although this method isn't the best method to use because some window titles can theoretically be the same, it works for our purposes now without complicating things further. Additionally, you need a method to start the `MessageWindow` class, so within the constructor of the main form, initialize the `Hashtable` object and add a method call to the `MessageWindow` method named `EnumWindows`, which was defined earlier. The `AddWindow` function and the updated constructor for the form should be similar to the following code:

```
public DeviceWindowsForm()
{
    InitializeComponent();

    hWndTable = new Hashtable();
    handler = new MessageHandler( this );

    // fill the listbox
    handler.EnumWindows();
}

public void AddWindow( IntPtr hWnd, string WindowTitle )
{
    // save window handle
    hWndTable[WindowTitle] = hWnd;

    // add to listbox
    listBox1.Items.Add( WindowTitle );
}
```

Last but not least is the button handler. At this point in the application, a user sees a large list of windows within the `ListBox`. The `EnumWindows` API method does not distinguish between visible and hidden windows, so even though no windows are visible, you still see a large amount of hidden windows within the `ListBox`. The button handler for the application allows the user to select a window title from the `ListBox` and force it to close by sending it an operating-system–defined message called `WM_CLOSE`. Instead of receiving messages with the `MessageWindow` and `Message` classes, you can send them also. To do so, create a new `Message` object by calling the static method `Message.Create` and passing a window handle, the message to send, and the associated `WParam` and `LParam` parameters of which both are `0` for the `WM_CLOSE` message. The window handle to send it to, if you recall, was stored in the `Hashtable` using the window title as the key.

Therefore, pass the selected `ListBox` item as the key to the `Hashtable` to retrieve its associated window handle. Finally, call the static method `MessageWindow.Send`, which sends the `WM_CLOSE` message to the target window:

```
private void btnClose_Click(object sender, System.EventArgs e)
{
    Message msg;

    // get selected hwnd
    IntPtr hwnd = (IntPtr) hWndTable[listBox1.SelectedItem.ToString()];

    // create the message to send
    msg = Message.Create( hwnd, WM_CLOSE, (IntPtr) 0, (IntPtr) 0 );

    // close the window
    MessageWindow.SendMessage( ref msg );

    // refresh listbox
    listBox1.Items.Clear();
    handler.EnumWindows();
}
```

Comments

Window messages drive the user interfaces of Windows. Although Windows Form applications shield you from having to learn all the intricacies, messages are still sent to your application and handled within the .NET Framework just like the code in this recipe. Another item that a developer using the .NET Framework rarely manages is Window handles. Each window created in the operating system is assigned a unique 32-bit value. The operating system uses this value as a pointer into its internally maintained handle table, which contains information about each window. A developer uses a window handle to interact with other windows within the system whenever information needs to be extracted from it, as in the `GetWindowText` method shown in this recipe, or a message needs to be sent to it, as in the `WM_CLOSE` message. Both the window handle and window message are packaged up with corresponding `WParam` and `LParam` values containing additional information into a `Message` class used by the .NET Compact Framework.

There is one additional thing to note about the code for this recipe dealing with the `GetWindowText` method called using `PInvoke`. In a desktop version of Windows such as Windows XP, the `GetWindowsText` method is contained within `user32.dll` library. For Pocket PC applications, there is no `user32.dll`. Instead, a lot of the methods are contained in the `coredll.dll` library contained within the device's ROM. Again, although the differences are small when changing from a desktop to a mobile-device environment, they are still worthy of pointing out.

26.6. Creating an IrDA Client

You want to create an Infrared Data Association (IrDA) client application that can communicate using infrared communication with a server.

Technique

The .NET Compact Framework contains the ability to communicate with other devices using an infrared (IR) connection, something the full .NET Framework doesn't have without resorting to pure `Socket` communications. This recipe and the next look at the process to both send and receive data using an infrared port on a mobile device. Additionally, we explain an IR chat application to demonstrate the concepts, and we use the terms *client* and *server* even though we create only one application. In the traditional sense of the words, a client is the portion that sends data, and a server is the portion that receives.

Sending data through an IR connection uses the .NET Compact Framework class named `IrDAClient` defined in the `System.Net.IrDA` assembly, to which you have to add a reference in your project. For the sample that goes along with this and the next recipe, the form contains a large, multiline read-only `TextBox` control used as the chat transcript; a smaller, single-line `TextBox`, which is used to enter a message; and a corresponding `Button` to send the data. The send portion of the application resides within the `Button`'s `Click` event handler.

The first step in sending data is to create an `IrDAClient`. Pass an `IrDAEndPoint` object, a `string` denoting the service name, or an empty parameter list. The `IrDAEndPoint` contains a `ServiceName` property, which is the equivalent of sending in a single string parameter to the constructor. This `ServiceName` can be anything you want, but the receiving device must be listening for that service name for a connection to be made. This process is similar to that of ports used in sockets but uses a unique string value instead of an integer. If a `ServiceName` is not specified, which means you are creating an `IrDAClient` with an empty parameter list, you can create the IR connection by calling the `Connect` method and passing in the `ServiceName` there. Listing 26.4 is the initial portion of the `Button` event handler. If no connection is made within a specified time period, an exception is thrown. Therefore, you create a loop to allow a certain number of retries before giving up.

Listing 26.4   **Using Infrared with Windows Forms**

```
using System;
using System.Collections;
using System.Windows.Forms;
using System.Data;
using System.Threading;
using System.Net;
using System.Net.Sockets;
```

Listing 26.4   **Continued**

```
using System.IO;
using System.Text;

namespace _7_IRChatClient
{
    public class Form1 : System.Windows.Forms.Form
    {
        private System.Windows.Forms.TextBox tbTranscript;
        private System.Windows.Forms.TextBox tbMessage;
        private System.Windows.Forms.Button btnSend;
        private System.Windows.Forms.MainMenu mainMenu1;
        private System.Windows.Forms.MenuItem menuItem1;
        private System.Windows.Forms.MenuItem mnuExit;

        // the name used for this IR service
        private string serviceType = "IRDA_CHAT";

        public Form1()
        {
            InitializeComponent();
        }

        /* Windows Form Designer Generated Code */

        private void AddMessage( string name, string message )
        {
            tbTranscript.Text += name + ": " + message + "\r\n";
            tbTranscript.ScrollToCaret();
        }

        private void btnSend_Click(object sender, System.EventArgs e)
        {
            int numTries = 0;
            const int numRetries = 5;
            IrDAClient client = null;   // the client to send data to

            // disable the send button and display the wait cursor
            btnSend.Enabled = false;
            Cursor.Current = Cursors.WaitCursor;

            do
            {
                try
                {
                    // find a device to send data to
```

Listing 26.4   **Continued**

```
        client = new IrDAClient( serviceType );
    }
    catch( Exception ex )
    {
        if( numTries >= numRetries-1 )
        {
            // add a message to the transcript TextBox
            AddMessage("Error","cannot send message-"+ex.Message);

            // enable button, reset cursor, clear message TextBox
            btnSend.Enabled = true;
            tbMessage.Text = "";
            Cursor.Current = Cursors.Default;
            return;
        }
    }

    numTries++;

} while( (client == null) && (numTries < numRetries ));

// to be continued...
```

At this point, if the code makes it past the do/while loop, a connection is made and data
cannot be sent. The IR classes were designed similarly to the Socket classes, which
means you utilize streams to send data to the other device. To get a Stream object, call
the GetStream method defined in the IrDAClient class. Next, call the Write method
from the Stream object passing a byte array, the offset to start at in the array, and the
number of total bytes to send. For this example, the application sends the text contained
in the message TextBox. To convert a string to a byte array, you use the GetBytes
method defined in the Encoding.ASCII class. After the data is sent, the Stream and
IrDAClient objects are closed and the application is reset and ready to send more data
whenever the user clicks the send button, as shown in Listing 26.5.

Listing 26.5   **Sending Data over Infrared**

```
Stream byteStream = null;
try
{
    byteStream = client.GetStream();
    byteStream.Write( Encoding.ASCII.GetBytes( tbMessage.Text ),
        0, tbMessage.Text.Length );
    AddMessage( "You", tbMessage.Text );
}
```

Listing 26.5 **Continued**

```
            finally
            {
                if( byteStream != null )
                    byteStream.Close();

                if( client != null )
                    client.Close();

                btnSend.Enabled = true;
                tbMessage.Text = "";
                Cursor.Current = Cursors.Default;
            }
        } // end btnSend_Click
```

Comments

Infrared communication between devices has been around for a number of years due to its immense popularity, especially for the transfer of contact information. Infrared on PDAs has given rise to a variety of different applications. For instance, some applications allow you to play multiplayer games by simply lining up the IR ports. Some applications even let you use your mobile device as a television remote control.

Chapter 15, "Sockets," described the notion of protocols. A *protocol* is simply a contract that is established between two systems for them to communicate effectively. The rules it enforces indicate what can and can't be sent between the two machines as well as the format of the data. This chapter developed an extremely simple protocol even though it didn't look like one. The protocol contained only two rules. The first rule was that a special service name must be used for IR chat application to communicate, and the name was arbitrarily chosen using a string value of IRDA_CHAT. The second rule concerned how data is transferred, which is by passing strings back and forth. Again, nothing major here and although everything is implied from the code, you should strive to establish a certain protocol when developing an application that utilizes IR communication. Additionally, if you are interested in communicating with another IR-capable device, you have to discover its service name and communicate using the protocol defined by that device.

26.7. Creating an IrDA Server

You want to create a server application that listens for incoming connection from an infrared port.

Technique

The last recipe created the send portion of an IR chat application. This recipe shows how to add the second piece of the equation, receiving data from an IR port. Receiving data uses an `IrDAListener` object that blocks until a connection is made, receives data, and then goes back into its blocking listening state. The blocking method is named `AcceptIrDAClient`, which, as its name suggests, returns an `IrDAClient` object that it has successfully connected to. Because this method is a blocking call, you want to use it within a secondary thread if your application uses a Windows Form. If you are continuing with the application created in the previous recipe, add two fields to the form class: an `IrDAListener` and a `Thread` that will be used for receiving data. Additionally, within the form constructor, create an instance of both objects. The `Thread` constructor accepts a `ThreadStart` delegate, which is shown following this recipe. At this point, your class variables and new constructor should appear as shown in Listing 26.6.

Listing 26.6   **Creating a Listener Thread**

```
using System;
using System.Threading;
using System.Net.Sockets;
using System.IO;
using System.Text;

namespace _7_IRChatClient
{
    public class Form1 : System.Windows.Forms.Form
    {
        private System.Windows.Forms.TextBox tbTranscript;
        private System.Windows.Forms.TextBox tbMessage;
        private System.Windows.Forms.Button btnSend;
        private System.Windows.Forms.MainMenu mainMenu1;
        private System.Windows.Forms.MenuItem menuItem1;
        private System.Windows.Forms.MenuItem mnuExit;
        private Thread listenerThread;
        private string serviceType = "IRDA_CHAT";
        IrDAListener listener;

        public Form1()
        {
            InitializeComponent();
```

Listing 26.6   **Continued**

```
            // create the IR listener
            listener = new IrDAListener( serviceType );

            // create the thread and start it
            listenerThread = new Thread( new ThreadStart(
                ListenerThreadMethod ));
            listenerThread.Start();
        }

        void ListenerThreadMethod()
        {
        }

        // continued...
}
```

The code passed a string value into the constructor of the `IrDAListener` constructor. This value is the service name that the listener will use when listening for incoming connections. In the previous recipe, a client wanting to send data creates an `IrDAClient` object passing this same string for the service name. As you can see, this method is quite similar to the methods used in sockets, but instead of integers being used for ports, strings are used in IR communication for service names.

The next step is to put the `IrDAListener` object in a blocked state while it listens for incoming connections. You call the `AcceptIrDAClient` method, which, as mentioned earlier, returns an `IrDAClient` object once a connection is made. At this point, the application is ready to receive data. To receive the incoming data from the connected client, call the `GetStream` method, which returns a `Stream` object. Next, call the `Read` method from the `Stream` object passing a byte array to fill; the offset into the array to start, which is normally 0; and the maximum bytes to read. Once this step is finished, you can close the `Stream` and `IrDAClient` objects and start listening for incoming connections again. Listing 26.7 demonstrates the techniques just described contained within the `Thread` delegate.

Listing 26.7   **Connecting and Communicating with Infrared Clients**

```
void ListenerThreadMethod()
{
    int bytesRead = 0;

    IrDAClient client = null;   // the connecting client

    Stream byteStream = null;
    byte[] buffer = new byte[1024];
```

Listing 26.7   **Continued**

```
    try
    {
        do
        {
            listener.Start();

            client = listener.AcceptIrDAClient();
            byteStream = client.GetStream();
            bytesRead = byteStream.Read( buffer, 0, 1024 );

            if( byteStream != null )
                byteStream.Close();

            if( client != null )
                client.Close();

            AddMessage( client.RemoteMachineName,
                Encoding.ASCII.GetString( buffer, 0, bytesRead ));
        } while (true);
    }
    finally
    {
        if( byteStream != null )
            byteStream.Close();

        if( client != null )
            client.Close();

        listener.Stop();
    }
}
```

Comments

This recipe and the last introduced the IrDAListener and IrDAClient classes. These two classes perform the majority of IR communications within the .NET Compact Framework. However, you can use another IR class to obtain more information about a connected client. The IrDADeviceInfo class allows you to get information about a device, such as its DeviceID, DeviceName, supported CharacterSet, and a value from the IrDAHints enumerate data type through the IrDADeviceInfo property Hints. These Hints indicate whether the device is a fax machine, PDA, printer, or computer, to name a few. However, devices aren't required to return that information, so you shouldn't use it as an indicator for what type of device you are discovering. You use the IrDADeviceInfo class in conjunction with an IrDAClient object. The IrDAClient class contains a method named `DiscoverDevices`, which returns an array of `IrDADeviceInfo` methods for any devices discovered in its IR range. Listing 26.8 uses an `IrDAClient` to discover any devices within range, and if it finds any, it places the information in the transcript `TextBox` for the application created in this recipe.

Listing 26.8   **Device Discovery Using Infrared**

```
private void mnuDevInfo_Click(object sender, System.EventArgs e)
{
    IrDAClient client = new IrDAClient();
    IrDADeviceInfo[] devices = client.DiscoverDevices(10);
    foreach( IrDADeviceInfo device in devices )
    {
        AddMessage( "Found", "DeviceID = " + FormatDeviceID(device.DeviceID) +
            " DeviceName: " + device.DeviceName +
            " Hints: " +  device.Hints.ToString() );
    }
}


private string FormatDeviceID( byte[] deviceID )
{
    string ret = "0x";

    for( int i = 0; i < 4; i++ )
    {
        ret += Convert.ToInt32(deviceID[i]).ToString("X");
    }

    return ret;
}
```

26.8. Building CAB Files for Application Distribution

You want to create an installation for mobile devices.

Technique

Installing an application to a mobile device is understandably more difficult than installing a desktop computer. You create the main packaging for a Smart Device Application using cabinet (CAB) files, which contain not only the program itself but also a device information file (INF) specifying the installation steps to take on the device.

Because devices can all use different processors, you must create CAB files for each supported processor. The .NET Framework was built with support for five processors, which means you need CAB files for each one. The Visual Studio .NET IDE has this support automatically built in. To create the necessary CAB file, highlight the project name within Solution Explorer and select Build, Build Cab File from the main menu. This step launches the CAB file creation tool named `cabwiz.exe`. After the process completes, the corresponding CAB files are placed in the CAB subdirectory of your project's main directory.

Although the ability to automatically generate CAB files for distribution is a nice feature added to the IDE, it creates only the necessary defaults without allowing you to customize the device installation. The default behavior is to place your application in the location specified in your project properties and to create a shortcut to that application in the Programs program group. To customize the application further, you have to edit the INF file that `cabwiz.exe` uses and then directly run `cabwiz.exe` to generate the CAB files again.

The following technique demonstrates a possible INF edit you can make and how to rerun the `cabwiz.exe` tool to regenerate the CAB files. To begin, find the folder named `obj/Debug` or `obj/Release` depending on which build mode you are in. In that folder, you find the INF file as well as a `.bat` file used to launch `cabwiz.exe`. You are going to edit the INF file to add a new Registry entry on the device.

Within the INF file, locate the recipe labeled `[DefaultInstall]` and add a new entry named `AddReg`, setting its value equal to `RegSettings`. The `DefaultInstall` recipe should appear as follows:

```
[DefaultInstall]
CEShortcuts=Shortcuts
CopyFiles=Files.Common
AddReg = RegSettings
```

Next, create a new section named `[RegSettings]`. When the device parses the INF file, it looks for the `AddReg` section and adds any Registry entries found within the corresponding section that you are about to create. The format for a Registry entry in the INF file uses the following syntax:

```
<registry key>, <registry subkey>, <value name>, <value type>, <value data>
```

The Registry key is a root Registry key, which you can specify using an acronym. For example, you can abbreviate `HKEY_LOCAL_MACHINE` using `HKLM`. The name for the value can be any string, and if you leave it empty, the default Registry value is filled in. Finally, the value type is an integer value specifying whether the value data is a string, `DWORD`, byte data, or multiple string value. The following example creates three Registry entries, one of which is a string and the other two `DWORD` values:

```
[RegSettings]
HKLM, Software\My Company\My Application,, 0x00010003, Copyright (c) 2003 My
Company
HKLM, Software\My Company\My Application, VersionMajor, 0x00010001, 1
HKLM, Software\My Company\My Application, VersionMinor, 0x00010001, 0
```

Registry entries are not created in the generated INF file that Visual Studio .NET creates, which is why we focused on them in this recipe. The INF file is logically organized, and determining the method to create shortcuts or additional files is a matter of following the same methods already present in the INF file.

When you finish editing the INF file, you can double-click on the `BuildCab.bat` file to regenerate the CAB files. One word of caution: If you use the Build Cab File menu item within Visual Studio .NET after editing the INF file, the changes you make are lost. Therefore, either back up the INF file after the changes are made or move the `BuildCab.bat` and INF file to another location and fix the path information before running it in the new location.

Comments

CAB files are created using an INF file. This INF file serves two purposes. The first is to tell the CAB file creation utility, `cabwiz.exe`, where the binary files for your application exist. This INF file is then placed within the CAB file itself when they are created to serve a secondary purpose. When the mobile device unpacks the CAB file when it's finished downloading, the INF file determines where the files go, which Registry settings to create, and whether any shortcuts need to be made.

26.9. Deploying Mobile Applications Using ActiveSync

You want to create an application installer that uses Microsoft ActiveSync.

Technique

The previous recipe demonstrated how to automatically generate CAB files for distribution as well as how to edit the generated INF to further customize the install. Although you can simply distribute the CAB files to users, they would have to manually copy the CAB files to their devices and then run them to start the installation. The *ActiveSync* utility provided for mobile devices running Microsoft operating systems allows you to provide automatic installation.

Assuming that you have already created the CAB files as outlined in the previous recipe, the next step is to create an INI file containing information used by ActiveSync. Fortunately, this file is quite a bit smaller than the INF and definitely much easier to create. You need two sections for the INI file; the first is called `[CEAppManager]` and contains a `Version` entry and a `Component` name, which is the same name as the next section. This next section contains three entries: a `Description`, which is displayed to the user during installation; the `Uninstall` entry, which is placed in the Add/Remove group in ActiveSync; and the `CabFiles` entry, which is a comma-delimited list of your application's CAB files created from the previous recipe. The full INI file should appear something like the following:

```
[CEAppManager]
Version     = 1.0
Component   = MyApp

[MyApp]
Description = My Application
Uninstall   = My Application
CabFiles    =
MyApp_PPC.ARM.CAB,MyApp_PPC.ARMV4.cab,MyApp_PPC.MIPS.cab,MyApp_PPC.SH3.cab
```

Once you create this file, create a normal installation application using one of the industry-standard installation programs or by simply creating one yourself. In any case, the install program needs to look for the file named `CeAppMgr.exe` and launch it passing the `INI` file created in this recipe on the command line. Rather than search through the file system looking for the `CeAppMgr.exe` application, you can query the Registry by looking at the value in the following key:

```
HKEY_LOCAL_MACHINE\SOFTWARE\Microsoft\Windows\CurrentVersion\App
Paths\CEAPPMGR.EXE
```

Comments

For a Smart Device Application, you can just give users the option to download the CAB file and run it on their devices. However, that isn't the most user friendly method. First, every user must know what type of processor he is running in his mobile device. Furthermore, he has to know how to transfer files from his desktop to a location on his device. If that weren't enough, he must then locate the CAB file once it's on the device and double-click it to start the installation. If any user is also accustomed to uninstalling applications on the device using the ActiveSync application from the desktop computer, he won't be able to use the manual CAB-copy method just described. Therefore, to create the best user experience possible, automate the installation as much as possible using the ActiveSync tool.

26.10. Creating Mobile ASP.NET Pages

You want to create ASP.NET pages that are targeted for mobile devices.

Technique

ASP.NET can allow you to create some pretty sophisticated Web sites, but for mobile devices that have small screens, your Web application might be unbearable to navigate. The Smart Device Extensions include ASP.NET Mobile Web Forms to allow you to create specific Web Forms tailored to small devices.

To create a new Mobile ASP.NET project, select the ASP.NET Mobile Web Application template from the New Project Wizard. Once you create the project, you are placed in the Web Form designer for mobile Web applications. One of the first differences you'll notice right away between Mobile ASP.NET pages and regular ASP.NET pages is the inability to use `GridLayout`. When the designer opens, you see a small window within the designer labeled `Form1`, which is where you place any necessary Mobile ASP.NET controls.

Designing a Mobile ASP.NET application follows the same procedures of designing a regular ASP.NET page. The toolbox window, however, displays a separate tab for mobile Web applications named Mobile Web Forms. A lot of the same controls from ASP.NET are included, but this tab adds some controls and removes other controls. For instance, the `DataGrid` cannot be displayed on a mobile device due to its propensity to become quite large when rendering. However, a new control named the `ObjectList` fills the void and is discussed in the next recipe. Along with the `ObjectList` control, some of the Mobile Web Form controls include the `PhoneCall`, `Form`, `TextView`, `Command`, and `DeviceSpecific` controls. This recipe and the following three recipes use each one of these controls.

As an example, this recipe creates a Mobile Web Application whose initial page gives a user a list of links to other areas within the site, which exercises a few of the Mobile Web Form controls. Therefore, you add four `Link` controls to the initial form. Mobile ASP.NET applications can offer a different method of Web site navigation. In ASP.NET, each form was associated with its own class. In mobile ASP.NET applications, you have the option of sharing the same class for all forms that are created. By dragging and dropping a `Form` control, you are in essence creating a new page for the application while still working within the same code-behind file. When the whole page is initially loaded, only the form that appears at the top of the designer window is displayed. To create a link to another form on the same page, drag and drop a `Link` control and sets its `NavigateUrl` property to the name of the form to display when the link is clicked.

The downloadable code for this recipe is available on the Sams Web site (`http://www.samspublishing.com`) and contains a control-panel form used to navigate through the different forms and a simple calculator form that performs arithmetic operations and uses form validation. This form in particular demonstrates that creating mobile Web forms is similar to creating full ASP.NET applications. The recipes that follow use the Mobile ASP.NET Web Form controls.

Comments

Browsing the Internet on a Pocket PC is not truly convenient because a majority of the Web sites are just too large to render on such a small screen. Mobile devices are seeing an explosion when it comes to Internet connectivity, and any large Web site should have mobile-device–specific pages, if not now, then very soon.

A feature you might want to consider adding to your ASP.NET-driven site is detecting mobile devices. In other words, if a user connects to the site using a desktop-based browser, you should serve up regular ASP.NET application pages. If, however, she connects with a mobile-device–based browser such as a Pocket IE or cell phone, you should serve up specific mobile Web pages. You can do so by creating an entry page, usually named `Default.aspx`, and creating code within the `Page_Load` handler to redirect a user based on her browser type. To detect whether a user is connecting with a mobile device, access the `Browser` object property named `IsMobileDevice` through the `Request` object, as shown in the code that follows. If `IsMobileDevice` returns `true`, then redirect the user to your mobile-device–specific pages, and if not, redirect her to the normal ASP.NET pages:

```
private void Page_Load(object sender, System.EventArgs e)
{

    if (Request.Browser["IsMobileDevice"] == "true" )
    {
        Response.Redirect("MobileDefault.aspx");
    }
    else
    {
        Response.Redirect("DesktopDefault.aspx");
    }
}
```

26.11. Using the Mobile ASP.NET `ObjectList` Control

You want to display data from a database using a control similar to the `DataGrid` control.

Technique

Mobile Web Forms do not contain a `DataGrid` control because a lot of the `DataGrid`'s functionality assumes a feature-rich browser is viewing the content. Instead, a new control named `ObjectList` allows you to display formatted data from a database. Assuming you have a Mobile Web Application project created and an initial form displayed in the Web Form Designer, drag and drop an `ObjectList` control from the toolbox to the form. Next, drag and drop a database table located in the Server Explorer from a data connection. This example uses the Northwind SQL database, and the table is the Products table.

Just as the Windows Form designer did when you created a Windows Form application, and the Web Form designer did when you created an ASP.NET application, dragging and dropping a table from the Server Explorer creates a connection and data adapter object. For the Products table, it corresponds to a `SqlConnection` and

SqlDataAdapter object. The next step is to generate a typed DataSet. Select the SqlDataAdapter object located in the bottom tray area of the Web Form designer, and click on the Generate Dataset verb located in the Property Browser. This step creates a typed DataSet object that you will databind the ObjectList control to.

To databind the ObjectList, select the control and specify the DataSet object to bind to using the DataSource property. Next, select the table within the DataSet that you want the ObjectList to display by setting the DataMember property. The last step is to write the code within your page handler as you did with ASP.NET projects—to fill the DataSet using the SqlDataAdapter and then to databind the ObjectList by calling the DataBind method, as shown in the following code:

```
private void Page_Load(object sender, System.EventArgs e)
{
    if( !Page.IsPostBack )
    {
        sqlDataAdapter1.Fill( productsDS1 );
        this.DataBind();
    }
}
```

At this point you can view the mobile Web form in a browser. By default, the ObjectList creates a single column whose header is the name of the primary-key column and a list of the values for that primary key using links. Clicking one of the links displays all the data for that specific record on a single page, with a link at the bottom to return to the master view. The next step is to change the default behavior so a list of product names appears rather than the ProductID column. Right-click on the ObjectList within the Web Form designer and select the Property Builder menu item. Select the General property page and move the PropertyName item from the list of Available Fields to the list of Selected Fields. Doing so overrides the default behavior of the ObjectList so only items within the Selected Fields list appear. Additionally, the first item in the list is rendered as a link to navigate to the detail page. When you run the mobile Web application now, you see a list of product names instead of their associated ID values, and clicking a product name displays more information for that product.

The last item to discuss as it relates to the ObjectList is the ability to edit items. For this example, you create a custom command that deletes an item from the ObjectList and subsequently from the SQL database. This procedure also uses the Property Builder dialog. Once the Property Builder dialog appears, click on the Commands property page. Next, click on the Create New Command button and give the command the name Delete. If the corresponding Text field is left blank, the text displayed will be the same as that of the command name.

The next step is to create an event handler for the Delete command. Select the ObjectList within the designer and add an event handler for the ItemCommand event using the Property Browser event view. Any items you add using the Property Builder will use the event handler you just created. To distinguish between the different

commands, you can access the `CommandName` property passed in through the
`ObjectListCommandEventArgs` object. For this example, the `CommandName` is `Delete`.
Therefore, whenever the `Delete` command is selected, perform the normal steps for
database updates by filling the `DataSet` to get the current data, find the corresponding
row to delete, remove it, and then update the database using the data adapter and rebind
the form controls. To determine the currently selected row in the `ObjectList` being
manipulated, you can use an indexer into the `ListItem` collection of the event argument
object. The index corresponds to the column within the table. In the example that follows, an index of `0` corresponds to the `ProductID` field of the `Products` table, which
you then use to find the corresponding row in the table by using the `FindByProductID`
method generated in the typed `DataSet` object. When the application runs, you can click
on a product name to view its detailed information. The bottom of the detail page contains a link named `Delete` and a link named `Back`. Clicking on the `Delete` link removes
that product from the database as shown in Listing 26.9.

Listing 26.9   **Responding to `ObjectList` Command Events**

```
private void ObjectList1_ItemCommand(object sender,
    System.Web.UI.MobileControls.ObjectListCommandEventArgs e)
{
    if( e.CommandName == "Delete" )
    {
        // get the current dataset
        sqlDataAdapter1.Fill( productsDS1, "Products");

        // find the correct row to delete
        ProductsDS.ProductsRow row =
            productsDS1.Products.FindByProductID( Int32.Parse(e.ListItem[0]) );

        // delete the row
        productsDS1.Products.RemoveProductsRow(row);

        // update the database and databind
        sqlDataAdapter1.Update( productsDS1, "Products");
        DataBind();
    }
}
```

Comments

The `DataGrid` is a powerful control, which unfortunately is a little too powerful to display on mobile Web browsers. The `ObjectList` uses a master/detail list to allow you to
navigate through the data of a database table using simple text rendering and hyperlinks
for navigation. Although not covered here, the `ObjectList` has a few other features

worth mentioning. Pagination is supported by the `ObjectList`. You access the Property Builder and set the number of items to display, which is normally 0 to display all items and the number of items to display per page. Additionally, you can customize the details page further by specifying your own fields in the Fields property page of the Property Builder. You have to make sure you uncheck the check box that automatically creates fields for you before adding your own. Each field that you add displays a value from the column in the database using the `DataField` selection box. You can also create a format string if, for instance, you want to display a certain field with a currency format. Finally, the `Title` field is the text that displays to the user to identify what the field denotes, such as Product Name or Product Price.

26.12. Querying Mobile Device Capabilities

You want to determine whether a connecting mobile device supports a certain technology or rendering method.

Technique

Mobile devices come in many forms, such as palmtops, dedicated Web devices, and cell phones. Because of the proliferation of all these devices, you occasionally have to tailor your site to work with a specific device. The `Device` property of the `MobilePage` class that your class derives from is a `MobileCapabilities` object. The `MobileCapabilities` class contains at least 72 different public properties that you can query to determine support for a certain technology. Listing 26.10 lists all the values for each property when a user connects to the page. To save your sanity, the code forgoes the painstakingly monotonous process of accessing each property individually. Rather, it uses reflection because that's what it's designed for, to dynamically retrieve all the public properties of the `MobileCapabilities` class. The final text is rendered onto a `TextView` mobile control.

Listing 26.10 **Enumerating Device Properties**

```
private void DeviceInformationForm_Load(object sender, System.EventArgs e)
{
    if( !Page.IsPostBack )
    {
        StringBuilder sb = new StringBuilder();

        // for each public property
        foreach( PropertyInfo prop in
            Device.GetType().GetProperties(
            BindingFlags.Instance | BindingFlags.Public) )
        {
            // only retrieve boolean properties
```

Listing 26.10   **Continued**

```
        if( prop.PropertyType != typeof(bool))
            continue;

        // print out property name and current value
        if( prop.GetValue(Device, null) != null )
            tvDeviceInfo.Text += "<b>" +
            prop.Name + "</b> = <em>" +
            prop.GetValue( Device, null ).ToString()+ "</em><br>";
    }
    }
}
```

Comments

If you run the mobile Web form containing the code in this recipe, you might be amazed. The .NET Compact Framework can determine several key pieces of information about a connecting mobile device that would be tremendously difficult and time-consuming to acquire without this support. The next recipe utilizes this information to support different rendering methods for specific classes of mobile devices.

26.13. Changing Mobile Web Form Output Using the `DeviceSpecific` Control

You want to change the content that is rendered to a client based on the mobile device capabilities.

Technique

The ASP.NET Mobile Web controls contain a special control called the `DeviceSpecific` control. The control itself is simply a container that allows you to define templates for specific mobile device capabilities. The following walkthrough demonstrates how to create content that looks different when viewed through a desktop browser, a Pocket PC browser, or on a cell phone.

After you create the ASP.NET Mobile Web Application project, drag and drop a `DeviceSpecific` control onto the Web form in the designer. The next step is to specify the different templates that this control supports. Each template is associated later with a specific device configuration. Once the page loads, the device configuration is checked against the configurations in the `DeviceSpecific` control, and if a match is found, the controls in that template are rendered. To add templates to the `DeviceSpecific` control, right-click on it and select the Templating Options menu item. The current list of templates in the Templating Options dialog will be blank, so click on the Edit button to add templates. The Applied Device Filters dialog lists a set of device configurations that are currently the most common and that you will more than likely use. The additional comments for this recipe explain how to add device filters.

For this example, the templates to add, in the order specified, include `isPocketIE`, `isHTML32`, and `supportsVoiceCalls`. The order in which you add these device filters is important. When the page loads, ASP.NET checks the first device filter, and if it makes a match, the corresponding template is rendered. For the three filters specified here, switching the `isHTML32` and `isPocketIE` causes Pocket PCs to render the `isHTML32` template because Pocket IE is a Win32 HTML browser.

Once you add the necessary device filters, you are ready to edit the associated templates. To edit a template for a single device filter, select that filter within the Templating Options dialog and close the dialog. Next, right-click on the `DeviceSpecific` class and choose the Edit Template, Header and Footer Templates menu item. You can then add ASP.NET mobile controls within the template. When you are finished, right-click on the `DeviceSpecific` control and select the End Template Editing item. You have to repeat this process for each device filter that you specified in the Templating Options, which means you have to select the next filter from the Templating Options dialog and repeat the process.

Comments

As mentioned in this recipe, the Web Form designer already contains a small subset of possible device filters that you can use. Some of them target certain technologies such as Pocket IE, whereas others specifically target actual mobile devices such as Nokia cell phones. You can add your own device filter by clicking on the Edit button of the Applied Device Filters dialog. This move brings up the Device Filter Editor, allowing you to create a custom filter based on a certain device capability. For instance, to add a device filter that detects whether a user is connecting using America Online (AOL), click on the New Device Filter button and give the filter a name of `isAOL`. In the `Compare` field of the `Attributes` section, select the `AOL` item and enter a value of `true` for the `Argument` field. Now whenever this filter is selected and a template is created for it, users who are using AOL will have specialized content rendered to them.

You can also use device filters to override individual properties for mobile Web controls. For instance, if you want users whose browsers support color to see a colorful label control, you can specify a specific property set for the `supportsColor` device filter. To do so, select the control that you want to edit and click on the button within the field for the `AppliedDeviceFilters` property in the Property Browser. Add any necessary device filters using the same technique discussed earlier in this recipe. For this example, add the `supportsColor` filter and close the dialog. Next, click on the button in the field for the `PropertyOverrides` property. The list of device filters displays in a `ComboBox` at the top of the dialog, and changing the device filter allows you to change the control's individual properties. Any property values you change only affect those devices that support the specified device filter.

26.14. Creating a `SqlServerCE` Database

You want to use a data from a SQL Server database installed on a mobile device.

Technique

Visual Studio .NET 2003 ships with a version of SQL Server designed to run on Windows CE and Pocket PC devices. The first step to create a database on the device is to copy SQL Server CE onto the device itself. The easiest way to do so is to create a new Smart Device Application and add a reference to the `System.Data.SqlServerCe` assembly. Once you build and deploy the application to the emulator or your device, the necessary binaries for `SqlServerCE` are also copied over. The examples covered in this and the next recipe assume that the SQL Server CE is running locally on the device. It is possible to do remote database connections with the .NET Compact Framework, but that topic is beyond the scope of this book. When you are ready to deploy your application to end users, the SQL Server CE CAB files are located in the following path:

```
<install drive>:\Program Files\Microsoft Visual Studio .NET 2003\
➥CompactFrameworkSDK\v1.0.5000
```

Additionally, you can use the techniques described in Recipe 26.8, "Building CAB Files for Application Distribution," to perform automatic installation of the CAB files.

Once you successfully transfer SQL Server CE to the device, you are ready to create a database. Run the Query Analyzer tool located in the Start menu with a link name of SQLCE Query. After the tool starts, click on the Databases item on the Objects tab and click on the Connect to Database toolbar located at the bottom of the window. This toolbar button has a green arrow on it to help distinguish it from the other button. Next, enter a name for the database, using an `.sdf` file extension and an optional password, and click on the New Database button.

After you create the database, expand the Databases node until you find the Tables node. Click on the new table toolbar button, which has a white plus sign, and enter a new table name. Within the Add Table dialog, you will also add any necessary columns. For this example and the next recipe, create a table named Catalog, which will hold information pertaining to a music collection. Click on the Insert Column button and add a column named ID. Because it will be a primary-key column, check the check box labeled Primary Key. To automatically increment this column, change the Identity value to `Yes` and enter the value `1` for the Identity Seed and Identity Inc fields.

Next, add a column named Title. The type for this column is `nvarchar` with an arbitrarily chosen length of 40. To ensure that the Title is specified when adding new items, uncheck the Allow Nulls check box. Finally, add another column named Artist using the same data type, but this time, leave the Allow Nulls check box checked.

Comments

Just as a small version of the .NET Framework was created for mobile devices, a small but powerful version of SQL Server was created. If you're like us, you tend to question technologies before using them to determine whether the path is clear before you dive right in. SQL Server CE Edition is one whose immediate benefits might not be particularly clear. After all, you can create a `DataSet` by simply reading in an XML file and a schema, so why not just use that? Consider the following scenario. You work as a developer for a company that wants to be able to take an inventory count at any time in the warehouse using a Pocket PC. The company maintains the current inventory of the items in the warehouse using a SQL database located on a large central server. By using SQL Server CE, you can create a Smart Device Application that updates a local database on the device, which will later be merged with the master database when you are finished. If you were to use other storage mechanisms, you would also have to create the additional toolset necessary to perform the database merge. With that in mind, the next recipe utilizes the database created in this recipe to add, delete, and modify the music catalog SQL Server CE database.

26.15. Using a SQL Server CE Database

You want to add, delete, and modify records in a SQL Server CE database.

Technique

This recipe continues where the last recipe left off. The last recipe created a database using SQL Server CE edition, which is used to hold song information. This recipe creates an application that lets you view that information as well as modify it.

To begin, create a new Smart Device Application. This application uses a `DataGrid`, but when you initially create the project, the `DataGrid` does not show up in the toolbox. To enable data controls, you must first add a reference to the SQL Server CE assembly named `System.Data.SqlServerCe`. After you add the reference, drag and drop a `DataGrid` control onto the device form.

Because the database is located on the device itself, you will be unable to use the Windows Form designer to automatically create the necessary data objects. Within the source file, create four fields to be used for SQL Server CE data access. These fields include a `SqlCeConnection` to connect to the database; a `SqlCeAdapter` to extract data from the database; a `SqlCeCommandBuilder` to automatically generated `INSERT`, `DELETE`, and `UPDATE` commands; and a `DataSet` to store the data from the database. One of these objects, the `DataSet`, is the same class used within ADO.NET applications. The other three are specific to SQL Server CE but are related to their SQL Server counterparts within the full .NET Framework. In fact, you'll notice that using these objects is exactly the same.

The first thing to do is create an instance of these objects, extract the database records, and bind the data to the `DataGrid` object. The procedures for this step are the same methods used in ADO.NET. First, you create a `SqlCeConnection` object, specifying a connection string. The connection string for a SQL Server CE database is much simpler than a regular SQL Server connection string. The only parameter you need, assuming you left the password field blank when you created the database, is the `Data Source` parameter. Its value is the location of the database, which by default is in the My Documents folder unless you specified otherwise. Next, create an instance of the `SqlCeDataAdapter` class. You can use a parameterless constructor because you will be associating the adapter with a `SqlCeCommand`. Therefore, set the `SelectCommand` property of the `SqlCeDataAdapter` object by creating a new `SqlCeCommand` object, passing in the `SELECT` statement and the connection object.

To automatically generate the `INSERT`, `UPDATE`, and `DELETE` commands, create an instance of the `SqlCeCommandBuilder` object, passing the data adapter as the parameter. Any time the `DataSet` object is updated, the data adapter uses the automatically generated commands to update the database when the `Update` method is called.

The last step is to create the `DataSet` object, fill it using the `DataAdapter`, and set the `DataSource` property of the `DataGrid` to the `Catalog` table of the `DataSet`. Listing 26.11 shows the form constructor for all of these steps.

Listing 26.11   Populating a `DataGrid` from a SQL Server CE Database

```
public Form1()
{
    InitializeComponent();

    sqlConnection = new SqlCeConnection(
        @"Data Source=/My Documents/MusicCatalog.sdf;" );

    string selectCmd  = "SELECT * From Catalog";

    // create the adapter
    sqlDataAdapter = new SqlCeDataAdapter();

    // assign select command
    sqlDataAdapter.SelectCommand = new SqlCeCommand(selectCmd, sqlConnection);

    cmdBuilder = new SqlCeCommandBuilder( sqlDataAdapter );

    // create dataset
    catalogDataSet = new DataSet("Catalog");

    // fill dataset
    sqlDataAdapter.Fill(catalogDataSet, "Catalog" );
```

Listing 26.11   **Continued**

```
    // databind datagrid
    dataGrid1.DataSource = catalogDataSet.Tables["Catalog"];
    sqlConnection.Close();


}
```

At this point, you can run your application and you see the `DataGrid` display the column headers for each column in the database table. However, unlike the `DataGrid` in the .NET Framework, you cannot directly edit cells in a Smart Device Application. You have to devise a way for users to edit the cells. For this application, create a menu item that when clicked automatically inserts a new record with some default values. Additionally, to enable editing of a cell, create a `TextBox` control at the bottom of the `DataGrid` with a corresponding button. To update a cell, therefore, the user selects a cell from the `DataGrid`, enters a new value in the `TextBox`, and clicks on the `Button` to make the change. The code to add a new row to the `DataGrid` as well as to update the underlying `DataSource` is as follows:

```
private void mnuAdd_Click(object sender, System.EventArgs e)
{
    DataRow newRow = catalogDataSet.Tables["Catalog"].NewRow();
    newRow["Title"] = "Song Title";
    newRow["Artist"] = "Artist";

    catalogDataSet.Tables["Catalog"].Rows.Add( newRow );
    sqlDataAdapter.Update( catalogDataSet, "Catalog" );
}
```

The `Button` event handler is where the database update code resides for individual cell editing. The first step is to figure out which cell the user has clicked within the `DataGrid`. Access the `CurrentCell` property of the `DataGrid`. This `DataGridCell` object contains information such as the value, row, and column that you need to update the underlying data source. Before that happens, the `DataGrid` cell data changes to reflect the new value. Next, you find the corresponding row within the `DataSet` by using the `CurrentRowIndex` value of the `DataGrid` as an indexer into the `Catalog` table rows. Once you find the row, you can use traditional dictionary-based access to set the individual columns within the row and finally update the data source using the data adapter, as shown in Listing 26.12.

Listing 26.12   **Updating a SQL Server CE Database**

```
private void btnChange_Click(object sender, System.EventArgs e)
{
    DataGridCell currentCell;
    string currentCellData;
```

Listing 26.12   **Continued**

```
    // Get the text to put into the current cell.
    currentCellData = tbNewValue.Text;

    // Get the current cell.
    currentCell = dataGrid1.CurrentCell;

    // Set the current cell's data.
    dataGrid1[currentCell.RowNumber,currentCell.ColumnNumber] = currentCellData;

    // update the data source
    DataRow updateRow =
        catalogDataSet.Tables["Catalog"].Rows[dataGrid1.CurrentRowIndex];

    updateRow["Title"] = dataGrid1[dataGrid1.CurrentRowIndex,1];
    updateRow["Artist"] = dataGrid1[dataGrid1.CurrentRowIndex,2];
    sqlDataAdapter.Update( catalogDataSet, "Catalog" );
}
```

The last thing to enable for the SQL Server CE database application is to delete a row. The procedure is much simpler than that for performing a database update. All you need is to find the corresponding row within the DataSet by once again using the CurrentRowIndex of the DataGrid. Once you find the row, call the Delete method from the DataRow object and update the data source using the data adapter:

```
private void mnuDelete_Click(object sender, System.EventArgs e)
{
    DataRow updateRow =
        catalogDataSet.Tables["Catalog"].Rows[dataGrid1.CurrentRowIndex];
    updateRow.Delete();
    sqlDataAdapter.Update( catalogDataSet, "Catalog" );
}
```

Comments

This recipe really demonstrates some of the cool things you can do with mobile devices and SQL Server CE. Both of the technologies involved, the .NET Compact Framework and the SQL Server CE Edition, might be small, but the functionality contained within them allows for unique and interesting application ideas. Although it might take a little more work because the designer and control support isn't as rich as it is in the full .NET Framework, you can still do a majority of the methods shown with the added benefit of being able to take it on the road with you.

VII

Appendixes

Visual Studio .NET IDE

A DEVELOPMENT ENVIRONMENT AS LARGE as Visual Studio .NET 2003 might seem a little daunting to those whose coding environment was restricted to straight text editors. The Integrated Development Environment (IDE) uses a series of tool windows that wrap around the most important window of them all, the source window. This appendix outlines the various facets of the IDE and how to organize it to obtain an environment more suited to your style.

Source Editing

The most important window you will work with in the IDE is the source code window. For sake of clarity, the source window also displays different designers based on the file format of the file being edited, but this discussion focuses on the source code window as it relates to C# source code files.

Code Outlining

Outlining is a feature that places logical code blocks into collapsible sections similar to that of a tree control. By default, the source code for new projects is displayed in its expanded state, except for code that is off limits such as Windows Form designer-generated code. By right-clicking within the source code window or selecting the Edit, Outlining pop-up menu from the main menu, you can view a list of outlining commands. The Toggle Outlining Expansion collapses a section to a single line and places an ellipsis at the end of that line or expands the section if it is already collapsed. This action is similar to clicking the tree node control along the left side of the source window.

The Toggle All Outlining command collapses all code blocks or expands them if they are already collapsed. Finally, the Collapse to Definitions item parses the source code file and collapses the code so that only method declarations are visible. For those who are familiar with C++, this view is similar to that of a header file. You can also disable outlining at any time by selecting the Stop Outlining menu item.

Outlining uses C# language constructs to determine regions to create. In other words, regions are created for matching braces, including those denoting a conditional control block such as an `if` statement or `do/while` block. You can also define your own regions by using the `#region` and `#endregion` preprocessor directives. The following example demonstrates how to create a region that can be collapsed for member variables within a class:

```
namespace _MyProject
{
    public class Form1 : System.Windows.Forms.Form
    {
        #region Windows Form Control Variables
        private System.Windows.Forms.DataGrid dataGrid1;
        private System.Windows.Forms.MenuItem menuItem1;
        private System.Windows.Forms.MenuItem mnuExit;
        #endregion
    }
}
```

IntelliSense

IntelliSense is the technology used by the IDE that displays help information within a tooltip or a selectable list box as you type in source code. For instance, entering a variable name that represents a class and following it with the dot operator for member access displays a list box that allows you to choose the proper class method or variable. As you continue typing, the list box changes to reflect the closest match based on the current typed characters. At any time the list box highlights the member you are looking for, press the Tab key to complete the word. You can additionally use the up- and down-arrow keys or PageUp and PageDown keys to navigate to the correct member.

As you enter a parenthesis denoting a method call, a specialized tooltip appears listing the possible method parameters. If any other overloaded versions of the method exist, you see an up/down control on the left side of the tooltip. You can use the up- and down-arrow keys to select the proper overloaded version that you want to use, and as you enter each parameter, the tooltip marks your location using a bold typeface.

IntelliSense also allows you to view information about a data type or method parameters at any time using the IntelliSense toolbar buttons or menu item accessed through the Edit menu. Clicking away for the current editing position while editing source code removes any tooltip or list box that is displayed. If you place your cursor back to that position and access one of the IntelliSense menu or toolbar items, the tooltip or list box reappears.

Bookmarks

Bookmarks allow you to mark positions within your code that you want to frequently access while working in your project. The bookmark commands appear on the toolbar, easily recognizable by a group of blue flags, or on the Edit main menu. If you position your cursor at a particular line in the source window and select the Toggle Bookmark command, a cyan colored marker appears in the left-side margin of the source code window. If you place an additional bookmark within the same file, you can switch between the locations by using the next and previous bookmark commands. They only navigate to bookmarks within the same source file, which means you are unable to toggle between two bookmarks if they are in different source files.

Creating Task List Shortcuts

The Task List window is generally used to display warnings and errors that arise whenever you compile your project. Clicking on the warning or error takes you to the corresponding line in the source code, allowing you to fix it. You can also use the source code window to create automatic entries within the task list to create shortcuts. To create a task list shortcut, place the cursor on the line to create the shortcut to and click on the Add Task List Shortcut menu item accessed through the Edit, Bookmarks menu. To view the list of shortcuts within the task list, right-click on the Task List window and select Show Tasks, Shortcuts.

You can also automatically create task list shortcuts by creating specialized comments. To automatically place a shortcut into the task list, add the single-line comment operator (//); followed by a task list keyword such as TODO, HACK, or UNDONE; followed by the text to display in the task list. You can optionally create your own keywords by clicking on Tools, Options from the main menu; selecting the Environment, Task List property page; and filling in the Name field with a new keyword. You can set the priority to low, medium, or high.

Tool Windows

Tool windows are the outlying windows surrounding the source code view which contain specialized functions and views that complement the item currently being edited.

Common Tool Windows

The following is a list of the default tool windows within the IDE and the functions that they perform:

- *Solution Explorer*—This window displays the hierarchical organization of the files within your project. The layout of the files directly mirrors the layout of the files on the file system. Additionally, deleting a file from the Solution Explorer also deletes the file from the hard drive. You can also remove a project from the Solution Explorer, but the files remain on the file system. By default, any supporting files for a file in your project are hidden, such as resource files for Windows Form projects. To view the extra files, click on the Show All Files button in the Solution Explorer window.

- *Class View*—This window displays all the data types within a project. Double-clicking on a class name, method, variable, interface, or other data type takes you to that type's definition within the source window. You can customize the layout of this window by clicking the organize toolbar button. For instance, selecting the Group by Type places all classes within a single group, and within each class a folder is created for all methods, variables, properties, delegates, and other language constructs.

- *Resource Window*—The Resource window displays any resources that you have created for your application. However, the Resource Window is used for Visual C++ resource files (`.rc`), which means that it is empty for C# projects.

- *Properties*—Otherwise known as the Property Browser, the Properties window uses a Property Grid .NET control and reflection techniques to show a list of properties for a selected type. For instance, selecting a `Button` control within the Window Form Designer displays the properties for the `Button` class, allowing you to change them as you see fit. You also use the Properties window to create event handlers for control events by selecting the lightning bolt icon within the Properties window toolbar.

- *Dynamic Help*—The first version of Visual Studio .NET introduced a unique concept of obtaining help, which automatically displays MSDN help items based on the current context you are editing in. For instance, clicking on the `class` keyword within the source code window displays relevant topics associated with creating and using classes.

- *Server Explorer*—The Server Explorer window displays any data connections that you have established within the IDE, allowing you to view and edit databases. For instance, installing SQL Server and creating data connections to a particular database allows you to edit the tables, perform database queries, and even edit stored procedures using the Visual Studio .NET Query Builder designer. Additionally, the Server Explorer displays local Windows-specific technologies related to the system such as performance counters, event logs, message queues, and services. You can add these items to a Windows Form application, and the necessary .NET object is created to interact with that item.

- *Toolbox*—The Toolbox window contains all the controls and components that you can use in a Windows application, ASP.NET Web application, and .NET applications that use the .NET Compact Framework. Several tabs are available within the toolbox, but you see only those that are relevant to the designer you are working in. In other words, if you are creating a Windows Form application, the Web Forms Toolbox tab is hidden from view. To view all the available tabs in the toolbox, right-click on it and select the Show All Tabs menu item.

Preset Layouts and Developer Profiles

Visual Studio .NET ships with several defined window layouts tailored to a particular developer's style and experience level. To access the list of profiles, select the Profiles tab from the Visual Studio .NET start page. The default profile is named Visual Studio Developer, but you can change the profile to appear more like Visual C++ 6.0, for instance, by setting the profile to Visual C++ Developer or more like Visual Basic 6.0 by setting the profile to Visual Basic Developer. Changing these profiles also changes the keyboard scheme, window layout, and help filter.

Docking

A docking window is a window that is anchored to a particular area of the IDE surrounding the main source view window. For instance, the Solution Explorer and Class View windows are docked along the top-right edge of the IDE with the Properties window and Dynamic Help along the bottom-right edge. You can change the location of the windows by dragging their toolbars and dropping them in a location. As you drag the windows, a gray rectangle shows the location of the window if it were dropped at that time. If multiple windows occupy the same space, a tab control allows you to tab between the different tool windows. To add a new item to a tab group, drag the toolbar of the window you want to dock onto the tab groups, and you see the outline of a new tab. You can also create a floating window, which is not anchored to the IDE. On the main development system, for instance, you might keep a floating output window that is displayed on a second monitor as well as a debug watch window.

Auto-Hiding

With so many available tool windows, the IDE can soon get cluttered, especially on monitors running in low resolutions. The Visual Studio .NET IDE allows you to auto-hide windows. Click on the upper-right push-pin button in the tool window's title bar to auto-hide that window. When you do so, the window collapses to the edge of the IDE and a tab appears with a label denoting the name of the tool window. If you hover your mouse over the tool window, it slides into place. If you auto-hide a tool window that is within a tab group, all the tab windows within that group collapse.

Visual Studio .NET Toolbars

The toolbars within Visual Studio .NET are logically organized by the functions they perform. You can view a list of all the available toolbars by right-clicking the area along the top of the IDE. Some toolbars automatically appear whenever you open a corresponding file or object within the IDE.

You can change the appearance and add new toolbar buttons by selecting Tools, Customize. Within the Customize dialog, you can create your own custom toolbars by clicking on the New button. A blank toolbar appears, ready for you to add buttons. To add a new toolbar button, click on the Commands tab within the Customize toolbox. Commands are grouped according to their category, and selecting a category displays the list of associated commands. After finding the command you want, simply drag and drop it from the Command tab to the toolbar that you want to place it on. You can also add buttons to the toolbars defined by the IDE. Visual Studio .NET features a macro-processing facility used for extensibility. You can assign these macros to toolbar buttons. To see the list of defined macros, select the Macros category.

B

.NET Debugging .Reference

To write any significant amount of code without ever creating a mistake is a near impossible task. In fact, most applications ship to customers with some defects still intact. Knowing how to use the debugger in Visual Studio .NET will help you pinpoint the problem more effectively. This appendix looks at the various methods to use while debugging as well as the associated debugger tool windows that provide additional information while you find problems in your code.

Working with Breakpoints

You use *breakpoints* to halt the execution of your program at a certain location in your code in order to inspect the values of any variables in your code as well as to view the order of statement execution, a process known as *stepping*. To add a breakpoint to a certain line, click in the left-side margin of the source window. A red dot appears at that location, and the corresponding statement is highlighted. If you later want to jump to the source code file where a certain breakpoint appears, you can use the Breakpoints tool window, which is accessible using the Debug, Windows menu item. You can also use this window to change the properties of the breakpoint if it is conditional.

Conditional Breakpoints

You can add *conditional breakpoints* that break only when a certain condition is met. To add a conditional breakpoint, right-click in the source window at the location to place the breakpoint and select New Breakpoint. Within the New Breakpoint dialog, click on the Condition button. The Breakpoint Condition dialog lets you enter a expression that is evaluated each time the program reaches that breakpoint. If the condition evaluates to `true`, then the program is halted at the breakpoint location. An example of where this is useful is a `for` loop. If you had a `for` loop that looped many times, but you were only interested in viewing the statement executions when the counter variable reaches a certain point, specify a breakpoint condition. The following code shows a `for` loop with a large range specified for the counter. To create a conditional breakpoint when the counter is above 100, use the expression i >= 100:

```
for( int i = 0; i < 1024; ++i )
{
    someArray[i] += someArray[i+1];
}
```

You can also add a breakpoint that only breaks after its location is passed a certain number of times. You use the same method described earlier, but instead of clicking the Condition button, click the Hit Count button. Within the Hit Count dialog, you can specify whether the breakpoint should stop execution all the time, only after a certain amount of hits occur, only when the hit count is a multiple of a certain number (useful, for instance, to only break every other hit), and if the hit count is greater than or equal to a certain value.

Debugging an Application

After you place any of the necessary breakpoints for your code, you can start debugging by pressing the F5 key or selecting Start Debug from the Build menu. Note that you don't have to build your project before debugging because the IDE performs that step before launching the debugger. The following sections introduce the various commands and tool windows that are at your disposal as you debug an application.

Stepping with the Keyboard

Stepping through code line-by-line to investigate the order of execution and the effect each statement makes to variables is the procedure used most when debugging. You use three methods to step through lines of source when debugging after a breakpoint is reached. Although you are more than welcome to use the stepping commands using the Debug menu within the main menu or using the Toolbar buttons, I recommend learning the three keyboard shortcuts to speed up the process without adding miles of cursor movement on your mouse.

The first method is stepping into statements, which you accomplish by pressing the F11 key. If the next statement to execute is a method call within your project, the debugger enters into the first executable line in that method and allows you to begin stepping through that method. If at any point you want to step out of the called method and return to the calling statement, press the key sequence Shift+F11. Execution commences at the next executing line in the calling method. If you want to simply execute a method without stepping into it, press the F10 key. The method runs, but the debugger does not enter into it, and the debugger stops at the next executing statement in your current location.

Using Watch Windows

Watch windows allow you to view the current state of a variable. If the variable is a primitive type, the watch window displays its value. If the variable is a class or struct, the watch window creates a treeview of that variable, allowing you to view the individual members. Additionally, if a member variable is also a complex data type, each of its members is contained within a child tree node as well. As you step through your code, the watch window updates any variables it is currently watching to reflect their new values.

There are a total of four different watch windows and a QuickWatch window. To display a watch window, click on Debug, Windows, Watch and select one of the four windows. To add a variable to the watch window, highlight the variable name within the source code window and drag and drop it into the watch window. The variable is always displayed regardless of your current position in the debugger. If the variable cannot be determined based on the current context, the watch window reflects that fact with an error message instead of the variable's value.

The watch windows are not only designed to contain variables. You can also create a watch for a certain statement as long as the statement does not contain method calls. The statement can contain any number of variables with associated properties in addition to indexer values for collection types.

The QuickWatch window is a modal dialog window that allows you to quickly inspect the value of a variable or statement. To access the QuickWatch window, highlight the item to view, right-click on it, and select the QuickWatch menu item. Using this window is similar to the other watch windows but to continue debugging, you must close the window.

Viewing the Call Stack

As your application is executing, a stack called the Call Stack follows the current position of the executing context with regards to the current method being executed. Whenever a method is entered, its address is placed on top of the stack with the calling method directly underneath it. When a breakpoint is hit, you can view the current call stack by selecting Debug, Windows, Call Stack. The top line of the window represents the method you are currently debugging, and each subsequent line represents the method that was currently executing before the current method was called. You can double-click any method within the call stack, and if the method is contained within your project code, the corresponding line in the source code for that method is displayed. Even though you might see method names that are contained within the .NET Framework assemblies, you cannot view the corresponding source code.

Debugging with Exceptions

If you are debugging an application and an exception is thrown but not handled, the debugger displays a message asking you to break at that location, continue, or abort the debugging process. If you click on the Break button, you are placed at the location the exception occurred.

You can also customize the debugger to break whenever any exceptions are thrown regardless of whether they are caught by accessing the Exceptions window through the Debug menu item. All the possible .NET exceptions and WIN32 exceptions appear in a treeview control. You can select a group of exceptions such as Common Language Runtime Exceptions and change the corresponding behavior the debugger should take when the exception is thrown. You can also target a specific exception by expanding the group the exception is within and selecting the exception name. You can then change the properties using the radio button settings for that exception only.

Additional Debugging Tool Windows

Two additional tool windows available when debugging behave similarly to the watch windows, but their functionality is automated by the debugger. The Locals window displays all the variables defined within the current executing context. In other words, the Locals window displays all the local parameters accessible from the current method being executed.

The Autos window is similar to that of the Locals window, but it limits the visibility of the current locals. Rather than display all the local variables within the currently executing method, it only displays those that are being currently accessed within the current statement and those that were accessed in the previous statement. You can immediately see a before and after snapshot of a variable after it is accessed by a statement.

Index

G

O

How can we make this index more useful? Email us at indexes@samspublishing.com

How can we make this index more useful? Email us at indexes@samspublishing.com

Your Guide to Computer Technology

www.informit.com

Developer's Library

Essential references for programming professionals

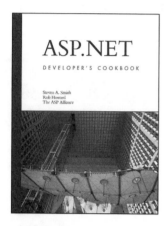

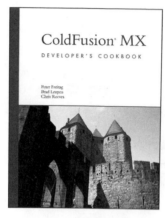

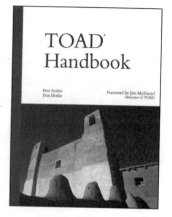

ASP.NET
DEVELOPER'S COOKBOOK

Steven Smith
Rob Howard
ISBN: 0-672-32524-1
$35.99 US

ColdFusion MX
DEVELOPER'S COOKBOOK

Peter Freitag
Brad Leupen
Chris Reeves
ISBN: 0-672-32462-8
$35.99 US

TOAD Handbook

Bert Scalzo
Dan Hotka
ISBN: 0-672-32486-5
$29.99 US

OTHER DEVELOPER'S LIBRARY TITLES

JavaServer Pages
DEVELOPER'S HANDBOOK

Nick Todd
Mark Szolkowski
ISBN: 0-672-32438-5
$49.99 US

XSL Formatting Objects
DEVELOPER'S HANDBOOK

Doug Lovell
ISBN: 0-672-32281-1
$49.99 US

HTTP
DEVELOPER'S HANDBOOK

Chris Shiflett
ISBN: 0-672-32454-7
$39.99 US

PostgreSQL
DEVELOPER'S HANDBOOK

Ewald Geschwinde
Hans–Juergen
Schoenig
ISBN: 0-672-32260-9
$44.99

PRICES SUBJECT TO CHANGE

DEVELOPER'S LIBRARY

www.developers-library.com